D1621019

WEBSTER'S
CONCISE
ENGLISH
DICTIONARY

WEBSTER'S
CONCISE
ENGLISH
DICTIONARY

Books
Are Fun®Ltd

Reader's
Digest. Company

This edition published 2004 for Books Are Fun by Geddes & Grosset,
David Dale House, New Lanark ML11 9DJ, Scotland

© 2004 Geddes & Grosset

ISBN 1 84205 416 3

Printed and bound in Poland, OZGraf S.A.

A

aback' *adv:*—**taken aback** surprised.

aban'don *vb* 1 to give up. 2 to depart from for ever, desert:—*n* freedom from care.

aban'doned *adj* 1 deserted. 2 immoral, shameless.

abase' *vb* to humble:—*n* **abase'ment**.

abashed' *adj* embarrassed, ashamed.

abate' *vb* to lessen:—*n* **abate'ment**.

abattoir [a-bat-wär'] *n* a place where animals are killed before being sold as meat.

abb'ess *n* the chief nun in a convent.

abb'ey *n* 1 a monastery or convent. 2 a church, once part of a monastery or convent.

abb'ot *n* the chief monk in a monastery.

abbrev'iate *vb* to shorten:—*n* **abbrevia'tion**.

ab'dicate *vb* to give up high office, esp a throne:—*n* **abdica'tion**.

ab'domen *n* the part of the body between the breast and thighs:—*adj* **abdom'inal**.

abduct' *vb* to kidnap:—*n* **abduc'tion**:—*n* **abduc'tor**.

aberra'tion *n* 1 a wandering from the right or usual way. 2 a wandering of the mind.

abet' *vb* to help or encourage, esp in evil:—*n* **abet'tor**.

abey'ance *n:*—**in abeyance** out of use for the time being.

abhor' *vb* to loathe:—*n* **abhor'rence**.

abhor'rent *adj* loathsome.

abide' *vb* 1 to put up with:—**abide by** to obey, to remain true to.

abid'ing *adj* lasting.

abil'ity *n* 1 skill or power to do a thing. 2 cleverness.

ab'ject *adj* miserable, wretched.

abjure' *vb* to swear to give up.

ablaze' *adj and adv* on fire, in flames.

ab'le *adj* 1 having skill or power to do a thing. 2 clever:—*adv* **ab'ly**.

ablu'tion *n* washing of the body.

abnor'mal *adj* different from the usual:—*adv* **abnor'mally**.

abnormal'ity *n* unusual quality.

aboard' *adv and prep* on board, on a ship, train, airplane, etc.

abode' *n* (*fml* or *hum*) house, home.

abol'ish *vb* to put an end to, to do away with.

aboli'tion *n* putting an end to something:—*n* **aboli'tionist**.

abom'inable *adj* hateful.

abom'inate *vb* to hate very much:—**abomina'tion**.

Aborig'inal *n* any of the original inhabitants of Australia.

aborigines [ab-ô-'riſ-in-eez] *npl* the original inhabitants of a country.

abor'tive *adj* unsuccessful because done too soon.

abound' *vb* to be plentiful.

about' *adv and prep* 1 concerning. 2 around. 3 near to. 4 nearly. 5 on the point of.

above' *adv and prep* 1 over. 2 higher (than).

above'board' *adj* honest, fair.

abra'sion *n* an injury caused by rubbing or scraping.

abreast' *adv* side by side:—**abreast of the times** up-to-date.

abridge' *vb* to make shorter:—*n* **bridg(e)'-ment**.

abroad' *adv* 1 out of one's country. 2 far and wide.

ab'rogate *vb* to do away with; to cancel (a law):—*n* **abroga'tion**.

abrupt' *adj* 1 sudden, hasty. 2 discourteous:—*adv* **abrupt'ly**:—*n* **abrupt'ness**.

ab'scess *n* a boil, a gathering of pus in some part of the body.

abscond' *vb* to run away secretly and suddenly, esp after doing wrong.

absence *see* **absent**[2].

ab'sent[1] *adj* not present.

absent'[2] *vb* to keep away:—*n* **ab'sence**.

absentee' *n* one who is not present.

ab'sent-mind'ed *adj* not thinking of what one is doing.

ab'solute *adj* 1 complete. 2 free from controls or conditions:—*adv* **ab'solutely**.

absorb' *vb* 1 to soak up. 2 to take up all the attention of.

absorp'tion *n* 1 act of absorbing. 2 full attention.

abstain' *vb* 1 to keep oneself from, to hold back from. 2 not to vote:—*n* **abstain'er**:—*n* **absten'tion**.

absurd' *adj* foolish:—*n* **absurd'ity**.

abund'ance *n* more than enough, plenty:—*adj* **abund'ant**:—*adv* **abund'antly**.

abuse [a-bûz'] *vb* 1 to make wrong use of. 2 to ill-treat, to maltreat, esp physically or sexually. 3 to use insulting language:—*n* **abuse** [a-bûs'].

abys'mal *adj* very great.

abyss' *n* a very deep pit or ravine.

academ'ic *adj* of or concerning education, esp in a college or university.

acad'emy *n* 1 a school for special studies. 2 a society for advancing arts and sciences.

accel'erate *vb* to increase speed:—*n* **accelera'tion**.

accel'erator *n* a device that controls the speed of a motorcar.

ac'cent *n* 1 a special emphasis given to part of a word. 2 the mark that indicates such emphasis. 3 a way of speaking peculiar to certain persons or groups:—*vb* **accent'** to emphasize a certain part of a word.

accept' *vb* 1 to receive something offered. 2 to regard as true, reasonable, satisfactory, etc:—*n* **accept'ance**.

ac'cess *n* a way or means of approach.

access'ible *adj* 1 easily approached. 2 easily reached:—*n* **accessibil'ity**.

access'ory *n* 1 an assistant, esp in crime. 2 an additional part or tool. 3 an additional item worn with a woman's clothes.

ac'cident *n* 1 an unexpected happening. 2 an unexpected event that causes damage or injury:—*adj* **acciden'tal**.

accom'modate *vb* 1 to provide lodgings for. 2 to have space for. 3 to supply with. 4 to make suitable, to adapt.

accom'modating *adj* obliging.

accommoda'tion *n* lodgings.

accom'panist *n* one who plays the accompaniment for a singer or player.

accompany [ak-kum'-pê-ni] *vb* 1 to go with. 2 to join a singer or player by playing a musical instrument.

accom'plice *n* a helper, esp in crime.

accom'plish *vb* to perform successfully.

accom'plishment *n* 1 something done successfully. 2 completion.

accord' *n* agreement:—**of one's own accord** by one's own wish.

accord'ing to *prep* 1 in keeping with. 2 as stated by.

account' *vb* (*fml*) to consider, to reckon:—*n* 1 a statement of money received and paid, a bill. 2 a report, description:—**account for** to give an explanation of:—**of no account** of no importance:—**on account of** because of.

account'able *adj* responsible.

account'ancy *n* the work of an accountant.

account'ant *n* one who keeps or examines money accounts.

9

accum'ulate *vb* 1 to increase, to heap up. 2 to collect.

ac'curacy *n* exactness, precision.

ac'curate *adj* 1 correct, exact. 2 correct, careful:—*adv* **ac'curately**.

accusa'tion *n* a charge brought against anyone.

accuse' *vb* to charge with wrongdoing:—*n* **accus'er**.

accused' *n* one charged with wrongdoing.

accus'tomed *adj* 1 usual. 2 used (to), familiar with.

ace [ās] *n* 1 one at cards, dice, or dominoes. 2 someone good at sports.

ache [āk] *vb* to be in or to give prolonged pain:—*n* a prolonged or throbbing pain.

achieve' *vb* 1 to succeed in doing. 2 to gain.

achieve'ment *n* 1 something done successfully. 2 a feat.

a'cid *adj* sour, sharp to the taste:—*n* a sour substance.

acknowledge [ak-nâ'-lèj] *vb* 1 to admit as true. 2 to admit the receipt of:—*n* **acknow'ledgement**.

acne [ak'-nee] *n* a skin disease.

a'corn *n* the fruit or seed of the oak tree.

acous'tics *npl* the science of sound.

acquaint' *vb* 1 to make familiar with. 2 to inform.

acquaint'ance *n* 1 a person one knows. 2 knowledge.

acquire' *vb* to gain, to obtain.

acquisi'tion *n* 1 the act of acquiring. 2 something acquired.

acquis'itive *adj* eager to obtain and possess:—*n* **acquis'itiveness**.

acquit' *vb* 1 to declare innocent. 2 to conduct oneself.

acquit'tal *n* a setting free.

acre [ā'-kèr] *n* a measure of land (= 4046.9 square metres or 4840 square yards).

ac'rid *adj* sharp and bitter in taste or smell.

ac'robat *n* a tight-rope or trapeze artiste:—*adj* **acrobat'ic**:— *npl* **acrobat'ics**.

act *vb* 1 to do. 2 to conduct oneself. 3 to perform on the stage. 4 to produce an effect:—*n* 1 a deed. 2 a law. 3 a part of a play.

ac'tion *n* 1 something done. 2 a movement. 3 the producing of an effect. 4 the events in a narrative or drama. 5 a battle. 6 a lawsuit.

ac'tive *adj* 1 energetic. 2 taking part, involved. 3 being in action, working, operative.

activ'ity *n* 1 energy. 2 occupation or pastime.

ac'tor *n* a man who performs in a play.

ac'tress *n* a woman who performs in a play.

ac'tual *adj* real, not imaginary. 2 true.

ac'tually *adv* really, as a matter of fact.

acute' *adj* 1 coming to a sharp point. 2 sharp-witted. 3 (of emotions or diseases) intense but short-lasting:—*adv* **acute'ly**.

adapt' *vb* 1 to make suitable, to fit to a different use. 2 to change, adjust.

add *vb* 1 to join one thing to another. 2 to increase. 3 to say further.

ad'der *n* a small poisonous snake.

ad'dict *n* a person who is dependent on and so unable to give up a habit, esp a harmful one such as drug-taking.

addict'ed *adj* dependent on, unable to give up:—*n* **addic'tion**.

addi'tion *n* 1 act of adding. 2 something added:—*adj* **addi'tional**.

address' *vb* 1 to speak to. 2 to direct a letter. 3 to direct one's attention or energy to:—*n* **address'**, **ad'dress** 1 the place where a person lives or works. 2 the directions on a letter or envelope. 3 a formal talk. 4 skill.

adequate [a'-dee-kwàt] *adj* 1 enough. 2 satisfactory:—*adv* **ad'equately**:—*n* **ad'equacy**.

adhe'sive *adj* sticky:—*n* a sticky substance, glue.

ad'jective *n* a word that describes a noun:—*adj* **adjecti'val** [ad-jek-tī'-vèl]:—*adv* **adjecti'vally**.

adjudicate [ad-jū'-di-kāt] *vb* to act as a judge in a competition, etc.

adjust' *vb* 1 to set right. 2 to put in order:—*adj* **adjust'able**:— *n* **adjust'ment**.

admin'ister *vb* 1 to manage, to govern. 2 to carry out. 3 (*fml*) to give.

administra'tion *n* 1 the management of a business or a government. 2 people involved in this:—*adj* **admin'istrative**.

ad'mirable *adj* deserving admiration or praise:—*adv* **ad'mirably**.

ad'miral *n* the highest rank of naval officer.

admira'tion *n* a feeling of pleasure and respect.

admire' *vb* to think very highly of:—*adj* **admir'er**.

admis'sion *n* 1 permission to enter. 2 the amount payable for entry. 3 a confession.

admit' *vb* 1 to allow to enter. 2 to accept as true or just. 3 to confess.

admit'tance *n* (*fml*) right or permission to enter.

admit'tedly *adv* it cannot be denied.

adopt' *vb* 1 to take as one's own. 2 to take over and use. 3 to choose formally:—*n* **adop'tion**.

ador'able *adj* lovable.

adore' *vb* 1 to worship. 2 to love or like very much:— *n* **adora'tion**.

adorn' *vb* to decorate, to make beautiful.

ad'ult, adult' *adj* 1 grown-up. 2 suitable or designed for adults:—*n* **ad'ult** a grown-up person.

advance' *vb* 1 to put forward. 2 to go forward. 3 to help promote. 4 to lend:—*n* 1 a forward movement. 2 progress. 3 a loan (of money), esp a payment made before the normal time. 4 increase:—*n* **in advance** in front; before.

advanced' *adj* 1 far on (in life, time, etc). 2 at a high level, not elementary. 3 modern and new, and sometimes not yet generally accepted.

advantage [ad-vàn'-têj] *n* 1 a better position or something that puts one in a better position. 2 gain, profit, benefit.

adven'ture *n* an exciting or dangerous deed or undertaking.

adven'turous *adj* 1 daring, eager for adventure. 2 dangerous, involving risk.

ad'verb *n* a word that modifies the meaning of a verb, an adjective, or another adverb:—*adj* **adver'bial**.

ad'verse *adj* acting against, unfavorable:—*adv* **ad'versely**.

adver'sity *n* misfortune.

ad'vert short for **advertisement**.

advertise' *vb* to make known to the public:—*n* **ad'vertiser** or **advertis'er**.

adver'tisement *n* an announcement to the public.

advice' *n* 1 a helpful opinion offered to another. 2 a formal letter, etc, giving information.

advis'able *adj* wise; correct in the circumstances:— *n* **advisabil'ity**.

advise' *vb* 1 to give advice. 2 to inform.

advis'er *n* one who gives advice.

advis'ory *adj* for the purpose of giving advice.

ad'vocate *vb* to recommend, to speak in favor of:—*n* 1 one who speaks for another. 2 someone who pleads a case in court.

aeon, eon [ee'-on] *n* an age, a period of time too long to be measured.

aerial [ā'-ri-al] *adj* of or from the air:—*n* an antenna for receiving radio waves or TV signals.

aer'osol *n* 1 a liquid under pressure in a container that is released in a fine spray. 2 the container for this.

affair' n 1 business. 2 a matter, a concern. 3 happenings or events connected with a particular person or thing. 4 a love affair.

affect' vb 1 to act upon. 2 to move the feelings. 3 to pretend.

affect'ed adj full of affectation.

affect'ing adj pathetic.

affecta'tion n manner or behavior that is not natural, pretense.

affec'tion n fondness, love.

affec'tionate adj loving:—adv **affec'tionately**.

affir'mative adj answering 'yes'.

afflict' vb to cause pain, distress, etc, to.—n **afflic'tion**.

af'fluence n wealth.

affluent adj wealthy.

afford' vb 1 to be able to pay for. 2 to be able to do, spend, etc, something without trouble, loss, etc. 3 (fml) to give.

afloat' adj and adv floating.

afraid' adj frightened.

af'ter adv, prep 1 later in time (than). 2 behind.

af'termath n the period of time, or consequences, following an unpleasant or unfortunate event.

afternoon' n the time from noon to evening.

af'terthought n 1 a fresh thought after an act or speech. 2 something added or done later, not part of an original plan.

af'terward adv later.

again [ê-gen'] adv once more.

against [ê-genst'] prep 1 in opposition to. 2 supported by.

age n 1 the length of time a person or thing has lived or existed. 2 (inf) a long time. 3 the state of being old. 4 a particular period in history:—vb 1 to grow old. 2 to make old.

aged adj 1 [a'-jêd] old. 2 [âjd] at the age of.

age'less adj never becoming old.

a'gency n the office or business of an agent.

a'gent n 1 someone or something that acts. 2 a person who acts on behalf of someone else.

agglomera'tion n a heap.

ag'gravate vb 1 to make worse. 2 (inf) to make angry:—n **ag'gravating**.—n **aggrava'tion**.

ag'gregate n a total.

aggress'ion n 1 an attack. 2 hostile feelings.

aggress'ive adj 1 always ready to attack, quarrelsome. 2 forceful, determined:—adv **aggress'ively**.

agile [a'-djîl] adj quick of movement, nimble:—n **agil'ity**.

ag'itate vb 1 to excite, to make anxious. 2 to try to stir up public feeling. 3 (fml) to shake:—n **agita'tion**.

ago' adv in the past.

agog' adj eager, excited.

a'gony n 1 great pain. 2 great distress.

agree' vb 1 to be of the same opinion. 2 to be alike. 3 to suit.

agree'able adj 1 pleasant. 2 ready to agree:—adv **agree'ably**.

agree'ment n 1 sameness of opinion. 2 likeness. 3 a contract.

agricul'ture n the science of cultivating the land, farming:—adj **agricul'tural**.

ahead' adv 1 in front. 2 forward, for the future.

aid vb to help:—n help.

ail'ment n a minor illness.

aim vb 1 to point a weapon (at). 2 to intend, to try:—n 1 the act of aiming a weapon. 2 intention, goal, purpose.

aim'less adj without purpose.

air n 1 the mixture of gases composing the earth's atmosphere. 2 a light breeze. 3 a tune. 4 manner. 5 pl a manner that is not genuine:—vb 1 to expose to fresh air. 2 to expose to warm air, to dry. 3 to speak openly about.

air'borne adj 1 carried by air. 2 in flight.

air'craft n (pl **air'craft**) a flying machine.

air'gun n a gun worked by releasing compressed air.

air'line n a company providing regular aircraft services.

air'plane n a heavier-than-air flying machine with wings.

air'port n a station for passenger aircraft.

air'ship n an aircraft kept aloft by a gas-filled balloon and driven by a motor.

air'tight adj so sealed that air can pass neither in nor out.

aisle [îl] n 1 the side part of a church, often separated from the central part by a row of pillars. 2 a passage in a church.

ajar' adv partly open.

akim'bo adv with the hand on the hip and the elbow outwards.

alarm' n 1 a warning of danger. 2 sudden fear:—vb to frighten.

alarm'ing adj frightening:—adv **alarm'ingly**.

alas' interj a cry of grief or pity.

al'bum n 1 a blank book into which may be put autographs, photographs, stamps, etc. 2 a long-playing record.

al'cohol n 1 pure spirit. 2 strong drink containing such spirit.

alcohol'ic n someone who is addicted to alcohol:—adj having to do with alcohol.

al'cove n a recess, a section of a room, etc, that is set back from the main part.

ale n a light-colored beer.

alert' adj 1 attentive. 2 quick:—n warning of danger:—n **alert'ness**.

alfal'fa n a green plant used as cattle food.

al'gebra n a method of calculation in which letters and symbols are used to represent numbers:—adj **algebraic** [-ā'-ik].

alias [ā'-li-as] adv otherwise:—n a false name.

alibi [a'-li-bî] n the plea that one was elsewhere when a crime was committed.

alien [ā'-li-yên] adj 1 foreign. 2 different, strange:—n 1 a foreigner, a person who is not a naturalized citizen of the country where he or she is living. 2 a being from another world.

alight'[1] vb 1 to get down (from). 2 to settle upon.

alight'[2] adv on fire.

align [a-lîn'] vb 1 to put in line, to straighten. 2 to join, ally oneself with:—n **align'ment**.

alike' adj like, similar:—adv in the same way.

alive' adj 1 living. 2 lively. 3 aware of.

all adj 1 every one of. 2 the whole of:—n 1 everyone. 2 everything:—adv wholly, entirely.

allege [al-ledj'] vb to state without proof:—n **allega'tion**.

allegiance n loyalty.

al'lergy n a reaction of the body to some substance:—adj **aller'gic**.

alley [al'-lä] n a narrow walk or passage.

alliance [al-lî'-êns] n a union between families, governments, etc.

allied see **ally**.

al'ligator n a type of crocodile.

al'locate vb to share out, to distribute:—n **alloca'tion**.

allot' vb (**allot'ted**, **allot'ting**) to give a share, to distribute:—n **allot'ment**.

allow' vb 1 to permit. 2 to set aside.

allow'ance n a sum of money granted for a special purpose:—**make allowance for** take into consideration.

al'loy n a mixture of metals.

allure' vb to attract:—n attraction, charm:—n **allure'ment**:—adj **allur'ing**.

ally [al-lî'] vb to join with another for a special purpose (e.g. by marriage or by treaty):—adj **allied** [al-lîd']:—n **al'ly** 1 a helper. 2 a nation bound to another by treaty of friendship.

almond [a'-månd] n the nut of the almond tree.

al'most adv nearly.

alms [ämz] npl money given to the poor.

aloft' adv high up in the air.

alone' adj, adv 1 without company. 2 taken by itself.

along'side adv and prep by the side of.

aloof' adv apart, distant:—adj distant, cool:—n **aloof'ness**.

aloud' adv so as can be heard.

al'phabet n the set of letters used in writing a language:—adj **alphabet'ical**.

al'pine adj having to do with high mountains, esp the Swiss Alps.

al'ready adv 1 before this time, previously. 2 now or before the expected time.

al'tar [âl'-têr] n 1 a raised place or table on which sacrifices are offered. 2 a communion table.

al'ter [âl'-têr] vb to change:—n **altera'tion**.

al'ternate [âl-têr'-n ĕt] adj 1 first one coming, then the other. 2 every second:—adj **alter'nately**:—vb **alternate** [âl'-têr-n ât] 1 to do, use, cause, arrange, etc, by turns. 2 to happen by turns:—n **alterna'tion**.

alter'native n 1 a choice between two things. 2 (inf) a choice of two or more possibilities:—adj offering such a choice:—adv **alter'natively**.

although' conj though.

al'titude n height.

altogeth'er adv 1 wholly. 2 including everything. 3 on the whole.

al'truism n acting to please others, not oneself:—n **al'truist**:—adj **altruis'tic**.

alumin'um n a soft, white, light metal.

al'ways adv at all times.

amal'gamate vb to unite, to join together:—n **amalgama'tion**.

am'ateur [am'-at-ûr or am'-atêr] n 1 one who takes part in any activity for the love of it, not for money. 2 a person without skill or expertise in something:—n **am'ateurism**.

amateur'ish adj inexpert, unskillful.

amaze' vb to astonish:—n **amaze'ment**.

am'azon n a tall strong woman.

ambas'sador n a high-ranking official appointed to represent his or her government in a foreign country:—adj **ambassado'rial**.

ambig'uous adj having more than one meaning:—n **ambigu'ity**.

am'bit n 1 the space round about. 2 limits.

ambi'tion [am-bish'-ĕn] n 1 desire for power, determination to succeed. 2 a goal, aim:—adj **ambi'tious**.

am'ble vb 1 to walk at an easy pace. 2 (of a four-legged animal) to move the two right legs together then the two left:—n 1 an easy pace. 2 a slow walk:—n **am'bler**.

am'bulance n a vehicle for carrying the sick or injured.

am'bush n 1 a body of people so hidden as to be able to make a surprise attack on an approaching enemy. 2 the place where such people hide. 3 a surprise attack made by people in hiding:—vb to lie in wait, to attack from an ambush.

amen'able [a-mee'-nĕ-bĕl] adj ready to be guided or influenced.

amend' vb 1 (fml) to change for the better. 2 to correct. 3 to alter slightly:—**make amends** make up for a wrong done.

amend'ment n 1 improvement. 2 an alteration (e.g. in a law).

ami'able [âm'-i-ĕbĕl] adj friendly, pleasant:—n **amiabil'ity**.

am'icable [a'-mik-ĕbĕl] adj friendly.

amid', amidst' preps in the middle of, amongst.

amiss' adv wrong:—**take amiss** to take offense at.

am'ity n friendship.

ammuni'tion n 1 powder, bullets, shells, etc. 2 facts, etc, used against someone in an argument, etc.

am'nesty n a general pardon.

amok' adv:—**to run amok** to go mad with the desire to kill.

among', amongst' preps 1 in the middle of. 2 in shares or parts to each person. 3 in the group of.

am'orous adj feeling or expressing love or sexual desire.

amount' vb 1 to add up to. 2 to be equal to:—n the sum total.

amphib'ian [am-fib'-i-an] n 1 a creature that can live both on land and in water. 2 a vehicle designed to move over land or water. 3 an aircraft that can take off from or land on land or water:—adj **amphib'ious**.

am'ple adj 1 large. 2 enough, sufficient, more than enough.

am'plifier n an instrument for making sounds louder.

am'ply adv fully, sufficiently.

am'putate vb to cut off (a limb):—n **amputa'tion**.

amuse' vb 1 to entertain, to give pleasure. 2 to make laugh or smile:—adj **amus'ing**.

amuse'ment n 1 pleasure, entertainment. 2 entertainment, pastime.

anach'ronism [an-ak'-ro-nizm] n 1 the mistake of placing a person or thing in the wrong period of time. 2 a thing or custom that is far behind the fashion.

an'agram n a word formed by arranging the letters of a word in a new order.

an'alog, an'alogue n 1 a word or thing corresponding in certain respects to something else. 2 an object or quantity used to measure another quantity:—adj **analo'gous**.

anal'ogy n 1 likeness. 2 the process of reasoning based on such similarity:—adjs **analog'ical, analo'gical**.

anal'ysis [a-na'-li-sis] n 1 (pl **ana'lyses**) 1 the process of analyzing. 2 a statement of the results of this. 3 short for **psycho-analysis**:—adj **analyt'ical**.

an'alyst n one who analyzes, esp in chemistry.

an'alyze vb to break a thing up into its parts or elements.

an'archy n 1 lawlessness. 2 absence of government:—adj **anarchic** [a-nar'-kick]:—n **an'archist**.

anat'omy n the study of the way the body is put together.

an'cestor [an'-ses-têr] n forefather, a person from whom one is descended:—adj **ances'tral**.

an'cestry n line of forefathers.

anchor [an'-kêr] n 1 a heavy iron hook that grips the sea bed and holds a ship at rest in the water. 2 a person or thing that provides support, stability, or security:—vb 1 to hold fast by an anchor. 2 to drop an anchor:—**to weigh anchor** to take up an anchor before sailing.

an'chorage n a place where a ship can anchor.

an'cient [ân'-shênt] adj 1 old, existing since early times. 2 belonging to old times. 3 (inf) very old:—**the ancients** those who lived long ago, esp the Greeks and Romans.

ancillary [an-sil'-ê-ri] adj supporting, helping, subsidiary.

an'ecdote n a short, interesting, or amusing story about a person or event.

anaesthetic [an-ês-thet'-ik] n a substance that causes loss of feeling for a time, either in the whole body (**general anaesthetic**) or in a limited area of the body, such as a leg (**local anaesthetic**):—also adj:—vb **anaesthetize** [an-ees'-thêt-îz].

anaesthetist [an-ees'-thêt-ist] n one who gives anaesthetics.

angel [ân'-jĕl] n 1 in Christianity, a spirit created to serve God. 2 a very good and helpful person:—adj **angel'ic**.

an'ger n a feeling of rage or fury:—vb to enrage.

angina [an-jî'-na] n a disease of the heart, causing sudden, sharp pains.

ang'le n 1 the space between two meeting lines. 2 a corner. 3 point of view.

Ang'lican (n) adj (a member) of the Anglican Church.

Anglican Communion n a group of Christian Churches in various countries, including the Episcopal Church, that are in full communion.

ang'ling n the art of fishing with a rod:—n **ang'ler**.

Ang'lo- prefix English; of England.

ang'ry adj feeling or showing anger:—adv **ang'rily**.

anguish [ang'-gwish] n very great pain, of body or mind.

ang'ular adj 1 sharp-cornered. 2 thin and bony.

an'imal n 1 a living being with the power to feel and to move at will. 2 such a living being other than human beings. 3 a four-footed creature, as distinct from a bird, fish, or insect. 4 a wild or uncivilized person.

an'imate vb 1 to give life to. 2 to enliven, to make lively and interesting:—adj living.

anima'tion n liveliness, activity.

animos'ity n strong dislike, hatred, enmity.

ank'le n the joint that connects the foot with the leg.

an'nex vb to attach, esp to something larger:—n **annexa'tion**:—n a part added to or situated near a building.

annihilate [an-nī'-il-ât] vb to destroy completely:—n **annihila'tion**.

anniver'sary n the yearly return of the date on which some event occurred and is remembered.

announce' vb to make known:—n **announce'ment**.

annoy' vb to vex; to tease; to be troubled by something one dislikes:—n **annoy'ance**.

an'nual adj 1 yearly. 2 happening every year or only once a year:—n 1 a plant lasting for only one year. 2 a book of which a new edition is published yearly:—adv **an'nually**.

annul' vb (**annul'led, annul'ling**) to declare that something is not valid, to cancel:—n **annul'ment**.

anon' abbr of **anonymous**.

anonymous [a-non'-im-ês] adj nameless, of unknown name:—n **anonym'ity**.

answer [än'-sêr] vb 1 to reply to. 2 to be suitable, to fit. 3 to accept blame or punishment. 4 to be responsible to:—n 1 a reply. 2 a solution (to a problem).

an'swerable adj open to blame for.

antagonis'tic adj opposed to, hostile.

Antarc'tic adj of South Polar regions.

an'telope n a graceful, delicate animal like the deer.

anten'na n 1 (pl **anten'nae**) the feeler of an insect. 2 (pl **anten'nas**) a wire or rod, etc, for receiving radio waves or TV signals.

an'them n a hymn or song of praise to God.

anthol'ogy n a collection of pieces of poetry or prose by different authors.

anthropol'ogy n the study of human beings in relation to their surroundings.

an'ti- prefix against.

antibiot'ic n a substance produced by living things, used in medicine to destroy bacteria that cause disease:—also adj.

antic'ipate vb 1 to expect. 2 to take action in advance of. 3 to foresee:—n **anticipa'tion**.

anticli'max n an unexpectedly dull ending to a striking series of events.

an'tics npl absurd or exaggerated behavior.

an'tidote n a medicine that counteracts the effects of poison or disease.

antip'athy n dislike, opposition to.

antipodes [an-ti'-po-dez] npl places on the surface of the earth exactly opposite each other.

antiqua'rian n one who studies things of an earlier period in history:—also adj.

antiquary [an'-tik-wa-ri] n an antiquarian.

an'tiquated adj old-fashioned, out of date.

antique [an-teek'] adj 1 made in an earlier period and usu valuable. 2 (fml) connected with ancient times:—n a piece of furniture, jewelry, etc, made in an earlier period and considered valuable.

antisep'tic adj having the power to kill germs:—n an antiseptic substance.

ant'ler n a branch of a stag's horn.

an'tonym n a word meaning the opposite of another word.

anxious [ang'-shus] adj worried about what will happen or has happened:—n **anxiety** [ang-zī'-ê-ti].

apart' adv separately.

apart'ment n 1 a home occupying one story or part of a story of a building. 2 a room.

a'pathy n lack of feeling or interest:—adj **apathet'ic**.

ape n a tailless monkey (e.g. chimpanzee, gorilla, orangutan, gibbon):—vb to imitate exactly.

ap'erture n an opening, a hole.

apiary [â'-pi-êr-i] n a place where bees are kept, a beehive.

apiece' adv to or for each one.

apologet'ic adj making excuses, expressing regret.

apol'ogize vb to express regret for a fault or error, to say one is sorry.

apol'ogy n an admission that wrong has been done, an expression of regret.

apostrophe [a-pos'-tro-fi] n a mark (') indicating the possessive case or omission of certain letters.

appall [ap-pâl'] vb (**appalled', appal'ling**) to shock, to horrify.

appall'ing adj shocking, terrible, horrific.

apparatus [ap-pa-râ'-tês] n 1 tools or equipment for doing work. 2 organization, system.

apparent [ap-pâ'-rê nt or ap-pa'-rênt] adj 1 easily seen, evident. 2 seeming but not necessarily real.

appar'ently adv evidently, seemingly.

appari'tion n 1 someone or something that appears suddenly. 2 a ghost.

appeal' vb 1 to make an earnest and strong request for. 2 to carry (a law case) to a higher court. 3 to interest, to please:—also n.

appear' vb 1 to come into sight. 2 to seem:—n **appear'ance**.

appendici'tis n a painful disease of the appendix, usu requiring surgical removal.

appen'dix n (pl **appen'dixes** or **appen'dices**) 1 information added at the end of a book. 2 a short, closed tube leading off the bowels.

ap'petite n desire to have something, esp food or pleasure.

appetiz'ing adj increasing the desire for food.

applaud' vb to praise by clapping or shouting:—n **applause'**.

ap'ple n a round, firm, fleshy, edible fruit:—**apple of the eye** a person or object held very dear.

appli'ance n an instrument intended for some particular use.

ap'plicant n one who asks for, a person who applies for or makes a formal request for.

applica'tion n 1 the act of applying. 2 a formal request. 3 perseverance, hard work.

apply' vb 1 to put or spread on. 2 to use. 3 to pay attention (to), to concentrate. 4 to ask for, to put in a formal request for. 5 to concern or be relevant to.

appoint' vb 1 to choose for a job or position. 2 (fml) to fix or decide on.

appoint'ment n 1 a post or position. 2 a meeting arranged for a certain time.

appre′ciate *vb* 1 to recognize the value or good qualities of, to enjoy. 2 to understand fully, to recognize. 3 to be grateful for. 4 to rise in value.

apprecia′tion *n* 1 a good or just opinion of. 2 gratitude. 3 understanding. 4 increase in value.

appre′ciative *adj* 1 willing to understand and praise justly. 2 grateful:—*adv* **appre′ciatively.**

apprehend′ *vb* (*fml*) to arrest, to seize.

apprehen′sion *n* 1 (*fml*) fear, dread. 2 (*fml*) arrest, seizure. 3 (*fml*) understanding.

apprehen′sive *adj* afraid of what may happen, anxious.

apprent′ice *n* one who is learning a trade or skill while working at it:—*vb* to bind by agreement to serve as an apprentice.

approach′ *vb* 1 to move nearer (to). 2 to seek an opportunity to speak to someone:—*n* 1 act of approaching. 2 the way leading to a place.

approach′able *adj* 1 able to be approached. 2 easy to speak to.

appro′priate *vb* 1 to take and use as one's own. 2 to set apart for a particular purpose or use:—*adj* suitable:—*ns* **appro′priation, appro′priateness.**

approve′ *vb* 1 to think well of, to accept as good. 2 to agree to, to accept:—*n* **approv′al:—on approval** for a period of trial before purchase.

approx′imate *vb* to come near to:—*adj* nearly correct.

approx′imately *adv* nearly.

apricot [āp′-ri-kot] *n* an orange-yellow fruit of the peach family.

A′pril *n* the fourth month of the year.

a′pron *n* a garment or cloth worn in front to protect the clothes.

apt *adj* 1 suitable, appropriate. 2 ready to learn. 3 having a tendency to.

apt′ly *adv* fitly.

apt′itude *n* skill, cleverness.

apt′ness *n* suitability.

aquarium [a-kwē′-ri-um] *n* (*pl* **aquariums**) a tank for (live) fish and water animals and water plants.

aqua′tic *adj* 1 living or growing in water. 2 taking place in water.

ar′able *adj* fit for plowing.

ar′bitrate *vb* to act as an umpire or referee, esp in a dispute:—*n* **ar′bitrator.**

arbitra′tion *n* the settling of a dispute by an arbitrator.

arc *n* 1 a curve. 2 a part of the circumference of a circle.

arcade′ *n* 1 a covered walk. 2 a covered street containing stores.

arch *n* a curved structure, usu supporting a bridge or roof.

archeology [ar-kä-ol′-odj-i] *n* the study of the remains and monuments of ancient times:—*adj* **archeolog′ical:—** *n* **archeol′ogist.**

arch′er *n* one able to use a bow and arrow.

arch′ery *n* the art of shooting with bow and arrow.

architect [ar′-ki-tekt] *n* 1 one who plans buildings. 2 a person who plans, designs, or creates something.

architec′ture *n* 1 the art or science, planning, or designing buildings. 2 a special fashion in building:—*adj* **architec′tural.**

archives [ar′-kīvz] *npl* 1 historical records. 2 the place where they are kept:—*n* **archivist.**

arc′tic *adj* very cold.

ar′dent *adj* eager, enthusiastic, passionate:—*adv* **ar′dently.**

ar′duous *adj* difficult, requiring much effort.

ar′ea *n* 1 any open space, place, region. 2 a subject, topic, or activity. 3 the extent of a surface. 4 an enclosed court, esp a sunken one between a house and the street.

ar′gue *vb* 1 to give reasons for believing something to be true. 2 to discuss in an unfriendly or quarrelsome way. 3 to quarrel:—*adj* **ar′guable.**

ar′gument *n* 1 reasons for holding a belief. 2 a dispute, an unfriendly discussion. 3 a quarrel. 4 a summary of a book.

argumen′tative *adj* given to discussing or disputing.

arise′ *vb* (*pt* **arose′**, *pp* **aris′en**) 1 to come into being, to appear. 2 to result from. 3 (*old*) to get up.

aris′tocrat *n* a person of noble birth:—*adj* **aristocrat′ic.**

arith′metic *n* the science of numbers; the art of working with numbers:—*adj* **arithmet′ical.**

arm *n* 1 one of the upper limbs, the part of the body from the shoulder to the hand. 2 anything resembling this. 3 the part of a garment that covers the arm. 4 power. 5 *pl* **arms** weapons or armor used in fighting. 6 *pl* the badge of a noble family, town, etc:—*vb* **arm** 1 to take up weapons. 2 to provide with weapons.

ar′mor *n* 1 protective covering. 2 (*old*) a metal covering worn by soldiers to protect their bodies. 3 the tank force of an army.

ar′mory *n* a place for keeping arms.

arm′pit *n* the hollow under the shoulder, between the arm and the body.

arm′y *n* 1 a large number of soldiers organized for war. 2 a large number of persons engaged on a common task.

aro′ma *n* a pleasant smell.

aroma′tic *adj* sweet-smelling.

around′ *prep* 1 on all sides of or in a circle, about. 2 here and there, at several places. 3 approximately. 4 near to:—*adv* 1 on every side, here and there. 2 in the surrounding area. 3 available. 4 in the opposite direction.

arouse′ *vb* 1 to stir up. 2 to make awake or active.

arrange′ *vb* 1 to put into order. 2 to make plans, to make preparations for:—*n* **arrange′ment.**

arrest′ *vb* 1 to take as prisoner, esp in the name of the law. 2 (*fml*) to catch or attract. 3 to stop:—*n* 1 the act of stopping. 2 the act of arresting in the name of the law.

arriv′al *n* 1 the act of arriving. 2 one who arrives.

arrive′ *vb* 1 to come. 2 to reach.

ar′rogant *adj* proud, haughty:—*n* **ar′rogance.**

ar′row *n* a pointed stick or similar missile for shooting from a bow.

ar′son *n* the crime of setting fire to property on purpose.

art *n* 1 a particular ability or skill. 2 (*fml*) cunning, trickery. 3 the practice of painting, sculpture, architecture, etc. 4 examples of painting, sculpture, etc:—**the Arts** subjects of study that are intended to broaden the mind rather than (or as well as) to teach practical skill.

ar′tery *n* a tube carrying blood from the heart.

art′ful *adj* deceitful, cunning:—*adv* **art′fully.**

ar′tichoke *n* 1 (**globe artichoke**) a tall plant, somewhat like a thistle, part of the leaves of which can be eaten. 2 (**Jerusalem artichoke**) a type of sunflower with edible underground stems.

ar′ticle *n* 1 a thing. 2 an essay on a single topic in a newspaper, periodical, or encyclopedia. 3 a single item in a list or statement (e.g. a treaty). 4 *pl* a written agreement.

articulate [ar-tik′-û-lêt] *adj* 1 distinct, clear. 2 able to express oneself clearly:—*vb* [ar-tik′-û-lât] 1 to join together. 2 to speak distinctly.

artific′ial *adj* 1 man-made, so not natural. 2 not genuine, unnatural:—*n* **artificial′ity.**

artil′lery *n* 1 big guns. 2 the part of an army that cares for and fires such guns.

ar′tist *n* 1 a professional painter. 2 one skilled in some art. 3 an artiste.

artiste [ar-teest'] *n* a public entertainer.
artis'tic *adj* 1 having to do with art or artists. 2 having or showing love for what is beautiful.
ascend' *vb* (*fml*) 1 to go upwards. 2 to climb.
ascen'sion *n* act of rising.
ascent' *n* (*fml*) 1 act of going up. 2 an upward slope.
ash[1] *n* a tree.
ash[2] *n* or **ash'es** *npl* the dust left after anything has been burned.
ashamed' *adj* feeling shame.
ash'en *adj* grayish-white like ashes, very pale.
ashore' *adv* on or to land.
aside' *adv* 1 on one side. 2 to one side, apart.
ask *vb* 1 to request. 2 to inquire.
askew [as-kû'] *adv* to one side, crookedly.
asleep' *adj and adv* sleeping.
as'pect *n* 1 (*fml*) appearance. 2 the direction in which a building, etc, faces. 3 a particular part or feature of something.
asphyx'iate *vb* to choke, to suffocate:—*n* **asphyxia'tion**.
as'pirin *n* a drug that relieves pain.
ass [as] *n* 1 a donkey. 2 a foolish person.
assail'ant *n* an attacker.
assass'in *n* one who kills by surprise or secretly.
assass'inate *vb* to murder by surprise or treachery, often for political reasons:—*n* **assassina'tion**.
assault' *n* a sudden violent attack:—*vb* to attack.
assem'ble *vb* 1 to bring or put together. 2 to come together.
assem'bly *n* a gathering of people to discuss and take decisions.
assent' *vb* to agree.
assert' *vb* to state firmly:—**to assert oneself** to stand up for one's rights.
asser'tive *adj* confident, tending to assert oneself.
assess' *vb* 1 to fix an amount payable. 2 to estimate the value, worth, quality, etc, of:—*n* **assess'or**.
assess'ment *n* the amount or value fixed.
as'sets *npl* the entire property of a person or company:—**an asset** a help, an advantage.
assid'uous *adj* 1 steadily attentive, careful. 2 hard-working, diligent.
assign' *vb* 1 to give as a share, duty, task, etc. 2 to appoint. 3 to fix, to name.
assigna'tion *n* an appointment to meet, esp secretly.
assign'ment *n* the share or amount (of work, etc) given to a person or group.
assist' *vb* to help.
assis'tance *n* help, aid.
assis'tant *n* 1 a helper. 2 a person who serves in a store, etc.
associate [as-sô'-shee-ât] *vb* 1 to keep company with, to join with. 2 to join or connect in the mind:—*n* a companion, a partner, a colleague.
assort'ed *adj* mixed:—**ill-assorted** badly matched.
assort'ment *n* a mixed collection.
assuage [as-swâj'] *vb* to make less, to ease.
assume' *vb* 1 to take for granted. 2 to take over. 3 (*fml*) to put on, to pretend. 4 (*fml*) to take on, to begin to have.
assump'tion *n* 1 act of assuming. 2 something supposed, but not proved, to be true.
assur'ance *n* 1 confidence. 2 a promise. 3 a form of life insurance.
assure' *vb* 1 to make certain. 2 to tell as a sure fact, to state positively.
asthma [as'-ma or as'-thma] *n* a disease marked by difficulty in breathing:—*adj* **asthmat'ic**.
aston'ish *vb* to surprise greatly, to amaze:—*n* **aston'ishment**.
astound' *vb* to shock with surprise, to surprise greatly.
astray' *adv* out of the right way.

astride' *adv* with the legs apart or on each side of a thing.
astrol'ogy *n* the study of the stars in order to learn about future events:—*n* **astrol'oger**.
as'tronaut *n* a member of the crew of a spaceship.
astronom'ical *adj* 1 connected with astronomy. 2 very great.
astron'omy *n* the scientific study of the stars:—*n* **astron'omer**.
astute' *adj* clever, shrewd:—*n* **astute'ness**.
ate *pt of* **eat**.
ath'lete *n* one good at sports, esp outdoor sports.
athlet'ic *adj* 1 having to do with sport or athletics. 2 physically strong and active.
athlet'ics *npl* field sports (e.g. running, jumping, etc).
at'las *n* a book of maps.
at'mosphere *n* 1 the air surrounding the earth. 2 the gas surrounding any star. 3 the air in a particular place. 4 the feelings given rise to by an incident, story, etc, mood.
atmospher'ic *adj* 1 connected with the air. 2 creating a certain atmosphere.
attach' *vb* to join (by tying, sticking, etc).
attached' *adj* 1 joined on to. 2 fond of.
attach'ment *n* 1 something joined on. 2 fondness. 3 a file sent with an email.
attack' *vb* 1 to use force against, to begin to fight against. 2 to speak or act strongly against. 3 to begin to deal with vigorously, to tackle:—*also n*:—*n* **attack'er**.
attain' *vb* to reach.
attain'able *adj* able to be reached.
attempt' *vb* to try to do:—*n* an effort.
attend' *vb* 1 to be present at. 2 to take care of. 3 (*fml*) to fix the mind on. 4 to wait on.
attend'ance *n* 1 presence. 2 the persons present.
attend'ant *n* 1 one who waits on. 2 a servant.
atten'tion *n* 1 care. 2 heed, notice. 3 concentration.
atten'tive *adj* giving attention, paying heed.
at'tic *n* a room just under the roof of a house.
attire' *vb* to dress:—*n* dress.
at'titude *n* 1 position of the body. 2 way of thinking or behaving.
attract' *vb* 1 to cause to come nearer. 2 to cause to like or desire. 3 to arouse.
attrac'tion *n* 1 the act of attracting. 2 the power to attract. 3 something that attracts.
attrac'tive *adj* 1 having the power to attract, interesting, pleasing, etc. 2 good-looking, pretty, handsome.
attrib'ute *vb* 1 to think of as being caused by. 2 to regard as being made, written, etc, by:—*n* **at'tribute** a quality, characteristic.
attune' *vb* to make to agree, bring into harmony.
au'burn *adj* reddish-brown.
auc'tion *n* a public sale at which an object is sold to the person offering the highest price.
auctioneer' *n* the person who conducts the sale at an auction.
auda'cious *adj* 1 bold, daring. 2 bold, shameless:—*n* **audac'ity**.
aud'ible *adj* able to be heard:—*n* **audibil'ity**.
aud'ience *n* 1 the people who listen (e.g. to a speech, concert, etc). 2 an interview granted by a ruler or person of high authority.
audi'tion *n* a test given to an actor or singer to see how good he or she is.
augment' *vb* to increase:—*n* **augmenta'tion**.
Au'gust *n* the eighth month of the year.
aunt [änt] *n* the sister of one's mother or father.
au'ral *adj* having to do with the ear or hearing.
austere' *adj* 1 simple and severe. 2 stern. 3 plain, without decoration:—*n* **auster'ity**.

authen'tic *adj* true, genuine:—*n* **authentic'ity**.

authen'ticate *vb* to show the authenticity of, to prove genuine.

auth'or *n* **1** a writer of books, etc. **2** (*fml*) a person who creates or begins something:—*n* **auth'orship**.

author'itative *adj* **1** having or showing power. **2** reliable, providing trustworthy information.

author'ity *n* **1** the power or right to rule or give orders. **2** a person or group of persons having this power or right.

auth'orize *vb* to give to another the right or power to do something.

auto *abbr* an automobile.

auto- *prefix* self.

autobiog'raphy *n* the story of a person's life written by himself or herself:—*adj* **autobiog'raphical**.

aut'ograph *n* a person's own handwriting or signature.

automat'ic *adj* **1** working by itself. **2** done without thought:—*adv* **automat'ically**.

aut'omobile *n* a usu four-wheeled vehicle powered by an internal combustion engine.

autop'sy *n* an examination of a dead body to discover the cause of death.

au'tumn *n* **1** fall, one of the four seasons of the year, between summer and winter. **2** a stage of life resembling this.

autum'nal *adj* having to do with autumn.

auxil'iary *n* a person or thing that helps:—*also adj*.

avail'able *adj* at hand if wanted.

av'alanche [av'-al-änsh] *n* **1** a great mass of snow, earth, and ice sliding down a mountain. **2** a great amount.

av'arice *n* greed for gain and riches:—*adj* **avaric'ious**.

avenge' *vb* to take revenge for a wrong:—*n* **aven'ger**.

av'enue *n* **1** a way of approach. **2** a broad street. **3** a double row of trees, with or without a road between them.

av'erage *n* the figure found by dividing the total of a set of numbers by the number of numbers in the set:—*adj* **1** calculated by finding the average of various amounts, etc. **2** ordinary:—*vb* to find the average.

averse' *adj* not in favor of.

aver'sion *n* **1** dislike. **2** something disliked.

aviary [ā'-vi-ér i] *n* a place for keeping birds.

avia'tion *n* the science of flying aircraft.

av'id *adj* eager, keen:—*n* **avid'ity**.

avoid' *vb* to keep away from:—*adj* **avoid'able**:—*n* **avoid'ance**.

await' *vb* (*fml*) to wait for.

awake' *vb* (*pt* **awoke'**, *pp* **awok'en**) **1** (*fml*) to rouse from sleep. **2** (*fml*) to stop sleeping. **3** to stir up, to rouse:—*adj* **1** not sleeping. **2** aware of, conscious of.

awak'en *vb* **1** to awake. **2** to rouse.

award' *vb* to give after judgment or examination:—*n* what is awarded, a prize.

aware' *adj* **1** having knowledge of, interested, concerned. **2** conscious of.

awe *n* fear mixed with respect or wonder.

aw'ful *adj* **1** very bad or unpleasant, terrible. **2** (*inf*) very great. **3** (*old or lit*) causing awe.

aw'fully *adv* (*inf*) very.

awk'ward *adj* **1** clumsy, unskilled. **2** difficult to use or deal with. **3** inconvenient:—*adv* **awk'wardly**.

awn'ing *n* a covering, usu of canvas, to provide shelter from sun or rain.

ax *n* (*pl* **ax'es**) a tool for hewing or chopping.

ax'is *n* (*pl* **ax'es**) the straight line, real or imaginary, on which a body turns.

azure [ā'-zhèr] *adj* sky-blue:—*n* **1** a bright blue color. **2** the sky.

B

bab′ble vb **1** to make indistinct sounds. **2** to chatter continuously and without making much sense. **3** to make a sound, as of running water:—n **1** indistinct sounds. **2** foolish chatter. **3** murmur, as of a stream.

ba′bel n **1** (with cap) in the Bible, the tower in Shinar (Genesis 11). **2** a confused noise.

baboon′ n a type of large monkey.

ba′by n **1** a newborn child or infant. **2** a very young animal. **3** (inf) a girl or young woman. **4** a personal project.

baby carriage n a four-wheeled carriage for a baby.

ba′chelor n **1** an unmarried man. **2** on who has passed certain college examinations.

bacillus [ba-sil′ēs] n (pl **bacilli** [ba-sil′-ī]) a type of bacterium causing disease.

back n part of the body, that which is behind:—also adj and adv:—vb **1** to go or move backwards. **2** to support:—n **back′er**.

back′bone n **1** the spine. **2** firmness. **3** the chief support.

back′gammon n an indoor game played with draftsmen and dice.

back′ground n **1** the area behind the principal persons in a picture, scene, or conversation. **2** a series of events connected with or leading up to something. **3** a person's origins, upbringing, education, etc.

back′ward adj **1** toward the back. **2** less advanced in mind or body than is normal for one's age. **3** behind others in progress. **4** shy, reserved:—adv (also **back′wards**) **1** toward the back. **2** with the back foremost. **3** in a way opposite the usual. **4** into a less good or favorable state or condition. **5** into the past:—n **back′wardness**.

bac′on n pig's flesh, salted and dried.

bacteria [bak-tee′-ri-a] npl (sing **bacte′rium**) very tiny living things that are often the cause of disease.

badge n something worn as a sign of membership, office, rank, etc.

bad′ger n a night animal that lives in a burrow:—vb to worry, to pester.

bad′minton n a game like tennis played with shuttlecocks as balls.

baf′fle vb **1** to puzzle, to bewilder. **2** to make someone's efforts useless:—n **baf′flement**.

bag n **1** a container. **2** the number of birds or animals shot on one outing:—vb (**bagged′, bag′ging**) **1** to put into a bag. **2** (inf) to take possession of. **3** to catch or kill. **4** to hang loosely, to bulge.

bag′gage n luggage.

bag′gy adj **1** loose. **2** out of shape.

bag′pipes npl a musical wind instrument in which a bag serves as bellows.

bail[1] n **1** one ready to pay a sum of money to obtain freedom for a person charged with a crime until the day of his or her trial. **2** the sum so charged, which is lost if the person does not appear for trial:—also vb.

bail[2] see **bale**[2].

bait n **1** food to trap or attract animals or fish. **2** a temptation:—vb **1** to put bait on a hook or in a trap. **2** to torment.

bake vb **1** to dry and harden by fire. **2** to cook in an oven.

bak′er n one who makes or sells bread.

bak′ery n a place where bread is made.

bal′ance n **1** a pair of weighing scales. **2** equality of weight, power, etc. **3** a state of physical steadiness. **4** a state of mental or emotional steadiness. **5** the difference between the amount of money possessed and the amount owed:—vb **1** to make equal. **2** to keep steady or upright. **3** to add up two

sides of an account to show the difference between them:—**in the balance** doubtful; about to be decided.

bal′cony n **1** a railed platform outside a window or along the wall of a building. **2** an upper floor in a hall or theatre.

bald adj **1** without hair. **2** bare, without the usual or required covering. **3** plain:—n **bald′ness**.

bale[1] n a large bundle or package.

bale[2], **bail** vb to throw water out of a boat, a little at a time.

balk [bäk] vb **1** to stop short of, to be reluctant or unwilling to be involved in. **2** to prevent.

ball[1] n **1** anything round in shape. **2** a round or roundish object used in games. **3** a rounded part of something.

ball[2] n a party held for the purpose of dancing:—n **ball′room**.

bal′lad n **1** a simple poem relating a popular incident. **2** a short, romantic song.

ballerina n a female ballet dancer.

ballet [bal′-ā] n a performance in which dancing, actions, and music are combined to tell a story.

balloon′ n **1** a small brightly colored rubber bag that can be blown up and used as a toy or as a decoration at parties, etc. **2** originally, a large bag of light material that floats in the air when filled with air or light gas, often equipped with a basket for carrying passengers. **3** a balloon-shaped line enclosing speech or thoughts in a strip cartoon:—vb **1** to inflate. **2** to swell, expand. **3** to travel in a balloon.

bal′lot n a way of voting secretly by putting marked cards into a box:—also vb.

balm [bäm] n something that heals or soothes.

bal′uster n any of the small posts of a railing, as on a staircase.

bal′ustrade n a row of balusters joined by a rail.

bamboo′ n a giant tropical reed from which canes, etc, are made.

ban n an order forbidding something:—vb (**banned′, ban′ning**) to forbid.

band[1] n **1** anything used to bind or tie together. **2** a strip of cloth around anything.

band[2] n a group of persons united for a purpose, esp to play music together:—vb to join (together).

ban′dage n a strip of cloth used in dressing a wound or injury:—also vb.

ban′dit n an outlaw, a robber.

ban′dy, ban′dy-legged adjs having legs curving outwards.

bang n **1** a sudden loud noise. **2** a blow or knock. **3** pl hair cut straight cross the forehead to form a fringe:—vb **1** to close with a bang. **2** to hit or strike violently, often making a loud noise. **3** to make a sudden loud noise.

ban′gle n a ring worn on the wrist or ankle.

ban′ish vb **1** to order to leave the country. **2** to drive away:—n **ban′ishment**.

ban′ister n a post or row of posts supporting a rail at the side of a staircase.

bank n **1** a ridge or mound of earth, etc. **2** the ground at the side of a river, lake, etc. **3** a place where money is put for safekeeping:—vb **1** to heap up. **2** to cover a fire with small coal to make it burn slowly. **3** to put money in a bank.

bank′rupt n one who is unable to pay his or her debts:—also adj:—n **bank′ruptcy**.

ban′ner n a flag.

ban′quet n a feast.

bapt′ism n **1** the ceremony by which one is received into the Christian Church. **2** a first experience of something, an initiation:—adj **baptis′mal**.

17

baptize' *vb* **1** to dip in or sprinkle with water as a sign of being received as a Christian. **2** to christen or give a name to.

bar *n* **1** a solid piece of wood, metal, etc, that is longer than it is wide. **2** a length of wood or metal across a door or window to keep it shut or prevent entrance through it. **3** an obstacle. **4** the bank of sand, etc, at the mouth of a river that hinders entrance. **5** a counter at which food or drink may be bought and consumed. **6** a counter at which alcoholic drinks are served. **7** a place where alcoholic drinks are sold. **8** the rail behind which a prisoner stands in a court of law. **9** all the lawyers in a court. **10** (*with cap*) lawyers collectively, the legal profession. **11** a division in music:—*vb* (**barred', bar'ring**) **1** to fasten with a bar or belt. **2** to hinder or prevent. **3** to forbid, to ban:—*prep* except.

barbar'ian *n* an uncivilized person.

bar'becue *n* **1** a framework on which meat, etc, may be cooked over a charcoal fire, usu outside. **2** a large outdoor party where food is cooked on a barbecue:—*vb* to cook on a barbecue.

bar'ber *n* a man's hairdresser.

bare *adj* **1** uncovered. **2** empty. **3** naked:—*vb* to uncover, to expose.

bare'back *adj, adv* without a saddle.

bare'faced *adj* shameless.

bare'ly *adv* **1** only just. **2** scarcely.

bar'gain *n* **1** an agreement about buying and selling. **2** an agreement. **3** something bought cheaply:—*vb* **1** to argue about the price before paying. **2** to make an agreement:—**into the bargain** in addition.

barge *n* a flat-bottomed boat for carrying cargoes on inland waters:—*vb* to move clumsily and often rudely.

bar'itone *n* a male singing voice that can go neither very high nor very low.

bark¹ *n* the outer covering of a tree:—*vb* to scrape the skin off.

bark² *n* the noise made by a dog, wolf, etc:—*also vb.*

bar'ley *n* a grain used for making malt.

barn *n* a farm building for the storage of grain, hay, etc.

baro'meter *n* **1** an instrument for measuring air pressure, thus showing what the weather may be. **2** something that indicates change.

bar'on *n* **1** a British nobleman of the lowest rank. **2** a powerful businessman.

bar'rack *n* (*usu pl*) a building for housing soldiers:—*vb* to shout insults to.

bar'rel *n* **1** a round wooden cask or container with flat ends and curved sides. **2** the tube of a gun.

bar'ren *adj* **1** producing no fruit or seed. **2** (*old*) unable to produce young, infertile. **3** unable to produce crops. **4** useless, not productive:—*n* **bar'renness**.

bar'ricade *n* a barrier, often temporary and quickly constructed, to prevent people passing or entering:—*also vb.*

bar'rier *n* **1** a kind of fence put up to control or restrain. **2** an obstacle. **3** something that separates or keeps people apart.

bar'row *n* a small hand-cart.

bar'ter *n* trade by exchange of goods instead of money payments:—*vb* to trade by barter, to exchange.

base¹ *n* **1** that on which a thing stands or is built up. **2** the place in which a fleet or army keeps its main stores and offices. **3** a fixed point in certain games:—*vb* **1** to use as a foundation. **2** to establish, to place.

base² *adj* low, worthless, vile:—*adv* **base'ly**.

base'ball *n* a game played with bat and ball.

base'less *adj* without foundation, groundless.

base'line *n* **1** the line at each end of a games court marking the line of play. **2** (*baseball*) the line between two consecutive bases. **3** a measured line in a survey.

base'man (*pl* **base'men**) *n* (*baseball*) a fielder placed at the first, second, and third bases respectively.

base'ment *n* the part of a building that is below ground level.

bash'ful *adj* modest, shy.

bas'ic *adj* **1** providing a foundation or beginning. **2** without more than is necessary, simple, plain.

bas'in *n* **1** a deep broad dish. **2** a hollow place containing water. **3** a dock. **4** the land drained by a river.

bas'is *n* (*pl* **bas'es**) that on which a thing is built up, the foundation or beginning.

bask *vb* **1** to lie in the sun. **2** to enjoy.

bas'ket *n* a container made of thin sticks or coarse grass plaited together.

bass¹ [bās] *n* **1** the lowest part in music. **2** the lowest male voice.

bass² *n* a type of fish.

bassoon' *n* a musical wind instrument, with low notes only.

bat¹ *n* a piece of wood prepared for striking a ball in certain games:—*vb* (**bat'ting, bat'ted**) to use the bat for striking the ball.

bat² *n* a flying creature with a body like a mouse and large wings.

batch *n* **1** a quantity of bread, etc, baked at one time. **2** a set or group.

bath *n* **1** act of washing the body. **2** a bathtub. **3** a large tank in which one can swim:—*vb* to wash the body in a bathtub.

bathe *vb* **1** to apply water to in order to clean. **2** to go for a swim:—*n* act of swimming or playing in water:—*n* **bath'er**.

bath'robe *n* a loose garment worn over night clothes or underclothes, a dressing gown.

bath'tub *n* a large vessel in which the body is washed.

bat'on *n* **1** a short stick used by the conductor of a band or choir. **2** a short club carried by police officers as a weapon. **3** a stick passed by one member of a team of runners to the next runner in a relay race.

batsman see **bat**.

battal'ion *n* a body of infantry, about 1000 strong.

bat'ter¹ *vb* to beat with violence:—*n* a paste of flour and liquid mixed together for cooking.

bat'ter² *n* (*baseball, etc*) a player who bats.

bat'tery *n* **1** a group of guns and the people who serve them. **2** a number of connected cells for providing or storing electric current. **3** a violent attack.

bat'tle *n* **1** a fight between armies, fleets, etc. **2** a struggle:—*vb* to fight or struggle.

bat'tlement *n* the top wall of a castle, with openings through which weapons can be aimed.

bawl *vb* to shout or cry loudly:—*also n.*

bay¹ *n* **1** an inlet of the sea. **2** a recess in a wall.

bay² *n* the laurel tree.

bay³ *n* the bark of a dog, the low cry of a hunting dog:—**to stand at bay** to stop running away and turn to defend oneself:—**to keep at bay** to keep at a safe distance:—*vb* to give the bark or cry of a dog.

bay'onet *n* a dagger-like weapon for fixing on to a rifle:—*vb* to stab with a bayonet.

bazaar' *n* **1** in the East, a marketplace or group of stores. **2** a sale of articles held to raise money for a special purpose.

beach' *n* the shore of a sea or lake:—*vb* to run or pull (a vessel) on to a beach.

bea'con *n* **1** a signal fire. **2** a hill on which a beacon could be lighted. **3** a signal of danger.

bead *n* **1** a small object, usu round, of glass or other material, with a hole through it for a string. **2** a drop or bubble. **3** *pl* a rosary.

beak *n* the bill of a bird.

beak'er *n* **1** a large drinking cup. **2** a glass vessel used in scientific experiments.

beam n 1 a thick piece of wood. 2 a main timber in a building. 3 the greatest breadth of a ship. 4 a ray of light. 5 radio waves sent out in one particular direction, as a ray:—vb to smile brightly.

bean n a plant whose seed or seed pod is eaten as a vegetable.

bear[1] vb (pt **bore**, pp **borne**) 1 (fml) to carry. 2 to put up with. 3 to support. 4 to have or show. 5 to move. 6 (pp **born**) to bring into existence. 7 (pp **borne**) to produce.

bear[2] n a wild animal with long hair and claws.

beard [beerd] n the hair on the chin and lower jaw:—vb to defy openly.

bear'er n a carrier.

bear'ing n 1 the way a person holds himself or herself or behaves. 2 direction. 3 connection, influence. 4 usu pl one's position, orientation. 5 a device on a heraldic shield.

beast n 1 a four-footed animal. 2 a person who behaves in an animal-like way, a hateful person:—adj **beast'ly:**— n **beast'liness**.

beat vb (pt **beat**, pp **beat'en**) 1 to strike several times. 2 to defeat or win against. 3 to throb:—n 1 a repeated stroke. 2 a police officer's round. 3 a regular rhythm (e.g the pulse, a drum).

beauty [bû´-ti] n 1 that which is pleasing to the senses. 2 a beautiful woman. 3 (inf) a very fine specimen. 4 (inf) advantage:—adj **beau'tiful**.

beav'er n 1 an animal that can live both on land and in water. 2 the fur of the beaver.

beck'on vb to make a sign inviting a person to approach.

become vb (pt **became'**, pp **become'**) 1 to come to be. 2 to suit.

becom'ing adj 1 (fml) fitting, suitable, appropriate. 2 suiting the wearer.

bed n 1 a thing to sleep or rest on. 2 the channel of a river. 3 a piece of ground prepared for growing flowers, plants, etc.

bedclothes npl, **bed'ding** n covers on a bed.

bed'lam n a scene of noisy uproar and confusion.

bedrag'gled adj wet and dirty, muddy.

bed'ridden adj having to stay permanently in bed.

bed'room n a room for sleeping in.

bee n a flying, honey-making insect.

beech n a type of tree:—n **beech'nut**.

beef n the flesh of an ox or cow.

bee'hive n a place where bees are kept, often dome-shaped.

bee'line n the shortest way:—**make a beeline for** to go directly and quickly toward.

beer n a drink made from barley and hops.

beet n a plant with a root eaten as a vegetable (also **sugar beet**).

bee'tle n a common insect:—vb (inf) to hurry, to scurry.

befriend' vb to act as a friend to, to be kind to.

beg vb (**begged**, **beg'ging**) 1 to ask for money. 2 to ask earnestly:—**beg the question** to take a fact for granted without proving its truth.

beg'gar n one who asks for money or food.

begin' vb (pt **began'**, pp **begun'**, prp **begin'ning**) 1 to start. 2 to be the first to do or take the first step in doing.

begin'ner n one starting to learn.

begrudge' vb 1 to give unwillingly. 2 to envy someone the possession of.

behalf' n:—**on behalf of** in the name of.

behave' vb 1 to conduct oneself. 2 to conduct oneself well. 3 to act.

behav'ior n conduct.

behead' vb to cut off the head.

belat'ed adj too late.

belay' vb on ships, to secure a rope by winding it around something.

belch vb to send out forcefully, esp wind through the mouth.

bel'fry n a bell tower.

belief' n 1 faith. 2 trust. 3 opinion.

believe' vb 1 to accept as true or real. 2 to trust. 3 to have faith, esp in God. 4 to think:—adj **believ'able**.

belit'tle vb to make to seem small or unimportant.

bell n a hollow metal vessel that gives a ringing sound when struck.

belligerent [bel-li'-jė-rėnt] adj 1 angry and ready to fight or quarrel. 2 (fml) taking part in war:—n a nation or person taking part in war.

bel'low vb 1 to shout loudly. 2 to roar:—also n.

bel'lows npl an instrument that makes a draft of air by forcing wind out of an airtight compartment.

bel'ly n the part of the human body between the breast and thighs.

belong' vb 1 to be the property (of). 2 to be a member. 3 to be connected with.

belong'ings npl the things that are one's own property.

beloved [bė-luv'-ė d or bė-luvd'] adj greatly loved:—n one who is greatly loved.

belt n 1 a strap or band for putting around the waist. 2 a leather band used to carry the motion of one wheel on to another in a piece of machinery. 3 a space that is much longer than it is broad. 4 an area that has a particular quality or characteristic. 5 (inf) an act of hitting, a blow:—vb 1 to put on a belt. 2 to hit with a strap. 3 to hit, to attack with blows:—**below the belt** 1 below the waistline. 2 unfair.

bench n 1 a long seat. 2 a work table. 3 the seat of a judge in court. 4 judges as a body.

bend vb (pt, pp **bent**) 1 to curve. 2 to make to curve. 3 to incline the body. 4 (fml) to direct:—n 1 a curving turn on a road. 2 an angle.

benefac'tor n one who gives help to another:—f **bene-fac'tress**.

beneficial [be-nė-fish'-ėl] adj helpful, having a good effect.

ben'efit n 1 advantage, gain. 2 reward:—vb 1 to do good to. 2 to be of advantage to.

bene'volent adj kindly, generous.

benign [bė-nin'] adj 1 kindly, gentle. 2 not malignant, not cancerous:—adv **benign'ly**.

bent[1] pt, pp of **bend**.

bent[2] n a natural skill in or liking for.

benzene [ben'-zeen] n a colorless liquid obtained from coal tar.

benzine [ben'-zeen] n a type of gasoline.

bequeath' vb to leave by will.

bequest' n the money or property left by will, a legacy.

bereaved adj having lost by death a near relative:—n one who has lost a relative by death.

beret [be'-rā] n a round flat cap with no peak or brim.

ber'ry n a small fruit containing seeds.

ber'serk adj 1 uncontrollably angry. 2 behaving in a frenzied, violent manner.

berth n 1 the place where a ship lies when at anchor or in dock. 2 a place for sleeping in a ship or train:—vb to moor a ship:—**give a wide berth to** keep well clear of.

besiege' vb 1 to surround a fortress with soldiers in order to bring about its capture. 2 to surround, to crowd around. 3 to overwhelm:—n **besieg'er**.

best adj (superl of **good**) good in the utmost degree:—vb to do better than, to win against.

bestow' vb (fml) to give (to).

bet n money put down in support of an opinion, to be either lost or returned with interest, a wager:—vb (**betting, bet**) to stake money in a bet.

betray' vb 1 to give up to an enemy. 2 to be false to, to, to a traitor to. 3 to reveal, to show:—n **betray'er.**

between prep 1 the space, time, etc, separating (two things). 2 connecting from one to the other.

betwixt' prep between.

bev'erage n a drink.

beware' vb to be cautious or careful of.

bewil'der vb to puzzle, to confuse:—adj **bewil'dering:**—n **bewil'derment.**

bewitch' vb 1 to put under a spell. 2 to charm, to fascinate:—n **bewitch'ment.**

beyond' prep on the farther side of:—adv at a distance.

bias [bī'-ês] n 1 the greater weight on one side of a bowl that causes it to roll off the straight. 2 an unreasonable dislike. 3 a preference. 4 in dressmaking, a line across the weave of a fabric:—vb to incline to one side, to prejudice.

bi'ased adj prejudiced.

bib n a cloth tied under a child's chin to keep him or her clean while eating.

Bib'le n the holy Scriptures of the Christian religion:—adj **bib'lical.**

bicentenary [bī-sen-tee'-nê-ri] n the two hundredth year (after a certain event).

biceps [bī'-seps] n a muscle in the upper part of the arm.

bick'er vb to quarrel frequently over unimportant things.

bi'cycle n a machine with two wheels that can be ridden on:—also vb.

bid vb (pt **bid** or **bade**, pp **bid'den** or **bid**, prp **bid'ding**) 1 to offer. 2 to ask, to order:—n 1 an offer of money, esp at a sale. 2 a strong effort.

bid'dable adj obedient.

bid'der n one offering a price.

biennial [bī-en'-ni-êl] adj 1 lasting for two years. 2 happening every second year:—n a plant that flowers only in its second year, then dies:—adv **bien'nially.**

big'amy n the state of having two wives or two husbands at the same time:—n **big'amist**:—adj **big'amous.**

bight n a bay.

big'ot n one who accepts without question certain beliefs and condemns the different beliefs held by others:—adj **big'oted**:—n **big'otry.**

bilingual [bī-ling'-gwêl] adj able to speak two languages.

bill[1] n 1 (old) a battle-ax with a long handle. 2 a tool for pruning. 3 the beak of a bird.

bill[2] n 1 the form of a proposed law, as put before parliament for discussion. 2 a piece of paper money. 3 a statement of money owed for things bought. 4 a printed notice:—vb to advertise by bills.

bill'board n a large panel designed to carry outdoor advertising, a hoarding.

billiards [bil'-yardz] n a game, played on a cloth-covered table, with cues and balls.

bil'lion n one thousand millions.

bil'low n a great wave of the sea:—vb to swell out:—adj **bil'lowy.**

bil'ly-goat' n a male goat.

bin n 1 a large box for corn, meal, etc. 2 a container for rubbish.

bind vb (pt, pp **bound**) 1 to tie. 2 to fasten together. 3 to cover (a book). 4 to put an edging on. 5 (fml) to put under an obligation:—**bind oneself** to promise.

binoc'ulars npl a pair of short telescopes fitted together for outdoor use.

biog'raphy n the written life story of a person:—adj **biograph'ical.**

bio'logy n the study of life and living creatures:—adj **biolog'ical**:—n **bio'logist.**

birch n 1 a tree. 2 a bundle of sticks tied together at one end and used for flogging:—vb to flog with a birch.

bird n a creature with feathers and wings that usu flies.

birth n 1 the act of being born. 2 the beginning.

birth'day n the day on which one is born, or its anniversary.

birth'mark n a mark on the body from birth.

birth'right n any right one possesses by birth.

bis'cuit n a dry bread made into flat, crisp cakes.

bisect' vb (fml) to cut into two equal parts.

bish'op n in some churches, the chief clergyman of a district.

bis'muth n a reddish-white metal.

bison [bī'-sên] n a type of wild ox.

bit n 1 a small piece. 2 a piece of. 3 part. 4 a tool for boring holes. 5 the metal bar attached to the bridle and put in the mouth of a horse.

bite vb (pt **bit**, pp **bit'ten**) 1 to cut, pierce, etc, with the teeth. 2 to take the bait:—n 1 the amount bitten off. 2 the wound made by biting. 3 a taking of bait by fish.

bit'ter adj 1 sharp to the taste. 2 severe, piercing. 3 painful. 4 feeling or showing hatred, hostility, envy, disappointment, etc:—adv **bit'terly**:—n **bit'terness.**

biweek'ly adj 1 happening once every two weeks. 2 twice in one week.

bizarre [bi-zär'] adj strange, peculiar, weird.

black n 1 a dark color like coal. 2 a member of one of the dark-skinned races of people:—also adj:—n 1 to make black. 2 to clean with black polish. 3 to impose a ban on, to refuse to handle:—n **black'ness.**

black'bird n a type of thrush.

black'board n a dark-colored board used for writing on with a light-colored chalk.

blackguard [bla'-gärd] n a rascal, a very bad person.

black'mail vb to obtain money by threatening to reveal a secret:—also n:—n **black'mailer.**

black'smith n a metal-worker who works with iron.

blad'der n a bag-like part of the body in which urine collects.

blade n 1 a leaf (of grass, corn, etc). 2 the cutting part of a sword or knife. 3 the flat part of an oar.

blame vb 1 to find fault with. 2 to regard as guilty or responsible:—n 1 fault. 2 guilt:—adjs **blame'less, blame'worthy.**

bland adj 1 so mild as to be almost tasteless. 2 so mild or gentle as to be without personality or emotion.

blank adj 1 not written or marked. 2 empty, without expression:—n an empty space.

blank verse n poetry with no rhymes.

blan'ket n 1 a woolen, etc, covering for a bed. 2 a covering.

blare vb to make a loud sound:—also n.

blaspheme [blas-feem'] vb 1 to speak mockingly or disrespectfully of God. 2 to swear or curse:—ns **blasphem'er, blas'phemy**:—adj **blas'phemous.**

blast n 1 a sudden, strong gust of wind. 2 a loud sound. 3 an explosion:—vb 1 to blow up or break up by explosion. 2 to make a loud noise. 3 (old or lit) to cause to wither. 4 to ruin. 5 (inf) to criticize severely.

blatant [blā'-tênt] adj very obvious.

blaze n 1 a bright fire or flame. 2 a bright glow of light or color. 3 a large, often dangerous, fire. 4 an outburst:—vb 1 to burn brightly. 2 to shine like a flame.

blaz'er n a kind of jacket.

bleach vb 1 to make white or whiter. 2 to become white:—n a substance that bleaches.

bleak *adj* 1 dreary, cold. 2 not hopeful or encouraging:— *n* **bleak'ness**.

blear'y-eyed *adj* with eyes unable to see properly.

bleat *vb* to cry, as a sheep:—*also n*.

bleed *vb* (*pt, pp* **bled**) to lose blood.

blem'ish *n* a stain, a fault.

blend *vb* to mix together:—*n* a mixture.

bless *vb* 1 to pronounce holy. 2 to ask God's favor for.

bless'ing *n* 1 a thing that brings happiness. 2 a prayer.

blight *n* 1 a disease in plants that causes them to wither. 2 a cause of ruin:—*vb* 1 to cause to wither. 2 to ruin.

blind *adj* 1 having no sight. 2 unable or unwilling to understand. 3 closed at one end:—*n* 1 window shade. 2 (*inf*) a pretense:—*vb* 1 to make blind. 2 to dazzle:—*adv* **blind'ly**:— *n* **blind'ness**.

blind'fold *vb* to cover the eyes with a bandage:—*also adj*.

blink *vb* 1 to wink. 2 to twinkle:—*n* 1 a glimpse. 2 a quick gleam of light.

bliss *n* great happiness.

bliss'ful *adj* very happy.

blis'ter *n* a bag of skin containing watery matter:—*vb* to raise a blister.

bliz'zard *n* a violent storm of wind and snow.

block *n* 1 a solid piece of wood, stone, etc. 2 the piece of wood on which people were beheaded. 3 a group of connected buildings. 4 a piece of wood in which a pulley is placed. 5 an obstacle:—*vb* to stop the way.

blond *adj* having fair hair and skin:—*f* **blonde**:—*also ns*.

blood *n* the red liquid in the bodies of people and animals. 2 family or race.

blood'shed *n* the spilling of blood, slaughter.

blood'shot *adj* (*of the eye*) red and inflamed with blood.

blood'thirsty *adj* eager to shed blood, taking pleasure in killing.

blood vessel *n* a vein or artery.

blood'y *adj* 1 bleeding, covered with blood. 2 stained with blood. 3 with much death or killing.

bloom *n* 1 a blossom, a flower. 2 the state of flowering. 3 freshness, perfection:—*vb* to blossom.

blot *n* 1 a spot or stain, often of ink. 2 disgrace. 3 something that spoils something beautiful or good.

blouse *n* a loose upper garment.

blow[1] *vb* (*pt* **blew**, *pp* **blown**) 1 to cause air to move. 2 to breathe hard (at or into). 3 to pant:—*vb* **blow up** to destroy by explosives.

blow[2] *n* 1 a stroke. 2 a misfortune.

blue *n* a primary color, as that of the sky on a clear day.

blue'print *n* 1 a photographic print of a plan for a structure. 2 a detailed plan or scheme.

bluff *n* 1 a cliff, a steep headland. 2 a pretense:—*adj* frank and abrupt but good-natured:—*vb* to try to deceive by a show of boldness.

blun'der *vb* 1 to make a foolish mistake. 2 to stumble about or into something:—*also n*.

blunt *adj* 1 not sharp. 2 short and plain in speech. 3 outspoken:—*vb* 1 to make less sharp. 2 to weaken.

blur *n* 1 an indistinct mass. 2 a stain, a blot, a smear:—*vb* (**blurred'**, **blur'ring**) to make unclear.

blurt *vb* to speak suddenly or thoughtlessly.

blush *vb* to become red in the face from shame, modesty, etc:—*n* the reddening of the face so caused:—*adv* **blush'ingly**.

blus'ter *vb* 1 (*of wind*) to blow violently. 2 to talk boastfully, noisily, or threateningly:—*n* boastful, noisy, or threatening talk.

bo'a *n* 1 a snake that kills by crushing its victim. 2 a scarf of fur or feathers.

boar *n* 1 a male pig. 2 a wild pig.

board *n* 1 a long, broad strip of timber. 2 food. 3 persons who meet at a council table. 4 the deck of a ship. 5 *pl* the stage. 6 a flat surface, often marked with a pattern, on which certain games are played:—*vb* 1 to cover with boards. 2 to supply with food and accommodation. 3 to take meals, and usu have accommodation, in. 4 to enter a ship. 5 to get on to.

board'er *n* one who receives board and lodging at an agreed price.

board'ing house *n* a house where board and lodging may be obtained.

board'ing school *n* a school in which pupils live as boarders.

boast *vb* 1 to speak with too much pride about oneself or one's belongings, etc. 2 to possess (something to be proud of):—*n* proud speech; a proud claim.

boat *n* a ship, esp a small one:—*vb* to go in a boat.

bob *vb* (**bobbed'**, **bob'bing**) 1 to move up and down quickly. 2 to cut short:—*also n*.

bod'ice *n* 1 a woman's tight-fitting, sleeveless garment worn on the upper body. 2 the upper part of a woman's dress.

bod'ily *adj* having to do with the body:—*adv* by taking hold of the body.

bod'kin *n* 1 a needle-like instrument for piercing holes. 2 a blunt needle with a large eye for threading tape through a hem.

bod'y *n* 1 the physical structure of a human being or animal. 2 the main part of anything. 3 a group of persons. 4 a dead body, a corpse.

bod'yguard *n* a guard to protect a person from attack.

bog *n* soft, wet ground, a marsh.

bog'us *adj* not genuine, sham.

boil[1] *vb* 1 to bubble from the action of heat. 2 to cook in boiling water:—*n* **boil'er**.

boil[2] *n* a painful swelling containing poisonous matter.

bois'terous *adj* 1 stormy. 2 noisy and cheerful.

bold *adj* 1 daring, brave. 2 large and clear.

bolt *n* 1 an arrow. 2 a thunderbolt. 3 a bar of a door:—*vb* 1 to fasten with a bolt. 2 to run away. 3 to eat too quickly.

bomb *n* a hollow metal missile containing high explosive, gas, etc:—*vb* 1 to attack with bombs. 2 to fail.

bombard' *vb* 1 to fire many guns at. 2 to direct many questions, statements of criticism, etc, at:—*n* **bombard'ment**.

bond *n* 1 that which binds. 2 a written agreement, esp to pay money. 3 a government store in which goods are kept until the taxes on them are paid. 4 (*fml*) *pl* chains, fetters.

bone *n* 1 the hard substance forming the skeleton of human beings and animals. 2 any one of the pieces of this:—*vb* to take out the bones from.

bon'fire *n* a large, open-air fire.

bon'net *n* 1 a headdress. 2 a hat fastened over the head by ribbons. 3 a soft cap.

bonus [bō-nês] *n* an extra payment, made for a special effort or services.

booby prize *n* a prize given to the worst performer.

booby trap *n* a trap hidden in a place so obvious that no one suspects it.

book[1] *n* printed matter, bound between covers.

book[2] *vb* to reserve in advance.

book'keeper *n* one who keeps accounts:—*n* **book'keeping**.

book'maker *n* (*also* (*inf*) **bookie**) one who makes his or her living by betting.

book'worm *n* one who reads a great deal.

boom¹ n a long deep noise:—also vb.

boom² n a time of rapid increase or growth:—vb to increase or grow quickly.

boom'erang n a curved throwing stick that returns to the thrower, used by Australian Aborigines:—also vb.

boon n an advantage, a blessing.

boon'docks npl (inf) 1 a wild inhospitable area. 2 a dull region.

boor n a rough, ill-mannered person:—adj **boor'ish**.

boot n 1 a covering for the foot and lower leg. 2 a patch for mending a tire:—vb to kick.

booth n 1 a tent at a fair. 2 a covered stall at a market. 3 a small, enclosed structure.

boot'y n 1 goods seized and divided by victors after battle. 2 goods taken by thieves.

bor'der n 1 the outer edge of anything. 2 the boundary between two countries. 3 a flowerbed around a lawn, etc:—vb to be next to:—**border (up)on** to come close to, to be almost.

bore¹ vb to make a hole in:—n 1 the hole made by boring. 2 greatest breadth of a tube, esp of a gun.

bore² vb to weary by uninteresting talk, etc:—n a person whose talk is wearisome:—adj **bo'ring**.

bored adj weary and dissatisfied with one's circumstances.

bore'dom n the state of being bored.

born pp of **bear**, sense 6.

borne pp of **bear**, senses 1–5, 7.

bor'row vb to ask or receive as a loan:—n **bor'rower**.

bosom [bŏ'-sĕm] n 1 the breast. 2 (lit or fml) the heart:—adj close, well-loved.

boss¹ n a knob.

boss² n (inf) a master, a manager:—vb 1 to be in charge. 2 to order about.

bot'any n the science or study of plants:—adjs **botan'ic, botan'ical**:—n **bot'anist**.

both'er vb 1 to annoy. 2 to trouble oneself:—n a trouble.

bot'tle n 1 a container, usu. of glass, with a narrow neck. 2 (inf) courage, boldness:—vb to put into bottles.

bot'tom n 1 the lowest part. 2 the buttocks:—adj lowest:—adj **bot'tomless**.

bough [bou] n (fml) the branch of a tree.

bought pt of **buy**.

boul'der n a large smooth stone.

bounce vb to jump or rebound suddenly:—also n.

bounc'ing adj big, strong.

bound¹ n a limit or boundary beyond which one must not go:—vb to form a limit or boundary.

bound² vb to jump, to leap:—also n.

bound³ adj 1 on the way to. 2 (pt of **bind**). 3 obliged. 4 sure (to do something). 5 tied. 6 covered.

boun'dary n 1 an outer limit. 2 a border.

bouquet [bŏ'-kā] n a bunch of flowers.

bout n 1 a period of action. 2 an attack (of illness). 3 a contest.

bow¹ [bou] vb 1 to bend, esp in respect or greeting. 2 to lower:—n a bending of the head or body in respect of greeting.

bow² [bō] n 1 a weapon for shooting arrows. 2 a looped knot. 3 a stick for playing a stringed instrument (e.g. the violin).

bow'els npl 1 the inside of the body, the intestines. 2 the organ by means of which waste matter is expelled from the body.

bowl¹ [bōl] n a round dish or basin.

bowl² [bōl] n 1 a heavy wooden ball. 2 pl the game played with such balls:—vb 1 to play bowls. 2 to deliver the ball in ball games.

bowl'er¹ n one who bowls.

bowl'er², **bowl'er hat** n a round stiff hat.

box¹ n 1 a case or container. 2 in a theater, a separate compartment with seats overlooking the stage:—vb to put in a box.

box² vb 1 to strike. 2 to fight in sport, wearing padded gloves:—n **box'er**.

Boxing Day n the day after Christmas Day.

box'room n a storage room in a house.

boy n 1 a male child. 2 a young male person:—n **boy'hood**.

boy'cott vb to refuse to have any dealings with:—also n.

bra n (abbr of **brassiere**) a woman's supporting undergarment worn over the breasts.

brace n 1 a support. 2 a pair or a couple. 3 a boring tool:—vb to steady or prepare oneself.

brace'let n an ornament for the wrist.

brac'ing adj giving strength.

brack'en n a type of fern.

brack'et n 1 a support for something fixed to a wall. 2 pl marks in printing to enclose a word, as { }, [ ] or ( ):—vb 1 to enclose in brackets. 2 to link or connect.

brag n a boast:—vb (**bragged', brag'ging**) to boast.

braid vb to twist together into one:—n 1 a plait of cords or hair so twisted together. 2 a narrow edging of decorated tape.

brain n 1 the soft matter within the skull, the center of the nervous system. 2 cleverness, intelligence. 3 (inf) someone very clever or intelligent:—vb to dash the brains out.

brake n 1 a large wagon. 2 an apparatus for slowing or stopping a vehicle:—vb to apply the brake.

branch n 1 a shoot growing out of the trunk or one of the boughs of a tree. 2 a connected part of a larger body (e.g. office, store, bank, etc):—vb to divide into branches:—**branch out** 1 to begin something new. 2 to expand.

brand n 1 (fml) a burning piece of wood. 2 a mark made with a hot iron to identify cattle, etc. 3 a trademark, a special make of article. 4 variety:—vb 1 to mark with a hot iron. 2 to mark down (as being bad).

bran'dish vb to wave, to shake.

bran'dy n a strong drink made from wine.

brass n 1 an alloy of copper and zinc. 2 (inf) impudence. 3 (inf) money:—adj **brass'y**.

brass'iere see **bra**.

brat n an ill-mannered child.

brave adj courageous, daring:—vb 1 to defy. 2 to face with courage:—n a North American Indian warrior.

brav'ery n courage, daring.

brawn'y adj muscular, strong.

bray vb to make a loud, harsh sound, as an ass:—also n.

braz'en adj 1 made of brass. 2 impudent, bold:—vb to face boldly and impudently.

breach n 1 act of breaking. 2 (fml) a gap. 3 a fault. 4 a quarrel, separation:—vb to make a gap or opening in.

bread n a food made from flour or meal and baked.

breadth n the distance from side to side, width.

break vb (pt **broke**, pp **bro'ken**) 1 to separate into two or more parts, usu by force. 2 to become unusable or in need of repair. 3 to tame. 4 to fail to keep. 5 to tell gently. 6 to go with force. 7 to do better than:—n 1 an opening. 2 a separation. 3 a pause. 4 a short vacation:—adj **break'able**.

breakfast [brek'-fĕst] n the first meal in the day:—vb to eat breakfast.

breast n (fml) the front part of the body from the neck to the stomach, the chest. 2 each of the milk-producing glands in a female:—vb 1 to face. 2 to touch. 3 to come to the top of.

breath n 1 the air taken into and put out from the lungs. 2 a gentle breeze.

breathe *vb* **1** to take air into one's lungs and put it out again. **2** (*fml*) to live. **3** (*fml*) to whisper.

breed *vb* (*pt, pp* **bred**) **1** to produce young. **2** to keep (animals) for the purpose of breeding young. **3** to be the cause of:—*n* a type, variety, species.

breeze *n* a light wind.

brev'ity *n* (*fml*) shortness.

brew *vb* **1** to make (beer). **2** to be about to start:—*n* the mixture made by brewing:—*n* **brew'er**.

brew'ery *n* a factory where beer is made.

bribe *n* a reward offered to win unfairly favor or preference:—*vb* to win over by bribes:—*n* **brib'ery**.

bride *n* a woman about to be married or newly married.

bride'groom *n* a man about to be married or newly married.

bridge[1] *n* **1** a roadway built across a river, etc. **2** the small deck for a ship's captain. **3** the piece of wood that supports the strings of a violin, etc:—*vb* **1** to build a bridge over. **2** to close a gap or pause to make a connection.

bridge[2] *n* a card game.

bri'dle *n* **1** the head straps and metal bit by which a horse is guided. **2** a check:—*vb* to put a bridle on.

brief *n* a summary of a law case for use in court:—*adj* short:—*vb* to provide with a summary of the facts.

brief'case *n* a case for carrying papers.

bright *adj* **1** shining. **2** strong, vivid. **3** lively, cheerful. **4** clever:—*n* **bright'ness**.

bright'en *vb* to make or become bright.

brill'iant *adj* **1** sparkling. **2** very bright. **3** very clever:—*n* a diamond:—*ns* **brill'iance, brill'iancy**.

brim *n* **1** the rim. **2** the edge.

brine *n* salt water.

bring *vb* **1** (*pt, pp* **brought**) **1** to fetch, to carry. **2** to cause:— **bring about** to cause to happen:—**bring off** to succeed:— **bring up 1** to rear, to educate. **2** to raise (a subject for discussion).

brink *n* **1** the edge of a steep place. **2** the edge, the point.

brisk *adj* keen; lively:—*adv* **brisk'ly**:—*n* **brisk'ness**.

bris'tle *n* a short, stiff hair:—*vb* to stand on end.

brit'tle *adj* hard but easily broken.

broach *vb* **1** (*fml*) to open up. **2** to begin to speak of.

broad [brâd] *adj* **1** wide. **2** not detailed, general. **3** (*of speech*) with a strong local accent:—*n* **broad'ness**.

broad'cast *vb* (*pt, pp* **broad'cast**) **1** to make widely known. **2** to send out by radio or TV. **3** to scatter widely:—*also n*.

broad'en *vb* to make or become broad or broader.

broad'-mind'ed *adj* ready to listen to and consider opinions different from one's own, liberal.

brochure [bro'-shör] *n* a small book, pamphlet.

broil *vb* to cook by exposure to direct heat, to grill:— *n* **broil'er**.

bronchi'tis *n* an illness affecting the windpipe to the lungs.

bronze *n* an alloy of copper and tin. **2** a reddish-brown color:—*vb* to give or become a reddish-brown color.

brooch *n* an ornamental pin.

brood *vb* **1** to sit on eggs. **2** to think deeply or anxiously about:—*n* **1** children. **2** a family of young birds.

brook *n* a small stream.

broom *n* **1** a plant with yellow flowers. **2** a brush, esp one of twigs.

broom'stick *n* the handle of a broom.

broth'er *n* (*pl* **broth'ers** or (*old or relig*) **breth'ren**) **1** a son of the same parents. **2** a member of the same group.

brought *pt of* **bring**.

brow *n* **1** the forehead. **2** the jutting-out edge of a cliff or hill.

brown *adj* of a dark color:—*also n*:—*vb* to make or become brown.

browse *vb* **1** to feed upon. **2** to glance through a book.

brows'er *n* **1** one who browses. **2** a computer program that accesses websites on the Internet.

bruise *n* a dark spot on the skin, caused by a knock:—*vb* to cause a bruise on.

brunet, brunette [brü-net'] *ns* a woman with dark brown hair.

brush *n* **1** an instrument for cleaning, sweeping, or smoothing. **2** an instrument for putting paint on to something. **3** the tail of a fox. **4** small trees and bushes. **5** a short battle. **6** (*inf*) a slight disagreement or hostile encounter:—*vb* **1** to clean with a brush. **2** to touch lightly.

brute *n* **1** an animal. **2** (*inf*) a cruel person.

bub'ble *n* a film of water or other liquid, containing air:—*vb* to form bubbles:—*adj* **bub'bly**.

buc'caneer *n* a pirate.

buck *n* **1** a male deer, goat, rabbit, etc. **2** (*inf*) a dashing young man. **3** (*inf*) a dollar.

bucka'roo *n* a cowboy.

buck'et *n* a vessel for carrying water.

buck'le *n* a fastener for joining the ends of a belt or band:—*vb* **1** to fasten. **2** to bend out of shape.

bud *n* a leaf or flower before it opens:—*vb* (**bud'ded, bud'ding**) to put out buds.

budgerigar [bu-jé-ri-gä r'] *n* a type of small parrot that can be trained to talk.

bud'get *n* **1** a statement of government taxation and intended spending for the coming year. **2** a plan to ensure that household expenses or those of a firm or organization will not be greater than income:—*vb* **1** to make such a plan. **2** to allow for something in a budget.

buf'falo *n* (*pl* **buf'faloes**) **1** a type of ox of Asia and America. **2** a popular name for the bison.

buffet[1] [budd-wt] *n* (*inf*) a blow, a slap:—*also vb*.

buffet[2] [bu-fä] *n* **1** a counter at which refreshments may be obtained. **2** a meal, often cold, set out on tables so that people can help themselves.

buffoon' *n* **1** a clown. **2** a person who plays the fool:— *n* **buffoon'ery**.

bug *n* **1** a bloodsucking insect. **2** any insect. **3** (*inf*) an infection. **4** (*inf*) a hidden microphone used to record people's conversations secretly. **5** (*inf*) a defect, as in a machine:—*vb* (**bugged', bug'ging**) (*inf*) **1** to install or use a hidden microphone. **2** (*inf*) to annoy.

bu'gle *n* **1** a hunting horn. **2** a trumpet:—*n* **bug'ler**.

build [bild] *vb* (*pt, pp* **built**) to put together materials in order to make something, to construct:—*n* **build'er**.

build'ing *n* the thing built.

bulb *n* **1** the round root of certain flowers. **2** a pear-shaped glass globe surrounding the element of an electric light.

bulge *n* a swelling:—*vb* to swell out:—*adj* **bulg'y**.

bulk *n* **1** size, esp of large things. **2** the main part:—**in bulk** in a large quantity:—*vb* to make fuller, to increase in size.

bulk'y *adj* very large and awkward to move or carry.

bull *n* the male ox, elephant, whale, etc.

bull'dozer *n* a heavy tractor for clearing away obstacles and making land level:—*vb* **bull'doze**.

bul'let *n* a lead ball shot from a rifle or pistol.

bul'letin *n* **1** a short, official report of news. **2** a printed information sheet or newspaper.

bulletin (bulletin board) *n* **1** a board on which bulletins are posted. **2** in computing, a place on the Internet where messages can be left.

bull'ock n. a young bull.

bull's-eye' n 1 the center of a target. 2 a shot that hits it. 3 a type of sweet.

bul'ly n a person who uses his or her strength to hurt or terrify those who are weaker:—vb (**bul'lying, bul'lied**) to intimidate, oppress, or hurt.

bul'rush n a tall weed.

bump n 1 a heavy blow, or the dull noise made by it. 2 a lump caused by a blow:—vb to knock against.

bum'per n 1 (old) a full glass or cup. 2 a fender on a motor vehicle:—adj unusually large or full.

bun n 1 a small cake. 2 a rounded mass of hair.

bunch n 1 a group or collection of things of the same kind. 2 (inf) a group of people:—vb to come or put together in groups or bunches.

bun'dle n 1 a collection of things tied together:—vb 1 to tie in a bundle. 2 to force to go in a hurry.

bun'galow n a low house, usu of one story.

bun'gle vb to do badly or clumsily:—also n.

bunk n 1 a narrow bed, esp in a ship. 2 one of a pair of beds placed one above the other.

buoy [boi] n an object floating in a fixed position to show ships the safe course:—vb 1 to keep afloat. 2 to support, to keep high. 3 to raise the spirits of.

buoy'ant adj 1 floating, able to float easily. 2 cheerful, optimistic:—n **buoy'ancy**.

bur'den n 1 a load. 2 the chorus of a song. 3 the leading idea (of):—vb to load heavily.

bur'glar n a thief who breaks into a house.

bur'glarize vb to commit burglary.

bur'glary n the crime of housebreaking.

bur'gle vb to commit burglary.

bur'ial n the act of putting into a grave.

bur'lap n a coarse fabric made of hemp, etc.

bur'lesque n a comic or mocking imitation, a parody, caricature:—also adj and vb.

bur'ly adj stout, big, and strong.

burn vb (pt, pp **burnt** or **burned**) 1 to be alight, to give out heat. 2 to be on fire. 3 to destroy or damage by fire. 4 to hurt or injure by fire. 5 to be very hot. 6 to feel great anger, passion, etc:—n a hurt caused by fire.

burn'er n the part of a stove, etc, from which the flame comes.

bur'row n a hole in the earth made by certain animals, e.g. rabbits, foxes, etc:—vb 1 to make by digging. 2 to search for something.

bur'sar n the person in charge of the finances of a school or college.

burst vb (pt, pp **burst**) 1 to break in pieces. 2 to rush, to go suddenly or violently:—n a sudden outbreak.

bur'y vb 1 to put into a grave. 2 to put under ground.

bus n (short for **omnibus**) a large road vehicle for carrying passengers:—vb (**bused, bu'sing** or **bussed, bus'sing**) to transport by bus.

bush n 1 a small low tree. 2 wild, uncleared country; forest country.

bush'el n a measure (8 gallons) for grain, etc.

bush'y adj 1 full of bushes. 2 thick-growing.

bus'iness n 1 one's work or job. 2 trade and commerce. 3 a matter that concerns a particular person.

bust n 1 the shoulders and breast. 2 a statue showing only the head, shoulders, and breast of a person.

bus'tle¹ vb to move about busily and often fussily:—n noisy movement, hurry.

bus'tle² n a frame or pad once worn to hold out the back of a woman's skirt.

bus'y adj 1 always doing something. 2 at work, engaged in a job, etc. 3 full of people, traffic, etc:—vb to occupy:—adv **bus'ily**.

but'cher n 1 one who kills and sells animals for food. 2 a cruel killer:—vb 1 to kill for food. 2 to kill cruelly.

but'ler n the chief manservant in a household, formerly in charge of the wine cellar.

butt¹ n 1 a large barrel. 2 the thicker end of a thing:—vb to strike with the head or horns.

butt² n 1 a mark to be shot at. 2 the mound behind the targets for rifle practice. 3 a person who is always being made fun of.

but'ter n an oily food made from milk.

but'terfly n 1 an insect with large colorful wings. 2 a frivolous unreliable person.

but'ton n 1 a knob or disk to fasten one part of a garment to another. 2 something shaped like a button, esp a knob or switch on an electrical appliance. 3 pl a boy servant in uniform:—vb to fasten with buttons.

but'tonhole n 1 a hole for a button. 2 a flower worn in a buttonhole:—vb to stop and hold in conversation.

bux'om adj jolly, plump.

buy vb (pt, pp **bought**) to obtain by paying for.

buy'er n 1 one who buys. 2 one whose job is to buy goods.

buzz n a humming noise:—also vb.

buz'zard n a type of hawk.

by and by adv soon.

by'-election n an election held to fill an elective position with an unexpired term.

by'law n a law made by a local body and applying to the area in which the body has authority.

by'pass n a road around a town to avoid busy areas:—vb to go around, to avoid.

by'-product n something made in the course of making a more important article.

C

cab n 1 (old) a horse carriage for public hire. 2 the driver's part of a railroad locomotive or a truck. 3 a taxi.

cab'bage n a kind of common vegetable with eatable green leaves.

cab'in n 1 a small simple house, a hut. 2 a room on a ship for accommodation of passengers. 3 the space available for passengers or crew on an aircraft. 4 the covered part of a yacht.

cab'inet n 1 a display case. 2 a piece of furniture with drawers. 3 a case or container for radio, TV, etc. 4 the chief ministers or advisers in a government.

cab'le n 1 a strong rope, often of wire. 2 a chain. 3 an undersea telegraph line. 4 a bundle of electric wires enclosed in a pipe. 5 a message sent by cable.—vb to send a message by cable.

ca'boose n 1 the guard's car at the rear of a freight train. 2 a kitchen on a ship's deck.

cacao [ka-kä'-ö or ka-kä'-ö] n the tree from whose seeds chocolate and cocoa are made.

cack'le n 1 the sound of the hen or goose. 2 noisy chatter. 3 loud unpleasant laughter.—also vb.

cac'tus n (pl **cac'ti**) a thick prickly plant.

cad n a dishonorable fellow.

cada'ver n the dead body of a human being, a corpse.

ca'fé n a tea or coffee house, a diner.

cafeteria [ka-fä-tee'-ri-a] n a restaurant with a self-service bar.

caffeine [ka'-feen] n a drug, present in tea and coffee.

cage n 1 a box, with one or more walls consisting of bars or wire-netting, in which animals or birds may be kept. 2 a lift for taking miners down a mine:—vb. to shut up in a cage or prison.

cait'iff n (old) a villain.

cajole' vb to persuade by flattery, to coax:—n **cajol'ery**.

cake n 1 a sweetened bread. 2 a type of biscuit. 3 a small flat lump.

calam'ity n 1 a disaster. 2 a serious misfortune:—adj **calam'itous**.

cal'cium n the metal found in chalk or lime.

cal'culate vb 1 to work with numbers. 2 to estimate. 3 to count on, to rely on.

cal'culating adj 1 far-seeing. 2 self-centered.

calcula'tion n 1 the art of counting. 2 a sum.

cal'endar n 1 a table showing the relation of the days of the week to the dates of a particular year. 2 a daily record of events or business appointments.

calf n (pl **calves**) the young of the cow, elephant, whale, etc.

calf[2] n (pl **calves**) the fleshy part at the back of the leg below the knee.

cal'iber n 1 the breadth of the inside of a gun barrel. 2 quality, ability.

cal'ipers npl an instrument for measuring round objects.

caliper splint n a splint fitted to the leg to help a lame person to walk.

call vb 1 to name. 2 to cry out. 3 to ask to come. 4 to make a short visit:—n 1 a cry. 2 a short visit. 3 a telephone call. 4 need, demand:—a **close call** a narrow escape.

callig'raphy n 1 handwriting. 2 the art of writing well.

call'ing n (fml) profession or employment.

cal'lous adj hardened, unfeeling, insensitive:—n **cal'lousness**.

cal'low adj immature, lacking experience.

calm adj 1 quiet, still. 2 unexcited, not agitated:—n 1 stillness. 2 freedom from excitement:—vb to make calm:—n **calm'ness**.

cal'orie n 1 a measure of heat. 2 a unit for measuring the energy value of food.

calve vb to give birth to a calf.

---

calves see **calf**[1], **calf**[2].

cam'ber n a slightly curving surface, as on a road.

cam'el n an animal of the desert, with one hump (called dromedary) or two humps (called bactrian) that can store water.

cam'era n an apparatus for taking photographs:—**in camera** in secret.

cam'isole n a woman's light undergarment worn on the upper part of the body.

camp n 1 a place where people live in tents, caravans, huts, etc. 2 a group of tents, huts, or other kinds of temporary shelter:—vb to stay in or set up a camp.

campaign' n 1 a battle or series of battles in a war. 2 any series of actions, meetings, etc, directed to one purpose:—vb to take part in or conduct a campaign.

cam'per n 1 a vehicle equipped with domestic items. 2 one who camps.

can[1] vb (also **is**, are) able.

can[2] n a small metal container:—vb (**canned'**, **can'ning**) to put into cans to preserve.

canal' n a man-made waterway.

cana'ry n a songbird often kept as a cage bird:—adj bright yellow.

can'cel vb 1 to cross out. 2 to put off:—n **cancella'tion**.

can'cer n 1 a harmful, sometimes fatal growth in the body. 2 a growing evil.

can'did adj saying what one thinks, frank:—adv **can'didly**.

can'didate n 1 one who offers himself or herself for a post or for election. 2 one who sits an examination:—n **can'didature**.

can'dle n a bar of wax or tallow containing a wick for lighting.

can'dlestick n a holder for a candle.

can'dor n frankness.

can'dy n 1 sugar hardened by boiling. 2 a solid confection of sugar or syrup with flavoring, fruit, nuts, etc:—vb to preserve by boiling with sugar.

cane n 1 a hard hollow reed, as bamboo, sugarcane, etc. 2 an easily bent stick. 3 a walking stick:—vb to beat with a cane.

cane sugar n sugar from the sugarcane.

can'ine adj having to do with dogs:—n one of the pointed teeth in the front of the mouth (also **canine tooth**).

can'ker n 1 a quickly spreading sore. 2 a disease of plants. 3 any growing evil.

can'nibal n 1 a person who eats human flesh. 2 an animal that eats flesh of its own species:—n **can'nibalism**.

can'non n a large gun.

canoe [ka-nö'] n a light boat moved by paddles:—also vb.

can'on n 1 a law, esp of the Church. 2 a member of the clergy with duties in a cathedral.

can'onize vb to recognize as a saint.

can'opy n a hanging cover forming a shelter above a throne, bed, etc.

cantank'erous adj cross and unreasonable.

canteen' n 1 a refreshment store in a camp, factory, office, etc. 2 a box containing a set of knives, forks, and spoons. 3 a flask for carrying water.

can'ter vb to gallop, but not very quickly:—also n.

can'to n a division of a long poem.

can'ton n a district with certain rights of local government, as in Switzerland.

can'vas n 1 a coarse cloth. 2 the sails of a ship. 3 an oil painting.

can'vass vb to go around asking for votes or orders:—n **can'vasser**.

25

can'yon n a pass between cliffs, a ravine.

cap n 1 a covering for the head with no brim or only part of one. 2 a cover or top piece:—vb (**capped, cap'ping**) 1 to put a cap on. 2 to improve on. 3 to choose for a team. 4 to impose an upper limit on.

cap'able adj 1 able to. 2 likely to. 3 able to do things well, competent, efficient:—n **capabil'ity**.

capa'cious adj wide, roomy.

capac'ity n 1 ability to hold or contain. 2 ability to produce, perform, experience, etc. 3 (fml) position.

cape[1] n a short cloak for covering the shoulders, a sleeveless cloak.

cape[2] n a headland.

cap'er vb to jump about playfully:—n 1 a jump or leap. 2 a prank, a mischievous act.

cap'ital adj 1 chief. 2 punishable by death. 3 (inf) excellent:—n 1 the top of a column or pillar. 2 the chief city of a country, etc. 3 money, esp when used for business. 4 a large letter, as used first in proper names.

capital punishment n punishment by death.

capit'ulate vb to surrender on conditions:—n **capitula'tion**.

capsize' vb to upset or overturn.

cap'sule n 1 a hollow pill containing medicine. 2 the part of a spacecraft containing the instruments and crew.

cap'tain n 1 a commander. 2 an officer. 3 a leader:—also vb.

caption [kap'-shèn] n the heading over (or under) a newspaper report or picture.

cap'tivate vb to charm, to fascinate.

cap'tive n a prisoner.

captiv'ity n the state of being a prisoner.

cap'tor n one who takes prisoner.

cap'ture vb 1 to take prisoner, to catch. 2 to take control of:—n 1 act of taking prisoner. 2 the thing so taken.

car n 1 a wheeled vehicle. 2 an automobile. 3 a carriage.

car'digan n a knitted woolen jacket with buttons.

care n 1 worry. 2 attention. 3 supervision:—vb 1 to be concerned or interested. 2 to look after. 3 to have a liking or love (for).

career' n 1 one's work or profession in life:—vb to go at full speed.

care'ful adj 1 taking trouble. 2 cautious:—adv **care'fully**.

care'less adj taking little or no trouble:—adv **care'lessly**:—n **care'lessness**.

caress' vb to touch or stroke lovingly:—also n.

caret n a sign (/) to show something has been missed out in writing.

care'taker n a janitor.

car'go n goods carried by a ship, airplane, etc.

car'icature n a picture that shows people or things as worse or uglier than they really are, to make others laugh at them:—vb to draw a caricature:—n **caricatur'ist**.

car'nival n 1 a time of feasting and merriment. 2 an entertainment given largely by skilled acrobats and trained animals, a circus.

car'nivore n a flesh-eating animal:—adj **carniv'orous**.

car'ol n a song of joy, esp one sung at Christmas:—vb to sing joyfully.

car'penter n one who makes the wooden framework for houses, ships, etc:—n **car'pentry**.

car'pet n 1 a thick covering of wool or other material for a floor. 2 a covering:—vb 1 to cover with a carpet. 2 to cover. 3 (inf) to scold, to reprimand.

car'riage n 1 act of carrying. 2 the price of carrying. 3 the way one stands or moves. 4 a vehicle with wheels.

car'rier n 1 one who carries or transports goods. 2 anyone or anything that carries.

carrier pigeon n a pigeon used for carrying letters.

car'rot n a reddish root vegetable.

car'ry vb 1 to take from one place to another. 2 to go from one place to another. 3 to have or hold:—**carry on** 1 to continue to do. 2 to behave badly or in an uncontrolled manner:—**carry out** to perform.

cart n a wheeled vehicle or wagon for carrying goods:—vb to carry by cart.

car'tel n an association of business firms to coordinate production, prices, etc, to avoid competition and maximize profits.

car'ton n a cardboard box.

cartoon' n a comic drawing:—n **cartoon'ist**.

car'tridge n the container for the explosive that fires the bullet or shell from a gun.

carve vb 1 to cut into a special shape. 2 to make by cutting wood or stone. 3 to cut into slices.

case[1] n 1 a box or container. 2 a covering. 3 a suitcase. 4 a piece of furniture for displaying or containing things.

case[2] n 1 an event, instance, or example. 2 a person having medical, etc, treatment. 3 a statement of facts and arguments or reasons. 4 a question to be decided in a court of law, a lawsuit.

cash n 1 coins or paper money, not checks, etc. 2 immediate payment rather than by credit or installment plan. 3 (inf) money generally:—vb to turn into money.

casino [ka-see'-no] n a hall for dancing or gambling.

cask n a barrel.

cas'ket n a jewel case.

cass'erole n 1 a heat-resisting dish in which food can be cooked in an oven and then served at table. 2 the food so prepared.

cast vb (pt, pp **cast**) 1 to throw. 2 to throw off. 3 to shape (melted metal) in a mold. 4 to give parts to actors in:—n 1 a throw. 2 a squint (in the eye). 3 a model made in a mold. 4 the actors in a play.

cast'away n a shipwrecked person.

cast iron n iron that has been melted and shaped in a mold:—adj very strong.

cas'tle n 1 a large building, usu one made strong against attack. 2 a piece in chess:—**castles in the air** a daydream.

cas'tor, cas'ter n 1 a small jar or bottle with holes in the top for sprinkling salt, sugar, etc. 2 a small wheel on a piece of furniture, making it easy to move.

casual [ka'-zhü-êl] adj 1 happening by accident. 2 not regular. 3 uninterested. 4 not careful, not thorough. 5 informal:—adv **cas'ually**.

cas'ualty n 1 an accident. 2 an injured or wounded person. 3 something that is damaged or destroyed as a result of an event.

cat n 1 a common domestic animal with soft fur and sharp claws. 2 a genus of wild animals.

cat'alog n 1 a complete list arranged in a special order so that the items can be found easily:—vb to make a list.

cat'apult n 1 (old) a machine used for hurling heavy stones in war. 2 a slingshot.

cat'aract n 1 a waterfall. 2 a disease of the eye, causing gradual loss of sight.

catarrh' n the fluid coming from the nose and eyes of a person with a cold.

catas'trophe [-fã] n a sudden great disaster:—adj **catastroph'ic**.

catch vb (pt, pp **caught**) 1 to take and hold. 2 to capture. 3 to become accidentally attached or held. 4 to surprise in the act of. 5 to succeed in hearing. 6 to get by infection. 7 to be in time for, to get on:—n 1 the act of catching. 2 the number of fish caught at one time. 3 a fastener. 4 a snag. 5 a song in which the same words and tune are repeated by several singers starting at different times.

catch'up n ketchup.

categor'ical adj definite:—adv **categor'ically**.

cat'egory n a class or group of things in a system of grouping.

cat'er vb 1 to supply with food and drinks, esp at social occasions. 2 to provide what is needed or desired by:—n **cat'erer**.

cat'erpillar n the worm-like grub of the butterfly and other insects.

cathe'dral n the chief church in a district in which a bishop has his throne.

cath'olic adj wide-ranging, broad, including many different things:—n **catholic'ity**.

Cath'olic n a member of the Roman Catholic Church:—also adj.

cat'kin n the furry blossom of the willow, hazel, etc.

catsup n ketchup.

cat'tle npl cows, bulls, and oxen.

caught pt of **catch**.

caul'dron n a large boiling pot.

caul'iflower n a type of cabbage, of which the white flower is eaten as a vegetable.

cause n 1 something or someone that produces an effect or result. 2 the reason for an action, a motive. 3 a purpose, aim:—vb to make happen.

caus'tic adj 1 burning. 2 bitter, severe, sarcastic:—adv **caus'tically**.

cau'tion n 1 carefulness, esp in order to avoid risk or danger. 2 warning:—vb 1 to warn against possible danger. 2 to give a warning to, often with the threat of future punishment.

cau'tious adj careful, showing caution.

cavalcade' n a procession (originally, of people on horseback).

cav'alry n combat troops originally mounted on horseback.

cave n a hollow place under the ground or in a rock:—**cave in** to fall in over a hollow.

cave'man n 1 (old) one who, in the earliest times, lived in a cave. 2 a man with very rough manners, esp toward women.

cav'ern n a large cave.

caviar(e)' n a dish made from the roe (eggs) of the sturgeon and similar fish.

cav'ity n 1 a hollow place. 2 a hole.

CD n (abbr of **compact disk**) a small mirrored plastic disk storing data, music, or images that are read optically by a laser beam.

cease vb 1 to stop. 2 to come to an end.

ce'dar n 1 a large cone-bearing tree. 2 its wood.

ceil'ing n 1 the inside roof of a room. 2 the greatest height to which a particular aircraft can climb. 3 an upper limit.

cel'ebrate vb 1 to perform (a religious ceremony). 2 to honor an event by feasting and rejoicing:—n **celebra'tion**.

cel'ebrated adj famous.

celeb'rity n a famous person.

celes'tial adj 1 heavenly. 2 having to do with the sky.

cell n 1 a small, bare room, esp in a prison or monastery. 2 a compartment in a honeycomb. 3 a single unit of the living matter of the body. 4 a unit of an electric battery. 5 a small group of people working for the same end.

cello short for **violoncello**.

Cel'lophane n trademark a transparent wrapping material.

cell phone n a portable telephone operated by microwave radio.

cement' n any powder that, mixed with liquid, forms a solid material used to make things stick together:—vb 1 to join with cement. 2 to unite closely.

cem'etery n a place where bodies are buried.

cen'sor n one who examines letters, books, films, etc, to see if they contain anything harmful to society:—also vb:—n **cen'sorship**.

cen'sus n 1 an official regular counting of a country's population. 2 an official counting of other things.

cent n 1 a hundred (e.g. ten per cent). 2 a coin that is one hundredth part of a dollar.

centenary [sen-teen'-ēr-i] n the hundredth year after a certain event.

centen'nial adj happening once every hundred years.

cen'ter n 1 the middle point or part of anything. 2 a place where certain activities or facilities are concentrated. 3 a political position that is not extreme:—vb 1 to put into the middle. 2 to collect or concentrate at or around.

cent'igrade adj divided into one hundred degrees.

cent'imetre n one hundredth part of a meter.

cent'ipede n an insect with many feet.

cen'tral adj 1 in the middle. 2 chief.

cen'tury n 1 a period of a hundred years. 2 a set of a hundred.

ce'real adj having to do with grain. 2 any grain that can be eaten. 3 food made from such grain, often eaten at breakfast.

ceremo'nial adj having to do with a ceremony:—n the actions connected with a ceremony.

ceremo'nious adj (fml) full of ceremony, very formal.

cer'emony n 1 the performing of certain actions in a fixed order for a religious or other serious purpose. 2 formal behavior, formality.

cer'tain adj 1 sure. 2 particular.

cer'tainly adv 1 undoubtedly. 2 willingly.

cer'tainty n 1 the state of being certain or sure. 2 that which is certain.

certif'icate n a written statement of fact.

cer'tify vb 1 to confirm formally the truth of a statement. 2 to officially declare insane.

chain n 1 a number of metal rings joined together to form a rope. 2 a number of connected facts or events, a series. 3 a measure of length (22 yards). 4 a range (of mountains):—vb to bind or fasten with a chain.

chair n 1 a movable seat with a back. 2 chairperson. 3 the seat or place of an official (e.g. of a professor in a university or a person controlling a meeting). 4 a professorship:—vb 1 to be in charge of (a meeting). 2 to carry shoulder-high as a sign of honor.

chair'man, chair'person, chair'woman n one who presides at or controls a meeting.

chalet [sha'-lã] n 1 a wooden house or hut with a steeply sloping roof, common in Switzerland. 2 a wooden house or hut used by vacationers, etc.

chalk n 1 a soft white limestone. 2 a pencil of chalk used for writing on a blackboard:—vb to mark with chalk:—adj **chalk'y**.

chal'lenge vb 1 to call on another to fight or play a match to see who is the better. 2 to doubt the truth of:—n 1 the daring of another to a contest. **2** an order given by a sentry to stop and say who one is. **3** a statement or action that questions or disputes something. **4** a difficult or stimulating task:— *n* **chal'lenger**.

cham'ber *n* **1** (*old*) a room. **2** a room in which an assembly, such as a parliament, meets. **3** an administrative group. **4** the part of a gun in which the cartridge is held.

champagne [sham-pân'] *n* a type of sparkling French wine.

cham'pion *n* **1** one who has beaten all his or her rivals or opponents. **2** one who fights for a certain cause, or for another person:—*vb* to defend or support.

cham'pionship *n* **1** a series of contests or matches to discover the champion. **2** the state of being a champion.

chance *n* **1** accident. **2** opportunity. **3** risk:—*vb* **1** (*fml*) to happen. **2** to risk:—*adj* accidental.

chandelier [shan-de-leer'] *n* a hanging frame with branches to hold lamps (formerly candles).

change *vb* **1** to become different. **2** to make different. **3** to put or take one thing in place of another, to exchange:—*n* **1** a difference or alteration. **2** money given in return for money received. **3** small coin:—*adjs* **change'able, change'less**.

chan'nel *n* **1** the course of a river. **2** the deep part of a river where ships can sail safely. **3** a narrow sea.

chant *vb* **1** to sing. **2** to recite slowly in a singing voice:— *n* **1** a song. **2** a way of singing sacred music.

cha'os *n* utter confusion, muddle.

chaos theory *n* (*physics*) the theory that the behavior of dynamic systems is haphazard rather than mathematical.

chaot'ic *adj* completely without order or arrangement.

chap *n* (*inf*) a man, a fellow.

chap'el *n* **1** a small church. **2** a private church.

chaperon [sha'-pê-rôn] *n* **1** (*esp formerly*) an older woman who accompanies a younger one when she goes out. **2** a person who supervises young people on an outing:—*vb* to act as chaperon to.

chap'ter *n* a division of a book.

char' *vb* (**charred'**, **char'ring**) **1** to burn in part. **2** to burn the outside.

char² *n* a red-bellied fish allied to the salmon.

char'acter *n* **1** a letter or figure or, as in Chinese, a sign standing for a whole word. **2** a person's nature as known by words, deeds, etc. **3** a reputation. **4** a person in a story or play. **5** (*inf*) an odd, humorous or interesting person. **6** (*inf*) a person.

characteris'tic *n* a single point in a person's character, a special and recognizable quality in someone or something:— *adj* typical.

char'acterize *vb* **1** to be characteristic or typical of. **2** (*fml*) to describe as.

char'coal *n* partly burnt wood used as fuel.

charge *vb* **1** to ask a price. **2** to accuse. **3** to rush. **4** to attack at speed. **5** to fill with electricity. **6** (*fml*) to load, fill. **7** to tell a person to do something as a duty:—*n* **1** a load of electricity. **2** a price. **3** a duty, esp that of a clergyman. **4** a violent attack. **5** an accusation:—*adj* **charge'able:—take charge** to take command, take control.

char'iot *n* **1** (*old*) a horse-drawn cart used in war. **2** a state carriage.

char'ity *n* **1** love as a Christian duty. **2** kindness to others. **3** generosity in giving to the poor:—*adj* **char'itable**.

charm *n* **1** a magic spell. **2** an object or words possessing magical power. **3** attractiveness of character, a pleasant quality. **4** *pl* (*fml*) beauty:—*vb* **1** to put under a spell. **2** to delight.

chart *n* **1** a map, esp one for sailors. **2** a paper showing a graph or diagram.

char'ter *n* a written paper granting certain rights:—*vb* to hire.

chase *vb* **1** to run after. **2** to drive away:—*n* a pursuit, a hunt.

chasm *n* **1** a wide deep crack in the surface of the earth, a gorge. **2** a wide gap or difference of opinion, attitudes, feelings, etc.

chastise' *vb* to punish by beating:—*n* **chastise'ment**.

chas'tity *n* purity.

chat *vb* (**chat'ted, chat'ing**) to talk about unimportant matters:—*n* a friendly talk.

chat'ter *vb* **1** to talk quickly and continuously, usu about something unimportant. **2** to make meaningless sounds:— *also n*:—*n* **chat'terer**.

chauffeur [shô'-fér or shô-fer'] *n* a person employed to drive someone's car:—*also vb*.

cheap *adj* **1** of a low price. **2** of little value.

cheap'en *vb* to lessen the price or value of.

cheat *vb* to deceive, to use unfair means:—*n* **1** a trick. **2** one who cheats.

check¹ *vb* **1** to stop. **2** to slow down. **3** to scold. **4** to look at something to see if it is correct or in order:—*n* **1** a sudden halt or obstacle. **2** a control. **3** a ticket to prove ownership:—*adj* divided into or marked by squares.

check² *n* a written order to a banker to pay out a sum of money from one's bank account.

check'ered *adj* **1** marked with a variegated pattern. **2** having a career marked by fluctuating fortunes.

check'ers *npl* a game in which round pieces are moved about on a squared board.

cheek *n* **1** the side of the face. **2** (*inf*) impudence.

cheek'y *adj* impudent.

cheep *n* **1** a faint squeak, a chirp. **2** a sound:—*also vb*.

cheer *n* **1** (*old*) mood, disposition. **2** food. **3** a shout of joy or encouragement:—*vb* **1** to brighten up. **2** to encourage, esp by shouts.

cheer'ful *adj* **1** happy and lively. **2** bright and attractive.

cheese *n* a solid savory food made from milk.

chef *n* a professional cook.

chem'ical *adj* having to do with chemistry:—*n* a substance studied in chemistry.

chem'istry *n* the science that separates and studies the substance of which all things are made up:—*n* **chem'ist**.

cher'ish *vb* **1** to treat lovingly, to hold dear. **2** to keep in the mind or heart.

cher'ry *n* **1** a small fruit. **2** a tree bearing cherries.

cher'ub *n* (*pl* **cher'ubs** *or* **cher'ubim**) an angel pictured as a winged child.

chess *n* a game of skill, played on a checkered board.

chest *n* **1** a large strong box. **2** the bony upper part of the body, from the shoulders to the waist.

chest'nut *n* **1** a nut. **2** a tree bearing chestnuts. **3** a reddish-brown horse. **4** (*inf*) a joke long known to all:—*adj* reddish-brown.

chew *vb* to crush with the teeth.

chick, chick'en *n* a young fowl.

chick'enpox *n* an infectious disease involving fever and red itchy spots, usu affecting children.

chide *vb* to scold.

chief *adj* **1** highest in rank. **2** most important, main:—*n* a head, a leader:—*adv* **chief'ly**.

child *n* (*pl* **chil'dren**) **1** a boy or girl. **2** a son or daughter:— *n* **child'hood**.

child'ish *adj* **1** like a child. **2** silly, immature.

children *see* **child**.

chill *n* **1** coldness. **2** an illness caused by cold. **3** coldness of manner, unfriendliness:—*vb* **1** to make cold. **2** to make cold without freezing. **3** to discourage:—*adj* cold.

chill'y *adj* 1 cold. 2 unfriendly.

chime *n* 1 the sound of a bell. 2 the music of bells. 3 *pl* a set of bells:—*vb* to ring musically:—**chime in** to agree.

chim'ney *n* 1 a passage by which smoke may escape. 2 a narrow crack in the side of a mountain.

chimpanzee' *n* a type of ape of Africa.

chi'na *n* 1 a fine thin earthenware. 2 cups, plates, etc, made of this.

chink *n* a very narrow opening.

chip *n* 1 a small piece. 2 a counter or token used in games. 3 *pl* French fries:—*vb* (**chipped'**, **chip'ping**) 1 to cut into small pieces. 2 to break off a small piece, often accidentally.

chirp *vb* to make a short sharp whistling sound:—*also n*.

chis'el *n* a tool used for cutting or chipping wood, stone, etc:—*also vb*.

chiv'alry *n* good manners, esp toward women:—*adjs* **chival'ric**, **chiv'alrous**.

chlor'ophyll, **chlor'ophyl** *n* the green coloring matter of plants.

chock'-full *adj* (*inf*) completely filled.

choc'olate *n* a drink or sweetmeat made from cacao seeds:—*adj* chocolate-colored, i.e. dark brown.

choice *n* 1 act of choosing. 2 that which is chosen:—*adj* very good, excellent.

choir [kwīr] *n* 1 a group of singers. 2 the part of the church where the choir sits.

choke *vb* 1 to be unable to breathe. 2 to prevent breathing by pressing the windpipe. 3 to block up:—*n* 1 a fit of choking or its sound. 2 a valve that controls the flow of air in a carburetor.

choose *vb* (*pt* **chose**, *pp* **cho'sen**) to take what one prefers.

chop *vb* (**chopped'**, **chop'ping**) 1 to cut with a quick strong blow. 2 to cut into pieces:—*n* a piece of pork or mutton on a rib bone.

chop'sticks *npl* two small sticks used by the Chinese instead of a knife and fork.

chor'al *adj* having to do with a chorus or choir.

chord [kord] *n* the playing of several musical notes at once in harmony.

chore *n* an odd job about the house.

chori'zo *n* a spicy pork sausage.

chor'us *n* 1 a group of singers and dancers. 2 a song or part of a song in which all may join:—*vb* to sing or speak together.

chough [chuf] *n* a red-legged bird of the crow family.

christen [kris'-ēn] *vb* 1 to baptize. 2 to name:—*n* **chris'tening**.

Chris'tian *adj* having to do with Christ and his teaching:—*n* a follower of Christ.

Christian name *n* the name given at christening.

Christmas [kris'-mês] *n* December 25, the day each year on which the birth of Christ is celebrated.

chron'ic *adj* lasting for a long time.

chronolog'ical *adj* arranged in order of time.

chrysalis [kris'-ēl-is] *n* an early stage in the life of a flying insect, when it is shut up in a shell-like cover until its wings grow.

chub *n* a freshwater fish.

chub'by *adj* plump.

chuck'le *vb* to laugh quietly:—*also n*.

chum[1] *n* chopped meal, etc, used as bait for fish.

chum[2] *n* a type of Pacific salmon.

chum[3] *n* (*inf*) a close friend:—*adj* **chum'my**.

chunk *n* a thick piece.

church *n* a building set aside by Christians for the worship of God.

church'yard *n* a burial ground around a church.

chur'lish *adj* ill-mannered and bad-tempered:—*n* **chur'lishness**.

chute [shöt] *n* 1 a waterfall. 2 a sloping passage or slide.

ci'der *n* a strong drink made from apple juice.

cigar' *n* a roll of tobacco leaves for smoking.

cigarette', **cigaret'** *n* tobacco finely cut and rolled in thin paper for smoking.

cin'der *n* burned coal.

cin'ema *n* 1 a movie theater. 2 the making of films.

cin'namon *n* 1 an East Indian tree. 2 a spice made from its bark, used in cooking.

cir'cle *n* 1 a perfectly round figure. 2 a group of people:—*vb* 1 to move around. 2 to draw a circle around.

circuit [sēr'-kēt] *n* 1 a path around. 2 the act of moving around. 3 the path of an electric current. 4 a chain or association, e.g. of movie theaters, controlled by one management. 5 sporting events attended regularly by the same competitors and at the same venue. 6 a motor-racing track.

cir'cular *adj* round:—*n* a letter, copies of which are sent to many people.

cir'culate *vb* 1 to move in a circle or a fixed path. 2 to pass around, to spread. 3 to pass from one person to another.

circula'tion *n* 1 the act of circulating. 2 the movement of the blood through the body. 3 the number of readers (of a newspaper, etc).

circum'ference *n* the line marking the limits of a circle.

cir'cumstance *n* 1 a condition relating to or connected with an act or event. 2 *pl* state of affairs, position (often financial).

circumvent' *vb* to evade, bypass, outwit.

cir'cus *n* 1 a carnival. 2 a building or group of houses arranged in a circle.

cirrus [sir'-ês] *n* (*pl* **cir'ri**) a high, fleecy type of cloud.

cis'tern *n* a tank for storing water.

cite *vb* 1 to call to appear in court. 2 to quote. 3 to give as an example.

cit'izen *n* 1 an inhabitant of a city. 2 a member of a state.

cit'rus *adj* of a group of related fruits, including the lemon, orange, lime, and grapefruit.

cit'y *n* a large town.

civ'ic *adj* 1 having to do with a city. 2 having to do with citizens or citizenship.

civ'il *adj* 1 having to do with citizens. 2 having to do with those citizens who are members of neither the armed forces nor the clergy. 3 polite:—*adv* **civ'illy**.

civil'ian *n* one not in the armed forces.

civil'ity *n* politeness.

civiliza'tion *n* 1 a well-organized and refined society. 2 the state of being civilized.

civ'ilize *vb* 1 to teach how to live in a properly organized society. 2 to make more polite and well-mannered:—*adj* **civ'ilized**.

civil war *n* a war between citizens of the same state.

clad *pp of* **clothe**.

claim *vb* to demand as a right:—*also n*.

claim'ant *n* one who claims.

clam'ber *vb* to climb with difficulty, to scramble:—*also n*.

clam'my *adj* damp and sticky.

clamp *n* an instrument used for holding things firmly together:—*vb* to fasten with a clamp.

clan *n* a group of families related by blood and ruled by a chief:—*n* **clans'man**.

clang *n* a loud ringing sound, as of metal against metal:—*vb* to make this noise.

clank *n* a short sharp sound:—*also vb*.

clap *vb* (**clapped'**, **clap'ping**) 1 to smack the hands together noisily. 2 to slap or tap, usu in a friendly way. 3 to put suddenly and quickly:—*n* **1** the noise made by clapping the hands. **2** a sudden sound (e.g. of thunder).

clar'ify *vb* to make clear or clearer:—*n* **clarifica'tion**.

clarinet [kla'-ri-net *or* kla-ri-net'] *n* a musical wind instrument, usu of wood:—*n* **clar'inet'ist**.

clar'ity *n* clearness.

clash *n* **1** to strike together noisily. **2** to disagree strongly about. **3** (*of events*) to happen at the same time:—*n* **1** the loud noise of two objects coming violently together. **2** a quarrel.

clasp *n* **1** a metal fastener. **2** a firm hold:—*vb* **1** to fasten. **2** to hold firmly.

class *n* **1** a group of persons or things of the same kind. **2** a group of students. **3** a rank, a standard of excellence. **4** the system according to which people are divided into social groups. **5** one of these groups:—*vb* to put in a class, to regard as being of a certain type.

clas'sic *adj* of the best kind or standard:—*n* **1** a great writer or book. **2** *pl* Greek and Latin literature.

clas'sical *adj* **1** classic. **2** having to do with Greek and Latin literature.

clas'sify *vb* to arrange in classes:—*n* **classifica'tion**.

clat'ter *vb* to make rattling noises:—*n* a rattling noise.

claw *n* **1** the hooked nail of a bird or animal. **2** a foot with such nails:—*vb* to scratch or tear with claws or nails.

clay *n* a moist sticky earth that hardens when dried:—*adj* **clay'ey**.

clean *adj* **1** free from dirt. **2** pure, free from guilt, evil, crime, etc. **3** complete:—*adv* completely:—*vb* to remove dirt, dust, etc, from:—*n* **clean'er**:—*n* **clean'ness**.

clear *adj* **1** easy to hear, see, or understand. **2** bright. **3** free from difficulties or obstacles. **4** obvious:—*vb* **1** to make or become clear. **2** to prove innocent. **3** to remove difficulties or obstacles from. **4** to pass through or over:—*adv* **clear'ly**.

clef *n* a mark to show the pitch in music.

cleft *n* a crack, a split.

clench *vb* to press tightly together.

cler'gy *n* the ministers and priests of the Christian religion.

cler'gyman *n* a minister.

cler'ical *adj* **1** having to do with the clergy. **2** having to do with a clerk.

clerk [klark] *n* an office employee doing written work.

clev'er *adj* **1** able to learn quickly. **2** able to do things well with the hands, skillful:—*adv* **clev'erly**:—*n* **clev'erness**.

click *n* a light sharp sound:—*also vb*.

cli'ent *n* **1** a customer. **2** one who employs a member of some profession.

cliff *n* a high steep rock face.

cli'mate *n* the usual weather conditions of a place:—*adj* **clima'tic**.

cli'max *n* the highest or most exciting point, the most dramatic moment:—*adj* **climac'tic**.

climb *vb* to go up, using the hands and feet:—*n* **climb'er**.

cling *vb* (*pt, pp* **clung**) **1** to stick to. **2** to hold firmly to.

clin'ic *n* **1** a building or a part of a hospital for people needing special treatment or advice. **2** a place where medical specialists practice as a group. **3** the teaching of medicine by treating patients in the presence of students:—*adj* **clin'ical**.

clink *n* a sharp thin ringing sound:—*also vb*.

clip[1] *n* (**clipped'**, **clip'ping**) to cut:—*n* **1** the thing clipped. **2** a sharp blow.

clip[2] *n* a fastener:—*vb* (**clipped'**, **clip'ping**) to fasten together.

cloak *n* **1** a loose outer garment. **2** a means of hiding (some activity):—*vb* **1** to cover as with a cloak. **2** to conceal.

clock *n* **1** an instrument for telling the time. **2** an ornamental pattern on the side of a sock or stocking.

clock'wise *adj* going round in the direction of the hands of a clock.

clock'work *n* machinery like that of a clock:—**like clockwork** regularly and smoothly.

clog *n* a shoe with a wooden sole:—*vb* (**clogged'**, **clog'ging**) to block, to choke.

close[1] [klōz] *vb* **1** to shut. **2** to finish. **3** to bring or come near together:—*n* the end.

close[2] [klōs] *adj* **1** shut in. **2** stuffy. **3** near. **4** near, not far. **5** mean.

clos'et *n* a large cupboard for hanging clothes or storing things.

clot *n* a soft lump formed from liquid:—*vb* (**clot'ted**, **clot'ting**) **1** to form into clots. **2** to thicken.

cloth *n* a material made by weaving threads of wool, cotton, etc.

clothe [klō(th)z] *vb* to put clothes on.

clothes [klō(th)z] *npl* garments.

cloud *n* **1** a mass of water vapor floating high up in the air. **2** a great many. **3** a cause of gloom or trouble:—*vb* to darken:—*adjs* **cloud'y**, **cloud'less**.

clown *n* **1** a fool. **2** one who plays the fool to amuse others:—*vb* to play the fool.

club *n* **1** a heavy stick. **2** a golf stick. **3** a group of people who meet for a common purpose. **4** their meeting place. **5** *pl* a suit of playing cards:—*vb* (**clubbed'**, **club'bing**) **1** to beat with a club. **2** to join together.

cluck *n* the sound made by a hen.

clue *n* a fact that, when understood, helps one to find the answer to a problem, a hint.

clum'sy *adj* **1** awkward in movement, shape, etc. **2** badly done:—*n* **clum'siness**.

clus'ter *n* a number of things growing very close together, a closely packed group:—*vb* to grow or stand close together.

clutch *vb* **1** to seize. **2** to hold tightly:—*n* **1** a firm hold. **2** *pl* power, control. **3** eggs being hatched at one sitting. **4** in an automobile, a lever that puts an engine in or out of action.

co- *prefix* together.

coach *n* **1** (*old*) a closed four-wheeled horse carriage. **2** a railroad vehicle that carries passengers. **3** a bus. **4** a private teacher. **5** one who trains athletes:—*vb* **1** to give private lessons. **2** to prepare (someone) for a contest.

coal *n* a black substance dug from a coal mine, used as fuel for fires.

coal tar *n* a black liquid made from coal.

coarse *adj* **1** rough. **2** rude, vulgar, not refined:—*adv* **coarse'ly**:—*n* **coarse'ness**.

coast *n* the side of the land next the sea:—*vb* **1** to sail alongside the coast. **2** to move without the use of power. **3** to go on without much effort:—*adj* **coast'al**.

coast'guard *n* an organization that monitors the coast and provides help for ships in difficulty, prevents smuggling, etc.

coat *n* **1** an outer garment with sleeves. **2** the natural cover of an animal (e.g. hair, wool, fur). **3** anything that covers:—*vb* to cover.

coat of arms *n* the heraldic bearings of a family, city, institution, etc.

coax *vb* to get someone to do something by speaking kindly or petting.

cob'ble *n* a cobblestone.

cob'bler *n* a mender of shoes.

cob'blestone *n* a rounded stone used in paving roads.

cob'ra *n* a poisonous snake found in India.

cob'web *n* the spider's web.

cock *n* **1** the adult male of the domestic fowl. **2** a tap. **3** the hammer of a gun:—*vb* **1** to turn upwards, to tilt. **2** to raise, to cause to stand up. **3** (*of a gun*) to draw back the hammer before firing.

cockatoo' *n* a type of parrot.

cock'erel *n* a young cock.

cock'pit *n* the pilot's place in an aircraft.

cock'roach *n* the black beetle.

co'co *n* a tropical palm tree, on which the coconut grows.

co'coa *n* **1** a powder made from cacao seeds. **2** a drink made from this powder.

co'conut *n* the fruit of the coco palm.

cocoon' *n* a silky case spun by many insects in the chrysalis state.

cod *n* a large sea fish.

cod'dle *vb* **1** to pet, to treat with too much care. **2** to cook gently.

code *n* **1** a collection of laws, rules, or signals. **2** a method of sending secret messages by using signs or words.

codicil [kod'-i-sil] *n* a note added at the end of a will.

cof'fee *n* a drink made from the seeds of the coffee tree.

cof'fer *n* a strong box for holding money or valuable things.

cof'fin *n* a box in which a dead body is put for burial.

cog *n* the tooth of a wheel.

coher'ent *adj* clear and logical:—*n* **coher'ence.**

coil *vb* to wind in a series of rings:—*n* a ring or rings into which a rope, etc, is wound.

coin *n* a metal piece of money:—*vb* **1** to make money out of metal. **2** to invent.

coincide' *vb* (*fml*) **1** to happen at the same time. **2** to be in agreement.

coin'cidence *n* the accidental happening of one event at the same time as another:—*adjs* **coin'cident, coinciden'tal**

cold *adj* **1** not hot or warm. **2** without emotion or passion, unenthusiastic. **3** unfriendly:—*n* **1** absence of heat. **2** an illness caused by cold.

cold-blood'ed *adj* **1** having blood colder than the air or water, as fish, snakes, etc. **2** completely unfeeling, cruel.

cold'ness *n* **1** absence of heat. **2** lack of feeling. **3** unfriendliness.

collab'orate *vb* **1** to work with another, esp in writing or study. **2** to work with another to betray secrets, etc:—*ns* **collabora'tion, collab'orator.**

collapse' *n* **1** a fall. **2** a sudden loss of consciousness. **3** a failure:—*vb* **1** to fall down. **2** to fall down unconscious. **3** to fail.

col'lar *n* **1** the part of clothing that covers or surrounds the neck. **2** a strap or band put around the neck of an animal:—*vb* (*inf*) to take hold of, to seize.

col'league *n* a fellow worker.

collect' *vb* **1** to bring together. **2** to come together. **3** to gather and keep things of the same kind. **4** to obtain money by contributions.

collec'tion *n* **1** act of collecting. **2** the things collected. **3** the gathering of money for a special purpose:—*n* **collec'tor.**

collec'tive *adj* taken as a whole, joint:—*n* a collective enterprise, as a farm:—*adv* **collec'tively.**

col'lege *n* **1** a society of learned or professional people. **2** a part of a university where students live and are taught. **3** a place of further education.

collide' *vb* to run into, to strike against:—*n* **colli'sion.**

col'lie *n* a sheepdog.

col'liery *n* a coal mine.

col'on *n* **1** a mark of punctuation (:). **2** a part of the bowel.

colonel [kėr'-nėl] *n* the officer commanding a regiment of soldiers.

col'ony *n* **1** a community of settlers in a new land. **2** the place in which they settle.

col'or *n* **1** a quality that objects have and that can be seen only when light falls on them. **2** paint. **3** redness (of the face).

4 a skin color varying with race. **5** vividness. **6** *pl* a flag:—*vb* **1** to paint, to put color on or into. **2** to give interesting qualities to, to exaggerate. **3** to affect. **4** to blush.

col'or-blind *adj* unable to see the difference between colors or certain colors.

colos'sal *adj* very big, gigantic.

col'umn *n* **1** a pillar used to support or ornament a building. **2** something similar in shape. **3** a body of troops standing one behind the other in one or more lines. **4** a row of numbers, one below the other. **5** a narrow division of a page:—*adj* **colum'nar.**

co'ma *n* a long-continuing unconscious state.

comb *n* **1** a toothed instrument for disentangling and arranging hair, wool, etc. **2** the crest of a cockerel:—*vb* to disentangle or arrange with a comb.

combina'tion *n* a joining together, a union.

combine' *vb* to join together.

come [kum] *vb* (*pt* came, *pp* come) to move toward (*opposite of* go):—*vb* **com'ing:—come across** to discover (something) by accident:—**come to pass** (*old or fml*) to happen.

come'dian *n* **1** a performer who tells jokes, a comic. **2** one who is always trying to make others laugh:—*f* **comedienne'**.

com'edy *n* **1** a light or amusing play with a happy ending. **2** an amusing happening, the amusing side of something.

com'et *n* a bright heavenly body, seen only rarely, with a tail of light.

com'fort *vb* to give comfort to, to cheer (someone) up:—*n* **1** the state of being free from anxiety, worry, pain, etc, and having one's physical needs satisfied, ease. **2** something that satisfies one's physical needs. **3** strength, hope, sympathy, etc. **4** the cause of comfort to others.

com'fortable *adj* **1** at ease, free from anxiety, worry, etc. **2** providing comfort, soft and restful, relaxing.

com'ic *adj* **1** having to do with comedy. **2** amusing, laughable:—*also n.*

com'ical *adj* funny, amusing.

com'ma *n* a mark of punctuation (,).

command' *vb* **1** to order. **2** to be in charge (of). **3** to control. **4** to overlook (a place):—*n* **1** an order. **2** mastery.

command'ment *n* an order, a law.

commem'orate *vb* to make people remember something by holding a service or doing something special:—*n* **commemora'tion.**

commence' *vb* (*fml*) to begin:—*n* **commence'ment.**

commend' *vb* to praise.

com'ment *vb* **1** to say something about, to remark on. **2** to write notes in explanation of:—*n* **1** a remark. **2** an explanation.

com'mentary *n* **1** a series of remarks or notes. **2** a book explaining another book. **3** a spoken description of an event as it happens.

com'mentator *n* **1** one who comments. **2** the writer or speaker of a commentary.

com'merce *n* the buying and selling of goods, trade.

commer'cial *adj* **1** having to do with trade or commerce. **2** profit-making.

commis'sion *n* **1** act of committing. **2** an order for a work of art. **3** a group of people appointed to study and report on a particular matter. **4** money paid to someone who has helped to arrange a business deal:—*vb* to give an order or request to, to appoint.

commit' *vb* (**commit'ted, commit'ting**) **1** to perform or do, esp something illegal. **2** to make a certain agreement (that one will do something). **3** to give (someone) into care. **4** (*fml*) to put in or on.

commit'ment n 1 the act of committing. 2 a promise, a duty, an obligation. 3 state of being dedicated or devoted.

commit'tal n the act of committing, esp of sending someone to prison, etc.

commit'tee n a group of people appointed from a larger body to manage its affairs or perform a particular duty.

commod'ity n (often pl) a thing produced to be sold, an article of commerce.

com'mon adj 1 belonging to everyone, of no special rank or quality. 2 found everywhere. 3 ordinary. 4 frequent. 5 rough, vulgar, regarded as being low-class. 6 (of a noun) applying to any of a class.

common sense n practical good sense, knowledge of how to act in everyday matters.

commo'tion n disorder.

com'munal adj shared by all.

commun'icate vb 1 to make known to, to tell. 2 to get in touch with. 3 to make known information, ideas, feelings, etc, clearly to others. 4 to pass (something) to another.

communica'tion n 1 a message. 2 a means of communicating.

commun'icative adj talkative, ready to give information.

commun'ion n fellowship—**Holy Communion** the sacrament of the Lord's Supper.

commun'ity n the whole body of the people living in a city, district, country, etc.

commute' vb to travel daily from the place where one lives to another place where one works.

commu'ter n one who commutes.

compact[1] adj 1 tightly packed, firm. 2 fitted neatly together in a small space. 3 short, concise:—n **compact'ness**.

compact disk see CD.

compan'ion n 1 a friend, a person, etc, who regularly accompanies another. 2 one who goes with or accompanies. 3 a person employed to live with someone and keep him or her company. 4 one of a matching pair or set of things—n **pan'ionship**.

compan'ionable adj liking company.

com'pany n 1 a number of people gathered together by chance or invitation. 2 being together with another or others. 3 a group of persons who have put together money to run a business. 4 a group of people working together. 5 a body of soldiers commanded by a captain. 6 the crew of a ship.

compare' vb 1 to consider things together to see how they are like and how different. 2 to point out the likeness between.

compar'ison n 1 act of comparing. 2 likeness, similarity.

compart'ment n 1 a part (e.g. of a drawer) divided off from the rest. 2 one of the small rooms in a railroad coach.

compass [kum-pès] n 1 a direction-finding instrument containing a magnetic needle. 2 scope. 3 pl **com'passes** an instrument for drawing circles.

compas'sion n pity, sympathy.

compas'sionate adj feeling or showing pity.

compat'ible adj 1 able to exist together peacefully. 2 in agreement with.

compel' vb (**compelled'**, **compel'ling**) to make to do, to force:—adj **compel'ling**.

compensa'tion n something given to make up for harm or injury.

compete' vb 1 to try to do better than one's fellows in work, games, etc. 2 to take part in the hope of winning a prize.

com'petence, com'petency ns ability, skill.

com'petent adj 1 good at one's job. 2 well done. 3 (fml) having the necessary powers:—adv **com'petently**.

competi'tion n 1 the act of competing, rivalry. 2 a contest for which a prize is offered. 3 people competing for a prize, etc.

compet'itive adj encouraging competition or rivalry.

compet'itor n 1 one who competes. 2 a rival.

compile' vb to collect (facts and figures, etc) and put together in a book:—n **compil'er**:—n **compila'tion**.

complain' vb 1 to grumble. 2 to say that one is not satisfied.

complaint' n 1 a grumble. 2 an expression of dissatisfaction. 3 an illness. 4 an accusation.

complete' adj 1 finished. 2 whole. 3 perfect:—vb 1 to finish. 2 to make whole:—n **comple'tion**.

com'plex adj 1 having many parts. 2 not simple:—n a group of connected or similar things.

comple'xion n the color of the face.

com'plicated adj 1 difficult to understand. 2 confusing because of having many parts.

complica'tion n 1 a confused state of affairs. 2 an event or fact that makes things more difficult.

com'pliment n 1 praise, a flattering remark. 2 pl (fml) good wishes:—vb to praise, to express admiration.

complimen'tary adj 1 flattering, showing admiration. 2 free.

compo'nent n a part necessary to the whole object:—also adj.

compose' vb 1 to make up by putting together. 2 to write. 3 to calm.

compos'er n one who writes music.

composi'tion n 1 act of putting together. 2 the arrangement of parts to form a pleasing whole. 3 the thing composed or written. 4 a mixture.

com'post n rotting vegetable matter, etc, used as a fertilizer.

com'pound[1] adj made up of two or more parts:—n a mixture of two or more substances.

com'pound[2] n the yard or garden around a building.

comprehend' vb to understand.

comprehen'sion n the power of understanding.

comprehen'sive adj taking in as much as possible.

compress' vb to press together, to press together into a smaller space:—n **com'press** a soft pad:—n **compres'sion**.

com'promise vb 1 to reach agreement by giving way on certain points. 2 to leave open to suspicion or criticism:—n an agreement reached when each party gives way on certain points.

compul'sory adj forced, compelled.

compute' vb (fml) to calculate or estimate:—n **computa'tion**.

comput'er n an electronic machine capable of storing and processing large amounts of information and of doing calculations.

con vb (**conned'**, **con'ning**) (inf) to deceive, to trick.

con'cave adj hollow, curved inwards (like a saucer).

conceal' vb to hide, to keep from others.

conceal'ment n 1 act of concealing. 2 hiding place.

concede' vb 1 to admit as true. 2 to give up.

conceit' n too high an opinion of oneself.

conceit'ed adj too proud of oneself, vain.

conceiv'able adj able to be thought of or imagined.

conceive' vb 1 to grasp clearly with the mind. 2 to imagine. 3 to become pregnant.

con'centrate vb 1 to bring together to one point. 2 to bring all the powers of the mind to bear on. 3 to make a substance stronger by reducing its volume. 4 to pack tightly:—n a concentrated substance:—n **concentra'tion**.

con'cept n a general idea.

concern' vb 1 to have to do with. 2 to take interest. 3 (fml) to be anxious about:—n 1 an affair. 2 interest. 3 anxiety. 4 a business.

concern'ing *prep* having to do with, about.

con'cert *n* 1 a musical entertainment. 2 harmony. 3 agreement.—**in concert** 1 working together. 2 (*musicians*) playing together.

conces'sion *n* 1 the action of giving up. 2 a thing conceded, a favor. 3 a discount.

concise' *adj* short and to the point, brief:—*n* **concise'ness**.

conclude' *n* 1 (*fml*) to end, to bring to an end. 2 to arrange, to settle on. 3 to come to believe after consideration of the facts.

conclu'sion *n* 1 (*fml*) end. 2 the idea finally reached after thinking something out.

conclu'sive *adj* convincing, putting an end to doubt.

con'crete *adj* 1 solid, having a real bodily existence (unlike an idea). 2 definite:—*n* a mixture of cement, sand, and gravel with water.

concur'rent *adj* happening at the same time:—*adv* **concur'rently**.

concus'sion *n* a temporary injury caused to the brain by a violent blow on the head.

condemn' *vb* 1 to blame. 2 to find guilty. 3 to name a punishment for a guilty person:—*n* **condemna'tion**.

condense' *vb* 1 to make shorter or smaller. 2 to make a substance more solid (e.g. change vapor into liquids):—*n* **condensa'tion**.

condescend' *vb* to agree to do something supposedly beneath one's dignity, usu in an ungracious, patronizing manner:—*adj* **condescend'ing**:—*n* **condescen'sion**.

con'diment *n* anything sharp-tasting eaten with food to bring out its flavor or taste.

condi'tion *n* 1 state. 2 something that must be or happen before something else can take place:—*adj* **condi'tional**.

conduct' *vb* 1 to lead, to guide. 2 to carry. 3 to direct. 4 (*fml*) to behave:—*n* **con'duct** behavior.

conduct'or *n* 1 the director of an orchestra. 2 a substance that passes on heat or electricity to something else.

cone *n* 1 a figure with a circular base and a pointed top. 2 the fruit of pines and firs. 3 any object shaped like a cone.

confec'tion *n* 1 candy, ice cream, preserves, etc. 2 anything too fanciful or ornate:—*n* **confec'tionery**.

confed'erate *adj* joined together by agreement:—*n* **confedera'tion**.

confer' *vb* (**conferred'**, **confer'ring**) 1 to talk together. 2 to give.

con'ference *n* a meeting held to discuss matters.

confess' *vb* 1 to own up to, to admit. 2 to tell one's sins to a priest.

confes'sion *n* an account of the wrong one has done.

confet'ti *n* small pieces of colored paper thrown at newly married people.

confide' *vb* to give or tell something to a person one trusts.

con'fidence *n* 1 trust. 2 belief in one's own abilities.

con'fident *adj* having no fear of failure:—*adv* **con'fidently**.

confiden'tial *adj* 1 trusted. 2 secret:—*adv* **confiden'tially**.

configura'tion *n* (*fml*) shape.

confine' *vb* 1 to shut up. 2 to keep within limits:—*n* a limit, a boundary.

confirm' *vb* 1 to say that something is undoubtedly certain or true. 2 to give final approval to.

confirma'tion *n* 1 proof. 2 the ceremony or sacrament by which one becomes a full member of certain churches.

confirmed' *adj* settled, habitual.

con'fiscate *vb* to seize a person's private property, esp as a punishment:—*n* **confisca'tion**.

con'flict *n* 1 a state of disagreement. 2 a fight:—*vb* **conflict'** to disagree, to clash.

conform' *vb* 1 to act or think like most other people, to accept the laws and customs of the time or place. 2 to obey, to be in accordance with.

conform'ity *n* behavior, attitudes, etc, that are the same as most people's.

confound' *vb* to surprise.

confront' *vb* to meet face to face:—*n* **confronta'tion**.

confuse' *vb* 1 to put into disorder, to muddle. 2 to puzzle, to bewilder. 3 to mistake one person or thing for another.

confu'sion *n* 1 disorder. 2 puzzlement, bewilderment.

congeal' *vb* 1 to freeze. 2 to become solid and stiff.

congen'ital *adj* dating from birth.

conger [kon(g)'-gėr] *n* a sea eel.

congest'ed *adj* 1 overcrowded. 2 too full of blood:—*n* **congest'ion**.

conglomera'tion *n* a mixed collection.

congrat'ulate *vb* to express pleasure at another's success, a happy event, etc:—*n* **congratula'tion**:—*adj* **congra'tulatory**.

con'gregate *vb* to meet together, to form a crowd.

congrega'tion *n* a gathering of people, esp at a church service.

con'gress *n* 1 a formal meeting to settle questions. 2 (*with cap*) the parliament of the USA, comprising the Senate and the House of Representatives.

con'ic, **con'ical** *adjs* cone-shaped.

con'ifer *n* a cone-bearing tree:—*adj* **conif'erous**.

conjec'ture *vb* to guess, to suppose.

conjure [kun'-jėr] *vb* to do magic, to do tricks so skillfully that the onlooker cannot see how they are done:—*n* **con'jurer**.

connect' *vb* 1 to join together. 2 to see that a thing or idea is related to another, to associate in the mind:—**well-connec'ted** related to important or powerful people.

connec'tion *n* 1 something that joins. 2 a relation by blood or marriage. 3 something that makes one think of a certain person, place, event, etc, when one sees another.

connive' *vb* to pretend not to see wrongdoing:—*n* **conni'vance**.

connoisseur [kon-ês-sèr'] *n* one with good knowledge of something and the ability to tell what is bad from what is good.

con'quer *vb* 1 to win by war. 2 to defeat. 3 to overcome:—*n* **con'queror**.

con'quest *n* 1 act of conquering. 2 the thing gained by force.

con'science *n* one's sense of right and wrong.

conscien'tious *adj* careful to do one's duty at work:—*n* **conscien'tiousness**.

con'scious *adj* 1 knowing what is going on around one. 2 aware:—*n* **con'sciousness**.

consec'utive *adj* following one after the other, in the correct order.

consent' *vb* to agree, to give one's permission:—*n* agreement, permission.

con'sequence *n* 1 a result, an effect. 2 importance.

conser'vative *adj* disliking change.

conser'vatory *n* a glasshouse for plants, a greenhouse.

conserve' *vb* to keep (something) as it is. 2 to keep from being wasted:—*n* a fruit preserved in sugar, jam:—*n* **conserva'tion**.

consid'er *vb* 1 to think about. 2 to think seriously. 3 to take into account. 4 to regard as.

consid'erable *adj* fairly large, great.

consid'erate *adj* thoughtful for others.

considera'tion *n* 1 serious thought. 2 thought for others and their feelings. 3 a payment or reward.

consid'ering *prep* allowing for.

consist' *vb* to be made up of.

consist'ency *n* 1 degree of thickness. 2 the quality of being consistent.

consis'tent *adj* **1** fixed, having a regular pattern. **2** agreeing with. **3** always thinking or acting on the same principles.

consola'tion *n* **1** comfort. **2** a person or thing that brings comfort in sorrow or sadness.

console' *vb* to comfort in sorrow:—*adj* **consol'atory**.

con'sonant *n* a speech sound or letter other than a vowel:—*adj* in agreement with.

conspic'uous *adj* easily seen, very noticeable.

conspir'acy *n* **1** a coming together to plan wrongdoing. **2** a plot.

conspire' *vb* **1** to plan secretly together to do something unlawful. **2** to unite:—*n* **conspir'ator**.

con'stable *n* **1** the lowest rank of police officer in some countries. **2** (*old*) a governor of a royal castle.

con'stant *adj* **1** never stopping. **2** unchanging. **3** (*fml*) faithful, loyal:—*n* **con'stancy**.

con'stantly *adv* **1** again and again, nearly always, regularly. **2** without stopping.

constella'tion *n* a group of stars.

con'stipated *adj* having difficulty in clearing the bowels:—*n* **constipa'tion**.

constit'uency *n* **1** a body of electors. **2** the voters in a particular district or area:—*n* **constit'uent**.

constitu'tion *n* **1** the way something is made up. **2** the general health of the body. **3** the body of law in keeping with which a country is governed.

constrict' *vb* **1** to make smaller or narrower, to make tight. **2** to prevent free movement:—*n* **constric'tion**.

construct' *vb* **1** to build. **2** to make by putting the parts together.

construc'tion *n* **1** act of constructing. **2** the thing constructed. **3** the way of arranging words to give a certain meaning. **4** (*fml*) meaning.

construc'tive *adj* useful and helpful.

consult' *vb* **1** to ask advice, information, or help from. **2** to discuss matters with. **3** to look up:—*n* **consulta'tion**.

consul'tant *n* one able to advise, esp a doctor who is an expert in one branch of medicine.

consume' *vb* **1** to eat. **2** to use up.

consum'er *n* one who buys or uses.

consump'tion *n* **1** the act of using. **2** the amount used.

con'tact *n* **1** touch. **2** communication:—*vb* to get in touch with, to communicate with.

contag'ious *adj* (*of disease*) able to be passed on by touch, quickly spreading to others:—*n* **contag'ion**.

contain' *vb* **1** to have in it. **2** to keep control of.

contain'er *n* anything made in order to hold something else in it.

contam'inate *vb* **1** to make dirty, infected, or impure, to pollute:—*n* **contamina'tion**.

con'template *vb* **1** to look at thoughtfully. **2** to think deeply about. **3** to think of doing:—*n* **contempla'tion**.

contem'porary *adj* **1** belonging to the same time. **2** modern:—*n* one who lives at the same time as another.

contempt' *n* the feeling that another person or thing is worthless and to be looked down on, scorn.

contempt'ible *adj* deserving to be looked down on.

contempt'uous *adj* showing contempt.

con'tent'¹ *n* that which is in something else.

content'² *adj* satisfied, pleased, not wanting more than one has:—*also vb and n:—n* **content'ment**.

contest' *vb* **1** to try to prove wrong. **2** to try hard to gain:—*n* **con'test 1** a struggle. **2** a competition.

contes'tant *n* one who contests.

con'text *n* **1** the part of a book from which a shorter passage has been taken. **2** circumstances, surrounding conditions.

con'tinent'¹ *n* one of the large land masses in the world (e.g. Africa).

con'tinent'² *adj* **1** able to control urination and defecation. **2** practicing self-restraint, chaste.

continent'al *adj* having to do with a continent.

contin'ual *adj* **1** going on all the time. **2** happening again and again, repeated.

contin'ue *vb* **1** to go on doing. **2** to carry on with later. **3** to go or move further. **4** to remain.

contin'uous *adj* **1** never stopping. **2** unbroken.

contort' *vb* to twist out of shape.

con'tour *n* **1** an outline, a shape. **2** a line drawn on a map through all places of the same height.

contract' *vb* **1** to make smaller or shorter. **2** to make or become smaller or shorter. **3** to begin to have:—*n* **con'tract** a legal written agreement.

contrac'tion *n* **1** something becoming smaller or shorter. **2** a shortened form.

contract'or *n* one who undertakes to do certain jobs.

contradict' *vb* **1** to say the opposite. **2** to say that something is not true:—*n* **contradic'tion**.

contradic'tory *adj* saying the opposite.

contrap'tion *n* an unusual machine or instrument.

con'trary [kon'-tra-ri *or* kon-trā'-ri] *adj* **1** opposite. **2** always choosing to act differently from others, difficult to deal with:—*n* **con'trary** the opposite.

contrast' *vb* **1** to put things together to show clearly the differences between them. **2** to appear very different from:—*n* **con'trast** a clear difference.

contrib'ute *vb* **1** to give part of what is needed. **2** to write something for:—*ns* **contribu'tion, contrib'utor**.

contrib'utory *adj* giving a share, helping.

con'trite *adj* showing or feeling guilt or sorrow:—*n* **contri'tion**.

contri'vance *n* **1** act of contriving. **2** an invention, an apparatus.

contrive' *vb* **1** to succeed in, usu with difficulty. **2** to succeed in bringing about, usu with difficulty.

control' *n* **1** power over the movements and actions of another person or thing. **2** power over one's own thoughts and feelings (self-control). **3** *pl* those parts of a machine that start, stop, or change the movement of all other parts:—*vb* (**controlled', control'ling**) **1** to have power or authority over. **2** to direct the movements of. **3** to hold back, to restrain. **4** to regulate, to cause to keep to a fixed standard:—*n* **control'ler**.

controver'sial *adj* causing controversy.

con'troversy *n* disagreement, dispute.

contu'sion *n* (*fml*) a bad bruise.

convalesce' *vb* to recover gradually after an illness:—*n* **convales'cence:—adj, n** **convales'cent**.

conve'nience *n* **1** quality of being convenient. **2** comfort.

conve'nient *adj* **1** suitable, not causing trouble or difficulty. **2** easy to reach, accessible. **3** easy to use or manage.

con'vent *n* a house of nuns:—*adj* **conven'tual**.

conven'tion *n* **1** a large meeting called for a special purpose. **2** an agreement. **3** a way of behaving that has been in use for so long that it is regarded as necessary, a custom.

conven'tional *adj* **1** following convention. **2** accepting the manners and ideas of others, not original.

converge' *vb* to come from different directions toward one point:—*n* **conver'gence:—adj** **conver'gent**.

conversa'tion *n* talk, speech with others.

converse'¹ *vb* to engage in conversation (with):—*n* familiar talk, conversation.

con'verse'² *n* the exact opposite:—*also adj.*

conver'sion n a change.

convert' vb 1 to change from one state or form to another. 2 to get another to change his or her ideas, esp on religion:—n **con'vert** one who has changed his or her beliefs or way of life.

convert'ible adj able to be changed into something else:—n an automobile with a folding or detachable roof.

con'vex adj curved outwards (like a saucer when upside down):—n **convex'ity**.

convey' vb 1 to carry, to take from one place to another. 2 to pass (e.g. property) from one person to another. 3 to make known.

convey'ance n any kind of vehicle that carries people or things.

convict' vb to prove guilty, esp in a court of law:—n **con'vict** a person imprisoned for a crime.

convic'tion n 1 a proving guilty. 2 a strong belief.

convince' vb to persuade a person that something is true.

convinc'ing adj 1 able to convince. 2 clear.

convulse' vb 1 to shake violently. 2 to agitate, to disturb.

convul'sion n a fit, shaking.

coo vb to make a sound, as a dove:—also n.

cook vb to prepare food by heating it:—n one who prepares food for eating.

cook'ery n the art of preparing food.

cook'ie n a sweet biscuit.

cool adj slightly cold, pleasantly cold. 2 calm, not easily excited:—vb 1 to make or become colder. 2 to become calmer or less keen:—n **cool'ness**.

cool'ly adv calmly, without excitement.

coop n a cage for hens or small animals:—vb to shut up in a small space.

coop'erate, co-op'erate vb to work or act together:—n **coopera'tion, co-opera'tion**.

coop'erative, co-op'erative adj willing to work with others, helpful. 2 made, done, etc, by people working together:—n an organization or enterprise owned by, and operated for the benefit of, those using its services.

cope vb to deal with, esp successfully.

cop'ing n the top row of stones on a wall.

co'pious adj plentiful.

cop'per n a reddish metal.

cop'pice, copse ns a small wood, a group of bushes growing close together.

copse see **coppice**.

cop'y n 1 a thing done or made in exactly the same way as another. 2 a single example of a newspaper, magazine, book, etc. 3 written material given to the printer for printing:—vb to imitate, to make a copy of.

cop'yright n the right, given to one person or publisher only, to print and sell books, music or pictures for a certain number of years.

cor'al n a rock-like material built up under the sea from the skeletons of tiny creatures (polyps).

cord n 1 a thin rope, a thick string. 2 a length of electrical cable or flex attached to an electrical apparatus. 3 a part of the body resembling this.

cor'dial adj 1 very friendly. 2 heartfelt:—n a refreshing drink.

cordill'era n a continuous ridge or chain of mountains.

cor'don n a line of soldiers, police, etc, to prevent people from entering an area:—vb to surround with a cordon.

core n 1 the central part of a fruit in which the seeds are stored. 2 the innermost part, the most important part.

cork n 1 the cork tree or its bark. 2 a stopper made from cork:—vb to stop a bottle with a cork.

cork'screw n an instrument for taking the cork out of a bottle.

corn n 1 a grain-bearing plant, as wheat, oats, etc. 2 the seeds of cereal plants, maize. 3(inf) something corny:—vb to put salt on to preserve.

corn[2] n a hard painful growth on the toe or foot.

cor'nea n the transparent covering of the eyeball.

cor'ner n 1 the meeting place of two walls. 2 a bend in a road. 3 a difficult position:—vb 1 to drive into a position from which there is no escape. 2 to put into a difficult situation. 3 to gain sole control of.

corn'starch n a flour made from corn used for thickening sauces.

corn'y adj (inf) overly sentimental, unsophisticated.

corol'la n the petals of a flower.

corona'tion n the crowning of a king or queen.

cor'oner n an officer of the law who holds an inquiry in the case of sudden or violent death.

cor'poral[1] adj (fml) having to do with the body.

corporal[2] n the lowest officer in the army.

corporal punishment n punishing by beating the body.

cor'porate adj 1 forming one group. 2 of or shared by all the members of a group:—adv **cor'porately**.

corpora'tion n 1 a group of people allowed by the law to act as one person in certain cases (e.g. in business matters). 2 (inf) fatness in the middle of the body.

corps [kôr or kär] n 1 a large body of soldiers, a division of an army. 2 a group of people working together for one purpose.

corpse n the dead body of a human being, a cadaver.

correct' adj right, having no mistakes:—vb 1 to set right, to remove mistakes from. 2 to point out or mark mistakes:—n **correct'ness**.

correc'tion n 1 act of correcting. 2 the right thing put in place of a mistake.

correspond' vb 1 to write letters to. 2 to fit in with, to agree with. 3 to be like, to be the equivalent of.

correspond'ence n 1 all the letters a person or office sends or receives. 2 likeness.

correspond'ent n 1 one who writes letters to another. 2 one who sends special reports to a newspaper.

correspond'ing adj like or similar.

cor'ridor n an indoor passage.

corrode' vb to eat or wear away slowly:—n **corro'sion**.

corro'sive adj able to eat away:—also n.

corrupt' vb to make or become evil or morally bad:—adj 1 evil. 2 ready to act dishonestly for money:—n **corrup'tion**:—adv **corrupt'ly**.

cortege [kor-tezh'] n a procession, as at a funeral.

cosmet'ic n something used to make the face and hair more beautiful:—adj 1 intended to improve the appearance. 2 dealing only with outside appearances.

cos'mic adj having to do with the universe.

cosmopol'itan adj 1 consisting of people from many different parts of the world. 2 having or showing wide experience of different peoples and places.

cos'mos n the whole universe.

cos'set vb to treat with great or too much kindness, to pamper.

cost vb (pt, pp **cost**) 1 to be on sale at a certain price. 2 to cause loss or suffering:—n 1 the price of something. 2 loss. 3 pl the money needed to pay for a lawsuit.

cost'ly adj having a high price, dear.

cos'tume n 1 the clothes worn in a special place or at a special time. 2 a woman's jacket and skirt, a suit.

cot n a bed with movable sides for a child.

cot'tage n a small house.

cot'ton n 1 a soft white substance got from the cotton plant. 2 thread or cloth made of cotton:—also adj.

couch [kowch] vb (fml) to put into words:—n a sofa, something on which one lies.

cough [kof] vb 1 to force air noisily from the throat, often to clear it:—n 1 a noisy forcing of the air from the throat. 2 an illness marked by frequent coughing.

coun'cil n a number of people chosen to make decisions for a larger number.

coun'cilor n a member of a council.

coun'sel n 1 (fml) advice. 2 professional advice given by a counselor. 3 the lawyer who presents a case in a law court:—vb to advise.

coun'selor n an adviser, one who gives (professional) advice on a variety of personal problems.

count[1] vb 1 to number. 2 to consider (as). 3 to matter:—n a numbering.

count[2] n a foreign noble.

coun'tenance n the face.

coun'ter n 1 a person or thing that counts. 2 a small flat object used in some games instead of money. 3 the table in a store across which goods are sold:—vb to act in order to oppose or defend oneself against.

counteract' vb to undo or prevent the effect of by opposite action.

counterclockwise adv going round in the direction opposite to the hands of a clock.

counterfeit [kown'-têr-feet] vb 1 to copy or imitate in order to deceive. 2 (fml) to pretend:—adj 1 not real. 2 made like, in order to deceive. 3 pretended:—n something copied, not real or true.

countermand' vb to withdraw an order or give an opposite order to replace it.

coun'terpart n a person or thing almost exactly the same as another.

count'less adj too many to be counted.

coun'try n 1 the land of one nation or people. 2 the land outside and away from cities. 3 an area or stretch of land:—adj having to do with the country rather than the town.

coun'tryman n 1 one living away from cities. 2 one belonging to the same nation.

coun'tryside n country areas.

coun'ty n a part of a country, operated for administrative purposes.

coup [kö] n a sudden successful action.

coupé n a covered two-seater automobile.

couple [kup'-êl] n 1 (inf) two. 2 a man and his wife:—vb 1 to join. 2 to link or associate with.

cou'pon n 1 a ticket that can be exchanged for money or goods. 2 an entry form.

cour'age n bravery.

coura'geous adj brave, fearless.

cour'ier n 1 a messenger. 2 a guide in charge of a party of travelers.

course n 1 the way along which a thing moves or runs. 2 the ground on which a race is run or golf is played. 3 a number of lectures or lessons given for the same purpose. 4 a row of stones, all at the same height, in a wall. 5 part of a meal served at the one time:—vb 1 to hunt, esp hares, with dogs. 2 (fml) to move quickly.

court n 1 a place marked out for tennis, squash rackets, etc. 2 a king and queen and all their advisers and attendants. 3 the building in which judges hear cases and give decisions. 4 all the judges and officials in a court of law. 5 attentions paid to someone to gain favor:—vb 1 to pay attention to a woman with a view to marrying her. 2 (fml) to try to gain. 3 to act in a way that is likely to bring about (something unpleasant).

courteous [kêrt'-yês] adj polite, considerate and respectful.

courtesy [kêr'-tê-si] n politeness, good manners.

court'yard n an open space shut in by walls or houses on every side.

cous'in n the child of an uncle or aunt.

cove n a small bay.

cov'er vb 1 to spread over. 2 to protect. 3 to wrap (up). 4 to include:—also n.

covet [kuv'-êt] vb to want to have something belonging to another:—adj cov'etous:—n cov'etousness.

cow n the female of certain animals (e.g. of the ox, elephant, whale).

cow'ard n one easily frightened.

cow'ardice n fear of danger.

cow'ardly adj having no bravery.

cow'boy n a man who looks after cattle on a ranch.

cow'er vb to crouch or shrink back out of fear.

coy adj 1 shy, bashful, esp excessively so. 2 reluctant to give information:—adv coy'ly.

co'zy adj pleasantly comfortable or warm:—n a teapot or egg cover:—adv co'zily.

crab n 1 a ten-legged sea creature with a shell. 2 a wild apple, a sour-tasting apple.

crab'bed adj bad-tempered, cross.

crack n 1 a sudden sharp noise. 2 a break in which the parts remain together. 3 a sharp blow:—also vb:—adj very good.

crack'er n 1 a small firework. 2 a crisp biscuit.

crack'le vb to go on making short sharp noises, to rustle:—n the act or sound of crackling.

cra'dle n a baby's bed that can be rocked.

craft n 1 cleverness, esp in deceiving. 2 a trade needing special skill. 3 a ship or airplane.

crafts'man n a skilled workman, esp with the hands:—ns crafts(s)'manship.

craft'y adj good at deceiving, cunning:—adv craft'ily.

crag n a steep, rough rock:—adj crag'gy.

cram vb (crammed', cram'ming) 1 to fill very full. 2 to learn many facts for an examination.

cramp n a sudden sharp pain in a muscle:—vb to prevent free movement, to hinder.

crane n 1 a long-legged, long-necked water bird. 2 a machine for raising heavy weights:—vb to stretch out one's neck.

crank n 1 in machines, a part that changes a movement of one shape into that of another. 2 a person with fixed obsessive ideas:—vb to turn or wind.

cra'nium n (fml) the skull.

cran'ny n a small narrow opening, a crack.

crash vb 1 to fall with a loud noise. 2 to dash violently against something:—n 1 the loud noise of a breakage or collision. 2 the sudden failure of a business.

crass adj very stupid, insensitive.

crate n a large box or packing case, with spaces between the boards.

cra'ter n 1 the bowl-shaped mouth of a volcano. 2 a deep wide hole in the earth.

crave vb 1 to beg for. 2 to desire very much.

crav'ing n a strong desire.

crawl vb 1 to move with the body on or near the ground, to move on the hands and knees. 2 to move slowly:—n 1 act of crawling. 2 a stroke in swimming.

cray'on n a stick of colored chalk, a colored pencil:—vb to draw with crayons.

craze vb to drive mad:—n a popular fashion, a temporary enthusiasm or fad.

craz'y adj 1 (inf) mad. 2 very enthusiastic, liking very much.

creak vb to make a harsh squeaking sound:—also n:—adj **creak'y**.

cream n 1 the oily part of the milk that rises to the top and from which butter is made. 2 the best of anything. 3 a cream-like substance for rubbing into the skin. 4 the color of cream.

cream'y adj like cream.

crease n a mark made by folding, crushing, or pressing.

create [kree-āt'] vb 1 to bring into existence. 2 to make.

crea'tion n 1 act of creating. 2 anything made or invented.

crea'tive adj 1 involving creation. 2 able to create or invent, producing original ideas and works.

crea'tor n one who creates or invents:—**the Creator** God.

creature [kree'-tyèr] n anything created, esp human beings, animals, etc.

cred'ible adj able to be believed:—n **credibil'ity**.

cred'it n 1 belief, trust in. 2 approval or praise. 3 a cause of honor. 4 a system of buying goods or services and paying for them later. 5 the quality of being able to pay debts. 6 the money a person has in a bank:—vb 1 to believe. 2 to sell or lend in trust. 3 to write in on the credit side of an account. 4 to consider as having (a good quality).

cred'itor n one to whom money is owed.

creep vb (pt, pp **crept**) 1 to move with the body on or near the ground. 2 to move slowly and silently. 3 to shiver with horror.

creep'er adj a plant that grows along the ground or up walls, trees, etc.

cre'mate vb to burn (a corpse) to ashes:—n **crema'tion**.

crepe [krep] n a soft light cloth with a finely lined and folded surface.

cres'cent n 1 the shape of the moon in its first and last quarter. 2 a narrow tapering curve. 3 a curving street:—adj shaped like a crescent.

crest n 1 a tuft or comb on the head of certain birds. 2 a bunch of feathers on the top of a helmet. 3 a sign or badge of family, seen on coats of arms, writing paper, etc. 4 the top of a slope, wave, etc:—vb to get to the top of.

crew n 1 the sailors of a ship. 2 a gang.

crib n a baby's bed.

crick n a painful stiffness, esp of the neck:—vb to cause this.

crick'et¹ n a small jumping insect.

crick'et² n an outdoor game played with a bat and ball:—n **crick'eter**.

crime n a breaking of the law.

crim'inal adj 1 against the law. 2 wrong, wicked:—n one who breaks the law.

crim'son n a deep red color:—also adj:—vb to make or become red.

cringe vb 1 to shrink back in fear. 2 to behave too humbly toward.

crip'ple n one who is unable to use some or all of his limbs:—vb 1 to make unable to move freely, to make lame. 2 to make less strong, less efficient, etc.

cris'is n (pl **crises** [krī'-seez]) 1 a turning point at which things must become either better or worse. 2 a very serious state of affairs.

crisp adj 1 hard but easily broken. 2 tight. 3 fresh and firm. 4 firm and clear. 5 dry and clear:—vb to curl or twist:—adv **crisp'ly**.

crit'ic n 1 one who judges something by pointing out its good and bad points. 2 one who finds fault, a person who expresses dislike and disapproval of.

crit'ical adj 1 pointing out both good and bad. 2 hard to please, ready to find fault. 3 having to do with a crisis. 4 most important.

crit'icism n 1 judgment. 2 fault-finding.

crit'icize vb 1 to point out the good and bad in. 2 to find fault with.

croak vb to make a low hoarse noise in the throat:—adj **croak'y**.

crock'ery n earthenware or china cups, plates, and other dishes.

croc'odile n a large reptile that can live both in water and on land.

crook n 1 a bend, curve. 2 a stick, hook-shaped at one end, as carried by a shepherd or bishop. 3 (inf) a dishonest person, a criminal:—vb to bend, to shape like a hook.

crook'ed adj 1 not straight, twisted. 2 dishonest, illegal. 3 dishonest, not to be trusted:—n **crook'edness**.

crop n 1 a pocket in the throat of birds in which the food is partly digested before passing to the stomach. 2 a riding whip. 3 the whole amount of grain, fruit, etc, growing or gathered at one place or time. 4 a short haircut:—vb (**cropped'**, **crop'ping**) 1 to cut short. 2 to bite off. 3 to sow or gather (a crop):—**crop up** to turn up unexpectedly.

cross n 1 a mark made by drawing one straight line across another, e.g. +, x. 2 one piece of wood fastened across another in the shape of a cross. 3 anything made in the shape of a cross. 4 the sign of the Christian religion. 5(old) a cross-shaped wooden frame to which criminals were fixed as a punishment. 6 a place where roads meet. 7 a monument in the shape of a cross. 8 a source of suffering or sorrow. 9 an animal or plant that is the offspring of different breeds or varieties:—vb 1 to draw a line through or across. 2 to go from one side to the other side. 3 to pass across each other. 4 to put or place something across or over something of the same type. 5 to hinder, to obstruct:—adj angry, bad-tempered.

cross-coun'try adj going across fields, etc, instead of along roads.

cross-exam'ine vb to ask a person questions about a statement he or she has made to test its truth, esp in a court of law:—n **cross-examina'tion**.

cros'sing n a place at which one may cross a street, river, etc.

cross-ques'tion vb to cross-examine.

cross'roads n the place where two roads cross.

cross'word n a word puzzle with squares and clues.

crow n 1 a large black bird. 2 the cry of a cock. 3 a baby's cry of pleasure:—vb 1 to cry like a cock. 2 (of a baby) to make sounds expressing pleasure. 3 (inf) to boast:—**as the crow flies** following the straightest and shortest way from one place to another.

crow'bar n a bar of iron used to raise heavy objects.

crowd n a large number of people gathered together, esp in a small space:—vb 1 to come together in large numbers. 2 to fill too full by coming together in.

crowd'ed adj full of people or objects.

crown n 1 an ornamental head-covering worn by a king or queen as a sign of office. 2 a wreath worn on the head. 3 the top of certain things:—vb 1 to put a crown on. 2 to finish with a success. 3 (inf) to hit on the head.

crucial [krö'-sh-ẽl] adj of the greatest importance, needing a clear decision.

cruci'fix n a cross with the sculptured figure of Christ.

cru'cify *vb* 1 to put to death by fastening on a cross. 2 to treat cruelly:—*n* **crucifix'ion**.

crude *adj* 1 rough. 2 in the natural state. 3 coarse, vulgar, not refined:—*n* **crud'ity**.

crude oil *n* a heavy oil obtained from under the surface of the earth, petroleum.

cru'el *adj* 1 taking pleasure in making others suffer, hard-hearted. 2 causing pain:—*n* **cru'elty**.

cruise [krōōz] *vb* 1 to sail here and there, often now for pleasure. 2 to travel at the speed that uses up least fuel:—also *n*.

crumb *n* a very small bit, esp of bread. 2 a small piece.

crum'ble *vb* 1 to break into small bits or dust. 2 to fall to pieces or into dust. 3 gradually to get into a poor state and come to an end.

crum'ple *vb* 1 to press into many folds, to crush out of shape. 2 to fall down suddenly. 3 to collapse, to fail:—also *n*.

crunch *vb* to crush noisily with the teeth:—also *n*.

crush *vb* 1 to squeeze or press together with force. 2 to press out of shape. 3 to defeat completely:—*n* the crowding together of things or persons.

crust *n* the hard outside of anything (e.g. bread):—*vb* to cover with a crust.

crust'y *adj* 1 having a crust. 2 short-tempered:—*adv* **crust'ily**.

crutch *n* a stick, with a top made to fit under the armpits, to support lame people. 2 a person or thing that provides help and support.

crux *n* the most important or difficult part of a matter, issue, etc.

cry *vb* 1 to make shrill loud sounds of weeping, joy, etc. 2 to weep. 3 to shout:—also *n*.

cry'ing *adj* needing to be put right.

crys'tal *n* 1 a clear, bright glass. 2 a hard glassy-looking stone. 3 one of the regular shapes in which the atoms of certain bodies are arranged:—also *adj*:—*adj* **crys'talline**.

crys'tallize *vb* 1 to form into crystals. 2 to make or become clear or definite:—*n* **crys'tallization**.

cub *n* the young of certain animals (e.g. the bear, fox, etc).

cube *n* a solid body with six equal square sides.

cu'bicle *n* 1 a small bedroom in a dormitory or large sleeping room. 2 a compartment in a larger room.

cuckoo [kŏŏ-kō] *n* a bird that lays its eggs in the nests of other birds.

cu'cumber *n* a creeping plant with a long green fruit much used in salads.

cud'dle *vb* 1 to hug lovingly. 2 to lie close and comfortably.

cue *n* 1 a word or sign that reminds a person of what to say or do next. 2 the long stick used for striking the balls in pool, etc.

cuff[1] *n* the part of a sleeve near the wrist.

cuff[2] *n* a blow:—also *vb*.

cul-de-sac [kŏl-dĕ-sak] *n* a street closed at one end.

cul'inary *adj* having to do with cooking.

cul'prit *n* a wrongdoer, one accused of a crime.

cul'tivate *vb* 1 to prepare (land) for the growing of crops. 2 to make to grow. 3 to improve (the mind):—*n* **cultiva'tion**:—*n* **cul'tivator**.

cul'ture *n* 1 the character of an age and people as seen in customs, arts, etc. 2 learning and good taste. 3 the rearing of creatures or growing of plants in conditions not natural to them:—*adj* **cul'tural**.

cum'bersome *adj* 1 heavy and difficult to move. 2 slow and inefficient.

cu'mulus *n* a mass of white rounded cloud.

cun'ning *adj* 1 clever, skilful, craft. 2 good at deceiving. 3 clever:—*n* skill, deceit.

cup *n* a small drinking vessel:—*vb* (**cupped'**, **cup'ping**) to put into the shape of a cup.

cupboard [kub'-ẽrd] *n* a shelved place for storing food, dishes, etc.

cur *n* 1 a dog of no fixed breed, a mongrel. 2 a low mean person.

cu'rate *n* a member of clergy who assists a vicar or priest.

curb *vb* to restrain, to check, to keep in subjection:—*n* 1 that which checks, restrains, or subdues. 2 a line of raised stones forming the edge of a sidewalk.

cur'dle *vb* to thicken, to become solid.

cure *n* 1 act of healing. 2 that which heals or gives back health. 3 (*fml*) the care of souls:—*vb* 1 to heal. 2 to preserve meat, fish, etc.

cur'few *n* 1 (*old*) a bell rung in the evening as a signal to put out all lights. 2 a military order for people to be indoors and keep the streets empty after a certain hour. 3 the time at which people have to be indoors.

curios'ity *n* 1 the desire to learn, or to find out about. 2 a rare or strange object.

cu'rious *adj* 1 wanting to learn. 2 wanting to know the private affairs of others. 3 strange.

curl *vb* 1 to form into ringlets. 2 to twist around and around. 3 to play at the game of curling:—*n* a ringlet.

cur'rant *n* 1 a small dried grape. 2 a type of berry growing on certain shrubs.

cur'rency *n* 1 the money in present use in a country. 2 the state of being widely known.

cur'rent *adj* 1 in general use. 2 belonging to the present time:—*n* 1 a stream of water or air moving in a certain direction. 2 a flow of electricity.

cur'ry[1] *n* a dish of meat, vegetables, etc, cooked with a hot-tasting sauce.

cur'ry[2] *vb*:—**curry favor** to try to win the favor of another by pleasing.

curse *vb* 1 to use bad language. 2 to call down harm and evil upon:—*n* the wish that another may suffer harm and evil. 2 a great evil or cause of suffering. 3 a swear word.

cur'sor *n* a flashing indicator on a computer screen.

cur'sory *adj* quick, careless.

curt *adj* 1 abrupt, rude. 2 brief, abrupt:—*n* **curt'ness**.

cur'tain *n* a cloth hung up to darken, or to hide things behind it:—*also vb*.

curve *n* 1 a line that is not straight and that changes direction without angles. 2 something shaped like this:—*vb* to bend into a curve.

cush'ion *n* 1 a cloth bag, filled with soft material, for sitting, leaning, or kneeling on. 2 anything that takes the force of a blow or shock:—*vb* to lessen a blow or shock.

cus'tard *n* a dish of milk, eggs, and sugar, baked or boiled.

cus'tody *n* 1 care. 2 safekeeping. 3 imprisonment.

cus'tom *n* 1 the usual way of doing something. 2 something done often as a habit. 3 the buying of certain things at one particular store, etc. 4 *pl* the taxes payable on goods brought into a country. 5 *pl* the office where such taxes are paid, the officials collecting them.

cus'tomary *adj* usual.

cus'tomer *n* one who usu buys things (in a particular store).

cut *vb* (**cut**, **cut'ting**) 1 to make an opening with a sharp instrument. 2 to divide into pieces with a sharp instrument. 3 to shorten or shape by cutting. 4 to divide a pack of cards. 5 to lessen. 6 to refuse to speak to:—*n* 1 an opening made by cutting. 2 a wound. 3 the way a thing is shaped. 4 a lessening. 5 a piece of meat.

cut'lery *n* silverware.

cut'ting *adj* hurting the feelings:—*n* **1** a piece of a plant cut off for replanting. **2** a piece cut out of a newspaper. **3** a passage cut through rock for a road or railroad.

cy'cle *n* **1** a series of events that are regularly repeated in the same order. **2** a number of stories, songs, etc, about the same person or event. **3** (*inf*) a bicycle:—*vb* to ride a bicycle.

cy'clist *n* one who rides a bicycle.

cyl'inder *n* **1** a solid or hollow shape with circular ends and straight sides. **2** an object or container shaped like this:—*adj* **cylin'drical**.

cym'bal *n* one of two brass plates used as a musical instrument and struck together to make a clanging noise.

cynic [sin'-ik] *adj* one who believes that people do not do things for good or kindly reasons but for their own advantage:—*also adj:*—*adj* **cyn'ical:**—*n* **cyn'icism**.

D

dab *vb* (**dabbed', dab'bing**) to touch or hit gently with something soft or damp:—*n* 1 a gentle touch. 2 a small lump of anything soft or damp. 3 a flatfish.

dab'ble *vb* 1 to splash, to wet. 2 to take up in a small way:— *n* **dab'bler**.

dachshund [däks'hünt] *n* a small dog with a long body and short legs.

dag'ger *n* a short sharp-pointed sword.

dai'ly *adj* happening every day:—*also adv:*—*n* a daily newspaper.

dain'ty *adj* small, delicate, and pretty.

dain'tily *adv* 1 in a dainty way. 2 with very great care:— *n* **dain'tiness**.

dai'ry *n* a place where milk is sold, or made into butter or cheese.

dais [dā'-is] *n* a low platform.

dal'ly *vb* 1 to move slowly or waste time. 2 to play with toy with:—*n* **dal'liance**.

dam *n* a wall to stop or control the flow of water:—*vb* (**dammed', dam'ming**) to keep back by a dam.

dam'age *n* 1 injury, harm. 2 *pl* money paid to make up for loss or harm:—*vb* to harm.

damn *vb* 1 to send to everlasting punishment. 2 to condemn, to declare to be bad. 3 to curse:—*n* a curse.

dam'nable *adj* hateful, terrible, deserving to be condemned or disapproved of.

damna'tion *n* everlasting punishment.

damp *adj* slightly wet:—*n* slight wetness:—*vb* to make slightly wet:—*n* **damp'ness**.

damp'en *vb* 1 to make or become damp. 2 to make less strong, etc.

dance *vb* 1 to move in time to music. 2 to move in a lively way:—*n* 1 act of dancing. 2 a social gathering for the purpose of dancing:—*n* **danc'er**.

dan'ger *n* 1 the risk of hurt or harm. 2 something that may cause harm, injury, death, etc.

dan'gerous *adj* full of risks.

dan'gle *vb* to hang loosely.

dap'ple, dap'pled *adjs* marked with spots of a different shade.

dare *vb* 1 to be brave enough (to), to undertake to do. 2 to challenge:—*n* a challenge.

dar'ing *adj* brave, fearless:—*n* courage.

dark *adj* 1 without light. 2 having black or brown hair. 3 evil:— *n* **dark'ness**.

dark'en *vb* to make or become darker.

dar'ling *n* one dearly loved:—*also adj*.

dart *n* 1 a pointed weapon thrown by hand. 2 a sudden quick movement. 3 in needlework, a small pleat. 4 *pl* a game in which darts are thrown at a target:—*vb* to move quickly.

dash *vb* 1 to run quickly. 2 to smash against. 3 to discourage:— *n* 1 a quick movement. 2 a small amount. 3 a mark of punctuation (—).

dash'board *n* the instrument panel in an automobile.

dash'ing *adj* 1 active, showy. 2 smart.

data *npl* (now often regarded as a singular noun) a known fact or piece of information.

date[1] *n* 1 the month, day, and/or year in which something happened or is going to happen. 2 (*inf*) an arrangement to meet at a certain time, esp with a member of the opposite sex:—*vb* 1 to write the date on. 2 (*inf*) to make a date, to see with a member of the opposite sex:—**date from** to have a beginning at a certain time:—**out of date** no longer in use.

date[2] *n* the eatable fruit of the date palm.

daughter [dä'-tèr] *n* a female child.

daugh'ter-in-law *n* (*pl* **daugh'ters-in-law**) the wife of a son.

daunt *vb* to make less brave, to discourage.

daw'dle *vb* to move slowly, often stopping, to waste time.

dawn *vb* to grow light:—*n* 1 the beginning of day. 2 a beginning:—**dawn upon** to become clear eventually.

day *n* 1 daylight. 2 twenty-four hours.

day'dream *vb* to dream while awake:—*also n*.

daze *vb* to confuse, to bewilder:—*n* confusion.

daz'zle *vb* 1 to prevent from seeing clearly with strong light. 2 to confuse or impress.

dead *adj* 1 without life. 2 dull, lifeless. 3 absolute, complete. 4 not working:—*adv* 1 completely. 2 straight:—*n* 1 a dead person. 2 the quietest time.

dead'ly *adj* 1 causing death. 2 (*inf*) very boring:— *n* **dead'liness**.

deaf *adj* 1 unable to hear. 2 unwilling to listen:—*n* **deaf'ness**.

deaf'en *vb* to make deaf.

deal *n* 1 an amount. 2 the giving out of playing cards. 3 a business agreement:—*vb* (*pt, pp* **dealt**) 1 to give out (cards). 2 to cope with, to handle. 3 to do business with.

deal'er *n* 1 one who buys and sells. 2 one who gives out playing cards in a game.

dear *adj* 1 well loved. 2 high in price:—*n* a loved person:—*adv* dearly:—*n* **dear'ness**.

dear'ly *adv* 1 with great affection. 2 at a high price.

dearth *n* want, scarcity.

death *n* state of being dead.

debar' *vb* (**debarred', debar'ring**) to shut out from.

debat'able *adj* doubtful, open to question.

debate' *n* 1 an argument. 2 the formal discussion of a question in public:—*vb* 1 to argue. 2 to discuss.

deb'it *n* the written note in an account book of a sum owed:— *vb* to note the sum owed.

debris [deb'-ree] *n* 1 the remains of something broken, destroyed, etc, wreckage. 2 trash, litter, etc.

debt *n* anything owed.

debt'or *n* one who owes.

dec'ade *n* a period of ten years.

dec'agon *n* a figure with ten sides:—*adj* **decag'onal**.

decant'er *n* a bottle with a stopper from which wine or spirits is served.

decap'itate *vb* to cut off the head of:—*n* **decapita'tion**.

decay' *vb* 1 to go rotten. 2 to fall into ruin:—*also n*.

decease' *n* (*fml*) death:—*vb* to die:—*also n*.

deceased' *adj* dead:—*n* a dead person.

deceit' *n* anything said or done to deceive, trickery:—*adj* **deceit'ful**.

deceive' *vb* to make someone believe what is not true, to trick:—*n* **deceiv'er**.

Decem'ber *n* the twelfth month of the year.

decency see **decent**.

de'cent *adj* 1 proper, not shocking. 2 reasonable, satisfactory:—*n* **de'cency**.

decep'tion *n* 1 act of deceiving. 2 a trick, pretense:—*adj* **decep'tive**.

decide' *vb* 1 to make up one's mind. 2 to settle a question, etc.

decid'ed *adj* 1 firm. 2 definite.

decid'uous *adj* having leaves that fall off in autumn.

40

dec'imal adj counted by tens, hundreds, etc:—n a fraction worked out to the nearest tenth, hundredth, etc.

decimal system n a system of weights, measures, and money based on multiplying and dividing by ten.

deciph'er vb to work out the meaning of.

decis'ion n 1 act of deciding. 2 a judgment.

declare' vb 1 to make known, to announce. 2 to state firmly:—n declara'tion.

decline' vb 1 to refuse. 2 to slope downwards. 3 to become worse or weaker. 4 to give the cases of a noun or adjective:—n a gradual worsening or weakening.

decompose' vb to decay, to rot:—n decomposi'tion.

dec'orate vb 1 to make beautiful or ornamental. 2 to put wallpaper, paint, etc, on the walls of. 3 to give a badge or medal of honor to:—n decora'tion.

de'coy n anything intended to lead people, animals, etc, into a trap.

decrease' vb to become or make less:—n de'crease a lessening.

decree' n 1 an order or law. 2 a judgment at law:—vb to make a decree.

ded'icate vb 1 to set apart for a special purpose. 2 to offer to God. 3 to write another's name at the beginning of a book to show that one thinks highly of him or her:—n dedica'tion:—adj ded'icatory.

deduce' vb to work out a truth from things already known:—adj deduc'tive.

deduct' vb to subtract, to take away.

deduc'tion n 1 an amount taken away. 2 a conclusion worked out from things already known.

deed n 1 that which is done, an act. 2 a written agreement.

deep adj 1 going far down. 2 difficult to understand. 3 strongly felt. 4 cunning. 5 (of sounds) low in pitch. 6 (of color) strong, dark, intense:—n the sea.

deep'en vb to become or make deep.

deer n a swift-moving animal with hooves and horns (e.g. the stag, reindeer, etc).

deface' vb to damage, to spoil the appearance of:—n deface'ment.

defam'atory adj doing harm to a person's good name.

defame' vb to speak ill of unfairly:—n defama'tion.

default' n 1 failure to do what is necessary. 2 failure to pay a debt:—also vb:—n default'er.

defeat' vb 1 to beat in a fight or contest. 2 to make to fail:—n a lost fight or contest.

de'fect[1] n a fault or flaw.

defect'[2] vb to desert a country, army, group, or political party to join an opposing one:—n defec'tion.

defec'tive adj 1 below average or normal. 2 faulty.

defend' vb 1 to protect or guard against attack. 2 to give reasons in support of one's ideas. 3 to present the case for an accused person.

defend'ant n in law, the person accused.

defense' n 1 act of holding off an attack. 2 that which protects. 3 the arguments in favor of an accused person, esp in a court of law.

defens'ive adj 1 suitable for defense, protecting. 2 ready to defend from attack:—n state of defending.

defer' vb (deferred', defer'ring) to put off until later:—n defer'ment.

deferen'tial adj respectful.

defi'ance n defiant behavior.

defi'ant adj fearlessly and boldly refusing to obey.

defic'iency n lack, want.

deficient [de-fish'-ênt] adj lacking something, not having something one should have.

deficit [def'-is-it] n the amount by which a sum of money falls short of what is needed, a shortage.

define' vb 1 to mark out the limits of. 2 to explain exactly.

def'inite adj fixed, certain.

defini'tion n an exact meaning or explanation.

deformed' adj badly or unnaturally shaped:—n deform'ity.

defraud' vb to cheat.

deft adj skilful:—n deft'ness.

defunct' adj dead, out of existence.

defy' vb 1 to challenge. 2 to refuse to obey or to respect. 3 to care nothing for.

degree' n 1 a step or stage. 2 (old) a rank. 3 a unit of measurement for heat, angles, etc. 4 the title given by a university to those who reach a certain standard of learning.

de'hydrate vb 1 to take the water out of. 2 to lose water from the body.

deign [dān] vb to do something as if it were a favour.

deity [dee'-i-ti] n a god or goddess:—the Deity God.

deject'ed adj sad, discouraged:—n dejec'tion.

delay' vb 1 to put off till later. 2 to make late. 3 to wait before going on:—also n.

del'egate vb 1 to send a person to act or speak for others. 2 to give certain powers to another:—n one acting or speaking for others.

delete' vb to rub out, to cross out:—n dele'tion.

deleterious [del-i-teer'-i-us] adj hurtful.

delib'erate [-āt] adj 1 (fml) to think over carefully, to consider. 2 to talk over:—adj [-ēt] 1 done on purpose. 2 slow.

del'icate adj 1 fine, easily hurt or damaged. 2 fine, dainty. 3 not very healthy, easily made ill. 4 light, subtle:—n del'icacy.

delic'ious adj very pleasing, esp to the taste.

delight' n great joy or pleasure:—vb to gladden, to give great joy.

delight'ful adj causing delight, pleasant.

delir'ious adj 1 wandering in the mind. 2 highly excited:—n delir'ium.

deliv'er vb 1 (fml) to set free, to hand over. 2 to make (a speech). 3 to aim.

deliv'erance n setting free, rescue.

deliv'ery n 1 childbirth. 2 a giving out of letters. 3 manner of speaking in public.

dell n a small valley.

del'ta n the land between the branches of a river with two or more mouths.

delude' vb to deceive, to trick.

del'uge n a great flood.

delu'sion n a mistaken belief.

delve vb (old) to dig, to search deeply.

demand' vb 1 to ask for firmly or sharply. 2 to require or need:—n 1 a claim. 2 a pressing request.

dem'i- prefix half.

demise' n 1 (fml) death. 2 end, often due to failure.

democ'racy n 1 government by the people. 2 a state that is governed by the people or by persons elected by the people.

dem'ocrat n one who believes in democracy:—adj democrat'ic.

demol'ish vb 1 to pull down. 2 to destroy:—n demoli'tion.

de'mon n an evil spirit, a devil.

dem'onstrate vb 1 to show. 2 to show how something works. 3 to take part in a public show of strong feeling or opinion, often with marching, large signs, etc.

demonstra'tion n 1 a proof. 2 actions taken by a crowd to show their feelings. 3 a display to show how something works.

demon'strative adj 1 indicating the person or thing referred to. 2 quick to show feelings, showing feelings openly.

dem'onstrator n one who shows how something works.

demor'alize vb to weaken the courage or self-confidence of:—n **demoraliza'tion**.

demure' adj serious and modest in manner:—n **demure'ness**.

den n 1 the home (cave, hole, etc) of a wild beast. 2 a secret meeting place. 3 (inf) a small room for studying in.

denial see **deny**.

denigrate [den'-i-grāt] vb to speak ill of, to belittle:—n **denigra'tion**.

den'im n a cotton material used for overalls, etc.

denomina'tion n 1 (fml) a name. 2 a class or unit of measurement or money. 3 all those sharing the same religious beliefs.

denom'inator n the number below the line in a vulgar fraction.

dense adj 1 thick. 2 closely packed. 3 stupid.

dens'ity n the thickness of anything.

dent n a hollow made by a blow or by pressure on the surface:—also vb.

dent'al adj having to do with the teeth.

dent'ist n one who takes out or repairs bad teeth, makes false teeth, and in general cares for the teeth of others:—n **dent'istry**.

dent'ure n a set of artificial teeth.

denuda'tion n the wearing away by the weather of the surface of the earth, and the laying bare of rocks underneath it.

denude' vb to make bare or naked, to strip.

denunciation see **denounce**.

deny' vb 1 to say that something is not true. 2 to refuse:—n **deni'al**.

deod'orant n a liquid or powder that takes away or hides bad smells.

depart' vb 1 (fml) to go away, to set out. 2 to cease to follow. 3 (fml) to die:—n **depart'ure**.

depart'ment n a separate part of a firm, etc.

departure see **depart**.

depend' vb 1 to be likely to happen only under certain conditions. 2 to trust, to rely on. 3 to need for one's support.

depend'able adj trustworthy.

depend'ant n one who looks to another for support or livelihood.

depend'ence n the state of depending.

depend'ency n a country governed by another country.

depend'ent adj 1 relying on another for support. 2 to be decided by.

depict' vb 1 to describe. 2 to draw, paint, etc.

deplor'able adj very bad, regrettable.

deplore' vb to regret, to express disapproval of.

deport' vb 1 to send a person out of the country in punishment. 2 (fml) to behave (oneself).

deporta'tion n act of sending out of the country.

deport'ment n (fml) the manner in which one stands, moves, etc.

depose' vb to remove from high office or the throne.

depos'it vb 1 (fml) to lay down. 2 to put in a safe place:—n 1 an amount paid into a bank. 2 a first payment toward a larger amount. 3 solid matter in liquid, collecting at the bottom.

depot [dep'-ō] n 1 a storehouse. 2 a military station or headquarters. 3 a garage for buses.

depreciate [de-prē'-shi-āt] vb 1 to lower the value of. 2 (fml) to represent as being of little value:—n **deprecia'tion**.

depress' vb 1 to press down, to lower. 2 to make sad.

depress'ion n 1 gloom, sadness. 2 a hollow. 3 low atmospheric pressure, causing unsettled or stormy weather.

depriva'tion n 1 loss. 2 want, hardship.

deprive' vb to take away from.

depth n 1 deepness. 2 strength (of feeling).

depths npl the deepest or most central parts.

deputa'tion n a group of persons speaking or acting for others.

dep'utize vb to take the place of, to act for.

dep'uty n one acting for another.

deranged' adj mad, insane.

der'elict adj left as useless:—also n.

derisive [de-rī'-siv] adj mocking.

deriva'tion n the history of a word back to its earliest known form.

derive' vb 1 to obtain from. 2 to come from.

derog'atory adj insulting, indicating disapproval and scorn.

descend' vb 1 (fml) to climb down. 2 to attack. 3 to have as an ancestor.

descend'ant n one having a certain person as an ancestor.

descent' n 1 (fml) act of climbing down. 2 a slope. 3 a sudden attack. 4 a line of ancestors.

describe' vb 1 to tell what happened. 2 to tell what a thing or person is like:—n **descrip'tion**:—adj **descrip'tive**.

des'ert[1] adj without inhabitants:—n a large area of barren, often sandy, land.

desert'[2] vb 1 to leave, to run away from. 2 to go away from (one's duty):—n **deser'tion**.

desert'er n one who leaves the army, navy, etc, without permission.

deserve' vb to be worthy of:—adj **deserv'ing**.

deser'vedly adv justly.

design' vb 1 to make a plan of. 2 to plan, to intend:—n 1 a plan or drawing of something to be made. 2 a plan, a purpose. 3 a pattern.

des'ignate vb 1 to name. 2 to point out. 3 to appoint to a particular post or position:—adj appointed to a post but not yet in it.

design'ing adj always planning cunningly or to gain advantage.

desir'able adj 1 much wanted. 2 arousing longing for:—n **desirabil'ity**.

desire' vb 1 (fml) to wish for, to long for. 2 to be sexually attracted to:—n 1 a longing, a wish. 2 a strong wish for sexual relations. 3 something or someone that is desired.

desk n a table for reading or writing at.

des'olate adj 1 deserted and miserable. 2 miserable, lonely:—vb to lay waste.

despair' vb to be without hope, to give up hope:—n hopelessness.

des'perate adj 1 hopeless, and therefore ready to take risks. 2 without hope. 3 urgent and despairing:—n **despera'tion**.

despise' vb to look down upon, to consider worthless.

despite' prep in spite of.

despond'ent adj without hope, downcast:—n **despond'ency**.

des'pot n a tyrant:—adj **despot'ic**.

dessert' n the sweet course at the end of a meal.

destina'tion n the place to which a person or thing is going.

des'tiny n a power that seems to arrange people's lives in advance, fate.

destroy' vb 1 to break to pieces. 2 to ruin. 3 to kill.

destroy'er n 1 one who destroys. 2 a fast-moving warship.

destruc'tion n 1 act of destroying. 2 ruin. 3 death.

destruc'tive adj 1 causing ruin. 2 unhelpful.

detach' vb 1 to unfasten. 2 to take away from the rest.

detach'able adj able to be detached.

detached *adj* separate, not joined to others.

detach'ment *n* 1 a group of soldiers taken away from a larger group. 2 freedom from prejudice, impartiality.

detail *vb* 1 (*fml*) to give a very full account or description. 2 to set apart for a particular job:—*n* **de'tail, detail'** a small part or item.

detain' *vb* 1 to prevent from leaving or doing something, to delay. 2 to arrest, to keep in custody:—*n* **deten'tion**.

detect' *vb* 1 to find out, to notice, to discover. 2 to investigate and solve:—*n* **detec'tion**.

detec'tive *n* one whose job it is to find those guilty of crimes.

detention *see* **detain**.

deter' *vb* (**deterred', deter'ring**) to keep from, to discourage.

deter'iorate *vb* to become worse.

determina'tion *n* strength of will, firmness.

deter'mined *adj* strong-willed.

deter'rent *n* something that keeps people from acting in a certain way:—*also adj*.

detest' *vb* to hate, to loathe:—*adj* **detest'able**:—*n* **detesta'tion**.

de'tour *n* 1 a roundabout way. 2 a turning aside from the main route (e.g. to avoid an obstacle).

dev'astate *vb* 1 to lay waste. 2 to overwhelm with grief or disappointment:—*n* **devasta'tion**.

devel'op *vb* 1 to grow bigger or better. 2 to make to grow bigger or better. 3 in photography, to treat a film with chemicals to make the picture appear.

devel'opment *n* 1 growth. 2 a stage of growth. 3 a new product or invention.

de'viate *vb* to turn aside.

devia'tion *n* a turning aside from the normal or expected course.

device' *n* 1 a plan, scheme, trick. 2 an invention, a tool or mechanism. 3 an emblem or sign.

dev'il *n* 1 an evil spirit. 2 Satan. 3 a very wicked person. 4 one who does detailed or routine work for a professional person (e.g. a lawyer, printer, etc).

de'vious *adj* 1 roundabout, indirect. 2 not direct, not straightforward and honest.

devise' *vb* to plan, to invent, to work out, esp cleverly.

devoid' *adj* lacking in, free from.

devote' *vb* to give up wholly to.

devot'ed *adj* loving.

devotee' [dev-o-tee'] *n* a very keen follower.

devo'tion *n* 1 great love, dedication. 2 (*fml*) prayer.

devour' *vb* 1 to eat greedily. 2 to destroy. 3 to possess completely. 4 to read eagerly.

devout' *adj* 1 given to prayer and worship, religious. 2 sincere, deeply felt.

dew *n* tiny drops of water that fall on the ground when air cools during the night:—*adj* **dew'y**.

dexter'ity *n* cleverness with the hands, skill:—*adj* **dex'terous**.

diagnose' *vb* to decide by examining a sick person the kind of illness that he or she has:—*n* **diagnos'is**.

diag'onal *adj* going from corner to corner:—*n* a line joining opposite corners.

di'agram *n* a plan or sketch, a drawing made to help to explain something.

di'al *n* 1 the face of a watch or clock. 2 the numbered disk or pad by means of which one rings a telephone number:—*vb* to ring a telephone number.

di'alect *n* the way of speaking in a particular part of a country.

di'alog, di'alogue *ns* a conversation between two or more people.

diam'eter *n* a straight line passing from one side of a circle to the other through its center:—**diametrically opposed** exactly opposite.

di'aper *n* a towel put round a baby's bottom to keep it clean.

di'ary *n* a book in which one writes something every day, a calendar.

dice *pl of* **die**²:—*vb* to cut into pieces shaped like cubes.

dictate' *vb* 1 to speak aloud something to be written down by another. 2 to give orders, to order about. 3 to fix, to determine:—*n* **dicta'tion**.

dicta'tor *n* one person with complete power of government:—*n* **dicta'torship**.

dic'tionary *n* a book in which words are arranged in alphabetical order and their meanings and other information about them given.

die¹ *vb* 1 to stop living. 2 to fade away.

die² *n* 1 (*pl* **dice**) a small cube, its sides marked with numbers from 1 to 6, used in games of chance. 2 (*pl* **dies**) a stamp for marking designs on paper, coins, etc.

dies'el engine *n* an engine that works by burning heavy oil.

di'et *n* 1 food, the type of food on which one lives. 2 a course of limited foods designed to lose weight, treat a medical condition, etc:—*vb* to eat certain foods only, esp in order to lose weight.

di'etary *adj* concerning diet.

dietet'ic *adj* having to do with diet:—*n* **dieti'cian**.

dif'fer *vb* 1 to be unlike. 2 to disagree.

dif'ference *n* 1 unlikeness. 2 a disagreement, a quarrel.

dif'ferent *adj* 1 unlike, not the same. 2 (*inf*) unusual, special.

differen'tiate *vb* 1 to see or point out the difference between. 2 to make different. 3 to treat differently.

dif'ficult *adj* 1 hard to do. 2 hard to please. 3 troublesome:—*n* **dif'ficulty**.

dig *vb* (**digged', dig'ging**) 1 to turn up earth or soil. 2 to prod. 3 (*inf*) to search:—*n* a prod, a sharp push:—*n* **dig'ger**.

digest' *vb* 1 to dissolve in the stomach. 2 to think over and understand fully:—*n* **di'gest** (*fml*) a summary, a short account.

diges'tion *n* the process of digesting food.

dig'it *n* 1 a human finger or toe. 2 any figure from 0 to 9.

dig'ital *adj* 1 of, having, or using digits. 2 using numbers rather than a dial to display measurements. 3 representing data as a series of numerical values.

digitalis [di-dji-tā'-lis] *n* a drug made from the foxglove.

dig'nified *adj* noble in manner, stately.

dig'nify *vb* 1 to give grace or nobility to. 2 to give an important-sounding name to something.

dig'nity *n* 1 goodness and nobleness of character, worthiness. 2 seriousness, calmness, formality. 3 high rank.

digress' *vb* to speak or write on a subject other than the one being considered:—*n* **digres'sion**.

dike, dyke *n* 1 a ditch or wall. 2 a bank built up to hold back the sea or floods.

dilate' *vb* 1 to become larger or wider. 2 to cause to become larger or wider.—*ns* **dilata'tion, dila'tion**.

dil'atory *adj* slow, given to wasting time.

dil'igent *adj* very careful, painstaking, hardworking:—*n* **dil'igence**.

dilute' *vb* to water down, to reduce in strength by adding water or another liquid.

dim *adj* 1 faint, not bright. 2 indistinct. 3 (*inf*) not bright, not understanding clearly:—*vb* (**dimmed', dim'ming**) to make or become dim.

dimen'sion *n* 1 the measure of length, breadth, and depth. 2 (*often pl*) size, extent.

dimin'ish *vb* to make or become less.

din *n* a continued loud noise.

dine *vb* to eat dinner.

din'er n 1 one who dines. 2 an inexpensive restaurant serving light meals.

din'gy adj dull, dirty-looking, faded:—n **din'giness**.

din'ner n the principal meal of the day.

dinosaur [dī'-no-sôr] n a very large lizard-like animal of prehistoric times.

dint n:—**by dint of** by means of.

dip vb (**dipped', dip'ping**) 1 to put into liquid for a moment. 2 to lower sheep into a liquid that disinfects them or kills insects. 3 to lower for a short time. 4 to take a sudden downward slope:—n 1 (inf) a quick wetting, a bathe. 2 a liquid or semi-liquid substance into which something is dipped. 3 a cleansing liquid for dipping sheep. 4 a downward slope.

diplo'ma n a printed paper showing that a person has passed certain examinations.

diplo'macy n 1 the discussing of affairs and making of agreements with foreign countries. 2 the ability to get people to do things without annoying them:—n **dip'lomat**.

diplomat'ic adj tactful.

dire adj very great, extreme, terrible.

direct' adj 1 straight. 2 without any other reason or circumstances coming between. 3 saying openly what one thinks:—vb 1 to point or aim at. 2 to show or tell the way to. 3 to control. 4 (fml) to order.

direc'tion n 1 the way in which one is looking, pointing, going, etc. 2 control. 3 an order. 4 an address. 5 pl information as to how to do something.

direct'ly adv 1 in a direct manner. 2 at once, very soon.

direct'or n 1 one of a group of people who manage a business, etc. 2 a person in charge of putting on a play or making a film.

direct'ory n a book containing people's names, addresses, telephone numbers, etc.

dirge n a song of mourning, a lament.

dirt n 1 anything not clean. 2 (inf) gossip, scandal. 3 (inf) something obscene.

dir'ty adj 1 unclean. 2 mean or unfair. 3 (inf) obscene. 4 (of weather) nasty:—also vb.

disa'ble vb to cripple:—ns **disabil'ity**, **disa'blement**.

disadvan'tage n something unfavorable or harmful to one's interests, a drawback:—adj **disadvantage'ous**.

disadvan'taged adj suffering from a disadvantage, esp with regard to one's economic situation, family background, etc.

disagree' vb 1 to differ. 2 to have different opinions, etc. 3 to quarrel. 4 to have a bad effect on:—n **disagree'ment**.

disagree'able adj unpleasant.

disappear' vb 1 to go out of sight. 2 to leave or become lost, esp suddenly or without explanation. 3 to cease to exist:—n **disappear'ance**.

disappoint' vb 1 to fail to do what is hoped or expected. 2 to cause sorrow by failure:—n **disappoint'ment**.

disapprove' vb 1 to believe that something is wrong or bad:—n.

disas'ter n 1 a great misfortune. 2 an accident affecting many people or causing much damage. 3 a complete failure:—adj **disas'trous**.

disband' vb to break up and separate:—n **disband'ment**.

disbelieve' vb to refuse to believe:—n **disbelief'**.

disburse' vb (fml) to pay out money:—n **disburse'ment**.

disc see **disk**.

discharge' vb 1 to unload. 2 to set free. 3 to fire. 4 to send away. 5 to give or send out. 6 to do, to carry out. 7 to pay:—n **dis'charge** 1 act of discharging. 2 the matter coming from a sore or wound.

dis'cipline n 1 training of mind or character. 2 ordered behavior. 3 punishment. 4 a branch of knowledge:—vb 1 to train to be obedient. 2 to punish.

disclaim' vb to refuse to accept, to say that one has nothing to do with.

disclose' vb 1 to make known. 2 to uncover.

discom'fort n the fact or state of being uncomfortable:—vb to make uncomfortable.

disconcert' vb to make uneasy.

disconnect' vb 1 to unfasten. 2 to break the connection.

discon'solate adj sad, disappointed.

discontent' n the state of not being satisfied, displeasure:—adj **discontent'ed**:—n **discontent'ment**.

discontin'ue vb to stop or put an end to.

dis'cord n 1 two or more notes of music that sound unpleasing when played together. 2 (fml) disagreement, quarreling:—adj **discord'ant**.

dis'count n a reduction in the cost or price of, a concession:—vb **discount'** 1 to give a discount. 2 to regard as unimportant or untrue.

discour'age vb 1 to dishearten. 2 to persuade not to do:—n **discour'agement**.

discourt'eous adj rude, impolite:—n **discourt'esy**.

discov'er vb 1 to find. 2 to find out.

discov'ery n 1 act of finding. 2 the thing found (out).

discred'itable adj shameful.

discreet' adj thinking carefully before acting or speaking, cautious, not saying anything that is likely to cause trouble.

discrep'ancy n the difference between what a thing is and what it ought to be or is said to be.

discre'tion n 1 discreetness. 2 judgment, caution.

discrim'inate vb 1 to see differences, however small. 2 to show judgment:—n **discrimina'tion**.

discrim'inating adj having good judgment.

discuss' vb to talk about, to consider:—n **discus'sion**.

disdain' vb to look down upon, to be too proud to, to refuse because of pride:—n scorn:—adj **disdain'ful**.

disease' n an illness or unhealthy condition.

disembark' vb to put or go on land from a ship:—n **disembarka'tion**.

disentan'gle vb to take the knots out of.

disfa'vor n dislike, lack of approval.

disfig'ure vb to spoil the appearance of:—n **disfig'urement**.

disgrace' n 1 shame, loss of favor or respect. 2 a person or thing that should cause shame:—vb to bring shame or dishonor upon.

disgrace'ful adj shameful.

disguise' vb to change the appearance of, to change so as not to be recognized:—n changed dress or appearance so as not to be recognized.

disgust' n strong dislike, loathing:—vb to cause to loathe or hate.

disgust'ing adj sickening.

dish n 1 a broad open vessel for serving food. 2 a particular kind of food. 3 food mixed and prepared for the table:—vb to put into a dish:—**dish out** 1 to distribute and give out. 2 (inf) to give out generously.

dishearten' vb to discourage.

dishon'est adj not honest:—n **dishon'esty**.

dishon'orable adj not honorable, shameful.

disillu'sion vb to free from a wrong idea or belief:—n **disillu'sionment**.

disinclined' adj unwilling.

disinfec'tant adj destroying germs, killing infection:—n a disinfectant substance.

disinher'it *vb* 1 to take from a son or daughter the right to receive anything by the will of a dead parent.

disin'tegrate *vb* 1 to break up into parts. 2 to fall to pieces:— *n* **disintegra'tion**.

disin'terested *adj* favoring no side.

disk *n* 1 a circular plate, coated with magnetic material, on which data can be recorded in a form that can be used by a computer. 2 a round flat object (*also* **disc**). 3 a phonograph record (*also* **disc**). 4 a layer of cartilage between the bones of the spine (*also* **disc**).

dislike' *vb* not to like:—*also n.*

dis'locate *vb* 1 to put out of joint. 2 (*fml*) to throw into disorder:—*n* **disloca'tion.**

dislodge' *vb* to move from its place.

disloy'al *adj* 1 unfaithful. 2 not true to:—*n* **disloy'alty.**

dis'mal *adj* dark, gloomy.

dismay' *vb* to make afraid, anxious, discouraged, etc:—*also n.*

dismiss' *vb* 1 to send away. 2 to send away from one's job:— *n* **dismiss'sal.**

dismount' *vb* to get down from a horse, etc.

disobey' *vb* to refuse to do what one is told:—*n* **disobed'ience**:—*adj* **disobed'ient.**

disor'der *vb* to put things out of their places, to untidy:— *n* 1 untidiness. 2 disturbance, riot. 3 illness, disease.

disor'derly *adj* 1 untidy. 2 out of control.

disor'ganize *vb* to put out of order, to throw into confusion:—*n* **disorganiza'tion.**

disown' *vb* to refuse to have anything to do with, to refuse to acknowledge as belonging to oneself.

dispatch' *vb* 1 to send. 2 (*old*) to kill. 3 (*fml*) to do quickly:—*n* 1 act of sending off. 2 a written official report.

dispel' *vb* (**dispelled'**, **dispel'ling**) to drive away, to make disappear.

dispense' *vb* 1 (*fml*) to give out. 2 to prepare and give out (medicines):—**dispense with** to do without.

dispensa'tion *n* a permission, often from the church, not to do something.

dispens'er *n* 1 one who prepares medicines. 2 a machine from which something can be obtained by the insertion of money.

disperse' *vb* to scatter:—*ns* **dispers'al, disper'sion.**

display' *vb* 1 to show. 2 to put where it can be easily seen:—*n* 1 show. 2 a parade. 3 an exhibition.

displease' *vb* to anger, to annoy.

displeas'ure *n* annoyance.

dispos'al *n* 1 act of getting rid of. 2 the way that people or things are arranged. 3 use.

dispose' *vb* 1 (*fml*) to arrange. 2 (*fml*) to make willing. 3 to get rid of.

dispropor'tionate *adj* too great (or too small) in the circumstances.

disprove' *vb* to prove to be false.

dispute' *vb* 1 to argue, to quarrel. 2 to refuse to agree with, to question the truth or rightness of:—*also n.*

disqual'ify *vb* 1 to make unable. 2 to put out of a competition, etc, usu for breaking a rule:—*n* **disqualifica'tion.**

disqui'et *n* anxiety:—*vb* to make anxious:—*n* **disqui'etude.**

disregard' *vb* to take no notice of:—*n* neglect.

disrepair' *n* a bad state resulting from lack of repairs.

disrep'utable *adj* 1 having a bad character. 2 in a bad condition, shabby.

disrepute' *n* disgrace, bad reputation.

disrespect' *n* rudeness, failure to behave in a proper way:— *adj* **disrespect'ful.**

disrupt' *vb* to put into a state of disorder:—*n* **disrup'tion.**

dissat'isfied *adj* not satisfied, discontented.

dissect' *vb* 1 to cut into separate parts in order to examine. 2 to study carefully:—*n* **dissec'tion.**

dissim'ilar *adj* unlike.

disso'ciate *vb* 1 to separate from. 2 to refuse to be connected with:—*n* **dissocia'tion.**

dissolve' *vb* 1 to make or become liquid by placing in liquid. 2 to break up, to put an end to.

dissuade' *vb* to advise not to do:—*n* **dissua'sion**:—*adj* **dissua'sive.**

dis'tance *n* 1 being far off. 2 the space between two points or places. 3 (*fml*) unfriendliness.

dis'tant *adj* 1 far off. 2 not close. 3 cold or unfriendly in manner.

distaste' *n* dislike.

distaste'ful *adj* unpleasant.

distend' *vb* to stretch, to swell:—*n* **disten'sion.**

distill' *vb* 1 to fall in drops. 2 to purify a substance by heating it until it turns into vapor, and then cooling the vapor until it becomes liquid.

distinct' *adj* 1 separate. 2 easily heard, seen, etc.

distinc'tive *adj* different in a special way.

distinct'ness *n* clearness.

disting'uish *vb* 1 to see or point out the differences (between). 2 to make different. 3 to make (oneself) outstanding. 4 to see, to make out.

disting'uished *adj* famous.

distort' *vb* 1 to twist out of shape. 2 to give a false meaning to:—*n* **distor'tion.**

distract' *vb* to draw the attention away.

distress' *n* 1 great pain or anxiety. 2 suffering caused by lack of money. 3 danger:—*vb* to cause anxiety, sorrow, or pain.

distrib'ute *vb* 1 to give out, to give each his or her share. 2 to spread out widely:—*n* **distribu'tion.**

dis'trict *n* 1 part of a country. 2 an area marked off for some special purpose.

distrust' *vb* to have no confidence or belief in:—*n* doubt, suspicion:—*adj* **distrust'ful.**

disturb' *vb* 1 to throw into disorder. 2 to trouble. 3 to interrupt.

disturb'ance *n* 1 disorder, riot. 2 disarrangement. 3 an interruption. 4 mental illness.

ditch *n* a long narrow trench for carrying away water:—*vb* to make a ditch.

dive *vb* 1 to plunge into water head first. 2 to move quickly downward:—*n* 1 a plunge. 2 a sudden downward move.

diverge' *vb* 1 to go off in a different direction, to branch in different directions:—*n* **diver'gence**:—*adj* **diver'gent.**

diver'sion *n* 1 (*fml*) amusement. 2 something that distracts the attention. 3 detour.

divers'ity *n* difference, variety.

divert' *vb* 1 to turn in another direction. 2 to draw away. 3 to amuse.

divide' *vb* 1 to break up into parts. 2 to share out. 3 to separate. 4 in arithmetic, to see how many times one number is contained in another.

div'idend *n* 1 a number to be divided. 2 a share of profit. 3 the rate at which the profits of a company are divided among stockholders.

divine' *adj* 1 of or belonging to God. 2 (*inf*) extremely good:—*n* a clergyman:—*vb* 1 to foretell, to guess. 2 to learn or discover by intuition, insight:—*n* **divina'tion.**

divin'ity *n* 1 a god. 2 the study of religion.

divis'ible *adj* able to be divided.

divi'sion *n* 1 act of dividing. 2 one of the parts into which something is divided. 3 disagreement. 4 a large army group.

divi'sional *adj* having to do with a division.

divi'sor *n* the number by which another number (the **dividend**) is divided in a sum.

divorce' *n* 1 legal permission to separate from one's married partner and to marry someone else if so desired. 2 separation.—*vb* 1 officially to end a marriage. 2 to separate.

divulge' *vb* to make known, to reveal.

diz'zy *adj* giddy, having the feeling that everything is spinning around:—*n* **diz'ziness**.

do[1] *vb* (*pt* **did**, *pp* **done**) 1 to perform, to carry out. 2 to attend to. 3 to act or behave. 4 to be enough or suitable.

do[2] *see* **ditto**.

do'cile *adj* easily managed, controlled, or influenced, quiet:—*n* **docil'ity**.

dock[1] *n* 1 an enclosure in a harbor where enough water can be kept to float a ship when it is being loaded or unloaded, repaired, etc. 2 a platform from which trucks, etc, are loaded and unloaded. 3 the box in which prisoners stand in a court of law:—*vb* 1 to sail into dock.

doc'tor *n* 1 one who is qualified by medical training to tend the sick and injured. 2 one who receives a degree granted by universities to those learned in a certain field:—*vb* 1 to give medical treatment to. 2 to make different in order to deceive, to tamper with.

doc'ument *n* a written or printed paper that can be used as proof:—*vb* to bring forward written evidence.

documen'tary *adj* 1 having to do with documents. 2 giving facts and explanations:—*n* a nonfiction film.

dod'der *vb* to move unsteadily or shakily.

dodge *vb* 1 to make a quick movement to avoid someone or something. 2 to avoid by cleverness or trickery:—*n* 1 a quick movement aside. 2 a trick.

doe *n* the female of many animals (e.g. deer, rabbit, etc).

dog *n* 1 a common domestic animal. 2 (*hum or contemp*) a fellow:—*vb* (**dogged', dog'ging**) to follow closely, to pursue.

dog'-eared *adj* having the corners of the pages turned down.

dog'ged *adj* determined, unwilling to give in:—*n* **dog'gedness**.

dog'gerel *n* bad poetry.

dog'ma *n* (*pl* **dog'mas, dog'mata**) 1 a belief taught or held as true, esp by a church. 2 a doctrine, belief.

dogmat'ic *adj* 1 relating to dogma. 2 holding one's beliefs very strongly and expecting other people to accept them without question:—*n* **dog'matism**.

dog rose *n* the wild rose.

doll *n* a toy in the shape of a person.

dol'lar *n* an American, Australian, or Canadian coin (= 100 cents).

dol'lop *n* (*inf*) a lump, esp of something soft.

dol'phin *n* a sea animal like the porpoise, belonging to the whale family.

dome *n* 1 a rounded top on a building. 2 something of this shape:—*adj* **domed**.

domes'tic *adj* 1 belonging to or having to do with the house. 2 concerning one's personal or home life. 3 tame and living with or used to people. 4 having to do with one's own country. 5 (*inf*) interested in and good at cooking, housework, etc:—*n* a house servant.

domes'ticated *adj* 1 accustomed to living near and being used by people. 2 fond of and/or good at doing jobs associated with running a house.

dom'inant *adj* 1 controlling others. 2 most important:—*n* **dom'inance**.

dom'inate *vb* 1 to have complete control over. 2 to be most important. 3 to rise high above:—*n* **domina'tion**.

domineer' *vb* to bully.

donate' *vb* to give, esp to a charity, etc, to contribute:—*n* **dona'tion**.

done *pp* of **do**:—*adj* (*inf*) utterly exhausted.

do'nor *n* 1 one who gives or contributes. 2 a person who provides blood for transfusion, organs for transplantation, etc.

doom *n* death, ruin, destruction, terrible and inevitable fate:—*vb* to cause to suffer something unavoidable and terrible, such as death, ruin, or destruction.

dor'mant *adj* not at present active.

dor'mer *n* a small window in a sloping roof.

dor'mitory *n* a sleeping room with many beds.

dor'mouse *n* (*pl* **dor'mice**) a small mouse-like animal that sleeps in winter.

dose *n* the amount of medicine given at one time:—*vb* to give medicine to.

dot *n* a small point or mark:—*vb* (**dot'ted, dot'ting**) to mark with dots:—**dotted with** having (things) placed here and there.

dote *vb* to show great fondness of, esp in a foolish way.

doub'le *adj* 1 twice as much as usual or normal. 2 for two people. 3 forming a pair. 4 combining two things or qualities:—*n* 1 twice the amount. 2 a person or thing looking the same as another. 3 a glass of spirits holding twice the standard amount. 4 a running pace:—*vb* 1 to multiply by two, to cause to become twice as large or numerous. 2 to fold in two. 3 to have two uses, jobs, etc:—*adv* **doub'ly**:—**dou'ble back** to turn back in the opposite direction, esp unexpectedly.

doub'le-bass' *n* a large, low-toned stringed musical instrument.

double-deal'ing *n* deceit, dishonesty:—*adj* devious, not to be trusted.

doubt *vb* to be uncertain about, to be unwilling to believe or trust:—*n* 1 a feeling of uncertainty. 2 distrust:—*adj* **doubt'ful**:—*adv* **doubt'less**.

dough [dō] *n* 1 flour moistened with water and pressed into a paste ready for baking. 2 (*inf*) money.

dove *n* a bird of the pigeon family.

dow'dy *adj* badly or shabbily dressed, unfashionable, drab:—*n* **dow'diness**.

down[1] *prep* in a descending direction in, on, along, or through:—*adv* 1 from a higher to a lower position, to a lying or sitting position. 2 toward or to the ground, floor, or bottom. 3 to or in a lower status or in a worse condition. 4 from an earlier time. 5 in cash. 6 to or in a state of less activity:—*adj* 1 occupying a low position, esp lying on the ground. 2 depressed:—*n* 1 a down. 2 (*inf*) a dislike:—*vb* 1 to go or cause to go or come down. 2 to defeat. 3 to swallow.

down[2] *n* the fine soft feathers of a bird:—*adj* **down'y**.

down'-and-out' *adj* having no job and often no money:—*n* a down-and-out person.

down'cast *adj* directed downwards. 2 sad, in low spirits.

down'fall *n* 1 ruin, fall from power, prosperity, etc. 2 a heavy fall of rain.

down'right *adj* thorough, complete.

doze *vb* to be half asleep:—*n* light sleep.

doz'en *n* twelve.

drab *adj* 1 of a dull grayish-brown color. 2 dull, uninteresting.

draft *n* 1 a number of soldiers picked to go somewhere on duty. 2 a written order to pay money. 3 a rough copy or plan of work to be done. 4 the amount taken in one drink. 5 a stream of air through a room. 6 the depth a ship sinks in water:—*vb* 1 to prepare a plan or rough copy. 2 to pick and send off.

draft'y *adj* cold because of a stream of air.

drag *vb* (**dragged', drag'ging**) 1 to pull along with force. 2 to trail on the ground. 3 (*inf*) to go very slowly. 4 to search underwater with hooks or a net:—*n* anything that causes to go slowly.

drag'on *n* 1 in fables, a winged monster. 2 a fierce, stern person.

drain *vb* 1 to draw off liquid by pipes, ditches, etc. 2 to empty completely. 3 to cause to become dry as liquid flows away:—*n* a pipe or channel to carry away liquid.

drake *n* a male duck.

dram'a *n* 1 a play. 2 plays as a branch of literature and as a performing art. 3 an exciting event, a series of exciting events. 4 excitement.

dramat'ic *adj* 1 having to do with drama. 2 sudden or exciting. 3 showing too much feeling or emotion.

drape *vb* 1 to decorate with cloth. 2 to cause to rest loosely:—*npl* cloths hung up to darken or hide things behind.

dras'tic *adj* acting with strength or violence, thorough.

draw *vb* (*pt* **drew**, *pp* **drawn**) 1 to pull along or toward. 2 to move toward or away from. 3 to attract. 4 to receive money (as wages, for a check, etc). 5 to make a picture or pictures of, usu with a pencil, crayons, etc. 6 (of a game or contest) to end with nobody winning. 7 (of a ship) to sink to a certain depth in the water:—*n* 1 an attraction. 2 a game or contest won by nobody. 3 the selecting of winning tickets in a raffle, lottery, etc:—**draw the line at** to refuse to have anything to do with:—**draw up** 1 to stop. 2 to prepare, esp in writing.

draw'back *n* a disadvantage.

draw'er *n* a sliding box or container in a table, cupboard, etc.

draw'ing *n* 1 a picture made with a pencil, crayons, etc. 2 the art of making such pictures.

draw'ing room *n* a sitting room, esp a large one in which guests are received.

drawl *vb* to speak slowly or lazily:—*also n.*

dread *n* fear, terror:—*adj* causing great fear, terrible:—*vb* to fear greatly.

dread'ful *adj* 1 terrible. 2 very unpleasant, bad.

dream *n* 1 the ideas or fancies passing through the mind of a person sleeping. 2 memories of the past or thoughts of what may happen. 3 state of being occupied with one's thoughts, daydream. 4 (*inf*) a beautiful or wonderful person or thing:—*vb* (*pt, pp* **dreamt** or **dreamed**) 1 to have dreams. 2 to imagine.

drear'y *adj* cheerless, gloomy.

dregs *npl* tiny pieces of matter that sink to the foot of a standing liquid.

drench *vb* 1 to make very wet. 2 to force (an animal) to drink.

dress *vb* 1 to put on clothes. 2 to wear evening or formal dress. 3 to straighten, to set in order. 4 to bandage. 5 to prepare for use:—*n* 1 clothing. 2 a woman's outer garment:—**dress up** 1 to put on the clothes of another person, nation, etc. 2 to put on one's best clothes.

dress'ing *n* 1 the ointments, bandages, etc, put on a wound. 2 something put on as a covering. 3 sauce for food, esp a mixture of oil and vinegar, etc, for putting on salads.

dress'ing gown *n* a loose garment worn over night clothes or underclothes, a bathrobe.

drib'ble *vb* 1 to fall or let fall in small drops. 2 to allow saliva to run from the mouth. 3 to keep a moving ball under control by little kicks or taps.

drift *n* 1 that which is driven by wind (e.g. snow, sand) or water (e.g. seaweed). 2 meaning:—*vb* 1 to be driven by wind or water current. 2 to do something aimlessly.

drill *n* 1 a tool for boring holes. 2 training practice. 3 procedures to be followed in a certain situation, such as an emergency:—*vb* 1 to make holes with a drill. 2 to teach something by making learners do it again and again. 3 to practice military exercises.

drink *vb* (*pt* **drank**, *pp* **drunk**) 1 to swallow (a liquid). 2 to take alcoholic liquids, esp in too great amounts:—*n* 1 an act of drinking. 2 a liquid suitable for drinking. 3 alcoholic liquids. 4 a glass of alcoholic liquid.

drip *vb* (**dripped'**, **drip'ping**) to fall or let fall in drops:—*n* a drop.

drive *vb* (*pt* **drove**, *pp* **driv'en**) 1 to control or guide (an automobile, etc). 2 to ride in an automobile or other vehicle. 3 to force or urge along. 4 to hit hard:—*n* 1 a ride in a carriage or automobile. 2 a private road up to a house. 3 a hard hit (at a ball). 4 energy.

driv'er *n* 1 one who drives. 2 a golf club with a wooden head.

driz'zle *vb* to rain in small drops:—*n* a fine rain.

drom'edary *see* **camel**.

droop *vb* 1 to hang down. 2 to become weak:—*also n.*

drop *n* 1 a very small amount of liquid. 2 the act of falling. 3 the distance that one may fall. 4 a small hard piece of candy:—*vb* (**dropped'**, **drop'ping**) 1 to fall or let fall in drops. 2 to fall or let fall. 3 to fall or cause to fall to a lower level or amount. 4 to stop seeing, talking about, doing, etc.

drought [drout] *n* a long spell of dry weather, lack of rain, dryness.

drown *vb* 1 to die under water by water filling the lungs. 2 to kill by keeping under water. 3 to flood, to submerge. 4 to put too much liquid in or on. 5 to prevent from being heard by making a noise.

drow'sy *adj* sleepy:—*n* **drow'siness**.

drud'gery *n* dull or hard work.

drug *n* 1 any substance used as or in a medicine. 2 a substance that causes sleep or loss of feeling, esp a habit-forming one:—*vb* (**drugged'**, **drug'ging**) to give drugs to in order to make insensible.

drug'store *n* a store in which medicines are made up and sold:—*n* **drug'gist**.

drum *n* 1 a musical instrument in which skin is stretched tightly over the ends of a box and then beaten to produce a booming sound. 2 the tight skin across the inside of the ear. 3 something shaped like a drum:—*vb* (**drummed'**, **drum'ming**) 1 to beat a drum. 2 to make a noise by beating or tapping:—*n* **drum'mer**.

drunk *adj* overcome or overexcited by too much strong drink:—*n* **drunk'enness**.

dry *adj* 1 not wet or damp. 2 with little rainfall. 3 not legally allowed to sell alcohol. 4 not sweet. 5 (*inf*) thirsty. 6 uninteresting. 7 (of humor) quiet, not easily noticed:—*vb* to make or become dry:—*adv* **dri'ly, dry'ly:**—*n* **dry'ness**.

du'al *adj* consisting of two, double:—*n* **dual'ity**.

du'bious *adj* 1 feeling doubt. 2 causing doubt, of uncertain worth, etc, possibly dishonest:—*n* **dubiety** [dû-bî'-ĕ-ti].

duch'ess *n* the wife or widow of a duke.

duch'y *n* 1 the lands of a duke. 2 a country ruled by a duke.

duck[1] *n* a type of common waterfowl, both domestic and wild, whose flesh is used as a food.

duck[2] *vb* 1 to plunge or dip under water. 2 to bend to avoid something or to avoid being seen. 3 to avoid or dodge.

duck'ling *n* a young duck.

dude *n* a city person on vacation on a ranch.

due *adj* 1 owed. 2 proper. 3 expected:—*adv* directly:—*n* 1 an amount owed. 2 a right. 3 *pl* a sum payable:—**due to** caused by.

du'el *n* 1 an arranged fight between two armed people. 2 a contest or struggle between two people:—*also vb.*

dug *see* **dig**.

duke *n* the highest rank of nobleman.

dull *adj* 1 slow, stupid. 2 uninteresting. 3 cloudy, sunless, gloomy. 4 not bright. 5 not sharp:—*vb* to make dull, to blunt:—*n* **dull'ness**.

du'ly adv **1** properly, fitly. **2** at the due and proper time.

dumb adj **1** unable to speak. **2** silent. **3** (inf) stupid, unintelligent:—n **dumb'ness**.

dumbfound' vb to astonish greatly.

dum'my n **1** a model of the human figure, used for displaying or fitting clothes. **2** an imitation article:—adj pretended, not real.

dump vb **1** to throw away, to get rid of. **2** (inf) to let fall or set down heavily. **3** in computing, to transfer data to another storage medium. **4** in football, to throw a pass to either end of the offensive line:—n **1** a store. **2** (inf) a dirty, untidy, or uninteresting place. **3** (inf) pl low spirits.

dump'ling n a food consisting of a thick paste, sometimes rolled into balls, or sometimes filled with fruit or meat.

dunce n a slow learner, a stupid pupil.

dune n a low sand hill, esp on the seashore.

dung n the waste matter passed from the bodies of animals:—vb to mix dung with earth to fertilize it.

dun'geon n a dark prison, an underground prison cell.

du'plex n an apartment on two floors, or a house divided into two separate dwellings.

dur'able adj **1** lasting, hard-wearing. **2** lasting or able to last:—n **durabil'ity**.

dura'tion n the time for which a thing lasts.

du'ring prep **1** in the course of. **2** throughout the time of.

dusk n partial darkness, twilight.

dust n tiny dry particles of earth or matter:—vb **1** to remove dust. **2** to sprinkle with powder:—adj **dust'y**.

dust'er n **1** a cloth for removing dust, etc. **2** a light full-length coat.

du'tiful adj obedient, careful to do one's duty.

du'ty n **1** that which one ought to do. **2** an action or task requiring to be done, esp one attached to a job. **3** a tax on goods.

dwarf n (pl **dwarfs** or **dwarves**) **1** a person, animal, or plant much smaller than is the average. **2** in fairy tales, a creature like a very small man who has magical powers:—adj undersized, very small:—vb to make seem small:—adj **dwarf'ish**.

dwell vb (pt, pp **dwelt** or **dwelled'**) **1** (old or lit) to live in. **2** to talk or think much about.

dwin'dle vb to grow gradually less.

dye vb to give a new color to, to stain:—n a coloring substance:—n **dy'er**.

dyke see **dike**.

dynam'ic adjective, energetic.

dyn'amite n a powerful explosive.

E

each *pron, adj* every one taken singly or separately.

eag'er *adj* full of desire, keen:—*n* **eag'erness**.

eag'le *n* a large bird of prey.

ear[1] *n* 1 the organ of hearing. 2 the ability to hear the difference between sounds. 3 attention.

ear[2] *n* a head or spike of corn.

earl *n* a British nobleman.

ear'ly *adj* 1 before the time arranged. 2 near the beginning. 3 belonging to the first stages of development, etc. 4 (*fml*) soon:—*adv* 1 near the beginning (of a period of time, etc). 2 sooner than usual, sooner than expected, sooner than often, etc.

earn *vb* 1 to get (money) in return for work. 2 to deserve.

ear'nest *adj* 1 serious. 2 determined:—*n* **ear'nestness:—in earnest** meaning what one says.

earn'ings *npl* wages, money paid for work done.

ear'ring *n* an ornament worn on the ear.

earth *n* 1 the planet on which we live. 2 the world, as opposed to heaven. 3 the dry land, the ground or soil. 4 the hole of a fox, badger, etc. 5 the wire connecting an electrical apparatus to the ground:—*vb* to connect an electrical apparatus to the ground.

earth'enware *n* dishes or other vessels made of baked clay, pottery.

earth'ly *adj* having to do with the world, of worldly rather than heavenly things.

earth'quake *n* a shaking movement of the surface of the earth.

earth'y *adj* 1 like or of earth. 2 coarse, not refined.

ease *n* 1 freedom from anxiety or pain. 2 lack of difficulty. 3 freedom from work, rest, comfort. 4 naturalness:—*vb* 1 to lessen. 2 to move gently or gradually.

eas'el *n* a stand to hold a picture, blackboard, etc, upright.

east *n adj and adv* one of the four chief points of the compass, the direction in which the sun rises:—*adjs* **east'ern**, **east'ward:—the East** the countries of Asia.

East'er *n* a religious feast during which Christians commemorate the rising of Christ from the dead.

east'erly *adj* from or toward the east.

eas'y *adj* 1 not difficult. 2 free from anxiety or pain. 3 comfortable. 4 relaxed, leisurely.

eat *vb* (*pt* **ate**, *pp* **eat'en**) 1 to chew and swallow, as food. 2 to wear away.

eaves *npl* that part of the roof that comes out beyond the walls.

eaves'drop *vb* (**eaves'dropped, eaves'dropping**) to try to hear what others are saying to each other privately:—*n* **eaves'dropper**.

ebb *n* 1 the flowing back of the tide. 2 a falling away or weakening:—*vb* 1 to flow back. 2 to grow less, weak, faint, etc.

eccentric [ek-sen'-trik] *adj* odd, strange.

echo [e'-kō] *n* (*pl* **e'choes**) 1 the repeating of a sound by the reflection of sound waves from a surface. 2 an imitation:—*vb* 1 to repeat, to throw back a sound. 2 to imitate.

eclipse' *n* 1 the cutting off of the light from the sun by the moon coming between it and the earth. 2 the darkening of the face of the moon by the earth coming between it and the sun. 3 a failure caused by the unexpected success of another:—*vb* 1 to cut off the light from, to darken. 2 to make another seem inferior by outdoing.

ecol'ogy *n* 1 the science of the life of things in their physical surroundings. 2 the relation of plants and living creatures to each other and to their surroundings:—*adj* **ecolog'ical**.

econo'mic *adj* 1 having to do with economics. 2 designed to give a profit.

econo'mical *adj* careful with money, not wasteful.

econo'mics *n* the study of the means of increasing the wealth of a community or nation.

econ'omist *n* one who studies economics.

econ'omize *vb* to spend or use carefully, to save, to be economical.

econ'omy *n* 1 careful management of the wealth, money, goods, etc, of a home, business, or country. 2 sparing use of money.

ec'stasy *n* great delight or joy.

ecstat'ic *adj* delighted, carried away by joy.

ed'dy *n* a whirling current of water or air, a whirlpool or whirlwind:—*vb* to move in eddies.

E'den *n* (in the Old Testament) the garden of Adam and Eve, paradise.

edge *n* 1 the sharp side of a blade. 2 a border or boundary. 3 keenness, sharpness:—*vb* 1 to move gradually, esp with small sideways movements. 2 to put a border on.

edge'ways, edge'wise *adjs* sideways.

ed'ible *adj* able or fit to be eaten.

edi'tion *n* the number of copies of a book or newspaper published at one time.

ed'itor *n* 1 one who edits. 2 one who collects the material for a newspaper or magazine and selects what is to be published or who is in charge of a newspaper or part of a newspaper.

ed'ucate *vb* to teach or train.

educa'tion *n* 1 the process of learning and training. 2 instruction, as in schools, colleges, and universities. 3 a course or type of instruction. 4 the theory and practice of teaching:—*adj* **educa'tional**.

eel *n* a snake-like fish.

ee'rie *adj* strange and frightening.

effect' *n* 1 result, power to bring about a change. 2 impression. 3 *pl* goods, property. 4 *pl* the imitation of natural lighting and sounds in a play, film, etc:—*vb* to bring about, to succeed in doing, to produce.

effec'tive *adj* 1 doing what is intended or desired, successful. 2 striking. 3 actual, real. 4 in operation, working.

effem'inate *adj* womanish, unmanly:—*n* **effem'inacy**.

efferves'cent *adj* 1 bubbling, sparkling. 2 lively and enthusiastic.

effic'ient *adj* 1 able to do what is necessary or intended without wasting time, energy, etc. 2 good at one's job, capable:—*n* **effic'iency**.

eff'igy *n* a likeness in the form of a picture, statue, or carving.

eff'ort *n* 1 an energetic attempt. 2 the making use of strength or ability.

effront'ery *n* open impudence, shameless rudeness.

egg[1] *n* (*pl* **e'choes**) 1 an object covered with a hard brittle shell, laid by a bird, reptile, etc, from which a young one is hatched. 2 such an object laid by the domestic hen used as food. 3 in the female mammal, the cell from which the young is formed, the ovum.

egg on *vb* to try to get somebody (to do something), to urge, to encourage.

egg'plant *n* a smooth, dark-purple fruit used as a vegetable.

eg'oist *n* a selfish person:—*n* **eg'oism**.

eg'otist *n* one always talking of himself or herself:—*n* **eg'otism**.

ei'derdown *n* a warm cotton fabric with a woolen nap.

49

ei'ther *pron and adj* one or other of two.

eject' *vb* to throw out.

ejec'tion *n* act of throwing out.

eke *vb*:—**eke out 1** to cause to last longer. **2** to manage with difficulty to make (a living, etc).

elab'orate *adj* worked out with great care. **2** having many parts. **3** very decorative:—*vb* **1** to work out very carefully, to add to and improve upon. **2** to explain fully:—*n* **elabora'tion**.

elas'tic *adj* able to stretch or be stretched easily but returning immediately to its former shape:—*n* a strip of material lined with rubber to make it elastic.

elate' *vb* to make very glad or proud:—*n* **ela'tion**.

el'bow *n* **1** the joint between the forearm and upper arm. **2** a sharp bend or corner:—*vb* to push with the elbow.

eld'er[1] *adj* older.

eld'er[2] *n* a small tree with purple berries.

eld'erly *adj* old or getting old.

eld'est *adj* oldest.

elect' *vb* **1** (*fml*) to choose. **2** to choose by voting:—*adj* chosen.

elec'tion *n* act of choosing, esp by vote.

elec'tor *n* one with the right to vote.

elec'toral *adj* having to do with electors.

elec'torate *n* all those having the right to vote on a certain occasion.

elec'tric *adj* **1** having to do with electricity. **2** exciting, thrilling:—*npl* electric fittings.

elec'trical *adj* having to do with electricity, worked by electricity.

electri'cian *n* one who works with electricity or electrical apparatus.

electric'ity *n* an energy produced by chemical or other action, a natural force that can be harnessed to give heat, light, and power.

elec'trify *vb* **1** to put electricity into. **2** to thrill.

elec'trocute *vb* to kill by electricity:—*n* **electrocu'tion**.

elec'tron *n* the negative electrical unit in an atom.

electron'ic *adj* **1** of or worked by streams of electrons flowing through semiconductor devices, vacuum or gas. **2** of or concerned with electrons or electronics.

electronic mail *see* **email**.

electron'ics *n* **1** the study, development, and application of electronic devices. **2** *pl* electronic circuits.

el'egant *adj* **1** graceful, smart, stylish. **2** stylish, polished:—*n* **el'egance**.

el'egy *n* a mourning or sorrowful poem.

el'ement *n* **1** a necessary part. **2** a substance that cannot be broken down into any other substances and from which all other things are made up. **3** *pl* knowledge without which a subject cannot be properly understood. **4** *pl* nature, the weather.

elemen'tal *adj* **1** having to do with elements, like the powers of nature. **2** basic.

elemen'tary *adj* **1** having to do with the beginning. **2** simple, easy.

el'ephant *n* a large very thick-skinned animal with a trunk and ivory tusks:—**white elephant** a gift or purchase that turns out to be of no use, a useless possession that is troublesome to keep up or retain.

el'evate *vb* **1** (*fml*) to make finer, better, more educated, etc. **2** to raise to a higher place or rank.

el'evator *n* a machine by which people or goods are carried from floor to floor of a building.

elf *n* (*pl* **elves**) in fairy tales, a mischievous fairy:—*adjs* **elf'in**, **elf'ish**.

elk *n* a type of large deer.

el'igible *adj* able to be chosen, suitable:—*n* **eligibil'ity**.

elim'inate *vb* to get rid of:—*n* **elimina'tion**.

élite [â-leet'] *n* a group that is at a higher level, professionally, socially, or in ability, etc.

ellipse' *n* an oval figure.

elm *n* a type of tree.

elocu'tion *n* the art or way of speaking well.

elope' *vb* to leave home secretly with one's lover:—*n* **elope'ment**.

el'oquent *adj* **1** able to speak well, esp in public, and express one's ideas and opinions effectively. **2** showing or using such an ability:—*n* **el'oquence**.

else *adj* **1** besides, also. **2** other than that already mentioned.

elsewhere' *adv* in another place.

elu'sive *adj* **1** hard to remember, express, identify, etc. **2** hard to catch or track down.

elves *see* **elf**.

ema'ciate *vb* to become or make very thin, to waste away:—*n* **emacia'tion**.

email, e-mail *n* (*short for* **electronic mail**) messages, etc, sent and received via computer terminals:—*also vb*.

embalm' *vb* to preserve a dead body with spices.

embank'ment *n* a mound of stones and earth built to shut in a river or to carry a road, railroad, etc, over low ground.

embar'go *n* (*pl* **embar'goes**) an official order forbidding something, esp trade with another country.

embark *vb* **1** to put or go on board ship. **2** to start (upon):—*n* **embarka'tion**.

embarr'ass *vb* **1** to cause to feel shy or uncomfortable. **2** to involve in difficulties:—*n* **embarr'assment**.

em'bassy *n* the house of an ambassador.

embell'ish *vb* **1** to make beautiful. **2** to make more interesting, etc, by adding exaggerated or untrue details:—*n* **embell'ishment**.

em'bers *npl* **1** live cinders of a dying fire. **2** the fading remains.

embezz'le *vb* to steal money that one has been trusted with by other people:—*n* **embezz'lement**.

em'blem *n* an object that is regarded as a sign of something:—*adjs* **emblema'tic**, **emblemat'ical**.

embod'iment *n* a living example.

embrace' *vb* **1** to hold in the arms, to hug. **2** to include:—*n* a holding in the arms.

embroi'der *vb* **1** to decorate with needlework. **2** to add interesting or exaggerated details to a story.

embroi'dery *n* **1** the art of decorating with needlework. **2** the act of adding interesting or exaggerated detail to. **3** decorative needlework.

embryo [em'-brö-ö] *n* the form of any creature before it is born or grows.

emend' *vb* to correct.

em'erald *n* a bright green precious stone:—*adj* bright green.

emerge' *vb* **1** to come out. **2** to become known:—*n* **emer'gence**:—*adj* **emer'gent**.

emer'gency *n* a state of affairs requiring immediate action.

em'igrant *n* one who emigrates:—*also adj*.

em'igrate *vb* to leave one's country and go to live in another:—*n* **emigra'tion**.

em'inent *adj* distinguished, very well known.

emit' *vb* (**emit'ted**, **emit'ting**) to send or give out:—*n* **emis'sion**.

emo'tion *n* **1** strong or deep feeling. **2** the moving or upsetting of the mind or feelings.

emo'tional *adj* **1** of the emotions. **2** causing or showing deep feelings. **3** easily moved by emotion.

em'peror *n* the ruler of an empire:—*f* **em'press**.

em'phasis *n* (*pl* **em'phases**) 1 the added force with which certain words or parts of words are spoken. 2 special meaning, value, importance, etc.

em'phasize *vb* 1 to say with emphasis. 2 to call attention to specially, to stress.

empha'tic *adj* forceful, firm, and definite.

em'pire *n* a group of countries under the rule of one of their number.

employ' *vb* 1 to give work to. 2 (*inf*) to use.

employ'ee, employee' *n* one paid to work for another person or for a firm.

employ'er *n* one who gives work to another.

employ'ment *n* job, occupation.

empow'er *vb* to give the right or power to.

empress *see* **emperor**.

emp'ty *adj* having nothing inside:—*vb* 1 to take everything out of. 2 to become empty:—*n* **emp'tiness**.

empyre'an *n* (*fml*) the sky:—*also adj*.

emu [ee-mû] *n* a large Australian flightless bird.

em'ulate *vb* (*fml*) to try to be as good as or better than.

ena'ble *vb* to give the power or means to do something.

enact' *vb* 1 to lay down by law, to pass a law. 2 to act, perform.

enam'el *n* 1 a smooth, glossy coating put on metals or wood to preserve or decorate them. 2 the outer covering of the teeth:—*vb* to cover with enamel.

enchant' *vb* 1 (*old*) to put a magic spell on. 2 to delight:—*n* **enchant'er**:—*f* **enchant'ress**:—*n* **enchant'ment**.

encir'cle *vb* to surround:—*n* **encir'clement**.

enclose' *vb* 1 to shut in, to fence in. 2 to send with a letter.

enclo'sure *n* 1 a space shut or fenced in. 2 something sent with a letter.

encore [on(g)-kôr] *adv* again, once more:—*n* 1 a call to a performer to repeat something or perform something else. 2 the repetition of part of a performance or a further performance by the same person or people given after a performance.

encoun'ter *n* 1 a meeting, esp an unexpected one. 2 a fight or quarrel:—*vb* to meet.

encour'age *vb* 1 to make bold. 2 to urge on:—*n* **encour'agement**.

encycloped'ia *n* a book or set of books containing information about every subject or about every branch of one subject.

encycloped'ic *adj* very detailed or complete.

end *n* 1 the last part of anything. 2 death. 3 purpose or aim:—*vb* to bring or come to an end.

endan'ger *vb* to put in danger.

endear'ment *n* an act or word showing love.

endeav'or [en-dev'ér] *vb* to try, to try hard:—*n* attempt, effort.

endem'ic *adj* found specially among one people or in one place.

end'less *adj* 1 having no end. 2 seemingly having no end.

endur'ance *n* the ability to endure or bear patiently.

endure' *vb* 1 (*fml*) to last. 2 to bear patiently. 3 to put up with.

en'emy *n* 1 one who is unfriendly, one who acts against another. 2 those with whom one is at war:—*also adj*.

energet'ic *adj* active, powerful, vigorous.

en'ergy *n* active power, force, vigor.

enforce' *n* to cause to be obeyed or carried out:—*n* **enforce'ment**.

engage' *vb* 1 (*fml*) to bind oneself by a promise, to promise. 2 to begin to employ. 3 to begin fighting. 4 to busy (oneself) with. 5 to attract and keep.

engag'ing *adj* pleasing, attractive.

engage'ment *n* 1 a promise to marry. 2 an arrangement to meet someone, an appointment. 3 a battle.

en'gine *n* 1 a machine that produces power. 2 a railroad locomotive.

engineer' *n* 1 one who looks after engines. 2 one who makes or designs machinery, roads, bridges, etc:—*vb* to arrange for or cause something to happen, usu by clever, cunning, or secret means.

engineer'ing *n* the science of making and using machines.

engrain' *n* to make sink deeply in.

engrave' *vb* 1 to cut or carve on metal, stone, wood, etc. 2 to cut a picture on a metal plate in order to print copies of it.

engrav'ing *n* a print from an engraved plate.

engross' *vb* to take up one's whole time or attention:—*n* **engross'ment**.

enhance' *vb* to increase in amount, value, importance, etc, to increase, to improve:—*n* **enhance'ment**.

enjoy' *vb* 1 to take pleasure in. 2 to possess:—*adj* **enjoy'able**:—*n* **enjoy'ment**.

enlarge' *vb* 1 (*fml*) to make larger. 2 to reproduce (a photograph) on a larger scale. 3 to talk at length about.

enlarge'ment *n* 1 act of making larger. 2 a larger copy of a photograph.

enlight'en *vb* (*fml*) to give more and correct information or knowledge about:—*n* **enlight'enment**.

en'mity *n* ill-will, hatred, hostility.

enor'mous *adj* huge, very large.

enrage' *vb* to make very angry.

enroll' *vb* 1 to write (a name) in a list. 2 to join or become a member:—*n* **enroll'ment**.

ensem'ble [ä(ng)-säm'-bèl] *n* 1 a group of musicians regularly performing together. 2 clothing made up of several items, an outfit.

ensue' *vb* to follow upon, to result from.

ensure' *vb* to make sure.

entan'gle *vb* 1 to cause to become twisted, tangled, or caught. 2 to get into difficulties or complications.

en'ter *vb* 1 to go or come into. 2 to become a member of. 3 to put down in writing.

en'terprise *n* 1 an undertaking or project, esp one that is difficult or daring. 2 willingness to take risks or to try out new ideas.

en'terprising *adj* having or showing enterprise.

entertain' *vb* 1 to receive as a guest. 2 to please, to amuse. 3 (*fml*) to consider.

entertain'ment *n* 1 the act of entertaining. 2 amusement. 3 something that entertains, such as a public performance.

enthrall' *vb* to delight, to enchant:—*n* **enthrall'ment**.

enthuse' *vb* to be, become, or cause to be enthusiastic, to show enthusiasm.

enthu'siasm *n* great eagerness, keenness.

enthu'siast *n* one who is very keen.

enthusias'tic *adj* full of enthusiasm.

entice' *vb* to tempt, to attract by offering something:—*n* **entice'ment**:—*adj* **entic'ing**.

entire' *adj* whole, complete:—*adv* **entire'ly**.

enti'tle *vb* 1 to give a right to. 2 to give a name to.

en'tity *n* 1 existence. 2 anything that exists.

en'trails *npl* the bowels, the internal organs of the body.

entrance'[1] *vb* to delight, to fill with wonder.

en'trance[2] *n* 1 coming or going in. 2 a place by which one enters (e.g. a door or gate).

en'trant *n* one who puts his or her name in for or joins.

entreat' *vb* (*fml*) to ask earnestly.

entreat'y *n* an earnest request.

entrust' *vb* to give into the care of.

en'try n **1** act of entering. **2** a way in. **3** something written in a diary, cash book, etc.

en'velop vb to cover or surround completely.

en'velope n a wrapper or cover, esp one made of paper for a letter.

en'viable adj causing envy, very desirable.

en'vious adj full of envy, jealous.

envir'onment n **1** surroundings. **2** all the conditions and surroundings that influence human character.

en'voy n a messenger, esp one sent to speak for his or her government in another country.

en'vy n **1** a feeling of discontent caused by someone else's good fortune or success, esp when one would like these for oneself. **2** something that causes envy:—vb to feel envy toward or at.

eon, aeon [ee'-on] n an age, a period of time too long to be measured.

ephemeral [e-fem'-er-êl or e-feem'-êr-êl] adj lasting for only a short time.

ep'ic n **1** a long poem telling of heroic deeds. **2** a story, film, etc, dealing with heroic deeds and exciting adventures:—adj of or like an epic, heroic, in the grand style.

epidem'ic n a disease or condition that attacks many people at the same time.

ep'ilogue n a part or section added at the end of a book, program, etc.

epis'copal adj having to do with bishops.

Episcopal Church n the branch of the Anglican Communion in the USA and Scotland.

ep'isode n **1** a particular event or a series of events that is separate from but forms part of a larger whole. **2** a part of a radio or TV serial that is broadcast at one time.

ep'itaph n words referring to a dead person, inscribed on his or her tombstone.

e'poch n a period of time in history, life, etc, esp one in which important events occurred. **2** the start of such a period.

equable [ek'-wa-bêl] adj **1** calm, even-tempered. **2** not changing suddenly, neither very hot nor very cold.

e'qual adj **1** the same in size, number, value, etc. **2** able (to do something):—n a person the same as another in rank or ability:—vb to be equal.

equal'ity n the state of being equal.

e'qualize vb to make or become equal.

equa'tion n a statement that two things are equal.

equa'tor n an imaginary line around the earth, halfway between the poles.

eques'trian adj **1** on horseback. **2** having to do with horse riding:—n a horseman or horsewoman.

e'qui- prefix equal.

equidis'tant adj equally distant.

equilat'eral adj having all sides equal.

equilib'rium n **1** a balance between equal weights. **2** steadiness. **3** balanced state of the mind, emotions, etc.

equine [e'-kwin] adj of or like a horse.

equip' vb (equipped', equip'ping) to give the things necessary for doing a job, to fit out.

equip'ment n outfit, the set of things needed for a particular activity.

equiv'alent adj equal in value, amount, meaning, etc:—n an equivalent thing.

equiv'ocal adj of doubtful meaning, capable of meaning two or more things.

era [e'-ra] n **1** a long period of time, starting from some important or particular event. **2** a period of time marked by an important event or events.

erad'icate vb to root out, to destroy completely:—n eradica'tion.

erase' vb to rub out, to remove.

erect' adj standing up straight:—vb **1** to build. **2** to set upright:—n erec'tion.

er'mine n **1** a type of weasel. **2** its white winter fur.

erode' vb to destroy or wear away gradually:—n ero'sion.

err vb (fml) to make a mistake, to do wrong.

err'and n **1** a short journey made to give a message, deliver goods, etc, to someone. **2** the purpose of such a journey.

erra'tic adj not steady, irregular, uneven, unpredictable.

er'ror n a mistake. **2** the state of being mistaken.

erupt' vb to break or burst out.

erup'tion n act of breaking or bursting out (e.g. of a volcano).

es'calate vb **1** to rise (as if on a moving staircase). **2** to increase in intensity.

es'calator n a moving staircase.

es'capade n a foolish or risky adventure.

escape' vb **1** to get out of the way of, to avoid. **2** to free oneself from. **3** to leak. **4** to avoid being noticed, remembered, etc:—n **1** act of escaping. **2** a leak.

escort' vb to go with as a guard, as a partner, to show the way or as an honor:—n es'cort **1** a guard, a bodyguard. **2** a partner, a companion.

Es'kimo n a former name for the Inuit.

esoter'ic adj (fml) understood by few people.

espar'to n a type of grass used for making paper.

espe'cially adv specially, particularly, markedly.

espionage [es'-pi-on-azh] n spying.

esplanade [es'-pla-nâd] n **1** a public walk along the sea front. **2** a level space for walking.

es'say n a written composition.

es'sayist n one who writes essays.

es'sence n **1** the nature or necessary part of anything. **2** a substance obtained from a plant, etc, in concentrated form.

essen'tial adj **1** necessary, very important, that cannot be done without. **2** of the basic or inner nature of something, fundamental.

estab'lish vb **1** to set up. **2** to place or fix in a position, etc, usu permanently. **3** to prove, to show to be true.

estab'lishment n **1** act of setting up. **2** a group of people employed in an organization, the staff of a household. **3** a place of business, the premises of a business organization or large institution:—the Establishment the people holding important positions in a country, community, etc, and usu supporting traditional ways, etc.

estate' n **1** all one's property and money. **2** area of land, esp in the country, with one owner.

esteem' vb to think highly of:—n respect, regard.

es'timate vb **1** to judge size, amount, etc, roughly, to guess. **2** to calculate the probable cost of:—n **1** an opinion. **2** a judgment as to the value or cost of a thing.

estima'tion n **1** judgment. **2** opinion.

es'tuary n the mouth of a river as far as the tide flows up it.

etch vb to cut a picture on a metal plate by use of acids in order to print copies of it.

etch'ing n a picture printed by etching.

eter'nal adj **1** everlasting, without beginning or end. **2** seeming never to stop.

eter'nity n **1** everlasting existence, with no beginning and no end, unending life after death. **2** (inf) a very long time.

eth'ical adj **1** having to do with right and wrong. **2** relating to ethics.

eth'ics n **1** the study of right and wrong. **2** rules or principles of behavior.

eth'nic *adj* having to do with human races or their customs, food, dress, etc.

etiquette [e'-ti-ket] *n* the rules of polite behavior, good manners.

eu'logy *n (fml)* praise.

euphemism [ŭ'-fem-izm] *n* the use of mild words or phrases to say something unpleasant (e.g. *fairy tale* for *lie*).

euthanasia [ū-than-ā'-zi-a] *n* painless killing, esp of a person suffering from a painful incurable disease.

evac'uate *vb* 1 to go away from (a place). 2 *(fml)* to make empty. 3 to send to a place of safety in wartime:—*n* **evacua'tion**.

evade' *vb* 1 to keep oneself away from. 2 to dodge, to find a way of not doing something, esp by using trickery, deception, etc. 3 to refuse to answer directly:—*n* **eva'sion**.

eval'uate *vb* to work out the value of:—*n* **evalua'tion**.

evap'orate *vb* 1 to turn into vapor and disappear. 2 to disappear—*n* **evapora'tion**.

evasion *see* **evade**.

eva'sive *adj* 1 having the purpose of evading. 2 not straightforward, not frank.

eve *n* 1 the day before. 3 the time before an important event.

e'ven *adj* 1 level. 2 smooth. 3 equal. 4 able to be divided by two. 5 calm:—*adv* just:—*vb* 1 to make smooth or level. 2 to make equal—*n* **e'venness**.

e'vening *n* the close of day.

event' *n* 1 anything that happens, an incident. 2 a single race or contest at sports or races.

even'tual *adj* happening as a result, final.

even'tually *adv* finally, at length.

ev'er *adv* always, at all times.

ev'ergreen *n* a tree or plant that has green leaves all the year around:—*adj* always green.

everlast'ing *adj* 1 never ending. 2 seemingly without end, frequent.

evermore' *adv* for ever.

ev'ery *adj* each one.

ev'eryday *adj* 1 happening every day. 2 usual, ordinary.

evict' *vb* to put out of a house or off land by order of a court:—*n* **evic'tion**.

ev'idence *n* 1 information given to show a fact is true. 2 the statement made by a witness in a court of law.

ev'ident *adj* clear, easily understood, obvious.

e'vil *adj* 1 wicked, bad, sinful. 2 unpleasant, nasty:—*n* 1 wickedness. 2 anything bad or harmful.

evolu'tion *n* the belief that life began in lower forms of creature and that these gradually changed over millions of years into the highest forms, such as humans.

ewe [ū] *n* a female sheep.

exact' *adj* 1 absolutely correct, accurate in every detail. 2 showing or taking great care:—*vb* 1 to force to make payment. 2 to demand and obtain.

exact'ing *adj* needing much work or attention.

exag'gerate *vb* 1 to speak or think of something as being better or more (or worse or less) than it really is. 2 to go beyond the truth in describing something:—*n* **exaggera'tion**.

exam'ine *vb* 1 to look at closely and carefully in order to find out something. 2 to question. 3 to test the knowledge of a learner by questions:—*n* **examina'tion**:—*n* **exam'iner**.

exam'ple *n* 1 one thing chosen to show what others of the same kind are like, a model. 2 a person or thing deserving to be imitated.

ex'cavate *vb* 1 to uncover by digging. 2 to dig up, to hollow out:—*n* **ex'cavator**.

exceed' *vb* 1 to go beyond. 2 to be greater or more numerous than.

exceed'ingly *adv* very, extremely.

excel' *vb* (**excelled'**, **excel'ling**) to do very well at, to get exceptionally good at.

ex'cellence *n* perfection, great merit.

ex'cellent *adj* very good, of a very high standard.

except' *vb (fml)* to leave out.

except'², **excepting** *preps* leaving out.

excep'tion *n* a person or thing that does not follow the rule:—**take exception** to object.

excep'tional *adj* different from others, unusual, remarkable:—*adv* **excep'tionally**.

excess' *n* 1 too much. 2 the amount by which a thing is too much.

exces'sive *adj* more than is right or correct.

exchange' *vb* 1 to give one thing and receive another in its place:—*n* 1 the act of exchanging. 2 a place where merchants meet to do business. 3 the changing of the money of one country into that of another.

exche'quer *n* that part of the government that looks after the nation's money.

excit'able *adj* easily excited.

excite' *vb* 1 to stir up feelings of happiness, expectation, etc. 2 to rouse:—*n* **excite'ment**.

exclaim' *vb* to cry out suddenly:—*adj* **exclam'atory**.

exclama'tion *n* a word or words said suddenly or with feeling.

exclamation mark *n* a mark of punctuation (!).

exclude' *vb* 1 to shut out. 2 to leave out. 3 to leave out, not to include:—*n* **exclu'sion**.

exclu'sive *adj* 1 open to certain people only. 2 sole. 3 not shared:—*adv* **exclu'sively**.

excommuni'cate *vb* 1 to bar from association with a church. 2 to exclude from fellowship:—*n* **excommuni'cation**.

ex'crement *n* waste matter put out from the body.

excrete' *vb* to put out what is useless from the body:—*adj* **excre'tory**.

excru'ciating *adj* 1 very great, intense. 2 terrible, very bad.

excur'sion *n* a trip made for pleasure, an outing.

excuse' [eks-kūz'] *vb* 1 to let off. 2 to forgive, to overlook. 3 to give reasons showing or intended to show that someone or something cannot be blamed:—*n* [eks-kūs'] a reason given for failure or wrongdoing:—*adj* **excus'able**.

ex'ecute *vb* 1 to perform. 2 to carry out. 3 to put to death by law.

execu'tion *n* 1 the carrying out, performance, etc, of something. 2 skill in performing music. 3 the act of putting to death by order of the law.

execu'tioner *n* an officer who puts to death condemned criminals.

exec'utive *adj* concerned with making and carrying out decisions, esp in business:—*n* one involved in the management of a firm.

exem'plary *adj* 1 admirable, worth copying, giving a good example. 2 *(fml)* serving as a warning.

exempt' *vb* to free from, to let off:—*adj* free:—*n* **exemp'tion**.

ex'ercise *n* 1 an action performed to strengthen the body or part of the body. 2 a piece of work done for practice. 3 training. 4 use:—*vb* 1 to use, to employ. 2 to perform some kind of physical exercises. 3 to give exercise to, to train.

exert' *vb* to apply:—**exert oneself** to try hard.

exer'tion *n* effort.

exhale' *vb* to breathe out—*n* **exhala'tion**.

exhaust' vb **1** to use up completely. **2** to tire out. **3** to say everything possible about:—n **1** a passage by which used steam or gases are carried away from an engine. **2** these gases.

exhaus'tion n **1** the state of being tired out. **2** lack of any strength.

exhaus'tive adj very thorough, complete.

exhib'it vb **1** to show in public. **2** (fml) to display, to show:—n a thing shown in public.

exhibi'tion n **1** act of exhibiting. **2** a collection of many things brought together to be shown to the public.

exhil'arate vb to make lively or happy:—n **exhilara'tion**.

ex'ile n **1** long or unwilling absence from one's home or country. **2** a person living in a country other than his or her own:—vb to send someone out of his or her own country as a punishment.

exist' vb **1** to be. **2** to live:—n **exis'tence**:—adj **exis'tent**.

ex'it n **1** a way out. **2** a going out:—also vb.

exor'bitant adj far too much, far too great:—n **exorb'itance**.

exot'ic adj **1** foreign, introduced from another country. **2** striking and unusual.

expand' vb **1** to make or become larger. **2** to spread out.

expanse' n a wide area.

expan'sion n act of expanding.

expan'sive adj **1** wide. **2** ready to talk freely.

expatriate [eks-pā'-tri-āt] n one living or working in a country other than his or her own.

expect' vb **1** to wait for. **2** to think it likely that something will happen. **3** to require as a right or duty.

expec'tant adj hopeful, waiting for something to happen:—ns **expec'tancy, expec'tance**.

expecta'tion n **1** hope that something will happen. **2** that which is expected.

expe'dient adj **1** wise or desirable in a particular case. **2** bringing immediate advantage, although not necessarily right or moral:—n a plan or action that solves an immediate difficulty.

expedite [eks'-ped-īt] vb to make happen more quickly.

expedi'tion n a journey made for a particular purpose.

expel' vb (**expelled', expel'ling**) **1** to drive out. **2** to force to go away. **3** to dismiss officially from a school, club, etc:—n **expul'sion**.

expend' vb to spend, to use up.

expen'diture n **1** the amount spent. **2** the act of spending.

expense' n **1** cost. **2** spending of money, etc.

expen'sive adj dear, costing much.

expe'rience n **1** a happening in one's own life. **2** knowledge gained from one's own life or work:—vb **1** to meet with. **2** to feel. **3** to undergo.

exper'iment n something done so that the results may be studied, a test:—vb to do an experiment:—adj **experimen'tal**.

expert' adj very skillful:—n **ex'pert** one having special skill or knowledge.

expira'tion n (fml) **1** act of breathing out. **2** end.

expire' vb **1** (fml) to die. **2** to come to an end.

expi'ry n end.

explain' vb **1** to make clear. **2** to give reasons for.

explana'tion n a statement of the meaning of or the reasons for.

expletive [eks-plee'-tiv] n a swear word.

explicit [eks-plis'-it] adj **1** stating exactly what is meant. **2** with full details, with nothing hidden.

explode' vb **1** to burst or blow up with a loud noise. **2** to show to be untrue, to destroy.

ex'ploit n a brave or outstanding deed:—vb to make use of, esp for selfish reasons:—n **exploita'tion**.

explore' vb **1** to examine closely. **2** to travel through a country to find out all about it:—n **explora'tion**:—n **explor'er**.

explo'sion n **1** going off or bursting with a loud noise. **2** an outburst.

explo'sive adj able to cause an explosion:—n any substance that will explode.

export' vb to send goods to another country:—n **ex'port** an article that is exported:—n **exporta'tion**.

expose' vb **1** to uncover. **2** to make known the truth about. **3** to allow light to fall on (a photographic film).

expo'sure n **1** act of exposing. **2** the effect on the body of being out in cold weather for a long time.

express' vb **1** to put into words, to state. **2** to make known by words or actions:—adj **1** swift. **2** clearly stated:—n a fast train.

expres'sion n **1** a word or phrase. **2** the look on one's face. **3** ability to read, play music, etc, with meaning or feeling.

express'ive adj with feeling or meaning.

expulsion see expel.

ex'quisite, exquis'ite adj beautiful and delicate, very fine.

extant' adj still existing.

extend' vb **1** to stretch out. **2** to reach or stretch. **3** to offer. **4** to make longer or bigger.

exten'sion n **1** an addition. **2** an additional period of time.

exten'sive adj **1** large. **2** wide, wide-ranging.

extent' n **1** the area or length to which something extends. **2** amount, degree.

exte'rior adj outer:—n the outside.

exter'minate vb to kill to the last one, to destroy completely:—n **extermina'tion**.

exter'nal adj on the outside.

extinct' adj **1** no longer found in existence. **2** no longer burning.

exting'uish vb **1** to put out. **2** to put an end to.

extort' vb to take from by force or threats:—n **extor'tion**.

extor'tionate adj far too expensive.

ex'tra adj additional, more than is usual, expected, or necessary:—adv more than usually:—n something additional.

extract' vb **1** to draw, take, or pull out. **2** to select a passage from a book:—n **ex'tract 1** a passage taken from a book. **2** a substance drawn from a material and containing all its qualities.

extrac'tion n **1** act of drawing out. **2** connection with a certain family or race.

extraor'dinary adj **1** very unusual, remarkable. **2** (fml) additional to what is usual or ordinary.

extrav'agance n **1** wastefulness. **2** wasteful spending.

extrav'agant adj **1** spending or using a great deal, wasteful. **2** spending foolishly. **3** foolish and improbable.

extreme' adj **1** farthest away. **2** greatest possible. **3** far from moderate, going beyond the limits, not sharing the views of the majority. **4** intense, strong, not ordinary or usual:—n **1** the end, the farthest point. **2** something as far or as different as possible from something else. **3** the greatest or highest degree.

extrem'ity n **1** the farthest point. **2** (fml) a situation of great misfortune, distress, or danger.

exu'berant adj in high spirits:—n **exu'berance**.

exude' vb to ooze out, to give off.

exult' vb to rejoice very much, to express joy:—adj **exul'tant**:—n **exulta'tion**.

eye n **1** the organ by means of which we see. **2** a small hole in a needle:—vb to look at, to watch closely.

eye'glasses npl spectacles.

eye'witness n one who sees an event happen.

F

fab'ric n **1** the framework of a building. **2** manufactured cloth.

fab'ulous adj **1** (fml) existing only in legend. **2** (inf) wonderful, marvelous, very good.

face n **1** the front part of the head, from forehead to chin. **2** the front part of anything:—vb **1** to stand looking toward, to turn toward. **2** to meet or encounter boldly. **3** to cover with a surface of different material.

facetious [fa-see'-shês] adj intended to make people laugh or to be amusing, often in an inappropriate situation:— n **face'tiousness**.

facil'ity n pl the means or conditions for doing something easily.

facsimile [fak-sim'-l-li] n **1** an exact copy. **2** an image produced by fax.

fact n **1** something known to be true or to have happened. **2** truth.

fac'tor n **1** a cause, element. **2** a number that goes exactly into another number.

fac'tory n a building where large quantities of goods are made.

fac'tual adj having to do with facts.

fade n **1** to lose color. **2** to disappear gradually.

fail vb **1** not to succeed. **2** to break down. **3** to disappoint. **4** to owe so much money that one cannot pay one's debts.

fail'ing n a fault, a weakness.

fail'ure n **1** lack of success. **2** one who has not succeeded. **3** a breakdown.

faint vb to become weak, to fall down unconscious:—n act of falling down unconscious:—adj **1** weak, dizzy. **2** lacking clearness or brightness. **3** slight.

fair[1] adj **1** light in color, having light-colored hair. **2** quite good. **3** just. **4** (of weather) not rainy. **5** (old or lit) attractive.

fair[2] n **1** a market or sale, often with shows and amusements. **2** a trade exhibition.

fair'ly adv quite.

fair'ness n justice.

fair'y n an imaginary small being, supposed to have magic powers.

faith n **1** trust, belief in God. **2** trust, confidence. **3** religion. **4** one's word of honor.

faith'ful adj **1** true to one's friends or one's promises. **2** loyal to one's marriage vows. **3** true to the facts of an original.

fake n someone or something that deceives by looking other than he, she, or it is:—vb **1** to change something so that it falsely appears better, more valuable, etc. **2** to copy something so as to deceive. **3** (inf) to pretend.

fal'con n a bird of prey trained to hunt smaller birds.

fall vb (pt fell, pp fallen) **1** to drop down. **2** to become less or lower. **3** to hang down. **4** to happen or occur. **5** to enter into a certain state or condition. **6** to be taken by an enemy. **7** to be killed in battle:—n **1** a drop or descent. **2** lessening or lowering. **3** loss of power. **4** a waterfall. **5** one of the four seasons of the year, between summer and winter, autumn:—**fall back** to go back:—**fall on** or **upon** to attack:—**fall out** (inf) to quarrel:—**fall through** to fail.

fallacy [fal'-ê-si] n a wrong idea or belief, usu one that is generally believed to be true, a false reasoning:—adj **falla'cious**.

false adj **1** not true. **2** disloyal. **3** not real, artificial:—ns **false'ness, fals'ity**.

falter [fâl'-ter] vb **1** to speak or say in an uncertain or hesitant way. **2** to stumble.

fame n the state of being well known for what one has done.

famil'iar adj **1** well known because often seen. **2** having good knowledge of. **3** too friendly, disrespectful:—n a close friend:—n **familiar'ity**.

fam'ily n **1** a household, parents and children. **2** one's children. **3** people descended from the same ancestors. **4** a group of things in some way related to each other (e.g. races, animals, etc.).

family tree n a table showing the growth of a family from a pair of common ancestors.

fam'ine n a great shortage of food.

fam'ous adj well known to all.

fan[1] n an instrument or machine causing a current of air:—vb (**fanned', fan'ning**) to move the air with a fan:—**fan out** to spread out over a wider front.

fan[2] n a keen follower or supporter.

fanat'ic n one who holds a belief, esp a religious or political belief, so strongly that he or she can neither discuss it reasonably nor think well of those who disagree with it:—n **fanat'icism**.

fan'cy n **1** a false idea or belief, something imagined. **2** a sudden desire. **3** a liking for, often a romantic one:—adj not plain, decorated:—vb **1** (fml) to imagine. **2** (inf) to like. **3** to be romantically or sexually attracted to.

fang n the tooth of an animal.

fantas'tic adj **1** strange or weird. **2** created in the mind, fanciful, unrealistic. **3** (inf) very large. **4** (inf) very good, excellent.

fan'tasy n **1** a highly imaginative composition. **2** an unusual or far-fetched idea, a dream.

far adj distant:—adv at a distance in time, space, or degree.

farce n **1** a stage play intended only to arouse laughter. **2** a laughable or ridiculous situation.

fare vb (fml or old) to be or do (ill or well):—n **1** food. **2** the cost of a travel ticket.

farewell' interj goodbye.

farm n an area of land prepared for crops and herds by one owner:—vb to use land as a farm:—n **farm'er**:—**farm out** to give out to be done by others.

fas'cinate vb to attract or interest very strongly, to charm:—n **fascina'tion**.

fash'ion n **1** the way in which a thing is done or made. **2** the kinds of clothes popular at a certain time:—vb to shape, to make.

fash'ionable adj **1** following a style that is currently popular. **2** used or visited by people following a current fashion.

fast[1] vb to do without food, esp for religious reasons:—n act or time of fasting.

fast[2] adj **1** firm, fixed. **2** quick, swift:—adv **1** firmly. **2** quickly. **3** (old) near.

fasten [fas'-ên] vb **1** to fix firmly. **2** to fix to.

fat adj well fed, fleshy:—n **1** an oily substance in animal bodies. **2** this substance or the oily substance found in some plants when in solid or almost solid form, used as a food or in cooking.

fatal [fā'-têl] adj causing death.

fatal'ity n **1** death caused by accident, war, etc. **2** (fml) deadliness.

fate n **1** an imaginary power that is supposed to decide future events before they happen. **2** what will happen to one in the future.

fa'ther n **1** a male parent. **2** a person who begins, invents, or first makes something. **3** a priest:—vb **1** to be the father of. **2** to start an idea or movement.

fatigue [fa-teeg'] n **1** weariness, great tiredness. **2** an unpleasant or tiring job:—vb to tire out.

fat'ty adj containing fat.

fau'cet n a short pipe containing a stopper that can be opened by a handle to allow liquid to flow out, a tap.

fault n 1 a mistake. 2 a weakness in character. 3 an imperfection, something wrong with something. 4 a break in rock that then drops below the rest:—*adj* **fault'less**.

fault'y *adj* having a fault, imperfect.

fa'vor n 1 a feeling of kindness or approval toward. 2 an act done out of kindness:—*vb* 1 (*fml*) to show more kindness to one than to another. 2 to prefer. 3 to give an advantage.

fa'vorable *adj* kindly, helpful.

fa'vorite n a person or thing preferred to others:—*also adj*.

fawn[1] n a young deer. 2 a yellowish-brown color:—*adj* yellowish-brown.

fawn[2] *vb* to flatter or behave like a slave to gain another's favor:—*adj* **fawn'ing**.

fax n (*short for* **facsimile transmission**) a system of transmitting a written, printed, or pictorial document over the phone system by scanning it and reproducing the image after transmission:—*also vb*.

fear n dread, terror, anxiety:—*also vb*.

fear'ful *adj* 1 apprehensive and afraid. 2 terrible. 3 (*inf*) very bad, very great.

fear'less *adj* unafraid.

feast n 1 a meal with plenty of good things to eat and drink. 2 something extremely pleasing. 3 a day or period of time kept in memory of a religious event, such as Christmas:—*vb* 1 to eat well. 2 to provide a good meal for others.

feath'er[1] n one of the growths that cover a bird's body:—*vb* to line or cover with feathers:—**feather one's nest** to make a profit for oneself out of work done for others.

feath'er[2] *vb* in rowing, to turn the oar so as to lessen air resistance.

fea'ture n 1 an outstanding part of anything. 2 a special long article in a newspaper. 3 *pl* the face:—*vb* to give or have a position, main part or important one.

Feb'ruary n the second month of the year.

fee n 1 a payment made for special professional services, a charge or payment. 2 money paid for entering or being taught in a school, college, etc.

fee'ble *adj* very weak:—n. **fee'bleness**.

feed *vb* (*pt, pp* **fed**) 1 to give food to. 2 to eat. 3 to provide what is necessary for. 4 to put into:—n food.

feel *vb* (*pt, pp* **felt**) 1 to touch. 2 to find out by touching. 3 to experience or be aware of. 4 to believe or consider. 5 to be moved by, to have pity:—n the sense of touch, a quality as revealed by touch.

feel'er n 1 the thread-like organ of touch of an insect. 2 something said to try to get others to give their opinions.

feel'ing n 1 the sense of touch. 2 emotion. 3 kindness for others. 4 an impression or belief:—*adj* able to understand the emotions of others.

feet *see* **foot**.

feign [fān] *vb* to pretend.

feline [fee'-līn] *adj* 1 cat-like. 2 of the cat family.

fell *vb* to cut down, to knock down.

fell'ow n 1 one of a pair. 2 a companion and an equal. 3 (*inf*) a man.

felt[1] *pt and pp of* **feel**.

felt[2] n a coarse cloth made of wool and hair.

fe'male n a girl or woman. 2 an animal or bird that can bear offspring:—*also adj*.

fem'inine *adj* 1 having the qualities considered suitable or essential for a woman. 2 of a woman.

fem'inism n the belief that men and women should have equal rights:—n **fem'inist**.

feminin'ity n the state of being female or womanly.

fence n 1 a wall made of wood or of wooden posts and wire to enclose a field. 2 (*inf*) a receiver of stolen goods:—*vb* 1 to put a fence around. 2 to take part in sword-play. 3 to avoid giving direct answers to questions, esp by quibbling over minor points:—**sit on the fence** to give no decision either way, to be neutral.

fenc'ing n 1 the materials for making a fence. 2 sword-play as a sport.

fend *vb* 1 to keep off, to turn aside. 2 to look after.

fen'der n 1 a guard around a fireplace. 2 a rope pad to protect the side of a ship. 3 a protective bar at the front and back of an motor vehicle. 4 a metal shield over the wheel of a bicycle to catch the mud thrown up by it.

ferment' *vb* 1 to cause or undergo a chemical change that causes solids to break up and mix and liquids to froth and bubble. 2 to excite:—n **fer'ment**:—n **fermenta'tion**.

fern n a plant with no flowers and feathery leaves.

fero'cious *adj* fierce, cruel, savage:—n **fero'city**.

fer'ret n a small weasel-like animal used to hunt rabbits:—*vb* 1 to search busily and persistently. 2 to find something carefully hidden.

fer'ry *vb* 1 to carry over water in a boat or airplane. 2 to transport:—n 1 a boat that ferries. 2 the place where a ferry crosses.

fer'tile *adj* 1 able to produce much, fruitful. 2 inventive:—n **fertil'ity**.

fer'tilize *vb* to make fertile or fruitful.

fer'vent *adj* eager, very keen, sincere.

fer'vor n keenness, strength of feeling.

fes'ter *vb* (*of a wound*) to become full of poisonous matter, to become infected.

fes'tival n 1 a day or number of days spent in joy, merry-making, etc. 2 a season of plays, films, concerts, etc.

fes'tive *adj* gay, joyous.

festiv'ity n gaiety, merrymaking.

fetch *vb* 1 to go and bring. 2 to be sold for.

fête [fet] n a day of public enjoyment and entertainment held usu out of doors and often to collect money for a special purpose:—*vb* to honor (as if) with a fête.

fett'er n a chain for the feet:—*vb* 1 to fasten with fetters. 2 to hinder, to restrain.

fett'le n condition, fitness.

feud [fūd] n lasting quarreling or strife between persons or families or clans, etc:—*also vb*.

fe'ver n 1 a disease causing great heat in the body. 2 an abnormally high body temperature. 3 excitement.

fe'vered, fe'verish *adjs* 1 hot with fever. 2 excited.

fiancé [fee-än(g)'-sā] n a man engaged to be married:—*f* **fiancée**.

fias'co n (*pl* **fias'coes**) a complete failure, a laughable failure.

fib n a not very serious lie or untruth:—*vb* (**fibbed', fib'bing**) to tell untruths:—n **fib'ber**.

fi'ber n a thread-like part of an animal or plant. 2 a material made of fibers.

fick'le *adj* quickly changing, not faithful:—n **fick'leness**.

fic'tion n 1 a made-up story. 2 the art of writing stories. 3 novels.

ficti'tious *adj* imaginary, invented.

fid'dle n a violin:—*vb* 1 to play the violin. 2 to play about with. 3 to prepare or alter dishonestly to one's own advantage:—n **fidd'ler**.

fidel'ity n 1 faithfulness, loyalty. 2 exactness.

fid'get *vb* to move about restlessly:—*also n*.

field n 1 open country. 2 an enclosed area of ground. 3 a battlefield. 4 a sports ground:—*vb* to catch and return a ball.

field hockey *see* hockey.

fiend *n* 1 a devil. 2 a very cruel person:—*adj* **fiend'ish**.

fierce *adj* wild, angry:—*n* **fierce'ness**.

fiery [fi'-ri] *adj* 1 having to do with fire. 2 easily angered or excited.

fig *n* the fig tree or its fruit.

fight *vb* (*pt, pp* **fought**) 1 to use force against another. 2 to take part in war or battle. 3 to quarrel, to argue. 4 to try hard to succeed:—*n* 1 a struggle in which force is used, a battle. 2 a hard effort.

fig'ment *n*:—**figment of one's imagination** something that one has imagined and that has no reality.

fig'ure *n* 1 the shape of the body. 2 a person. 3 lines drawn to show a shape, a geometrical shape. 4 a number from 0 to 9. 5 a price. 6 a diagram or illustration:—*vb* 1 to work out the answer to a sum or problem. 2 to appear. 3 (*inf*) to think or consider.

figure of speech *n* the use of words in an unusual meaning or order to express ideas with greater clarity or feeling.

file[1] *n* 1 a number of papers arranged in order. 2 any device that keeps them in order. 3 a row of persons one behind the other:—*vb* 1 to put in place in a file. 2 to walk in file.

file[2] *n* a tool with a rough face for smoothing or cutting:—*vb* to smooth or cut away with a file.

fill *vb* 1 to make full. 2 to become full. 3 to stop up. 4 to occupy:—*n* as much as fills or satisfies, often to a great extent.

fill'et *n* boneless meat or fish:—*vb* to take the bones out of.

film *n* 1 a thin skin or covering. 2 the thin roll of celluloid on which the pictures are taken by a camera. 3 a movie:—*vb* to photograph or make a film of.

film star *n* a popular film actor or actress.

fil'ter *n* a strainer, a device through which liquid is passed to cleanse it:—*vb* 1 to cleanse or separate by passing through a filter.

filth *n* 1 dirt, foulness. 2 evil talk, obscene literature.

filth'y *adj* 1 very dirty. 2 disgusting, obscene.

fin *n* a small wing-like organ by means of which a fish swims.

fi'nal *adj* 1 last. 2 putting an end to:—*n* **final'ity**:—*adv* **fi'nally**.

fi'nance *n* 1 money matters. 2 *pl* money resources:—*vb* **finance'** to find or provide the money for:—*adj* **finan'cial**.

find *vb* (*pt, pp* **found**) 1 to come upon what one is looking for. 2 to discover. 3 to decide after inquiry:—*n* a valuable discovery.

fine[1] *adj* 1 very thin or small. 2 excellent. 3 delicate, beautiful. 4 bright, sunny. 5 healthy. 6 slight.

fine[2] *n* money paid as a punishment:—*vb* to punish by fine.

fing'er *n* one of the five points that extend from the hand or glove:—*vb* to touch with the fingers:—**have at one's finger-tips** to have ready knowledge of.

fing'erprint *n* 1 the mark made by the tips of the fingers. 2 an ink print of the lines on the fingertips for identification purposes.

fin'ish *vb* 1 to bring to an end. 2 to come to an end:—*n* 1 the end. 2 extra touches to make perfect.

fir *n* a cone-bearing (coniferous) tree.

fire *n* 1 something burning giving out heat and light. 2 an apparatus for heating. 3 (*fml*) keenness:—*vb* 1 to set on fire. 2 to bake (pottery). 3 to cause to explode. 4 to arouse keenness. 5 (*inf*) to dismiss (from a job).

fire'arm *n* a gun, rifle, or pistol.

fire en'gine *n* an engine or pump for putting out fires.

fire escape *n* a long ladder or steps by which people may escape from a burning building.

fire'place *n* a framed opening in the wall of a house to hold a fire.

fire'works *npl* toy explosives (e.g. rockets, squibs, etc) set off in the dark for show.

firm[1] *adj* 1 steady, not easily moved. 2 determined:—*n* **firm'ness**.

firm[2] *n* a business company organized to manufacture or trade in goods.

fir'mament *n* the sky of heavens.

first *adj* the first:—*adv* 1 before all others. 2 before doing anything else.

first aid *n* treatment given to an injured person before the doctor arrives, simple medical attention.

first floor *n* the story of a building on the same level as the ground.

fish *n* an animal with gills and fins, living in water:—*vb* 1 to try to catch fish. 2 (*inf*) to search for.

fish'monger *n* one who buys and sells fish.

fish'y *adj* 1 of or like fish. 2 doubtful, arousing suspicion.

fist *n* the hand tightly shut.

fit[1] *adj* 1 suitable, proper, right. 2 in good health:—*n* the particular way in which something fits:—*vb* (**fit'ted, fit'ting**) 1 to be of the right size. 2 to suit. 3 to make suitable.

fit[2] *n* 1 a sudden attack of illness, fainting, etc. 2 a sudden feeling.

fit'ness *n* suitability.

fit'ting *adj* suitable, proper:—*n* a thing fixed in position

fix *vb* 1 to make firm. 2 to arrange. 3 to fasten. 4 to repair. 5 (*inf*) to arrange the result of dishonestly:—*n* (*inf*) a difficulty.

fixed *adj* firm, not moving or changing:—*adv* **fix'edly**.

fix'ture *n* 1 anything fastened in place. 2 an arrangement to play a game, etc, on a certain date.

fizz *vb* to release or give off many bubbles:—*n* 1 bubbles of gas in a liquid. 2 the sound of fizzing.

flab'bergast *vb* to astonish.

flab'by *adj* 1 soft, hanging loosely. 2 having soft loose flesh:—*n* **flab'biness**.

flag *n* 1 a square or oblong piece of material with a pattern on it representing a country, party, association, etc. 2 a colored cloth or paper used as a sign or signal:—*vb* (**flagged', flag'ging**) 1 to signal with flags. 2 to cause a vehicle to stop by signaling to the driver.

flag'on *n* a large or wide bottle.

flagrant [flā'-grēnt] *adj* done without concealment, shameless.

flair *n* 1 a natural ability. 2 style, stylishness, an original and attractive quality.

flake *n* 1 a small thin piece of anything, esp a small loose piece that has broken off something. 2 a very light piece (e.g. of snow):—*vb* to come off in flakes:—*adj* **flak'y**.

flamboy'ant *adj* 1 very brightly colored or decorated. 2 showy and confident.

flame *n* a tongue of fire, a blaze:—*vb* 1 to burn brightly. 2 (*inf*) to become suddenly angry.

flamm'able *adj* easily set on fire.

flan'nel *n* 1 a soft woolen cloth. 2 a wash cloth.

flap *n* 1 anything fixed at one end and hanging loose, esp part of a garment. 2 the sound made by such a thing when it moves. 3 (*inf*) panic, agitation:—*vb* (**flapped', flap'ping**) 1 to flutter, to move up and down, to make a sound as of fluttering. 2 (*inf*) to get into a panic, to become confused or excited.

flare *vb* 1 to blaze up, to burn brightly but unsteadily. 2 to spread outward:—*n* 1 a bright unsteady light. 2 a light used as a signal. 3 a gradual widening out, esp of a skirt.

flash *n* 1 a quick or sudden gleam. 2 (*fig*) a moment. 3 anything lasting for a very short time. 4 flashlight:—*vb* 1 to shine out suddenly. 2 to move very quickly.

flash'light n 1 an electric light carried in the hand, a torch. 2 a device for producing a short burst of electric light used to take photographs in the dark.

flask n 1 a kind of bottle. 2 a pocket bottle. 3 a vacuum flask.

flat adj 1 level. 2 uninteresting, dull, and lifeless. 3 (of music) below the right note. 4 lying full length. 5 deflated, without enough air in it. 6 emphatic, firm. 7 no longer fizzy:— n 1 a level area. 2 the flat part or side. 3 apartment. 4 a musical sign showing that a note is to be played a semitone lower. 5 a flat tire:—n **flat'ness**.

flat'ten vb to make flat.

flat'ter vb 1 to praise over much or insincerely. 2 to make appear better than is true:—n **flat'terer**.

flat'tery n insincere praise.

fla'vor n 1 a taste. 2 the taste special to a thing:—vb to add something to a dish in order to improve its taste.

flaw n 1 a crack, a defect, imperfection. 2 any weakness that makes a person or thing less than perfect, less effective, etc:— adj **flaw'less**.

flea n a small, jumping, bloodsucking insect.

flee vb (pt, pp **fled**) to run away, to run away from.

fleece n 1 the wooly coat of a sheep or similar animal. 2 something that resembles this in appearance or warmth:—vb 1 to remove wool from. 2 to defraud.

fleet n a large number of ships, automobiles, airplanes, etc, together.

fleet'ing adj (fml) passing quickly.

flesh n the soft substance that covers the bones of an animal to form its body. 2 this as food. 3 the eatable part of fruit. 4 the body.

flew pt of **fly**.

flex vb to bend:—n a cord of rubber-covered wires used to carry electric currents.

flex'ible adj 1 easily bent. 2 easily changed, adaptable. 3 willing and able to change according to circumstances, adaptable:—n **flexibil'ity**.

flick'er vb 1 to shine or burn unsteadily. 2 to flutter, to move quickly and lightly.

flier see **fly**.

flight n 1 the act of flying. 2 the act of running away. 3 the movement or path of a thing through the air. 4 a journey made by air. 5 a number of birds flying together. 6 a set of stairs or steps.

flim'sy adj 1 thin. 2 not strong, easily broken or destroyed. 3 weak.

flinch vb to draw back in fear or pain.

fling vb (pt, pp **flung**) to throw.

flint n 1 a hard stone. 2 a piece of hard mineral from which sparks can be struck.

flip vb (**flipped'**, **flip'ping**) 1 to turn over lightly but sharply. 2 toss:—also n.

flip'pant adj not serious, disrespectful:—n **flip'pancy**.

flirt vb 1 to show interest in for a time only. 2 to behave toward another as if attracted by or in order to attract:—n one who plays at making love:—n **flirta'tion**.

flit vb (**flit'ted**, **flit'ting**) 1 to move quickly and lightly. 2 to vacate (a premises) stealthily:—also n.

float vb 1 to remain on the surface of a liquid. 2 to suggest, to put forward.

flock' n 1 a company of birds or animals. 2 a number of people together. 3 a congregation:—vb to come together in a crowd.

flock' n a tuft or flake of wool. 2 waste wool used for stuffing cushions, etc.

floe n a large sheet of floating ice.

flog vb (**flogged'**, **flog'ging**) to beat, to thrash:—n **flog'ging**.

flood n 1 an overflowing of water on to dry land. 2 a rush (of water, people, etc). 3 the flowing in of the tide:—vb 1 to overflow, to cover or become covered with water. 2 to put too much water, fuel, etc, on or in.

floor n 1 the bottom surface of a room on which one walks. 2 any bottom surface. 3 all the rooms, etc, on the same level of a building.

flop vb (**flopped'**, **flop'ping**) 1 to sit or fall down heavily or loosely. 2 to hang or swing heavily or loosely. 3 to fail completely, to be unsuccessful:—n a complete failure.

flor'al adj having to do with flowers.

flor'ist n one who grows or sells flowers.

floss n waxed thread for cleaning between the teeth:—also vb.

flounce' vb to move sharply or quickly:—also n.

flounce' n a gathered strip of cloth sewn by its upper edge around a skirt or dress and left hanging.

flour n the meal of wheat, etc, ground into powder.

flourish [flur'-ish] vb 1 to get on well, to be very successful, to prosper. 2 to grow well, to bloom. 3 to wave about in a showy manner:—n 1 spoken words or handwriting that attract attention by being unusual. 2 a sudden short burst of music. 3 a bold sweeping movement or gesture.

flow [flō] vb 1 to move steadily and easily, as water. 2 to proceed evenly and continuously. 3 to fall or hang down loosely and freely. 4 to be plentiful:—n 1 a flowing movement, a stream. 2 the rise of the tide. 3 a continuous stream or supply.

flow'er n 1 a blossom. 2 the best part of:—vb 1 to blossom or bloom.

flow'ery adj 1 full of flowers. 2 patterned with flowers. 3 ornate, over-elaborate.

fluc'tuate vb 1 to rise and fall, as a wave. 2 to vary, to change continually and irregularly:—n **fluctua'tion**.

flu'ent adj able to speak or write quickly and easily:— n **flu'ency**.

fluff n any soft or feathery material.

fluff'y adj like fluff, soft and downy.

flu'id adj 1 able to flow, flowing. 2 able to change quickly. 3 smooth and graceful:—n any substance that flows, as liquid or gas.

fluid ounce n one sixteenth of a pint.

fluorescence [flō-ér-es'-êns] n a quality in certain substances that enables them to give very bright light for quite low expenditure of electricity.

fluoresc'ent adj having or showing fluorescence.

flur'ry n 1 confused movement. 2 a sudden rush of air, rain, etc:—vb to make anxious or confused.

flush vb 1 to become suddenly red in the face. 2 to cleanse by a flow of water:—n 1 a sudden redness in the face. 2 freshness, vigor:—adj level.

flus'ter vb to make confused.

flute n a wooden musical wind instrument.

flutt'er vb 1 to move the wings up and down without flying. 2 move about quickly:—n 1 quick movement. 2 (inf) excitement. 3 (inf) a bet, a gamble.

fly vb (pt **flew**, pp **flown**) 1 to move through the air on wings. 2 to travel by airplane. 3 to move quickly. 4 to run away:— n 1 a common flying insect. 2 a fishing hook covered with feathers to make it look like a fly. 3 a flap, esp that closing the entrance to a tent:—n **fli'er**, **fly'er**.

foal n a young horse or ass:—vb to give birth to a foal.

foam n bubbles on the top of liquid, froth:—vb to gather or produce foam.

fob vb (**fobbed'**, **fob'bing**) to get rid of another by giving him or her something of little value.

fo′cus *n* (*pl* **foci** [fō′-ki] or **fo′cuses**) **1** a point at which rays of light meet. **2** a center of interest or attention:—*vb* **1** to bring to bear on one point. **2** to get a clear image in the lens of a camera before taking a photograph.

fod′der *n* dried food for cattle.

foe *n* (*fml*) an enemy.

fog *n* a thick mist.

fog′gy *adj* **1** misty. **2** confused, vague.

foi′ble *n* (*fml*) a weakness in character.

foil[1] *n* **1** a very thin sheet of metal. **2** anything placed alongside something else to make it show to advantage.

foil[2] *n* a blunt sword used in fencing.

foist *vb* by a trick, to get rid of something worthless or unwanted to another.

fold[1] *vb* **1** to bend one part of a thing over to cover another part. **2** to enclose:—*n* **1** a line or crease made by folding. **2** the part doubled over.

fold[2] *n* a place where sheep are kept.

fold′er *n* a stiff cover for holding papers, etc.

fo′liage *n* (*fml*) the leaves of trees.

folk *n* **1** (*inf*) people. **2** the people of a country or a particular part of a country. **3** (*inf*) *pl* relatives, parents.

fol′low *vb* **1** to go or come after. **2** to be next in order to. **3** to go along. **4** to accept as a leader or a teacher. **5** to result from. **6** to understand.

fol′lower *n* a supporter.

fol′lowing *n* all one's supporters:—*adj* next in order.

fol′ly *n* **1** foolishness. **2** a foolish act.

fond *adj* **1** having a love or liking for. **2** loving:—*n* **fond′ness**.

fon′dle *vb* to stroke, to touch lovingly.

font *n* **1** a receptacle for holy water. **2** a set of printing type.

food *n* that which can be eaten.

fool *n* **1** a silly or stupid person. **2** (*old*) a jester:—*vb* **1** to deceive. **2** to behave as if one were a fool.

foolhar′dy *adj* foolishly bold, taking unnecessary risks, reckless.

fool′ish *adj* silly, stupid:—*n* **fool′ishness**.

fools′cap *n* large size of writing paper, 16 × 13 inches.

foot *n* (*pl* **feet**) **1** the part of the leg below the ankle. **2** the lowest part of anything. **3** a measure of length equal to 12 inches.

foot′ball *n* **1** a large ball for kicking. **2** a ball game for a team of eleven players played with an oval ball.

foot′ing *n* **1** a safe place for the feet. **2** balance. **3** foundation, basis. **4** relationship.

foot′lights *npl* lights on the floor at the front of the stage in a theater.

foot′note *n* a note at the foot of a page.

foot′print *n* the mark left by a foot.

foot′step *n* the sound or mark made by the foot of someone walking.

for′ay *n* **1** a raid. **2** a vigorous but brief attempt to be involved in a different activity, profession, etc:—*also vb*.

for′bear[2] *n* an ancestor.

forbid′ *vb* (*pt* **forbade′**, *pp* **forbid′den**) to order not to do.

forbid′ding *adj* rather frightening.

force *n* **1** strength, power. **2** violence. **3** an organized body of people. **4** *pl* the army, navy, and airforce. **5** a person or thing that has great power:—*vb* **1** to make (somebody do something). **2** to get something by strength, violence, or effort. **3** to grow plants out of season under artificial conditions.

forced *adj* unnatural, strained.

for′cible *adj* done by force.

ford *n* a place where a river is shallow enough to be crossed:—*vb* to wade across.

fore *adj* and *adv* in front:—*n* the front:—*interj* a warning cry in golf.

fore- *prefix* **1** in front. **2** beforehand.

fore′arm *n* the arm from the elbow to the wrist.

forebod′ing *n* a feeling that evil is going to happen.

fore′cast *vb* (*pt, pp* **fore′cast**) to say what will happen in the future:—*also n*.

fore′father *n* an ancestor.

fore′front *n* the front part.

forego *see* **forgo**.

forego′ing *adj* earlier, previous.

fore′ground *n* **1** the nearest objects shown in a picture. **2** the nearest part of a view.

forehead [for′-id] *n* the part of the face above the eyebrows.

for′eign *adj* **1** belonging to or concerning another country. **2** strange. **3** out of place.

for′eigner *n* a person from a country other than one's own.

fore′most *adj* **1** most famous, best. **2** most important.

foren′sic *adj* having to do with the law or courts of law.

fore′runner *n* **1** (*old*) one who goes before with a message or announcement. **2** an ancestor. **3** a person or thing that comes before another.

foresee′ *vb* (*pt* **foresaw′**, *pp* **foreseen′**) to see what is going to happen.

for′est *n* a large area covered by trees and undergrowth.

for′estry *n* the study of planting and looking after forests.

foretell′ *vb* (*pt, pp* **foretold′**) to say what will happen in future, to prophesy.

forewarn′ *vb* to warn in advance.

for′feit *vb* to lose or give up a right as a punishment:—*n* that which is so lost or given up, a fine.

forge *vt* **1** to beat hot metal into shape. **2** to make by hard effort. **3** to imitate something in order to deceive.

forg′ery *n* **1** act of imitating something dishonestly, esp another's writing. **2** the imitation so made.

forget′ *vb* (*pt* **forgot′**, *pp* **forgot′ten**) to fail to remember.

forget′ful *adj* bad at remembering:—*n* **forget′fulness**.

forgive′ *vb* **1** to pardon. **2** to stop being angry or bitter toward, to stop blaming or wanting to punish:—*n* **forgive′ness**:—*adj* **forgiv′able**.

forgiv′ing *adj* quick to forgive.

forgo′, **forego′** *vb* to give up, to do without.

fork *n* **1** an instrument with two or more pointed prongs used for digging, eating, etc. **2** a place where two roads meet. **3** where a tree or branch divides:—*vb* **1** to raise or dig with a fork. **2** to divide into branches.

form *n* **1** shape. **2** a paper so printed that a message or information can be written in prepared spaces. **3** kind. **4** a long bench. **5** a class in school. **6** arrangement. **7** a fixed way of doing things:—*vb* **1** to make, to cause to take shape. **2** to come into existence, to take shape.

form′al *adj* **1** following the accepted rules or customs. **2** stiff in manner.

formal′ity *n* **1** stiffness of manner. **2** something done only to carry out a rule. **3** care to follow rules and customs.

form′er *adj* earlier, past:—*pron* the person or thing previously mentioned.

form′erly *adv* in earlier times.

for′midable *adj* **1** to be feared. **2** difficult.

form′ula *n* (*pl* **form′ulae** or **form′ulas**) **1** a fixed arrangement of words. **2** a rule in arithmetic set down with signs or letters so that it can be used for any sum. **3** in chemistry, the use of signs or letters to show how substances, etc, are made up. **4** a statement of a principle accepted to cover differences of opinion.

forsake′ *vb* (*pt* **forsook′**, *pp* **forsak′en**) to give up, to abandon.

fort *n* a place prepared for defense against an enemy.

forte¹ [for'-tā] n one's strong point.

forte² [for'-tā] adv (mus) loudly.

forth adv 1 onward in time, place, or order. 2 out.

forthcom'ing adj 1 about to happen, coming soon. 2 open, responsive.

forth'right adj saying what one thinks.

fortifica'tion n anything built or dug to protect defenders.

fort'ress n a place prepared with strong defenses against attackers.

for'tunate adj lucky.

for'tune n 1 luck, chance. 2 wealth, a large amount of money. 3 the supposed power that affects one's life.

for'ward adv toward the front (also **for'wards**):—adj 1 advancing. 2 near the front. 3 in advance. 4 developing more quickly than usual. 5 bold, not shy:—vb 1 to help forward. 2 to send on.

foss'il n the remains of a plant or animal that have hardened into stone and so been preserved in shape in rock or earth.

foster vb 1 to look after for a time, to bring up a child that is not one's own. 2 to encourage.

foul adj 1 dirty, disgusting. 2 stormy. 3 against the rules. 4 nasty. 5 obscene, bad:—vb 1 to make or become dirty. 2 to become entangled. 3 to break the rules of a game:—n an act against the rules of a game.

found¹ pt of find.

found² vb 1 to start from the beginning, to set up. 2 to give money to start a school, hospital, etc:—n found'er.

founda'tion n the lowest part of a building upon which the walls stand.

foun'der vb 1 to fill with water and sink. 2 to come to nothing, to fail.

fount n 1 a source. 2 a printing font.

foun'tain n 1 a spring of water. 2 a jet of water thrown into the air from a pipe. 3 (fml) a beginning or source.

four-way n the place where two roads cross.

fowl n a bird, esp the farmyard cock or hen.

fox n 1 a dog-like animal with red fur and a bushy tail. 2 a cunning or deceitful person.

foyer [foi'yā] n a lobby.

fracas [fra'-kä] n an uproar, a noisy quarrel.

frac'tion n 1 a part of a whole. 2 a small part. 3 in arithmetic, part of a whole number, e.g. ¹/₂, ¹/₄, etc.

frac'ture n 1 a break. 2 the breaking of a bone:—vb to break, to suffer a fracture.

fra'gile adj 1 easily broken. 2 not strong.

frag'ment n 1 a part broken off. 2 a small part:—vb **fragment'** to break into fragments.

fra'grance n a sweet smell, perfume.

fra'grant adj sweet-smelling.

frail adj 1 weak, feeble, delicate. 2 (old) easily tempted to do wrong.

frame vb 1 to make, to construct. 2 to put in a frame. 3 (inf) to cause someone to seem guilty of a crime:—n 1 the supports around which the rest of a thing is built. 2 the border of metal, wood, etc, placed around a picture. 3 the body.

frame'work n the supports around which the rest of a thing is built.

frank adj 1 saying what one really thinks. 2 open, honest-looking:—n frank'ness.

fran'tic adj 1 very anxious or worried. 2 wildly excited, hurried.

frater'nal adj brotherly.

fraud n 1 dishonesty. 2 a deceiving trick. 3 a person who deceives.

fraud'ulent adj dishonest.

fraught adj 1 full of, loaded. 2 tense.

fray vb 1 to wear away by rubbing. 2 to become worn at the edges. 3 to upset, to exasperate.

freak n 1 a living creature of unnatural form. 2 a strange, unexpected happening:—adj strange, unusual.

freak'ish adj very unusual, strange

freck'le, n a brownish-yellow spot on the skin:—adj freck'led.

free adj 1 at liberty, able to do what one wants. 2 not forced or persuaded to act, think, speak, etc, in a particular way. 3 not occupied. 4 generous. 5 costing nothing. 6 open, frank:—n 1 to set at liberty. 2 to set free from.

free'dom n 1 the state of being at liberty. 2 the right to act, think, speak, etc, as one pleases without interference. 3 the state of being without. 4 the unrestricted use of something.

free trade n the exchanging of goods without making a customs charge on imports.

free'way n a fast road with several lanes.

freeze vb (pt froze, pp froz'en) 1 to harden because of cold. 2 to become or make into ice. 3 to be very cold. 4 to make (food) very cold so as to preserve it. 5 to become suddenly still.

freez'er n a compartment or container that freezes and preserves food for long periods.

freight [frāt] n 1 the cargo of a ship. 2 goods carried on a train. 3 the cost of transporting goods:—vb 1 to load with freight. 2 to send by freight.

French fries npl small pieces of deep-fried potato.

fren'zied adj wild, uncontrolled.

fren'zy n 1 a sudden attack of madness. 2 uncontrollable excitement or feeling.

fre'quency n 1 the number of times something happens. 2 the number of waves, vibrations, etc, per second.

fre'quent adj happening often, common:—vb **frequent** [free-kwent'] to visit often.

fresh adj 1 new. 2 not tired. 3 cool. 4 not stale. 5 not frozen or canned. 6 not salted.

fret vb (fret'ted, fret'ting) 1 to wear away by rubbing. 2 to worry, to be anxious, to be discontented.

fret'ful adj troubled, peevish, irritable.

fric'tion n 1 rubbing, a rubbing together. 2 disagreement.

Friday n the sixth day of the week.

friend n a close companion.

friend'ly adj 1 kind. 2 fond of or liking one another:—n friend'liness.

friend'ship n the state of being friends.

fright n a sudden feeling of fear, a shock.

fright'en vb to make afraid.

fright'ful adj 1 dreadful, causing fear. 2 (inf) very bad, dreadful.

frill n 1 a loose ornamental edging of cloth gathered or pleated at one end and sewn on to a garment. 2 an unnecessary ornament:—adj frill'y.

fringe n 1 an ornamental edging of hanging threads. 2 hair arranged to fall over the forehead. 3 the edge:—vb to border.

frisk'y adj playful, active.

friv'olous adj 1 interested only in amusement. 2 not taking important matters seriously, flippant. 3 not serious, playful, light-hearted:—n frivol'ity.

frizz vb to curl.

fro adv:—to and fro forward and back again.

frock n 1 a woman's outer garment. 2 the long loose-sleeved gown worn by a monk, etc.

frog n a four-footed land and water creature.

frol'ic vb (frol'icked, frol'icking) to play about, to dance or jump about happily:—n a trick played for fun, lively amusement.

front *n* **1** the forward part of anything. **2** in war, the place where the fighting is going on:—*also adj*:—*vb* to face, to stand before.

fron′tier *n* the boundary between one country and another.

frost *n* frozen dew or moisture freezing:—*vb* **1** to cover with frost. **2** to cover with frosting. **3** to treat glass so that it cannot be seen through.

frost′bite *n* injury caused to the body by very severe cold:—*adj* **frost′bitten.**

frost′ing *n* a mixture of fine powdery sugar with liquid used to cover cakes.

frost′y *adj* **1** covered with frost. **2** cold because of frost. **3** unfriendly.

froth *n* a mass of tiny bubbles on the surface of liquid, foam:—*vb* to throw up froth:—*adj* **froth′y.**

frown *vb* **1** to wrinkle the forehead, to scowl, to look angry:—*also n*:—**frown on** to discourage, to disapprove of.

fru′gal *adj* **1** careful, not wasteful. **2** very small, meager:—*n* **frugal′ity.**

fruit *n* **1** the part of a plant that produces the seed, esp when eaten as a food. **2** result.

fruit′ful *adj* having good results.

frustrate′ *vb* **1** to make to fail. **2** to cause to have feelings of disappointment or dissatisfaction:—*n* **frustra′tion.**

fry[1] *vb* to cook in fat:—*n* (*pl* **fries**) anything fried.

fry[2] *n* (*pl* **fry**) a young fish.

fuchsia [fū′-sha] *n* a shrub with long hanging bell-shaped flowers.

fudge *n* a soft sweet.

fuel [fū′-ĕl] *n* **1** material to keep a fire going. **2** material used for producing heat or power by burning.

fu′gitive *n* one who is running away.

fulfill′ *vb* **1** to carry out successfully, to complete. **2** to satisfy, to meet:—*n* **fulfill′ment.**

full *adj* **1** holding as much as possible. **2** complete:—*n* **full′ness.**

fum′ble *vb* **1** to feel for something one cannot see. **2** to handle clumsily.

fume *n* smoke, vapor,

fun *n* merriment, amusement, enjoyment.

func′tion *n* **1** the work that a thing is made or planned to perform, use. **2** duties. **3** (*fml*) a public ceremony or party:—*vb* **1** to work as intended. **2** to act.

fund *n* **1** an amount laid aside till needed. **2** money collected or kept for a purpose.

fundamen′tal *adj* having to do with the beginning or most necessary parts of something, of great importance:—*also n.*

fu′neral *n* **1** burial of the dead. **2** the ceremonies performed at burial.

fun′gus *n* (*pl* **fun′gi** or **fun′guses**) **1** a mushroom, toadstool, or similar plant. **2** an unhealthy growth on an animal or plant.

fun′nel *n* **1** a hollow cone used for pouring liquids into bottles etc. **2** a passage by which smoke, etc, escapes.

fun′ny *adj* **1** amusing, humorous. **2** strange, odd.

fur *n* **1** the short soft hair of certain animals. **2** the skin of an animal with the hair still attached, used as a garment. **3** a coating (e.g. on the tongue).

furious *see* **fury.**

furl *vb* to roll up (a sail, flag, etc).

fur′nace *n* an enclosed place in which great heat can be produced by fire.

fur′nish *vb* **1** to provide what is necessary. **2** to put tables, chairs, beds, and other necessary articles in a house.

fur′niture *n* the articles (tables, chairs, etc) needed in a house or office.

fur′row *n* **1** the trench cut in the earth by a plow. **2** a wrinkle:—*vb* **1** to plow. **2** to wrinkle.

fur′ry *adj* covered with fur.

fur′ther *adv* **1** besides. **2** farther:—*adj* **1** more distant. **2** more:—*vb* to help forward.

fur′thermore *adv* besides, in addition.

fur′tive *adj* stealthy, done secretly.

fu′ry *n* rage, great anger:—*adj* **fu′rious.**

fuse[1] *vb* **1** to melt by heat. **2** to melt together as a result of great heat. **3** (*of an electrical appliance or circuit*) to stop working or cause to stop working because of the melting of a fuse. **4** to join together:—*n* easily melted wire used to complete an electric current.

fuse[2], **fuze** *n* a tube of slow-burning substance used to explode shells, bombs, dynamite, etc.

fu′sion *n* **1** act of melting. **2** a joining together to make one.

fuss *n* anxiety or excitement over unimportant things.

fuss′y *adj* worrying over details, hard to please.

fus′ty *adj* stuffy, having a stale smell.

fu′tile *adj* having no useful result:—*n* **futil′ity.**

fu′ture *adj* about to happen, coming:—*n* the time to come.

fuze *see* **fuse**[2].

fuzz *n* a mass of fine light hair or similar substance.

fuzz′y *adj* **1** covered in fuzz. **2** not clear, blurred.

G

ga'ble n the pointed top to the end wall of a building with a sloping roof.

gad'get n a small useful tool or machine.

gag vb (**gagged', gag'ging**) to stop somebody speaking by forcibly stopping the mouth:—n 1 something put in the mouth to prevent speech. 2 a joke.

gag'gle n 1 a flock of geese. 2 a disorderly group of people.

gai'ety n fun, enjoyment.

gaily see **gay**.

gain vb 1 to obtain. 2 to have an increase in. 3 to reduce between oneself and someone or something. 4 (fml) to reach:—n profit, advantage.

gal'axy n 1 a belt of stars stretching across the sky (e.g. the Milky Way). 2 a company of well-known, impressive, etc, people.

gale n a strong wind.

gall[1] [găl] n(inf) impudence.

gall[2] vb to annoy or irritate.

gal'lant adj (fml) brave, noble:—adj **gallant'** (esp old) polite and attentive to women:—also n.

gal'lantry n 1 (fml) bravery. 2 (esp old) politeness to women.

gal'lery n 1 a raised floor over part of a church, theater, etc. 2 a narrow passage in a mine. 3 a room in which pictures, etc, are displayed.

gal'ley n 1 (old) a long low ship with sails and oars. 2 a ship's kitchen.

gal'lon n a measure for liquids or grain (= 8 pints or 4.546 liters).

gal'lop n a horse's fastest speed:—vb 1 to go at a gallop. 2 (inf) to move or do very quickly.

gal'lows n or npl a wooden frame for hanging criminals.

galore' adj in plenty.

galosh' n a covering to protect shoes in wet weather.

gal'vanize vb to rouse to activity.

gam'bit n 1 in chess, opening moves in which one piece is given up to gain a strong position for others. 2 (often **opening gambit**) a starting move, action, remark, etc.

gam'ble vb 1 to play for money, to bet. 2 to take risks:—n a risk:—n **gam'bler**:—n **gam'bling**.

gam'bol vb to jump about playfully:—also n.

game n 1 a sporting contest. 2 a single part of a set into which a game is divided. 3 an amusement or diversion, a pastime. 4 (inf) a scheme, a trick. 5 birds or animals hunted for sport:—adj 1 brave, plucky. 2 willing, ready:—vb to gamble.

game'keeper n one who looks after birds or animals that are to be hunted.

gam'mon n the end piece of a side of bacon, salted and smoked:—vb to talk nonsense, to deceive.

gam'ut n 1 the musical scale. 2 all the known musical notes. 3 whole range of anything.

gan'der n a male goose.

gang n 1 a group of people working on the same job. 2 a group of criminals working together.

gang'ster n a member of an organized gang of criminals.

gang'way n 1 a movable footbridge from a ship to the shore. 2 a passage between rows of seats.

gap n 1 an opening. 2 space.

gape vb 1 to stare open-mouthed. 2 to be wide open.

gar'age n 1 a building in which an automobile can be kept. 2 a place where automobiles are repaired.

garbage n 1 waste food, rubbish. 2 (inf) nonsense, rubbish.

garbage can n a container for household trash.

gar'bled adj mixed up and muddled.

gar'den n a piece of land on which flowers or vegetables are grown:—vb to look after a garden, often as a hobby:—n **gar'dener**.

gargan'tuan adj huge, gigantic.

gar'gle vb to wash the throat with a mouthful of liquid by blowing it up and down in the back of the mouth:—n a liquid prepared for gargling.

gar'ish adj flashy, unpleasantly bright.

gar'land n a wreath of flowers:—vb to decorate with a garland.

gar'lic n a plant with a strong-smelling bulb used in cookery.

gar'ment n (fml) any article of clothing.

gar'nish vb to decorate.

gar'nishing n that which decorates, decoration.

garr'ison n the soldiers sent to a place to defend it:—vb to send soldiers to defend.

gar'ter n a band of elastic to hold up a stocking.

gas n 1 matter in the form of an air-like vapor. 2 any of various gases or mixtures of gases used as fuel. 3 the vapor given off by a substance at a certain heat. 4 gasoline.

gash n a wide deep wound or cut:—vb to cut deep.

to heat or light a house.

gas'oline n a light oil obtained by refining petroleum.

gasp vb 1 to breathe with difficulty, to pant. 2 to draw in the breath suddenly through the mouth:—n the act or sound of gasping.

gas'sy adj full of gas, fizzy.

gas'tric adj having to do with the stomach.

gastron'omy n the art of good eating.

gate n 1 a movable frame of wood, iron, etc, to close an opening in a wall or fence. 2 an entrance or way out, esp in an airport. 3 the number of people who pay to see a game. 4 the total sum of money paid for entrance to a sports ground.

gath'er vb 1 to bring or come together. 2 to collect, to pick. 3 to draw cloth together in small folds. 4 to come to the conclusion:—n a fold in cloth held in position by thread.

gath'ering n 1 a meeting. 2 (old) a sore containing infected matter.

gaudy [gă'-di] adj showy, flashy, too bright:—n **gau'diness**.

gauge [găj] vb 1 to measure. 2 to make an estimate of. 3 to make a judgment about, to judge:—n 1 a measuring rod. 2 a measuring instrument. 3 the distance between the two rails of a railroad. 4 a help to guessing accurately.

gaunt adj very thin, haggard.

gauze n a light cloth that one can see through.

gawk'y adj clumsy, awkward.

gay adj 1 homosexual. 2 lively, fond of enjoyment, cheerful:—adv **gai'ly**.

gaze vb to look hard at without looking away:—n a fixed look.

gazetteer' n a book listing places in alphabetical order and telling where they can be found on a map.

gear n 1 the set of tools, equipment, etc, used for a particular job, sport, expedition, etc. 2 any arrangement of levers, toothed wheels, etc, that passes motion from one part of a machine to another.

geese see **goose**.

gem n 1 a precious stone. 2 anything or anyone that is thought to be especially good.

gen'der *n* in grammar, a grouping of nouns roughly according to the sex (masculine, feminine, or neuter) of the things they name.

gene *n* any of the basic elements of heredity passed from parents to their offspring that cause the offspring to have certain features that the parents have.

genealogy [jee-nee-al'-o-ji] *n* the tracing of the history of a family to discover all its ancestors and branches:—**genealog'ical**.

gen'era *see* **genus**.

gen'eral *adj* 1 including every one of a class or group. 2 not specialized. 3 common, usual, normal. 4 taken as a whole, overall. 5 widespread, public. 6 without details:—*n* 1 a high-ranking army officer. 2 the commander of an army.

gen'eralize *vb* 1 to work out from a few facts an idea that covers a great number of cases. 2 to talk in general terms without details:—*n* **generaliza'tion**.

gen'erally *adv* in most cases.

gen'erate *vb* to bring into life, to produce, to be the cause of.

genera'tion *n* 1 the act of bringing into existence or producing. 2 a single step in family descent. 3 people living at the same time.

generic *see* **genus**.

gen'erous *adj* 1 giving or given freely and gladly. 2 ready to see the good in others:—*n* **generos'ity**.

genet'ic *adj* of genes, of genetics.

genet'ics *n* the science of breeding and family characteristics.

ge'nius *n* 1 extraordinary skill or ability. 2 a person of extraordinary intelligence. 3 (*inf*) a natural ability.

geno'cide *n* the systematic killing of a whole race of people.

gen'tle *adj* 1 (*old*) well born. 2 not rough or violent in manner, unwilling to hurt anyone:—*n* **gen'tleness**:—*adv* **gen'tly**.

gen'tleman *n* a well-mannered, kindly man.

gen'tlemanly *adj* well mannered.

gen'uine *adj* 1 true, real. 2 sincere, without pretense or dishonesty:—*n* **gen'uineness**.

gen'us *n* (*pl* **gen'era**) a kind or class of animals, plants, etc, with certain characteristics in common:—*adj* **gener'ic**.

geog'raphy *n* the study of the surface of the earth and its climate, peoples, cities, etc:—*n* **geog'rapher**:—*adjs* **geograph'ic(al)**.

geol'ogy *n* the study of the rocks, etc, forming the earth's crust:—*n* **geol'ogist**:—*adj* **geolog'ical**.

geom'etry *n* a branch of mathematics dealing with the measurement of lines, figures, and solids:—*adjs* **geomet'ric**, **geomet'rical**.

germ *n* 1 a tiny living cell that has the power to grow into a plant or animal. 2 the beginning of anything. 3 a very small living thing that carries disease.

ger'minate *vb* to begin to grow.

gesta'tion *n* 1 the carrying of a child in the womb. 2 the coming to birth from the stage of a seed. 3 gradual development.

ges'ture *n* 1 a movement of the hands, head, etc, to express feeling. 2 an action showing one's attitude or intentions:—*vb* to make a gesture.

get *vb* (**got**, **get'ting**, *pp* **got'ten** *or* **got**) 1 to obtain. 2 to reach. 3 to become.

ghast'ly *adj* 1 (*fml or lit*) deathly pale. 2 horrible, terrible. 3 (*inf*) very bad, ugly, etc. 4 (*inf*) unwell, upset:—*n* **ghast'liness**.

ghost *n* the spirit of a dead person appearing to one living:—*adjs* **ghost'like**, **ghost'ly**:—*n* **ghost'liness**.

gi'ant *n* 1 in fairy stories, a huge man. 2 a person of unusually great height and size. 3 a person of very great ability or importance:—*f* **gi'antess**.

gib'berish *n* nonsense, meaningless words.

gibe *vb* to mock, to jeer at:—*also n*.

gid'dy *adj* 1 dizzy. 2 changeable, not serious in character, fond of amusement:—*n* **gid'diness**.

gift *n* 1 a present. 2 a natural ability to do something:—*vb* to give as a present.

gift'ed *adj* having exceptional natural ability.

gig *n* 1 (*old*) a light two-wheeled carriage. 2 (*inf*) a single booking for a jazz or pop band, etc, a single night's performance.

gigan'tic *adj* huge, giant-like.

gig'gle *vb* to laugh quietly but in a silly way.

gild *vb* to cover with gold:—*n* **gild'ing**.

gill[1] [gil] *n* the organ through which a fish breathes.

gill[2] [gil] *n* a liquid measure equal to a quarter of a pint

gilt *adj* covered with gold or gold paint:—*n* the gold or imitation of gold used in gilding.

gim'mick *n* an ingenious gadget or device to attract attention.

gin *n* an alcoholic drink flavored with juniper berries.

gin'ger *n* 1 a hot-tasting root used as a spice. 2 a reddish-yellow color:—*vb* to stir up, to enliven.

gin'gerbread *n* molasses cake flavored with ginger.

gin'gerly *adv* carefully, cautiously.

gip'sy *same as* **gyp'sy**.

giraffe' *n* an African animal with a very long neck and long legs.

gir'der *n* a heavy beam of iron or steel used to bridge an open space when building.

gir'dle *n* a kind of belt.

girl *n* 1 a female child. 2 a young woman. 3 a daughter:—*n* **girl'hood**.

girl'ish *adj* like or of a girl.

girth *n* 1 the measurement around the waist. 2 the distance around something cylindrical in shape.

gist [jist] *n* the meaning, the most important part.

give *vb* (*pt* **gave**, *pp* **given**) 1 to make a present of. 2 to hand over to. 3 to allow. 4 to utter. 5 to produce. 6 to organize, to hold. 7 to yield, bend, break, etc:—*n* **giv'er**:—**give away** 1 to give as a gift. 2 to tell something secret:—**give ground** to go backward:—**give in** to admit defeat:—**give out** to report:—**give up** 1 to leave to be taken by others. 2 to stop. 3 to lose hope:—**give way** 1 to stop in order to allow someone or something to pass. 2 to be replaced by. 3 to break and fall:—**give and take**.

glacier [glas'-i-êr] *n* a large slow-moving river of ice.

glad *adj* pleased, cheerful:—*n* **glad'ness**.

glad'den *vb* to make glad.

glam'or, glam'our *n* apparent charm and attractiveness that depend entirely on outer appearance, dress, etc:—*adj* **glam'orous**.

glance *n* a quick look:—*vb* 1 to look at for a moment. 2 to hit the side of something and fly off in another direction. 3 to gleam.

gland *n* an organ in the body that produces certain fluids necessary to the health of the body:—*adj* **glan'dular**.

glare *n* 1 a dazzling light. 2 an angry or fierce look:—*also vb*.

glass *n* 1 hard, easily broken transparent material. 2 a mirror. 3 a glass drinking vessel. 4 *pl* a pair of spectacles:—*adj* made of glass.

glass'y *adj* 1 like glass. 2 lifeless, having a fixed expression.

glaze *vb* 1 to fit with glass. 2 to cover with a smooth shiny surface. 3 to become fixed or glassy-looking:—*n* a smooth shiny surface.

gleam *n* 1 a small ray of light, esp one that disappears quickly. 2 a temporary appearance of some quality:—*vb* 1 to shine softly. 2 to be expressed with a sudden light, to be bright.

glee n 1 pleasure, joy. 2 a song with several different parts to be sung together.

glee'ful adj joyful.

glide vb to move smoothly.

glid'er n an aircraft with no engine.

glim'mer n 1 a low and unsteady light 2 a slight sign or amount.

glimpse n a quick or passing view of:—vb to see for a moment only.

glint vb to flash, to sparkle:—n 1 a brief flash of light. 2 a brief indication.

glist'en vb (esp of wet or polished surfaces) to shine, to give a bright, steady light, to sparkle:—also n.

glit'ter vb to sparkle, to give a bright flickering light:—also n.

gloat vb to look at with greedy or evil enjoyment.

globe n 1 a ball, a sphere. 2 anything ball-shaped. 3 the earth. 4 a map of the earth printed on to a ball.

gloom n 1 darkness. 2 sadness.

gloom'y adj 1 dark, dim. 2 sad-looking, depressed.

glor'ious adj 1 splendid, magnificent. 2 famous.

glor'y n 1 honor, fame. 2 brightness, beauty, splendor. 3 worship, adoration. 4 a special cause for pride, respect, honor, etc;—vb to take pride in, to rejoice.

gloss n a bright or shiny surface:—vb to give a shine to.

gloss'y adj smooth and shining.

glove n a covering of cloth or leather for the hand, each finger being separately covered.

glow vb 1 to give out light and heat but no flame. 2 to look or feel warm or red:—n 1 a bright steady light. 2 a warm look or feeling. 3 a good feeling.

glow'er vb to give an angry look.

glue n a sticky substance used for sticking things together:—vb to stick with glue.

glum adj 1 sad, gloomy. 2 downcast.

glut vb (**glut'ted, glut'ting**) to supply with more than is needed:—vb too great an amount.

glutt'on n 1 one who eats too much. 2 (inf) a person who is always ready for more.

glutt'onous adj greedy, too fond of food.

glutt'ony n a fondness for eating a good deal, love of food.

gnarled [narled'] adj twisted and having a rough surface.

gnash [nash] vb to strike the teeth together, to grind the teeth.

gnaw [nå] vb 1 to keep on biting at in order to wear away gradually. 2 to cause continued distress to.

gnome [nōm] n in fairytales, a mischievous fairy supposed to live underground.

go vb (pt **went**, pp **gone**) 1 to move. 2 to become:—n **go'ing—go for** to attack—**go hard with** (fml) to turn out badly for:—**go in for** to take interest in:—**go under** to fail.

goad n a sharply pointed stick to urge forward cattle:—vb 1 to urge on, to prod. 2 to annoy.

goal n 1 an aim, target, object of one's efforts. 2 in some games, the wooden frame through which players try to pass the ball. 3 a score at football, hockey, etc.

goat n an animal with horns, related to the sheep.

gob'ble vb 1 to eat quickly. 2 to make a noise like a turkey.

gob'lin n in fairytales, a mischievous fairy.

God n the Creator of the world, the Supreme Being:—n **god** any being worshipped for having more than human powers.

godd'ess n 1 a female god. 2 a woman of superior charms or excellence.

god'send n an unexpected piece of good luck.

gog'gles npl a type of eyeglasses, esp those worn to protect the eyes.

gold n 1 a precious metal. 2 wealth, money. 3 the color of gold.

gold'en adj 1 made of gold. 2 of the color of gold. 3 valuable.

golden raisin n a dried white grape used in cooking.

golden wedding n the fiftieth anniversary of marriage.

gold'smith n a worker in gold.

golf n an outdoor game played with clubs and a hard ball:—also vb.

gon'dola n 1 a long narrow boat used on the canals of Venice. 2 the passenger compartment of an airship. 3 a set of shelves in a store for displaying goods.

gone pp of **go**.

gong n a flat metal plate that makes a ringing sound when struck.

good adj 1 right, morally acceptable, virtuous. 2 of a high quality. 3 pleasant, agreeable, welcome. 4 fit, competent. 5 well behaved. 6 kindly. 7 clever. 8 fit to be eaten. 9 beneficial:—npl **goods** 1 movable property. 2 things for buying or selling.

goodbye' n and interj a farewell greeting.

good-for-noth'ing adj useless, worthless:—also n.

good-look'ing adj handsome.

good-na'tured adj kindly.

good'ness n the quality of being good.

goodwill' n 1 kindly feeling. 2 the good name and popularity of a store or business.

goose n (pl **geese**) 1 a web-footed farmyard fowl. 2 (fml or old) a foolish person.

goose'berry n 1 a thorny shrub. 2 its eatable berry. 3 an unwanted third person when two people, esp lovers, want to be alone.

gore[1] vb to wound with a tusk or horn.

gore[2] n (fml or lit) blood from a dead or wounded person, esp when formed into solid lumps:—adj **gor'y**.

gorge n 1 (old) the throat. 2 a deep narrow pass between hills—**make one's gorge rise** to sicken, to fill with disgust—vb to overeat, to eat greedily.

gor'geous adj 1 splendid, magnificent, richly decorated or colored. 2 (inf) very beautiful and glamorous. 3 (inf) giving much pleasure, marvelous.

gorill'a n a large ape.

gory see **gore**.

gos'ling n a young goose.

gos'pel n 1 the teaching of Jesus Christ. 2 the story of the life of Christ in the New Testament. 3 any complete system of beliefs. 4 (inf) the truth. 5 religious music in a popular or folk style and black in origin.

gos'sip n 1 one who likes to hear and spread news about the private affairs of others. 2 idle talk:—vb 1 to spread stories about others. 2 to talk idly or chatter, often about other people.

gourmet [gŏr'-mä] n one who is a good judge of wines and food.

gov'ern vb 1 to control and direct the affairs of. 2 to control, to guide, to influence. 3 to exercise restraint over, to control.

gov'erness n a woman who looks after and teaches children in their home.

gov'ernment n 1 the act or way of ruling. 2 the group of people who direct the affairs of a country:—adj **governmen'tal**.

gov'ernor n 1 a person who is elected as head of a state. 2 a member of the committee of people who govern a school, hospital, etc.

gown n 1 a woman's dress, usu formal. 2 a long robe worn by members of clergy, teachers, lawyers, etc.

grab vb (**grabbed', grab'bing**) 1 to take hold of with a sudden quick movement. 2 to get or take something quickly and sometimes unfairly.

grace n 1 the mercy or kindness of God. 2 a sense of what is right or decent. 3 a delay allowed as a favor. 4 beauty and effortlessness of movement. 5 a short prayer said at meal times. 6 a title of respect used to archbishops, etc:—n 1 to honor. 2 to adorn.

grace'ful adj beautiful in appearance or movement.

gra'cious adj kind, pleasant, polite.

grade n 1 a placing in an order according to one's merit, rank, performance, etc. 2 rank:—vb to arrange in grades.

grade crossing n a place where a railroad crosses the surface of a road.

gra'dient n 1 a slope. 2 steepness of a slope.

grad'ual adj slow and steady, little by little.

graft vb 1 to fix a piece cut from one plant on to another so that it grows into it. 2 to put skin cut from one part of the body on to another part. 3 to replace an organ of the body by one belonging to someone else, to transplant:—n 1 the cutting or skin so grafted. 2 (inf) the getting of money or advantage dishonestly.

grain n 1 a seed of wheat, corn, etc. 2 corn in general. 3 a very small hard particle. 4 a very small amount. 5 the smallest measure of weight (1 pound = 7000 grains). 6 the pattern of markings in wood, leather, etc:—vb to imitate the grain of wood when painting doors, etc.

gram n the basic unit of weight in the metric system.

gram'mar n the science of the correct use of language.

grammat'ical adj correct in grammar.

gram'ophone n a phonograph.

grand adj 1 noble, magnificent, splendid. 2 important, proud, too proud. 3 (inf) pleasant. 4 wonderful, highly respected. 5 magnificed.

grand'father n the father of one's father or mother:—f **grand'mother**:—also **grand'-parent**, **grand'child**, **grand'son**, **grand'daughter**.

grand pia'no n a large piano in which the strings are horizontal.

grand'stand n rows of seats built on a rising slope to allow people a good view of a sports contest:—vb to show off:—n **grandstand'er**.

gran'ite n a hard rock.

gran'ny n (inf) a grandmother.

grant vb 1 to give, to agree to, to allow. 2 (fml) to admit as true:—n something allowed or given, esp money given for a certain purpose.

gran'ule n a small grain.

grape n the fruit of the vine.

grape'fruit n a large yellow sharp-tasting fruit.

graph n a diagram in which different numbers, quantities, etc, are shown by dots on a piece of squared paper, and then joined up by lines so that they can be easily compared.

graph'ic adj 1 pertaining to a graph or graphics. 2 so well told that the events, etc, can be seen in the mind's eye.

graph'ics n or npl 1 the use of drawings and lettering. 2 the drawings, illustrations, etc, used in a newspaper, magazine, TV program, etc. 3 information displayed in the form of diagrams, illustrations, and animation on a computer monitor.

grap'ple vb 1 to fight hand to hand, to take hold of and struggle with. 2 to struggle with.

grasp vb 1 to take firm hold of. 2 to understand:—n 1 firm hold. 2 reach. 3 understanding.

grasp'ing adj mean, always wanting more money.

grass n a common plant that covers the ground, usu green.

grass'hopper n a small jumping insect.

grate[1] n a metal frame in a fireplace for holding the fire.

grate[2] vb 1 to break down by rubbing on something rough. 2 to make a harsh sound, as of metal rubbing on metal. 3 to annoy, to irritate.

grate'ful adj thankful.

grat'ify vb 1 to please. 2 to satisfy.

grat'ing n a framework of metal bars.

grat'itude n thankfulness.

grave[1] n the hole dug in the earth for a dead body.

grave[2] adj serious, important.

grav'el n 1 small stones or pebbles. 2 a mixture of small stones and sand used to make the surface of roads and paths.

grave'yard n a piece of land set aside for graves.

grav'itate vb to move in a certain direction as if drawn there by some force:—n **gravita'tion**.

grav'ity n 1 seriousness, importance. 2 (fml) weight. 3 the force drawing bodies toward the center of the earth.

gra'vy n the juice got from meat when it is being cooked, often thickened and served as a sauce with the meat.

gray adj black mixed with white in color:—also n.

graze[1] vb 1 to touch or rub against lightly in passing. 2 to scrape along the surface:—n 1 a passing touch. 2 a scraping of the skin.

graze[2] vb to eat growing grass.

grease n 1 fat in a soft state. 2 fatty or oily matter:—vb to smear with grease:—adj **greas'y**.

great adj 1 large in amount, number, or size. 2 important. 3 famous. 4 long in time. 5 more than is usual. 6 noble. 7 possessed and made full use of extraordinary ability:—n **great'ness**.

great-grand'father n the father of one of one's grandparents:—f **great-grand'mother**:—also **great-grand'parent**, **great-grand'child**, etc.

greed n 1 the desire to have more and more for oneself. 2 love of eating.

greed'y adj always wanting more than one has:—n **greed'iness**.

green adj 1 the color of grass. 2 fresh, not ripe. 3 inexperienced:—n 1 green color. 2 a piece of ground covered with grass. 3 pl green vegetables (e.g. cabbage):—n **green'ness**.

green'house n a heated building, mainly of glass, for growing plants.

greet vb 1 to welcome. 2 to speak or send good wishes to someone. 3 to receive.

greet'ing n 1 welcome. 2 pl good wishes.

grenade' n a small bomb thrown by hand.

grew see **grow**.

grey adj gray.

grey'hound n a lean fast-running dog used in racing.

grid n a framework of metal bars.

grid'dle n a flat iron plate for baking cakes, etc, on a fire or the top of a stove.

grid'iron n 1 a framework of iron bars used for cooking meat over a fire. 2 anything resembling this, such as a field for football.

grief n great sorrow:—**come to grief** to fail, to suffer a misfortune.

griev'ance n a cause of complaint.

grieve vb 1 to sorrow, to mourn. 2 (fml) to cause sorrow.

grill n 1 a framework of metal bars used in cooking, a device on a cooker that directs heat downward for cooking meat, toasting bread, etc. 2 food cooked on a grill, a grille:—vb 1 to cook on a grill. 2 (inf) to question intensively.

grille n a framework of metal bars fitted into a counter, a door, or outside a window.

grim adj 1 angry-looking, unsmiling. 2 unpleasant, depressing. 3 severe, harsh. 4 stubborn, determined:—n **grim'ness**.

grimace [gri-mās'] vb to twist the face to show one's feelings:—also n.

grime n dirt, filth:—adj **grim'y**.

grin vb (**grinned', grin'ning**) to smile widely in pleasure:—also n.

grind vb (pt, pp **ground**) 1 to rub or crush to powder. 2 to sharpen by rubbing. 3 to press together noisily. 4 (inf) to work hard:—n hard and uninteresting work.

grip n (**gripped', grip'ping**) 1 to take a firm hold of, to hold very tightly. 2 to seize the attention of:—n a firm or tight hold.

gris'ly adj dreadful, frightening.

grit n 1 grains of sand or dust. 2 courage, determination:—vb (**grit'ted, grit'ting**) 1 to press (the teeth) tightly together. 2 to spread grit on roads.

groan vb to utter a low, deep sound expressing pain or anxiety:—also n.

gro'cer n one who sells dry and canned foods, tea, sugar, and household supplies.

gro'ceries npl goods sold by a grocer.

grog'gy adj not steady on the feet, weak.

groom n 1 a person who cares for horses. 2 a man who is being married.

groove n a long narrow hollow, as that made by a tool in wood:—vb to make a groove in.

grope vb to feel for something unseen by feeling with one's hands.

gross adj 1 fat and overfed. 2 coarse, vulgar, impolite. 3 very noticeable, glaringly obvious. 4 whole, complete, total:—n 1 twelve dozen. 2 the whole.

gross'ness n rudeness, vulgarity.

ground[1] n 1 the surface of the earth, land. 2 a piece of land used for a particular purpose. 3 (often pl) a reason. 4 pl the tiny pieces of matter that sink to the bottom of a liquid. 5 pl the land surrounding a large house, etc:—vb 1 (of a ship) to run ashore. 2 (of an airplane) to come to or keep on the ground. 3 to base. 4 to teach the basic facts to.

ground[2] pt of **grind**.

ground'ing n knowledge of the elementary part of a subject.

ground'work n work that must be done well in the beginning if later work on the subject or task is to succeed.

group n 1 a number of persons or things taken together. 2 a set of people who play or sing together:—vb to put or go into a group.

grov'el vb 1 to lie face downward in humility or fear. 2 to humble oneself, to behave with humility.

grow vb (pt **grew**, pp **grown**) 1 to become bigger. 2 (of plants) to have life. 3 to become. 4 to plant and rear:—n **growth**.

growl vb to utter a low harsh sound, as a dog when angry:—also n.

grown-up n a fully grown person.

growth see **grow**.

grub n the form of an insect when it comes out of the egg.

grub'by adj dirty.

grudge vb 1 to be unwilling to give. 2 to be displeased by another's success, to envy:—n a deep feeling of ill-will, dislike, resentment, etc.

gruff adj deep and rough.

grum'ble vb to complain, to express discontent:—also n:—n **grum'bler**.

grunt vb to make a noise like a pig:—also n.

guarantee [ga-rên-tee'] n 1 a promise to pay money on behalf of another person if that person fails to pay money he or she has promised to pay. 2 one who undertakes to see that another keeps his promise, esp to repay money, a guarantor. 3 a promise, usu in the form of a written state-

ment, that if an article bought is unsatisfactory, it will be repaired or replaced. 4 a thing that makes something likely or certain:—vb 1 to promise. 2 to undertake to see that a promise is kept.

guard vb 1 to watch over, to protect. 2 to defend against attack:—n 1 something that protects. 2 a person, such as a soldier or prison officer, who watches over a person or place to prevent escape, attack, etc. 3 a group of persons whose duty it is to watch over and defend something or someone. 4 the official in charge of a train. 5 a position in which one can defend or protect oneself, a state of watchfulness.

guar'dian n 1 (fml) a keeper. 2 a person who has the legal duty to take care of a child.

guess vb 1 to put forward an opinion or solution without knowing the facts. 2 (inf) to suppose, to consider likely:—n opinion or judgment that may be wrong as it is formed on insufficient knowledge.

guest n 1 a visitor to a house. 2 one staying in a hotel.

guffaw' vb to laugh loudly or rudely:—also n.

guide vb 1 to lead to the place desired. 2 to show the way. 3 to direct, to influence:—n 1 one who shows the way. 2 an adviser, a person who directs or influences one's behavior. 3 a guidebook. 4 one who leads people around a place, pointing out things of interest. 5 a thing that helps one to form an opinion or make a calculation.

guide'book n a book describing a place and giving information about it.

guile n (fml) deceit, trickery, cunning skill:—adjs **guile'ful**, **guile'less**.

guillotine [gil'-o-teen] n 1 a machine formerly used in France for beheading persons. 2 a machine for cutting paper.

guilt n 1 the fact of having done wrong, the fact of having committed a crime. 2 blame or responsibility for wrongdoing. 3 a sense of shame, uneasiness, etc, caused by the knowledge of having done wrong:—adj **guilt'less**.

guilt'y adj 1 having done wrong, having broken a law. 2 responsible for behavior that is morally wrong or socially unacceptable. 3 feeling or showing a sense of guilt or shame.

guin'ea pig n 1 a small animal like a rabbit. 2 a person made use of for the purpose of an experiment.

guitar' n a six-stringed musical instrument.

gulf n 1 an inlet of the sea, a long bay. 2 a deep hollow. 3 an area of serious disagreement or separation.

gull n a long-winged sea bird.

gull'ible adj easily deceived.

gull'y n a deep channel worn by running water.

gulp vb 1 to eat quickly, to swallow in large mouthfuls. 2 to make a swallowing movement:—also n.

gum[1] n the flesh in which the teeth are set.

gum[2] n 1 the sticky juice of trees. 2 a liquid used for sticking things together:—vb (**gummed', gum'ming**) to stick with gum.

gump'tion n common sense, quick brains.

gun n any weapon that fires bullets or shells by means of explosive:—vb (**gunned', gun'ning**) to shoot or hunt with a gun.

gun'powder n a type of explosive.

gur'gle vb 1 to flow with a bubbling sound. 2 to make a noise resembling this:—also n.

gush n a sudden or strong flow:—vb 1 to flow out strongly. 2 to talk as if one felt something very deeply, to speak insincerely.

gust n a sudden violent rush of wind.

gut n 1 a tube in the body that takes the waste matter from the stomach. 2 a strong cord used for violin strings, etc:—vb (**gut'ted, gut'ting**) **1** to take out the inner parts. **2** to remove or destroy all except the walls of a building.

gut'ter n **1** a passage at the edge of a roof or at the side of the road to carry away water. **2** the lowest poorest level of society.

gut'tural adj made or seeming to be made in the throat, harsh.

guy[1] n a rope to steady anything.

guy[2] n **1** (inf) a strange-looking or strangely dressed person. **2** (inf) a person. **3** a figure of Guy Fawkes burned on November 5 in Britain in memory of the time when he tried to blow up the Houses of Parliament in 1605.

gymna'sium n a room or hall fitted out for bodily exercise.

gym'nast n one skilled in gymnastics:—adj **gymnas'tic**.

gymnas'tics npl exercises to develop the muscles of the body.

gynecol'ogy n the branch of medicine that deals with diseases of women:—n **gynecolo'gist**.

gyp'sy n a member of a wandering people.

H

hab'it n 1 a fixed way of doing something without having to think about it first, one's ordinary way of doing things, something that a person does usu or regularly. 2 dress, esp of a monk or rider.

hab'itable adj that may be lived in.

hab'itat n the place or surroundings in which a plant or animal is usu found.

habita'tion n 1 the act of living in a place. 2 the place where one lives.

habit'ual adj 1 usual. 2 having formed a certain habit.

hack vb 1 to cut roughly or unevenly. 2 to kick:—n a cut, a kick.

hack'neyed adj overused and therefore uninteresting.

hag n an ugly old woman.

hag'gard adj pale, thin-faced, and tired-looking.

hag'gle vb to try to get a seller to lower his or her price.

hail[1] n 1 frozen rain. 2 a shower of anything:—vb 1 to rain hail. 2 to pour down.

hail[2] vb 1 to call to, to greet. 2 to shout to a person to try to catch his or her attention:—interj a call of greeting:—**hail from** to come from.

hair n any or all of the thread-like growths covering the skin of people and animals:—adjs **hair'less, hair'y**:—**to split hairs** to point out differences so slight that they could be overlooked.

hair'dresser n one who cuts, arranges, etc, hair.

half n (pl **halves**) one of two equal parts—also adj.

half'-brother n a brother by one parent only.

half'-heart'ed adj lacking enthusiasm, not eager.

half'-sister n a sister by one parent only.

half-wit'ted adj 1 weak in mind. 2 foolish, idiotic.

hall n 1 a large public room. 2 the room or passage at the entrance to a house. 3 a large country house.

hallo', hello', hullo' interjs a greeting.

hallucina'tion n 1 the experiencing of seeing something that is not there. 2 something imagined as though it is really there.

ha'lo n 1 a circle of light around the sun or moon. 2 a colored ring round the head of a holy person in a painting.

halt vb to stop:—n 1 a stopping place. 2 a stop.

halt'er n 1 a rope or strap fitted on to the head of a horse for leading it. 2 a rope for hanging a person.

halve vb to cut or break into halves.

halves see **half**.

ham n 1 the back of the thigh. 2 the thigh of a pig salted and dried and used as food. 3 (inf) a bad actor who exaggerates his or her actions and speech.

ham'let n a small village.

ham'mer n 1 a tool for driving nails, beating metal, etc. 2 part of a machine or apparatus that strikes:—vb 1 to drive or beat with a hammer. 2 to strike hard:—**hammer and tongs** with all one's strength.

ham'mock n a bed of a strip of canvas or network hung up at the ends.

ham'per[1] n a large basket.

ham'per[2] vb to prevent from moving freely.

ham'ster n a rodent like a small rat, often kept as a pet.

hand n 1 the end of the arm below the wrist. 2 a worker. 3 a sailor on a ship. 4 the cards given to one player in a card game. 5 one's style of writing. 6 the pointer of a clock or watch. 7 a measure of four inches used in measuring a horse's height at the shoulder. 8 a share, a part, an influence:—vb to give with the hand.—**hand in glove with** in league with:—**hand-to-hand** at close quarters:—**hand-**to-mouth with only just enough money to live on with nothing for the future:—**out of hand** out of control:—**upper hand** control:—**to wash one's hands of** to refuse to have anything to do with.

hand'bag n a small bag carried by people to contain their personal possessions.

hand'cuff vb to put handcuffs on:—npl **hand'cuffs** metal rings joined by a chain, locked on the wrists of prisoners.

hand'icap vb (**hand'icapped, hand'icapping**) 1 in sports or races to give a certain advantage to weaker competitors so that they have an equal chance of winning. 2 to hinder, to put at a disadvantage:—n 1 in sports or games, an arrangement that allows all competitors to start with an equal chance of winning. 2 a hindrance, a disadvantage. 3 a physical or mental disability.

hand'kerchief n a cloth for wiping the nose.

hand'le vb 1 to feel, use, or hold with the hand. 2 to deal with:—n that part of a thing made to be held in the hand.

hand'lebar n the bent rod with which one steers a bicycle.

hand'some adj 1 good-looking. 2 generous.

hand'writing n the way one writes.

hand'y adj 1 clever in using one's hands, skillful. 2 useful and simple. 3 ready, available. 4 near:—n **hand'iness**.

hang vb (pt, pp **hung**) 1 to fix one part to something above and allow the rest to drop. 2 to remain steady in the air, as certain birds. 3 to let fall. 4 (pt, pp **hanged'**) to kill a criminal by putting a rope round the neck and then letting him or her drop suddenly so that the neck is broken.

hank'er vb to desire greatly, to long for.

haphaz'ard adj chance, unplanned:—adv **haphaz'ardly**.

hap'pen vb 1 to take place. 2 to come about by chance.

hap'pening n an event.

hap'py adj 1 lucky. 2 pleased, joyous. 3 pleasant, joyful. 4 suitable:—adv **hap'pily**:—n **hap'piness**.

har'ass vb 1 to attack again and again. 2 to worry or disturb constantly or frequently.

har'bor n 1 a place of safety for ships. 2 a place of shelter:—vb 1 to give shelter. 2 to keep in the mind.

hard adj 1 firm, solid. 2 unfeeling, unkind, cruel. 3 difficult. 4 harsh, severe:—adv 1 with force. 2 with great effort. 3 close. 4 with great attention:—**hard of hearing** fairly deaf.

hard'en vb to make hard or harder.

hard-heart'ed adj unfeeling, having no pity.

hard'ly adv 1 almost not. 2 only just, not really. 3 with difficulty.

hard'ness n the state of being hard.

hard'ship n poor or difficult conditions.

hard'ware n 1 household articles made of metal. 2 the mechanical and electronic components of a computer system.

hardware store n where hardware is sold.

hard'y adj 1 strong, tough. 2 (old) bold.

hare n a fast-running animal with rabbit-like ears and long hind legs.

hare'brained adj thoughtless, rash.

harem [hā'-rēm or ha-reem'] n 1 in Muslim countries, the part of the house where the women live. 2 the women themselves.

hark vb to listen:—**hark back** 1 to begin speaking again about something already discussed. 2 to mention events or subjects of an earlier time.

har'lequin n a kind of clown, dressed in a suit of colors and often wearing a mask.

harm n hurt, damage, wrong:—also vb:—adjs **harm'ful, harm'less**.

harmo'nious adj 1 pleasant-sounding. 2 friendly. 3 pleasant to the eye.

harmo'nium n a musical wind instrument, like a small organ.

har'mony n 1 agreement, friendship. 2 the pleasant effect made by parts combining into a whole. 3 the playing at one time of musical notes that are pleasant when sounded together. 4 pleasant sound.

har'ness n the straps, etc, by which a horse is fastened to its load:—vb to put a harness on.

harp n a stringed musical instrument played by the fingers:— also vb:—ns **harp'ist**, **harp'er**:—**harp on** to keep on talking about one subject.

harpoon' n a long spear used in hunting whales:—vb to strike with a harpoon.

har'ridan n a bad-tempered old woman.

har'rowing adj very distressing.

harsh adj 1 rough and unpleasant to hear, see, etc. 2 unkind, severe, cruel.

har'vest n 1 the time when the ripe crops are cut and gathered in. 2 the crops so gathered:—vb to cut and gather in:—n **har'vester**.

haste n speed, hurry.

hast'y adj 1 done in a hurry. 2 done too quickly, rash. 3 quick to lose one's temper.

hat n a head-covering.

hatch¹ vb 1 to produce (young) from eggs. 2 to break out of the egg. 3 to work out in secret:—n the young hatched from eggs.

hatch² n 1 an open space in a wall or roof or the deck of a ship. 2 a half door.

hat'chet n a small ax:—**bury the hatchet** to end a quarrel.

hate vb to dislike greatly:—n great dislike.

hate'ful adj deserving or causing hate.

ha'tred n great dislike.

hat'-trick n the scoring of three successive points, victories, etc.

haugh'ty adj proud, behaving as if one were better than others:—n **haugh'tiness**.

haul vb 1 to pull by force, to drag. 2 to transport by truck, etc:— n 1 a pull. 2 an amount taken or caught (e.g. of fish).

haul'er n a person or business that transports goods by road.

haunt vb 1 to visit again and again, to go often to. 2 to visit as a ghost. 3 to be always in the thoughts of someone:—n a place often visited.

haunt'ed adj visited by ghosts.

have vb (pt, pp **had**; indicative **I have, he has; we, they have**) 1 to possess, to own, to hold. 2 to be forced (to do):— **to have to do with** to be concerned in.

ha'ven n 1 (old) a harbor. 2 (fml) a place of safety, a shelter.

hav'oc n destruction, ruin.

hawk¹ n a bird of prey:—vb to hunt with a hawk.

hawk² vb 1 to sell from door to door. 2 to try to get people interested in:—n **hawk'er**.

hay n grass cut and dried.

hay fever n an illness caused by dust or pollen.

hay'stack, hay'rick ns a large pile of hay.

hay'wire adj (inf) disordered.

haz'ard n risk:—vb 1 to risk. 2 to put in danger. 3 to put forward.

haz'ardous adj risky.

haze n 1 a thin mist. 2 vagueness of mind.

ha'zel n 1 a tree with eatable nuts. 2 a reddish-brown color.

haz'y adj 1 misty. 2 not clear. 3 doubtful:—n **haz'iness**.

head n 1 the top part of the body. 2 a person's mind. 3 a chief person, a head teacher. 4 the top or front part. 5 a division in an essay or speech. 6 the beginning of a stream:—vb 1 to lead. 2 to be first. 3 to direct. 4 to strike (a ball) with the head:—adj 1 belonging to the head. 2 chief, principal. 3 coming from the front.

head'ache n pain in the head.

head'dress n a covering for the head.

head'gear n a covering for the head.

head'ing n the words written at the top of a page or above a piece of writing.

head'lamp n a light at the front, esp of a motor vehicle.

head'land n a piece of high land jutting out into the sea.

head'line n the line in large print above a piece of news in a newspaper.

headmas'ter n the male head of a school:—f **headmis'tress**.

head'quarters n the office of those who are in control or command.

head'stone n the stone placed over a dead person's grave in his or her memory.

head'strong adj determined to have one's own way.

head'way n advance, improvement.

heal vb to make or become well or healthy.

health n 1 the state of being well. 2 the state of being free from illness.

health'y adj 1 having good health. 2 causing good health.

heap n a number of things lying one on top of another:—vb to put one on top of another.

hear vb (pt, pp **heard**) 1 to perceive sounds by the ear. 2 to listen.

hear'ing n 1 the power to hear sounds. 2 the distance at which one can be heard. 3 the examining of evidence by a judge.

hear'say n what people say though not perhaps the truth, gossip.

hearse n a car or carriage for a coffin at a funeral.

heart n 1 the organ that keeps the blood flowing through the body. 2 the central or most important part of anything. 3 the center of a person's thoughts and emotions. 4 the cause of life in anything. 5 enthusiasm, determination. 6 kindly feelings, esp love. 7 pl a suit of playing cards. 8 a thing shaped like a heart:—**learn by heart** to memorize.

hearth n 1 the floor of a fireplace. 2 the place beside a fire.

heart'y adj 1 cheerful, sometimes too cheerful. 2 sincere. 3 healthy. 4 large.

heat n 1 hotness, warmth. 2 anger, excitement. 3 a division of a race from which the winners go on to the final:—vb to make or become warm or hot.

heath'en n one who knows nothing of God:—also adj.

heave vb 1 to lift, to raise with effort. 2 to move up and down regularly. 3 to pull hard. 4 to utter with effort:—n 1 an upward throw. 2 a pull.

hea'ven n 1 the sky. 2 the dwelling place of the gods. 3 in some religions the happy place where the good go after death.

hea'venly adj 1 having to do with heaven or the sky. 2 (inf) delightful.

hea'vy adj 1 having weight, of great weight. 2 of more than the usual size, amount, force, etc. 3 dull, dark, and cloudy. 4 sleepy. 5 sad. 6 difficult to digest. 7 busy, full of activity:— n **hea'viness**.

hedge n 1 a fence of bushes, shrubs, etc. 2 means of defense or protection:—vb 1 to surround with a hedge. 2 to avoid giving a clear, direct answer.

hedge'hog n a small animal covered with prickles, that can roll itself into a ball.

heed vb to pay attention to, to notice:—n care, attention.

heel n **1** the back part of the foot. **2** the part of a shoe, etc, under the heel of the foot:—vb **1** to strike with the heel. **2** to put a heel on:—**bring to heel** to get control over:—**down at heel** poorly or untidily dressed.

hef'ty adj **1** rather heavy, big, and strong. **2** large and heavy. **3** powerful. **4** (inf) large, substantial.

height n **1** the distance from top to bottom. **2** the state of being high. **3** a high place. **4** a hill. **5** the highest degree of something.

height'en vb **1** to make higher. **2** to increase.

heir n **1** one who receives property or a title after the death of the previous owner:—f **heir'ess**.

heir'loom n a valuable object that has been the property of a family for many generations.

hel'icopter n a type of airplane with propellers that enable it to go straight up or down.

he'lium n a very light gas.

hell n **1** in some religions, the place where the wicked suffer after death. **2** everlasting banishment from God. **3** a place of great evil or suffering.

hello see **hallo**.

helm n a steering wheel or handle on a ship:—**at the helm** in control or command.

hel'met n a protective covering for the head.

help n **1** to aid, to assist. **2** to give what is needed. **3** to serve someone in a store. **4** to make it easier for something to happen. **5** to avoid (doing):—n aid, assistance:—n **help'er**.

help'ful adj **1** willing to help. **2** useful.

help'ing n one's share of a dish of food.

hem n the border of a garment folded back and sewn:—vb (**hemmed**, **hem'ming**) to sew a hem.

hem'isphere n **1** half of the world. **2** a map showing half of the world.

hen n a female bird, esp a farmyard fowl.

hence adv **1** (old) from this place. **2** (fml) from this time on. **3** for this reason.

henceforth', **hencefor'ward** advs (fml) from this time on.

hen'pecked adj ordered about by one's wife.

hep'tagon n a seven-sided figure.

her'ald n **1** (old) one who makes important announcements to the public. **3** a sign of something to come:—vb **1** to announce the approach of someone or something. **2** to be a sign of.

her'aldry n the study of coats of arms and the history of families:—adj **heral'dic**.

herb [erb] n **1** any plant whose stem dies away during the winter. **2** a plant used for medicine or flavoring food.

herb'al adj of herbs.

herb'alist n one who studies or sells herbs.

herbiv'orous adj eating grass or herbs.

herd n **1** a flock of animals. **2** a large crowd of people. **3** a herdsman:—vb **1** (inf) to crowd or collect together. **2** to look after a herd. **3** to drive.

hered'itary adj passed on from parents to children.

hered'ity n the passing on of qualities of character, etc, from parents to children.

her'esy n an opinion that contradicts accepted ideas, esp in religion.

her'etic n one who teaches a heresy:—adj **heret'ical**.

her'itage n **1** that which is passed on to one by one's parents. **2** things that have been passed on from earlier generations.

hermet'ically adv so tightly (sealed) as to keep out all air.

her'mit n one who lives alone or away from other people, originally for religious reasons.

he'ro n (pl **he'roes**) **1** a brave person, someone admired for his brave deeds. **2** the chief character in a play or novel:—f **her'oine**.

hero'ic adj **1** brave. **2** to do with heroes.

her'oin n a habit-forming drug obtained from opium.

heroine see **hero**.

her'oism n bravery.

her'on n a water bird with long legs and neck.

her'ring n a small sea fish used as food.

hes'itance, **hes'itancy**, **hesita'tion** ns doubt, act of hesitating, indecision.

hes'itant adj doubtful, undecided.

hes'itate vb **1** to stop for a moment before doing something or speaking. **2** to be undecided.

hex'agon n a six-sided figure:—adj **hexag'onal**.

hi'bernate vb to pass the winter in sleep, as certain animals do:—n **hiberna'tion**.

hic'cup n **1** a sudden short stoppage of the breath. **2** the sound caused by this. **3** a small delay or interruption:—vb (**hic'cuped**, **hic'cuping**) to have hiccups.

hide¹ vb (**hid**, pp **hid'den**) **1** to put or keep out of sight. **2** to keep secret.

hide² n the skin of an animal.

hid'eous adj **1** frightful. **2** very ugly.

hide'out n a place to hide.

hid'ing n a thrashing, a beating.

hi'erarchy n an arrangement in order, putting the most important first.

hig'gledy-pig'gledy adj, adv (inf) very untidy, in disorder.

high adj **1** being a certain distance up. **2** being above normal level. **3** raised above. **4** of important rank. **5** morally good. **6** dear (in price). **7** (of meat) not fresh:—also adv:

high'brow adj **1** interested only in things requiring great learning. **2** relating to things requiring great learning:—also n.

high'-hand'ed adj using power without thought for the rights or feelings of others.

high'lands npl the mountainous part of a country.

high'ly adv greatly, very.

high'ly strung', **high'-strung** adjs very nervous, easily excited.

high'ness n a title of honor given to sons or daughters of kings or queens.

high'road n a main road.

high school n a school educating up to an advanced standard.

high seas npl the open seas.

high water n high tide.

high'way n a public road.

high'wayman n (old) one who attacks and robs travelers.

hike vb to go on a long walk in the country, esp over rough ground:—n **hik'er**.

hila'rious adj extremely amusing:—n **hilar'ity**.

hill n a low mountain.

hill'y adj abounding with hills.

hind¹ n a female deer.

hind² adj at the back.

hin'der vb to stop or delay the advance or development of, to put difficulties in the way of.

hin'drance n something or someone that makes action or progress difficult.

hinge n a folding joint to which a door or lid is fixed so that it can turn on it:—vb **1** to fix hinges to. **2** to depend on.

hint vb to suggest indirectly:—n **1** an indirect suggestion. **2** a helpful suggestion. **3** a small amount.

hip¹ n the upper part of the thigh.

hip² n the fruit of the wild rose.

hippopot'amus *n* (*pl* **hippopot'amuses** *or* **hippopot'ami**) a large wild river animal found in Africa.

hire *n* 1 the hiring of something. 2 the money paid for the use of a thing or for the work of another:—*vb* 1 to get the use of a thing by paying for it. 2 to lend to another for payment.

hiss *vb* to make a sound like that of the letter *s*, often as a sign of disapproval:—*n* the act or sound of hissing.

histor'ian *n* a writer of history.

histor'ic *adj* of outstanding importance.

histor'ical *adj* having to do with history.

his'tory *n* 1 the study of past events. 2 an accurate account of past events, conditions, ideas, etc.

hit *vb* (**hit**, **hit'ting**) 1 to strike. 2 to reach, to arrive at:—*n* 1 a blow. 2 a success.

hitch *vb* 1 to hook or fasten (on to). 2 to try to get a ride in someone else's vehicle:—*n* 1 a jerk, a pull. 2 a type of knot. 3 a difficulty, a snag.

hith'er *adv* (*fml or old*) to this place:—**hither and thither** back and forward, here and there.

hith'erto *adv* (*fml*) until now.

hive *n* 1 a home made for bees. 2 a place of great activity.

hoar *n* white frost:—*adj* hoary.

hoard *n* a hidden store:—*vb* 1 to store secretly. 2 to collect, to lay in a store of.

hoard'ing *n* a high wooden fence on which posters are often stuck.

hoarse *adj* having a rough or husky voice.

hoax *n* a trick or joke intended to deceive:—*vb* to deceive, to trick.

hob *n* 1 an iron shelf at the side of a fireplace for pots, etc. 2 a flat surface on a cooker incorporating hot plates or burners.

hob'ble *vb* 1 to limp. 2 to tie the legs of a horse to one another to stop it running away.

hob'by *n* a favorite subject or interest for one's spare time, an interesting pastime.

hob'goblin *n* in fairy stories, a mischievous fairy.

ho'bo *n* (*pl* **ho'boes, ho'bos**) a migrant laborer, a tramp.

hock'ey *n* 1 an outdoor team game played with a ball and sticks curved at the end (**field hockey**). 2 an indoor or outdoor team game played on ice with curved sticks and a flat disk called a puck (**ice hockey**).

hoe *n* a garden tool for loosening the earth around plants:—*vb* to dig with a hoe.

hog *n* 1 a pig. 2 a greedy or filthy person.

hoist *vb* to lift, to raise, esp by some apparatus:—*n* a lift for goods.

hold *vb* (*pt, pp* **held**) 1 to have or take in the hand(s) or arms. 2 to bear the weight of, to support. 3 to be able to contain. 4 to have (an opinion). 5 to cause to take place:—*n* 1 grasp. 2 the lowest part of a ship, where the cargo is stored:—**hold forth** (*fml*) to speak in public or at length:—**hold one's own** to keep one's advantages without gaining any more:—**hold up** 1 to attack and rob. 2 to delay, to hinder. 3 to last. 4 to raise. 5 to support:—**hold with** to agree with.

hold'er *n* one who holds or possesses.

hold'ing *n* 1 a small rented farm. 2 the amount possessed.

hole *n* 1 a hollow or empty space in something solid. 2 an opening. 3 an animal's den. 4 (*inf*) a difficulty:—*vb* to make a hole in.

hole'-and-cor'ner *adj* secret and dishonest.

hol'iday *n* a day or period of rest or amusement.

ho'liness *n* the state of being holy:—**Holiness** a title given to the pope.

holl'ow *adj* 1 not solid. 2 empty inside. 3 worthless. 4 not sincere. 5 sounding as if coming from a hollow place, echoing:—*n* 1 a sunken place, something hollow. 2 a low

place between folds, ridges, etc. 3 a valley:—*vb* 1 to make hollow. 2 to take out the inside leaving the surrounds.

holly *n* a prickly evergreen tree with red berries.

hol'ograph *n* a document wholly in one's own handwriting.

ho'ly *adj* 1 good and trying to be perfect in the service of God. 2 set aside for the service of God.

hom'age *n* 1 (*old*) the promise to do certain duties for an overlord. 2 respect, things said or done to show great respect.

home *n* 1 one's house, the place where one lives. 2 where one was born, the place where a person or thing originally comes from. 3 a place where children without parents, old people, people who are ill, etc, are looked after:—*adj* 1 having to do with one's home. 2 made or done at home:—*adv* to or at home.

home'ly *adj* 1 plain, simple. 2 like home, comfortable.

homeopath'ic *adj* having to do with homeopathy.

homeopathy [hō-mi-op'-thi] *n* the curing of diseases by giving medicine that would cause a mild form of the disease in a healthy person.

home'sick *adj* having a longing for home:—*n* **home'sickness**.

hom'icide *n* 1 the act of killing another human being. 2 one who kills another human being: —*adj* **homici'dal**.

hone *n* a smooth stone for sharpening knives, etc:—*vb* 1 to sharpen on a hone. 2 to sharpen or make effective.

honest [on'-st] *adj* 1 free from deceit, upright, truthful, not cheating, stealing, etc. 2 open and frank. 3 typical of an honest person, open. 4 true:—*n* **hon'esty**.

honey [hun'-i] *n* a sweet fluid collected by bees, etc, from flowers.

hon'eycomb *n* the waxy cells in which bees store their honey.

hon'eymoon *n* the holiday taken by a newly married couple immediately after marriage:—*also vb*.

honor [on'-or] *n* 1 good name, reputation. 2 high principles and standards of behavior. 3 glory. 4 a person or thing that brings pride or glory. 5 a title of respect used when talking to or about certain important people such as judges, mayors, etc. 6 respect:—*vb* 1 to respect. 2 to raise in rank or dignity. 3 to pay (a bill) when due.

hon'orable *adj* 1 worthy of respect or honor. 2 honest, of high principles. 3 just. 4 a title of respect.

hon'orary *adj* 1 unpaid. 2 given to a person as a mark of respect for his or her ability.

hood *n* 1 a covering for the head and neck. 2 anything hood-shaped. 3 the metal cover of an automobile engine.

hood'wink *vb* to deceive.

hoof *n* (*pl* **hooves** *or* **hoofs**) the horny part of the foot in certain animals.

hook *n* a piece of metal or plastic bent for catching hold or for hanging things on:—*vb* to catch, hold, or fasten with a hook:—*adj* **hooked**:—**by hook or by crook** by any means, fair or unfair.

hool'igan *n* a lawless young person:—*n* **hool'iganism**.

hoop *n* 1 a band of metal around a cask. 2 a large ring of wood, metal, etc.

Hoosi'er *n* a nickname used for someone from Indiana.

hoot *vb* 1 to cry as an owl. 2 to make a loud noise of laughter or disapproval. 3 to sound a horn:—*n* 1 the cry of an owl. 2 the sound of a hooter. 3 a shout of laughter or disapproval.

hoot'er *n* 1 a steam whistle. 2 an instrument that makes a hooting sound.

hooves *see* **hoof**.

hop *vb* (**hopped**, **hop'ping**) 1 to jump on one leg. 2 to jump:—*n* a jump, esp on one leg.

hope *vb* to wish and expect what is good in future:—*n* a wish or expectation for the future.

hope'ful adj **1** full of hope. **2** giving cause for hope.

hope'less adj **1** without hope. **2** giving no cause for hope. **3** (inf) poor, not good.

horde n a huge crowd.

hori'zon n **1** the line along which earth and sky seem to meet. **2** the breadth of one's understanding and experience.

horizon'tal adj parallel to the horizon, flat, level.

horn n **1** a hard pointed growth on the heads of some animals. **2** anything shaped like a horn (e.g. snail's feelers). **3** a musical wind instrument. **4** on an automobile, an instrument that makes warning noises:—adj made of horn.

hor'rible adj **1** causing horror, dreadful, terrible. **2** (inf) unpleasant, nasty.

hor'rid adj **1** (fml) horrible, dreadful. **2** (inf) horrible, unpleasant, nasty.

hor'rify vb to shock.

hor'ror n **1** terror, great fear or dislike. **2** (inf) a disagreeable person or thing.

horse n **1** an animal that can be used for riding on or pulling loads. **2** a padded block on four legs used by gymnasts in vaulting.

horse chest'nut n **1** a type of tree. **2** its nut.

horse'play n rough play.

horse'power n the pulling power of a horse taken as a measure of power.

horse'radish n a plant with a sharp-tasting eatable root used for a sauce or relish.

horse sense n common sense.

horse'shoe n **1** a curved iron shoe for horses. **2** anything of this shape.

hors'y adj **1** having to do with horses. **2** resembling a horse.

hor'ticulture n the art or science of gardening or growing flowers, vegetables, etc.

hose n **1** (fml) stockings, socks, etc. **2** a movable pipe of rubber plastic, etc, for carrying water:—vb to spray with a hose.

hos'pice n a hospital for sufferers of incurable diseases.

hos'pitable adj kind to guests and visitors.

hos'pital n a building for the care of the sick.

hospital'ity n kindness to guests and visitors, often including refreshments.

host[1] n one who receives guests:—f **host'ess**: —vb to act as a host (to a party, TV show, etc).

host[2] n **1** (old) an army. **2** a very large number.

hos'tage n one held prisoner until certain conditions have been carried out.

hos'tel n a building in which persons away from home (students, travelers, etc) may pay to stay if they agree to keep its rules.

hostess see host.

hos'tile adj **1** unfriendly. **2** having to do with an enemy.

hostil'ity n **1** unfriendliness. **2** enmity. **3** pl warfare.

hot adj **1** very warm. **2** easily excited. **3** having a sharp, burning taste.

hotel' n a building where people may live and eat when away from home, an inn.

hot-tem'pered adj easily angered.

hound n **1** a hunting dog. **2** (inf) a rascal:—vb to hunt:—**hound out** to drive out.

hour [our] n **1** (old) sixty minutes. **2** the 24th part of a day. **3** the time fixed for doing something, the time at which something is usu done.

hour'ly adj happening every hour.

house n **1** a building in which people, often a family, live. **2** a place used for a particular purpose. **3** a theater audience. **4** a business firm. **5** a school boarding house:—vb [houz] **1** to provide a house for. **2** to shelter.

house'boat n a boat used as a home.

house'hold n all who live in a house:—adj having to do with a house or those who live in it.

house'holder n one who owns or rents a house.

house'keeper n a person in charge of a house.

house'warming n the first party given after going to live in a new house.

house'wife n a woman who works at home looking after her house and family and cooking, cleaning, etc.

hov'el n a poor, dirty house.

hov'er vb **1** to stay in the air without moving. **2** to stay near, to loiter.

hov'ercraft n a type of vehicle or boat that can skim over the surface of smooth land or water on a cushion of air.

howev'er adv **1** in whatever way. **2** no matter how. **3** yet.

howl vb **1** to give a long, loud cry, as a dog or wolf. **2** to wail, to cry:—also n.

hub n **1** the central part of a wheel. **2** a center of interest or activity.

hud'dle vb to crowd together:—n a close crowd.

hue[1] n (fml or lit) color.

hue[2] n:—**hue and cry** a noisy protest.

hug vb (hugged', hug'ging) **1** to hold tightly in the arms, to take lovingly in the arms. **2** to keep close to:—n a close grip, an embrace.

huge adj very big, enormous:—n **huge'ness**.

hulk'ing adj big and awkward.

hull n **1** the outer covering of a grain or seed. **2** the frame or body of a ship.—vb to strip off the husk.

hullo see hallo.

hum vb (hummed', hum'ming) **1** to make a buzzing sound. **2** to sing without words or with the mouth closed:—n **1** a buzzing noise. **2** the noise made by a flying bee.

hu'man adj having to do with mankind.

humane' adj kindly, merciful.

humanita'rian n one who works to lessen human suffering: —also adj.

human'ity n **1** all mankind. **2** kindness, feeling for others.

hum'ble adj thinking oneself unimportant, not proud, seeking no praise:—vb **1** to make humble. **2** to lessen the importance or power of:—adv **humb'ly**.

hu'mid adj moist, damp.

humid'ity n dampness, the amount of moisture in the air.

humil'iate vb to lessen the importance or power of, to lower the dignity or pride of:—n **humilia'tion**.

humil'ity n the state of being humble.

hu'mor n **1** a comical or amusing quality. **2** a state of mind, mood.

hu'morous adj **1** funny, amusing. **2** having or displaying a sense of humor.

hump n a rounded lump, esp on the back.

hunch n **1** a rounded hump, esp on the back. **2** (inf) an intuitive feeling, a hint.

hun'dred n ten times ten:—adj **hun'dredth**.

hun'dredweight n a measure of weight = 110 pounds (abbr cwt).

hun'ger n **1** a strong desire for food. **2** lack of food. **3** any strong desire:—vb **1** (old) to feel hunger. **2** to desire greatly.

hun'gry adj **1** needing food, feeling or showing hunger. **2** having a strong need or desire for.

hunk n (inf) a large piece.

hunt vb **1** to chase wild animals in order to kill or capture them. **2** to look for. **3** to follow in order to catch:—n **1** the act of hunting. **2** a group of people who meet to hunt wild animals.

hunt'er n one who hunts (f **hunt'ress**).

hur'dle n 1 a gate-like movable frame of wood or metal. 2 a wooden frame over which people or horses must jump in certain races. 3 hindrance, obstacle.

hurl vb to throw with force.

hur'ly-bur'ly n confusion, great noise.

hurrah' interj a cry of joy.

hur'ricane n a violent storm, a very strong wind.

hur'ried adj done quickly, often too quickly, hasty.

hur'ry vb 1 to do or go quickly. 2 to make to go quickly:— n haste, speed.

hurt vb (pt, pp **hurt**) 1 to cause pain to, to wound, to injure. 2 to upset:— n (fml) 1 a wound, an injury. 2 harm.

hurt'ful adj harmful.

hurt'le vb to move with force and speed through the air.

hus'band n a married man:—vb to use or spend carefully.

hush n silence, stillness:—vb 1 to make silent, to quieten. 2 to become silent:—**hush up** to prevent something becoming generally known:—interj quiet! silence!

husk n the dry outer covering of a grain or seed, or of certain fruits.

husk'y adj 1 hoarse, dry and rough. 2 hefty, strong.

hust'le vb 1 to hurry. 2 to push roughly:—also n.

hut n a small, roughly built house, a wooden shed.

hutch n a box-like cage for rabbits.

hy'brid n a plant or animal resulting from the mixing of two different kinds or species, a mongrel:—adj bred from two different kinds.

hy'drant n a pipe from the main water pipe of a street from which water (e.g. for a hose) may be drawn direct.

hydraul'ic adj worked by the pressure of water or other liquid.

hy'dro- prefix having to do with water.

hydroelec'tric adj having to do with electricity obtained by water power.

hy'drogen n an invisible gas with no color or smell that with oxygen forms water.

hydropho'bia n 1 rabies. 2 fear of water. 3 the inability to swallow water.

hyena [hi-ee'-nä] n a dog-like animal that eats dead flesh.

hy'giene n 1 the study of clean and healthy living. 2 clean and healthy living.

hygien'ic adj having to do with hygiene, clean.

hymn [him] n a song of praise, esp to God.

hym'nal n a book of hymns.

hyper'bole n a figure of speech by which a statement is exaggerated in a striking way.

hy'phen n a short dash (-) between syllables or between words joined to express a single idea.

hypno'sis n a sleep-like state in obedience to the will of another who can then make the sleeper do as he or she says.

hypnot'ic adj producing sleep.

hyp'notism n the art of producing hypnosis.

hyp'notist n one who has the power to hypnotize others.

hyp'notize vb to will a person into a sleep-like state and to perform certain actions while in it.

hypochondriac [hi'-pô-k on'-dri-ak] n one who is always worried about the state of his or her health, one who thinks he or she is ill:—n **hy'pochon'dria**.

hypoc'risy n the pretense of being good or of having beliefs or feelings that one does not have.

hyp'ocrite n one who pretends to be good but is not so, a person who says one thing and does another.

hypoder'mic adj 1 under the skin. 2 used for injecting a drug under the skin:—n a medical instrument for injecting a drug under the skin.

hyste'ria n 1 a disorder of the nerves, causing a person to laugh or cry violently without reason, have imaginary illnesses, etc. 2 lack of control, uncontrolled excitement.

hyster'ics n 1 a fit of hysteria. 2 (inf) an uncontrollable fit of laughter.

hyster'ical adj 1 suffering from hysteria. 2 caused by hysteria. 3 (inf) very funny.

ice n 1 frozen water. 2 an ice cream:—vb 1 to cool in ice. 2 to cover with frosting.

ice'berg n a great mass of ice floating in the sea.

ice'box n an apparatus for preserving food, etc, by keeping it cold.

ice cream n cream or a mixture of creamy substances flavored and frozen.

ice hockey see **hockey**.

i'cicle n a long, hanging pointed piece of ice formed by the freezing of falling water.

i'cing n frosting.

i'con n a religious picture or statue, an image.

i'cy adj 1 very cold. 2 covered with ice. 3 unfriendly.

ide'a n 1 a plan, thought, or suggestion. 2 a picture in the mind. 3 an opinion or belief.

ide'al n 1 a perfect example. 2 (too) high principles or perfect standards, a person's standard of behavior, etc:—adj 1 perfect. 2 extremely suitable. 3 expressing possible perfection that is unlikely to exist.

iden'tical adj 1 the very same. 2 the same, exactly alike.

identifica'tion n 1 act of recognizing. 2 something that is proof of or a sign of identity. 3 the feeling that one shares ideas, feelings, etc, with another person.

iden'tify vb 1 to think of as being the same. 2 to recognize as being a certain person or thing. 3 to discover or recognize.

iden'tity n who a person is.

id'iom n a group of words that together have an unexpected meaning.

idiomat'ic adj 1 having an unusual or unexpected meaning. 2 having to do with everyday speech.

id'iot n 1 (old or fml) a person with very low intelligence. 2 foolish or stupid person.

i'dle adj 1 doing nothing, not working, not in use. 2 lazy. 3 having no effect or results:—vb 1 (fml) to be idle, to do nothing. 2 (of a machine) to run without doing work:—n **i'dleness**:—n **i'dler**:—adv **i'dly**.

i'dol n 1 a statue or other object that is worshipped. 2 a person regarded with too great love and respect.

i'dolize vb to love or admire very greatly.

idyll'ic adj 1 perfectly happy, pleasant. 2 charming, picturesque.

ig'loo n an Inuit house made of frozen snow.

ignite' vb 1 to set fire to. 2 to catch fire.

igni'tion n 1 act of setting fire to. 2 the part of a motor engine that sets fire to the fuel that drives the engine.

igno'ble adj 1 (fml) mean, dishonorable. 2 (old) of low birth.

ig'norance n 1 want of knowledge. 2 lack of.

ig'norant adj 1 having little or no knowledge. 2 unaware of.

ignore' vb to take no notice of, to refuse to pay attention to.

ill adj 1 sick. 2 bad. 3 evil, harmful:—n 1 evil, harm. 2 trouble:—adv badly.

ill'-advised' adj unwise

ille'gal adj against the law:—n **illegal'ity**.

illeg'ible adj that cannot be read, badly written.

illegit'imate adj born of unmarried parents:—n **illegit'imacy**.

illic'it adj unlawful, against the law.

illit'erate adj 1 unable to read or write. 2 uneducated:—n **illit'eracy**.

ill'-mann'ered adj rude, impolite.

ill nat'ure n bad temper.

ill'ness n sickness, the state of being unwell.

illog'ical adj 1 not using reasoning, not reasonable. 2 against the rules of reasoning.

ill'-tem'pered adj having a bad temper, angry.

ill-treat' vb 1 to handle roughly. 2 to behave roughly to, to be cruel to.

illum'inate vb 1 (old) to light up. 2 (of books, etc) to decorate with bright colors. 3 to explain, to make clear.

illumina'tion n (fml) 1 a light. 2 decorative lights. 3 a picture or decoration painted on a page of a book. 4 explanation, clarification.

illu'sion n 1 deception. 2 a wrong belief.

ill'ustrate vb 1 to make clear by examples. 2 to provide pictures for a book or magazine.

illustra'tion n 1 an example that makes something easier to understand or demonstrates something. 2 a picture in a book or magazine.

illus'trious adj (fml) famous.

im'age n 1 a likeness, form. 2 a likeness or copy of a person, etc, made of stone, wood, etc. 3 a picture formed of an object in front of a mirror or lens. 4 a picture in the mind.

imag'inary adj existing in the mind only.

imagina'tion n 1 the power of inventing stories, persons, etc, creative ability. 2 the power of forming pictures in the mind. 3 the seeing or hearing of things that do not exist.

imag'inative adj 1 having a good imagination. 2 demonstrating imagination.

imag'ine vb 1 to form a picture in the mind. 2 to form ideas of things that do not exist or of events that have not happened. 3 to suppose.

imbecile [im'-be-seel] n a fool, an idiot.

im'itate vb 1 to copy, to try to be, behave, or look the same as:—n **im'itator**.

imita'tion n 1 act of imitating. 2 a copy.

immac'ulate adj spotless.

immate'rial adj unimportant.

immature' adj 1 unripe. 2 not fully grown. 3 lacking experience and wisdom:—n **immatur'ity**.

immeas'urable adj huge.

imme'diate adj 1 happening at once. 2 direct, without anyone or anything coming between. 3 near, close.

imme'diately adv 1 at once. 2 closely.

immense' adj huge:—n **immens'ity**.

immerse' vb 1 to put into water. 2 to give one's whole attention to:—n **immer'sion**.

im'migrant n one who immigrates.

im'migrate vb (fml) to enter a country not one's own and settle there:—n **immigra'sion**.

immor'al adj wrong, evil, wicked:—n **immoral'ity**.

immor'tal adj 1 living for ever. 2 famous for all time.

immortal'ity n 1 everlasting life. 2 undying fame.

immune' adj 1 free from, specially protected from. 2 not to be infected by:—n **immun'ity**.

im'munize vb to inject disease germs into the blood stream to cause a mild attack of an illness, so making the person immune from it.

imp n 1 in fairy tales, an evil spirit. 2 a mischievous child.

im'pact n 1 the force with which one thing strikes another. 2 a collision. 3 a strong effect or impression.

impair' vb to make worse, to weaken.

impart' vb (fml) 1 to tell. 2 to give.

impar'tial adj fair, just, not taking sides.

impass'able adj unable to be passed or crossed.

impass'ive adj 1 not showing strong feeling. 2 calm, unexcited.

impa'tient *adj* not willing to wait, easily angered by delay:— *n* **impa'tience.**

impeach' *vb* 1 to charge with a crime, esp treason. 2 (*fml*) to raise doubts about:—*n* **impeach'ment.**

impecc'able *adj* faultless.

impecu'nious *adj* (*fml or hum*) having no money, poor.

impede' *vb* 1 to prevent from moving freely. 2 to delay.

imped'iment *n* 1 something that prevents or delays movement. 2 a physical or nervous condition that makes it difficult to speak clearly.

impend'ing *adj* about to happen.

imper'ative *adj* 1 commanding. 2 necessary, urgent.

imper'fect *adj* having faults, not perfect.

imperfec'tion *n* a fault, a flaw.

impe'rial *adj* 1 having to do with an empire or emperor, royal. 2 (*of weights and measures*) according to the non-metric imperial system.

imperial system *n* a non-metric system of weights and measures established by statute in Britain.

imper'sonal *adj* not influenced by personal feelings.

imper'sonate *vb* to pretend to be someone else:—*n* **imper'sona'tor.**

imper'tinent *adj* cheeky, purposely disrespectful:— *n* **imper'tinence.**

imperturb'able *adj* calm, not easily excited or worried.

imper'vious *adj* 1 that cannot be passed through. 2 taking no notice (of).

impet'uous *adj* acting without thinking first, rash, hasty:— *n* **impetuos'ity.**

im'petus *n* 1 the force with which something moves. 2 energy.

impinge' *vb* 1 to come into contact with, to make an impression on. 2 to interfere with, to trespass on.

imp'ish *adj* mischievous.

implant' *vb* 1 to plant firmly. 2 to place in. 3 to teach.

im'plement *n* a tool, an instrument:—*vb* **implement'** to put into practice.

im'plicate *vb* to show that a person is involved or connected with (an affair), to mix up in.

implica'tion *n* something hinted at but not said openly.

impli'cit *adj* 1 understood but not said. 2 unquestioning, without doubts.

implore' *vb* to ask earnestly, to beg.

imply' *vb* to suggest something without saying it openly, to hint.

import' *vb* to bring in goods from abroad:—*n* **im'port** something brought in from abroad:—*n* **import'er.**

impor'tant *adj* 1 deserving great attention. 2 having results that affect many people. 3 having a high position:— *n* **impor'tance.**

impose' *vb* 1 to lay on (as a duty, tax, etc). 2 to make to accept:—**impose upon** to take advantage of, to exploit, to make unfair demands on.

impos'ing *adj* important-looking, stately.

imposi'tion *n* 1 the act of laying upon. 2 a tax. 3 an unfair demand. 4 a punishment exercise.

impos'sible *adj* not able to be done or achieved:—*n* **impossibil'ity.**

im'post *n* a tax, esp on imports.

impos'tor *n* one who deceives by pretending to be someone else, a deceiver.

imprac'ticable *adj* impossible to carry out, not able to be done:—*n* **impracticabil'ity.**

impress' *vb* 1 to mark by pressing into, to stamp. 2 to fix in the mind. 3 to stress, to emphasize the importance of.

impress'ion *n* 1 the mark left by pressing or stamping. 2 the number of copies of a book printed at one time. 3 an effect on the mind or feelings. 4 a not very clear idea or memory. 5 an attempt to copy in a humorous way someone else's voice, behavior, appearance, etc.

impress'ionable *adj* easily influenced.

impress'ionist *n* a person who does impressions of people, esp as a form of theatrical entertainment:—*adj* **impress'ive.**

impress'ive *adj* 1 important-looking. 2 causing deep feeling, such as admiration.

imprint' *vb* 1 to make a mark by pressing or printing. 2 to fix in the memory.

impris'on *vb* to put into prison, to shut in.

impris'onment *n* the act of imprisoning or the state of being imprisoned.

improb'able *adj* not likely:—*n* **improbabil'ity.**

impromp'tu *adj* not prepared:—*adv* without preparation.

improp'er *adj* 1 wrong. 2 not suitable, not polite. 3 indecent.

improper fraction *n* a fraction greater than 1 (e.g. $^1/_2$).

improve' *vb* to make or become better:—*n* **improve'ment.**

im'provise *vb* 1 to make something from material that is available. 2 to make something up at the moment required without preparation:—*n* **improvisa'tion.**

im'pudent *adj* disrespectful, cheeky:—*n* **im'pudence.**

im'pulse *n* 1 a force causing movement. 2 a sudden desire or decision to act at once.

impuls'ive *adj* 1 done without forethought. 2 acting without thinking first:—*n* **impuls'iveness.**

impure' *adj* 1 dirty, polluted. 2 mixed with something else. 3 sinful:—*n* **impur'ity.**

inabil'ity *n* lack of power, state of being unable.

inaccess'ible *adj* not to be reached or approached.

inacc'urate *adj* 1 not correct. 2 not exact:—*n* **inacc'uracy.**

inac'tive *adj* 1 not taking much exercise. 2 no longer working or operating. 3 not taking an active part.

inadequate [in-ad'-i-kwāt] *adj* 1 not good enough. 2 not sufficient:—*n* **inad'equacy.**

inadmiss'ible *adj* not able to be allowed.

inadver'tent *adj* 1 without care or attention. 2 unintentional:— *n* **inadver'tence.**

inadver'tently *adv* unintentionally.

ina'lienable *adj* that cannot be given or taken away.

inane' *adj* foolish, silly:—*n* **inan'ity.**

inappro'priate *adj* not suitable.

inapt' *adj* not suitable, not appropriate.

inartic'ulate *adj* 1 not clear. 2 unable to express oneself clearly.

inatten'tive *adj* not attending, neglectful.

inaud'ible *adj* that cannot be heard.

in'born *adj* apparently existing in one since birth, natural.

in'bred *adj* having become part of one's nature as a result of early training.

incap'able *adj* 1 not good at one's job. 2 not able, helpless:— *n* **incapabil'ity.**

incapac'itate *vb* to make unfit or unable.

incapac'ity *n* 1 unfitness. 2 lack of ability.

in'cense[1] *n* a mixture of spices burned to give a sweet-smelling smoke.

incense'[2] *vb* to make angry.

incen'tive *n* something for which one is prepared to work hard, a reason for action.

incess'ant *adj* not stopping,.

inch *n* the twelfth part of a foot in length:—*vb* to move a little at a time.

in'cidence *n* the extent or rate of frequency of something.

in'cident *n* 1 a happening, an event. 2 an event involving violence or lawbreaking.

inciden'tal *adj* 1 happening as a result, though not the most important one. 2 accompanying.

inciden'tally *adv* by the way.

incin'erator *n* a furnace for burning anything to ashes.

inci'sion *n* 1 act of cutting. 2 a cut, a deep cut.

inci'sive *adj* clear and sharp, to the point.

inci'sor *n* a cutting tooth in the front of the mouth.

incite' *vb* to stir up, to urge on:—*n* **incite'ment**.

inclina'tion *n* 1 a slope. 2 a bow. 3 a liking, preference. 4 a tendency.

incline' *vb* 1 to slope. 2 to bend. 3 to move gradually off the straight way:—**be inclined to** 1 to feel a desire or preference. 2 to have a tendency to:—*n* **in'cline** a slope.

include' *vb* to count as a part or member:—*n* **inclu'sion**.

inclu'sive *adj* including everything mentioned or understood.

incog'nito *adj* in disguise, under a false name.

incoher'ent *adj* not speaking or writing clearly, difficult to follow or understand:—*n* **incoher'ence**.

in'come *n* the money earned or gained.

income tax *n* the tax charged on income.

incom'parable *adj* 1 that cannot be equaled. 2 having no equal.

incompat'ible *adj* 1 unable to get on together. 2 not in agreement:—*n* **incompatibil'ity**.

incom'petent *adj* 1 unable to do one's job well, unskillful. 2 not good enough:—*ns* **incom'petence**, **incom'petency**.

incomprehen'sible *adj* that cannot be understood.

inconsid'erate *adj* having no thought for the feeling of others, thoughtless.

inconsis'tent *adj* 1 not agreeing with what was said or done before or elsewhere. 2 changeable, erratic. 3 contradictory:—*n* **inconsis'tency**.

inconspic'uous *adj* not easily seen.

incon'stant *adj* 1 often changing. 2 not always behaving in the same way:—*n* **incon'stancy**.

inconven'ience *n* trouble, annoyance:—*vb* (*fml*) to cause trouble or difficulty.

inconven'ient *adj* causing trouble, unsuitable.

incor'porate *vb* 1 to bring together in one. 2 to make to form a part of, to include:—*n* **incorpora'tion**.

incorrect' *adj* 1 wrong. 2 not according to accepted standards.

increase' *vb* to make or become greater in size or number:—*n* **in'crease** a rise in amount, numbers, or degree.

incred'ible *adj* 1 unbelievable, hard to believe. 2 amazing, wonderful:—*n* **incredibil'ity**.

incred'ulous *adj* not willing to believe, unbelieving:—*n* **incredu'lity**.

in'crement *n* an increase in money or value, often in salary.

incrim'inate *vb* to show that a person has taken part in a crime.

in'cubate *vb* 1 to sit on eggs, to keep eggs warm till the young come out of them. 2 (*of eggs*) to be kept warm until the young birds come out. 3 (*of a disease or infection*) to develop until signs of disease appear. 4 to be holding in one's body an infection that is going to develop into a disease:—*n* **in'cubation**.

in'cubator *n* 1 an apparatus for hatching eggs. 2 an apparatus for keeping alive prematurely born babies.

incur' *vb* (**incurred'**, **incur'ring**) 1 to bring upon oneself. 2 to fall into.

incur'able *adj* that cannot be cured.

indebt'ed *adj* owing thanks:—*n* **indebt'edness**.

inde'cent *adj* 1 not decent, morally offensive, improper. 2 not suitable, not in good taste:—*n* **inde'cency**.

indeci'pherable *adj* that cannot be read or made out.

indeci'sive *adj* 1 uncertain, having difficulty in making decisions. 2 settling nothing.

indeed' *adv* truly.

indefat'igable *adj* never becoming tired.

indefens'ible *adj* that should not be defended.

indefin'able *adj* that cannot be clearly described or explained.

indef'inite *adj* 1 not fixed or exact, without clearly marked outlines or limits. 2 not clear, not precise, vague.

indel'icate *adj* 1 slightly indecent, improper. 2 lacking in tact:—*n* **indel'icacy**.

indent' *vb* 1 to make a notch or zigzag in. 2 to begin a line in from the margin.

indenta'tion *n* 1 a notch or piece cut out of a straight edge. 2 the starting of a line in from the margin.

indepen'dence *n* freedom to act or think as one likes, freedom.

indepen'dent *adj* 1 thinking and acting for oneself. 2 free from control by others. 3 having enough money to live without working or being helped by others.

indescrib'able *adj* that cannot be described.

indestruc'tible *adj* that cannot be destroyed.

indeter'minate *adj* not fixed, uncertain.

in'dex *n* (*pl* **in'dices**) 1 the pointer on the dial or scale of an instrument. 2 something that indicates or points to. 3 (*pl* **in'dexes**) an alphabetical list of names, subjects, etc, at the end of a book.

Indian summer *n* a spell of fine warm weather in late fall.

in'dia-rub'ber *n* a piece of rubber used for erasing pencil marks.

in'dicate *vb* 1 to point out, to show. 2 to be a sign of. 3 to show to be necessary or desirable.

indica'tion *n* a sign.

indic'ative *adj* showing, being a sign of.

in'dicator *n* 1 a needle or pointer on a machine that indicates something or gives information about something. 2 a turn signal.

indiff'erence *n* lack of interest.

indiff'erent *adj* 1 taking no interest, not caring. 2 neither good nor bad.

indigest'ible *adj* not easily digested.

indiges'tion *n* illness or pain caused by failure to dissolve food properly in the stomach.

indig'nant *adj* angry, annoyed by what is unjust:—*n* **indigna'tion**.

indirect' *adj* 1 not leading straight to the destination, round-about. 2 not direct, not straightforward, not frank. 3 not intended, not directly aimed at.

indiscreet' *adj* 1 unwise, thoughtless. 2 done or said without thought of results.

indiscre'tion *n* 1 thoughtless behavior. 2 an act done without thought of its results.

indiscrim'inate *adj* taking no notice of differences, choosing without care.

indispens'able *adj* that cannot be done without.

indispu'table *adj* that cannot be denied or contradicted.

indistinct' *adj* not clear.

indisting'uishable *adj* that cannot be made out.

individ'ual *adj* 1 single. 2 intended for, used by, etc, one person only. 3 special to one person:—*n* 1 a single person. 2 (*inf*) a person.

individ'ualist *n* one who believes in doing things in his or her own way:—*n* **individ'ualism**.

individ'ually *adv* separately, one by one.

indivis'ible *adj* that cannot be divided.

indoc'trinate *vb* 1 to instruct in a belief. 2 to bring to accept a system of belief unquestioningly.

in'dolent *adj* lazy:—*n* **in'dolence**.

indoor *adj* done in a house or building.

indoors' *adv* within doors, inside a house.

indu'bitable *adj* that cannot be doubted.

induce' *vb* 1 to lead on to do, to persuade. 2 to bring about.

induce'ment *n* something that leads one to try to do something, an attractive reason for doing something.

indulge' *vb* 1 to take pleasure in something, without trying to control oneself. 2 to give in to the wishes of.

indul'gent *adj* kindly, easygoing, ready to give in to the wishes of others.

indus'trial *adj* having to do with the manufacturing of goods.

indus'trialist *n* one who owns or runs an industrial organization.

indus'trious *adj* hard-working, busy.

in'dustry *n* 1 (*fml*) the ability to work hard. 2 in trade or commerce, the work that is done to make goods ready for selling, the manufacturing and selling of goods.

ined'ible *adj* that should not or cannot be eaten.

ineffec'tive *adj* useless, having no effect:—*n* **ineffec'tiveness**.

ineffec'tual *adj* 1 not having the desired effect. 2 not able to get things done.

inefficient [in-è-fish'-ént] *adj* 1 not good at one's job, unable to do the job required. 2 not producing results in the best, quickest, and cheapest way:—*n* **ineffic'iency**.

inel'igible *adj* not suitable to be chosen or to include.

inequal'ity *n* lack of equality, unevenness.

inert' *adj* 1 without the power to move. 2 not wanting to take action, not taking action. 3 not acting chemically when combined with other substances.

iner'tia *n* 1 unwillingness or inability to move. 2 the inability of matter to set itself in motion or to stop moving.

inessen'tial *adj* not necessary.

ines'timable *adj* (*fml*) 1 of very great value. 2 that cannot be valued.

inev'itable *adj* certain to happen:—*n* **inevitabil'ity**.

inexact' *adj* not quite correct:—*n* **inexact'itude**.

inexcus'able *adj* that cannot be forgiven or pardoned.

inexhaust'ible *adj* that cannot be used up or worn out.

inexpen'sive *adj* cheap, not dear.

inexpe'rience *n* lack of skill or practice:—*adj* **inexpe'rienced**.

inex'pert *adj* not skilled.

inex'plicable *adj* that cannot be explained.

inexpress'ible *adj* that cannot be put into words.

infall'ible *adj* 1 unable to make a mistake. 2 that cannot fail:—*n* **infallibil'ity**.

in'famous *adj* famous for something bad or wicked:—*n* **in'famy**.

in'fant *n* a very young child:—*n* **in'fancy**.

infect' *vb* 1 to pass on a disease to another. 2 to make impure by spreading disease into it. 3 to pass on or spread.

infec'tion *n* the passing on or spreading of disease, or anything harmful.

infec'tious *adj* that can be passed on to others.

infer' *vb* (**inferred'**, **infer'ring**) to work out an idea from the facts known.

infe'rior *adj* 1 of lesser value or importance. 2 of bad quality:—*n* a person lower in rank.

infidel'ity *n* disloyalty, unfaithfulness.

in'filtrate *vb* 1 to pass through, a few at a time. 2 to enter and secretly and gradually become part of, usu with an unfriendly purpose:—*n* **infiltra'tion**.

in'finite *adj* 1 having neither beginning nor end, limitless. 2 (*inf*) very great.

infin'ity *n* 1 space, time, or quantity that is without limit or is immeasurably great or small. 2 an indefinitely large number, quantity, or distance.

inflame' *vb* 1 to set on fire. 2 to excite. 3 to anger.

inflamm'able *adj* 1 flammable. 2 excitable.

inflamma'tion *n* a swelling on part of the body, accompanied by heat and pain.

inflate' *vb* 1 to puff up. 2 to make to swell by filling with air or gas. 3 to increase in price or value.

infla'tion *n* 1 act of inflating. 2 a situation in a country's economy where prices and wages keep forcing each other to increase:—*adj* **infla'tionary**.

inflex'ible *adj* 1 that cannot be bent, stiff and firm. 2 not easily changed. 3 not giving in:—*n* **inflexibil'ity**.

inflict' *vb* to force something unpleasant or unwanted on someone.

in'fluence *n* 1 the ability to affect other people or the course of events. 2 the power to make requests to those in authority:—*vb* to have an effect on.

influen'tial *adj* having power, important.

influen'za *n* a type of infectious illness, usu causing headache, fever, a cold, etc.

in'flux *n* (*fml*) a flowing in.

inform' *vb* 1 to tell, to give information. 2 to teach, to give knowledge to.

inform'al *adj* 1 without ceremony. 2 not bound by rules or accepted ways of behaving. 3 suitable for ordinary everyday situations:—*n* **informal'ity**.

informa'tion *n* facts told, knowledge in the form of facts, news, etc.

inform'er *n* one who gives away the plans of others.

infre'quent *adj* not happening often:—*n* **infre'quency**.

infu'riate *vb* to make very angry.

inge'nious *adj* 1 having good or new ideas, inventive. 2 cleverly thought out.

ingenu'ity *n* 1 cleverness, inventiveness. 2 the ability to invent, cleverness.

ingrained' *adj* fixed firmly in.

ingrat'itude *n* lack of thankfulness.

ingre'dient *n* one of the things in a mixture.

inhab'it *vb* to live in.

inhab'itant *n* one who lives in a certain place.

inhale' *vb* to breathe in.

inher'ent *adj* natural, existing in one since birth.

inher'it *vb* 1 to receive something from another at his or her death. 2 to receive certain qualities through one's parents:—*n* **inher'itor**.

inher'itance *n* that which is inherited.

inhib'it *vb* 1 to prevent or hinder, to hold back from doing. 2 to make someone reluctant or uncomfortable.

inhu'man *adj* cruel, merciless:—*n* **inhuman'ity**.

ini'tial *adj* first, happening at the beginning:—*vb* to mark or write one's initials:—*npl* the first letters of each of a person's names.

ini'tiative *n* 1 the ability to make decisions and take action without asking for help and advice. 2 the first movement or action that starts something happening.

inject' *vb* 1 to put into the bloodstream through a hollow needle. 2 to put in:—*n* **injec'tion**.

in'jure *vb* 1 to hurt. 2 to harm, to damage.

in'jury *n* 1 damage, harm, hurt. 2 a physical hurt or wound.

injus'tice *n* 1 unfairness. 2 an unfair act.

ink *n* a colored liquid used for writing or printing:—*vb* to mark with ink.

ink'ling *n* a hint, a slight idea.

in'land n the part of a country away from the sea coast or border:—adj **1** having to do with a country's own affairs. **2** away from the coast or border:—also adv.

in'let n a small bay.

in'mate n one living in a house, hospital, etc.

in'most adj farthest in.

inn n a house where travelers may pay to eat, drink, or stay for the night.

in'ner adj farther in.

in'nermost adj farthest in.

inn'ings n (pl **innings**) **1** (baseball) a team's turn at bat. **2** (cricket) the time spent batting or the score made by a player or a team.

inn'keeper n one who is in charge of an inn.

inn'ocence n freedom from blame or wickedness.

inn'ocent adj **1** not guilty. **2** having no knowledge or experience of evil.

innova'tion n a new way of doing something, a new thing or idea.

innu'merable adj too many to be counted.

inoc'ulate vb to infect slightly with the germs of a disease to prevent more serious infection:—n **inocula'tion**.

inoffen'sive adj not causing harm.

inop'erative adj not working.

in'quest n a legal inquiry to decide the cause of a person's sudden death.

inquire' vb **1** to ask. **2** to ask for information about. **3** to try to discover the facts of.

in'quiry n **1** a question. **2** a careful search for information, an investigation.

inquisi'tion n **1** (fml) an official inquiry. **2** (old) an examination consisting of a series of questions:—n **inquis'itor**.

insane' adj **1** mad. **2** (inf) very unwise.

insan'itary adj dirty, causing disease.

insan'ity n madness.

insatiable [in-sä'-shi-a-bèl] adj that cannot be satisfied, greedy.

inscrip'tion n words written on something, often as a tribute.

inscru'table adj that cannot be fully understood, mysterious.

in'sect n a tiny creature with a body divided into sections and usu with six legs.

insec'ticide n a liquid or powder for killing insects.

insectiv'orous adj insect-eating.

insecure' adj **1** anxious and unsure of oneself, lacking confidence. **2** (fml) not safe, likely to be lost. **3** (fml) not safe or firmly fixed:—n **insecur'ity**.

insen'sible adj unconscious.

insen'sitive adj **1** not noticing the feelings of others. **2** not quick to feel or notice.

insep'arable adj that cannot be put apart.

insert' vb to put in or among.

inser'tion n **1** something inserted. **2** the act of inserting.

in'shore adj and adv near the shore.

inside' n **1** the inner side or part. **2** pl (inf) the internal organs, stomach, bowels:—adj **1** internal. **2** known only to insiders, secret:—adv **1** on or in the inside, within, indoors. **2** (inf) in prison:—prep in or within.

insignif'icant adj of little importance:—**insignif'icance**.

insin'uate vb to hint in an unpleasant way.

insinua'tion n a sly hint.

insip'id adj **1** having no taste or flavor. **2** uninteresting, dull.

insist' vb **1** to state firmly, to demand or urge strongly. **2** to keep on saying.

insis'tent adj **1** firm. **2** wanting immediate attention:—n **insis'tence**.

in'solent adj rude, boldly insulting:—n **in'solence**.

insol'uble adj **1** impossible to dissolve. **2** that cannot be solved.

insol'vent adj not able to pay debts, having no money:—n **insol'vency**.

insom'nia n sleeplessness.

inspect' vb to look at closely, to examine.

inspec'tion n an examination.

inspec'tor n **1** one who inspects. **2** one who examines the work of others to see that it is done properly. **3** a rank of police officer.

inspira'tion n **1** a person or thing that encourages one to use one's powers. **2** the encouragement so given.

inspire' vb **1** to encourage someone with the desire and ability to take action by filling with eagerness, confidence, etc. **2** to be the origin of. **3** to arouse in someone.

install' vb **1** to place in office, esp with ceremony. **2** to put in place:—n **installa'tion**.

install'ment n **1** payment of part of a sum of money owed. **2** part of a serial story published or broadcast at one time.

installment plan n a method of paying for goods in regular installments.

in'stance n an example:—**for instance** for example:—vb to give or quote as an example.

in'stant adj **1** immediate. **2** concentrated or pre-cooked for quick preparation:—n **1** a moment. **2** the exact moment.

in'stantly adv at once.

instead' adv in place of.

in'stinct n a natural tendency to behave or react in a particular way and without having been taught.

instinc'tive adj done at once without thinking, natural.

institu'tion n **1** an organization, usu a long-established or well-respected one. **2** the building used by such an organization. **3** an accepted custom or tradition.

instruct' vb **1** to teach. **2** to order.

instruc'tion n **1** teaching. **2** an order. **3** pl information on how to use something correctly.

instruc'tor n a teacher, a coach.

in'strument n **1** a tool, esp one used for delicate work. **2** a device producing musical sound. **3** a device for measuring, recording, controlling, etc, esp in an aircraft.

insuff'erable adj that cannot be borne, unbearable.

insuffi'cient adj not enough:—n **insuffi'ciency**.

in'sulate vb **1** to keep apart. **2** to cover with rubber, etc, in order to prevent loss of electricity or heat:—n **insula'tion**.

in'sulator n a material that does not allow electricity or heat to pass through it.

insult' vb to speak rude or hurtful words to or of:—n **in'sult**.

insupport'able adj unbearable.

insure' vb to pay regular sums to a society on condition that one receives an agreed amount of money in case of loss, accident, death, etc:—n **insu'rance**.

insurrec'tion n a rebellion, a rising against the government.

intact' adj untouched, unharmed, with no part missing.

intan'gible adj **1** that cannot be touched. **2** not able to be clearly defined or understood.

in'tegral adj necessary to make something complete:—also n.

in'tegrate vb **1** to join in society as a whole, to mix freely with other groups. **2** to fit parts together to form a whole:—n **integra'tion**.

integ'rity n **1** the state of being whole and undivided, completeness. **2** honesty.

in'tellect n **1** the mind, the power to think and understand. **2** someone with great intellect.

intellec'tual adj **1** having a high intellect. **2** having to do with the intellect:—also n.

intell'igence n 1 cleverness, quickness of mind or understanding. 2 (fml) news.

intell'igent adj having a quick mind, clever.

intell'igible adj clear, that can be understood.

intend' vb to mean to.

intense' adj 1 very great. 2 very serious.

inten'sify vb to make greater or more severe.

inten'sity n 1 strength. 2 seriousness, earnestness.

intent' adj 1 attending carefully. 2 eager, planning or wanting to do something.—n (fml) purpose.

inten'tion n purpose, aim in doing something.

inten'tional adj done on purpose.

in'ter- prefix between, among.

interact' vb to act upon each other.—n interac'tion.

intercept' vb to stop or catch on the way from one place to another:—n intercep'tion.

interchange' vb 1 to change places with each other. 2 to give and receive in return.—n an exchange.

interchange'able adj that can be exchanged for each other.

in'terest n 1 something in which one takes part eagerly. 2 advantage. 3 eager attention. 4 concern. 5 the money paid for the use of a loan of money:—vb to gain the attention of.

in'teresting adj arousing interest.

interfere' vb 1 to get in the way of, to prevent from working or happening. 2 to force oneself into the affairs of others. 3 to touch or move something that one is not supposed to.

interfer'ence n 1 act of interfering. 2 the interruption of radio broadcasts by atmospherics or other broadcasts.

inte'rior adj 1 inner. 2 inland:—n 1 the inner part. 2 the inland part.

interjec'tion n 1 a short word expressing surprise, interest, disapproval, etc. 2 a remark made when another is speaking.

interlock' vb 1 to clasp or lock together. 2 to fit or fasten together.

in'terloper n one who enters a place in which he or she has no right to be.

in'terlude n 1 an interval between the acts of a play, etc. 2 the music or other entertainment provided during such an interval. 3 a period of time that comes between two events or activities.

interme'diate adj coming between two other things, in the middle.

intermis'sion n a short break in a play, concert, etc.

intermit'tent adj stopping for a time, then going on again, happening at intervals.

intern'[1] vb to detain and confine within an area, esp during wartime:—n intern'ment.

intern'[2] n 1 a doctor serving in a hospital, usu just after graduation from medical school. 2 an apprentice journalist, teacher, etc:—vb to serve as an intern.

inter'nal adj 1 having to do with the inside, esp of the body. 2 of one's own country.

internal combustion engine n an engine producing power by the explosion of a fuel-and-air mixture within the cylinders.

interna'tional adj having to do with several or many countries:—n a sporting contest between teams from different countries.

internecine [in-ter-nee'-sin] adj 1 causing death and destruction to both sides. 2 involving conflict within a group or organization.

Inter'net n the worldwide network that enables computers to connect to each other.

in'terplay n the action of one thing upon another.

inter'pret vb 1 to explain the meaning of. 2 to understand the meaning of to be. 3 to translate from one language into another.

interpreta'tion n 1 act of interpreting. 2 the meaning given to a work of art by a critic or performer.

inter'preter n one who translates from one speaker's language into another's.

inter'rogate vb to put questions to.

interroga'tion n the act of interrogating.

interrogation mark n the punctuation mark put after a direct question (?).

interrog'ative adj asking a question, having to do with questions:—n a word used in asking questions (e.g. why).

interrupt' vb 1 to break flow of speech or action. 2 to stop a person while he or she is saying or doing something. 3 (fml) to cut off.

interrup'tion n a remark or action that causes a stoppage.

intersect' vb to cut across each other.

intersec'tion n the point at which lines or roads cross each other.

intertwine' vb to twist together.

in'terval n 1 the time or distance between. 2 a break, a spell of free time. 3 an intermission. 4 the difference of pitch between two musical sounds.

intervene' vb 1 to interrupt, to interfere. 2 to be or to happen between (in time). 3 to happen so as to prevent something:—n interven'tion.

in'terview n 1 a meeting at which a person applying for a job is questioned. 2 a meeting with a person to get information or to do business:—also vb.

intes'tines npl the inner parts of the body, esp the bowels.

in'timacy n closeness, close relationship.

intimate [in'-ti-mêt] adj 1 having a close relationship. 2 having a close knowledge of:—n a close friend:—vb [in'-ti-mât] (fml) to make known.

intim'idate vb to make afraid, e.g. by making threats:—n intimida'tion.

intol'erable adj that cannot or should not be put up with.

intol'erant adj not willing to put up with actions or opinions different than one's own, narrow-minded:—n intol'erance.

intona'tion n the rise and fall of the voice while speaking.

intox'icate vb 1 to make drunk. 2 to excite greatly:—n intoxica'tion.

intran'sitive adj (of verbs) not taking an object.

intrep'id adj fearless, brave.

in'tricate adj having many small parts, complicated:—n in'tricacy.

intrigue [in-treeg'] n 1 a secret plot. 2 a secret love affair:—vb 1 to plot secretly. 2 to interest greatly.

introduce' vb 1 to bring in or put forward, esp something new. 2 to make one person known to another.

introduc'tion n 1 act of introducing. 2 a short section at the beginning of a book to make known its purpose.

introspec'tive adj thinking much about one's own actions and ideas:—n introspec'tion.

in'trovert n one who is always thinking about his or her own ideas and aims.

intrude' vb to come or go where one is not wanted:—n in'tru'sion.

intru'der n 1 one who intrudes. 2 a person who breaks into a house to steal, a burglar.

intui'tion n 1 immediate knowledge of the truth gained without having to think. 2 the ability to know things in this way:—adj intu'itive.

Inuit *n* a race of people living in the Arctic.

in'undate *vb* **1** to flow over. **2** to flood, to come in very large amounts.

invade' *vb* **1** to enter as an enemy, to attack. **2** to interfere with.

invalid' *n* a sick person.

inval'idate *vb* to make to have no value or effect.

inva'luable *adj* of very great value, more valuable than can be paid for.

inva'riable *adj* unchanging.

inva'sion *n* **1** entry into a country by enemy forces. **2** interference.

invent' *vb* **1** to think of and plan something new. **2** to make up:—*n* **inven'tor**.

inven'tion *n* **1** a thing thought of and made for the first time. **2** the ability to think out new ideas.

inven'tive *adj* good at thinking of new or unusual ideas.

in'ventory *n* a list of goods or articles.

inverse' *adj* opposite or reverse.

inver'sion *n* **1** act of turning upside down. **2** a change in the usual order of words in a sentence.

invert' *vb* to turn upside down, to turn the other way round.

inver'tebrate *adj* having no backbone:—*n* an animal without a backbone.

invest' *vb* **1** to mark someone's entry to rank or office by clothing him or her with the robes belonging to it. **2** to surround a fort with an army. **3** to lend money in order to increase it by interest or a share in profits.

inves'tigate *vb* to examine, to find out everything about:—*n* **inves'tigator.**

investiga'tion *n* an inquiry.

invest'ment *n* **1** the act of investing. **2** a sum of money invested. **3** the thing bought.

invig'orate *vb* to make strong or healthy, to refresh.

invin'cible *adj* that cannot be defeated:—*n* **invincibil'ity.**

invis'ible *adj* that cannot be seen:—*n* **invisibil'ity.**

invite' *vb* **1** to ask politely, to ask to come, esp as a guest. **2** to attract:—*n* **invita'tion.**

invit'ing *adj* attractive.

in'voice *n* **1** a list of goods sent to a buyer, with prices. **2** a list of work done and payment due:—*vb* to send an invoice.

invol'untary *adj* unintentional, done without conscious effort or intention.

involve' *vb* **1** to include. **2** to mix up in. **3** to cause as a result.

involved' *adj* complicated.

invul'nerable *adj* that cannot be wounded.

in'ward *adj* **1** inner. **2** having to do with the mind.

in'ward(s) *adv* toward the inside.

i'on *n* an electrically charged atom.

iota [i-ō'-ta] *n* **1** a Greek letter. **2** a tiny amount.

irate' *adj* very angry, furious.

irides'cent *adj* colored like the rainbow, brightly colored:—*n* **irides'cence.**

i'ris *n* **1** the colored circle of the eye. **2** a flowering plant. **3** the rainbow.

i'ron *n* **1** the most common of metals. **2** a tool or instrument made of iron, esp for smoothing clothes. **3** *pl* chains:—*adj*

1 made of iron. **2** strong, hard:—*vb* to smooth (clothes) with an iron.

iron'ic, iron'ical *adjs* expressing irony.

i'ronware *n* articles made of iron.

i'rony *n* **1** a remark made in such a way that the meaning is understood to be the opposite of what is said. **2** the result of an action that has the opposite effect to that intended.

irra'tional *adj* **1** not reasonable, not sensible. **2** not able to reason, not using reason.

irreg'ular *adj* **1** not in agreement with the rules, not according to accepted standards. **2** not straight or even. **3** not happening, etc, regularly:—*n* **irregular'ity.**

irrel'evant *adj* having nothing to do with the subject, not to the point:—*ns* **irrel'evance, irrel'evancy.**

irresist'ible *adj* **1** that cannot be resisted. **2** very strong. **3** very attractive, charming.

irrespec'tive *adj* not troubling about.

irrespon'sible *adj* not caring about the consequences of one's actions.

irr'igate *vb* to supply water to dry land by canals, etc:—*n* **irriga'tion.**

irr'itable *adj* easily angered or annoyed:—*n* **irritabil'ity.**

irr'itant *n* something that irritates.

irr'itate *vb* **1** to annoy, to anger. **2** to cause to itch:—*n* **irrita'tion.**

i'sland *n* a piece of land surrounded by water.

isle [il] *n* (*lit*) an island.

islet [i'-lêt] *n* a small island.

i'sobar *n* a line on a map joining places with equal atmospheric pressure.

i'solate *vb* **1** to place apart or alone. **2** to cut off. **3** to separate:—*n* **isola'tion.**

isosceles [i-so'-sê-leez] *adj* (*of a triangle*) having two sides equal.

i'sotherm *n* a line on a map joining places with equal temperature.

issue [i'-shö] *vb* **1** to go or come out. **2** to send out. **3** to flow out. **4** to give out. **5** to publish:—*vb* (*fml*) a result. **2** a question under discussion. **3** the number of books, papers, etc, published at one time.

isth'mus *n* a narrow neck of land joining two larger land masses.

ital'ic(s) *n* in printing, letters in sloping type (e.g. *italics*).

itch *n* **1** an irritation of the skin that causes a desire to scratch. **2** a longing:—*vb* **1** to feel an itch. **2** to feel a strong desire:—*adj* **itch'y.**

i'tem *n* **1** a single one out of a list or number of things. **2** a piece of news:—*adv* also, in the same way.

it'erate *vb* (*fml*) to repeat:—*n* **itera'tion.**

itin'erant *adj* not settling in any one place, moving from place to place.

itin'erary *n* a note of the places visited or to be visited on a journey.

i'vory *n* the hard white substance forming the tusks of elephants, etc:—*adj* of or like ivory, creamy white.

i'vy *n* an evergreen climbing plant.

J

jab *vb* (**jabbed'**, **jab'bing**) to prod or poke suddenly:—*n* **1** a sudden prod or poke. **2** (*inf*) an injection.

jab'ber *vb* to chatter, to speak quickly and indistinctly.

jack *n* **1** a tool for lifting heavy weights. **2** the small white ball aimed at in the game of bowls. **3** the knave in cards. **4** a young pike:—*vb* to raise with a jack.

jack'et *n* **1** a short coat. **2** a loose paper cover for a book.

jad'ed *adj* tired, bored, uninterested.

jag'ged *adj* having rough edges.

jag'uar *n* an animal like the leopard, found in South America.

jail *n* a prison.

jail'er *n* a prison guard.

jam¹ *n* fruit boiled with sugar to preserve it.

jam² *vb* (**jammed'**, **jam'ming**) **1** to squeeze in, to fix so tightly that movement is impossible, to wedge in. **2** to crowd full:—*n* a pile-up of traffic.

jan'gle *n* a harsh ringing noise:—*vb* **1** to make or cause to make a jangle. **2** (*inf*) to irritate.

jan'itor *n* **1** a doorkeeper. **2** one who looks after a building or place.

Jan'uary *n* the first month of the year.

jar *n* a glass or earthenware vessel with a wide mouth.

jar'gon *n* words special to a group or profession.

jaunt *n* a short pleasure trip.

jaun'ty *adj* cheerful-looking, confident

jaw *n* one of the bones in the mouth that hold the teeth.

jay *n* a bird of the crow family with brightly colored feathers.

jea'lous *adj* **1** disliking rivals in love, having feelings of dislike for any possible rivals. **2** disliking another because he or she is better off than oneself in some way, envious. **3** (*fml*) very careful of:—*n* **jea'lousy**.

jeans *npl* close-fitting trousers often made of denim.

jeep *n* a light truck, military or otherwise, for going over rough ground.

jeer *vb* to laugh or shout at disrespectfully, to mock:—*n* insulting words.

Jel'lo *n trademark* jelly.

jel'ly *n* **1** a sweet food made by boiling the juice of fruit with sugar and mixing with gelatin to make it set. **2** a type of preserved fruit. **3** a material that is in a state between solid and liquid.

jel'lyfish *n* a jelly-like sea creature.

jeopardize [je'-pêr-dî z] *vb* to put in danger, to risk.

jeopardy [je'-pêr-di] *n* danger.

jerk *vb* **1** to give a sudden pull or push. **2** to move suddenly and quickly:—*n* a sudden, quick movement.

jer'sey *n* **1** a close-fitting knitted upper garment. **2** a fine wool.

jest *n* a joke, something done or said in fun:—*vb* to joke.

jet *n* **1** a stream of liquid or gas forced through a narrow opening. **2** a spout through which a narrow stream of liquid or gas can be forced. **3** a jet plane.

jet'-black *adj* deep black.

jet plane *n* an airplane that is jet-propelled, i.e. driven forward by the force of jets of gas forced out to the rear.

jet'ty *n* **1** a wall built to protect a harbor from high seas.

jew'el *n* **1** a precious stone. **2** something valued highly.

jew'eler *n* one who buys and sells jewels.

jew'elry *n* jewels, personal ornaments, as rings, necklaces, etc.

jib *vb* (**jibbed'**, **jib'bing**) to object and refuse to proceed with.

jibe *same as* **gibe**.

jif'fy *n* (*inf*) a moment, an instant.

jig *n* a lively dance tune:—*also vb*.

jig'saw *n* a saw with a narrow fine-toothed blade for cutting irregular shapes.

jigsaw (puzzle) *n* a picture that has been cut into different shapes and the puzzle is to try to fit them together again.

jilt *vb* to leave someone after promising to love or marry him or her.

jin'gle *n* a light ringing noise made by metal against metal, as by small bells or coins:—*vb* to ring lightly, to clink.

job *n* **1** a piece of work. **2** one's employment.

jock'ey *n* a rider in horse races:—*vb* to persuade or manipulate a person gradually and skillfully into doing something

jodh'purs *npl* riding breeches reaching to the ankle.

jog *vb* (**jogged'**, **jog'ging**) **1** to nudge, to prod. **2** to walk or run at a slow, steady pace:—*n* **1** a nudge, a slight shake. **2** a slow walk or trot:—*n* **jog'ger**.

join *vb* **1** to put or fasten together. **2** to take part in with others. **3** to become a member of:—*n* a place where things join:—**join battle** to begin fighting.

join'er *n* a worker in wood, who makes furniture, etc.

joint *n* **1** a place at which two things meet or are fastened together. **2** a place where two things are joined but left the power of moving (e.g. as at the elbow or in a hinge). **3** (*inf*) a cheap bar or restaurant:—*adj* **1** shared between two or among all. **2** done by several together:—*also vb*.

joint'ly *adv* together.

joist *n* one of the beams of wood supporting the floor or ceiling.

joke *n* something said or done to cause laughter:—*also vb*.

jol'ly *adj* merry, cheerful.

jolt *vb* **1** to give a sudden jerk to. **2** to move along jerkily:—*n* **1** a sudden jerk. **2** a shock.

jostle [jos'-êl] *vb* to knock or push against.

jot *n* a small amount:—*vb* (**jot'ted**, **jot'ting**) to write down in short form.

journal [jur'-nêl] *n* **1** (*usu in titles*) a daily newspaper. **2** a weekly or monthly magazine. **3** a record of the events of every day.

jour'nalism *n* the work of preparing or writing for newspapers and magazines.

jour'nalist *n* one whose job is journalism.

jour'ney *n* a distance traveled, esp over land:—*vb* to travel.

jo'vial *adj* merry, joyful, cheerful:—*n* **jovial'ity**.

jowl *n* the jaw, the lower part of the cheek.

joy *n* **1** delight, gladness. **2** a cause of great happiness.

joy'ful, joy'ous *adjs* full of joy.

joy ride *n* (*inf*) a drive for pleasure in an automobile (often one that does not belong to the driver):—*vb* **joy'-ride**.

joy'stick *n* **1** the pilot's lever to control an airplane. **2** a control lever on a computer.

ju'bilant *adj* rejoicing greatly.

jubila'tion *n* triumphant joy.

ju'bilee *n* **1** a special anniversary of an event. **2** a celebration of this:—**golden jubilee** a fiftieth anniversary:—**silver jubilee** a twenty-fifth anniversary:—**diamond jubilee** a sixtieth anniversary.

judge *n* **1** one who presides in a court of law giving advice on matters of law and deciding on the punishment for guilty persons. **2** one asked to settle a disagreement:—*vb* **1** to act as judge in a court of law. **2** to decide, to give an opinion on. **3** to decide which is the best in a competition. **4** (*fml*) to criticize or blame someone.

judg'ment *n* **1** act or power of judging. **2** the decision given at the end of a law case. **3** good sense. **4** an opinion.

ju'do *n* a Japanese system of unarmed combat

jug *n* a pitcher.

jug'gle *vb* **1** to keep on throwing things up, catching them, and throwing them up again with great quickness of hand. **2** to change the arrangement of something in order to get a satisfactory result or to deceive:—*n* **jug'gler.**

juice *n* the liquid of a fruit or plant:—*adj* **juic'y.**

ju-jit'su *n* a form of self-defense first used in Japan.

Ju'ly *n* the seventh month of the year.

jum'ble *vb* to mix in an untidy heap:—*n* a muddle.

jump *vb* **1** to push off the ground with the feet so that the whole body moves through the air. **2** to make a sudden quick movement or start, as when surprised:—*n* **1** a leap. **2** a sudden, quick movement. **3** an obstacle to be jumped over:—**jump at** to accept willingly:—**jump to conclusions** to take things as true without waiting for proof.

jump'er *n* **1** one who jumps. **2** a sleeveless dress usu worn over blouse, etc. **3** a close-fitting garment put on over the head.

junc'tion *n* **1** (*fml*) a joining point. **2** a station where several railroad lines meet.

junc'ture *n* moment, point, stage.

June *n* the sixth month of the year.

jungle [jun(g)'-gĕl] *n* land, esp in the tropics, covered with trees and matted undergrowth.

ju'nior *adj* **1** younger. **2** lower in rank:—*also n.*

junk *n* old or unwanted things, rubbish.

junk food *n* a snack with little nutritional value.

ju'ror *n* a member of a jury.

ju'ry *n* a number of persons who have sworn to give a fair and honest opinion of the facts related in a law case.

just *adj* **1** right and fair. **2** honest, fair, moral. **3** reasonable, based on one's rights. **4** deserved:—*adv* **1** exactly. **2** on the point of. **3** quite. **4** merely, only. **5** barely. **6** very lately or recently.

jus'tice *n* **1** fairness or rightness in the treatment of other people. **2** a judge.

justifica'tion *n* a reason for doing something, a defense.

jus'tify *vb* to show that something is right, just, reasonable, or excusable.

jut *vb* (**jut'ted, jut'ting**) to stick out.

ju'venile *adj* **1** having to do with young people. **2** typical of young people, childish:—*n* a young person.

K

kangaroo' *n* an Australian mammal with a pouch for its young and long strong hind legs by means of which it jumps along.

kara'te *n* a Japanese form of unarmed combat using the feet, hands, and elbows.

keel *n* the long beam or girder along the bottom of a ship from which the whole frame is built up:—*vb* **keel over 1** to capsize. **2** (*inf*) to fall down, to collapse.

keen *adj* **1** sharp. **2** eager, very interested:—*n* **keen'ness**.

keep *vb* (*pt, pp* **kept**) **1** to have something without being required to give it back. **2** not to give or throw away, to preserve. **3** to remain in a certain state. **4** to have charge of, to look after. **5** to pay for and look after. **6** to hold back. **7** to carry out. **8** to go on doing. **9** (*inf*) to remain in good condition:—*n* **1** (*fml*) care. **2** a strong tower in the center of a castle. **3** (*inf*) maintenance, food, and lodging:—**keep at** to go on trying to do.

keep'er *n* one who keeps or looks after.

keep'ing *n* care, charge.

keep'sake *n* a gift valued because of the giver.

keg *n* a small barrel.

ken'nel *n* a house for dogs.

ker'nel *n* **1** the eatable part in the center of a nut or fruit stone. **2** the most important part.

kero'sene *n* a liquid mixture obtained from shale or coal and used as aircraft fuel, solvent, etc.

ketch *n* a small two-masted sailing vessel.

ketch'up *n* a thick smooth sauce usu made of tomatoes and spices.

ket'tle *n* a metal vessel, with a spout and handle, used for boiling water:—**pretty kettle of fish** a great difficulty.

key [kee] *n* **1** an instrument for opening locks, winding clocks, etc. **2** one of the levers struck by the fingers on a piano, typewriter, etc. **3** the relationship of the notes in which a tune is written. **4** something that when known enables one to work out a code, problem, etc. **5** a translation. **6** a general mood, tone, or style.

key'board *n* the set of levers struck by the fingers on a piano, typewriter, etc:—*vb* to use a keyboard.

key'hole *n* the hole through which a key is put in a lock.

khaki [kä'-kee] *adj* dust-colored:—*n* yellowish-brown cloth originally used in making army uniforms.

kick [kik] *vb* **1** to strike with the foot. **2** (*of a gun*) to jerk back when fired:—*n* **1** a blow given with the foot. **2** the recoil of a gun. **3** (*inf*) a thrill, a feeling of pleasure. **4** strength, effectiveness.

kid *n* **1** a young goat. **2** goatskin leather. **3** (*inf*) a child:—*vb* (**kid'ded, kid'ding**) (*inf*) to deceive in fun.

kid'nap *vb* to carry off a person by force:—*n* **kid'naper**.

kid'ney *n* **1** one of two glands that cleanse the blood and pass the waste liquid out of the body. **2** the kidneys of certain animals used as food.

kill *vb* **1** to put to death. **2** to put an end to.

kil'o- *prefix* one thousand.

kil'ogram *n* a measure of weight = 1000 grams (about 2$^1/_5$ pounds).

kil'ometer *n* a measure of length = 1000 meters (about $^5/_8$ mile).

kil'owatt *n* a measure of electric power = 1000 watts.

kind [kïnd] *n* **1** sort, type, variety. **2** nature, character:—*adj* thoughtful and friendly, generous:—*n* **kind'ness**.

kindergart'en *n* a class or school for very young children.

kin'dle *vb* **1** to set on fire, to light. **2** to stir up.

kind'ly *adj* kind, friendly:—*also adv*:—*n* **kind'liness**.

king *n* **1** the male ruler of a state. **2** a playing card with a king's picture. **3** a piece in chess.

king'dom *n* a state ruled over by a king.

kink *n* **1** a backward twist in a rope, chain, etc. **2** an unusual or strange way of thinking about things.

ki'osk *n* **1** a small hut or stall for the sale of things. **2** a public telephone booth.

kiss *vb* to touch with the lips as a sign of love or respect:—*also n*.

kit *n* all the tools, etc, needed to do a job.

kitch'en *n* the room in which cooking is done.

kitchenette' *n* a small kitchen.

kite *n* **1** a type of hawk. **2** a toy made of paper or cloth stretched on a tight framework, flown in the air at the end of a string.

kit'ten *n* a young cat.

ki'wi *n* **1** a wingless tailless bird of New Zealand. **2** the fruit of an Asian vine.

knack [nak] *n* knowledge of the right way to do a thing, skill gained by practice.

knave [nāv] *n* **1** a rascal, a dishonest rogue. **2** the third picture in a pack of cards, the jack.

knead [need] *vb* to press into a dough or paste.

knee *n* the joint between the upper and lower parts of the leg.

kneel *vb* (*pt, pp* **knelt** *or* **kneeled'**) to go down or rest on the knees.

knickerbock'ers *npl* baggy breeches fastened by a band at the knee.

knick'ers *npl* **1** a woman's undergarment with elastic round the waist, pants. **2** knickerbockers.

knick'-knack *n* a small or dainty ornament.

knife [nïf] *n* (*pl* **knives**) a tool with a sharp edge for cutting:—*vb* to stab with a knife.

knight [nït] *n* **1** in olden days, one of honorable rank. **2** a rank awarded for service to society, entitling the holder to be called Sir. **3** a piece in chess:—*vb* to make (someone) a knight:—*n* **knight'hood**.

knit *vb* (**knit'ted** *or* **knit, knit'ting**) **1** to make woolen thread into garments by means of needles. **2** to join closely.

knives *see* knife.

knob *n* **1** a rounded part sticking out from a surface. **2** the round handle of something. **3a** round control switch. **4** a small lump.

knock *vb* **1** to strike. **2** to rap on a door. **3** (*inf*) to criticize:—*n* **1** a blow. **2** a rap.

knock'er *n* a hammer attached to a door for knocking.

knot *n* **1** the twisting of two parts or pieces of string, etc, together so that they will not part until untied. **2** a hard piece of the wood of a tree, from which a branch grew out. **3** a small group of people. **4** a measure of speed at sea (about 1.15 miles per hour):—*vb* to tie in a knot.

know [nō] *vb* (*pt* **knew**, *pp* **known**) **1** to be aware of. **2** to have information or knowledge about. **3** to have learned and remember. **4** to be aware of the identity of, to be acquainted with. **5** to recognize or identify.

know'ledge *n* **1** that which is known, information. **2** the whole of what can be learned or found out.

knuck'le *n* a finger joint:—*vb* **knuckle down** to start working hard:—**knuckle under** to be forced to accept the authority of someone, to give in to.

knuck'le-dust'er *n* a blunt metal instrument fixed on the hand as a weapon.

koa'la *n* a small bear-like animal found in Australia.

L

la'bel n a piece of paper or card fixed to something to give information about it:—vb to fix a label to.

la'bor n 1 hard work. 2 childbirth. 3 all workers as a body:—also adj:—vb 1 to work hard. 2 to be employed to do hard and unskilled work. 3 to do something slowly or with difficulty.

lab'oratory n a workshop used for scientific experiments.

la'borer n a person who does unskilled work.

lace n 1 a cord used for tying opposite edges together. 2 an ornamental network of thread:—vb to fasten with a lace.

lack vb to want, to need, to be without:—n want, need.

lackadai'sical adj lacking energy or interest.

lacquer [la'-kêr] n 1 a varnish. 2 a substance used to keep hair in place:—vb to paint with lacquer.

lacrosse' n a team ball game played with long-handled rackets.

lad n a boy, a youth.

lad'der n 1 a frame of two poles or planks, joined by short crossbars, used as steps for going up or down. 2 something resembling a ladder in form or use.

lad'en adj loaded.

la'dle n a large long-handled spoon for lifting liquids:—vb to lift with a ladle.

la'dy n 1 a woman of rank or with good manners. 2 in Britain, the title of the wife of a knight or of a man of higher rank.

la'dybird n a small beetle, usu red with black spots.

lag vb (**lagged'**, **lag'ging**) 1 to go too slowly, not to keep pace with, to fall behind. 2 not to keep up with.

lager [lä'-gêr] n a light beer.

lagoon' n a shallow salt-water lake cut off from the sea by sandbanks or rocks.

laid pt of **lay**.

lair n a wild beast's den.

lake n a large stretch of water surrounded by land.

lamb n a young sheep.

lame adj unable to walk well because of an injured or badly formed leg. 2 not good, inadequate:—vb to make lame:—n lame'ness.

lament' vb 1 to show grief or sorrow for, to mourn for. 2 to express regret for:—n 1 the expressing of great grief. 2 a mournful song or tune:—n lamenta'tion.

lam'entable adj much to be regretted, extremely unsatisfactory.

lamp n any device producing light.

lance n a long spear used by horse soldiers:—vb 1 to wound or hit with a lance. 2 to cut open with a lancet.

land n 1 the solid part of the earth's surface. 2 country. 3 ground, soil:—vb to bring, put, or go ashore, to touch down.

land'ing n 1 the act of going ashore. 2 a place for going on shore. 3 the corridor opening on to the rooms at the top of a flight of stairs.

land'lady n 1 a woman who keeps an inn or boarding house. 2 a woman who rents out rooms, apartments, or houses.

land'lord n 1 a man who rents out rooms, apartments, or houses. 2 a man who keeps an inn or boarding house.

land'mark n 1 an easily recognized object from which travelers can tell where they are. 2 a very important event.

land'scape n 1 a view of the country seen from one position. 2 a picture of the countryside.

land'slide n the falling of a mass of earth, etc, down the side of a mountain.

lane n 1 a narrow road. 2 a narrow passage or alley between buildings. 3 any of the parallel parts into which roads are divided for a single line of traffic. 4 the route intended for or

regularly used by ships or aircraft. 5 a marked strip of track, water, etc, for a competitor in a race.

lan'guage n 1 meaningful speech. 2 the speech of one people. 3 words.

lan'guid adj weak, slow-moving.

lan'guish vb 1 to lose strength, to become weak. 2 to experience long suffering.

lank adj 1 tall and thin, lanky. 2 straight and limp.

lank'y adj ungracefully tall and thin.

lan'tern n a case, usu of glass, that encloses and protects a light.

lap¹ n 1 the seat formed by the knees and thighs of a person sitting. 2 one round of a course in a race.

lap² vb (**lapped'**, **lap'ping**) 1 to lick up. 2 to wash against in little waves:—n the sound made by small waves.

lap'dog n a small pet dog.

lapel' n the folded back part of the breast of a coat or jacket.

lapse n 1 a mistake, a small error or fault. 2 the passing (of time):—vb 1 to fall out of use. 2 to come to an end. 3 to pass gradually into a less active or less desirable state.

lar'ceny n stealing, theft.

lard n the fat of pigs, prepared for use in cooking.

lar'der n a room or cupboard for storing food.

large adj more than usual in size, number, or amount, big:—at large free, at liberty.

lark n 1 a songbird. 2 something done for fun:—vb to play tricks.

lar'va n (pl **lar'vae**) the form of an insect on coming out of the egg, a grub.

lar'ynx n the upper part of the windpipe, containing the vocal chords that produce the voice.

lash n 1 the cord of a whip. 2 a blow given with a whip:—vb 1 to whip, to strike hard or often. 2 to fasten by tying tightly.

lass n a girl.

lasso [las-ö'] n (pl **lassos'** or **lassoes'**) a rope with a running knot for catching animals:—vb to catch with a lasso.

last¹ adj 1 coming after all others. 2 latest. 3 final:—adv at the last time or place:—at last in the end.

last² vb 1 to go on. 2 to continue.

last name n a surname.

latch n a small piece of wood or metal for keeping a door shut:—vb to fasten with a latch.

latch'key n the key for the main door of a house.

late adj 1 arriving after the time fixed. 2 far on in time. 3 now dead. 4 recent:—adv after the time fixed:—n late'ness.

late'ly adv in recent times, recently.

lat'eral adj on, at, or from the side.

lath'er n 1 froth of soap and water. 2 froth from sweat:—vb 1 to cover with lather. 2 to become frothy.

Lat'in n the language of ancient Rome.

lat'itude n 1 distance north or south of the equator. 2 freedom from controls.

lat'ter adj 1 near the end of a period of time. 2 second of two just spoken of.

lat'terly adv recently, lately, in the last part of a period of time.

lat'tice n a network of crossed bars or strips as of wood:—adj lat'ticed.

laugh [laf] vb to make a sound expressing amusement or pleasure:—n the sound of laughing.

laugh'able adj causing people to laugh, ridiculous.

laugh'ing-stock n a person laughed at and made fun of by everyone.

laugh'ter n the act or sound of laughing.

84

launch vb 1 to put into motion, to send on its course. 2 to cause (a ship) to move into the water. 3 to put into action, to set going:—n 1 the act of launching. 2 a large motorboat.
laun'dry n a place where clothes, etc, are washed and ironed.
la'va n the melted rock emitted by a volcano.
lav'atory n a toilet.
lav'ender n 1 a plant with sweet-smelling flowers. 2 a light purple color.
lav'ish adj 1 giving freely, generous. 2 given or spent in great quantities:—vb to give or spend lavishly.
law n a rule or set of rules laid down for a people or a group of people by a person or persons with recognized authority.
law'-abid'ing adj obeying the law.
law court n a place where those who are said to have broken laws are brought before a judge.
law'ful adj allowed by law.
law'less adj not keeping the laws, wild.
lawn[1] n a stretch of carefully kept grass in a garden.
lawn[2] n a type of fine linen.
lawn'mower n a machine for cutting grass.
law'suit n claiming before a judge that another has broken the law.
lawn ten'nis n an outdoor game played with a ball and rackets.
law'yer n one skilled in the law.
lay[1] pt of **lie**.
lay[2] vb (pt, pp **laid**) 1 to cause to lie. 2 to place. 3 to make ready. 4 to produce eggs.
lay'er n an even spread of one substance over the surface of another.
lay'man n 1 one not a clergyman. 2 one not an expert or specialist.
laze vb to be lazy, to do nothing:—n **laz'iness**.
la'zy adj unwilling to work.
lead[1] [led] n 1 a soft heavy metal. 2 the stick of black lead or graphite in a pencil. 3 a piece of lead attached to a cord for finding the depth of water.
lead[2] [leed] vb (pt, pp **led**) 1 to go in front to show the way, to guide. 2 to act as a chief or commander. 3 to influence. 4 to spend (life) in a certain way:—n 1 a guiding suggestion or example. 2 a chief part. 3 the position ahead of all others. 4 a cord, etc, for leading a dog.
lead'er n 1 one who shows the way. 2 one who gives orders or takes charge. 3 a person or thing that is ahead of others 4 a newspaper article giving an opinion on a news item of interest (also **leading article**):—n **lead'ership**.
lead'ing adj chief, most important.
leaf n (pl **leaves**) 1 one of the thin, flat usu green blades growing out of the stem of a plant or the branch of a tree. 2 a single sheet of paper in a book with pages printed on both sides. 3 the movable part of a table-top or double door.
leaf'let n a printed sheet of paper, usu folded and free of charge, containing information.
league [leeg] n 1 a group of people or nations bound by agreement to help each other. 2 a group of sports clubs or players that play matches among themselves.
leak n 1 a hole by which water escapes (e.g. from a pipe) or enters a dry place. 2 a small accidental hole or crack through which something flows in or out. 3 the accidental or intentional making public of secret information:—vb 1 to let water in or out. 2 to get out through a hole or crack. 3 to make public that which is secret.
lean[1] vb (pt, pp **leaned** or **leant**) 1 to slope to one side. 2 to bend. 3 to rest against. 4 to have a preference for.
lean[2] adj 1 not having much fat. 2 thin, healthily thin:—n meat without fat:—n **lean'ness**.

lean'ing n preference, liking.
leap vb (pt, pp **leaped** or **leapt**) to jump:—n 1 a jump. 2 the height or distance jumped.
leap'frog n a game in which one player leaps over the others while they are bent double.
leap year n a year in which there are 366 days, occurring once every four years.
learn vb (pt, pp **learned** or **learnt**) 1 to gain knowledge or skill, to find out how to do something. 2 to come to understand, to realize. 3 to memorize, to fix in the memory.
learn'ed adj having much knowledge, gained by study.
learn'ing n knowledge gained by study.
leash n a cord or strap for leading animals:—vb to hold on a leash.
least adj smallest:—also n:—adv in the smallest degree.
lea'ther n material made by preparing animal skins in a certain way:—also adj:—vb (inf) to beat, to thrash.
leave n 1 permission. 2 permitted absence. 3 vacation. 4 farewell:—vb (pt, pp **left**) 1 to give to another at one's death. 2 to cause to be or remain in a particular state or condition. 3 to go without taking. 4 to depart. 5 to desert. 6 to entrust to another. 7 to allow to remain unused, not taken, uneaten, etc.
leaven [lev'-ėn] n 1 a substance mixed with dough to make it rise. 2 (fml) anything helping to bring change:—vb to act as leaven.
leaves see **leaf**.
leav'ings npl that which is left as useless.
lec'ture n 1 a talk on a certain subject. 2 a scolding:—vb 1 to give a lecture. 2 to scold:—n **lec'turer**.
led pt of **lead**.
leek n a vegetable with broad flat leaves.
leer vb to look at sideways in a sly or unpleasant way:—also n.
lees npl tiny bits of matter settling at the bottom of a vessel of liquid.
left[1] pp of **leave**.
left[2] n 1 the side opposite to the right. 2 in politics, the socialist party:—also adj.
left-hand'ed adj better able to use the left hand than the right.
leg n 1 one of the limbs on which an animal stands or moves. 2 a support for a table, chair, etc:—**pull a person's leg** to play a joke on someone.
leg'acy n that which is left to one by will.
leg'al adj 1 having to do with the law. 2 allowed by law.
leg'alize vb to make legal.
leg'end n an ancient story passed on by word of mouth.
leg'endary adj 1 having to do with ancient legends, famous in story, existing only in story. 2 very famous.
legg'ings npl a thick covering for the lower leg.
leg'gy adj (inf) having very long legs.
leg'ible adj possible to read:—n **legibil'ity**.
le'gion n 1 a Roman regiment or division (3000–6000 soldiers). 2 a great number.
legisla'tion n 1 the act of making laws. 2 the laws made.
legit'imacy n being legitimate.
legit'imate adj 1 allowed by law, lawful. 2 born of married parents.
lei'sure n spare time, time free from work.
lei'sured adj having plenty of spare time.
lei'surely adj slow, unhurried:—also adv.
lem'on n 1 a pale yellow sharp-tasting fruit. 2 the tree bearing this fruit. 3 a pale yellow color.
lemonade' n a drink made from or tasting of lemon juice.
lend vb (pt, pp **lent**) to give something to another on condition that it is returned after use:—n **lend'er**.

length *n* measurement from end to end of space or time:—**at length 1** at last. **2** taking a long time, in detail.

length'en *vb* to make or become longer.

length'ways, length'wise *advs* in the direction of the length.

length'y *adj* very long.

le'nient *adj* **1** merciful. **2** not severe:—*ns* **le'nience, le'niency**.

lens *n* a transparent substance, usu glass, with a surface curved in such a way that objects seen through it appear bigger or smaller.

len'til *n* the eatable seed of a pea-like plant.

leopard [lep'-êrd] *n* a large, spotted animal of the cat family.

less *adj* smaller, not so much:—*n* a smaller amount:—*adv* not so greatly, not so much.

less'en *vb* to make or become less.

less'er *adj* less, smaller.

less'on *n* **1** something that is learned or taught. **2** a period of teaching. **3** a passage read from the Bible. **4** an example.

lest *conj* (*fml or old*) **1** in order that . . . not. **2** for fear that.

let *vb* (**let, let'ting**) **1** to allow. **2** to allow the use of for rent or payment:—*n* the act of letting for rent.

le'thal *adj* causing death.

lethar'gic *adj* sleepy, slow-moving, lacking interest.

leth'argy *n* lack of energy and interest.

lett'er *n* **1** a sign standing for a sound. **2** a written message. **3** (*fml*) *pl* literature, learning:—**letter of credit** a letter allowing the holder to draw money when away from home:—**to the letter** exactly.

lett'ering *n* letters that have been drawn, painted, etc.

lett'uce *n* a plant whose leaves are used in salads.

lev'el *n* **1** a flat, even surface. **2** an instrument for finding out whether a thing is flat. **3** a general standard of quality or quantity. **4** a horizontal division or floor in a house, etc:—*adj* **1** flat. **2** even. **3** on the same line or height:—*vb* **1** to make flat. **2** to make equal. **3** to destroy, to demolish. **4** to aim.

level-head'ed *adj* sensible.

le'ver *n* a bar for raising heavy objects.

le'verage *n* power gained by the use of a lever.

lev'eret *n* a young hare.

liabil'ity *n* **1** debt. **2** the state of being liable. **3** something for which one is responsible.

li'able *adj* **1** likely to have to or suffer from. **2** legally responsible for. **3** likely to get, be punished with, etc.

liaison [lee-âz'-ên(g)] *n* a close connection or working association.

li'ar *n* one who tells lies.

li'bel *n* something written that damages a person's reputation:—*also vb*.

li'belous *adj* hurtful to one's reputation.

lib'eral *adj* **1** generous. **2** ready to accept new ideas:—*n* one who believes in greater political freedom.

lib'erate *vb* to set free:—*n* **libera'tion**.

lib'erator *n* one who sets free.

lib'ertine *n* (*fml*) one who openly leads a wicked, immoral life.

lib'erty *n* **1** freedom. **2** the right to do as one likes. **3** too great freedom of speech or action.

libra'rian *n* one in charge of a library.

li'brary *n* **1** a collection of books. **2** a room or building in which books are kept.

lice *see* **louse**.

li'cense *n* **1** a written permission to do or keep something. **2** (*fml*) too great freedom of action:—*vb* to give a license to.

lichen [lī'-ken] *n* a moss that grows on rocks, tree trunks, etc.

lick *vb* **1** to pass the tongue over. **2** to take (food or drink) into the mouth with the tongue. **3** (*inf*) to defeat. **4** (*inf*) to thrash:—*n* **1** act of passing the tongue over. **2** a blow.

lic'orice *n* **1** a black sweet-tasting root used in making medicines and sweets. **2** a kind of candy made from this.

lid *n* the movable cover of a pot, box, etc.

lie¹ *n* a statement that the maker knows to be untrue:—*vb* (**lied, ly'ing**) to tell a lie.

lie² *vb* (**lay, ly'ing, pp lain**) **1** to put the body full length upon. **2** to be or remain in a certain place:—*n* the way in which something lies.

lieu [lū] *n*:—**in lieu of** instead of.

lieutenant [lu-ten'-ênt] *n* **1** (*fml*) one who does the work of another, deputy. **2** a naval or army officer.

life *n* (*pl* **lives**) **1** the state of being alive. **2** the force existing in animals and plants that gives them the ability to change with the passing of time. **3** liveliness, activity. **4** the time one has been alive. **5** the story of one's life.

life-belt *n* a belt of a material that floats easily and so helps to prevent the wearer sinking when in water.

life'boat *n* a boat that goes to the help of those in danger at sea.

life buoy *n* an object that floats easily and to which ship-wrecked people can hold until help arrives.

life'guard *n* an expert swimmer employed to prevent drownings.

life'less *adj* **1** dead. **2** dull. **3** not lively.

life'like *adj* seeming to have life.

life'-size, life'-sized *adj* of the same size as the person or thing represented.

life'time *n* the length of time a person lives.

lift *vb* **1** to raise up higher. **2** to pay off (a mortgage, etc):—*n* **1** an elevator. **2** a free ride in a private vehicle.

lig'ament *n* a band of tough substance joining bones together at joints.

light¹ *n* **1** that which makes it possible for the eye to see things. **2** anything that gives light, as the sun, a lamp, etc. **3** knowledge, understanding. **4** brightness in the eyes or face:—*adj* **1** clear, not dark. **2** not deep or dark in color:—*vb* (*pt, pp* **lit**) to give light to, to set fire to.

light² *adj* **1** not heavy. **2** not difficult. **3** not severe. **4** small in amount. **5** not serious, for entertainment. **6** graceful. **7** happy, merry.

light³ *vb* to come upon by chance.

light'en¹ *vb* **1** to make bright. **2** to flash.

light'en² *vb* to make less heavy.

light'er *n* a device for setting something alight.

light'-head'ed *adj* giddy, dizzy.

light'-heart'ed *adj* **1** merry, cheerful. **2** not serious.

light'house *n* a tower with a light to guide ships.

light'ning *adj* the electric flash seen before thunder is heard.

light year *n* the distance light travels in a year.

like¹ *adj* nearly the same, resembling:—*prep* in the same way as:—*n* a person or thing nearly the same as or equal to another.

like² *vb* **1** to be pleased by. **2** to be fond of.

like'able, lik'able *adj* attractive, pleasant.

like'lihood *n* probability.

like'ly *adj* **1** probable. **2** suitable:—*adv* probably.

lik'en *vb* to compare.

like'ness *n* **1** resemblance. **2** a picture of a person.

likes *npl* things pleasing to one.

like'wise *adv* **1** in the same way. **2** also.

lik'ing *n* a fondness or preference for.

li'lac n 1 a type of small tree with light-purple or white flowers. 2 a light purple color:—adj light purple.

lilt vb to sing cheerfully:—n 1 a regular pattern of rising and falling sound. 2 a cheerful song. 3 a tune with a strongly marked rhythm.

li'ly n a flower grown from a bulb, often white in color.

limb [lim] n 1 an arm, leg, or wing. 2 a branch of a tree.

lime[1] n a white substance got by heating certain kinds of rock.

lime[2] n 1 a small lemon-like, yellowish-green fruit. 2 the tree bearing this fruit.

lime'light n:—**in the limelight** in a position in which one's doings are followed with interest by many people.

lime'stone n rock containing much lime.

lim'it n 1 a boundary. 2 that which one may not go past. 3 the greatest or smallest amount or number that is fixed as being correct, legal, necessary, desirable, etc:—vb to keep within bounds.

limita'tion n 1 that which limits. 2 inability to do something, weakness.

lim'ited adj 1 small in amount. 2 not very great, large, wide-ranging, etc.

limp[1] vb to walk lamely:—also n.

limp[2] adj 1 not stiff, drooping. 2 without energy or strength.

lim'pet n a shellfish that clings tightly to rocks.

lim'pid adj clear, transparent.

line n 1 a length of rope or cord. 2 a thin mark made with a pen, pencil, etc. 3 a row of persons or things. 4 a row of words on a page. 5 a short letter. 6 a railroad track. 7 an orderly line of persons waiting their turn. 8 ancestors and descendants. 9 a fleet of steamers, airplanes, etc, providing regular services. 10 (inf) the equator. 11 a telephone wire. 12 (inf) way of behaving or of earning one's living. 13 pl the positions of an army ready to attack or defend:—vb 1 to mark with lines. 2 to arrange in a row or rows. 3 to cover on the inside. 4 to form a line.

lin'ear adj having to do with lines.

lin'en n cloth made of flax.

li'ner n 1 a large ocean-going passenger ship. 2 something that lines.

lin'ger vb 1 to delay before going. 2 to stay about, to last or continue for a long time.

lin'guist n one skilled in foreign languages.

linguis'tic adj having to do with the study of languages.

lin'ing n the covering of the inside of something, such as a garment or box.

link n 1 one ring of a chain. 2 that which connects one thing with another:—vb to connect, to join.

lino'leum n a floor covering made of cloth coated with linseed oil.

lint n linen specially prepared for dressing open wounds.

li'on n 1 a large flesh-eating animal of the cat family. 2 a famous and important person:—f **li'oness—lion's share** the largest share.

lip n 1 either of the edges of the opening of the mouth. 2 the edge or brim of anything.

liq'uid adj 1 in the form of a liquid. 2 clear. 3 (of sounds) smooth and clear, as the letter r or l:—n a substance that flows and has no fixed shape, a substance that is not a solid or gas.

liq'uidate vb 1 to pay debts. 2 to close down a business when it has too many debts. 3 to put an end to, to get rid of, to destroy:—n **liquida'tion**.

liquor [li'-ker] n 1 strong drink, such as spirits. 2 the liquid produced from cooked food.

liquor store n a place where alcohol is sold for consumption off the premises.

lisp vb 1 to say the sound th for s when speaking. 2 to speak as a small child does:—also n.

list[1] n a series of names, numbers, etc, written down in order one after the other:—vb to write down in order.

list[2] vb to lean over to one side:—also n.

listen [lis'-ên] vb 1 to try to hear. 2 to pay attention to:—n **list'ener**.

list'less adj lacking energy, uninterested.

lit pt of **light**.

li'ter n in the metric system, a measure of liquid (about $1\frac{3}{4}$ pints).

lit'eracy n ability to read and write.

lit'eral adj 1 with each word given its ordinary meaning, word for word. 2 following the exact meaning without any exaggeration or anything added from the imagination:—adv **lit'erally**.

lit'erary adj having to do with literature or with writing as a career.

lit'erate adj able to read and write.

lit'erature n 1 the books, etc, written on a particular subject. 2 written works, esp those of lasting interest and of fine quality and artistic value.

lithe [liTH] adj able to bend or twist easily.

lit'ter n 1 the young of an animal born at one time. 2 scraps of paper and garbage lying about:—vb to make untidy, to scatter about.

lit'tle adj 1 small. 2 short. 3 young:—n 1 a small amount. 2 a short time:—adv not much.

live[1] vb 1 to have life, to exist, to be alive. 2 to continue to be alive. 3 to dwell, to have one's home. 4 to behave in a certain way. 5 to keep oneself alive, obtain the food or goods necessary for life. 6 to pass or spend one's life:—**live down** to live in a way that makes others overlook one's past faults.

live[2] adj 1 having life, alive. 2 full of energy, capable of becoming active. 3 heard or seen as the event takes place, not recorded. 4 burning.

live'lihood n the work by which one earns one's living.

live'ly adj active, energetic, cheerful:—n **live'liness**.

li'ven vb to make more cheerful.

liv'er n 1 an organ inside the body that helps to cleanse the blood. 2 this organ from certain animals used as food.

live'stock n animals kept on a farm.

liv'id adj 1 discolored, black and blue. 2 (inf) very angry.

liv'ing n 1 a means of providing oneself with what is necessary for life. 2 employment as a member of clergy in the Anglican Church.

liz'ard n a four-footed reptile with a long tail.

load vb 1 to put a burden on the back of an animal. 2 to put goods into a vehicle. 3 to put a heavy weight on. 4 to put ammunition into a gun. 5 to put film into a camera:—n 1 that which is carried. 2 a weight. 3 a cargo.

loaf[1] n (pl **loaves**) bread made into a shape convenient for selling.

loaf[2] vb to pass time without doing anything, to laze around:—n **loaf'er**.

loan n that which is lent.

loath adj unwilling.

loathe vb to hate.

loaves see **loaf**[1].

lob'by n an entrance hall.

lobe n the fleshy hanging part of the ear.

lob'ster n a long-tailed jointed shellfish.

lo'cal adj having to do with a particular place.

local'ity n a district, area, neighborhood.

lo'calize vb to keep to one place or district.

locate' vb 1 to find the place of. 2 to fix or set in a certain place.

loca'tion n 1 place. 2 the place where a story is filmed.

loch n 1 a lake, esp in Scotland. 2 an arm of the sea.

lock n 1 a fastening bolt moved by a key. 2 the part of a gun by which it is fired. 3 a section of a canal, enclosed by gates, in which the amount of water can be increased to raise a ship to a higher level, or vice versa. 4 a firm grasp. 5 a curl of hair:—vb 1 to fasten with lock and key. 2 to hold firmly. 3 to jam, to become fixed or blocked.

lock'er n a small cupboard with a lock.

lock'et n a small metal case, often containing a picture, worn on a chain around the neck as an ornament.

lock'smith n one who makes or repairs locks.

locomo'tive n a railroad engine.

lo'cust n a large grasshopper that feeds on and destroys crops.

lodge n 1 a small house originally for a gatekeeper at the entrance to a park, church, etc. 2 a house or cabin used occasionally for some seasonal activity:—vb 1 to put in a certain place. 2 to stay in another's house on payment. 3 to fix in:—**lodge a complaint** to make an official complaint.

lodg'er n one who stays in rented rooms in another's house.

lodg'ing n a place where one can stay on payment.

loft n 1 the space under the roof of a building. 2 a room over a stable or barn. 3 a gallery in a church, etc:—vb to send into a high curve.

loft'y adj 1 (lit) very high. 2 of high moral quality. 3 proud, haughty:—n **loft'iness**.

log n 1 a piece sawn from the trunk or one of the large branches of a tree. 2 an instrument for measuring the speed of ships. 3 an official written record of a journey.

log'arithms n numbers arranged in a table by referring to which calculations can be done quickly.

log'book n 1 a book in which the rate of progress of a ship is written daily. 2 an official written record of a journey.

log'gerheads npl:—**at loggerheads** quarreling.

lo'gic n 1 the art or science of reasoning. 2 a particular way of thinking or reasoning. 3 (inf) reasonable thinking, good sense.

lo'gical adj 1 having to do with logic. 2 well reasoned. 3 able to reason correctly.

loi'ter vb 1 to stand about idly. 2 to go slowly, often stopping.

loll vb 1 to sit back or lie lazily. 2 (of the tongue) to hang out.

loll'ipop n a sweetmeat on a stick.

lone adj alone, single, without others.

lone'ly adj sad because alone.

long adj 1 not short, in time or space. 2 having length, covering a certain distance from one end to the other or a certain time. 3 (of drinks) containing little or no alcohol and served in a long glass:—adv for a long time:—vb to want very much.

longev'ity n very long life.

long'ing n an eager desire.

lon'gitude n 1 length. 2 distance in degrees east or west of an imaginary line running through Greenwich (London).

long-sight'ed adj able to see distant objects more clearly than near ones.

long-suff'ering adj patient, ready to put up with troubles without complaint.

look vb 1 to turn the eyes toward so as to see. 2 to have a certain appearance. 3 to face in a certain direction:—n 1 act of looking. 2 a glance. 3 the appearance, esp of the face:—**look after** to take care of:—**look down on** to despise:—**look for** 1 to try to find. 2 to hope for:—**look on** to watch:—**look out**

1 to be careful. 2 to watch out for. 3 to search for and find, to choose:—**look over** to examine

look'ing glass n a mirror.

loom[1] n a machine for weaving cloth.

loom[2] vb 1 to appear gradually and dimly, as in the dark, to seem larger than natural. 2 to seem threateningly close.

loon[1] n a large fish-eating diving bird.

loon[2] n (inf) a clumsy, stupid, or crazy person.

loop n 1 a line that curves back and crosses itself. 2 a rope, cord, etc, that so curves:—vb 1 to make a loop. 2 to fasten in a loop.

loose adj 1 untied, not packed together in a box, etc. 2 free, at liberty. 3 not definite. 4 careless. 5 not tight. 6 indecent, immoral:—vb 1 to untie. 2 to set free.

loos'en vb to make or become loose or less tight.

loot n that which is stolen or carried off by force:—also vb.

lop vb (**lopped**, **lop'ping**) to cut off.

lop-sid'ed adj leaning to one side.

lord n 1 a master. 2 a ruler. 3 a noble. 4 a title of honor. 5 an owner:—vb to rule strictly or harshly.

lord'ly adj 1 proud, grand. 2 commanding.

lose [lûz] vb (pt, pp **lost**) 1 to cease to have. 2 to fail to keep in one's possession. 3 to be defeated in. 4 to fail to use, to waste. 5 to miss. 6 (of a watch or clock) to work too slowly. 7 to have less of:—**lose one's head** to become too excited to act sensibly.

loss n 1 act of losing. 2 that which is lost. 3 harm, damage:—**at a loss** not knowing what to do.

lost pt of **lose**.

lot n 1 one of a set of objects, a separate part. 2 a set of objects sold together at an auction. 3 the way of life that one has to follow. 4 a large number. 5 a piece of land.

lo'tion n a liquid for healing wounds, cleansing the skin, etc.

lott'ery n a game of chance in which prizes are shared out among those whose tickets are picked out in a public draw.

loud adj 1 easily heard. 2 noisy. 3 unpleasantly bright, showy.

loudspeak'er n a radio apparatus by which sound is transmitted and made louder when necessary.

lounge vb 1 to stand about lazily, to move lazily, to spend time in an idle way. 2 to sit or lie back in a comfortable position:—n 1 a comfortably furnished sitting room. 2 a public room in a hotel:—n **loung'er**.

lour same as **lower**[2].

louse n (pl **lice**) a wingless insect that lives on the bodies of animals.

lous'y adj 1 full of or covered with lice. 2 (inf) very bad, poor.

loutre see **lower**[2].

lout n a rude and clumsy fellow.

lov'able adj worthy of love.

love n 1 a strong liking for. 2 a feeling of desire for. 3 the person or thing loved. 4 (in some games) no score:—vb 1 to be fond of, to like. 2 to be strongly attracted to, to be in love with:—n **lov'er**.

love'ly adj 1 beautiful. 2 (inf) very pleasing:—n **love'liness**.

lov'ing adj full of love, fond.

low adj 1 not far above the ground. 2 not tall, not high. 3 small in degree, amount, etc. 4 not high in rank or position. 5 cheap. 6 vulgar, coarse. 7 dishonorable. 8 soft, not loud. 9 sad, unhappy.

low'er[1] adj 1 not so high. 2 to let or bring down. 3 to make of less value or worth.

low'er[2], **lour** vb 1 to frown. 2 to become dark.

low'land n low-lying or level country.

low'ly adj 1 (fml or hum) humble, not high in rank. 2 (old or lit) gentle in manner.

loy'al *adj* **1** faithful to one's friends, duty, etc. **2** true:—*n* **loy'alty**.

lu'bricate *vb* to oil something to make it run smoothly:—*ns* **lubrica'tion, lu'bricator**.

lu'cid *adj* clear, easily understood:—*n* **lucid'ity**.

luck *n* **1** the good or bad things that happen by chance, fate, fortune. **2** something good that happens by chance, good luck.

luck'less *adj* (*fml*) unfortunate.

luck'y *adj* fortunate, having good luck.

lu'crative *adj* bringing in much money or profit.

lu'dicrous *adj* funny, silly, and laughable.

lug *vb* (**lugged', lug'ging**) to pull, draw, or carry with difficulty.

lug'gage *n* a traveler's baggage.

luke'warm *adj* **1** quite warm, neither hot nor cold. **2** not eager.

lull *vb* **1** to calm. **2** to send to sleep:—*n* an interval of calm.

lull'aby *n* a song sung to a baby to make it sleep.

lum'ber *n* **1** unused or useless articles. **2** wood of trees cut into timber:—*vb* **1** to move heavily and clumsily. **2** to give someone an unpleasant or unwanted responsibility or task.

lu'minous *adj* shining, giving light.

lump *n* **1** a shapeless mass. **2** a hard swelling:—*vb* to put together as one, to consider together.

lump'y *adj* full of lumps.

lu'nacy *n* madness.

lu'nar *adj* having to do with the moon.

lu'natic *n* a mad person:—*adj* mad, insane, very foolish.

lunch *n* a midday meal:—*vb* to take lunch.

lung *n* one of the two bodily organs by means of which we breathe.

lunge *n* a sudden move or thrust forward:—*vb* to make a sudden onward movement.

lurch *vb* to roll or sway to one side:—*n* a sudden roll:—**leave in the lurch** to leave (someone) in difficulty.

lure *n* something that attracts or leads on:—*vb* to attract, to lead on, as by promise or gifts.

lu'rid *adj* **1** too brightly colored, too vivid. **2** horrifying, shocking.

lurk *vb* **1** to remain out of sight. **2** to lie hidden, to exist unseen.

luscious [lu'-shês] *adj* very sweet in taste.

lush *adj* growing very plentifully, thick.

lust *n* a strong desire:—*vb* to desire very much:—*adj* **lust'ful**.

lus'ter *n* **1** brightness. **2** glory. **3** dress material with a shiny surface.

lus'ty *adj* **1** strong and healthy, full of energy. **2** strong or loud.

luxu'riant *adj* growing in great plenty.

luxu'rious *adj* **1** fond of luxury. **2** splendid and affluent.

lux'ury *n* **1** great ease and comfort. **2** a desirable or pleasing thing that is not a necessity of life.

ly'ing *pres p of* **lie**:—*also adj*.

lynch *vb* to seize someone, judge him or her on the spot, and put to death without a proper trial.

lynx *n* an animal of the cat family noted for keen sight.

lyr'ic *n* **1** a short poem expressing the writer's feelings. **2** *pl* the words of a song.

M

ma'am *short for* **madam**.

macaro'ni *n* flour paste rolled into long tubes.

machine' *n* 1 any apparatus for producing power or doing work. 2 a system under which the work of different groups is directed to one end. 3 a vehicle.

machine gun *n* a gun that fires many bullets in a short time before it has to be reloaded.

machin'ery *n* 1 machines. 2 parts of a machine. 3 organization.

machin'ist *n* one who makes, looks after, or operates machinery.

mack'erel *n* an eatable sea fish.

mack'intosh *n* a waterproof overcoat.

mad *adj* 1 insane. 2 out of one's mind with anger, pain, etc. 3 (*inf*) very angry. 4 (*inf*) very unwise, crazy.

mad'am *n* the title used in addressing a woman politely.

madd'en *vb* to make mad.

mad'man *n* one who is mad.

mad'ness *n* 1 insanity. 2 folly.

mag'azine *n* 1 a store for firearms and explosives. 2 a weekly or monthly paper containing articles, stories, etc.

mag'got *n* the grub of certain insects, esp the fly or bluebottle.

ma'gic *n* 1 the art of controlling spirits, so gaining knowledge of the future or commanding certain things to happen, witchcraft. 2 the art of producing illusions by tricks or sleight of hand. 3 fascination:—**black magic** magic done with the aid of evil spirits.

ma'gic, ma'gical *adjs* 1 having to do with magic. 2 (*inf*) marvelous, very good.

magi'cian *n* 1 one with magic powers. 2 a person who practices the art of producing illusions by tricks or sleight of hand.

ma'gistrate *n* a public officer empowered to administer the law.

mag'net *n* 1 a piece of iron that attracts to it other pieces of iron and that when hung up points to the north. 2 a person or thing that attracts.

magnet'ic *adj* 1 acting like a magnet. 2 attractive.

mag'netism *n* 1 the power of the magnet. 2 the science that deals with the power of the magnet. 3 personal charm or attraction.

magnif'icent *adj* splendid, grand:—*n* **magnif'icence**.

mag'nify *vb* 1 to make appear larger, to exaggerate. 2 to praise.

mag'nifying glass *n* a glass with a curved surface that makes things appear larger.

mag'nitude *n* 1 greatness of size or extent. 2 importance.

mag'pie *n* a black and white bird of the crow family.

mahog'any *n* a reddish brown wood much used for furniture.

maid *n* a female servant.

maid'en *n* (*old*) a young unmarried woman.

maiden name *n* the last name of a married woman before marriage.

maiden voyage *n* the first voyage of a new ship.

mail¹ *n* 1 the postal service. 2 letters, parcels, etc, sent by post:—*vb* to send by post.

mail² *n* (*old*) armor.

mail'box *n* 1 a public box in which letters may be posted. 2 a box near a house for the occupant's mail.

mail'man *n* one who delivers letters.

maim *vb* to disable, to cripple.

main *adj* chief, principal:—*n* 1 the greater part. 2 the ocean. 3 a pipe under the street for water, gas etc. 4 strength.

main'land *n* land, as distinct from nearby islands.

main'ly *adv* chiefly.

maintain' *vb* 1 to feed and clothe. 2 to keep up. 3 to keep in good repair. 4 to defend a point of view.

main'tenance *n* upkeep, support.

maize *n* 1 corn. 2 a light yellow color.

majes'tic *adj* dignified, stately.

maj'esty *n* 1 grandeur, dignity. 2 the title given to a king or queen.

ma'jor *adj* 1 the greater in number, size, or quantity. 2 the more important:—*n* an army officer just above a captain in rank.

major'ity *n* 1 the greater number. 2 in voting, the amount by which the number of votes cast for one candidate exceeds that cast for another. 3 (*fml*) the age at which one may legally own property.

make *vb* (*pt, pp* **made**) 1 to create. 2 to construct by putting parts or substances together. 3 to cause to be. 4 to force. 5 to add up to. 6 to earn:—*n* 1 the way something is made. 2 shape:—**make for** to go toward:—**make good** to succeed, to do well:—**make off** to run away:—**make out** 1 to decipher. 2 (*inf*) to succeed:—**make up** 1 to invent (a story). 2 to put paint, powder, etc (on the face). 3 to bring (a quarrel) to an end, to try to become friendly again.

make'-believe *n* pretense:—*also vb*.

mak'er *n* one who makes.

make'shift *adj* used or done because nothing better can be found or thought of.

make'-up *n* 1 paint, powder, etc, for the face. 2 one's character.

male *adj* of the sex that can become a father:—*also n*.

malev'olent *adj* wishing harm to others, spiteful:—*n* **malev'olence**.

malformed' *adj* out of shape, wrongly shaped:—*n* **malforma'tion**.

mal'ice *n* pleasure in the misfortunes of others, spite, a desire to harm others.

mali'cious *adj* spiteful, full of malice.

malign [ma-lîn'] *vb* to speak ill of:—*adj* evil, harmful.

malig'nant *adj* 1 feeling great hatred. 2 very harmful. 3 able to cause death.

malin'gerer *n* a person who pretends to be ill in order to avoid duty.

mall *n* a shopping center.

malleable [ma'-li-êbl] *adj* 1 that which can be hammered into shape. 2 easily influenced.

mall'et *n* a wooden hammer.

malnutri'tion *n* a state caused by eating too little food or food that does not supply the needs of the body.

maltreat' *vb* to treat badly, to ill-use.

mama', mamma' *n* (*old*) mother.

mam'mal *n* an animal that suckles its young.

mam'moth *n* a type of large elephant, no longer existing:—*adj* huge.

man *n* (*pl* **men**) 1 the human race. 2 a human being. 3 a male human being. 4 (*inf*) a husband. 5 a male servant:—*vb* (**manned', man'ning**) to provide with people to go to or to be in the place where a duty is to be performed.

man'acle *n* an iron ring and chain used to fasten the hands of a prisoner:—*vb* to put manacles on.

man'age *vb* 1 to control, to be in charge of. 2 to succeed (in doing something).

man'ageable *adj* easily controlled.

man'agement *n* 1 control, direction. 2 the group of persons who control or run a business.

man'ager n one who controls a business or part of it:—f **man'ageress**.

manage'rial adj having to do with management of a business.

man'darin n a small orange.

man'datory adj compulsory.

mane n the long hair on the neck of certain animals.

maneuver [ma-nö´-vèr] n 1 a planned movement of armies or ships. 2 a skillful or cunning plan intended to make another behave as you want him or her to. 3 pl practice movements of armies or ships:—vb 1 to move armies or ships. 2 to move or act cunningly to gain one's ends.

mange n a skin disease of dogs, etc.

man'gle vb to cut or tear so as to be unrecognizable.

man'handle vb 1 to move by hand. 2 to treat roughly.

man'hole n a hole in the ground or floor through which a person may enter an underground shaft or tunnel.

man'hood n the state of being a man or of having the qualities of a man.

ma'nia n 1 madness. 2 a very great interest (in), an obsession.

ma'niac n a mad person.

man'icure n the care of the hands and fingernails:—also vb.

man'icurist n one whose job it is to care for hands and nails.

man'ifest adj (fml) easily seen or understood, obvious:—vb to show clearly.

manifes'to n a public announcement of future plans.

man'ifold adj (fml) many and different.

manip'ulate vb 1 to handle skillfully. 2 to manage skillfully (often in a dishonest way):—n **manipula'tion**.

man'ly adj having the qualities of a man.

mannequin [man´-i-kin] n 1 a woman employed to wear and display new dresses. 2 a life-size model of a human being used to display clothes.

man'ner n 1 the way in which anything is done or happens. 2 the way a person speaks or behaves to others.

man'nerism n a way of behaving, writing, etc, that has become a habit.

mann'ish adj like a man.

man'or n the land or house belonging to a lord.

man'sion n a large dwelling house.

man'slaughter n the unlawful but unintentional killing of a person.

man'telpiece, man'tel ns 1 an ornamental surround built on either side of and above a fireplace. 2 the shelf above a fireplace.

man'tle n 1 (old) a loose sleeveless cloak. 2 a cover on a gas or oil lamp that emits light:—vb to cloak, to cover.

man'ual adj done by hand:—n a small book containing all the important facts on a certain subject.

manufac'ture n 1 the making of goods or materials. 2 a article so made:—vb to make, esp by machinery, in large quantities:—n **manufac'turer**.

manure' n dung or any other substance used to make soil more fertile:—vb to treat with manure.

man'uscript n 1 a paper or book written by hand. 2 the written material sent by an author for publishing.

map n a plan of any part of the earth's surface:—vb (**mapped'**, **map'ping**) to make a map of:—**map out** to plan.

ma'ple n a tree from whose sap sugar is made.

mar vb (**marred'**, **mar'ring**) to spoil, to damage.

mar'ble n 1 a type of hard stone used for buildings, statues, etc. 2 a small ball of stone or glass used in children's games.

march vb to walk with a regular step:—n 1 movement of a body of soldiers on foot. 2 the distance walked. 3 music suitable for marching to.

March n the third month of the year.

mare n the female of the horse.

mar'garine n a substance made from vegetable or animal fat, often used instead of butter.

mar'gin n 1 the part of a page that is not usu printed or written on. 2 an amount more than is necessary, something extra.

mar'ginal adj 1 on or near the edge, border, or limit. 2 very small or unimportant.

marine' adj 1 having to do with the sea. 2 having to do with shipping.

mar'itime adj of or near the sea.

mark n 1 a sign, spot, or stamp that can be seen. 2 a thing aimed at. 3 a number or letter indicating the standard reached. 4 an acceptable level of quality. 5 a stain or dent. 6 an indication, a sign:—vb 1 to make a mark on. 2 to indicate by a mark the standard reached. 3 (old) to watch closely, to pay attention to. 4 to show the position of. 5 to be a sign of:—**mark time** 1 to move the legs up and down as if walking but without going backwards or forwards. 2 to fill in time.

marked adj noticeable, obvious.

mark'er n a person or thing used to mark a place.

mar'ket n 1 a public place for buying and selling. 2 a coming together of people to buy and sell. 2 a demand or need:—vb to sell in a market.

marks'man n one who shoots well.

maroon'[1] n a brownish-crimson color:—adj of this color.

maroon'[2] vb to abandon.

marquee [mar-kee´] n a large tent.

mar'riage n 1 the ceremony of marrying or being married. 2 life together as husband and wife.

mar'row n 1 a soft fatty matter filling the hollow parts of bones. 2 squash.

mar'ry vb 1 to join together as husband and wife. 2 to take as husband or wife.

marsh n low watery ground, a swamp:—adj **marsh'y**.

mar'shal n 1 in some armies and air forces, an officer of high rank. 2 in some states, a public official whose duties resemble those of a sheriff. 3 in some states, the chief police or fire officer:—vb to arrange in order.

marsu'pial n an animal that carries its young in a pouch.

mar'tial adj having to do with war.

mar'tyr n 1 one who suffers death for his or her beliefs. 2 one who suffers continuously from a certain illness:—vb to put to death for refusing to give up one's faith:—n **mar'tyrdom**.

mar'vel n a wonder:—vb to wonder (at), to feel astonishment.

mar'velous adj 1 wonderful, astonishing, extraordinary. 2 (inf) very good, excellent.

marzipan' n a sweet made from ground almonds, sugar, etc.

mas'cot n a person, animal, or thing supposed to bring good luck.

mas'culine adj 1 of the male sex. 2 manly. 3 like a man.

mash vb to crush food until it is soft.

mask n 1 a cover for the face or part of the face. 2 an animal or human face painted on paper, etc, and worn at parties or processions. 3 any means of concealing what is really going on. 4 a poetical play:—vb 1 to cover with a mask. 2 to hide.

ma'son n one skilled in shaping stone or building.

ma'sonry n stonework.

masquerade' n a ball at which masks are worn:—vb 1 to go in disguise. 2 to pretend to be another.

mass n 1 a lump or quantity of matter. 2 (often pl) a crowd. 4 the larger part:—vb 1 to gather into a mass. 2 to form a crowd.

mass'acre *n* the killing of large numbers of men, women, and children:—*vb* to kill in large numbers.

massage [ma-säj'] *n* rubbing and pressing the muscles to strengthen them or make them less stiff:—*also vb.*

mass'ive *adj* huge, big and heavy.

mast *n* on a ship, an upright pole on which sails may be set.

mas'ter *n* 1 one who is in charge or gives orders. 2 a male teacher. 3 an expert:—*vb* 1 to gain complete knowledge of. 2 to overcome:—**old master** a great painter of the past.

mas'terful *adj* used to giving orders.

mas'terly *adj* showing great skill.

mas'terpiece *n* the best piece of work done by an artist.

mat *n* 1 a small piece of coarse cloth or plaited fiber used as a floor covering or foot-wiper. 2 a piece of cloth or other material placed under a plate or dish:—*adj* without luster, dull:—*vb* (**matt'ed, matt'ing**) to twist together, to entangle.

match[1] *n* a small stick tipped with a substance that catches fire when rubbed on certain prepared surfaces.

match[2] *n* 1 a person or thing the same or nearly the same as another. 2 an equal. 3 a sporting contest or game. 4 a marriage:—*vb* 1 to be equal to. 2 to be like or to go well with something else.

match'maker *n* one who tries to arrange a marriage between others.

mate *n* 1 a companion, a colleague. 2 (*inf or hum*) a husband or wife. 3 a ship's officer below the master in rank. 4 one of a matched pair. 5 an animal with which another is paired for producing offspring:—*vb* to come together for breeding.

mate'rial *adj* 1 made of matter. 2 worldly, not spiritual. 3 (*fml*) important:—*n* 1 the substance out of which a thing is made. 2 cloth.

mate'rially *adv* to a large extent, considerably.

mate'rialize *vb* 1 to become real, to happen. 2 to appear.

mater'nal *adj* of or like a mother.

mater'nity *n* motherhood.

mathemat'ical *adj* having to do with mathematics.

mathemat'ics *n* the science of space and numbers:—*n* **mathemati'cian**

matinee [mat'-i-nā] *n* an afternoon performance in a theater.

mat'rimony *n* (*fml*) the state of marriage:—*adj* **matrimo'nial**.

ma'tron *n* 1 a wife or widow, esp one of mature appearance and manner. 2 a woman in charge of domestic and nursing arrangements in a school, hospital, or other institution.

matte *adj* dull, without shine.

matt'er *n* 1 that out of which all things are made. 2 a subject of conversation or writings. 3 affair. 4 the infected liquid contained in a wound or sore:—*vb* to be of importance.

matt'ress *n* a flat bag filled with soft material or light springs, placed under a sleeper for comfort.

mature' *adj* 1 ripe. 2 fully grown. 3 fully developed in body or mind:—*vb* 1 to ripen. 2 to become mature. 3 to be due in full.

matu'rity *n* 1 ripeness. 2 full growth or development.

maul *vb* 1 to injure badly. 2 to handle roughly.

mauve *n* a purple dye or color:—*adj* light purple.

max'imum *n* the greatest possible number or amount:—*also adj.*

May *n* the fifth month of the year.

may'be *adv* perhaps.

may'or *n* the chief administrative officer of a city or borough:—*f* **may'oress**

maze *n* 1 a confusing system of paths or passages through which it is difficult to find one's way. 2 a confusing network of streets, etc.

mea'dow *n* rich grassland.

mea'ger *adj* scanty, not enough.

meal[1] *n* food taken at one time.

meal[2] *n* grain ground to powder.

mean[1] *adj* 1 (*old or lit*) poor. 2 nasty, unkind over small things. 3 unwilling to spend or give away:—*n* **mean'ness**.

mean[2] *vb* (*pt, pp* **meant**) 1 to intend. 2 to have a certain purpose. 3 to express a certain idea.

mean[3] *adj* 1 middle. 2 halfway between numbers, amounts, extremes, etc, average:—*n* 1 the average. 2 a middle state. 3 *pl* that by which something is done or carried out. 4 *pl* money or property.

mean'ing *n* 1 the idea expressed by a word or words. 2 the sense in which something is intended to be understood:—*adjs* **mean'ingful, mean'ingless**.

mean'time *n* the time between two events:—*adv* meanwhile.

mean'while *n* the time between two events, meantime:—*adv* 1 in or during the intervening time. 2 at the same time.

mea'sles *n* an infectious disease with a red rash.

mea'sure *n* 1 a unit by which one expresses size, weight, etc. 2 size, weight, etc, so expressed. 3 an instrument used in finding size, weight, etc. 4 (*fml*) the regular rhythm of poetry or music. 5 (*old*) a dance. 6 a course of action. 7 a law proposed but not passed:—*vb* 1 to find out size quantity, etc, with an instrument. 2 to judge. 3 to weigh out:—*n* **mea'surement**.

meat *n* 1 the flesh of animals used as food. 2 the essence of something.

mechan'ic *n* one who looks after a machine.

mechan'ical *adj* 1 done or worked by machine. 2 having to do with machinery. 3 done by habit, done without awareness.

mech'anism *n* the machinery that makes something work.

med'al *n* a flat piece of metal with a picture or writing stamped on it, made in memory of some person or event or as a reward of merit.

med'dle *vb* to interfere:—*n* **med'dler**.

media *see* **medium**.

med'ical *adj* 1 having to do with medicine. 2 having to do with the work of a doctor, medicine or healing.

medica'tion *n* (*fml*) medicine, treatment by medicine.

med'icine *n* 1 the science of bringing the sick back to health. 2 any substance that cures or heals. 3 the science of curing or treating by means other than surgery.

medie'val *adj* having to do with the Middle Ages.

me'diocre *adj* not very good, ordinary:—*n* **medioc'rity**

med'itate *vb* 1 to think deeply about. 2 to spend short regular periods in deep, esp religious, thought.

medita'tion *n* deep thought.

me'dium *n* 1 (*pl* **me'dia**) the means by which something is done. 2 (*esp in pl*) a means by which news is made known. 3 (*pl* **me'diums**) one able to receive messages from spirits at a meeting held for that purpose:—*adj* middle or average in size, quality, etc.

med'ley *n* 1 a mixture. 2 a selection of tunes played as one item.

meek *adj* gentle, kind, unresisting.

meet *vb* (*pt, pp* **met**) 1 to come face to face with, often by chance. 2 to come together by arrangement. 3 to pay. 4 to satisfy. 5 to answer.

meet'ing *n* a coming together for a special purpose.

meg'aphone *n* a large trumpet for making the voice louder.

mel'ancholy *n* sadness, depression:—*also adj.*

mel'low *adj* 1 soft with ripeness. 2 made kindly by age:—*vb* to make or become mellow:—*n* **mell'owness**.

melo'dious *adj* sweet-sounding.

melodramat'ic *adj* more like a play than real life, theatrical, exaggerated.

mel'ody *n* **1** a tune. **2** the principal part in a piece of harmonized music.

mel'on *n* a large juicy fruit that grows on the ground.

melt *vb* **1** to make or become liquid by heat, to soften, to dissolve. **2** to disappear. **3** to make or become gentler.

mem'ber *n* (*fml or old*) a limb of the body. **2** one of a society or group.

mem'bership *n* **1** the state of being a member. **2** all the members of a society.

memen'to *n* an object kept or given to remind one of a person or event.

memo *see* **memorandum**.

memoir [mem'wär] *n* **1** a written account of past events. **2** *pl* the story of a person's life.

mem'orable *adj* worth remembering.

memoran'dum *n* (*pl* **memoran'da**) (*often abbreviated to* **me'mo**) a written note of something one wants to remember.

memo'rial *n* an object, often a monument, that helps people to remember a person or event.

mem'orize *vb* to learn by heart.

mem'ory *n* **1** the power of the mind to recall past events or to learn things by heart. **2** the mind's store of remembered things. **3** something remembered. **4** the part of a computer that stores information.

men'ace *n* **1** a threat, a person or thing likely to cause harm or danger. **2** a threat, a show of hostility:—*vb* (*fml*) to threaten.

men'acing *adj* **1** threatening to harm. **2** threatening-looking.

mend *vb* **1** to repair. **2** to improve. **3** (*inf*) to become well or healthy again:—*n* the hole or crack that has been mended.

me'nial *adj* humble, unskilled.

men'tal *adj* having to do with the mind

mental'ity *n* **1** mental power. **2** the way of thinking typical of a person, the character of a person's mind.

men'tion *vb* **1** to speak of, to refer to, to say the name of. **2** to say briefly or indirectly:—*n* a remark about or reference to.

men'u *n* **1** a list of foods that can be ordered for a meal in a restaurant. **2** a list of options on a computer display.

mer'cenary *adj* **1** working for money. **2** doing things only to obtain money, greedy for money:—*n* a soldier hired to fight for a country not his own.

mer'chandise *n* goods bought and sold.

mer'chant *n* one who buys and sells goods in large quantities.

mer'ciful *adj* showing mercy, forgiving.

mer'cy *n* kindness and pity, forgiveness, willingness not to punish.

mere *adj* no more or less than.

mere'ly *adv* only.

merge *vb* **1** to join together to make one. **2** to become part of a larger whole.

mer'it *n* **1** the quality of deserving praise or reward, worth or excellence. **2** good point. **3** *pl* good qualities:—*vb* to deserve.

mer'maid *n* an imaginary sea creature, half woman and half fish:—*also* **mer'man**.

mer'ry *adj* joyous, happy, full of fun:—*n* **mer'riment**.

mer'ry-go-round *n* a large revolving circular platform with seats in the shape of animals, etc, on which people may ride for amusement at a fair.

mesh *n* **1** the space between the threads of a net. **2** *pl* the threads of a net.

mes'merize *vb* to hold the complete attention of and make seemingly unable to move or speak.

mess[1] *n* **1** a muddle. **2** a dirty or untidy state:—*vb* **1** to make dirty or untidy. **2** to do badly or inefficiently.

mess[2] *n* **1** a company of people who take their meals together as in the armed services. **2** the place where they eat. **3** (*old*) a dish of food, esp soft or semi-liquid food:—*vb* to eat in mess.

mess'age *n* **1** information or news sent to another by word of mouth or in writing. **2** a piece of instruction, an important idea.

mess'enger *n* one who bears a message.

met *pt of* **meet**.

met'al *n* a class of substances, such as gold, copper, iron, tin, etc.

metal'lic *adj* of or like metal.

met'aphor *n* a way of comparing two things by identifying them and speaking about one as if it were the other:—*adjs* **metaphor'ic, metaphor'ical**.

me'teor *n* a shining body that can be seen moving across the sky, a shooting star.

meteor'ic *adj* rapid but often short-lasting.

me'teorite *n* a meteor that falls to earth as a piece of rock.

meteorolog'ical *adj* having to do with meteorology.

meteorol'ogy *n* the study or science of the earth's weather:— *n* **meteorol'ogist**.

me'ter *n* **1** an instrument for measuring things. **2** the systematic arrangement of stressed and unstressed syllables that give poetic rhythm. **3** a measure of length (≈ 39.37 inches) in the metric system.

meth'od *n* **1** a way of doing something. **2** an orderly way of arranging or doing things.

method'ical *adj* orderly in following a plan or system.

met'rical *adj* (*of poetry*) having a regular rhythm or meter.

metric system *n* a system of weights and measures in which each unit is divisible into 10 parts.

met'ronome *n* an instrument with a pendulum that can be set to mark time correctly for a musician.

metro'polis *n* (*fml or hum*) a large city, esp the capital.

met'tle *n* spirit, courage:—*adj* **mett'lesome:—on one's mettle** trying to do one's best.

mew, miaow *ns* the cry of a cat:—*vb* to emit a high-pitched cry, as a cat.

miaow *see* **mew**.

mice *see* **mouse**.

micro'meter *n* an instrument for measuring small distances.

mi'crophone *n* in a telephone or radio, the instrument by which the sound of the voice is changed into electric waves, used to make sounds louder.

mi'croscope *n* an instrument containing an arrangement of curved glasses by means of which very tiny objects can be seen larger and studied.

microscop'ic *adj* **1** very small, tiny, seen only with the help of a microscope. **2** (*inf*) tiny.

micro'wave *n* **1** an electromagnetic wave between 1 and 100 centimeters long. **2** (*inf*) a microwave oven:—*vb* to cook in a microwave oven.

mid *adj* having to do with the middle, in the middle of.

mid'day *n* noon or the time about noon.

mid'dle *adj* equally distant from the ends or limits:—*n* the center, the middle part or point.

mid'dle-aged' *adj* neither old nor young, between youth and old age.

Middle Ages *npl* the period between AD 500 and AD 1500 in history.

mid'dle class' *n* those who are well enough off to live in comfort but are neither wealthy nor of noble birth:—*adj* **mid'dle-class** having to do with the middle class.

mid'dling *adj* (*inf*) neither very good nor very bad, average.

midge n a small flying insect that bites.

mid´get n a very small or unusually small person.

mid´night n twelve o'clock at night.

mid´riff n the part of the body containing the muscles separating the stomach from the lungs.

midst n the middle.

mid´summer n the middle of summer.

mid´way n halfway:—also adv.

might n power, strength.

might´y adj 1 powerful, strong. 2 huge.

mi´grant n one who migrates:—also adj.

migrate´ vb 1 to move one's home from one land to another, to go from one place to another. 2 (of birds) to move to another place at the season when its climate is suitable:—n **migra´tion**.

migra´tory adj used to migrating.

mild adj 1 gentle, merciful, not severe. 2 calm. 3 (of weather) not cold:—n **mild´ness**.

mile n a measure of length (= 1760 yards or 1.6 kilometers).

mile´age n distance in miles.

mile´stone n 1 a stone by the roadside telling the distance in miles to places in the neighborhood. 2 a time at which one can consider the progress made.

mil´itant adj 1 fighting, warlike. 2 active in a campaign.

mil´itary adj having to do with soldiers or battles:—n the army, soldiers.

mil´itate vb 1 to act or stand (against). 2 to act as a reason against.

milk n 1 the secreted liquid on which female mammals feed their young. 2 such milk produced by cows or goats and drunk by humans or made into butter and cheese:—vb to draw milk from (e.g. a cow).

milk´tooth n one of a child's first set of teeth.

milk´y adj 1 like milk. 2 containing much milk.

Milky Way n a bright band across the night sky, made up of countless stars.

mill n 1 a machine for grinding corn, coffee, etc. 2 the building in which corn is ground into flour. 3 a factory:—vb 1 to grind. 2 to stamp a coin and cut grooves around its edge.

millen´nium n (pl **millen´nia** or **millen´niums**) a period of 1000 years.

mill´er n one who keeps a corn mill.

mill´et n a grass bearing eatable grain.

mil´ligram n the thousandth part of a gram.

mil´limeter n the thousandth part of a meter.

mil´liner n one who makes or sells ladies' hats.

mil´linery n hats made or sold by a milliner.

mil´lion n 1 a thousand thousand. 2 (inf) a very great many.

millionaire´ n one possessing a million or more dollars.

mime n 1 a play without words carried on by facial expressions, gestures, and actions. 2 using actions without language:—vb to act without speaking.

mim´ic vb (**mim´icked**, **mim´icking**) to imitate, esp in order to make fun of:—n one who imitates.

mince vb to cut into very small pieces.

mince´meat n 1 minced meat. 2 currants, etc, chopped up small and mixed with spices.

mind n 1 the power by which human beings understand, think, feel, will, etc. 2 a person of great mental ability. 3 memory:—vb 1 to take care of. 2 to take heed, to be careful. 3 to object to.

mine[1] poss pron belonging to me.

mine[2] n 1 a deep hole made in the earth so that minerals can be taken from beneath its surface. 2 a container filled with explosive charge to blow something up. 3 a person or place

from which much may be obtained:—vb 1 to make tunnels into and under the earth. 2 to dig for in a mine. 3 to place explosive mines in position. 4 to blow up with mines.

mi´ner n one who works in a mine.

min´eral n an inorganic substance found naturally in the earth and mined:—adj having to do with minerals.

mineral water n water that comes from a natural spring and contains minerals, sometimes sold still and sometimes carbonated.

mineral´ogy n the study of minerals:—n **mineral´ogist**.

min´gle vb 1 to mix together. 2 to mix with.

min´iature n a very small painting:—adj very small, tiny.

min´imize vb to make seem less important.

min´imum n the smallest amount possible.

min´ister n 1 a person in charge of a government department. 2 the principal representative of a government in another country. 3 a member of the clergy:—vb to give help, to serve.

min´istry n 1 the clergy. 2 a department of government in charge of a minister.

mink n a small stoat-like animal valued for its fur.

min´now n a very small freshwater fish.

mi´nor adj smaller, of less importance:—n a person under legal age.

minor´ity n 1 the state of being under age. 2 the smaller number in a group or assembly, less than half.

mint[1] n 1 a place where coins are made, esp by the government. 2 (inf) a large amount of money:—vb to make coins.

mint[2] n a sweet-smelling herb whose leaves are used as flavoring in cooking.

mi´nus prep less:—adj 1 less. 2 (inf) not having:—n the sign of subtraction (−).

minute[1] [mi-or mî-nût´] adj 1 very small. 2 exact.

minute[2] [mî´-nêt] n 1 the sixtieth part of an hour. 2 the sixtieth part of a degree. 3 a short time. 4 a written note or comment. 5 pl a short account of what was discussed and decided at a meeting:—vb to make a written note of.

mir´acle n 1 an extraordinary event brought about by the interference of God with the natural course of events. 2 any extraordinary event for which there is no known explanation.

mirac´ulous adj 1 caused by a miracle, marvelous. 2 amazing, extraordinary.

mirage [mi-räzh´] n imaginary objects (e.g. water, trees) that appear real to a traveler because of certain atmospheric conditions, such as shimmer caused by heat.

mir´ror n 1 a smooth surface that reflects images 2 a faithfully depiction:—vb to reflect as in a mirror.

mirth n laughter, merriment:—adjs **mirth´ful**, **mirth´less**.

misadven´ture n (fml or old) an unlucky happening.

misbehave´ vb to behave badly:—n **misbeha´vior**.

miscella´neous adj mixed, of different kinds.

mis´chief n 1 (fml) harm done on purpose. 2 children's naughtiness.

mis´chievous adj 1 harmful, intended to cause trouble. 2 naughty.

misdeed´ n (fml) a wrongful action, a crime.

misdemean´or n 1 an act that breaks the law, a petty crime. 2 an act of misbehavior.

misdirect´ vb to give wrong instructions to:—n **misdirec´tion**.

mi´ser n one who dislikes spending money.

mis´erable adj 1 very unhappy. 2 causing unhappiness or discomfort. 3 low in quality or quantity.

mi´serly adj very mean.

mis´ery n great unhappiness or suffering.

mis´fit n a person unsuited to his or her circumstances.

misfor´tune n 1 bad luck. 2 a piece of bad luck.

misgiv'ing *n* a feeling of fear, doubt or mistrust.

misgov'ern *vb* to rule badly:—*n* **misgov'ernment**.

misguid'ed *adj* showing bad judgment.

mis'hap *n* an unlucky event, usu not serious.

misjudge' *vb* to judge wrongly, to form a wrong opinion.

mislay' *vb* (*pt, pp* **mislaid'**) to put (something) down and forget where one has put it.

mislead' *vb* (*pt, pp* **misled'**) to deceive, to give the wrong idea to.

mis'print *n* a mistake in printing:—*vb* **misprint'**.

mispronounce' *vb* to pronounce wrongly:—*n* **mispronuncia'tion**.

misrule' *vb* to rule or govern badly:—*also n*.

miss *vb* 1 to fail to hit, find, meet, catch, or notice. 2 to leave out. 3 to regret the loss or absence of:—*n* a failure to hit or catch.

misshap'en *adj* badly formed, deformed, ugly.

mis'sile *n* 1 any object thrown or fired from a gun to do harm. 2 an explosive flying weapon with its own engine, which can be aimed at distant objects.

mis'sing *adj* lost.

mis'sion *n* 1 persons sent to carry out a certain task. 2 the task itself. 3 one's chief aim in life. 4 a group of persons sent to a foreign land to teach their religion. 5 the building(s) in which they live.

mis'sionary *n* one sent to a foreign land to teach his or her religion:—*also adj*.

misspell' *vb* to spell wrongly:—*n* **misspell'ing**.

mist *n* 1 rain in fine, tiny drops. 2 a cloud resting on the ground.

mistake' *vb* 1 to understand wrongly. 2 to confuse one person or thing with another:—*n* an error.

mistak'en *adj* in error, wrong.

mis'ter *n* the title put before a man's name (usu written **Mr**).

mis'tletoe *n* an evergreen plant with white berries.

mis'tress *n* 1 (usu written **Mrs** [mis'-ĕz]) the title put before the name of a married woman. 2 a woman having charge or control (of). 3 a woman teacher. 4 a woman who is the lover of a man and sometimes maintained by him but not married to him.

mistrust' *vb* to suspect, to doubt:—*also n*.

mist'y *adj* 1 darkened or clouded by mist. 2 not clear.

misunderstand' *vb* to take a wrong meaning from.

misunderstand'ing *n* a disagreement, esp one due to failure to see another's meaning or intention.

mite *n* 1 a type of very small insect. 2 a small child. 3 a very small amount.

mitt, mitt'en *ns* 1 a type of glove that covers the hand but not the fingers and thumb. 2 a glove without separate places for the fingers.

mix *vb* 1 to put together to form one. 2 to go together or blend successfully. 3 to join in (with others).

mixed *adj* 1 made up of different things or kinds. 2 relating to people of different sexes.

mix'ture *n* the result of mixing things or people together.

moan *vb* 1 to make a low sound of sorrow or pain. 2 (*inf*) to complain:—*also n*.

moat *n* a trench, often filled with water, around a castle or fort.

mob *n* a disorderly crowd.

mo'bile *adj* 1 that can be moved. 2 easily moved. 3 able to move easily, active.

mobil'ity *n* ability to move about.

mo'bilize *vb* 1 to call upon to serve as soldiers. 2 to organize for a particular reason:—*n* **mobiliza'tion**.

mocc'asin *n* a shoe or slipper made of deerskin or sheepskin.

mock *vb* 1 to make fun of. 2 to imitate in order to make appear foolish:—*adj* false, not real.

mock'ery *n* 1 the act of mocking. 2 a person or thing mocked.

mod'el *n* 1 a person or thing to be copied. 2 a copy, usu smaller, of a person or thing. 3 a small copy of (e.g. a building or ship made from the plan to show what the finished object will look like). 4 a living person who sits or stands still to let an artist draw him or her. 5 one employed to display clothes by wearing them. 6 an artificial figure used in display:—*adj* worth copying, perfect:—*vb* 1 to give shape to. 2 to make a model of. 3 to wear clothes to show to possible buyers:—*n* **mod'eling**.

mod'erate *vb* 1 to prevent from going to extremes. 2 to lessen:—*adj* 1 not going to extremes. 2 average.

modera'tion *n* avoidance of extremes, self-control.

mod'ern *adj* 1 belonging to the present day. 2 belonging to recent centuries. 3 up-to-date:—*n* **moder'nity**.

mod'ernize *vb* to bring up-to-date:—*n* **moderniza'tion**.

mod'est *adj* 1 not having too high an opinion of oneself. 2 not boastful. 3 decent. 4 not very large:—*n* **mod'esty**.

mod'ify *vb* 1 to alter in part. 2 to make less severe.

mo'hair *n* 1 the silky hair of an Angora goat. 2 the wool or cloth made from it.

moist *adj* slightly wet, damp.

moisten [moi'-sĕn] *vb* to make damp.

mois'ture *n* dampness, wetness caused by tiny drops of water in the atmosphere.

mo'lar *n* one of the back teeth that grind food.

mold[1] *n* a fluffy growth consisting of tiny plants on stale food or damp surfaces.

mold[2] *vb* 1 to work into a shape. 2 to shape or influence.

mold'y *adj* 1 covered with mold. 2 (*inf*) of little value, unpleasant, dull.

mole[1] *n* a dark spot on the human skin.

mole[2] *n* a small furry burrowing animal.

mol'ecule *n* the smallest particle of a substance that can exist while still retaining the chemical qualities of that substance:—*adj* **molec'ular**.

mole'hill *n* the heap of earth thrown up by a burrowing mole.

molest' *vb* 1 to disturb or annoy. 2 to make a bodily, often sexual, attack upon:—*n* **molesta'tion**.

moll'usk *n* a soft-bodied animal with a hard shell, as a snail, oyster, etc.

moll'ycoddle *vb* to take too great care of.

mol'ten *adj* 1 melted. 2 made by having been melted.

mom *n* (*inf*) mother.

mo'ment *n* 1 a very short time. 2 (*fml*) importance.

mo'mentary *adj* lasting only a moment.

momen'tous *adj* very important.

momen'tum *n* the force of a moving body.

mom'my *n* (*inf*) mother.

mon'arch *n* a single supreme ruler, a sovereign, a king or queen.

mon'archy *n* a state or system of government in which power is, in appearance or reality, in the hands of a single ruler.

mon'astery *n* a house for monks.

Mon'day *n* the second day of the week.

mon'etary *adj* having to do with money.

mon'ey *n* metal coins and printed bills used in making payments, buying and selling.

mon'eyed *adj* rich.

mon'eylen'der *n* one who lives by lending money on condition that interest is paid to him or her for the time of the loan.

mongrel [mung(g)'-grĕl] *adj* of mixed breed or race:—*n* a dog of mixed breed.

mon'itor *n* 1 in school, a senior pupil who helps to keep order. 2 an instrument that receives and shows continuous information about the working of something. 3 a screen for use with a computer. **4** a small screen in a TV studio showing the picture that is being broadcast at any given time.

monk *n* a man who, with the intention of devoting his life to prayer, joins a religious society and spends his life in a monastery.

mon'key *n* **1** an animal resembling a human being in shape. **2** (*inf*) a mischievous child:—*vb* to play about (with).

mono- *prefix* one.

mon'olog(ue) *n* a scene or play in which only one person speaks.

monop'olize *vb* **1** to have or obtain complete possession or control of. **2** to take up the whole of.

monop'oly *n* **1** complete control of the trade in a certain article by a single person or company. **2** possession of or control over something that is not shared by others.

mono'tone *n* **1** an utterance or musical tone without a change in pitch. **2** a tiresome sameness of style, color, etc.

monot'onous *adj* **1** dull from lack of variety. **2** in a monotone.

monot'ony *n* dullness, lack of variety, sameness.

monsoon' *n* a South Asian wind, blowing from the southwest in summer and the northeast in winter, usu bringing heavy rain.

mon'ster *n* **1** a huge frightening creature. **2** anything huge. **3** an unnaturally cruel or wicked person.

monstros'ity *n* something, usu large, that is very ugly.

month *n* one of the twelve periods of time into which the year is divided.

month'ly *adj* happening once a month or every month:—*also adv.*

mon'ument *n* a statue, stone, etc, set up in memory of a person or event.

mood *n* **1** a state of the mind and feelings, a person's temper at a certain time. **2** a state of bad temper. **3** in grammar, a verb form that tells whether the verb is used to express a command, desire, statement of fact, etc.

mood'y *adj* tending to change mood suddenly or often, often bad-tempered.

moon *n* **1** the heavenly body that moves around the earth and reflects the light of the sun. **2** any similar heavenly body that moves around a larger one:—*vb* (*inf*) to walk about in a dreamy way.

moor¹ *n* a large extent of poor land on which coarse grass, heather, etc, will grow, a heath.

moor² *vb* to fasten a ship by ropes, cables, etc.

moor'ing *n*, **moor'ings** *npl* **1** the ropes, cables, etc, by which a ship is fastened. **2** the place where a ship is so fastened.

moose *n* the largest of the deer family, native to North America.

mop *n* strips of coarse cloth, yarn, etc, fixed together to a handle and used for washing floors, etc:—*vb* (**mopped'**, **mop'ping**) to clean with a mop, to wipe.

mope *vb* to be gloomy or sad.

mor'al *adj* **1** having to do with what is right or wrong in action. **2** living according to the rules of right conduct:—*n* **1** the lesson to be learned from a story. **2** *pl* one's beliefs as to what is right or wrong in action. **3** *pl* standards of behavior.

morale [mo-räl'] *n* belief in one's ability to do what is asked of one, courage.

moral'ity *n* **1** moral principles. **2** a particular system of moral principles. **3** the quality of an action, as estimated by a standard of right and wrong.

mor'alize *vb* to discuss questions of morals.

mor'bid *adj* **1** unhealthy, diseased. **2** thinking too much about what is gloomy or disgusting:—*n* **morbid'ity.**

more *adj* greater in amount, number, etc:—*also n:—adv* **1** to a greater extent or degree. **2** again.

moreo'ver *adv* in addition, further.

morgue [morg] *n* a mortuary.

morn'ing *n* the early part of the day.

mor'on *n* (*inf*) a very stupid person:—*adj* **moron'ic.**

Morse code *n* a signaling code in which dots and dashes (or short and long sounds or flashes) represent the letters of the alphabet.

mor'sel *n* a small piece, a bite.

mor'tal *adj* **1** having to die. **2** causing death:—*n* a human being.

mortal'ity *n* **1** the state of being mortal. **2** the number who die from a certain cause.

mortgage [mor'-gej] *n* **1** giving to one who has lent money the control of certain property that he or she may sell if the loan is not repaid but must return when the loan is repaid in full:—*vb* to give control over property to another to obtain a loan.

morti'cian *n* one who manages funerals.

mor'tify *vb* **1** to make ashamed. **2** (*old*) to gain control over one's body by refusing its desires or causing it suffering:—*n* **mortifica'tion.**

mor'tuary *n* a building in which dead bodies are kept until burial.

mosaic [mô-zä'-ik] *n* a picture or design made by placing together differently colored pieces of glass, stone, etc.

mosque [mosk] *n* a Muslim place of worship.

mosqui'to *n* (*pl* **mosqui'toes**) a stinging insect that sometimes carries the germs of malaria.

moss *n* a tiny flowerless plant growing on walls, tree trunks, and in damp places (stones covered in moss).

moss'y *adj* overgrown with moss.

most *adj* greatest in number, amount, etc:—*also n:—adv* **1** in or to the greatest degree or extent. **2** very.

moth *n* **1** a winged insect that flies by night. **2** an insect that eats clothing.

mother [mu'-thèr] *n* **1** a female parent. **2** the female head of a convent of nuns:—*vb* to care for, as would a mother.

mo'therhood *n* the state of being a mother.

mo'ther-in-law *n* the mother of the person to whom one is married.

mo'therless *adj* having no mother.

mo'therly *adj* like a mother.

mo'ther tongue *n* one's native language.

mo'tion *n* **1** act of moving. **2** a movement. **3** an idea put to a meeting so that it can be voted on:—*vb* to make a movement as a sign.

motion picture *n* a film, movie.

mo'tionless *adj* unmoving.

mo'tivate *vb* to give a reason or urge to act.

mo'tive *adj* causing movement:—*n* a reason for doing something.

mot'ley *adj* **1** made up of different kinds. **2** (*old*) multicolored.

mo'tor *n* an engine that by changing power into motion drives a machine:—*adj* causing movement or motion:—*vb* to travel by automobile:—*n* **mo'torist.**

mo'tor bike *n* a bicycle driven by a motor:—*similarly* **mo'torboat, mo'tor car.**

mot'to *n* (*pl* **mot'toes**) **1** a wise saying that can be used as a rule of life. **2** the word or words on a coat of arms. **3** a printed saying or joke.

mould *same as* **mold.**

mound *n* **1** a low hill. **2** a heap of earth or stones.

mount *n* **1** (*usu in names*) a hill, a mountain. **2** an animal, esp a horse, for riding. **3** a card or paper surrounding a picture or photograph:—*vb* **1** to go up, to climb. **2** to get on to. **3** to place in position. **4** to get on horseback.

moun'tain *n* **1** a high hill. **2** a large heap.

mountaineer' *n* one who climbs mountains.

moun'tainous *adj* **1** having many mountains. **2** huge.

mount'ed *adj* on horseback.

mourn *vb* to show sorrow, to feel grief, esp after a loss or death:—*n* **mourn'er**.

mourn'ful *adj* sad, sorrowful.

mourn'ing *n* 1 sorrow, grief 2 black clothes worn as a sign of grief for another's death.

mouse *n* (*pl* **mice**) a small rodent animal found in houses or in the fields.

mouth *n* 1 the opening in the face for eating and uttering sounds. 2 the opening into anything hollow. 3 the part of a river where it flows into the sea.

mouth'ful *n* the amount placed in the mouth at one time.

mov'able, **move'able** *adjs* able to be moved.

move [môv] *vb* 1 to cause to change place or position. 2 to go from one place to another. 3 to change houses. 4 to set in motion. 5 to stir up the feelings. 6 to rouse to action. 7 at a meeting, to put forward an idea to be voted on:—*n* 1 a change of position or place. 2 a change of house. 3 an action. 4 in chess, etc, the act of moving a piece.

move'ment *n* 1 act of moving. 2 change of position. 3 a number of people working for the same purpose. 4 a complete part of a long musical work.

mo'vie *n* 1 a cinema film, motion picture. 2 *pl* the showing and making of films.

movie theater *n* a place where movies are shown.

mov'ing *adj* stirring up the feelings.

mow *vb* (*pp* **mown**) 1 to cut (grass). 2 to knock down, to kill in large numbers.

mow'er *n* a person or machine that mows.

much *adj* great in amount or quantity:—*n* a great amount:—*adv* greatly.

muck *n* (*inf*) wet filth, dirt:—*vb* (*inf*) 1 to dirty. 2 to make a mess of. 3 to spoil. 4 to bungle.

muck'y *adj* (*inf*) filthy.

mud *n* soft wet earth.

mud'dle *vb* 1 to confuse. 2 to mix up. 3 to act without plan:—*n* confusion, disorder.

mud'dle-head'ed *adj* unable to think clearly.

mud'dy *adj* covered with mud:—*vb* 1 to make dirty or muddy. 2 to make unclear.

mud'guard *n* a fender on a bicycle.

muff[1] *n* a cover of warm material for both hands.

muff[2] *vb* (*inf*) 1 to fail to hold. 2 to do badly.

muff'in *n* a small cup-shaped cake of sweet bread eaten hot with butter.

muf'fle *vb* 1 to wrap up to keep warm. 2 to deaden sound. 3 to make a sound less loud.

muf'fler *n* 1 a long warm scarf. 2 a device for reducing the noise of a vehicle exhaust.

mug *n* 1 a drinking vessel with a handle and more or less straight sides. 2 (*inf*) one easily made a fool of or cheated.

mug'gy *adj* unpleasantly warm and damp.

mule *n* 1 the offspring of an ass and a horse, supposedly famous for its stubbornness. 2 a machine for spinning cotton.

mul'ish *adj* stubborn:—*n* **mul'ishness**.

multi- *prefix* many.

mul'ticol'ored *adj* of many colors.

multilat'eral *adj* 1 having many sides. 2 (*fml*) concerning more than two groups.

mul'tiple *adj* 1 having or affecting many parts. 2 involving many things of the same kind:—*n* a number that contains another an exact number of times.

multiplica'tion *n* act of multiplying.

mul'tiply *vb* 1 to increase. 2 to find the number obtained by adding a number to itself a certain number of times.

mul'titude *n* 1 a great number. 2 (*old*) a crowd.

mum *adj* silent:—*n* (*inf*) mother.

mum'ble *vb* to speak in a low, indistinct voice.

mum'my[1] *n* (*inf*) mother.

mum'my[2] *n* a human body kept from decay by being treated with certain drugs and wrapped tightly in cloth:—*vb* **mum'mify**.

mumps *n* an infectious disease that causes swelling of the neck and face.

munch *vb* to chew noisily, to crush with teeth.

mun'dane *adj* ordinary, with nothing exciting or unusual.

muni'cipal *adj* having to do with a city or town.

mu'ral *n* a painting that is painted directly on to the walls of a building.

mur'der *n* act of unlawfully and intentionally killing another:—*also vb*:—*ns* **mur'derer**.

murk'y *adj* 1 dark, gloomy. 2 vague or obscure.

mur'mur *n* 1 a low, indistinct sound, as of running water. 2 a soft low continuous sound. 3 a grumble:—*vb* 1 to make a low indistinct sound. 2 to talk in a low voice. 3 to grumble.

muscle [mu'-sĕl] *n* the elastic fibers in the body that enable it to make movements.

mus'cular *adj* 1 having to do with muscles. 2 having well-developed muscles, strong.

muse *vb* to think deeply about, to ponder.

muse'um *n* a building in which objects of scientific, artistic, or literary interest are kept.

mush'room *n* an eatable plant with a soft whitish pulpy top:—*vb* to grow in size very rapidly.

mu'sic *n* 1 the art of arranging sounds to give melody or harmony. 2 the sounds so arranged when played, sung, or written down.

mu'sical *adj* 1 having to do with music. 2 pleasant-sounding.

musi'cian *n* one skilled in music.

musk *n* 1 a sweet-smelling substance obtained from the musk deer and used in making perfume. 2 a type of plant.

musk deer *n* a hornless deer found in Asia.

mus'ket *n* (*old*) a handgun formerly carried by soldiers:—*n* **musketeer'**.

mus'lin *n* a fine thin cotton cloth.

mus'sel *n* an eatable shellfish enclosed in a double shell.

mustache [mus-täsh'] *n* the hair growing on the upper lip.

mus'tard *n* 1 a plant with hot-tasting seeds. 2 a type of seasoning made from these for flavoring food, esp meat.

mus'ter *vb* 1 to bring together. 2 to call up, to gather:—*n* an assembling, as of troops, etc:—**pass muster** to be good enough.

mus'ty *adj* stale.

muta'tion *n* change, alteration.

mute *adj* 1 silent. 2 unable to speak. 3 not pronounced.

mu'ted *adj* 1 subdued. 2 soft in hue, shade, etc.

mu'tinous *adj* 1 taking part in a mutiny. 2 obstinate and sulky, as if going to disobey.

mu'tiny *n* refusal to obey those in charge, esp a rising of people in the armed services against their officers:—*also vb*.

mut'ter *vb* to speak in a low voice, without sounding the vowels clearly, esp with grumbling or insulting:—*also n*.

mut'ton *n* the flesh of sheep as meat.

mu'tual *adj* 1 common to or shared by two or more persons or parties. 2 given and received in the same degree by those concerned.

muz'zle *n* 1 the mouth and nose of an animal. 2 a cage or set of straps fastened on an animal's mouth to prevent it biting. 3 the open end of a gun:—*vb* 1 to put a muzzle on an animal's mouth. 2 to prevent from speaking freely.

muz'zy *adj* confused, dizzy.

myste'rious *adj* difficult to understand or explain.

mys'tery *n* **1** a religious truth that cannot be fully understood by the human mind. **2** anything difficult to understand or explain. **3** a secret way of doing something, known only to a few.

mys'tic *adj* having to do with religious mysteries or secrets:— *n* one who believes that through prayer or sympathy he or she has understood in part the mysteries of life and of the existence of God.

mys'tical *adj* mystic.

mys'ticism *n* the beliefs or practices of a mystic.

mys'tify *vb* to puzzle, to bewilder:—*n* **mystifica'tion**.

myth *n* **1** a story about the gods or goddesses of ancient peoples, esp one containing their beliefs about the facts of nature. **2** something that is popularly thought to be true but is not.

myth'ical *adj* existing in myths or legends, imaginary.

mythol'ogy *n* **1** a collection of myths. **2** the study of myths:— *adj* **mytholog'ical**.

N

nadir *n* [ná'-dèr] *n* the lowest point or condition.

nag *vb* (**nagged, nag'ging**) to keep on annoying or finding fault with.

nail *n* 1 the horny growth on the tips of the fingers or toes. 2 the claw of a bird or animal. 3 a thin piece of metal with a pointed end and a flattened head, used for joining together pieces of wood:—*vb* to fasten with a nail.

naïve [na-eev'] *adj* 1 simple and natural, innocent. 2 ignorantly simple, too trustful:—*n* **naïveté** [na-eev'-tä].

na'ked *adj* 1 wearing no clothes. 2 uncovered. 3 plain, unconcealed:—*n* **na'kedness**.

name *n* 1 the word by which a person or thing is known. 2 reputation:—*vb* 1 to give a name to. 2 to speak about by name.

name'ly *adv* that is to say.

name'sake *n* a person with the same name as another.

nan'ny *n* 1 a woman employed to take care of children, a children's nurse. 2 a female goat (*also* **nan'ny-goat**).

nap *n* a short sleep, a doze:—*vb* (**napped, nap'ping**) to take a short sleep:—**caught napping** taken by surprise.

nape *n* the back part of the neck.

nap'kin *n* 1 a small cloth used at table to keep the clothes clean. 2 a diaper.

narrate' *vb* to tell (a story).

nar'rative *adj* 1 telling a story. 2 having to do with storytelling:—*n* a story.

narra'tor *n* the teller of a story.

nar'row *adj* 1 not broad, measuring little from side to side. 2 (*also* **nar'row-mind'ed**) unwilling to accept new ideas or ways of doing things. 3 not extensive, not wide-ranging. 4 only just avoiding the opposite result:—*vb* to make or become narrow.

nar'rowly *adv* barely, only just.

na'sal *adj* having to do with the nose.

nastiness *see* **nasty**.

nas'ty *adj* 1 unpleasant. 2 dirty. 3 disagreeable. 4 unkind:—*n* **nas'tiness**.

na'tion *n* all the people belonging to one country and living under the same government.

na'tional *adj* 1 having to do with a nation. 2 of concern to all the people in a country.

na'tionalism *n* the policy or beliefs of a nationalist.

na'tionalist *n* 1 one who demands self-government for his or her country. 2 one who has great pride in and love of his or her country and considers it superior to others.

national'ity *n* membership of a particular nation.

na'tionalize *vb* to take land, mines, etc, away from private possessors and make them the property of the whole nation.

na'tive *adj* 1 of the place where one was born. 2 belonging to a country. 3 born in a person:—*n* 1 a person belonging to a place by birth. 2 (*now often considered offensive*) an original inhabitant of a place.

nat'ural *adj* 1 in agreement with the laws that seem to govern the universe and existence. 2 born in a person. 3 not caused by human beings. 4 without pretense, simple and direct. 5 normal. 6 real, genuine. 7 (*mus*) neither sharp nor flat.

natural history *n* the study of the earth and all that grows on it.

nat'uralist *n* one who studies plant and animal life.

nat'uralize *vb* to accept someone as a member of a nation to which he or she does not belong by birth:—*n* **naturaliza'tion**.

nat'urally *adv* 1 in a natural way. 2 of course.

na'ture *n* 1 all existing and happening in the universe that is not the work of human beings, such as the plants and animals

around us. 2 the sum of those qualities that make any creature or thing different from others. 3 the character of a person. 4 kind, sort.

naught *n* 1 nothing. 2 the figure 0.

naught'y *adj* mischievous, badly behaved:—*n* **naught'iness**.

nausea [nä'-zee-a] *n* 1 a feeling of sickness. 2 great disgust:—*adj* **nau'seous**.

nau'seate *vb* 1 to sicken. 2 to disgust.

nau'tical *adj* having to do with the sea, sailors, or ships.

na'val *adj* having to do with a navy or warships.

na'vel *n* a little hollow in the center of the belly.

nav'igate *vb* 1 to sail (a ship). 2 to work out the correct course for a ship, aircraft, etc, and direct it on that course.

naviga'tion *n* 1 the science of working out the course or position of a ship, aircraft, etc. 2 act of sailing a ship.

nav'igator *n* one who navigates.

na'vy *n* the warships of a nation, their crews, and equipment.

navy blue *adj* very dark blue.

near *adj* 1 close, not distant in time or place. 2 only just missed or avoided:—*prep* close to:—*adv* almost:—*vb* to approach.

near'ly *adv* almost.

near'-sight'ed *adj* short-sighted.

neat *adj* 1 tidily arranged. 2 skillfully done or made. 3 not mixed with anything weaker:—*n* **neat'ness**.

ne'cessary *adj* needed, unavoidable, that cannot be done without:—*adv* **necessar'ily**.

necess'itous *adj* (*fml*) poor, in need.

necess'ity *n* 1 that which one needs. 2 the condition of being necessary or unavoidable. 3 circumstances forcing one to act or behave in a certain way.

neck *n* 1 the part of the body joining the head to the shoulders. 2 the narrow part near the mouth of a bottle. 3 a narrow strip of land joining two larger masses of land:—**neck and neck** exactly level.

neck'lace *n* a string of beads or jewels worn around the neck.

nec'tar *n* 1 in Greek legend, the drink of the gods. 2 a sweet liquid found in flowers.

nec'tarine *n* a type of peach with a smooth skin.

need *n* 1 a want. 2 that which one requires. 3 poverty:—*vb* 1 to be in want of, to require. 2 to be obliged.

nee'dle *n* 1 a small sharply pointed piece of steel used for drawing thread through cloth in sewing. 2 a short pointed stick used for knitting wool. 3 a small metal pointer on a dial, compass, etc. 4 the long pointed leaf of a pine tree, fir, etc.

need'less *adj* unnecessary.

need'lework *n* sewing.

need'y *adj* poor, living in want.

ne'er-do-well *adj and n* good for nothing.

neg'ative *adj* 1 saying no. 2 criticizing but putting forward no alternative plan or idea:—*n* 1 a word like no, not, etc, expressing refusal or denial. 2 the image on a photographic film or plate in which light seems dark and shade light.

neglect' *vb* 1 to fail to take care of. 2 to leave undone. 3 to pay no or little attention to, to give too little care to:—*n* want of care or attention.

neglect'ful *adj* heedless, careless.

neg'ligence *n* carelessness, lack of proper care.

neg'ligent *adj* careless.

neg'ligible *adj* too little to bother about.

nego'tiate *vb* 1 to try to reach agreement, to bargain. 2 to arrange, usu after a long discussion. 3 to obtain or give

99

money for. **4** to pass (over, etc) successfully:—*n* **nego-tia'tion**:—*n* **nego'tiator**.

neigh *n* the cry of a horse:—*also vb*.

neigh'bor *n* **1** one living near. **2** a person living next door.

neigh'borhood *n* **1** the surrounding area or district. **2** a group of people and their homes forming a small area within a larger one.

neigh'boring *adj* close at hand, near.

neigh'borly *adj* friendly, helpful.

nei'ther *adj, pron, conj, adv* not either.

nem'esis *n* the punishment justly suffered by the wrongdoer.

ne'on *n* a gas that glows brightly when electricity passes through it.

ne'phew *n* the son of one's brother or sister.

nerve *n* **1** one of the thread-like fibers along which messages pass to and from the brain. **2** courage. **3** (*inf*) self-confidence, cheek. **4** *pl* excitement, nervousness:—*vb* to give strength.

ner'vous *adj* easily excited or upset, timid:—*n* **ner'vousness**.

nest *n* **1** a place built by a bird in which it lays its eggs and brings up its young. **2** the home built by certain small animals and insects. **3** a set of things that fit one inside another:—*vb* to build a nest and live in it.

nest egg *n* a sum of money laid aside for future use.

nes'tle *vb* **1** to lie close to. **2** to settle comfortably.

nest'ling *n* a bird too young to leave the nest.

net[1] *n* **1** crisscrossing strings knotted together at the crossing places. **2** an extent of this used for catching fish, animals, etc, and for many other purposes. **3** a fabric made like this:—*vb* (**net'ted, net'ting**) **1** to catch in a net. **2** to cover with a net. **3** to hit or kick into a net.

net[2] *adj* left after one has subtracted the amount due for taxes, expenses, etc:—*vb* (**net'ted, net'ting**) to bring in as profit.

net'ting *n* material made in the form of a net.

net'tle *n* a weed covered with stinging hairs:—*vb* to anger, to annoy.

net'work *n* **1** anything in which lines, roads, railroads, etc, cross and re-cross each other. **2** a widespread organization:—*vb* **1** to broadcast on a network. **2** to connect (computers, etc) so that information, devices, etc, can be shared.

neurolog'ical *adj* having to do with the nerves.

neurot'ic *adj* in a nervous state, unreasonably anxious or sensitive.

neu'ter *adj* neither masculine nor feminine.

neu'tral *adj* **1** not taking sides, neither for nor against, impartial. **2** not strong or definite:—*n* a neutral person or party.

neutral'ity *n* the state of being neutral.

nev'er *adv* at no time.

nevertheless' *adv* for all that.

new *adj* **1** never known before. **2** just bought or made, fresh. **3** changed from an earlier state, different:—*n* **new'ness**.

new'comer *n* one who has recently arrived.

new'ly *adv* recently.

news *n* **1** information about what is going on. **2** an account of recent events.

news'dealer *n* a storekeeper who sells newspapers.

news'paper *n* a number of printed sheets (usu issued daily) containing the latest news, articles, advertisements, etc.

next *adj* nearest:—*also adv, prep, n*.

nib *n* the point of a pen.

nib'ble *vb* to take small bites at:—*also n*.

nice *adj* **1** pleasing. **2** (*old*) particular when choosing, hard to please. **3** (*fml*) fine, delicate.

niche [nitsh] *n* **1** a hollow place in a wall for a statue, etc. **2** the work or place for which one is best suited.

nick *n* the small hollow left when a piece is cut or chipped out of something, a notch:—*vb* to cut notches in:—**in the nick of time** just in time.

nick'name *n* a name used instead of one's real name in friendship or mockery:—*vb* to give a nickname to.

nic'otine *n* a toxic oily liquid from tobacco.

niece *n* the daughter of one's brother or sister.

night *n* the time between sunset and sunrise, darkness.

night'cap *n* **1** a cap worn in bed. **2** a drink taken last thing at night.

night'dress *n* a garment worn in bed, esp by women and children.

night'ingale *n* a type of small bird that sings beautifully.

night'ly *adj* happening every night:—*adv* every night.

night'mare *n* a frightening dream.

night'stick *n* a police officer's baton.

night'-watch'man *n* one who looks after buildings, etc, by night.

nil *n* nothing.

nim'ble *adj* active, quick-moving.—*n* **nim'bleness**.

nip *vb* (**nipped', nip'ping**) **1** to pinch. **2** to bite. **3** to stop the growth:—*n* **1** a pinch. **2** biting cold. **3** a small drink:—**nip in the bud** to destroy at an early stage.

nip'ple *n* **1** the point of the breast. **2** anything so shaped. **3** a rubber stopper with a small hole in it through which liquid may pass, a teat.

nit *n* the egg of a louse or other small insect.

ni'trogen *n* a colorless gas that makes up about four-fifths of the air.—*adj* **nitro'genous**.

nit'wit *n* a foolish, worthless person.

nobil'ity *n* **1** goodness of character. **2** the nobles of a country.

no'ble *adj* **1** fine in character, honorable. **2** of high rank. **3** stately:—*n* a person of high rank.

no'body *n* no one. **2** (*inf*) a person of no importance.

noctur'nal *adj* **1** happening at night. **2** active by night.

nod *vb* (**nod'ded, nod'ding**) **1** to bow the head slightly. **2** to let the head drop forward in tiredness:—*n* a slight bow of the head.

noise *n* **1** a sound. **2** loud or unpleasant sounds, din:—*vb* (*fml or old*) to make public:—*adjs* **noise'less, nois'y**.

no'mad *n* **1** a wanderer. **2** a member of a tribe that is always on the move.

nomad'ic *adj* wandering.

nom'inal *adj* existing in name but not in reality.

nom'inate *vb* **1** to put forward another's name for a certain office. **2** to appoint:—*n* **nomina'tion**.

nom'inative *n* in grammar, the case of the subject of a verb.

nominee' *n* a person nominated.

nonagena'rian *n* one who is ninety years old or between ninety and a hundred.

non'chalant *adj* calm, unexcited, showing little interest, cool:—*n* **non'chalance**.

non-committ'al *adj* not definite, saying neither yes nor no.

nonconform'ist *n* **1** one who refuses to follow the accepted ways of doing things. **2** a Protestant who is not a member of the Episcopal Church:—*n* **nonconform'ity**.

non'descript *adj* not easily described, not very interesting.

nonen'tity *n* a person of no importance, a person of little ability or character.

nonplus' *vb* to puzzle completely, to leave speechless.

non'sense *n* foolish or meaningless words, ideas, etc.

nonsen'sical *adj* meaningless, absurd.

non'-stop *adj and adv* without any stop or pause.

noo'dle *n* a paste for cooking made from flour, water, and eggs.

nook *n* a corner.

noon n twelve o'clock, midday.

noose n a cord or rope with a loop at one end fastened by a running knot:—vb 1 to catch in a noose.

norm n the usual rule, an example or standard with which others may be compared.

nor'mal adj usual, according to what is expected, average:— n **normal'ity**.

north n 1 one of the chief points of the compass, opposite the midday sun as seen from the Northern Hemisphere. 2 the northern part of a country. 3 the northern regions of the world:—adj 1 having to do with the north. 2 of or from the north.

northeast' n the point of the compass halfway between north and east:—also adj.

north'erly, north'ern adjs 1 having to do with the north. 2 of or from the north.

north'ernmost adjs farthest to the north.

North Pole n the northern end of the earth, in the middle of the Arctic regions.

north'ward(s) adv toward the north.

northwest' n the point of the compass halfway between north and west:—also adj.

nose n 1 a jutting-out part of the face containing the organ of smell. 2 a sense of smell. 3 any jutting-out part in front of anything:—vb 1 to smell. 2 to find by smell. 3 to look or search around in. 4 to discover by searching. 5 to move slowly.

nostal'gia n a longing or feeling of fondness for things past:— adj **nostal'gic**.

nos'tril n one of the two openings of the nose.

no'table adj worthy of notice, deserving to be remembered:— n **notabil'ity**.

notch n a small V-shaped cut:—vb to make a notch in.

note n 1 a short letter. 2 a short written account of what is said or done. 3 a written explanation. 4 a single musical sound or the sign standing for it. 5 a piece of paper money, a bill. 6 fame, good reputation:—vb 1 to put down in writing. 2 to take notice of.

note'book n a book into which notes may be written.

not'ed adj famous, well-known.

note'worthy adj deserving to be noticed or remembered.

noth'ing n 1 no thing, not anything. 2 a thing of no importance.

no'tice n 1 a written or printed announcement. 2 warning. 3 attention. 4 advance information:—vb 1 to pay attention to. 2 to see.

no'ticeable adj 1 worthy of attention. 2 easily seen:—adv **no'ticeably**.

no'tify vb to inform, to make known:—n **notifica'tion**.

no'tion n 1 idea, opinion, view. 2 a sudden desire.

noto'rious adj well known for something bad.

nought same as **naught**.

noun n in grammar, a word that names a person or thing.

nour'ish vb to feed, to give what is needed to grow or stay healthy.

nour'ishment n food, esp food of value to health.

nov'el adj new and often of an unusual kind:—n a long story of which all or some of the events are imaginary.

nov'elty n 1 newness, the quality of being novel. 2 a new or unusual thing. 3 an unusual, small, cheap object.

Novem'ber n the eleventh month of the year.

nov'ice n a beginner.

now adv 1 at the present time. 2 at once.

now'adays adv in modern times.

no'where adv in no place.

noz'zle n a spout or pipe fitted on to the end of a hose, etc, to direct the liquid.

nu'cleus n (pl **nu'clei**) 1 the central part of an atom, seed, etc. 2 the central part of anything around which the rest grows up.

nude adj naked, wearing no clothes:—n a naked person.

nudge vb to push with the elbow:—also n.

nu'dity n nakedness.

nug'get n a lump, as of gold, silver, etc.

nuis'ance n a person, action, or thing that annoys.

null adj:—**null and void** having no legal force.

numb adj unable to feel:—vb to take away the power of feeling sensations.

num'ber n 1 a word or sign that tells how many. 2 a collection of several (persons, things, etc). 3 a single copy of a magazine, etc, printed at a particular time, an issue. 4 a piece of popular music or a popular song sung forming part of a longer performance:—vb 1 (fml) to reach as a total. 2 to give a number to. 3 to include.

nu'meral n a word or figure standing for a number.

nu'merate adj able to do arithmetic and mathematics:— n **numera'tion**.

nu'merator n in simple fractions, the number above the line which tells how many parts there are.

numer'ical adj having to do with numbers.

nu'merous adj many.

nun n a woman who joins a convent and vows to devote her life to the service of God.

nun'nery n a convent, a house for nuns.

nurse n one trained to look after the young, sick, or aged:—vb 1 to look after as a nurse. 2 to give milk from the breast, to suckle.

nurs'ery n 1 a room in a house for children to sleep or play in. 2 a place where young children are looked after. 3 a place where young plants are grown for sale.

nursery school n a school for young children of preschool age.

nursing home n a small private hospital for invalids, convalescent people, or old people unable to take care of themselves.

nut n 1 a fruit with a hard outer shell and an eatable kernel inside it. 2 the eatable kernel. 3 a screw that is turned on to one end of a bolt to fasten it:—**in a nutshell** in a few words.

nutri'tion n nourishment.

nutri'tious, nu'tritive adjs good for the health of the body.

nut'ty adj 1 tasting of nuts. 2 (inf) mad.

nuz'zle vb 1 to push or rub with the nose. 2 to press close up to.

ny'lon n 1 an artificial fiber for thread or cloth. 2 a stocking made from this.

O

oaf *n* a stupid or clumsy person.

oak *n* a hardwood tree that bears acorns.

oar *n* a pole with a flat broad end, used for rowing a boat.

oasis [ō-ā´-si s] *n* (*pl* **oa´ses** [ō-ā´-sez]) **1** a place in the desert where there is water and plants grow. **2** any place of shelter or relief.

oat *n*, **oats** *npl* a grain much used for food:—**sow one's wild oats** to live a life of unrestrained enjoyment when young.

oath *n* **1** a solemn promise, esp one made in God's name. **2** a swear word.

oat'meal *n* **1** oats ground to powder. **2** a food made from oatmeal boiled in water or milk to make a thick broth, porridge.

obe'dient *adj* willing to do what one is told:—*n* **obedience**.

obey' *vb* **1** to do what one is told. **2** to carry out.

object'ion *n* anything that can be perceived by the senses. **2** aim, purpose. **3** in grammar, a word governed by a verb or preposition:—*vb* **object' 1** to express dislike. **2** to speak against.

objec'tion *n* a reason against.

objec'tionable *adj* deserving to be disliked, unpleasant.

objec'tive *adj* not depending on, or influenced by, personal opinions:*n* aim, purpose.

object'or *n* one who objects.

obliga'tion *n* **1** a duty, a promise that must be kept. **2** gratitude due to another for kindness or help.

oblig'atory *adj* that has to be done (e.g. as a duty), compulsory.

oblige' *vb* **1** (*fml*) to force or make it necessary to do. **2** to do a kindness or service for.

oblig'ing *adj* ready to help, kind.

oblique [o-bleek´] *adj* **1** slanting. **2** indirect.

ob'long *n* **1** a four-sided figure with all angles right angles and one pair of sides longer than the other pair. **2** a figure or object so shaped.

o'boe *n* a wooden wind instrument:—*n* **o'boist**.

obscene' *adj* disgusting, indecent, esp sexual:—*n* **obscen'ity**.

obscure' *adj* **1** (*fml*) dark. **2** not clear in meaning. **3** not well known, not famous:—*vb* **1** to darken. **2** to hide from view. **3** to make more difficult.

obscu'rity *n* the state of being obscure.

obser'vance *n* **1** the act of observing. **2** the act of obeying.

obser'vant *adj* quick to notice things.

observa'tion *n* **1** the act, power, or habit of observing. **2** a remark.

obser'vatory *n* a place from which scientists study the stars, the planets, and the heavens.

observe' *vb* **1** (*fml*) to see, to notice. **2** to watch carefully. **3** to carry out. **4** to say, to make a remark.

obses'sion *n* an idea or interest that takes up all one's attention so that one never thinks of other things.

ob'solete *adj* no longer in use, out of date:— *n* **obsolescence**.

ob'stacle *n* that which is in the way and prevents progress.

ob'stinate *adj* **1** determined to hold to one's own opinions, etc, stubborn. **2** not easy to cure or remove:—*n* **ob'stinacy**.

obstruct' *vb* **1** to stop up. **2** to prevent from moving or acting freely.

obstruc'tion *n* **1** a cause of delay. **2** an obstacle.

obtain' *vb* **1** to get. **2** (*fml*) to be in use.

obtain'able *adj* that can be got.

ob'verse *n* the "heads" side of a coin.

ob'vious *adj* easily seen or understood.

occa'sion *n* **1** a particular time. **2** a special event. **3** (*fml*) a reason. **4** (*fml*) opportunity:—*vb* to cause.

occa'sional *adj* **1** happening now and then. **2** having to do with a particular event or occasion.

oc'cident (*fml*) *n* **1** the west, western regions or lands. **2** (*with cap*) the Western Hemisphere.

occult' *adj* secret, mysterious, having to do with magic.

oc'cupant, oc'cupier *ns* the person living in a house.

occupa'tion *n* **1** act of occupying. **2** the time during which a place is occupied. **3** one's job. **4** that which one is doing at a certain time.

oc'cupy *vb* **1** to take possession of. **2** to live in. **3** to fill. **4** to keep busy. **5** to take up space, time, etc).

occur' *vb* (**occurred', occur'ring 1** to happen. **2** to come to the mind. **3** to be found here and there.

occur'rence *n* a happening, an event.

ocean [ō´-shēn] *n* **1** the vast body of salt water surrounding the land on the earth. **2** a large sea:—*adj* **ocean'ic**.

oc'tagon *n* a figure or shape with eight angles and sides.

octag'onal *adj* eight-sided.

octet' *n* a group of eight singers or players of instruments.

Octo'ber *n* the tenth month of the year.

octogena'rian *n* one who is eighty years old or between eighty and ninety.

oc'topus *n* a sea creature with eight arms.

odd *adj* **1** (*of a number*) not even, that cannot be divided by two without leaving a remainder of one. **2** strange, unusual. **3** unmatched.

odd'ity *n* something strange or unusual, a queer person.

odd'ment *n* a piece left over.

odds *npl* the chances in favor of a certain happening or result:**odds and ends** extra pieces or things of various kinds.

o'dious *adj* hateful, disgusting.

o'dor *n* any smell, pleasant or unpleasant:—**in bad odor** unpopular.

off *adv* **1** away. **2** distant:—*adj* **1** not happening. **2** (*inf*) not fit to eat, bad, rotten:—*prep* away from, not on.

off'al *n* the inner organs of an animal sold as food or regarded as waste matter.

offend' *vb* **1** to displease, to hurt someone's feelings. **2** (*fml*) to do wrong. **3** to be unpleasant or disagreeable.

offen'der *n* **1** one who does wrong. **2** one who causes offense.

offense' *n* **1** a wrongful act. **2** hurt done to the feelings, a feeling that one has been insulted.

offen'sive *adj* **1** unpleasant. **2** insulting. **3** having to do with attack:—*n* an attack.

of'fer *vb* **1** to give one the chance of taking. **2** to say that one is willing (to do something). **3** to give as a sacrifice:—*n* **1** act of offering. **2** the thing or amount offered.

off'hand *adj* careless, thoughtless.

of'fice *n* **1** a special duty. **2** a room or building in which business is carried on.

of'ficer *n* one holding a post with certain powers or duties, esp in the armed forces.

offi'cial *adj* **1** having to do with an office or the duties attached to it. **2** given out or announced by those with the right to do so:—*n* one who holds a post with certain powers or duties.

offi'cious *adj* too eager to give orders or offer advice.

of'fing *n*:—**in the offing** not far off.

off'shoot *n* 1 a branch or shoot growing out from the main stem of a plant. 2 something growing out of something else.

off'spring *n* a child.

of'ten *adv* frequently.

o'gle *vb* to look sideways at, to look or stare at because of admiration or sexual attraction.

o'gre *n* in fairy tales, a man-eating giant:—*f* **o'gress**.

ohm [ōm] *n* the unit of measurement of electrical resistance.

oil *n* 1 a greasy liquid obtained from vegetable, animal, or mineral sources and used as a fuel, lubricant, etc. 2 *pl* oil paints or painting:—*vb* to put or drop oil on, as on the parts of a machine to make them work smoothly.

oil'y *adj* 1 covered with oil. 2 greasy.

oint'ment *n* an oily paste rubbed on the skin to heal cuts or sores.

old *adj* 1 not new. 2 aged. 3 belonging to the past. 4 not fresh.

old-fash'ioned *adj* out of date.

ol'ive *n* an evergreen tree bearing a small, sharptasting fruit, from which oil can be obtained. 2 its fruit, used as food:—*adj* yellowish-green:—*n* **ol'ive oil**.

ol'ive-skinned' *adj* having a yellowish-brown skin.

Olympic Games *npl* an international athletic contest held every four years, each time in a different country.

om'elet *n* eggs beaten and fried in a pan.

o'men *n* a sign of a future event, good or bad.

om'inous *adj* signifying future trouble or disaster.

omit' *vb* (**omit'ted, omit'ting**) 1 to fail to do. 2 to leave out:—*n* **omis'sion**.

om'nibus *n* (*fml*) a bus.

omnis'cient [om-nish'ent] *adj* knowing all things:—*n* **omnis'cience**.

omni'vorous *adj* 1 (*fml or hum*) eating all kinds of food. 2 taking in everything indiscriminately.

once *adv* 1 on one occasion only. 2 formerly: **once and for all** once and never again:—**at once** immediately.

on'coming *adj* approaching.

one *adj* single:—*pron* a person.

on'going *adj* continuing, continuing to develop.

onion [un'-yên] *n* a strong-smelling eatable bulb, much used in cooking.

on'looker *n* a spectator, one who looks at what is happening but takes no part in it.

on'rush *n* a rapid advance.

on'set *n* the first attack of or the beginning of.

on'shore *adj* toward the shore:—*adv* **onshore**.

on'slaught *n* a fierce attack.

on'ward *adj* forward:—*advs* **on'ward, onwards**.

ooze *n* soft mud, slime:—*vb* 1 to flow very slowly. 2 to have flowing from.

opacity *see* **opaque**.

opaque [o-pāk'] *adj* that cannot be seen through, letting no light through:—*n* **opa'city**.

o'pen *adj* 1 not shut, uncovered. 2 ready for business. 3 not hidden. 4 free from obstructions. 5 public. 6 sincere. 7 clear:—*vb* 1 to make or become open. 2 to unlock. 3 to begin.

o'pening *n* 1 beginning. 2 a gap, a way in or out. 3 an opportunity.

o'penly *adv* publicly, not secretly.

o'pen-mind'ed *adj* ready to consider new ideas, unprejudiced.

op'era *n* a musical drama in which all or some of the words are sung.

op'erate *vb* 1 (*of a machine*) to work or to cause to work. 2 (*of a surgeon*) to cut the body in order to cure or treat a diseased part.

op'erating room *n* a room in a hospital in which surgeons perform operations.

opera'tion *n* 1 action. 2 the way a thing works. 3 the cutting of the body by a doctor or surgeon to cure or treat a diseased part.

op'erative *adj* 1 in action. 2 having effect:—*n* a worker in a factory.

op'erator *n* one who looks after a machine.

opin'ion *n* 1 that which one thinks or believes about something. 2 judgment.

oppo'nent *n* an enemy, a person whom one tries to overcome in a game, argument, etc.

oppor'tune *adj* happening at the right time.

oppose' *vb* 1 to act or speak against. 2 to resist.

op'posite *adj* 1 facing. 2 in the same position on the other side. 3 different in every way:—*n* something in every way different:—*adv, prep* across from.

opposi'tion *n* 1 the act of going or speaking against, resistance. 2 (*often cap*) in parliament, the party that criticizes or resists the governing party.

oppress' *vb* 1 to govern harshly or unjustly, to treat cruelly. 2 to make gloomy or anxious:—*n* **oppression**.

oppres'sive *adj* 1 harsh and unjust. 2 (*of the weather*) hot and tiring.

op'tic, op'tical *adjs* having to do with sight or the eye(s).

opti'cian *n* one who makes or sells glasses for the eyes.

op'tics *n* the science of light or sight.

op'timism *n* the belief that all that happens is for the best, cheerful hope that all will go well.

op'timist *n* a cheerfully hopeful person.

optimis'tic *adj* having to do with or characterized by optimism.

op'tion *n* choice.

op'tional *adj* that may or may not be done by choice.

op'ulence *n* (*fml*) riches, wealth.

op'ulent *adj* (*fml*) rich, wealthy.

o'ral *adj* spoken, not written.

or'ange *n* 1 a juicy fruit with a reddish-yellow skin. 2 the tree bearing it. 3 its color, reddishyellow:—*adj* of orange color.

orang'utan' [-ûtan'] *n* a large man-like ape with long arms.

or'ator *n* a skilled public speaker.

or'bit *n* the curved path of a planet, a rocket, etc, around a larger heavenly body:—*also vb*.

or'chard *n* a field in which fruit trees are grown.

orchestra [or'-kis-tra] *n* a group of musicians skilled in different instruments who play together.

orches'tral *adj* suitable for performance by an orchestra.

orchestra seat *n* a first-floor seat in a theatre.

or'deal *n* 1 a difficult, painful experience.

or'der *n* 1 a methodical arrangement. 2 a command. 3 rank, class. 4 obedience to law. 5 tidiness. 6 an instruction to make or supply something (an order for books). 7 a body or brotherhood of people of the same rank, profession, etc, a religious brotherhood obeying a certain rule:—*vb* 1 to arrange. 2 to command. 3 to give an instruction to make or supply.

or'derly *adj* 1 tidy, well-arranged. 2 well-behaved:—*n* 1 a soldier who carries the orders and messages of an officer. 2 a hospital attendant.

or'dinary *adj* usual, common, not exceptional.

ore *n* rock from which metal is obtained.

or'gan *n* 1 part of an animal or plant that serves some special purpose. 2 a large musical instrument supplied with wind through pipes and played by a keyboard. 3 a means of conveying views or information to the public.

organ'ic *adj* 1 having to do with an organ. 2 produced by living organs. 3 grown without the use of artificial fertilizers.

or'ganism n 1 any living thing. 2 anything in which the parts all work together to serve one purpose.

or'ganist n one who plays the organ.

organiza'tion n 1 orderly arrangement. 2 a group of people working systematically to carry out a common purpose.

or'ganize vb 1 to put together in an orderly way, to make to work systematically. 2 to arrange.

or'gy n a wild or drunken feast.

or'ient[1] (fml) n 1 the east, the eastern regions, or lands. 2 (with cap the Eastern Hemisphere, the countries of Asia.

or'ient[2] vb 1 to find out north, south, east, and west from the point where one is standing. 2 to face in a particular direction. 3 to arrange or direct toward:—n **orienta'tion**.

Orien'talist n one who studies Eastern languages.

or'igin n 1 the place or point at which a thing begins, beginning. 2 cause.

orig'inal adj 1 new, not thought of before. 2 first in order. 3 ready to think or act in a new way. 4 not copied:—n 1 an original work of art, etc. 2 a creative or eccentric person.

original'ity n the ability to think or act in a new way.

orig'inate vb 1 to bring into being. 2 to come into being.

or'nament n that which decorates or makes more attractive:—vb ornament' to decorate:—n **ornamenta'tion**.

ornamen'tal adj decorative.

ornate' adj with a great deal of ornament, richly decorated.

ornithol'ogist n one who studies birds:—n **ornithology**.

or'phan n a child whose parents are dead:—vb to cause to become an orphan:—also adj.

or'phanage n a home for orphans.

or'thodox adj 1 having the same beliefs or opinions as most other people. 2 agreeing with accepted belief:—n **orthodoxy**.

ostenta'tion n the making of much show to attract attention, a showing off, rich display.

ostenta'tious adj showy, fond of display.

os'tracize vb to drive out of society, to refuse to have anything to do with:—n **os'tracism**.

os'trich n a large swift-running bird valued for its feathers.

oth'er adj 1 one of two things. 2 additional. 3 those not mentioned, present, etc.

oth'erwise adv 1 in a different way. 2 if this were not so.

ot'ter n a fish-eating animal of the weasel family.

ought vb should.

ounce n 1 a unit of weight (= ¹/16 pound). 2 one fluid ounce (= ¹/16 pint). 3 a small amount.

oust vb to put out, to drive out.

out adv 1 not inside. 2 away:—prep out of, out through, outside:—adj 1 external. 2 asleep or unconscious.

out'-and-out' adj thorough.

out'break n a sudden beginning, a breaking out.

out'burst n a bursting out, an explosion of anger.

out'cast adj driven away from one's home and friends:—n a person so driven away.

out'come n the result.

out'cry n widespread complaint.

outdo' vb to do better than.

out'door adj done in the open air.

outdoors' adv in the open air.

out'er adj 1 farther out. 2 outside.

out'ermost adj farthest out.

out'fit n 1 all the articles necessary for a certain job. 2 a set of articles of clothing.

out'going adj 1 departing, retiring. 2 sociable, forthcoming:—n 1 an outlay. 2 pl expenditure.

outgrow' vb 1 to grow taller than. 2 to grow too big or too old for.

out'house n a small house or building near the main one.

out'ing n a short trip made for pleasure.

outland'ish adj strange.

out'law n (old) one whose person and property are no longer protected by the law:—vb 1 to declare an outlaw. 2 to declare not legal:—n **outlawry**.

out'lay n money spent.

out'let n 1 an opening outward. 2 an activity that allows one to make use of one's powers or of a particular ability.

out'line n 1 a line showing the shape of a thing. 2 an account of the most important points, etc:—vb 1 to draw in outline. 2 to describe without giving details.

outlive' vb to live longer than.

out'look n 1 view. 2 what seems likely to happen in future. 3 point of view.

out'lying adj distant, far from the center.

outnum'ber vb to be greater in number than.

out-of-date' adj old-fashioned.

out-of-the-way' adj 1 not easily reached. 2 unusual.

out'patient n one who visits a hospital for treatment but does not stay there.

out'put n the total amount produced by a machine, factory, worker, etc.

out'rage n 1 a violent and wicked deed. 2 a deed that shocks or causes widespread anger:—vb 1 to injure. 2 to insult.

outrage'ous adj 1 shocking, wicked. 2 extravagantly unusual.

outright' adv 1 completely and at once. 2 openly, frankly:—adj complete.

out'set n beginning.

outshine' vb to do much better than.

out'side n 1 the outer part or parts. 2 the part farthest from the center:—adj 1 being on the outside, external. 2 outdoor. 3 slight:—adv on or to the outside:—prep on or to the exterior of, beyond.

outsid'er n 1 one who is not accepted as a member of a certain group. 2 one who is believed to have little chance of winning.

out'skirts npl the parts of a town or city farthest from the center.

outspo'ken adj saying just what one thinks, frank.

outstand'ing adj 1 exceptionally good. 2 (fml) still in existence.

out'ward adj 1 on the outside or surface. 2 away from a place:—advs out'ward, out'wards, outwardly.

outwit' (outwit'ting, outwit'ted) to outdo or overcome by greater cleverness, to deceive.

ova see ovum.

o'val adj egg-shaped:—n an oval shape or figure.

o'vary n 1 a bodily organ in which eggs are formed. 2 the seed case of a plant.

oven [uv'-én] n a small cupboard heated by a fire or stove and used for cooking.

o'ver prep 1 above. 2 across. 3 more than:—adv 1 above. 2 across. 3 from one side to the other or another. 4 more than the quantity assigned. 5 completed. 6 from beginning to end:—n the number of successive balls delivered by a bowler in cricket.

o'veralls npl a garment worn over one's usual clothes to keep them clean.

overbal'ance vb 1 to lean too much in one direction and fall. 2 to cause to fall in this way.

overbear'ing adj proud and commanding.

overboard' adv over the side of a ship.

overcast' adj clouded over.

o'vercoat n a warm outer garment.

overcome' vb 1 to defeat. 2 to get the better of.

overdo' vb 1 to do too much. 2 to cook for too long.

o'verdose *n* too large a dose:—*also vb.*

o'verdraft *n* the amount of money drawn from a bank in excess of what is available in an account.

overdraw' *vb* to take more from a bank than one has in one's account.

overdue' *adj* after the time fixed or due.

overflow' *vb* to flood, to flow over the edge or limits of:— *n* **1** what flows over the sides. **2** the amount by which something is too much.

overgrown' *adj* grown beyond normal size.

overhead' *adj and adv* in the sky, above.

o'verheads *npl* the costs of running a business.

overhear' *vb* to hear what one is not intended to hear.

overlap' *vb* to cover partly and go beyond it.

overlook' *vb* **1** to look down on from above. **2** to forgive, to let off without punishment. **3** not to notice, to miss.

overnight' *adv* during the night:—*adj* done in or lasting the night.

overpow'er *vb* to defeat by greater strength.

overpow'ering *adj* too great to bear.

overrate' *vb* to think a person or thing better than he, she, or it really is.

overrule' *vb* to use one's power to change the decision or judgement of another.

overrun' *vb* **1** to spread over in large numbers. **2** to continue beyond the expected time.

oversea(s)' *adj and adv* across the sea.

oversee' *vb* to direct the work of others:—*n* **overseer**.

oversha'dow *vb* to make seem less important.

o'versight *n* a mistake, a failure to do something.

oversleep' *vb* to sleep later than intended.

oversubscribed' *adj* with more wanted than is on sale.

overtake' *vb* to catch up with.

overthrow' *vb* to defeat, to remove from power:—*also n adj and adv.*

o'vertime *n* time worked beyond the regular hours:—*also adj and adv.*

overturn' *vb* **1** to turn upside down. **2** to make fall, to defeat, to ruin.

overweight' *adj* weighing more than the proper amount:— *n* excess weight.

overwhelm *vb* **1** to defeat utterly. **2** to overcome all ones powers, to make to feel helpless.

overwork' *vb* to work too hard:—*n* too much work.

overwrought' *adj* overexcited, too nervous.

ovoid *n* egg-shaped.

o'vum *n* (*pl* **o'va**) an egg.

owe *vb* **1** to be in debt to. **2** to be obliged to someone), to feel grateful to:—**owing to** because of.

owl *n* a night bird of prey.

own *adj* belonging to oneself:—*vb* **1** to possess. **2** (*fml*) to admit:—*n* **own'er**:—*n* **own'ership**.

ox *n* **1** a bull or cow. **2** *pl* **ox'en** cattle.

ox'ygen *n* a gas without color, taste, or smell that is present in air and water and is necessary for all life.

oxymo'ron *n* a figure of speech in which an adjective seems to contradict the noun it accompanies (e.g. busy idler).

oy'ster *n* an eatable shellfish with a double shell in which pearls are sometimes found.

o'zone *n* **1** a kind of colorless gas with a chlorine-like smell. **2** (*inf*) clean bracing air as found at the beach.

ozone layer *n* a layer of ozone in the stratosphere that absorbs ultraviolet rays from the sun.

P

pace n 1 a step with the foot. 2 the distance so covered. 3 speed:—vb to walk slowly and steadily.

pa'cifier n 1 a person or thing that pacifies. 2 a small rubber or plastic nipple for a baby to suck or chew on.

pa'cifism n one who works for the end of all war:— n pa'cifism.

pa'cify vb 1 to restore peace, to end a war in. 2 to calm, to soothe.

pack n 1 a bundle of things fastened or strapped together. 2 a set of playing cards. 3 a number of animals acting or hunting together. 4 a gang. 5 a mass of floating pieces of ice:—vb 1 to make into a bundle, to put something into a case, etc. 2 to fill. 3 to fill to overflowing.

pack'age n a parcel, a bundle.

pack'et n a small parcel.

pack'ing n the paper, cardboard, etc, used to protect goods being delivered.

pact n an agreement.

pad¹ n 1 a small cushion. 2 soft material used to protect or to alter shape. 3 sheets of paper fixed together. 4 the soft flesh on the foot of certain animals:—vb (**pad'ded, pad'ding**) 1 to fill out with soft material. 2 to make longer with unnecessary words.

pad² vb to walk steadily and usu softly.

pad'ding n 1 soft material used for stuffing or fitting out. 2 words, sentences, etc, put in merely to make longer.

pad'dle n 1 a short oar with a broad blade, sometimes at each end. 2 something resembling this used to hit, bit, or stir:—vb 1 to row with a paddle. 2 to walk in water with bare feet.

pad'dock n a small enclosed field. 2 an enclosure in which horses are assembled before a race.

pad'lock n a metal device that closes over two rings, thus fastening something:—vb to close with a padlock.

pa'gan n one who does not know about God, a heathen:— n pa'ganism.

page¹ n 1 a boy servant, usu uniformed, in a hotel, club, etc. 2 a boy attendant on a bride at a wedding. 3 (old) a boy attendant of a knight or nobleman.

page² n one side of a sheet of paper in a book, etc.

pageant [pa'-jènt] n 1 a performance or procession in which scenes from history are presented. 2 a fine display or show.

pail n an open vessel with a handle for carrying liquids.

pain n 1 suffering of body or mind. 2 pl trouble, care:—vb (fml) to cause suffering to:—adjs pain'ful, pain'less—on pain of death with death as a punishment.

pains'taking adj 1 very careful. 2 taking great trouble.

paint n a coloring substance spread over the surface of an object with a brush:—vb 1 to put on paint. 2 to paint a picture.

paint'er¹ n 1 one who paints. 2 an artist.

paint'er² n a rope for fastening a small boat.

paint'ing n a painted picture.

pair n 1 two things of the same kind, a set of two. 2 a couple, two people, animals, etc, often one of either sex, who are thought of as being together:—vb 1 to arrange in twos. 2 to join one to another.

paja'mas npl a sleeping suit.

pal n (inf) a friend, comrade.

pal'ace n a large and splendid house, esp the house of a king or queen.

pal'atable adj 1 pleasing to the taste. 2 pleasant, acceptable.

pal'ate n 1 the roof of the mouth. 2 the sense of taste, the ability to tell good food or wine from bad. 3 a taste or liking.

pala'tial adj large and splendid, like a palace.

pala'ver n 1 idle talk. 2 (inf) fuss:—vb to talk idly.

pale¹ n 1 a pointed stake of wood driven into the ground as part of a fence. 2 (old) a boundary.

pale² adj 1 lacking color, whitish. 2 not dark in color:—vb 1 to make or become pale.

palette [pal'-et] n a thin board on which an artist mixes paints.

pa'ling n a fence of stakes.

pall¹ n 1 the cloth spread over the coffin at a funeral. 2 a cloak.

pall² vb to become uninteresting through too much use.

pall'et n a wooden platform on which goods can be carried by a fork-lift truck.

pal'lid adj pale, white-faced.

pal'lor n paleness.

pal'ly adj (inf) friendly.

palm¹ [päm] n the inner part of the hand between the wrist and fingers:—vb palm off to get to accept something worthless.

palm² [päm] n a tall tropical tree with a crown of long broad leaves at the top of the trunk.

palm'ist n a person who claims to tell one's future from the lines on one's hand:—n palm'istry.

pal'pable adj 1 that can be touched. 2 (fml) plain, obvious.

paltry adj 1 mean. 2 contemptibly small, worthless.

pam'per vb to spoil by trying to please too much.

pam'phlet n a small paper-covered book.

pan n 1 a metal pot used for cooking. 2 the upper part of the skull. 3 the tray of a balance or set of scales. 4 a depression in the earth filled with water. 5 the bowl of a lavatory:—vb (**pan'ning, panned**) 1 to wash gold-bearing gravel with water. 2 (of a film camera) to follow an object. 3 (inf) to find fault with.—vb pan out to turn out, to result.

pan'cake n a thin cake of batter cooked in a pan or on a girdle.

pan'da n a large black and white animal found in China.

pandemo'nium n a scene of noisy disorder, uproar.

pan'der vb to give in to the desires of a person or group.

pane n a single piece of glass in a window.

pan'el n 1 a thin board fitted into the framework of a door or on a wall or ceiling. 2 a group of people who discuss or answer questions put to them by others.

pang n 1 a sudden sharp pain. 2 a sudden sharp feeling.

pan'handle¹ n a narrow projecting tongue of land.

pan'handle² vb 1 to prospect for gold. 2 (inf) to beg or obtain by begging.

pan'ic n 1 a sudden uncontrollable fear. 2 sudden fear spreading through a crowd and causing wild disorder:—also adj:— vb (**pan'icking, pan'icked**) to affect or be affected by panic.

pan'ic-strick'en adj filled with panic.

panora'ma n a wide view.

pan'sy n a large type of violet.

pant vb 1 to take short quick breaths. 2 to long for:—n a gasp.

pan'ther n a leopard, esp the black variety.

panti'hose n a light, close-fitting garment covering the lower trunk and legs.

pan'tomime n 1 an amusing Christmas entertainment with music and songs based on a story popular with children. 2 mime.

pan'try n 1 a small room for keeping food. 2 a room in which food, dishes, etc, are stored.

pants n 1 a garment originally for men, reaching from waist to ankles and covering each leg separately, trousers. 2 underpants.

pa′pal *adj* having to do with the pope.

pa′per *n* **1** a material made from wood pulp, rags, etc, and used for writing, printing, wrapping, etc. **2** a newspaper. **3** an essay. **4** a set of examination questions on a subject or part of a subject:—*vb* to cover with paper.

pa′perback *n* a soft book with a paper cover.

paper money *n* bank bills.

pa′perweight *n* a heavy object placed on top of loose papers to keep them in place.

papier mâché [pap′-yà mä′-shâ] *n* a substance consisting of paper pulp and used for making boxes, ornaments, etc.

par *n* **1** the state of being equal. **2** the normal value, amount or degree of something. **3** in golf, the number of strokes that should be taken on a round by a good player.

par′achute *n* an apparatus that, by opening like an umbrella, enables people to jump from an airplane and drop to earth safely:—*also vb.*

parade′ *n* **1** a public procession. **2** display, show. **3** soldiers, etc, standing in lines under the command of their officers:—*vb* **1** to show off. **2** to take up places in an orderly body (e.g. of soldiers). **3** to march in procession. **4** to walk up and down.

par′adise *n* **1** heaven. **2** (*inf*) a place or state of great happiness.

par′affin wax *n* a waxy substance obtained from shale or coal and used for making candles or made into oil for lamps, etc.

par′agraph *n* a distinct division of a piece of writing marked by having its first word slightly in from the left-hand margin.

par′akeet *n* a small parrot.

par′allel *adj* (*of lines*) at the same distance from each other at all points. **2** similar:—*n* **1** a like or similar example, a comparison. **2** one of the lines drawn on maps through all places at the same distance from the equator.

parallel′ogram *n* a four-sided figure whose opposite sides are parallel.

paral′ysis *n* a condition causing loss of feeling and the power to move in part of the body.

par′alyze *vb* **1** to make helpless or powerless. **2** to strike with paralysis.

par′apet *n* a safety wall at the side of a bridge, at the edge of a roof, etc.

par′asite *n* **1** one who lives at another's expense. **2** a plant or animal that lives on or in another:—*adj* **parasit′ic**.

par′asol *n* a sunshade in the form of an umbrella.

par′atroop(er) *n* a soldier trained to drop from an airplane by parachute.

par′cel *n* **1** a small bundle or package. **2** a small piece of land, esp part of a large piece:—*vb* **1** to divide into shares. **2** to wrap up in paper.

parch *vb* to dry up.

parched *adj* **1** dried out. **2** (*inf*) very thirsty.

par′don *vb* to forgive, to let off without punishment:—*n* forgiveness.

pare *vb* to cut off the skin or edge of.

pa′rent *n* a father or mother.

pa′rentage *n* parents and ancestors, birth.

paren′tal *adj* of a parent.

paren′thesis *n* (*pl* **paren′theses**) **1** a group of words put into the middle of a sentence, interrupting its sense and often enclosed in brackets. **2** brackets.

par′ish *n* **1** a district with its own church and priest or minister. **2** the people living in a parish:—*adj* having to do with a parish.

par′ing *n* a piece of skin cut off.

parish′ioner *n* a member of a parish or parish church.

par′ity *n* equality, the state of being equal.

park *n* **1** a large enclosed space of open ground around a country house. **2** an enclosed piece of ground for the use of the public. **3** a parking lot:—*vb* to leave (an automobile, etc) standing.

park′ing lot *n* a place where automobiles, etc, may be left.

park′way *n* an open landscaped highway.

par′liament *n* **1** an assembly that discusses and makes laws. **2** (*usu with cap*) the supreme governing and legislative body of various countries.

parliamenta′rian *n* an experienced member of parliament.

par′lor *n* **1** a sitting room. **2** a store providing some kind of personal service.

paro′chial *adj* **1** having to do with a parish. **2** narrow-minded.

par′ody *n* **1** a humorous imitation of a serious work of literature. **2** a weak and unsuccessful copy or absurd imitation:—*vb* **1** to make a parody of. **2** to imitate in order to make fun of.

parole′ *n* the release of a prisoner before the end of his or her sentence on condition that he or she does not break the law:—*also vb.*

parquet [par-kā] *n* flooring made of wooden bricks arranged to form a pattern.

par′rot *n* a brightly colored tropical bird able to imitate human speech.

pars′ley *n* a garden herb used in cooking.

par′son *n* a member of clergy.

part *n* **1** one of the pieces into which a thing can be divided. **2** some but not all. **3** the character played by an actor on the stage. **4** *pl* ability, talents:—*adj* and *adv* in part:—*vb* **1** to divide. **2** to separate:—*adv* **part′ly:—in good part** without being angry.

par′tial *adj* **1** in part only. **2** favoring one side or person. **3** fond (of).

partic′ipant, partic′ipator *ns* one who takes a part in.

partic′ipate *vb* to take part in, to have a share in:—*n* **participa′tion**.

par′ticle *n* a very small part.

partic′ular *adj* **1** different from others, special. **2** careful, exact. **3** difficult to please:—*n* a single fact, a detail.

part′ing *n* **1** separation. **2** act of going away or leaving. **3** the division made when the hair is brushed in two directions:—*adj* done when going away, final.

parti′tion *n* **1** a dividing wall or screen. **2** division. **3** a part divided off from the rest:—*vb* **1** to divide up. **2** to set up a dividing wall, etc.

part′ner *n* **1** one who works or plays with another in a certain undertaking, game, etc. **2** a husband or wife, someone with whom one lives or is in a long-term relationship:—*vb* to go with or give to as a partner.

part′nership *n* **1** the state of being partners. **2** a group of people working together for the same purpose. **3** people playing on the same side in a game.

part′-time *adj* for some of the time only.

par′ty *n* **1** a group of people who have the same or similar beliefs and opinions. **2** a group of people meeting for enjoyment. **3** one taking part:—*vb* to attend or give a party for.

pass *vb* **1** to go past. **2** to go on one's way. **3** to move (something) from one place or person to another. **4** to die. **5** (*of time*) to go by. **6** to spend (time). **7** to overtake. **8** to succeed at examination. **9** to recognize as good enough, to approve. **10** to utter. **11** to set up as by vote. **12** (*fml*) to be the cause for:—*n* **1** a narrow valley between mountains. **2** a written permission to visit certain places. **3** success in an examination:—**a pretty pass** a bad state of affairs.

pass′able *adj* **1** fairly good. **2** that can be crossed or traveled on.

pass'age n 1 a way through. 2 act of passing. 3 a journey, esp by sea. 4 a lane. 5 a corridor. 6 part of a book, poem, etc.

pass'enger n one traveling in a ship, train, etc.

pass'er-by n one who is walking past.

pass'ing adj 1 moving or going by. 2 lasting for a short time only.

passion [pa'-shēn] n 1 a strong feeling, such as love. 2 anger. 3 great enthusiasm.

pas'sionate adj 1 having or showing strong feelings. 2 very enthusiastic.

pass'ive adj 1 acted on. 2 showing no emotion, interest, etc. 3 unresisting:—n **passiv'ity**.

pass'port n a document giving a person permission to travel in foreign countries.

pass'word n 1 a secret word, knowledge of which shows that a person is friendly. 2 a sequence of characters required to access a computer program.

past adj 1 gone by. 2 belonging to an earlier time:—n 1 time gone by. 2 one's earlier life:—prep 1 beyond. 2 after:—adv by.

paste n 1 flour mixed with water, etc, to make dough for cooking. 2 a sticky mixture of this used as an adhesive. 3 food crushed so that it can be spread like butter. 4 the material of which imitation gems are made:—vb to stick with paste.

pas'tel n 1 a colored chalk or crayon. 2 a drawing done with pastel:—adj not bright.

pas'teurize vb to heat in order to kill all harmful germs.

pas'time n a hobby, a game, an interest for one's spare time.

past' master n an expert, one with great skill.

pas'tor n the minister of a church.

pas'toral adj 1 (fml) having to do with the country or country life. 2 having to do with a member of the clergy or his or her duties:—n a poem describing country life.

pas'try n 1 paste of flour, water, etc, made crisp by baking. 2 a pie or tart.

pas'ture n grassland where farm animals graze.

pasty [pãs'-ti] adj 1 like paste. 2 pallid and unhealthy in appearance.

pat n 1 a tap, a light touch. 2 a small lump:—vb (**pat'ted, pat'ting**) to tap, to hit lightly:—adj ready, coming too easily.

patch n 1 a piece of material sewed or put on to cover a hole. 2 a small piece of ground:—vb to mend by covering over.

patch'work n many small pieces of material sewn together.

patch'y adj 1 full of patches. 2 (inf) sometimes good, sometimes bad.

pa'tent n a written document giving someone the sole right to make or sell a new invention:—adj 1 protected by patent. 2 (fml) obvious, clear:—vb to obtain a patent for.

patent leather n a leather with a high gloss.

pater'nal adj 1 fatherly, like a father. 2 related by blood to one's father.

path n 1 a narrow way made by the treading of feet, a track. 2 the course followed by a person or thing.

pathet'ic adj sad, causing pity.

pathol'ogy n the study of diseases:—n **pathol'ogist**.

pa'tience n 1 the ability to suffer or wait long without complaining, calmness despite delay or difficulty. 2 a card game for one person.

pa'tient adj suffering delay, pain, irritation, etc, quietly and without complaining:—n a person receiving treatment from a doctor.

pa'triot n one who loves his or her country:—n **pa'triotism**.

patriot'ic adj loving one's country.

patrol' n 1 a group of men, ships, etc, sent out as a moving guard. 2 the act of patrolling:—vb (**patrolled', patrol'ling**) to move about on guard or to keep watch.

pa'tron n 1 one who encourages, helps, or protects. 2 a regular customer.

pat'ronize vb 1 to behave to another as if superior to him or her. 2 to be a regular customer of.

patron saint n a saint believed to give special protection.

pat'ter vb 1 to make a light tapping sound. 2 to run with quick light steps:—n the sound of pattering.

pat'tern n 1 a model that can be copied. 2 an example. 3 a design on cloth, a carpet, etc. 4 the way in which something happens or develops.

pat'ty n a little pie.

pau'per n a person too poor to support himself or herself.

pause vb to stop for a time:—n a short stop.

pave vb to make a road or path by laying down flat stones:—
pave the way for to prepare for.

pave'ment n a paved surface, esp on a public thoroughfare.

pavil'ion n a building on a playing field for the use of players and spectators.

paw n the foot of an animal that has claws.

pawn[1] n in chess, the piece of least value.

pawn[2] n a thing handed over in return for a loan of money and returned when the loan is repaid:—vb to hand over in return for money lent.

pawn'broker n one who lends money to those who pawn goods with him or her until the loan is repaid.

pay vb (pt, pp **paid**) 1 to give money for goods, service, etc. 2 to suffer for faults, crimes, etc. 3 to give. 4 to produce a profit. 5 to let run out:—n wages, salary:—**pay through the nose** (inf) to pay too much for something.

pay'able adj that must be paid.

payee' n one to whom money is to be paid.

pay'ment n 1 the act of paying. 2 the amount paid.

pea n 1 a climbing plant with pods containing round eatable seeds. 2 one of the seeds.

peace n 1 quiet, calm. 2 freedom from war or disorder. 3 the agreement to end a war.

peace'able adj fond of peace, not liking to fight or quarrel.

peace'ful adj 1 quiet, calm, untroubled. 2 without war.

peace'maker n one who tries to stop wars, disputes, etc.

peace' offering n something offered to bring about peace.

peach n a juicy fruit with a rough stone and soft velvety skin.

pea'cock n a bird the male of which has a large brightly colored spreading tail:—f **pea'hen**.

peak n 1 the highest point. 2 the pointed top of a mountain. 3 the jutting-out brim at the front of a cap.

peal n 1 a sudden noise. 2 the loud ringing of bells. 3 a set of bells for ringing together:—vb to sound or ring loudly.

pea'nut n 1 a plant with underground pods containing eatable seeds. 2 the pod or any of its seeds. 3 (pl) (inf) a trifling thing or amount.

pear n a juicy fruit narrower at one end than at the other.

pearl n a shining white jewel found in shellfish, esp oysters.

pea'sant n a person who works on the land, esp in a poor or underdeveloped area.

peb'ble n a small stone made round by the action of water.

peck vb 1 to strike with the beak. 2 to pick up with the beak. 3 to eat slowly in small mouthfuls, to nibble.

pecu'liar adj 1 strange, odd. 2 belonging to one person, place, or thing in particular and to no other.

peculiar'ity n 1 a quality, custom, etc, that belongs to a particular person, thing, etc. 2 an odd way of behaving.

ped'al n a lever worked by foot to control the working of a machine:—vb to work a pedal by foot.

ped'dle vb 1 to sell from door to door. 2 to sell (drugs, etc) illegally:—n **ped'dler**.

ped'estal n the block of stone at the base of a column or under a statue.

pedes'trian adj 1 going on foot. 2 dull, uninteresting:—n one who goes on foot.

ped'igree n 1 a written table showing one's ancestors. 2 one's ancestors:—adj of good birth.

peel vb 1 to strip off. 2 to cut the skin off a fruit or vegetable. 3 to come off, as does skin or the bark of a tree:—n skin, rind, bark.

peep vb 1 to look at through a narrow opening. 2 to look at for a moment only. 3 to begin to appear:—n 1 a quick or secret look. 2 a look through a narrow opening. 3 a first appearance.

peer¹ vb 1 to strain one's eyes to see. 2 to look closely.

peer² n 1 an equal, one's equal in age, ability, rank. 2 a noble:—f **peer'ess**.

peer'age n 1 all the nobles of a country. 2 the rank or title of a noble person.

peg n a nail, pin, or fastener:—vb (**pegged'**, **peg'ging**) to fasten with a peg:—**peg away** (inf) to keep on trying as hard as possible:—**take down a peg** to humble, to humiliate.

pel'ican n a water bird with a large beak containing a pouch for storing fish.

pel'let n 1 a small ball of anything. 2 one of a number of small lead balls packed in a cartridge and fired from a gun.

pelt¹ n the raw skin of an animal.

pelt² n 1 to attack by throwing things at. 2 (of rain) to fall heavily.

pen¹ n an instrument for writing in ink:—vb to write.

pen² n a small enclosure, esp for animals:—vb (**penned'**, **pen'ning**) to shut up in a small space.

penal'ize vb to impose a penalty.

pen'alty n 1 due punishment. 2 a disadvantage of some kind that most be suffered for breaking the rules.

pen'ance n punishment willingly accepted as a sign of sorrow for sin.

pen'cil n a writing or drawing instrument with a core of graphite or crayon:—vb to write or draw with pencil.

pen'dant n an ornament hanging from a necklace or bracelet.

pen'dent adj hanging, dangling.

pen'ding adj not yet decided:—prep waiting for.

pen'dulum n a swinging weight, as in a large clock.

pen'etrate vb 1 to pass through. 2 to make a hole in. 3 to reach the mind of.

pen'etrating adj 1 sharp. 2 far-seeing. 3 loud and clear.

pen friend n a person one gets to know through exchanging letters.

pen'guin n a web-footed bird with very short wings that it uses for swimming, not flying.

penicill'in n a kind of germ-killing drug obtained from mold.

penin'sula n a piece of land almost surrounded by water.

pen'itent adj sorrowful for having done wrong:—n one who is penitent:—n **pen'itence**.

pen'knife n a folding pocket knife.

pen name n a pretended name under which an author writes.

pen'nant, pen'non n a long narrow triangular flag.

pen'niless adj having no money.

pen'ny n (pl **pen'nies**) a coin worth one hundredth of a dollar.

pen'sion n money paid regularly to someone for the rest of his or her lifetime after he or she has stopped working or after some misfortune.

pen'sioner n one who receives a pension.

pen'tagon n a five-sided figure.

penul'timate adj (fml) the last but one.

pen'ury n (fml) poverty, want.

people [pee'-pêl] n 1 all those belonging to one nation or country. 2 the ordinary persons of a country and not their rulers, etc. 3 persons:—vb 1 to fill with people. 2 to inhabit.

pep'per n 1 a plant whose seeds are ground into a hot-tasting powder and used for flavoring food. 2 the powder so used.

pep'percorn n the seed of the pepper plant.

pep'permint n 1 a plant with sharp-tasting oil. 2 a sharp-tasting sweet.

per prep 1 for each. 2 during each. 3 (inf) according to.

perceive' vb to know through one of the senses, to see, to understand.

per cent adv in each hundred (%).

percen'tage n the number of cases in every hundred.

percep'tive adj 1 quick to notice or understand. 2 showing the ability to notice or understand.

perch¹ n a freshwater fish.

perch² n 1 the bar on which a bird stands when resting. 2 a high place. 3 a measure of length (5¹/2 yards):—vb 1 to rest on a bar or high place. 2 to put in a high position.

perchance' adv (old) perhaps.

per'colate vb 1 to pass slowly through. 2 to put through a strainer.

per'colator n 1 a strainer. 2 a coffee pot in which boiling water is passed through coffee grains until the coffee is strong enough to drink.

percus'sion n 1 the striking of one thing against another. 2 the sound thus made. 3 the drums and cymbals section of an orchestra.

peremp'tory adj short and commanding.

peren'nial adj 1 lasting for ever, continual. 2 (of a plant) growing again year after year:—n a perennial plant.

per'fect adj 1 without fault, excellent. 2 exact. 3 complete, utter:—vb **perfect'** to finish, to make perfect:—n **perfec'tion**.

per'forate vb to make a hole or row of holes through.

perfora'tion n a row of small holes, often to make tearing easy, as in sheets of stamps.

perform' vb 1 to do, to carry out. 2 to show in a theatre. 3 to act in a play.

perform'ance n 1 act of doing or carrying out. 2 that which is done. 3 the acting of a play or part.

perform'er n an actor, musician, etc.

perform'ing adj trained to act, to do tricks, etc.

per'fume n 1 a sweet smell. 2 a sweet-smelling liquid, scent:—vb **perfume'** 1 to put perfume on. 2 to give a pleasant smell to.

perfu'mery n 1 a place where perfumes are made or sold. 2 the art of making perfumes.

perfunc'tory adj done carelessly or without interest, badly done.

perhaps' adv it may be, possibly.

per'il n risk, danger.

per'ilous adj dangerous.

perim'eter n 1 the total length of the line(s) enclosing a certain space or figure. 2 the boundaries of a camp or piece of land.

pe'riod n 1 a certain length of time. 2 an age in history. 3 the dot or full stop marking the end of a sentence. 4 a time of menstruation.

period'ic adj happening at regular intervals.

period'ical n a newspaper or magazine that appears at regular intervals (e.g. of a week, month, etc):—adj periodic.

periph'ery n a boundary line.

per'iscope *n* an instrument in which mirrors are so arranged that one can see things on the surface of the land or sea when in a trench or submarine.

per'ish *vb* **1** to die. **2** to pass away completely. **3** to rot away.

per'ishable *adj* that will rot away under ordinary conditions.

per'jure *vb* to swear that something is true, knowing it to be untrue:—*n* **per'jurer**.

per'jury *n* the saying on oath that a statement is true when one knows it to be false.

perk[1] *vb* (*inf*) to cheer up.

perk[2] *n see* **perquisite**.

perk'y *adj* lively, cheerful:—*n* **perk'iness**.

per'manent *adj* lasting:—*n* **per'manence**.

permanent wave *n* an artificial wave in the hair.

permanent way *n* railroad track(s).

per'meable *adj* allowing liquid, gases, etc, to pass through.

per'meate *vb* to pass through, to spread through every part of.

permiss'ible *adj* (*fml*) that can be allowed.

permis'sion *n* leave, consent.

permis'sive *adj* (*fml*) allowing freedom.

permit' *vb* (**permit'ted, permit'ting**) to allow:—*n* **per'mit** a paper giving the holder the right to do certain things.

permuta'tion *n* **1** all the ways in which a series of things, numbers, etc, can be arranged. **2** one of these ways

perpendic'ular *adj* **1** at right angles. **2** upright:—*n* a line at right angles to another.

perpet'ual *adj* **1** lasting for ever. **2** continuing endlessly, uninterrupted.

perplex' *vb* to puzzle, to bewilder.

per'secute *vb* to ill-treat, esp because of one's beliefs, to treat cruelly:—*n* **persecu'tion**:—*n* **per'secutor**.

persever'ance *n* the quality of going on trying until one succeeds.

persevere' *vb* to keep on trying.

persist' *vb* **1** to keep on doing. **2** to last. **3** not to give in despite difficulty.

persis'tence *n* the quality of persisting, obstinacy.

persis'tent *adj* **1** keeping on trying, not giving in easily. **2** long, continuing.

per'son *n* **1** a human being, a man, woman or child. **2** (*fml*) one's body.

per'sonable *adj* good-looking.

per'sonage *n* a person of importance.

per'sonal *adj* **1** one's own private. **2** (*of remarks*) unkind.

personal'ity *n* **1** the union of qualities that makes one's character different from those of other people. **2** a strong, distinct character. **3** a well-known person. **4** *pl* unkind remarks about others.

per'sonally *adv* as far as one is concerned oneself.

person'ify *vb* **1** to speak or write of a thing, quality, etc, as if it were a human being. **2** to be a perfect example of:—*n* **personifica'tion**.

personnel' *n* the persons employed in a firm.

personnel officer *n* a person whose job it is to interview workers and look after their welfare.

perspec'tive *n* **1** the art of drawing objects on a flat surface so that they appear farther or nearer as they do to the eye. **2** (*fml*) a view.

perspire' *vb* to sweat:—*n* **perspira'tion**.

persuade' *vb* to convince a person or get him or her to do as one wants by argument.

persua'sion *n* **1** act of persuading. **2** (*fml*) a belief or set of beliefs. **3** a group holding certain beliefs.

persua'sive *adj* good at gaining the agreement of others, able to influence others.

pert *adj* forward, cheeky:—*n* **pert'ness**.

pertain' *vb* to belong, to have to do with.

per'tinent *adj* to the point, having to do with the subject:—*ns* **per'tinence, per'tinency**.

perturb' *vb* to make worried or anxious, to disturb.

perturba'tion *n* anxiety, worry.

pervade' *vb* to spread through.

perva'sive *adj* spreading through all parts.

perverse' *adj* **1** holding firmly to a wrong opinion. **2** continuing to do things that one knows to be wrong, unacceptable, or forbidden.

perver'sion *n* putting to a wrong or evil use.

pervert' *vb* **1** to put to a wrong use. **2** to teach wrong ways to:—*n* **per'vert** one who has formed unnatural habits.

pes'simism *n* the belief that things generally turn out for the worst:—*n* **pes'simist**.

pessimis'tic *adj* having to do with pessimism, gloomy.

pest *n* **1** something harmful. **2** a nuisance. **3** a destructive animal, insect, etc.

pes'ter *vb* to keep on annoying.

pet *n* **1** a favorite child. **2** a tame animal kept in the house as a companion:—*adj* best loved, favorite:—*vb* (**pet'ted, pet'ting**) **1** to treat lovingly. **2** to fondle.

pet'al *n* the leaf-shaped part of a flower.

pet aversion *n* what one dislikes most.

pe'ter *vb*:—**peter out** to stop or disappear gradually.

petite [pe-teet'] *adj* tiny, dainty.

peti'tion *n* **1** a request. **2** a written request signed by a number of people. **3** a prayer:—*vb* **1** to make a request to one able to grant it. **2** to put forward a written request:—*n* **peti'tioner**.

pet'rify *vb* **1** to turn into stone. **2** to terrify, to astound.

pet'rol *n* a light oil obtained from crude oil.

petro'leum *n* crude oil.

pet'ticoat *n* a woman's undergarment.

pet'ty *adj* **1** small, unimportant, trivial. **2** mean-spirited.

petty cash *n* money held in readiness to meet small expenses.

pet'ulant *adj* easily angered or annoyed, peevish:—*n* **pet'ulance**.

pew *n* a seat in a church.

pew'ter *n* a mixture of tin and lead.

phan'tom *n* a ghost.

phar'isee *n* (*inf*) a hypocrite.

phar'macy *n* **1** the making up of drugs or medicines. **2** a drugstore:—*n* **phar'macist**.

phase *n* **1** a distinct stage in growth or development. **2** apparent shape (e.g. of the moon).

phenom'enon *n* (*pl* **phenom'ena**) **1** any natural happening that can be perceived by the senses. **2** anything unusual or extraordinary.

phenom'enal *adj* unusual, extraordinary.

philan'thropy *n* love of humankind, shown by giving money, etc, to help those in need or to benefit the public:—*adj* **philanthrop'ic**:—*n* **philan'thropist**.

philat'ely *n* stamp collecting:—*n* **philat'elist**.

phil'istine *n* an uncultured person.

philos'opher *n* one who tries to find by reasoning the causes and laws of all things.

philosoph'ic(al) *adjs* **1** having to do with philosophy. **2** calm, not easily annoyed.

philos'ophy *n* **1** the study of the causes and laws of all things. **2** a particular way of thinking.

phlegm [flem] *n* **1** the thick slimy liquid coughed up from the throat. **2** coolness of temper, lack of excitement.

phlegmatic [fleg-mat'-ik] *adj* not easily excited.

pho'bia *n* an unreasoning fear or dread.

phoenix [fee'-niks] *n* in ancient fables, a bird said to burn itself and rise again from its ashes.

phone *the common short form of* **telephone**.

phonet'ic *adj* having to do with the sounds of speech or pronunciation:—*npl* **phonet'ics** the study of the sounds of speech.

pho'nic *adj* having to do with sound.

phono'graph *n* an instrument on which sound recorded on a specially prepared disk can be played back, a record-player.

pho'ny *adj* (*inf*) not genuine, not sincere, unreal.

phosphores'cent *adj* giving out a faint light in the dark.

phos'phorous *n* a yellowish substance, easily set alight, giving out a faint light.

photo *short for* **photograph**.

pho'tocopy *n* a photographed copy:—*also vb*.

photogen'ic *adj* suitable for photographing.

pho'tograph *n* (*abbr* **pho'to**) a picture taken with a camera by means of the action of light on specially prepared glass or celluloid:—*vb* to take a photograph:—*n* **photog'rapher**:—*adj* **photograph'ic**.

photog'raphy *n* the art of taking photographs.

Pho'tostat *n* trademark for a device for making photo-graphed copies:—*also vb*.

phrase *n* 1 a small group of connected words expressing a single idea. 2 (*mus*) a group of connected notes:—*vb* to express in words.

phraseology [frā-zee-ol'-o-ji] *n* a manner or style of expressing in words.

phys'ical *adj* 1 having to do with the body. 2 having to do with the natural world.

physical therapy *n* the treatment of disorders and dis-ease by physical and mechanical means:—*n* **physical therapist**.

physi'cian *n* a doctor, esp as opposed to a surgeon.

phys'ics *n* the study of matter, its properties, and the forces affecting it (e.g. heat, electricity, etc).

physiol'ogy *n* the study of living bodies, their organs, and the way they work:—*adj* **physiolog'ical**:—*n* **physiol'ogist**.

physique [fi-zeek'] *n* 1 the structure of a person's body. 2 strength of body.

pi'anist *n* one who plays on a piano.

pia'no, pianoforte [pi-a-nō-for'-ti] *ns* a musical instrument played by pressing down keys that cause little hammers to strike tuned strings.

pick¹ *vb* 1 to choose. 2 to pull or gather. 3 to eat by small mouthfuls. 4 to open (a lock) with a tool. 5 to steal from (a pocket):—*n* choice, the best:—**pick up** 1 to take up. 2 to learn as if by chance. 3 to come upon by chance.

pick² **pick'ax** *ns* a tool with a long pointed head, used for breaking up hard ground, etc.

pick'et *n* 1 a pointed wooden post. 2 a small group of soldiers acting as a guard. 3 a number of people on strike who try to prevent others from going to work:—*vb* 1 to send out soldiers, strikers, etc, on picket. 2 to tie to a post.

pick'le *n* 1 salt water or vinegar in which food is preserved. 2 (*inf*) a difficult or unpleasant situation. 3 *pl* vegetables preserved in vinegar:—*vb* to preserve by putting in salt water, vinegar, etc.

pick'pocket *n* one who steals from pockets.

pic'nic *n* an outing taken for pleasure, when meals are eaten out of doors:—*also vb* (**picnick'ing, picnicked'**).

picto'rial *adj* told or illustrated by pictures.

pic'ture *n* a painting, drawing, or other likeness, a portrait:—*vb* 1 to imagine clearly. 2 (*fml*) to represent in a painting.

picturesque' *adj* that would make a good picture, striking in appearance, beautiful.

pid'gin *n* a language using words and grammar from other languages.

pidgin English *n* pidgin based on English.

pie *n* meat or fruit in or under a crust of pastry.

pie'bald *adj* having patches of different colors, esp black and white, spotted.

piece *n* 1 a bit. 2 a distinct part. 3 a literary or musical composi-tion. 4 a gun. 5 a coin:—*vb* 1 to put (together). 2 to patch.

pied [pīd] *adj* (*fml*) of different colors, spotted.

pier [peer] *n* 1 a stone pillar supporting an arch, etc. 2 a stone or wooden platform or wall built out into the sea, often used as a landing place by boats.

pierce *vb* 1 to make a hole through. 2 to go through.

pierc'ing *adj* 1 high-sounding. 2 bright, intelligent-looking, staring.

pie'ty *n* love of prayer and religious ceremonies.

pig *n* 1 a common farm animal. 2 a rough block or bar of smelted metal:—*vb* (**pigged', pig'ging**) (*inf*) to live in dirty or untidy surroundings.

pi'geon *n* a dove.

pigeonhole *n* one of several compartments in a desk for storing papers, letters, etc.

pig-head'ed *adj* foolishly stubborn.

pig'ment *n* any substance used for coloring.

pig'my *same as* **pygmy**.

pig'sty *n* 1 an enclosure for pigs. 2 a filthy, untidy place.

pig'tail *n* a plait of hair hanging down the back of the head.

pike¹ *n* 1 a sharp point or spike. 2 the top of a spear:—*vb* to pierce or kill with a pike.

pike² *n* an eatable long-snouted fish.

pike³ *short for* **turnpike**.

pile¹ *n* a heap, mound:—*vb* to heap up.

pile² *n* the soft wooly hair on cloth, carpets, etc.

pile³ *n* a beam driven into the ground as part of the forces for a building.

pil'fer *vb* to steal small amounts or articles of small value:—*n* **pil'ferer**.

pil'grim *n* one who travels to a holy place for pious reasons.

pil'grimage *n* a journey made by a pilgrim.

pill *n* a tiny ball of medicine.

pill'age *n* (*fml*) the seizing and carrying off of enemy prop-erty after a battle, plunder, spoil:—*vb* to seize and carry off by force.

pill'ar *n* an upright of stone, wood, etc, for supporting an arch, roof, etc.

pill'ion *n* a seat at the back of the saddle of a motorcycle for a passenger.

pill'ow *n* a soft cushion for the head.

pill'owcase *n* the cover put over a pillow.

pi'lot *n* 1 one who guides a ship in and out of harbor. 2 one who steers an airplane:—*vb* 1 to guide, to show the way. 2 to steer an airplane.

pin *n* a short pointed bar of wire with a flattened head, used for fastening cloth, paper, etc. 2 a wooden, metal, or plastic peg. 3 a bolt:—*vb* (**pinned', pin'ning**) 1 to fasten a brooch. 2 to hold firmly (to):—**pins and needles** a tingling feeling in a limb.

pin'afore *n* a kind of dress with no covering for the arms, usu worn over a blouse or sweater.

pin'cers *npl* 1 a tool for gripping things firmly, used esp for pulling out nails. 2 claws (e.g. as of a crab).

pinch *vb* 1 to take or nip between the finger and thumb. 2 to squeeze the flesh until it hurts. 3 (*inf*) to steal:—*n* 1 the amount that can be taken between the finger and thumb. **2** a small amount. **3** need, distress.

pine¹ *n* a cone-bearing evergreen tree.

pine² *vb* **1** to waste away with sorrow, pain, etc. **2** to long for.

pine'apple *n* a cone-shaped tropical fruit.

ping *n* a sharp sound, as of a bullet in flight.

ping'-pong *n* **1** a name for table tennis. **2** *(with caps) trademark* for table tennis equipment.

pink *n* **1** a light red color. **2** the best of condition:—*also adj*.

pin'nacle *n* **1** a pointed tower or spire on a building. **2** a pointed mountain. **3** the highest point.

pint *n* a liquid measure equal to one quart or the eighth part of a gallon.

pioneer' *n* **1** one who goes before the main body to prepare the way, one who is the first to try out new ideas, etc. **2** an explorer:—*vb* **1** to begin. **2** to explore.

pi'ous *adj* loving and worshipping God, religious:—*n* **pi'ety**.

pip *n* seed of fruit.

pipe *n* **1** a musical wind instrument. **2** a long tube. **3** a tube with a bowl at one end for smoking tobacco. **4** a shrill voice. **5** a bird's note:—*vb* **1** to play upon a pipe. **2** to make (water, gas, etc) pass through pipes. **3** to speak in a shrill voice:—**piping hot** very hot.

pip'er *n* one who plays a pipe or bagpipes.

pi'racy *n* the crime of a pirate.

pi'rate *n* **1** one who attacks and robs ships at sea. **2** a person who does something without legal right:—*also vb*.

pirat'ical *adj* having to do with pirates.

pirouette' *vb* to turn round on the points of the toes, as a ballet-dancer:—*also n*.

pis'til *n* the seed-bearing part of a flower.

pis'tol *n* a small firearm fired with one hand.

pis'ton *n* a plug that fits closely into a hollow cylinder inside which it moves up and down.

pit *n* **1** a deep hole in the earth. **2** the passageway leading down to a mine. **3** a mine (for coal, etc). **4** the back seats on the ground floor of a theater:—*vb* (**pit'ted, pit'ting**) **1** to lay in a pit. **2** to set against in order to outdo.

pitch¹ *vb* **1** to set up. **2** to throw. **3** to fall heavily. **4** to set the keynote of (a tune). **5** *(of a ship)* to dip head-first down after rising on a wave:—*n* **1** a throw. **2** the highness or lowness of a note in music. **3** the ground marked out for a game:—**pitched battle** a set battle between two prepared armies.

pitch² *n* a thick dark substance obtained from tar.

pitch'er¹ *n* a deep vessel for holding liquids, with a handle.

pitch'er² *n* one who throws the ball to the batter in baseball.

pit'fall *n* a trap.

pith *n* **1** the soft center of the stem of a plant. **2** material just under the skin of an orange, etc. **3** the most important part.

pith'y *adj* short and to the point, forceful.

pit'iable *adj* deserving pity.

pit'tance *n* a small allowance or wage.

pit'ted *adj* marked with little hollows, as the skin after smallpox.

pit'y *n* sympathy for the pain or sorrow of others:—*vb* to feel sorry for:—*adjs* **pit'iful, pit'iless**.

piv'ot *n* **1** the pin on which anything (e.g. a wheel) turns. **2** the central point of anything:—*adj* **piv'otal**.

pix'ie, pix'y *n* a fairy.

pizza [peet'-zë] *n* a baked dough crust covered with cheese, tomatoes, etc.

plac'ard *n* a notice put up in a public place to announce or advertise something.

placate' *vb* to make calm or peaceful.

place *n* **1** an open space in a town. **2** a particular part of space. **3** a village, town, city, etc. **3** the post or position held by someone. **4** rank in society. **5** a passage in a book:—*vb* **1** to put or set. **2** to decide from where a thing comes or where it ought to be. **3** to recognize. **4** to find a job for.

plac'id *adj* calm, not easily angered or upset, gentle:—*n* **placid'ity**.

plague [plāg] *n* **1** a very infectious and dangerous disease. **2** *(inf)* a nuisance.

plaid [plad *or* plād] *n* **1** tartan. **2** a long wide piece of woolen cloth used as a cloak.

plain *adj* **1** clear, easily understood. **2** simple, bare, undecorated. **3** obvious:—*n* a stretch of level country.

plain' sail'ing *n* something easy.

plain'tive *adj* sad, expressing sorrow.

plait [plat, plât *or* pleet], **pleat** *ns* **1** a pigtail of intertwined hair. **2** a fold (e.g. in material):—*vb* **1** to twist together into a plait.

plan *n* **1** a drawing of the outlines made by an object on the ground, a map. **2** a scheme of what is to happen on a future occasion:—*vb* (**planned', plan'ning**) **1** to draw a plan of. **2** to arrange beforehand what should happen:—*n* **plan'ner**.

plane¹ *n* **1** a smooth or level surface. **2** a joiner's tool for giving wood a smooth surface. **3** *a common short form of* **airplane**:—*adj* level, smooth:—*vb* to make smooth.

plan'et *n* one of the heavenly bodies moving in orbit around the sun.

plank *n* a long flat piece of timber.

plant *n* **1** anything growing from the earth and feeding on it through its roots. **2** the machinery and equipment used in a factory:—*vb* **1** to put in the ground to grow. **2** to set firmly.

plaque [plăk] *n* **1** an ornamental plate of metal, etc. **2** a deposit of saliva and bacteria that forms on the teeth.

plas'ter *n* **1** a mixture of lime, water, and sand spread over the walls of buildings to make them smooth. **2** an adhesive bandage used for dressing wounds, etc:—*vb* **1** to cover with plaster. **2** to spread over the surface of:—**plaster of Paris** a quickly hardening plaster, used to support broken limbs.

plas'terer *n* one who plasters walls.

plas'tic *adj* easily shaped or molded:—*n* one of a group of man-made substances that can be molded into any shape.

plastic surgery *n* the reshaping of the human body by surgery.

plate *n* **1** a flat piece of metal, glass, etc. **2** a shallow dish for food. **3** gold and silver household articles. **4** a picture printed from an engraved piece of metal, etc:—*vb* to cover with a thin coat of metal.

pla'teau *n* an extent of high level land.

plate'-glass *n* large thick sheets of glass as used for store windows.

plat'form *n* **1** a raised part of the floor (for speakers, etc). **2** a bank built above ground level for those entering trains, etc. **3** statement of the aims of a group.

plat'inum *n* a valuable heavy grayish-white metal.

platt'er *n* a large flat plate or dish.

plau'sible *adj* that sounds convincing, seemingly true or truthful:—*n* **plausibil'ity**.

play *vb* **1** to amuse oneself. **2** to take part in a game. **3** to gamble. **4** to act a part in a drama. **5** to perform on a musical instrument. **6** to trifle:—*n* **1** free movement. **2** trifling amusement or sport. **3** gambling. **4** a drama.

play'er *n* **1** one who takes part in a sport or drama. **2** a musical performer.

play'ful *adj* fond of sport or amusement.

play'ground *n* a piece of ground set aside for children to play in.

play'mate *n* a childhood companion.

play'thing *n* a toy.

play'wright *n* one who writes plays.

plea *n* **1** an excuse. **2** an earnest request. **3** the prisoner's answer to the charge in a law court.

plead *vb* (*pt, pp* **plead'ed** *or* **pled**) **1** to request earnestly. **2** to put forward in excuse. **3** to present one's case or one's client's case in a law court.

pleas'ant *adj* agreeable, enjoyable.

please *vb* **1** to make happy or content. **2** to seem good to. **3** to be so kind as to.

plea'sure *n* **1** delight, joy. **2** will.

pledge *n* **1** an object handed over to another to keep until a debt has been paid back to him or her. **2** a solemn promise. **3** a toast:—*vb* **1** (*fml*) to give to keep until a debt has been repaid. **2** to promise solemnly. **3** to drink to the health of.

plen'tiful *adj* enough, more than enough.

plen'ty *n* all that is necessary, more than is necessary.

pli'able *adj* **1** easily bent. **2** easily influenced:—*n* **pliabil'ity**.

pli'ers *npl* a small tool for gripping things firmly and for cutting wire.

plight¹ *n* a condition, situation.

plight² *vb* (*fml or old*) to promise.

plod *vb* (**plod'ded, plod'ding**) to walk or work slowly and steadily.

plot *n* **1** a small piece of ground. **2** the planned arrangement of the events of a story, play, etc. **3** a secret plan against one or more persons:—*vb* (**plot'ted, plot'ting**) **1** to plan. **2** to form a plan against. **3** to mark out or set down on paper:—*n* **plot'ter**.

plow [plou] *n* an instrument for turning up soil before seeds are sown:—*vb* **1** to turn up with a plow. **2** to force a way through. **3** to work at laboriously.

pluck *vb* **1** to pick or gather. **2** to snatch. **3** to pull the feathers:—*n* **courage**.

pluck'y *adj* brave.

plug *n* an object that fits into a hole and stops it, a stopper:—*vb* (**plugged', plug'ging**) **1** to stop with a plug. **2** (*inf*) to publicize.

plum *n* **1** a common fruit. **2** a great prize.

plu'mage *n* the feathers of a bird.

plumb [plum] *adj* straight up and down:—*adv* **1** exactly. **2** straight up and down:—*vb* to measure depth.

plumber [plum'-ér] *n* a person skilled in mending or fitting pipes, taps, etc.

plumbing [plum'-ing] *n* **1** the work of a plumber. **2** all the pipes, taps, etc, in a house.

plume *n* **1** a feather. **2** an ornament of feathers in a hat.

plum'met *vb* to drop down, to plunge.

plump¹ *adj* fat and rounded:—*vb* to grow fat, to fatten:—*n* **plump'ness**.

plump² *vb* to choose.

plun'der *vb* to steal by force, to rob:—*n* that which is taken away by force.

plunge *vb* **1** to thrust into water. **2** to jump or dive into water. **3** to rush (into):—*n* **1** a dive. **2** act of rushing.

plu'ral *adj* more than one in number:—*n* the form(s) of a word indicating more than one.

plus *prep* with the addition of:—*adj* **1** more than. **2** to be added, extra:—*n* the sign (+) of addition.

ply'wood *n* strong board made up of several thin layers of wood stuck together.

poach *vb* to hunt unlawfully on another's land:—*n* **poach'er**.

pock'et *n* **1** a small bag attached to a garment, billiard table, suitcase, etc. **2** a hollow in earth or rock filled with metal ore:—*vb* **1** to put into a pocket. **2** to steal. **3** to conceal.

pocketbook *n* **1** a small holder or case for letters, money, credit cards, etc. **2** a woman's purse, a handbag. **3** a small, esp paperback, book.

pocket money *n* money carried about for immediate personal use.

pod *n* the covering of the seed of plants, such as peas, beans, etc.

podg'y *adj* (*inf*) short and fat.

po'em *n* a piece of writing set down in memorable language and in lines with a recognizable rhythm.

po'esy *n* (*fml*) **1** the art of writing poetry. **2** poetry.

po'et *n* one who writes poetry:—*f* **po'etess**.

poet'ic, poet'ical *adjs* **1** having to do with poetry. **2** suitable for poetry.

po'etry *n* ideas, feelings, etc, expressed in memorable words and rhythmical language.

point *n* **1** the sharp end of anything. **2** a headland. **3** a dot. **4** the exact place or time. **5** the purpose for which something is said or written. **6** a single stage in an argument or list. **7** the unit of scoring in certain games. **8** *pl* movable rails that enable a train to pass from one railroad line to another:—*vb* **1** to show the direction of with a finger, stick, etc. **2** to sharpen. **3** to aim:—**on the point of** about to.

point'ed *adj* **1** sharp. **2** meant to be understood in a certain way.

point'er *n* **1** a rod for pointing with. **2** a dog trained to point out game.

point'less *adj* having no meaning, having no sensible purpose.

poise *n* **1** balance. **2** calmness and good sense:—*vb* **1** to balance. **2** to hover.

poi'son *n* **1** any substance that, taken into a living creature (animal or vegetable), harms or kills it. **2** any idea, etc, that when spread through society causes standards of judgment to become lower:—*vb* **1** to give poison to. **2** to kill by poison.

poi'sonous *adj* **1** being or containing poison. **2** having a very harmful influence.

poke *vb* **1** to push with something pointed (e.g. a finger, stick, etc), to prod:—*n* a prod given with something pointed.

po'ker *n* **1** a metal rod for stirring the coal, etc, in a fire. **2** a card game, usu played for money.

po'ky *adj* (*inf*) small and confined.

po'lar *adj* of or near one of the poles of the earth.

polar bear *n* the white bear of Arctic regions.

pole¹ *n* **1** a long rod. **2** a long rounded post.

pole² *n* **1** one of the ends of the axis of the earth. **2** one of the points in the sky opposite the poles of the earth (**celestial poles**). **3** the end of either of the two arms of a magnet.

Pole Star *n* a particular star at or near the celestial North Pole, used for finding directions.

police' *n* a body of persons whose job is to keep public order and see that the law is kept:—*vb* to see that law and order are kept:—*ns* **police'man, police officer, police'woman**.

pol'icy *n* **1** the methods or plans of a government or party. **2** a course of action. **3** a written agreement with an insurance company.

pol'ish *vb* **1** to make smooth and shining by rubbing. **2** to improve, to refine:—*n* **1** a smooth shiny surface. **2** any substance rubbed on to make smooth and shiny.

polite' *adj* well mannered, refined:—*n* **polite'ness**.

polit'ical *adj* having to do with politics.

politi'cian *n* a person whose work is concerned with the public affairs or government of a country.

pol'itics *n* the art or study of government, political matters.

pol'ka *n* a quick lively dance.

poll *n* **1** an election. **2** the number of votes:—*vb* to vote

poll'en n the yellow dust on a flower, which, united to seeds, makes them grow.

poll'inate vb to make pollen unite with the seed:—n **pollina'tion**.

pollute' vb to make filthy:—n **pollu'tion**.

po'lo n a game like field hockey played on horseback.

pol'y- prefix many.

polyethyl'ene n an artificial plastic material resistant to chemicals and moisture.

pol'ygon n a figure with many sides.

pom'mel vb to beat hard, esp with the fists.

pomp n splendid show or display, grandeur.

pom'pous adj trying to appear dignified or important.

pond n a large pool of standing water.

pon'der vb (fml) to think deeply, to consider carefully.

pontif'icate vb (fml) to state one's opinions pompously, as if stating undoubted facts.

po'ny n a small horse.

poo'dle n a small pet dog with curly hair, often clipped to leave part of its body bare.

pool¹ n 1 a puddle. 2 a deep place in a stream or river. 3 an area of still water.

pool² n 1 all the money bet on a certain game or event. 2 a collection of goods, money, etc, given by many people for reselling, sharing out, etc. 3 a game played on a billiard table with six pockets:—vb to put together the goods, etc, of individuals for use by the whole group.

poop¹ n the back part of a ship, the stern.

poop² vb to tire, to become tired.

poor adj 1 having little money. 2 unfortunate. 3 bad.

poor'ly adj unwell.

pop n a sharp, low sound:—vb (**popped'**, **pop'ping**) 1 to make a sharp low sound. 2 to move quickly or suddenly.

pope n the head of the Roman Catholic church.

pop music n popular tunes of the day.

pop'py n a plant with brightly colored flowers.

pop'ular adj 1 having to do with the people. 2 well liked by most people.

popular'ity n the state of being liked by most people.

pop'ularize vb to make popular.

popula'tion n all the people living in a place.

por'celain n fine pottery.

porch n a roofed approach to a door.

por'cupine n an animal like the rat, covered with prickly quills.

pore¹ n a tiny opening, esp in the skin.

pore² vb:—**pore over** to study closely.

pork n the meat obtained from a pig.

pornog'raphy n indecent writings, paintings, etc:—adj **pornograph'ic**.

porpoise [por'-pês] n a sea animal about five feet long.

por'ridge n a food made from oatmeal boiled to make a thick broth.

port¹ n 1 a harbor. 2 a place with a harbor.

port² n an opening in the side of a ship.

port³ n the left side of a ship (looking forward), larboard.

port⁴ n a dark sweet red wine.

port'able adj able to be carried about.

por'tent n a sign of future evil.

por'ter n one who carries loads, baggage, etc, for others

portfo'lio n a case for carrying loose papers, drawings etc

port'hole n a small window in the side of a ship.

por'tion n 1 a share. 2 a helping. 3 the money and property given to a woman at the time of her marriage. 4 (fml or old) one's fate. 5 a part.

port'ly adj stout.

por'trait n 1 a picture of a person. 2 a good description.

portray' vb 1 to draw or paint. 2 to describe.

portray'al n the act of portraying

pose vb 1 to put. 2 to put on or take up a certain attitude. 3 to pretend to be what one is not:—n 1 position, attitude. 2 a pretence of being what one is not. 3 a false manner or attitude.

posi'tion n 1 place. 2 rank, grade. 3 job. 4 state of affairs. 5 a place occupied by troops during battle:—vb to place.

pos'itive adj 1 sure. 2 certain, definite. 3 confident. 4 greater than zero. 5 really existing. 6 active, leading to practical action.

pos'itively adv completely, really.

posse [po'-si] n a small body of people, esp police.

possess' vb 1 to have as one's own. 2 (fml) to control the mind of:—adj **possessed'**.

posses'sion n 1 the act of possessing. 2 ownership. 3 control by evil spirits.

posses'sive adj 1 showing possession. 2 liking to possess or own, unwilling to share. 3 in grammar, denoting a case, form or construction expressing possession.

possess'or n one who possesses.

possibil'ity n something possible.

poss'ible adj 1 that may be true. 2 that may exist. 3 that can be done.

poss'ibly adv perhaps, maybe.

post¹ n a strong pole or length of wood stuck upright in the ground:—vb to put up on a post, bulletin board, etc.

post² n 1 the system by which letters, parcels, etc, are carried from one place to another. 2 one's place of duty. 3 one's job:—vb 1 to put in a mailbox. 2 to send to a certain place of duty.

post- prefix after.

post'age n the charge for sending something by post.

post'al adj having to do with the carrying of letters, having to do with the post office.

post'card n a card on which a message may be written and posted without an envelope.

post'date' vb to put on a date later than the actual one.

post'er n a large printed notice for public display.

poste'rior adj (fml) 1 later. 2 placed behind:—n (inf) the buttocks.

poster'ity n one's descendants, later generations.

post'-haste' adv with all possible speed.

post'humous adj 1 born after the father's death. 2 published after the author's death.

post'-mor'tem adj after death:—n an examination of a body after death to find out the cause of death.

post office n 1 an office where stamps may be bought, letters posted, etc. 2 a public department handling the transmission of mail.

postpone' vb to put off till a later time:—n **postpone'ment**.

post'script n something extra written at the end of a letter after the signature.

pos'ture n a way of holding oneself

po'sy n a small bunch of flowers.

pot n 1 a vessel for cooking in. 2 a vessel for holding plants, liquids, etc:—vb (**pot'ted**, **pot'ting**) 1 to put in a pot. 2 to shoot at and kill.

pota'to n (pl **pota'toes**) a plant the swellings (tubers) of whose roots are eaten as vegetables.

po'tent adj strong, powerful.

poten'tial adj existing but not made use of, possible:—n the unrealized ability to do something.

pot'hole n 1 a hole in the surface of a road. 2 a deep hole in limestone.

po'tion n (lit) a dose, a liquid medicine.

pot luck' n 1 whatever food is ready. 2 what chance may send.

potpourri [pō'-pŏŏ'-ree] n 1 a mixture of dried pieces of sweet-smelling flowers and leaves. 2 a collection of different things.

pott'er[1] n one who makes earthenware vessels.

pott'er[2] vb to work slowly and without much attention.

pott'ery n 1 cups, plates, etc, made of earthenware. 2 a potter's workshop.

pouch n a small bag.

poul'try n farmyard fowls.

pounce n the claw of a bird:—vb 1 to jump on suddenly. 2 to attack suddenly.

pound[1] vb 1 to beat hard. 2 to crush into powder or small pieces. 3 to walk or run heavily.

pound[2] n 1 an enclosure for lost cattle. 2 a place for holding lost property until claimed.

pound[3] n 1 a unit of weight equal to 16 ounces. 2 a British unit of money.

pour [pŏr] vb 1 to cause to flow. 2 to flow strongly. 3 to rain heavily. 4 to move in great quantity or in large numbers.

pout vb to thrust out the lips in displeasure, to look sulky:—n a sulky look.

pov'erty n lack of money or goods, want, the state of being poor.

pow'der n 1 any substance in the form of tiny dry particles. 2 gunpowder:—vb 1 to make into a powder. 2 to put powder on.

pow'dery adj dust-like. 2 covered with powder.

pow'er n 1 the ability to act or do. 2 strength, force. 3 influence. 4 control. 5 a strong nation. 6 mechanical energy:—adjs **pow'erful, pow'erless.**

pow'er plant n a place where electrical power is generated.

prac'ticable adj that can be done, possible.

prac'tical adj 1 skillful in work, able to deal with things efficiently. 2 that can be carried out, useful. 3 concerned with action rather than with ideas:—adv **prac'tically.**

practical'ity n usefulness.

prac'tice n 1 (fml) habit, frequent use. 2 the doing of an action often to improve one's skill. 3 a doctor's or lawyer's business:—vb 1 to do frequently. 2 to do often in order to improve one's skill. 3 to carry on a profession.

practit'ioner n one who practices a profession.

prag'matic adj concerned with actual results.

prai'rie n an extent of level treeless grassland.

praise vb 1 to speak well of, to speak in honor of. 2 to worship, as by singing hymns, etc—n 1 an expression of credit or honor. 2 glory, worship expressed through song.

praise'worthy adj deserving to be spoken well of.

prance vb to walk in a showy manner.

prank n a trick played in fun.

prat'tle vb to talk much and foolishly, to chatter, as a young child:—n foolish or childish talk.

prawn n a shellfish like but larger than a shrimp.

pray vb 1 to beg for, to ask earnestly. 2 adv to speak to God in worship, thanksgiving, etc.

pray'er n 1 an earnest request. 2 words addressed to God in worship, thanksgiving, etc.

pre— prefix before.

preach vb to speak in public on a religious or sacred subject:—n **preach'er.**

prearrange' vb to arrange beforehand.

preca'rious adj uncertain, dangerous.

precau'tion n something done to prevent future trouble:—adj **precau'tionary.**

precede [pree'seed'] vb to come or go before in time, place, or importance.

pre'cedence n 1 being earlier in time. 2 greater importance. 3 order according to rank.

precedent [pre'-sĭd-ĕnt] n an earlier case that helps one to decide what to do in like circumstances.

preced'ing adj previous.

pre'cinct n 1 the land around and belonging to a church, government office, etc. 2 pl the grounds. 3 a part laid out for a particular use.

pre'cious adj 1 of great worth or value. 2 too deliberate, too concerned with perfection or unimportant detail.

prec'ipice n a very steep cliff.

precip'itate vb 1 to hasten. 2 to cause the solid matter in a liquid to sink to the foot—adj thoughtless, overhasty:—n the solid matter that settles at the bottom of a liquid.

precipita'tion n 1 too great haste. 2 rainfall.

precip'itous adj (fml) steep.

précis, precis [prā'-see] n a summary.

precise adj 1 exact, clearly expressed. 2 careful. 3 exact, particular, very:—n **preci'sion.**

preclude' vb (fml) to prevent from happening, to make impossible.

preco'cious adj (of a child) too clever for one's age, forward:—n **preco'city.**

precur'sor n a person or thing that comes before and leads to another.

pred'atory adj living by killing or robbing others.

pre'decessor n one who held a certain post before another.

predestina'tion n the belief that God has settled beforehand everything that is to happen, including the fate of people in afterlife.

predic'ament n a difficulty, an unpleasant situation.

predict' vb to say what will happen in the future, to foretell:—n **predic'tion.**

predisposi'tion n a tendency to be influenced or affected by.

predom'inance n 1 control. 2 superiority in numbers, etc.

predom'inant adj 1 outstanding. 2 largest.

pre-em'inent adj outstanding, better (or worse) than all others:—n **pre-em'inence.**

preen vb 1 (of birds) to trim the feathers with the beak. 2 to tidy one's hair, clothes, etc.

pref'ace n an explanatory passage at the beginning of a speech or book

prefer' vb (preferred', prefer'ring) to like better, to choose before others

pref'erable adj more likeable, chosen before others.

pref'erence n a liking for one more than another.

pre'fix n a meaningful syllable or word put at the beginning of a word to alter its meaning.

preg'nant adj 1 being with young. 2 full of. 3 full of meaning:—n **preg'nancy.**

prehistor'ic adj before the time of written records.

prej'udice n 1 an unreasonable feeling for or against. 2 an opinion formed without full knowledge of the facts:—vb to influence unreasonably for or against.

prejudi'cial adj (fml) harmful.

prelim'inary adj coming before what is really important, introductory:—also n.

prel'ude n 1 a piece of music played before and introducing the main musical work. 2 something done or happening before an event, helping to prepare one for it.

pre'mature adj 1 happening or done too soon. 2 before the natural or proper time.

premed'itate vb (fml) to plan beforehand.

pre'mier adj first, chief:—n a prime minister.

premi'ere n the first public performance of a play, film, etc:—also vb.

prem'ises npl a building, its outhouses, and grounds.

pre'mium n 1 the amount paid for an insurance policy. 2 a reward, esp an inducement to buy. 3 something given free or at a reduced price with a purchase:—**at a premium** of greater value than usual, difficult to obtain.

premoni'tion n a feeling that something particular is about to happen.

preoccupa'tion n a concern that prevents one thinking of other things.

preocc'upied adj thinking of other things.

prepara'tion n 1 the act of preparing. 2 something done to make ready. 3 that which is made ready.

prepar'atory adj helping to prepare, making ready for something that is to follow.

prepare' vb 1 to make ready. 2 to get oneself ready.

pre'paid adj paid in advance.

preposi'tion n in grammar, a word showing the relation between a noun or pronoun and another word.

prepossess'ing adj pleasing, attractive.

prepos'terous adj completely absurd, foolish.

prerog'ative n a special power or right.

prescribe' vb to order a certain medicine.

prescrip'tion n a written order by a doctor for a certain medicine.

pres'ence n 1 the state of being in the place required. 2 one's appearance and bearing:—**presence of mind** ability to behave calmly in face of difficulty or danger.

pres'ent' adj 1 in the place required or mentioned. 2 now existing or happening:—n the time in which we live.

pres'ent' n a gift:—vb **present'** 1 to give, to offer. 2 to introduce (one person to another). 3 to show. 4 to put forward. 5 to point (a rifle).

present'able adj fit to be seen or shown.

presenta'tion n 1 the act of handing over a present, esp in public. 2 something given by a group of people to mark a special occasion. 3 the way in which things are shown or arguments put forward.

pres'ently adv soon.

preserva'tion n the act of preserving. 2 safeguarding.

preserv'ative adj keeping from going bad.

preserve' vb 1 (fml) to keep from harm. 2 to keep from rotting or decaying. 3 to keep safe or in good condition:—n 1 fruit, etc, treated so as to prevent it from going bad, jam. 2 a place where animals, birds, etc, are protected.

pres'ident n the elected head of a republic, company, society, etc, a chairman.

press vb 1 to push on or against with force. 2 to squeeze. 3 to smooth and flatten. 4 to try to persuade:—n 1 a crowd. 2 a printing machine. 3 a machine for crushing or squeezing. 4 the newspapers.

press'ing adj urgent.

press'ure n 1 the act of pressing force. 2 forceful influence. 3 stress.

prestige' n good name, high reputation.

presum'ably adv apparently.

presume' vb 1 to take for granted, to accept as true without proof. 2 (fml) to act in a bold or forward way.

pretence' n 1 the act of pretending. 2 a deception. 3 a false claim.

pretend' vb 1 to make believe by words or actions that one is other than one really is. 2 to behave as if one were in other circumstances.

preten'sion n 1 a claim, true or false. 2 pretentiousness.

preten'tious adj claiming much for oneself, too proud.

pre'text n a pretended reason, an excuse.

prett'ty adj pleasing to the eye, attractive:—adv quite:—n **prett'iness**.

prevail' vb 1 to overcome, to prove better or stronger than. 2 to be in general use. 3 to persuade.

prevail'ing adj 1 common, most widely accepted, etc. 2 (of a wind) that usually blows over an area.

prevent' vb to stop from happening:—n **preven'tion**.

preven'tive adj helping to prevent:—also n.

pre'vious adj earlier, happening before.

prey [prā] n 1 an animal or bird hunted and killed by another animal or bird. 2 one who suffers (from):—vb 1 to hunt and kill for food. 2 to keep on attacking and robbing. 3 to trouble greatly.

price n 1 the money asked or paid for something on sale. 2 what must be done to obtain something.

price'less adj of great value.

prick vb 1 to stab lightly with the point of a needle, dagger, etc. 2 to make a tiny hole in. 3 to make to stand up straight:—n 1 a sharp point. 2 a tiny hole. 3 a sting. 4 a thorn.

pride n 1 a feeling of pleasure at one's own abilities, deeds, etc. 2 too great an opinion of oneself, one's deeds, etc. 3 the most valuable person or thing:—**pride oneself on** to take pleasure in.

priest n a clergyman, a minister of religion:—f **priest'ess**.

prim adj 1 stiff in manner, formal and correct. 2 neat, restrained.

pri'mary adj 1 first. 2 chief:—adv **primar'ily**.

primary colors npl the colors red, yellow, and blue, from which other colors may be made.

pri'mate n 1 an archbishop. 2 one of the highest kinds of animals, including men and monkeys.

prime adj 1 most important. 2 excellent in quality. 3 that cannot be divided by any smaller number:—n the best time:—vb 1 to provide with information. 2 to prepare for painting.

prime minister n the chief minister in a government.

prime number n a number that can be divided only by itself and the number 1.

prime'val adj having to do with the first ages of the world.

prim'itive adj 1 of the earliest times. 2 simple or rough.

prince n 1 a ruler. 2 the son of a king or emperor.

prin'cess n 1 the wife of a prince. 2 the daughter of a king or emperor.

prin'cipal adj chief, most important:—n 1 the head of a school, college, etc. 2 an amount of money lent at interest.

prin'cipally adv chiefly.

prin'ciple n 1 a general truth from which other truths follow. 2 a rule by which one lives.

print vb 1 to make a mark by pressure. 2 to reproduce letters, words, etc, on paper by use of type. 3 to publish in printed form. 4 to write without joining the letters. 5 to stamp. 6 to stamp a design on cloth. 7 to produce a picture from a photographic negative. 8 to write in large clear lettering:—n 1 a mark made by pressure. 2 letters, words, etc, reproduced on paper by use of type. 3 a copy of a picture taken from a photographic negative or engraving.

print'er n 1 one who prints books, newspapers, etc. 2 a machine that prints.

pri'or n earlier, previous.

prior'ity n 1 the state or right of coming before others in position or time. 2 something or someone that must be considered or dealt with first.

pris'on n a building in which convicted criminals are kept for a time.

pris'oner n 1 one kept in prison. 2 a person captured by the enemy in war.

pris'tine adj 1 former, of earlier times. 2 pure, undamaged, clean.

priv'acy n 1 undisturbed quiet. 2 secrecy.

pri'vate adj 1 belonging to oneself only, not open to other people. 2 not public. 3 secret:—n a common soldier who has not been promoted.

priv'ilege n 1 a right or advantage allowed to a certain person or group only. 2 advantage possessed because of social position, wealth, etc:—vb to allow a privilege to.

priv'y adj (fml) allowed to share knowledge hidden from others:

prize' n 1 something given as a reward for merit or good work. 2 that which is won by competition. 3 anything seized from an enemy:—vb to value highly.

prize' vb to force open, pry.

pro- prefix 1 before. 2 in favor of:—**pros and cons** reasons for and against.

probabil'ity n likelihood.

prob'able adj 1 likely to happen, likely to be true. 2 easy to believe.

prob'ably adv very likely.

proba'tion n 1 the testing of a person's conduct, work, or character. 2 a time of trial or testing, esp for a young person found guilty of a crime but not sentenced on condition that his or her conduct improves.

proba'tioner n one whose fitness for certain work is being tested

probation officer n one whose duty it is to watch over young persons on probation.

probe n vb to examine carefully, to inquire into thoroughly.

probity [pro'-bi-ti] n (fml) honesty, uprightness.

prob'lem n a question or difficulty to which the answer is hard to find.

problemat'ic(al) adj doubtful.

proce'dure n way of conducting business.

proceed' vb 1 to move forward. 2 to go on doing, to continue. 4 (fml) to go to law (against):—npl **pro'ceeds** money made on a particular occasion.

proceed'ing n 1 something happening. 2 a course of action.

pro'cess n 1 the way in which a thing is done or made. 2 a number of actions each of which brings one nearer to the desired end. 3 (fml) a law-court case.

proces'sion n a body of people moving forward in an orderly column.

proclaim' vb to announce publicly, to tell openly.

proclama'tion n a public announcement.

procure' vb (fml) to obtain.

prod vb (**prod'ded, prod'ding**) 1 to push with something pointed. 2 to nudge. 3 to urge into action:—also n.

prod'igy n a person of extraordinary abilities.

produce' vb 1 to bring forward, to bring into view. 2 to bear, to yield. 3 to cause or bring about. 4 to make or manufacture. 5 to give birth to. 6 to cause, to make (a line) longer:—n **prod'uce** things grown, crops.

produc'er n 1 a person or country that grows or makes certain things. 2 one who gets a play or TV program ready for performance.

prod'uct n 1 that which grows or is made. 2 result. 3 the number given by multiplying other numbers together.

produc'tion n 1 the act of making or growing. 2 the amount produced. 3 a performance or series of performances of a TV program, play, opera, etc.

produc'tive adj 1 fertile. 2 having results.

productiv'ity n the rate of producing something.

profess' vb 1 to say openly. 2 to claim skill or ability. 3 to declare one's beliefs. 4 to pretend.

profes'sion n 1 a public declaration. 2 an employment requiring special learning. 3 the people involved in such employment.

profes'sional adj 1 having to do with a profession. 2 paid for one's skill. 3 done for a living. 4 of a very high standard:—n one who makes his or her living by arts, sports, etc (opposite of **amateur**).

profes'sor n one who teaches in a college or university.

profi'cient adj highly skilled, expert:—n **profi'ciency**.

pro'file n 1 an outline, a short description. 2 a head or an outline of it in side view.

prof'it n 1 an advantage. 2 a gain, esp of money:—vb 1 to gain an advantage. 2 to be of use to.

prof'itable adj 1 bringing profit or gain. 2 useful.

profound' adj 1 deep. 2 showing much knowledge or intelligence. 3 intense.

profuse' adj very plentiful.

profu'sion n great plenty.

prog'eny n children.

pro'gram n 1 a plan or scheme. 2 a list of the items in a concert, etc. 3 a scheduled radio or TV broadcast. 4 a sequence of instructions fed into a computer:—vb 1 to prepare a plan or schedule. 2 to feed a program into a computer. 3 to write a program.

pro'gress n 1 movement forward, advance. 2 improvement:—vb **progress'** 1 to advance. 2 to improve.

progres'sion n 1 onward movement. 2 a steady and regular advance.

progres'sive adj 1 moving forward, advancing. 2 believing in trying new ideas and methods.

prohib'it vb 1 to forbid. 2 to prevent.

project' vb 1 to throw. 2 to plan. 3 to stick out. 4 to operate a projector:—n **pro'ject** 1 a plan. 2 a housing project.

projec'tion n 1 a part that sticks out. 2 the representation on a plane surface of part of the earth's surface. 3 a projected image. 4 an estimate of future possibilities based on a current trend. 5 a mental image externalized. 6 an unconscious attribution to another of one's own feelings and motives.

projection'ist n 1 one who operates a projector. 2 a mapmaker.

projec'tor n an apparatus for showing pictures on a screen.

prolif'ic adj producing much.

pro'logue n (fml) an introduction.

prolong' vb to make longer.

prolonged' adj very long.

prom'inence n the state or act of being prominent.

prom'inent adj 1 easily seen. 2 well known. 3 sticking out.

prom'ise vb 1 to say that one will do or not do something, to give one's word. 2 to give hope of a good result:—n 1 act of giving one's word. 2 a sign of future success.

prom'ising adj likely to do well in the future.

prom'ontory n a headland.

promote' vb 1 to raise to a higher position or rank. 2 to help on. 3 to help to start:—n **promo'tion**.

prompt adj 1 ready, quick to take action. 2 done without delay, quick:—vb 1 to try to get another to take action. 2 to help someone (esp an actor) who cannot remember what he or she ought to say.

prompt'er n one whose job it is to whisper words to an actor who cannot remember them.

prone adj 1 lying face downward. 2 inclined (to).

prong n the spike of a fork etc.

pro'noun *n* a word used instead of a noun.

pronounce' *vb* 1 to make the sound of. 2 to declare publicly. 3 to speak.

pronounced' *adj* very noticeable.

pronuncia'tion *n* the way of making the sounds of a language.

proof *n* 1 an argument, fact, etc, that shows clearly that something is true or untrue. 2 (*fml*) a test or trial. 3 (*in printing*) a first printing for correction before reprinting. 4 the statement of strength of some spirits, e.g. whiskey:—*adj* not affected by, able to resist.

prop *n* 1 a support. 2 a piece of stage equipment:—*vb* (**propped'**, **prop'ping**) to support, to hold up.

propagan'da *n* a plan for spreading certain ideas, beliefs etc, to large numbers of people.

propel' *vb* (**propelled'**, **propel'ling**) to drive or push forward.

propell'er *n* a revolving screw with sloping blades attached for moving forward ships, airplanes, etc.

propen'sity *n* a natural leaning or tendency to behave in a certain way.

prop'er *adj* 1 correct, suitable, decent, polite. 2 (*inf*) thorough, complete.

prop'erly *adv* 1 correctly, suitably. 2 strictly (speaking).

prop'erty *n* 1 anything owned, that which belongs to one. 2 one's land. 3 a quality or characteristic.

proph'ecy *n* 1 the foretelling of future events. 2 something foretold.

proph'esy *vb* to tell what will happen in the future, to foretell.

proph'et *n* 1 one who foretells the future. 2 one who tells people a message or command from God:—*adj* **prophet'ic**.

propi'tious *adj* (*fml*) signifying good luck.

propor'tion *n* 1 the size of a part when compared with the whole. 2 the size of one object, number, etc, when compared with that of another. 3 a share. 4 *pl* size.

propor'tional, propor'tionate *adjs* in correct or proper proportion.

propo'sal *n* 1 a suggestion or plan put forward. 2 an offer to marry.

propose' *vb* 1 to put forward for consideration. 2 to intend. 3 to offer to marry.

proposi'tion *n* 1 a plan or suggestion put forward. 2 an offer. 3 a statement, a statement that is to be proved true.

propri'etary *adj* 1 owned by a person or group of persons. 2 possessive.

propri'etor *n* an owner.

propri'ety *n* (*fml*) correctness of behavior.

propul'sion *n* a driving or pushing forward.

prosa'ic *adj* dull, commonplace, not poetic.

prose *n* 1 the language of ordinary speech and writing. 2 all writing not in verse.

pros'ecute *vb* 1 (*fml*) to carry on. 2 to accuse in a court of law:—*n* **prosecu'tion**.

pros'ecutor *n* the person who makes the accusation in a court of law.

pros'pect *n* 1 (*fml*) a view. 2 one's idea of what may happen in the future. 3 chance of future success:—*vb* **prospect'** to explore, to search for places where mines may be sunk for oil, metals, etc.

prospec'tive *adj* expected, probable.

prospec'tus *n* a written description of some undertaking or of the training offered by a school.

pros'per *vb* to do well, to succeed.

prosper'ity *n* success, good fortune.

pros'perous *adj* successful, well off.

pros'titute *vb* to put to a low or evil use:—*n* a person making a living by immoral means:—*n* **prostitu'tion**.

pros'trate *adj* 1 lying flat with the face to the ground. 2 exhausted:—*vb* 1 to throw flat on the ground. 2 to bow in reverence. 3 to tire out:—*n* **prostra'tion**.

protag'onist *n* 1 one playing a leading part in a drama or in an exciting situation in real life. 2 a leader. 3 someone taking part in a contest.

protect' *vb* to keep safe from danger, loss, etc, to defend.

protec'tion *n* 1 defense, watchful care. 2 the taxing of imported goods to protect home goods.

protec'tive *adj* giving defense, care, or safety.

protec'tor *n* a person or thing that protects.

protégé [pro'-tā-j ā] *n* (*fml*) one under the care of another.

protein [prō'-teen] *n* a substance contained in certain foods (e.g. meat, eggs) that helps the body to grow and become stronger.

protest' *vb* 1 to object. 2 to disapprove. 3 to declare:—*n* **pro'test** a statement of disagreement or disapproval.

Prot'estant *n* a member of one of the Christian groups separated from the Roman Catholic church at the Reformation:—*also adj*.

pro'totype *n* the first model from which others are copied, a pattern.

protract' *vb* to make long or longer.

protrac'tor *n* an instrument for measuring angles.

protrude *vb* (*fml*) to stick out.

protu'berant *adj* (*fml*) bulging out.

proud *adj* 1 having too high an opinion of oneself, one's deeds, or possessions. 2 rightly satisfied with oneself and what one has done.

prove *vb* 1 to show the truth of. 2 to turn out to be. 3 to test.

prov'erb *n* a popular truth or belief expressed in a short memorable sentence.

provide' *vb* 1 to supply what is needed. 2 to make ready beforehand, to prepare for:—*conj* **provi'ded (that)** on condition (that).

prov'idence *n* 1 care for the future, foresight. 2 God's care of his creatures.

prov'ince *n* 1 a division of a country. 2 *pl* all the parts of a country outside the capital.

provin'cial *adj* 1 like or in a province. 2 having limited or local interests, unsophisticated.

provi'sion *n* 1 something provided for the future. 2 *pl* food:—*vb* to supply with stores of food.

provi'sional *adj* for a time only, that may be changed.

provi'so *n* a condition.

provoca'tion *n* a cause of anger or annoyance.

provoke' *vb* 1 to make angry. 2 to give rise to.

prow *n* the front part of a ship or boat.

prow'ess *n* skill or ability.

prowl *vb* to keep moving about as if searching for something, to move quietly about looking for the chance to do mischief.

prowl'er *n* one who moves stealthily, esp a thief.

proxim'ity *n* nearness, neighborhood.

prox'y *n* 1 the right to act or vote for another. 2 one with the right to act or vote for another.

prude *n* a person who makes a show of being very modest and correct in behavior:—*n* **prud'ery**.

pru'dent *adj* thinking carefully before acting, wise, cautious.

prud'ish *adj* over-correct in behavior.

prune¹ *n* a dried plum.

prune² *vb* 1 to cut off the dead or overgrown parts of a tree. 2 to shorten by cutting out what is unnecessary.

pry¹ *vb* to inquire closely, esp into the secrets of others, to examine closely.

pry² *vb* to force open.

pseudo [sū́-dō] *adj* false, not real.

pseudonym [sū́-dō-n im] *n* a name used instead of one's real name (e.g. a pen name).

psychiatry [sī-kī́-ět-ri] *n* the treatment of diseases of the mind:—*n* **psychi′atrist**.

psychic [sī́-kik], **psy′chical** *adjs* 1 having to do with the mind. 2 *(of influences, forces)* that act on the mind and senses but have no physical cause. 3 *(of a person)* sensitive to these influences. 4 able to communicate with spirits.

psychology [sī-ko′-lo-dji] *n* 1 the study of the human mind. 2 the mental process of a person:—*adj* **psycholog′ical:**—*n* **psychol′ogist**.

pterodac′tyl *n* a prehistoric winged reptile known of from fossils.

pu′berty *n* the age by which a young person has fully developed all the characteristics of his or her sex.

pub′lic *adj* 1 open to all. 2 having to do with people in general. 3 well known:—*n* the people in general.

publica′tion *n* 1 the act of publishing. 2 a published book, magazine, or paper.

public′ity *n* 1 making something widely known, advertising. 2 the state of being well known:—*vb* **pub′licize**.

pub′lish *vb* 1 *(fml)* to make widely known. 2 to print for selling to the public.

pub′lisher *n* one who publishes books, etc.

puck′er *vb* to gather into small folds or wrinkles:—*n* a fold or wrinkle.

pud′ding *n* a soft sweet cooked food served at the end of a meal.

pud′dle *n* a small pool of dirty water:—*vb* to make watertight with clay.

puff *n* 1 a short sharp breath or gust of wind. 2 a small cloud of smoke, steam, etc, blown by a puff. 3 a soft pad for powdering the skin. 4 a kind of light pastry:—*vb* 1 to breathe quickly or heavily, as when short of breath. 2 to blow in small blasts. 3 to blow up, to swell. 4 to praise too highly.

puff′y *adj* blown out, swollen.

pugna′cious *adj (fml)* quarrelsome, fond of fighting:—*n* **pugna′city**.

pull *vb* 1 to draw toward one, to draw in the same direction as oneself. 2 to bring along behind one while moving. 3 to remove (flowers, etc) from the ground. 4 to gather.

pul′ley *n* a grooved wheel with a cord running over it used for raising weights.

pulp *n* 1 the soft juicy part of a fruit. 2 soft substance obtained by crushing rags, wood, etc, and made into paper:—*vb* to make into pulp, to become pulpy.

pul′pit *n* a raised platform enclosed by a half wall for preaching in church.

pulsate′ *vb* to beat or throb.

pulse¹ *n* 1 the throb of the heart or of the blood passing through the arteries. 2 a place on the body where the throb of the blood can be felt:—*vb* to beat or throb.

pulse² *n* the eatable seeds of peas, beans, lentils, etc.

pum′mel *vb* to keep on striking with the fist(s).

pump¹ *n* 1 a machine for raising water from a well. 2 a machine for raising any liquid to a higher level. 3 a machine for taking air out of or putting air into things:—*vb* 1 to work a pump. 2 to raise with a pump.

pump² *n* a light shoe for dancing.

pun *n* the witty or amusing use of a word like another in sound but different in meaning:—*vb* **(punned′, pun′ning)** to make a pun.

punch¹ *vb* 1 to strike with the fist. 2 to make a hole with a special tool or machine:—*n* 1 a blow with the fist. 2 a tool or machine for making holes.

punch² *n* a drink made from wine or spirit mixed with sugar, hot water, fruit, etc.

punc′tual *adj* 1 up to time, not late. 2 good at arriving at the correct time:—*n* **punctual′ity**.

punc′tuate *vb* 1 to divide up written work with full stops, commas, etc. 2 to interrupt repeatedly:—*n* **punctua′tion**.

punc′ture *n* a hole made by a sharp point:—*vb* to make a hole in, to pierce.

pun′gent *adj* sharp:—*n* **pun′gency**.

pun′ish *vb* 1 to cause someone to suffer for doing wrong. 2 to deal roughly with.

pun′ishment *n* pain, loss, etc, inflicted on a wrongdoer.

pu′ny *adj* small and weak.

pup *n* a puppy, a young dog.

pu′pa *n (pl* **pu′pae** *or* **pu′pas)** 1 a stage in the growth of an insect just before it develops wings. 2 an insect in this stage.

pu′pil *n* 1 one being taught, a learner. 2 the round opening in the center of the eye through which light passes.

pup′pet *n* 1 a doll whose movements are controlled by strings, etc. 2 one who obeys without question all the orders given him or her by another.

pup′pet show *n* a performance by puppets.

pup′py *n* a young dog.

pur′chase *vb* to buy:—*n* 1 the thing bought. 2 a position that allows one to apply all one's strength.

pur′chaser *n* a buyer.

pure *adj* 1 clear. 2 unmixed. 3 clean, free from dirt or harmful matter. 4 free from guilt or evil. 5 complete, absolute.

purée [pū́-rā] *n* food crushed to a pulp and passed through a sieve.

pure′ly *adv* 1 wholly. 2 only, merely.

purifica′tion *n* act of purifying.

pu′rify *vb* 1 to cleanse. 2 to make pure.

pu′ritan *n* one who is very strict in matters of morals or religion:—*adj* **puritan′ical:**—*n* **pu′ritanism**.

pu′rity *n* the state of being pure.

pur′ple *n* a color of red and blue mixed.

pur′pose *n* 1 the reason for an action, an intention or plan. 2 use or function.

pur′poseful *adj* 1 having a clear intention in mind. 2 determined.

pur′posely *adv* intentionally, on purpose.

purr *n* the low sound made by a cat when pleased:—*also vb*.

purse *n* 1 a small bag for money. 2 a sum of money offered as a prize. 3 a small bag carried by people to contain their personal possessions:—*vb* to pull in (the lips).

pursue′ *vb* 1 to follow in order to catch. 2 to carry on (an activity).

pursuit′ *n* the act of pursuing.

pus *n* yellow matter from an infected sore or wound.

push *vb* 1 to press against with force. 2 to move by force, to shove. 3 to try to make someone do something. 4 to sell illegally. 5 *(inf)* to promote, to advertise:—*n* 1 a shove. 2 strong effort. 3 *(inf)* energy. 4 an attack by a large army:—*n* **push′er**.

push′ing *adj* 1 energetic. 2 eager to get on.

puss, puss′y *ns (inf)* a cat.

put [pŭt] *vb* **(put, put′ting)** 1 to set down or move into a certain place. 2 to ask. 3 to express in words:—**put by** to keep for future use:—**put up** to give accommodation to:—**put up with** to bear without complaining:—*see also* **putt**.

pu′trid *adj* 1 *(fml)* rotten, decayed. 2 *(inf)* very bad, poor.

putt, put [put] *vb* (**putt'ed, putt'ing**) **1** to throw from the shoulder with a bent arm. **2** in golf, to hit the ball into the hole on the green:—*n* **1** act of throwing a weight in sport. **2** in golf a hit intended to send the ball into the hole.

putt'y *n* a paste made from chalk and linseed oil, used for fitting glass in windows, etc.

puz'zle *vb* **1** to present with a difficult problem or situation, to baffle, to perplex. **2** to think long and carefully about:—*n* **1** a difficult question or problem. **2** a toy intended to test one's skill or cleverness:—*n* **puz'zlement**.

pyg'my, pig'my *n* **1** a member of a race of very small people in Africa. **2** (*inf*) a very small person or animal:—*also adj*.

py'lon *n* a hollow skeleton pillar for carrying overhead cables.

pyr'amid *n* **1** a solid body with triangular sides meeting in a point at the top. **2** a monument of this shape.

pyre *n* a pile of wood, etc, on which a dead body is placed for burning.

py'thon *n* a large nonpoisonous snake that crushes its prey in its coils.

Q

quack[1] *n* the harsh cry of a duck:—*vb* to make the cry of a duck.

quack[2] *n* 1 one who pretends to knowledge or skill that he or she does not possess, esp in medicine. 2 (*inf*) a doctor:—*n* **quack'ery**.

quad- *prefix* four.

quadran'gle *n* a figure with four sides and four angles.

quadrilat'eral *n* a four-sided figure.

quad'ruped *n* (*fml*) an animal with four feet.

quad'ruple *adj* four times as great:—*vb* to make or become four times greater.

quad'ruplet *n* (*often abbreviated to* **quad**) one of four children born at one birth.

quag'mire *n* bog, marsh.

quail *vb* to bend or draw back in fear.

quaint *adj* unusual and old-fashioned, pleasingly strange.

quake *vb* to tremble.

qualifica'tion *n* 1 an ability, skill, etc, that fits a person for a certain post or occupation. 2 a remark that in some way alters a statement already made.

qual'ify *vb* 1 to achieve the standards required before one can enter a profession, fill a certain post, etc. 2 to make fit. 3 to change but not alter completely. 4 (*of an adjective*) to describe.

qual'ity *n* 1 a characteristic of a person or thing. 2 the degree to which something is good or excellent, a standard of excellence. 3 excellence. 4 (*old*) people of high rank.

qualm [kwäm] *n* doubt, a fear that one is about to do what is wrong.

quan'dary *n* a state of uncertainty, doubt as to what one ought to do.

quan'tity *n* 1 size, amount. 2 a large portion. 3 the length of a vowel sound.

quar'antine *n* a period of time during which a person, animal, or ship that may carry infection is kept apart.

quar'rel *n* an angry dispute or disagreement:—*vb* to exchange angry words with, to fall out.

quar'relsome *adj* fond of quarreling.

quar'ry[1] *n* that which one is trying to catch.

quar'ry[2] *n* a place from which stone, slate, etc, may be excavated.

quart *n* a measure of liquid equal to 2 pints or $1/4$ gallon.

quar'ter *n* 1 the fourth part of anything. 2 25 cents, or a coin of this value. 3 a measure of weight, $1/4$ hundredweight (25 pounds). 4 direction. 5 a district in a town. 6 a limb and the part where it joins the body. 7 mercy to an enemy defeated in battle. 8 (*in heraldry*) one of the four divisions of a shield. 9 *pl* lodgings:—*vb* to divide into four equal parts.

quar'terly *adj* happening every three months: —*also n*:—*adv* once every three months.

quartet(te)' *n* 1 a piece of music written for four performers. 2 a group of four singers or players. 3 a set or group of four.

quash *vb* 1 to set aside (an order or judgment). 2 to put down, to put an end to.

quasi- [kwä-zī *or* kwä'-zee] *prefix* almost, to some extent but not really.

qua'ver *vb* 1 to shake, to tremble. 2 to speak in a trembling, uncertain voice:—*n* a trembling of the voice.

quay [kee] *n* a landing place for the loading and unloading of ships.

que'asy *adj* feeling sick, easily made sick.

queen *n* 1 the wife of a king. 2 a female ruler of a country. 3 the female of the bee, ant, etc. 4 a picture playing card. 5 a piece in chess.

queen bee *n* the only female bee in a hive.

queen mother *n* a former queen who is the mother of the reigning king or queen.

queer *adj* 1 strange, unusual. 2 unwell:—*vb* to spoil.

quell *vb* 1 to put down completely, to crush. 2 to put an end to.

quench *vb* 1 to put out. 2 to satisfy.

query [kwee'-ri] *n* 1 a question. 2 a question mark (?):—*vb* to doubt.

quest (*fml or lit*) *n* a search.

ques'tion *n* 1 a request for news, information, knowledge, etc. 2 words spoken or arranged in such a way that an answer is called for. 3 a problem. 4 the matter under consideration:—*vb* 1 to ask questions. 2 to doubt.—*n* **ques'tioner**.

ques'tionable *adj* 1 doubtful. 2 open to suspicion.

questionnaire' *n* a set of written questions chosen for a particular purpose.

queue [kū] *n* 1 a line of persons awaiting their turn. 2 a pigtail:—*vb* to wait in line.

quib'ble *n* an objection or argument, esp an unimportant, trivial one:—*vb* to argue about small unimportant details.

quick *adj* 1 fast-moving. 2 clever. 3 done in a short time. 4 (*old*) living:—*n* the very tender flesh under the nails or just below the skin:—*adv* quickly.

quick'en *vb* 1 to give life to. 2 to become alive or lively. 3 to make or become faster.

quick'ly *adv* at once, rapidly.

quick'sand *n* loose wet sand into which anything of weight (e.g. ships, people) may sink.

quick'step *n* a quick ballroom dance, a quick fox-trot.

quid pro quo *n* something equivalent given in exchange for something else.

qui'et *adj* 1 at rest. 2 noiseless, not noisy. 3 calm, peaceful, gentle. 4 (*of colors*) not bright:—*n* 1 rest, peace. 2 silence:—*vb* 1 to calm. 2 to make silent.

qui'eten *vb* 1 to make or become quiet. 2 to remove or lessen.

qui'etness *n* rest, peace, silence.

quill *n* 1 a large feather from a goose or other bird, used as a pen. 2 one of the prickles on the back of a porcupine or hedgehog.

quilt *n* 1 a thick, warm bedcover. 2 a coverlet of two cloths sewn together with padding between:—*vb* to stitch together like a quilt, to make a quilt.

quintes'sence *n* the most perfect form of anything, the perfect type or example of:—*adj* **quintessen'tial**.

quintet(te)' *n* 1 a piece of music written for five performers. 2 a group of five singers or players. 3 a set or group of five.

quin'tuple *adj* five times as great:—*vb* to make or become five times greater.

quintup'let *n* (*often abbreviated to* **quin**) one of five children born at one birth.

quip *n* a joking or witty remark:—*vb* (**quipped'**, **quip'ping**) to make such remarks.

quirk *n* 1 a way of behaving or doing something peculiar to oneself. 2 a strange or unexpected happening:—*adj* **quirk'y**.

quit *vb* (**quit'ted** *or* **quit**, **quit'ting**) 1 to leave. 2 to give up.

quite *adv* 1 wholly. 2 fairly, rather.

quits *adj* on even terms, owing nothing to each other.

quiv′er *vb* to tremble:—*n* a shudder, a slight trembling.

quiz *vb* (**quizzed′, quiz′zing**) to examine by questioning:—*n* a number of questions set to test one's knowledge.

quo′ta *n* the share of the whole to which each member of a has a right.

quota′tion *n* **1** the words or passage quoted. **2** a price stated.

quotation marks *npl* punctuation marks ("" *or* '') placed at the beginning and end of a written quotation.

quote *vb* **1** to repeat or write down the exact words of another person, making it known that they are not one's own. **2** to say the price of:—*n* (*inf*) **1** a quotation. **2** a quotation mark.

quotid′ian *adj* (*fml*) daily.

quo′tient *n* the answer to a division sum.

R

rabbi [rab'-i] *n* one learned in the law and doctrine of the Jews, a Jewish priest.

rab'bit *n* **1** a small long-eared burrowing animal. **2** (*inf*) one who plays a game very badly.

rab'ble *n* a noisy or disorderly crowd.

ra'bid *adj* **1** fanatical. **2** (*of dogs*) suffering from rabies.

ra'bies *n* a disease that causes madness, and often death, in dogs and other animals.

race[1] *n* **1** a contest to see who can reach a given mark in the shortest time. **2** a strong, quick-moving current of water:—*vb* **1** to take part in a race. **2** to run or move quickly.

race[2] *n* **1** any of the main groups into which human beings can be divided according to their physical characteristics. **2** a group of people who share the same culture, language, etc

race'course, race'track *ns* the ground on which races are run.

ra'cial *adj* having to do with a race or nation.

rack *n* **1** a frame for holding articles. **2** (*old*) an instrument for torturing persons by stretching their joints:—*vb* **1** to cause great pain or trouble to. **2** (*old*) to torture on the rack.

rack'et[1] *n* a bat (usu a frame strung with crisscrossing cords) for playing tennis, etc. **2** *pl* (*also* **racquet'ball, rac'quets**) a game for two or four players played in a four-walled court.

rack'et[2] *n* **1** an uproar, a din. **2** a dishonest method of making a lot of money.

racquetball *n*, **racquets** *see* **racket**[1].

ra'dar *n* the sending out of radio signals to determine the position of ships, airplanes, etc.

ra'diance *n* brightness, brilliance.

ra'diant *adj* **1** sending out rays of light or heat. **2** glowing. **3** shining. **4** showing great joy or happiness.

ra'diate *vb* **1** to send out rays of light or heat. **2** to shine with (happiness, love, etc). **3** to send out or spread from a central point:—*n* **radia'tion**.

ra'diator *n* **1** an apparatus (an electric or gas fire, hot water pipes, etc) for warming a room by radiating heat. **2** an apparatus for cooling a vehicle engine.

rad'ical *adj* **1** having to do with the root or basic nature. **2** seeking great political, social, or economic change. **3** very thorough:—*n* one who desires to make far-reaching changes in society or in methods of government.

radii *see* **radius**.

ra'dio *n* **1** the sending or receiving of sounds through the air by electric waves. **2** an apparatus for receiving sound broadcast through the air by electric waves. **3** the radio broadcasting industry.

ra'dioac'tive *adj* giving off rays of force or energy that can be dangerous but can be used in medicine, etc:—*n* **ra'dioactiv'ity**.

ra'diother'apy *n* the treatment of disease by rays (e.g. X-rays):—*n* **ra'diother'apist**.

ra'dius *n* (*pl* **radii** [rā'-dee-ī]) **1** a straight line from the center of a circle to any point on the circumference. **2** a bone in the forearm.

raff'le *n* a sale in which people buy tickets for an article that is given to the person whose name or number is drawn by lottery:—*vb* to sell by raffle.

raft *n* logs fastened together to make a floating platform or a flat boat without sides.

raf'ter *n* one of the sloping beams supporting a roof.

rag *n* **1** a torn or tattered piece of cloth, a left-over piece of material. **2** *pl* old tattered clothes.

rage *n* **1** violent anger, fury. **2** inspiration. **3** something very popular or fashionable at a certain time:—*vb* **1** to be furious with anger. **2** to behave or talk violently.

rag'ged *adj* **1** torn or tattered. **2** wearing old tattered clothes. **3** rough-edged.

rag'time *n* a highly syncopated form of music, an early form of jazz.

raid *n* a sudden quick attack made by a group intending to return to their starting point:—*also vb*:—*n* **raid'er**.

rail[1] *n* **1** a level or sloping bar of wood or metal linking up a line of posts, banisters, etc. **2** a strip of metal molded to a certain shape and laid down as part of a railroad or streetcar line:—*vb* **1** to enclose with railings. **2** to send by railroad.

rail'ing *n* a fence made of posts some distance apart linked together by a rail.

rail'road *n* a track laid with parallel metal strips so molded that a locomotive can run on them.

rain *n* moisture falling from the clouds in drops:—*vb* **1** to fall in drops. **2** to fall or throw down in large numbers:—*ns* **rain'drop, rain'water**.

rain'bow *n* a semicircular colored band that often appears in the sky when the sun shines through raindrops.

rain'fall *n* the amount of rain that falls in a certain place during a certain length of time.

rain'y *adj* wet, raining.

raise *vb* **1** to lift upward, to move to a higher position. **2** to breed. **3** to make higher. **4** to cause to grow, to cultivate. **5** to increase in amount, size, etc. **6** to begin to talk about. **7** to collect. **8** to make louder. **9** to give up.

rai'sin *n* a dried grape.

rake *n* a metal or wooden toothed crossbar fixed to a pole and used for scraping the ground, pulling together cut grass or hay, smoothing the soil, etc:—*vb* **1** to scrape, pull together, smooth, etc, with a rake. **2** to search very carefully.

rall'y *vb* **1** to bring or come together again in one body. **2** to regain some of one's strength, health, etc, after weakness or illness. **3** to call upon for a greater effort:—*n* **1** a coming together in large numbers. **2** recovery of strength, health, good spirits, etc.

ram *n* a male sheep:—*vb* (**rammed'**, **ram'ming**) **1** to run into with great force. **2** to push down, into, or on to with great force. **3** to strike violently.

ram'ble *vb* **1** to walk as and where one likes for pleasure. **2** to grow in all directions. **3** to change from one subject to another in a foolish, purposeless way:—*n* a walk taken for pleasure.

ramp *n* a slope.

ram'page[1] *vb* to rush about, to rage:—*n* great anger or excitement.

ram'pant *adj* **1** uncontrolled. **2** growing uncontrollably. **3** in heraldry, standing on the hind legs.

ram'part *n* a defensive wall or mound of earth.

ram'shackle *adj* broken-down.

ranch *n* a large cattle farm.

ran'cid *adj* bad, unpleasant to taste or smell.

ran'dom *adj* without plan or purpose:—**at random** without plan or purpose.

range *vb* **1** to set in a line, to place in order. **2** (*fml*) to wander. **3** to extend. **4** to vary between certain limits:—*n* **1** a line or row, e.g. of mountains. **2** extent. **3** a variety. **4** the distance over which an object can be sent or thrown, sound carried, heard, etc. **5** a piece of ground for firing practice. **6** an enclosed kitchen fireplace for cooking and baking.

ran'ger n a keeper in a large park or forest.

rank n 1 a row or line. 2 a position of authority, a level of importance:—vb 1 to arrange in a row or line. 2 to put or be in a certain class or in an order of merit.

rank'le vb to go on causing anger or dislike.

ran'sack vb 1 to search thoroughly. 2 to plunder.

ran'som n a sum of money paid to free someone from captivity:—vb to pay to obtain freedom, to redeem.

rant vb to talk in a loud, uncontrolled manner, often using words for fine sound rather than meaning:—also n:—n **rant'er**.

rap n 1 a quick light blow, a knock. 2 (inf) talk, conversation. 3 a style of popular music in which (usu rhyming) words are spoken in a rhythmic chant over an instrumental backing:—vb (**rapped'**, **rap'ping**) to give a rap.

rape vb to assault sexually:—n act of raping.

rap'id adj very quick-moving:—n (usu pl) a quick-flowing stretch of river running downhill.

rapt adj giving one's whole mind.

rap'ture n (fml) delight, great joy.

rap'turous adj full of delight, very happy.

rare adj 1 uncommon, unusual. 2 very lightly cooked. 3 not thick. 4 very good. 5 valuable:—n **rare'ness**.

rare'ly adv seldom, not often.

rar'ity n 1 rareness. 2 a thing seldom met with.

ras'cal n 1 a rogue, a scoundrel. 2 a naughty child:—adj **ras'cally**.

rash¹ adj 1 acting without forethought. 2 foolishly daring:—n **rash'ness**.

rash² n a redness of the skin caused by illness or allergy.

rasp n a harsh, grating sound:—vb 1 to make a harsh, grating sound. 2 to say in a harsh voice.

rasp'berry n 1 a common shrub. 2 its eatable red berry.

rat n a gnawing animal like, but larger than, the mouse.

ratch'et n a toothed wheel with which a catch automatically engages as it is turned, preventing it from being turned in the reverse direction.

rate n 1 the amount of one thing measured by its relation to another. 2 speed. 3 price:—vb 1 (fml) to consider. 2 to value. 3 to assign to a position on a scale.

ra'ther adv 1 preferably, more willingly. 2 fairly, quite. 3 more exactly, more truly.

rat'ing n value or rank according to some kind of classification.

ra'tio n one number or amount considered in relation or proportion to another.

ra'tion n a fixed amount of something allowed every so often:—vb to limit to fixed amounts.

ra'tional adj 1 having the power to think things out. 2 reasonable, sensible.

ra'tionalize vb 1 to try to find reasons for all actions. 2 to explain as due to natural causes.

rat'tle vb 1 to make a number of short quick noises one after the other. 2 to shake something to cause such noises. 3 to speak or say quickly:—n 1 an instrument or toy for rattling. 2 a rattling sound.

rau'cous adj hoarse, harsh-sounding.

rav'age vb to lay waste, to plunder, to destroy far and wide:—n damage, destruction.

rave vb 1 to talk wildly or madly. 2 (inf) to praise very highly.

rav'en n a bird of prey of the crow family:—adj black.

rav'enous adj very hungry.

ravine' n a narrow valley with steep sides.

rav'ishing adj delightful, wonderful.

raw adj 1 uncooked. 2 sore. 3 cold and damp.

ray¹ n 1 a line of light, heat, etc, getting broader as it goes farther from its origin. 2 a little, a very small amount.

ray² n a species of flatfish.

ray'on n artificial silk.

raze vb to destroy completely.

ra'zor n an implement for shaving hair.

ra'zorblade n a very sharp blade for use in certain kinds of razor.

reach vb 1 to stretch out. 2 to stretch out a hand or arm for some purpose. 3 to obtain by stretching out for. 4 to arrive at, to get as far as. 5 to pass with the hand:—n 1 the distance one can extend the hand from the body. 2 a distance that can be easily traveled. 3 a straight stretch of river.

react' vb 1 to act, behave, or change in a certain way as a result of something said or done. 2 to do or think the opposite.

reac'tion n 1 action or behavior given rise to by something said or done. 2 opposition to progress. 3 in chemistry, the change in a substance when certain tests are made on it.

read [reed] vb (pt, pp **read** [red]) 1 to look at and understand. 2 to speak aloud what is written or printed. 3 to study. 4 to be written or worded.

read'ily adv willingly, cheerfully.

read'ing n 1 the study of books. 2 words read out from a book or written paper

read'y adj 1 prepared and fit for use. 2 quick. 3 willing:—n **read'iness**.

read'y-made adj (of clothes) not made specially for the person who buys them.

real adj 1 actually existing. 2 true, genuine, not false or fake. 3 utter, complete.

real estate n immovable property, land.

re'alism n the habit of taking a sensible, practical view of life.

re'alist n one who believes in realism.

realis'tic adj 1 life-like. 2 taking a sensible, practical view of life.

real'ity n 1 that which actually exists. 2 truth. 3 things as they actually are.

re'alize vb 1 to make real. 2 to understand fully. 3 to sell for money:—n **realiza'tion**.

re'ally adv 1 actually, in fact. 2 very.

realm [relm] n 1 (fml) a kingdom. 2 one particular aspect or sphere of life.

Re'altor n one who buys and sells real estate on behalf of others.

re'alty n real estate.

reap vb 1 to cut down (crops), to gather in. 2 to receive as a reward.

rear¹ n 1 the part behind. 2 the back part of an army or fleet.

rear² vb 1 to raise. 2 to bring up. 3 to breed. 4 to stand on the hind legs.

rear-ad'miral n a naval officer just below a vice-admiral in some navies.

rea'son n 1 the power to think things out. 2 good sense. 3 cause for acting or believing:—vb 1 to think out step by step. 2 to try to convince by arguing.

rea'sonable adj 1 sensible. 2 willing to listen to another's arguments. 3 not excessive.

rea'soning n 1 use of the power of reason. 2 arguments used to convince.

reassure' vb to take away the doubts or fears of:—n **reassur'ance**.

re'bate n part of a payment given back to the payer.

rebel' n one who revolts against authority:—vb **rebel'** (**rebelled'**, **rebel'ling**) 1 to take up arms (against). 2 to refuse to obey those in authority.

rebel'lion n open resistance to or fighting against authority.

rebel'lious adj 1 ready to rebel, disobedient. 2 fighting against authority.

rebuke' vb to scold, to find fault with:—n a scolding.

recall' vb 1 to remember. 2 to call back:—n an order to return.

recede' vb 1 to move back. 2 to slope back.

receipt' n 1 a written statement that a sum of money or an article has been received. 2 the act of receiving:—vb to mark as paid or received.

receive' vb 1 to come into possession of, to get. 2 to welcome. 3 to accept what one knows to be stolen.

receiv'er n 1 one who receives. 2 equipment that receives electronic signals. 3 a person appointed to manage or hold in trust property in bankruptcy or pending a lawsuit.

re'cent adj not long past:—adv **re'cently**.

recep'tacle n a place or vessel for holding things.

recep'tion n 1 the act of receiving or being received, the welcoming of guests. 2 a formal party. 3 welcome. 4 the quality of radio or TV signals.

recep'tionist n one employed by a hotel, doctor, business, etc, to receive guests, clients, callers, etc.

recess' n 1 an interval, a break from work. 2 part of a room set back into the wall.

reces'sion n a period of reduced trade and business activity.

recipe [re'-si-pi] n instructions on how to make or prepare a certain dish.

recip'ient n one who receives.

recip'rocal adj done by each of two parties to the other, affecting both equally.

reci'tal n 1 a detailed account. 2 a public musical performance, esp by one performer.

recita'tion n that which is recited (e.g. a poem).

recite' vb to repeat aloud from memory.

reck'less adj rash, heedless of danger.

reck'on vb 1 (fml) to count. 2 to consider. 3 to guess, to estimate.

reclaim' vb 1 to demand the return of. 2 to bring under cultivation waste land, land covered by the sea, etc:—n **reclama'tion**.

recline' vb to sit or lie back at one's ease.

recogni'tion n 1 act of recognizing. 2 acknowledgment.

recogniz'able adj that may be recognized.

recognize' vb 1 to know again. 2 to greet or salute. 3 to admit. 4 to accept. 5 to reward.

recoil' vb to go suddenly backward in horror, fear, etc.

recollect' vb to remember.

recollec'tion n 1 memory. 2 something remembered.

recommend' vb 1 to speak in praise of, to suggest that something or someone is good, suitable, etc. 2 to advise.

recommenda'tion n act of praising or speaking in favor of.

rec'ompense vb (fml) to pay back or reward for loss, effort, etc:—n repayment, reward.

rec'oncile vb 1 to make or become friendly again. 2 to make (oneself) accept something new or strange.

reconcile'ment, reconcilia'tion ns a renewal of friendship.

reconnais'sance n an examination of the nature of a piece of country, esp for military purposes (e.g. siting a camp, etc).

reconnoi'ter vb 1 to examine the enemy's position and seek information about strength, etc. 2 to examine unknown territory before crossing or settling on it.

record' vb 1 to put down in writing. 2 to preserve sounds or images by mechanical means on a flat disk, tape, etc. 3 to sing songs, play music, etc, that is recorded on a disk or tape:—n **rec'ord** 1 a recorded account. 2 a book containing written records, a register. 3 the best performance yet known in any type of contest. 4 a vinyl disk for playing on a record-player. 5 what is known about a person's past. 6 a criminal record.

record'er n 1 one who keeps registers or records. 2 a simple form of flute.

rec'ord-player n a machine for playing records.

recount' vb 1 to tell in detail. 2 to count again:—n **re'count** another counting, e.g. of votes after an election.

recoup' vb to get back all or part of a loss.

recover' vb 1 to cover again. 2 to get back, to regain. 3 to make or become better after illness or weakness.

recov'ery n 1 a return to health after illness. 2 the regaining of anything after losing some or all of it.

recrea'tion n 1 rest and amusement after work. 2 a sport, a pastime.

recrimina'tion n the act of accusing one's accuser.

recruit' n a new member:—vb to enlist new soldiers, members:—n **recruit'ment**.

rec'tangle n a four-sided figure with all its angles right angles and one pair of sides longer than the other:—adj **rect-ang'ular**.

rec'tify vb to put right, to correct:—n **rectifica'tion**.

rec'tor n in the Episcopal Church, a parish clergyman.

recu'perate vb to regain health or strength after illness:—n **recupera'tion**.

recur' vb (recurred', recur'ring) to happen again and again:—n **recur'rence**.

recur'rent adj happening or appearing again and again.

red adj 1 of a color like blood. 2 politically left:—n 1 the color red. 2 a socialist:—**see red** to become suddenly very angry.

Red Cross n an international organization that looks after sick and wounded in time of war and protects the rights of prisoners of war.

red'den vb 1 to make or become red. 2 to blush.

red'-hand'ed adj in the very act of doing wrong.

red herring n something mentioned that takes attention away from the subject being discussed.

red'-letter adj 1 marked in the calendar in red letters. 2 notable, memorable.

redoubt'able adj to be feared, deserving respect.

redress' vb to set right, to make up for:—n 1 the setting right of a wrong. 2 something given to make up for wrong done or loss caused.

red tape n overmuch attention to rules and regulations so that business is delayed.

reduce' vb 1 to make less, smaller, or less heavy. 2 to change into another and usu worse state, form, etc. 3 to bring or force to do something less pleasant, etc, than usual:—n **reduc'tion**.

redun'dant adj 1 more than necessary. 2 (of workers) no longer required and so dismissed:—n **redun'dancy**.

reed n 1 a tall grass-like water plant with a hollow stem. 2 that part of certain wind instruments that vibrates and so causes the sound when the instrument is blown.

reef n a ridge of rock or sand just above or just below the surface of the water.

reel n a frame or roller around which string, thread, photographic film, etc, may be wound:—vb 1 to wind on to a reel. 2 to stagger:—**reel off** to tell without stopping.

refer' vb (referred', refer'ring) 1 to pass (a matter) on to another for decision. 2 to look up a certain item in a book. 3 to make mention of. 4 to advise to consult elsewhere.

referee' n 1 one chosen to give a clear decision in case of doubt. 2 in games, a person who sees that the rules are kept. 3 one ready to supply information about the character, behavior, etc, of another.

ref'erence n 1 mention. 2 directions as to where to find certain items, passages, etc, in a book. 3 a letter giving information about the character, behavior, etc, of one applying for a job.

reference book n a book (e.g. a dictionary) that supplies information.

refine' vb 1 to purify. 2 to make more polite and civilized.

refine'ment n 1 the state of being purified. 2 politeness, good taste, etc.

reflect' vb 1 to throw back, esp rays of light or heat. 2 (of a mirror) to show the image of. 3 to think about carefully. 4 to be a cause of (praise or blame) for.

reflec'tion n 1 the act of reflecting (light, an image, etc). 2 the image seen in a mirror, etc. 3 a thought, deep or careful thought. 4 blame.

reflec'tive adj thoughtful.

re'flex n an involuntary response to a stimulus:—adj 1 (of an angle) more than 180 degrees. 2 (of a camera) with a full-size viewfinder using the main lens.

reflex'ive adj in grammar, referring back to the subject.

reform' vb 1 to make or become better. 2 to give up bad habits:—n a change for the better.

reform'er n one who calls for or brings about changes in politics, society, religion, etc.

refrain¹ vb 1 to hold (oneself) back from doing something.

refrain² n a line or phrase that is repeated several times in a song or poem, a tune.

refresh' vb to give new strength, energy, power, etc.

refresh'ment n a meal, a snack, a drink.

refrig'erate vb to make cold, to freeze:—n **refrigera'tion**.

refrig'erator n an apparatus for preserving food, etc, by keeping it cold, an icebox.

ref'uge n a shelter from danger or distress.

ref'ugee n one fleeing from danger, one who leaves his or her country to seek shelter in another.

refund' vb to repay:—n 1 the act of refunding. 2 the amount refunded.

refus'al n act of refusing.

refuse' vb 1 not to accept. 2 to say that one will not do or give something:—n **ref'use** garbage, that which is left as worthless.

regain' vb 1 to get possession of again. 2 to reach again.

re'gal adj of or like a king, royal, magnificent.

regard' vb 1 (fml) to look at. 2 to consider:—n 1 (fml) attention. 2 respect. 3 pl good wishes.

regard'ing prep concerning.

regard'less adj paying no attention, not caring about.

regime n [rā-zheem'] a method or system of government.

reg'iment n a body of soldiers consisting usu of several battalions.

re'gion n 1 a part of a country, often a large area of land. 2 neighborhood:—adj **re'gional**.

reg'ister n 1 an official list. 2 a book in which records (e.g. of births, deaths, school attendance, etc) are kept:—vb 1 to write down in a register. 2 to give details to an official for writing in a register. 3 to pay extra to ensure that a letter or parcel reaches its destination safely. 4 to show (what one is feeling).

registra'tion n act of registering.

reg'istry n an office where official records of births, deaths, marriages, etc, are kept.

regress' vb to move backward:—adj **regres'sive**.

regret' vb (regret'ted, regret'ting) to be sorry for what one has said or done:—n sorrow:—adj **regret'ful**.

regret'table adj unfortunate, unwelcome.

reg'ular adj 1 normal, usual. 2 done always in the same way or at the same time. 3 occurring, acting, etc, with equal amounts of space, time, etc, between. 4 the same on both or all sides:—n **regular'ity**.

reg'ulate vb 1 to control. 2 to alter (a machine) until it is working properly.

regula'tion n a rule, an order, an instruction:—adj as laid down in the rules.

rehear'sal n a practice before a performance.

rehearse' vb to practice, esp in preparation for public performance.

reign [rān] n 1 rule. 2 the time during which a king or queen has ruled:—vb 1 to rule as a sovereign. 2 to exist.

reimburse' vb to repay what someone has lost or spent:—n **reimburse'ment**.

rein [rān] n 1 the strap by which a driver or rider directs a horse. 2 control:—vb to check or control with the rein.

rein'deer n a deer found in northern parts of Europe and America.

reinforce'ments npl more or fresh troops, etc.

reinstate' vb to put back in a former position:—n **reinstate'ment**.

reit'erate vb to repeat again and again:—n **reitera'tion**.

reject' vb 1 to refuse to accept. 2 to throw back or away:—n **rejec'tion**.

rejoice' vb to express one's joy.

rejoin'der n an answer, a reply, esp a rude or angry one.

relapse' vb to fall back into evil or illness after improving:—also n.

relate' vb 1 (fml) to tell. 2 to show or see the connection between.

rela'tion n 1 a story, an account. 2 one belonging to the same family by birth or marriage. 3 a connection:—n **rela'tionship**.

rel'ative adj 1 considered in comparison with others. 2 having to do with:—n one belonging to the same family, by birth or marriage.

rel'atively adv 1 quite. 2 when compared with others.

relax' vb 1 to loosen. 2 to become less strict or severe. 3 to take a complete rest, to become less tense or worried.

relaxa'tion n 1 loosening. 2 rest, amusement after work. 3 making less severe.

release' vb 1 to set free. 2 to let go. 3 to unfasten. 4 to make public:—also n.

rel'egate vb to put down to a lower place:—n **relega'tion**.

relent' vb to give way.

relent'less adj 1 without pity. 2 continuous.

rel'evant adj having to do with the matter under consideration:—ns **rel'evance**.

reliabil'ity n trustworthiness.

reli'able adj able to be trusted.

reli'ance n trust, confidence.

reli'ant adj relying on, depending on.

rel'ic n 1 a souvenir. 2 something old-fashioned that still exists.

relief' n 1 complete or partial freeing from pain or worry. 2 one who takes another's place on duty. 3 a piece of sculpture in which the design stands out just beyond a flat surface. 4 a clear outline.

relieve' vb 1 to set free from or lessen (pain or worry). 2 to give help to. 3 to take another's place on duty.

reli'gion n 1 belief in and worship of a god or gods. 2 belief, faith.

reli'gious adj following a religion, holy.

relin'quish vb to give up.

rel'ish vb 1 to enjoy the taste of. 2 to like or enjoy:—n 1 a taste, flavor. 2 enjoyment. 3 a sharp-tasting sauce.

reluc'tant adj unwilling:—n **reluc'tance**.

rely' vb 1 to trust in. 2 to depend on.

remain' vb 1 to stay on in a place. 2 to be left over. 3 to continue to be.

remain'der n that which is left over or behind.

remains' npl 1 that which is left. 2 (fml) a dead body.

remand' vb to send back to prison while further inquiries are being made:—n 1 act of remanding. 2 the state of being remanded.

remark' vb 1 to say. 2 to comment (on):—n something said.

remark'able adj worthy of notice, extraordinary.

rem'edy n 1 a cure. 2 a medicine. 3 any way of putting right what is wrong:—vb 1 to cure. 2 to put right.

remem'ber vb 1 to keep in mind. 2 to recall to the mind. 3 to give greetings from another.

remind' vb to cause to remember.

remind'er n something that helps one to remember.

reminis'cence n 1 a memory of one's past. 2 the remembering of the past. 3 pl stories about one's past.

reminis'cent adj 1 remembering the past. 2 reminding of the past.

remiss' adj (fml) careless, negligent.

remis'sion n 1 the reduction of a prison sentence. 2 a period when an illness is less severe.

remitt'ance n a sum of money sent.

rem'nant n a small piece or part left over.

remorse' n great sorrow for having done wrong:—adj remorse'ful.

remorse'less adj feeling no remorse, pitiless.

remote' adj 1 distant, far away, out of the way. 2 not closely related. 3 not friendly, withdrawn. 4 slight.

remov'al n 1 act of removing. 2 a change of dwelling place.

remove' vb 1 to take from its place. 2 to take off. 3 to dismiss:—adj remov'able.

remunera'tion n pay, salary.

remu'nerative adj profitable, bringing in a lot of money.

ren'der vb 1 to give. 2 to perform in a certain way. 3 to translate. 4 to cause to be.

rendezvous [ro(ng)-dä-vö] n 1 (fml) an agreed meeting place. 2 a meeting.

renew' vb 1 to make new again. 2 to begin again:—n renew'al.

renounce' vb to give up:—n renuncia'tion.

ren'ovate vb to make like new, to repair and clean:—n renova'tion.

renowned' adj famous.

rent n a payment made for the use of land, a house, etc:—vb 1 to get the use of by paying rent. 2 to let or hire out for rent.

ren'tal n rent, the sum paid in rent.

renunciation see renounce.

repair' vb 1 to mend. 2 to put right, make up for. 3 to go:—n 1 returning to good condition, mending. 2 a mended place. 3 condition for using.

repartee' n a quick clever reply.

repay' vb to pay back.

repay'ment n 1 act of repaying. 2 the sum repaid.

repeal' vb to withdraw, to abolish:—also n.

repeat' vb 1 to do or say again. 2 to speak aloud something learned by heart.

repeat'edly adv again and again.

repel' vb (repelled', repell'ing) 1 to drive back. 2 to cause dislike.

repell'ent adj causing dislike or disgust:—n that which is able to repel or drive away something.

repent' vb to feel sorry for having said or done something:—n repen'tance:—adj repen'tant.

repeti'tion n 1 act of repeating. 2 saying from memory.

replace' vb 1 to put back in place. 2 to take the place of.

replace'ment n 1 act of replacing. 2 a person or thing taking the place of another.

replete' adj (fml) full:—n reple'tion.

rep'lica n 1 an exact copy of a work of art. 2 a reproduction, esp of a smaller size.

reply' vb to answer:—n an answer.

report' vb 1 to give as news or information, to tell. 2 to write an account of, esp for a newspaper. 3 to make a complaint about for having done wrong. 4 to tell someone in authority:—n 1 a spoken or written account of work performed. 2 an account of something that has been said or done, esp when written for a newspaper. 3 a rumor. 4 a loud noise.

report'er n one who reports for a newspaper or TV/radio broadcast.

repose' vb n 1 rest, sleep. 2 calmness.

represent' vb 1 to stand for, or make to stand for, as a sign or likeness. 2 to be a picture or statue of. 3 to have the right to speak or act for. 4 to describe or declare, perhaps falsely. 5 (fml) to be, to constitute. 6 to be the representative of (a company).

representa'tion n 1 the act of representing or being represented. 2 an image.

represen'tative adj typical, standing for others of the same class:—n 1 one who acts for another. 2 one who sells goods for a business firm. 3 an elected member of parliament.

repress' vb 1 to keep under control, to keep down, to restrain.

reprieve' vb 1 to let off punishment, to pardon:—also n.

rep'rimand n a severe scolding:—vb to scold severely.

reproach' vb to accuse of a fault, to blame:—n 1 scolding, blame. 2 something that brings shame.

reproach'ful adj accusing, shameful.

reproduce' vb 1 to cause to be heard, seen, or done again. 2 to increase by having offspring:—n reproduc'tion:—adj reproduc'tive.

rep'tile n a class of cold-blooded animals that crawl or creep (e.g. snake, lizard).

repub'lic n a state entirely governed by elected persons, there being no sovereign.

repulse' vb (fml) 1 to drive back. 2 to refuse sharply:—n 1 a defeat. 2 a refusal.

repul'sion n dislike, disgust.

repul'sive adj hateful, disgusting.

reputa'tion n 1 one's good name, one's character as seen by other people. 2 fame.

rep'utable adj having a good name, respectable.

reput'ed adj supposed (to be).

reput'edly adv as is commonly supposed.

request' vb to ask for:—n 1 the act of asking for something. 2 a favor asked for.

requiem [rek'-wi-em] n a mass for the dead.

require' vb 1 to need. 2 to demand by right, to order.

require'ment n 1 a need, something needed. 2 a necessary condition.

res'cue vb to save from danger or evil:—n act of rescuing:—n res'cuer.

research' n careful study to discover new facts.

resem'ble vb to be like:—n resem'blance.

resent' vb to be angered by, to take as an insult.

resent'ful adj showing resentment.

resent'ment n anger, indignation.

reserva'tion n 1 something kept back. 2 a condition. 3 land set aside for some special purpose. 4 a booked place or seat.

reserve' vb 1 (fml) to keep back for future use. 2 to order or book for future use:—n 1 something kept back for future use. 2 shyness, unwillingness to show one's feelings.

reserved' adj shy, not showing what one is thinking or feeling.

res'ervoir n 1 a place where the water supply of a city is stored. 2 a store.

res'idence n dwelling, house.

residen'tial adj 1 suitable for living in. 2 (of a district) having many houses.

res'idue n the remainder, what is left over.

resign' vb 1 to give up. 2 to give up an office or post. 3 to accept with complaint:—n resigna'tion.

resigned' adj accepting trouble with no complaint, patient.

resist' vb 1 to stand against, to fight against. 2 to face or allow oneself not to accept.

resis'tance n the act or power of resisting, opposition.

res'olute adj determined, bold, having the mind made up.

resolu'tion n 1 determination. 2 a firm intention. 3 a proposal for a meeting to vote on. 4 (fml) the act of solving.

resolve' vb 1 to determine. 2 to break up into parts or elements. 3 to solve:—n 1 a fixed purpose. 2 determination.

res'onant adj 1 echoing. 2 deep-sounding:—n res'onance.

resort' vb to turn to:—n 1 a source of help. 2 a place where people go to on vacation.

resound'ing adj 1 echoing. 2 very great.

resource' n 1 ability to think out clever plans. 2 a means of obtaining help. 3 (often pl) a source of economic wealth, esp of a country.

resource'ful adj full of clever plans.

respect' vb 1 to think highly of. 2 to pay attention to:—n 1 honor. 2 care or attention. 3 pl good wishes.

respectabil'ity n 1 state of deserving respect. 2 decency.

respec'table adj 1 deserving respect, decent 2 large enough, good enough, etc.

respect'ful adj showing respect.

respect'ing prep (fml) having to do with.

respec'tive adj each to his or her own.

respec'tively adv belonging to each in the order already mentioned.

res'pite n a pause, an interval.

respond' vb 1 to answer. 2 to do as a reaction to something that has been done.

response' n 1 an answer, a reply. 2 a reaction.

respon'sible adj 1 able to be trusted. 2 having to say or explain what one has done. 3 being the cause of something:—n responsibil'ity.

respon'sive adj quick to react.

rest[1] n 1 a pause in work. 2 inactivity. 3 sleep. 4 a support or prop:—vb 1 to cease from action. 2 to stop work for a time. 3 to be still or quiet. 4 to sleep or repose. 5 to be supported (by).

rest[2] n that which is left, the remainder.

restaurant [res'-tê-ro(ng)] n a place where one may buy and eat meals.

rest'ful adj peaceful, quiet.

rest'ive adj unable to keep still, impatient.

rest'less adj 1 always on the move. 2 not able to stay still.

restore' vb 1 to bring back. 2 to put back. 3 to make strong again. 4 to bring back to an earlier state or condition:—n restora'tion.

restrain' vb to hold back, to check.

restraint' n 1 self-control. 2 lack of freedom.

restrict' vb to set limits to, to keep down (the number or amount of).

restric'tion n a rule or condition that lessens freedom.

result' n 1 that which happens as the effect of something else, the outcome. 2 the final score in a sports contest:—vb 1 to follow as the effect of a cause. 2 to end (in).

result'ant adj following as a result.

resume' vb (fml) to begin again.

resump'tion n act of resuming.

resus'citate vb to bring back to life or consciousness:—n resuscita'tion.

retail n the sale of goods in small quantities.

retain' vb 1 to hold back. 2 to continue to use, have, remember, etc. 3 to engage someone's services by paying a fee in advance.

retal'iate vb to return like for like, to get one's own back:—n retalia'tion.

retch vb to try to vomit:—also n.

ret'icent adj unwilling to speak to others, silent:—n ret'icence.

ret'ina n the inner layer of the eye.

ret'inue n all the followers or attendants of a person of high rank.

retire' vb 1 (fml) to go back or away. 2 to leave one's work for ever because of old age, illness, etc. 3 to go to bed:—n retire'ment.

retired' adj 1 having given up one's business or profession. 2 out-of-the-way, quiet.

retir'ing adj shy, not fond of company.

retort' vb to reply quickly or sharply:—n a quick or sharp reply.

retrace' vb to go back over again.

retract' vb to take back what one has said:—n retrac'tion.

retreat' n 1 (of an army) to move back away from the enemy:—n 1 act of retreating. 2 a quiet, out-of-the-way place, a place of peace and safety

retribu'tion n just punishment for wrong done.

retrieve' vb 1 to find again. 2 to find and bring back

ret'ro- prefix backward.

ret'rograde adj leading to a worse state of affairs.

retrogres'sive adj 1 backward. 2 becoming worse.

retrospec'tive adj looking back to the past.

return' vb 1 to come or go back. 2 to give or send back. 3 to elect to parliament:—n 1 a coming or going back. 2 what is given or sent back. 3 profit.

reu'nion n a meeting again of old friends or comrades.

reunite' vb to join together again.

reveal' vb 1 to show what was hidden. 2 to make known.

revela'tion n 1 act of making known. 2 a surprising discovery or piece of information.

rev'elry n noisy feasting or merrymaking.

revenge' n making someone suffer for a wrong done to another, repaying evil with evil:—also vb:—adj revenge'ful.

rev'enue n money made by a person, business, or state.

rever'berate vb to echo:—n reverbera'tion.

rev'erence n respect and admiration.

rev'erie n 1 a daydream. 2 a state of dreamy thought.

reverse' vb 1 to turn back to the front or upside down. 2 to go or move backward. 3 to change to the opposite:—n 1 a defeat. 2 a failure. 3 the opposite. 4 the back of a coin, medal, etc:—adj 1 opposite. 2 back.

rever'sible adj 1 able to be reversed. 2 that can be turned outside in.

rever'sion n going back to a former owner or condition.

revert' vb to go back to a former condition, custom, or subject.

review' vb 1 to look over again, to consider with a view to changing. 2 to inspect. 3 to write one's opinion of (books, plays, etc):—n 1 a looking back on the past. 2 reconsideration or revision. 3 an article in a newspaper, magazine, etc, giving an opinion on a book, play, etc

revise' vb to go over again and correct or improve:—n revis'er.

revi'sion n act of revising.

revi'val n 1 act of reviving. 2 the arousing of fresh enthusiasm for.

revive' vb 1 to bring back to life, health, or consciousness. 2 to bring back to use or an active state. 3 to give new vigor or energy to.

revoke' vb to do away with, to withdraw.

revolt' vb 1 to rebel. 2 to shock or disgust:—n a rebellion, a rising against the government.

revolt'ing adj disgusting, shocking.

revolu'tion n 1 one complete turn of a wheel, etc. 2 a complete change. 3 a movement or rebellion as a result of which a new method of government is introduced.

revolu'tionary adj desiring to bring about a complete change:—n one who works for a complete change of government.

revolve' vb 1 to turn around and around. 2 to move around a center or axis.

revol'ver n a pistol able to fire several shots without reloading.

revul'sion n a sudden complete change of feeling, disgust.

reward' n 1 something given in return for work done, good behavior, bravery, etc. 2 a sum of money offered for finding or helping to track a criminal, lost or stolen property, etc:—vb to give as a reward.

rhino'ceros n a large thick-skinned animal with a horn (or two horns) on its nose.

rhu'barb n a garden plant with juicy stalks eatable when cooked and roots sometimes used in medicines.

rhyme [rīm] n 1 sameness of sound at the ends of words or lines of poetry. 2 a word that rhymes with another. 3 a poem with rhymes:—vb 1 to find words ending in the same sound(s). 2 to end in the same sound(s) as. 3 to write poetry.

rhythm n 1 the regular beat of words (esp in poetry), music, or dancing. 2 a regular repeated pattern of movements, graceful motion.

rhyth'mic, rhyth'mical adjs having a regular beat, regular.

rib n 1 one of the curved bones of the breast. 2 a low narrow ridge or raised part of a material.

rib'bon n a narrow decorative band of silk or other material.

rice n a white eatable grain much grown in hot countries, esp in river valleys.

rich adj 1 having much money, wealthy. 2 fertile. 3 valuable. 4 plentiful. 5 containing much fat or sugar. 6 deep, strong.

rich'es npl wealth.

rich'ly adv 1 in a rich manner. 2 with riches.

rick'ety adj shaky, unsteady.

rid vb (**rid** or **rid'ded**, **rid'ding**) to make free from, to clear.

rid'dle n a puzzling question.

ride vb (pt **rode**, pp **rid'den**) 1 to be carried on the back of an animal or on a vehicle. 2 to be able to ride on and control a horse, bicycle, etc. 3 to float at anchor:—n a trip on an animal's back or in a vehicle.

rid'er n 1 one who rides. 2 something added to what has already been said or written.

ridge n 1 a long narrow hill. 2 the raised part between two lower parts. 3 a mountain range.

rid'icule n mockery:—vb to mock, to make fun of.

ridic'ulous adj deserving to be laughed at, absurd.

rife adj found everywhere or in large numbers or quantities, extremely common.

riff'-raff n low, badly behaved people.

ri'fle¹ n a handgun with a grooved barrel that makes the bullet spin in flight.

ri'fle² vb to search through and steal anything valuable.

rift vb to split:—n 1 a split or crack in the ground. 2 a disagreement between two friends.

rig vb (**rigged', rig'ging**) 1 to provide clothes. 2 to provide tools or equipment. 3 to set up. 4 to arrange wrongfully to produce a desired result.

right [rīt] adj 1 correct. 2 true. 3 just, morally correct. 4 straight. 5 on the side of the right hand. 6 in good condition. 7 suitable, appropriate:—vb 1 to put back in position, to set in order. 2 to mend, to correct:—n 1 that which is correct, good, or true. 2 something to which one has a just claim. 3 the right-hand side. 4 in politics, the party or group holding the more traditional, conservative beliefs:—adv 1 straight. 2 exactly. 3 to the right-hand side.

right angle n an angle of 90 degrees.

righteous [rī'-tyēs] adj virtuous:—n **righ'teousness**.

right'ful adj lawful, just.

right'ly adv 1 justly. 2 correctly.

rig'id adj 1 that cannot be bent. 2 stern, strict, not willing to change. 3 not to be changed:—n **rigid'ity**.

rig'or n harsh inflexibility, severity, strictness:—adj **ri'gorous**.

rigor mor'tis the stiffening of the body after death.

rim n 1 the outer hoop of a wheel. 2 the outer edge, brim.

rime n white frost or hoarfrost.

rind n 1 the skin of some fruits. 2 the skin of bacon, cheese, etc. 3 the bark of trees.

ring¹ n 1 anything in the form of a circle. 2 a hoop of gold or other metal for the finger. 3 a space enclosed by ropes for a boxing match:—vb (pt, pp **ringed'**) 1 to surround, to encircle.

ring² vb (pt **rang**, pp **rung**) 1 to make a clear sound as a bell. 2 to cause a bell to sound. 3 to echo:—n the sound of a bell.

ring'leader n the leader of a gang.

ring'let n a long curl of hair.

rink n 1 a level stretch of ice for skating or curling. 2 a floor for roller-skating. 3 a level piece of ground for playing bowls.

rinse vb to put in clean water to remove soap.

ri'ot n 1 a noisy or violent disorder caused by a crowd. 2 (inf) something or someone very funny. 3 a bright and splendid show.

rip vb (**ripped', rip'ping**) to tear or cut open, to strip off:—n a tear, a rent.

ripe adj 1 ready to be gathered or picked, ready for eating. 2 suitable or ready for:—n **ripe'ness**.

ri'pen vb 1 to become ripe. 2 to cause to become ripe.

rip'ple n 1 the sound of shallow water running over stones. 2 a sound resembling this:—vb to flow with a murmuring sound.

rise vb (pt **rose**, pp **ri'sen**) 1 to get up from bed. 2 to stand up. 3 to go upward. 4 to increase. 5 to rebel. 6 to move to a higher position. 7 (of a river) to have its source or beginning:—n 1 an increase. 2 an upward slope. 3 a small hill:—**give rise to** to cause or bring.

risk n 1 danger. 2 possible harm or loss:—vb 1 to put in danger, to lay open to the possibility of loss. 2 to take the chance of something bad or unpleasant happening.

risk'y adj dangerous.

rite n an order or arrangement of proceedings fixed by rule or custom.

rit'ual adj having to do with or done as a rite:—n a set of rites.

ri'val n 1 one who is trying to do better than another. 2 a competitor for the same prize:—vb to be as good or nearly as good as:—n **ri'valry**.

riv'er n a large running stream of water.

riv'et n a bolt driven through metal plates, etc, to fasten them together and then hammered flat at both ends:—vb 1 to fasten with rivets. 2 to fix (the eyes or mind) firmly upon.

road n 1 a prepared public way for traveling on. 2 a street. 3 a way. 4 pl a place near the shore where ships may anchor.

roam vb to wander about.

roar vb to give a roar:—n 1 a loud shout or cry. 2 the full loud cry of a large animal.

roast vb to cook before a fire or in an oven:—n roasted meat, esp a large piece of meat containing a bone.

rob vb (**robbed, rob'bing**) to steal from:—n **rob'ber**.

rob'bery n the act of robbing.

robe n a long, loose-fitting garment.

rob'in, rob'in red'breast n a small red-breasted bird.

rob'ot n a machine made to carry out certain tasks usu done by people.

robust' adj healthy and strong.

rock[1] vb 1 to move from side to side, or backward and forward in turn. 2 to sway from side to side.

rock[2] n 1 the hard, solid part of the earth's crust. 2 a large mass or piece of stone. 3 a type of candy made in sticks.

rock'er n a curved piece of wood fastened to the foot of a chair, cradle, etc, to enable it to rock.

rock'et n 1 a firework that flies up into the air as it is burning out, often used as a signal. 2 a cylinder that is propelled through the air by a backward jet of gas. 3 a spacecraft launched in this way.

rock garden n part of a garden consisting of a heap of earth and large stones or small rocks with plants growing between them.

rock'y adj 1 full of rocks. 2 hard as rock. 3 shaky.

rod n 1 a straight slender stick or bar. 2 a measure of length (= $5^1/2$ yards).

ro'dent n any animal that gnaws, e.g. a mouse.

roe n 1 a female deer. 2 a small type of deer.

rogue [rōg] n 1 a dishonest person. 2 a naughty mischievous child.

role n 1 the part played by an actor. 2 one's actions or duties.

roll vb 1 to move by going around and around, like a wheel or ball. 2 to rock or sway from side to side. 3 to flatten with a roller. 4 to make a loud long noise:—n 1 paper, cloth, etc, rolled into the form of a cylinder. 2 a list of names. 3 a very small loaf of bread. 4 a turning or rocking movement.

roll call n the calling over of a list of names.

roll'er n 1 anything made in the form of a cylinder so that it can turn around and around easily (for flattening something). 2 a long swelling wave.

roll'er skate n a skate mounted on small wheels:—vb **roll'er-skate.**

Ro'man adj having to do with Rome.

Roman Catholic n a member of that part of the Christian church that is governed by the Pope, the Bishop of Rome.

romance' n 1 a story of wonderful or fanciful events. 2 a love story. 3 a love affair:—adj (of a language) derived from Latin:—vb 1 to fix firmly. 2 to tell lies.

Roman numerals npl numbers represented by letters (e.g. IV, V, VI for 4, 5, 6, etc).

roman'tic adj 1 imaginative, fanciful. 2 showing feelings of love. 3 dealing with love.

roman type n ordinary upright type (not italics).

Rom'any n 1 a gypsy. 2 the gypsy language:—also adj.

romp vb 1 to play roughly or noisily. 2 to go swiftly and easily.—n rough or noisy play.

roof n 1 the outside upper covering of a house, building, vehicle, etc. 2 the upper part of the mouth.

rook n 1 a black bird of the crow family. 2 a piece in chess.

room n 1 an apartment in a house. 2 space. 3 space for free movement. 4 scope. 5 pl lodgings.

roost n the pole on which birds rest at night:—vb to rest or sleep on a roost.

root n 1 the part of a plant that is fixed in the earth and draws nourishment from the soil. 2 the beginning or origin. 3 a word from which other words are formed. 4 a factor of a number that when multiplied by itself gives the original number:—vb 1 to take root. 2 to fix firmly. 3 to search about for.

rope n a strong thick cord, made by twisting together strands of hemp, wire, etc:—vb 1 to fasten with a rope. 2 to mark off with a rope.

ro'sary n in the Roman Catholic Church, a series of prayers or a string of beads each of which represents a prayer in the series.

rose n 1 a beautiful, sweet-smelling flower growing on a thorny shrub. 2 a shrub bearing roses. 3 a light red or pink color. 4 a nozzle full of holes at the end of the spout of a watering can.

rosette' n a badge, like a rose in shape, made of ribbon

ros'ter n a list showing the order in which people are to go on duty.

ros'y adj 1 red. 2 giving cause for hope.

rot vb (**rot'ted, rot'ting**) 1 to go bad from age or lack of use, to decay. 2 to cause to decay:—n 1 decay. 2 (inf) nonsense.

ro'ta n a roster.

rota'tion n 1 movement around a center or axis. 2 a regular order repeated again and again.

rot'ten adj 1 decaying, having gone bad. 2 (inf) mean.

rough [ruf] adj 1 not smooth, uneven. 2 wild, stormy. 3 not polite. 4 not gentle. 5 coarse, violent. 6 badly finished. 7 not exact:—n a violent, badly behaved person.

rough'en vb to make or become rough.

roulette' n a gambling game played on a revolving board with a ball that falls into one of a number of holes when the board ceases spinning.

round adj like a ball or circle in shape:—n 1 a round object. 2 a duty visit to all the places under one's care. 3 a division of a boxing match. 4 a complete part of a knockout competition (e.g. in football). 5 a game of golf. 6 a spell or outburst:—adv 1 in the opposite direction. 2 in a circle. 3 from one person to another. 4 from place to place:—prep 1 on every side of. 2 with a circular movement about.

round'about n 1 a merry-go-round. 2 a traffic circle:—adj 1 indirect. 2 using too many words.

rouse vb 1 to awaken. 2 to stir up to action.

rous'ing adj stirring, exciting.

rout vb to defeat and put to disordered flight:—n 1 a disorderly and hasty retreat after a defeat. 2 a complete defeat.

route [röt] n a way from one place to another.

routine' n a regular way or order of doing things.

rove vb 1 to wander about. 2 to wander.

row[1] [rō] n a line of people or things.

row[2] [rō] vb to move a boat by means of oars:—n 1 a spell of rowing. 2 a trip in a boat moved by oars.

row[3] [rou] n 1 noise, disturbance. 2 a quarrel:—vb (inf) to quarrel.

row'dy adj noisy and quarrelsome:—n a rowdy person.

roy'al adj 1 having to do with a king or queen. 2 splendid, kingly.

roy'alty n 1 a royal person or persons. 2 a share of the profits paid to authors, inventors, etc, for the use of their work.

rub vb (**rubbed, rub'bing**) to move one thing against another.

rub'ber n 1 a tough elastic substance made from the juice of certain tropical trees. 2 a piece of rubber used to remove marks by rubbing.

rub'bish n 1 that which is thrown away as useless, useless material. 2 nonsense.

rub'ble n broken pieces of bricks or stones.

ruck'sack n a bag carried on the back and held by straps over the shoulders.

rud'der *n* a flat hinged plate at the stern of a ship or the tail of an aircraft for steering.

rud'dy *adj* **1** reddish. **2** a healthy red.

rude *adj* impolite.

rudimen'tary *adj* simple, elementary, undeveloped.

ru'diments *npl* simple but necessary things to be learned about a subject before it can be studied thoroughly.

rue[1] *vb* (*fml*) to be sorry for.

rue[2] *n* an evergreen plant with bitter-tasting leaves.

rue'ful *adj* sorrowful, regretful.

ruff'ian *n* a violent lawbreaker.

ruff'le *vb* **1** to disturb the smoothness of, to disarrange. **2** to anger or annoy:—*n* a frill.

rug *n* **1** a mat for the floor. **2** a thick woolen coverlet or blanket.

rug'by *n* a form of football in which the ball, oval in shape, may be carried in the hands.

rug'ged *adj* **1** rough, uneven. **2** strong.

ru'in *n* **1** destruction. **2** downfall, overthrow, state of having lost everything of value. **3** remains of an old buildings (*often pl*):—*vb* **1** to destroy. **2** to cause to lose everything of value.

rule *n* **1** government. **2** a regulation or order. **3** an official or accepted standard. **4** the usual way that something happens:—*vb* **1** to govern, to manage. **2** to give an official decision. **3** to draw a straight line with the help of a ruler.

rul'er *n* **1** one who governs or reigns. **2** a flat rod for measuring length.

rul'ing *adj* greatest, controlling:—*n* a decision.

rum *n* spirit made from sugar cane.

rum'ble *vb* to make a low rolling noise:—*also n*.

ru'minant *n* an animal that chews the cud.

rum'mage *vb* to search untidily:—*also n*.

rummage sale *n* a sale of second-hand goods often to raise money for charity.

ru'mor *n* **1** a widely known story that may not be true. **2** common talk, gossip.

rum'ple *vb* to crease.

rum'pus *n* a noisy disturbance or quarrel.

run *vb* (**ran, run'ning,** *pp* **run**) **1** to move quickly. **2** to move from one place to another. **3** to take part in a race. **4** to flow. **5** to organize or manage. **6** to smuggle. **7** to last or con-tinue:—*n* **1** act of running. **2** a trip or journey. **3** the length of time for which something runs. **4** a widespread demand for. **5** an enclosed place for animals or fowls. **6** a tear that runs up or down a stocking or pantihose. **7** the unit of scoring in base-ball, etc:—**run down 1** to say bad things about. **2** to stop working because of lack of power (e.g. because a spring is unwound):—**run over 1** to knock over in a vehicle. **2** to over-flow. **3** to exceed a limit. **4** to rehearse quickly.

rung *n* a step of a ladder.

run'ner *n* **1** one who runs. **2** a messenger. **3** a long spreading stem of a plant. **4** a long narrow cloth for a table or carpet for a stair. **5** any device on which something slips or slides along.

run'ner-up *n* the person or team second to the winner.

run'ning *adj* **1** going on all the time. **2** in succession:—*n* **1** the act of moving quickly. **2** that which runs or flows:—**in the running** with a chance of success.

run'way *n* a flat road along which an aircraft runs before taking off or after landing.

rup'ture *n* **1** a clean break. **2** a quarrel or disagreement. **3** the thrusting of part of the intestine through the muscles of the abdomen:—*vb* **1** to break. **2** to thrust. **3** to quarrel.

ru'ral *adj* having to do with the country.

ruse *n* a trick.

rush *vb* **1** to move quickly and with force. **2** to capture by a sudden quick attack. **3** to do hastily. **4** to make another hurry:—*n* **1** a fast and forceful move. **2** a sudden advance. **3** hurry. **4** a sudden demand.

rust *n* the red coating formed on iron and steel left in a damp place:—*vb* to decay by gathering rust.

rus'tic *adj* (*fml*) having to do with the country or country people.

rus'tle[1] *vb* to make a low whispering sound:—*also n*.

rus'tle[2] *vb* to steal (cattle):—*n* **rus'tler**.

rust'y *adj* **1** covered with rust. **2** out of practice.

rut *n* a deep track made by a wheel.

rutabag'a *n* a plant with a bulbous root used as food and fodder.

ruth'less *adj* cruel, merciless.

rye *n* **1** a grain used for making flour and whiskey. **2** a whiskey made from rye.

S

Sab'bath n a day of rest and worship.

sabbati'cal n a year's leave from a teaching post for research or travel.

sac n a bag of liquid inside an animal or plant.

sachet [sa'-shā] n a small sealed envelope or bag used to contain shampoo, perfume, etc.

sack n 1 a bag made of coarse cloth for holding flour, wool, etc. 2 (inf) dismissal from a job (old):—vb 1 (inf) to dismiss someone from his or her job.

sac'red adj holy, set apart for the service of God.

sac'rifice n 1 an offering to a god. 2 the act of giving up of one's own with something desirable. 3 something given up in this way:—vb 1 to make an offering to God. 2 to give up something held dear:—adj sacrifi'cial.

sac'rilege n disrespectful or insulting treatment of something holy:—adj sacrileg'ious.

sad adj sorrowful.

sad'den vb to make sad.

sad'dle n a seat for a rider on a horse or bicycle:—vb 1 to put a saddle on. 2 to give (to another) something troublesome:—**in the saddle** in control.

safari n a hunting expedition.

safe adj 1 out of harm or danger. 2 not likely to cause harm, danger, or risk:—n a strong box or room for valuables:—adv **safe'ly**.

safe'guard n a protection:—also vb.

safe'ty n freedom from harm or loss.

sag vb (**sagged', sag'ging**) 1 to sink in the middle. 2 to droop.

saga [sä'-gä] n a very long story with many episodes.

said pt of **say**.

sail n 1 a canvas spread to catch the wind. 2 a trip in a boat. 3 the arm of a windmill:—vb 1 to travel on water. 2 to move along without effort.

sail'or n a seaman.

saint n a very good person:—adj **saint'ly**.

sake n:—**for the sake of** in order to get:—**for my sake** in order to please me.

sal'ad n a dish of lettuce and other raw vegetables, sometimes including meat, fish, cheese, or fruit, usu served with a dressing.

sal'ary n the fixed sum of money paid to someone for work over an agreed length of time, usu a month or a year.

sale n 1 the act of selling. 2 the exchange of anything for money. 3 a selling of goods more cheaply than usual.

sales'man, sales'woman, sales'person ns a person engaged in selling.

saline [sä'-līn] adj containing salt.

sali'va n the liquid that keeps the mouth moist, spittle:—adj **sali'vary**.

salmon [sam'-ŏn] n a large fish with pinkish flesh and silver scales, greatly valued for food and sport.

salon [saÍ-o(ng)] n 1 a reception room. 2 a building or room used for a particular business, such as hairdressing, the selling of fashionable clothes, etc.

saloon' n 1 a large public room in a passenger ship. 2 a place where alcoholic drink is sold and drunk.

salt n 1 a white mineral substance, obtained from sea water or by mining, used to give flavor to or to preserve food. 2 a compound produced by the action of acid on the hydrogen atoms of metals. 3 an experienced sailor:—vb to flavor or preserve with salt:—adj containing or tasting of salt:—adj **salt'y**.

salute vb 1 to greet. 2 to make a gesture of respect by raising the right hand to the forehead or cap, firing artillery, etc:—

n 1 the gesture of respect made by saluting. 2 the firing of guns as a welcome or mark of respect.

sal'vage vb to save from destruction, shipwreck, fire, etc.

salva'tion n 1 the saving from sin and the punishment due to it. 2 the means of this.

same adj in no way different:—n the same person or thing:—adv in a like manner.

same'ness n lack of change or variety.

sam'ple n a part or piece given to show what the whole is like:—vb to try something to see what it is like.

sanc'tion n 1 permission. 2 a punishment or penalty imposed to make people obey a law:—vb to permit.

sanc'tuary n 1 a place where one is safe from pursuit or attack. 2 a place providing protection, such as a reserve for wildlife.

sand n 1 a dust made of tiny particles of rock, shell, etc. 2 pl a desert.

san'dal n a type of shoe to protect the sole, leaving the upper part of the foot largely or wholly uncovered except by cross-straps, etc.

sand'paper n paper made rough by a coat of sand, used for smoothing and polishing.

sand'stone n a stone made up of sand pressed together.

sand'wich n two slices of bread with meat, paste, cheese, salad, etc, between:—vb to fit between two other things.

sand'y adj 1 covered with sand. 2 yellowish-red in color.

sane adj 1 sound in mind. 2 sensible.

san'itary adj having to do with health or cleanliness.

sanita'tion n 1 the process or methods of keeping places clean and hygienic. 2 a drainage or sewage system.

san'ity n 1 soundness of mind. 2 good sense.

sap n the juice that flows in plants, trees, etc, and nourishes the various parts:—vb (**sapped', sap'ping**) to weaken gradually.

sapphire [sa'-fīr] n 1 a precious stone of a rich blue color. 2 its color:—also adj.

sar'casm n a mocking remark intended to hurt another's feelings.

sarcas'tic adj 1 given to sarcasm. 2 mocking, scornful.

sardine' n a small fish of the herring family.

sash[1] n an ornamental scarf worn around the waist or across the body over one shoulder.

sash[2] n a window frame.

Sa'tan n the Devil.

satan'ic adj having to do with the Devil.

satch'el n a little bag worn on the shoulder or back for carrying books, etc.

sat'ellite n 1 a body that moves through the heavens in orbit around a larger body, including artificial bodies launched into orbit. 2 a country that is totally in the power of another.

sat'in n a silk cloth that is shiny on one side.

sat'ire n a composition in prose or verse in which persons, customs, actions, etc, are mocked and made to appear ridiculous.

satir'ical adj holding up to scorn.

satisfac'tion n 1 contentment. 2 the feeling of having enough.

satisfac'tory adj 1 good enough. 2 quite good.

sat'isfy vb 1 to give all that is requested or expected. 2 to be enough. 3 to convince.

sat'urate vb to soak something so thoroughly that it cannot take in any more liquid:—n satura'tion.

Sat'urday n the seventh day of the week.

132

sauce n 1 a liquid, either savory or sweet, poured on foods to improve or bring out the flavor. 2 (inf) cheek, impudence.

sauce'pan n a cooking pot with a lid and handle.

sau'cer n a small plate placed under a cup.

sau'cy adj rude, cheeky.

saun'ter vb to walk slowly, to stroll:—also n.

saus'age n a roll of minced meat in a thin skin.

sav'age adj 1 wild, untamed, or uncivilized. 2 fierce, cruel:—n 1 a member of a savage tribe. 2 a very cruel person.

save vb 1 to rescue from danger or harm. 2 to keep for future use. 3 to keep money instead of spending it:—prep except.

sa'ving npl money put aside for future use.

sa'vior n 1 one who saves from danger or harm. 2 (with cap) Jesus Christ.

sa'vory adj 1 tasty, arousing appetite. 2 salty or sharp rather than sweet.

saw¹ n a tool with a toothed edge for cutting wood, etc:—vb to cut with a saw.

saw² pt of **see**.

sax'ophone n a brass wind instrument with keys.

say vb (pt **said**) 1 to utter in words, to speak. 2 to state:—n the right to give an opinion.

say'ing n a proverb, a remark commonly made.

scab n a crust that forms over a healing sore.

scaf'fold n the platform on which criminals are executed.

scaf'folding n a framework of poles, etc, to support platforms from which people can work above ground level (e.g. when building a house).

scald vb to burn with hot liquid:—n a burn caused by hot liquid.

scale¹ n one of the thin flakes or flat plates on the skin of fish, reptiles, etc.

scale² n 1 the pan of a weighing machine. 2 (often pl) a balance or weighing machine.

scale³ n 1 a series of successive musical notes between one note and its octave. 2 the size of a map compared with the extent of the area it represents. 3 a measure. 4 a system of units for measuring. 5 a system of grading. 6 size, extent:—vb to climb.

scalp n the skin and hairs on top of the head:—vb to cut off the scalp.

scal'y adj covered with scales, like a fish.

scamp n a rascal.

scam'per vb to run quickly or hurriedly, as if afraid:—n a quick or hurried run.

scan vb (**scanned'**, **scan'ning**) 1 to examine closely or carefully. 2 to obtain an image of an internal part (of the body) by using e.g. X-rays, ultrasonic waves. 3 to mark the weak and strong syllables in a line of poetry.

scan'dal n 1 widespread talk about someone's wrongdoings, real or supposed. 2 a disgrace. 3 disgraceful behavior that gives rise to widespread talk.

scan'dalous adj disgraceful.

scape'goat n one who takes the blame for wrong done by others.

scar n the mark left by a healed wound:—vb (**scarred'**, **scar'ring**) to leave or cause a scar.

scarce adj 1 few and hard to find. 2 not enough.

scarce'ly adv hardly, surely not.

scarc'ity n shortage, lack of what is necessary.

scare vb to frighten:—n a fright, panic.

scare'crow n anything (e.g. a dummy man) set up to frighten away birds.

scarf n (pl **scarves**) a strip of material worn around the neck and over the shoulders.

scar'let n a bright red color:—also adj.

scath'ing adj hurtful, bitter.

scatt'er vb 1 to throw about on all sides. 2 to go away or drive in different directions.

scatt'erbrain n a foolish person:—adj **scatt'erbrained**.

scenario [shä-nē′-ri-o] n a written outline of the main incidents in a play or film.

scene [seen] n 1 the place where something happens. 2 what one can see before one from a certain viewpoint. 3 a distinct part of a play. 4 a painted background set up on the stage to represent the place of the action. 5 a quarrel or open show of strong feeling:—**behind the scenes** in private.

scen'ery n 1 the painted backgrounds set up during a play to represent the places of the action. 2 the general appearance of a countryside.

sce'nic adj picturesque.

scent n 1 a smell, esp a pleasant one. 2 the smell of an animal left on its tracks. 3 the sense of smell:—vb 1 to smell out. 2 to find by smelling. 3 to make smell pleasant.

schedule [ske′-dûl] n 1 a list of details. 2 a list of classes, giving times when they begin an end, a timetable:—vb to plan.

scheme [skeem] n 1 a plan of what is to be done. 2 a plot:—vb 1 to plan. 2 to plot:—n **sche'mer**.

scholar [skol′-êr] n 1 a learned person. 2 a student.

schol'arly adj learned.

school¹ [skül] n an institution in which instruction is given:—ns **school'master**, **school'mistress**, **school'teacher**.

school² [skül] n a large number of fish of the same kind swimming together, a shoal.

sci'ence n 1 all that is known about a subject, arranged in a systematic manner. 2 the study of the laws and principles of nature. 3 trained skill.

scientif'ic adj 1 having to do with science. 2 done in a systematic manner.

sci'entist n one learned in one of the sciences.

sciss'ors n a cutting instrument consisting of two blades moving on a central pin.

scoff vb to mock (at):—n mocking words, a jeer.

scold vb to find fault with, to rebuke:—n **scold'ing**.

scoop vb 1 to gather and lift up, as with the hands. 2 to hollow out with a knife, etc:—n 1 a deep shovel for lifting grain, earth from a hole, etc. 2 a piece of important news known only to one newspaper.

scope n 1 freedom of movement, thought, etc, within certain limits. 2 the range of matters being dealt with. 3 opportunity.

scorch vb 1 to burn the outside of. 2 to singe or blacken by burning.

scorch'ing adj 1 very hot. 2 very fast.

score n 1 a set of twenty. 2 a mark or line cut on the surface of. 3 a note of what is to be paid. 4 in games, the runs, goals, points, etc, made by those taking part. 5 a piece of music written down to show the parts played by different instruments:—vb 1 to make marks or scratches on the surface of. 2 to gain an advantage. 3 to keep the score of a game. 4 to arrange music in a score:—**score off** to strike out:—**score' off** to get the better off:—n **scor'er**.

scorn vb 1 to feel contempt for. 2 to refuse to have anything to do with:—n contempt, complete lack of respect for.

scorn'ful adj mocking, full of contempt.

scoun'drel n a thoroughly wicked person, a rascal.

scour¹ vb to clean or brighten by rubbing.

scour² vb to go back and forward over, searching carefully.

scourge [skurj] n 1 a whip. 2 a cause of great trouble or suffering:—vb 1 to whip. 2 to make suffer greatly.

scout n 1 one sent in front to see what lies ahead and bring back news. 2 a person employed to find new talent:—vb 1 to go out as a scout. 2 to search or explore.

scowl *vb* to lower the brows and wrinkle the forehead in anger or disapproval:—*also n.*

scrag′gy *adj* thin and bony.

scram′ble *vb* 1 to climb using both hands and feet. 2 to move awkwardly or with difficulty. 3 to struggle to obtain:—*n* a pushing and struggling for something.

scrap *n* 1 a small piece. 2 *pl* what is left over:—(**scrapped′, scrap′ping**) to throw away as no longer useful.

scrape *vb* 1 to clean by rubbing with an edged instrument. 2 to make a harsh, unpleasant sound by rubbing along. 3 to save or gather with difficulty:—*n* 1 a scratch. 2 something caused by scraping or its sound. 3 (*inf*) a small fight. 4 (*inf*) a difficult situation.

scrap heap *n* a place for waste material, a rubbish heap.

scrap′py *adj* made up of bits and pieces.

scratch *vb* 1 to mark or wound the surface with something pointed. 2 to rub with the nails to stop itching. 3 to tear with the nails or claws. 4 to rub out. 5 to withdraw from a competition or contest:—*n* a slight mark or wound, esp one made by scratching:—*adj* 1 without a plus or minus handicap. 2 put together hastily:—**up to scratch** as good as usual.

scrawl *vb* to write untidily or carelessly:—*n* untidy or careless handwriting.

scream *vb* to shout in a loud, high-pitched voice, to shriek:—*also n.*

screech *vb* to utter a loud high-pitched cry:—*also n.*

screen *n* 1 a movable piece of furniture like a section of a fence that can be used to break a draft, to conceal part of a room, etc. 2 a wooden division in a building. 3 a surface on which a motion picture is shown. 4 the front glass surface of a TV, word processor, etc, on which pictures or items of information are shown. 5 a sieve for separating smaller pieces of coal, etc, from larger:—*vb* 1 to protect. 2 to hide. 3 to put through a test. 4 to show on film or TV.

screw *n* 1 a type of nail with a spiral thread so that it can be twisted into wood, etc, instead of hammered. 2 the propeller of a ship. 3 a twist or turn:—*vb* 1 to fasten by means of a screw. 2 to twist.

scrib′ble *vb* to write carelessly or hurriedly:—*n* something written quickly or carelessly.

scrimp *vb* to give or use too little.

script *n* 1 handwriting. 2 a printing type like handwriting. 3 a written outline of the incidents in a film. 4 the text of a broadcast talk or play.

scroll *n* a roll of parchment or paper.

scrub *vb* (**scrubbed′, scrub′bing**) 1 to clean by rubbing hard, esp with a stiff brush. 2 (*inf*) to cancel, to remove.

scruff *n* the back of the neck.

scruff′y *adj* shabby, untidy.

scru′pulous *adj* very careful.

scrutineer′ *n* one who scrutinizes.

scru′tinize *vb* to examine closely or carefully.

scru′tiny *n* a close or careful examination.

scuf′fle *n* a confused or disorderly struggle.

scull′ery *n* a room in which pots, dishes, etc, are washed.

sculp′tor *n* one skilled in sculpture.

sculp′ture *n* 1 the art of carving in wood, stone, etc. 2 a work of sculpture.

scum *n* 1 dirt and froth that gathers on the surface of liquid. 2 wicked or worthless people.

scur′ry *vb* to run hurriedly:—*also n.*

scur′vy *n* a disease caused by lack of fresh fruit or vegetables:—*adj* mean, nasty.

scut′tle *vb* to run away hurriedly.

scythe [sīth] *n* a tool consisting of a long, curving, very sharp blade set at an angle to a long handle, used for cutting grass, etc.

sea *n* 1 the salt water that covers much of the earth's surface. 2 a large extent of this. 3 the ocean or part of it. 4 the swell of the sea. 5 a large amount or extent of anything:—**at sea** 1 on the sea. 2 puzzled.

sea′faring *adj* going to sea.

sea′going *adj* able to sail across the sea to other lands.

seal¹ *n* 1 wax with a design, etc, stamped on it, used to fasten shut envelopes, boxes, etc. 2 a stamp with a design, initials, etc, engraved on it. 3 a substance or thing that closes, fixes, or prevents leakage:—*vb* 1 to fasten with a seal. 2 to close firmly. 3 to make airtight. 4 to confirm.

seal² *n* a sea animal valued for its oil and fur.

sea level *n* the level of the sea's surface at half-tide.

sea lion *n* a large seal.

seam *n* 1 the line made by the stitches joining two pieces of cloth. 2 a vein of metal, coal, etc.

sear *vb* to burn with powerful heat

search *vb* to look for, to explore, to examine in order to find:—*n* act of looking for, an inquiry, an examination:—*n* **search′er.**

search′ing *adj* thorough, testing thoroughly.

search′light *n* a powerful electric lamp able to throw a beam of light on distant objects.

sea′side *n* the land near or beside the sea.

sea′son¹ *n* 1 one of the divisions of the year into four (e.g. winter). 2 a time of the year noted for a particular activity.

sea′son² *vb* 1 to make (wood) hard and fit for use by drying gradually. 2 to add something to food to give it a good taste.

sea′sonable *adj* suitable to the season of the year.

sea′sonal *adj* having to do with one or all of the seasons.

sea′soning *n* anything added to food to bring out or improve its taste.

seat *n* 1 anything on which one sits. 2 a place of furniture for sitting on. 3 a place as member of a council. 4 the place where something is carried on:—*vb* 1 to place on a seat. 2 to have or provide seats for.

se′cede *vb* to withdraw formally one's membership of a society, etc.

seces′sion *n* act of seceding.

seclud′ed *adj* 1 out of the way. 2 private, quiet.

seclu′sion *n* quietness and privacy.

sec′ond *adj* coming immediately after the first:—*n* 1 one who comes after the first. 2 one who supports and assists another in a fight or duel. 3 the sixtieth part of a minute. 4 *npl* goods that because of some flaw are sold more cheaply:—*vb* 1 to support. 2 to assist:—*vb* **second′** to transfer from normal duties to other duties.

sec′ondary *adj* 1 of less importance. 2 (*of education*) more advanced, usu for children over 12.

sec′ond-hand *adj* not new, having been used by another.

sec′ond sight *n* the ability to see things happening elsewhere or to foresee the future.

se′crecy *n* 1 the habit of keeping information to oneself. 2 concealment.

se′cret *adj* 1 hidden from others. 2 known or told to few. 3 private:—*n* 1 a piece of information kept from others. 2 privacy

sec′retary *n* 1 one whose job it is to deal with letters and help to carry on the day-to-day business of his or her employer. 2 a high government official or minister.

secrete′ *vb* 1 to hide away. 2 to produce a substance or fluid within the body by means of glands or other organs.

secre'tion n **1** the act of secreting. **2** the substance or fluid secreted (e.g. saliva).

se'cretive adj **1** keeping information to oneself. **2** fond of concealing things.

sect n a body of persons holding the same beliefs, esp in religion.

sec'tion n **1** a distinct part. **2** a part cut off. **3** the shape of the flat face exposed when something solid is cut clean through.

sec'tor n **1** part of a circle between two radii. **2** one of the parts into which an area is divided. **3** part of a field of activity.

sec'ular adj **1** having to do with this world (not with heaven), not sacred. **2** having to do with lay, not church, affairs.

secure' adj **1** free from care or danger. **2** safe:—vb **1** to make safe. **2** to fasten securely. **3** to seize and hold firmly.

secur'ity n **1** safety. **2** something given as proof of one's intention to repay a loan. **3** pl documents stating that one has lent a sum of money to a business, etc, and is entitled to receive interest on it.

sedan' n an automobile with no division between driver and passengers.

sedate' adj calm and dignified.

sed'ative adj having a calming effect:—n a sedative drug.

sed'entary adj inactive, requiring much sitting.

sed'iment n the particles of matter that sink to the bottom of liquid.

seduce' vb to persuade someone to do what is wrong or immoral.

see vb (pt **saw**, pp **seen**) **1** to perceive with the eye. **2** to notice. **3** to understand. **4** to visit or interview.

seed n the grain or germ from which, when placed in the ground, a new plant grows:—vb to produce seed:—**go to seed**, **run to seed** (of a plant) to shoot up too quickly. **2** to deteriorate.

seed'ling n a young plant grown from a seed.

seed'y adj **1** shabby. **2** unwell.

seek vb (pt, pp **sought**) **1** to look for. **2** to try to get, to ask.

seem vb to appear to be, look as if.

seem'ing adj having the appearance of, apparent.

seem'ly adj proper, fitting, decent.

see'saw n **1** a plank that is balanced in the middle and on which children sit at either end so that when one end goes up the other one goes down. **2** the act of moving up and down or back and forth:—adj moving up and down like a seesaw:—vb **1** to play on a seesaw. **2** to move up and down or back and forth.

seethe vb **1** to boil. **2** to be full of anger, excitement, etc.

seg'ment n **1** a piece cut off. **2** part of a circle cut off by a straight line:—vb to cut into segments.

seg'regate vb to set apart or separate from others:—n **segrega'tion**.

seize vb **1** to take by force. **2** to take firm hold of.

sel'dom adv rarely.

select' vb to choose, to pick out:—adj specially chosen:—n **select'or**.

selec'tion n **1** act of choosing. **2** what is chosen.

selec'tive adj choosing carefully, rejecting what is not wanted.

self n (pl **selves**) one's own person or interest.

self-cen'tered adj selfish, thinking chiefly of oneself and one's interests.

self-con'fident adj sure of oneself and one's powers.

self-con'scious adj thinking about oneself too much, shy because one thinks others are watching one.

self-control' n the ability to control one's temper, etc.

self-esteem' n a high opinion of oneself, conceit.

self-ev'ident adj obvious, needing no proof.

self-impor'tant adj full of one's own importance, pompous:—n **self-impor'tance**.

self-imposed' adj undertaken of one's own free will.

self-in'terest n thought of one's own advantage only, selfishness.

self'ish adj thinking only of oneself and one's own advantage:—n **self'ishness**.

self-made adj successful or wealthy as a result of one's own efforts.

self-possessed' adj cool, calm:—n **self-posses'sion**.

self-respect' n proper care of one's own character and reputation.

self-right'eous adj too aware of what one supposes to be one's own goodness.

self-sat'isfied adj pleased with oneself or one's actions, etc, conceited.

self-ser'vice adj (of a store, restaurant, etc) helping oneself:—also n.

self-suffi'cient adj needing no help from others.

sell vb (pt, pp **sold**) to give in exchange for money.

sell'er n one who sells.

selves see **self**.

semes'ter n an academic or school half-year.

sem'i- prefix half

sem'icircle n a half circle:—adj **semicir'cular**.

sem'icolon n a mark of punctuation (;).

semiconduc'tor n a substance in a transmitter, as silicon, used to control the flow of current.

sem'i-detached' adj (of a house) joined to the next house on one side but not on the other:—also n **duplex**.

sen'ate n **1** the upper house of the lawmaking assembly in certain countries. **2** (with cap) the upper branch of a two-body legislature in the United States, France, etc.

sen'ator n a member of a senate.

send vb (pt, pp **sent**) **1** to have taken from one place to another. **2** to order to go:—n **sen'der**.—**send for** to order to be brought, to summon.

se'nile adj weak in the mind from old age:—n **senil'ity**.

se'nior adj **1** older. **2** higher in rank or importance:—n **1** one older. **2** one having longer service or higher rank:—n **senior'ity**.

sensa'tion n **1** the ability to perceive through the senses, feeling. **2** an impression that cannot be described. **3** great excitement. **4** an event that causes great excitement.

sensa'tional adj causing great excitement.

sense n **1** one of the five powers (sight, hearing, taste, smell, touch) by which we gain knowledge of things outside ourselves. **2** wisdom in everyday things. **3** understanding. **4** meaning.

sense'less adj **1** foolish, pointless. **2** unconscious.

sen'sible adj **1** having or showing good judgment, wise. **2** aware. **3** practical.

sen'sitive adj **1** quick to feel things. **2** easily hurt or damaged. **3** able to feel emotions keenly:—n **sensitiv'ity**.

sen'tence n **1** a group of words, grammatically correct and making complete sense. **2** a judgment given in a court of law. **3** the punishment given to a wrongdoer by a judge:—vb to state the punishment due to a wrongdoer.

sen'timent n **1** what one feels or thinks about something. **2** an expression of feeling. **3** tender or kindly feeling.

sentimen'tal adj **1** showing, causing, etc, excessive tender feeling or emotion. **2** concerning the emotions rather than reason:—n **sentimental'ity**.

sen'try n a soldier on guard.

sep'al n one of the leaves growing underneath the petals of a flower.

sep'arate vb 1 to put apart. 2 to go away from. 3 to stop living together. 4 to go different ways. 5 to divide into parts:—adj unconnected, distinct, apart.

separa'tion n 1 act of separating. 2 an agreement by a married couple to live apart from each other.

Septem'ber n the ninth month of the year.

sep'tic adj infected and poisoned by germs.

se'quel n 1 that which follows, a result or consequence. 2 a novel, film, etc, that continues the story of an earlier one.

se'quence n a number of things, events, etc, following each other in a natural or correct order.

serene' adj calm, undisturbed.

seren'ity n calmness, peace.

sergeant [sar'-jĕnt] n 1 an army rank. 2 a rank in the police.

se'rial n a story published or broadcast in parts or installments:—adj 1 happening in a series. 2 in successive parts.

se'ries n (pl **se'ries**) a number of things arranged in a definite order.

se'rious adj 1 thoughtful. 2 important. 3 likely to cause danger.

ser'mon n a talk given by a priest or minister in church on a religious subject.

ser'pent n a snake.

serrat'ed adj having notches like the edge of a saw.

ser'vant n one who works for and obeys another

serve vb 1 to work for and obey. 2 to hand food to at table. 3 to supply with (food, etc). 4 to be helpful. 5 to be of use instead of. 6 (in tennis) to hit the ball into play.

ser'vice n 1 the work of a servant or employee. 2 time spent in the forces, police, etc. 3 use, help. 4 a religious ceremony. 5 a set of dishes for use at table. 6 in tennis, the hit intended to put the ball into play. 7 pl the armed forces.

ser'viceable adj useful.

serviette' n a small cloth used at table to keep the clothes clean.

ses'sion n 1 a meeting or sitting of a court or assembly. 2 a school year.

set vb (**set**, **set'ting**) 1 to put. 2 to fix in position. 3 to put to music. 4 to become hard or solid. 5 (of the sun, etc) to sink below the horizon:—n 1 a number of things of the same kind. 2 a group of people with similar interests. 3 a group of games in a tennis match:—adj fixed, regular.

set'back n something that hinders.

settee' n a sofa.

set'ting n 1 surroundings. 2 background. 3 music written to go with certain words.

set'tle n a bench with arms and a high back:—vb 1 to set up home in a certain place. 2 to come to rest on. 3 to put an end to by giving a decision or judgment. 4 to make or become quiet or calm. 5 to pay (a bill, etc). 6 to sink to the bottom of.

set'tlement n 1 a decision or judgment that ends a dispute. 2 money or property given to someone under certain conditions. 3 payment of a bill. 4 a colony.

sev'er vb 1 to cut or tear apart or off. 2 to break:—n **sev'erance**.

sev'eral adj 1 more than two but not very many. 2 separate, various.

severe' adj 1 strict, harsh. 2 plain and undecorated. 3 very cold:—n **sever'ity**.

sew [sō] vb (pt **sewed'**, pp **sewn**) to join by means of needle and thread.

sewage [sō'-êj] n waste matter.

sewer [sō'-êr] n an underground drain to carry away waste matter, waste matter, etc.

sex n 1 the state of being male or female. 2 the qualities by which an animal or plant is seen to be male or female. 3 sexual intercourse.

sextet' n a musical composition for six voices.

sex'ual adj having to do with sex.

shab'by adj 1 untidy through much wear, threadbare, dressed in threadbare clothes. 2 mean, ungenerous:—n **shab'biness**.

shack n a hut.

shack'le vb 1 to fasten with a chain. 2 to restrict freedom of action or speech:—npl **shack'les** chains for fastening the limbs.

shade vb 1 to protect from light or sun. 2 to darken. 3 to color:—n 1 any device that protects from light or sun, a window screen. 2 a place in a shadow cast by the sun, half-darkness. 3 a slight difference. 4 a little. 5 a ghost.

sha'dow n 1 a dark patch on the ground caused by the breaking of rays of light by a body. 2 shade. 3 one who follows another around. 4 a ghost:—vb to follow someone closely without his or her knowing it.

shad'y adj 1 protected from light or sun. 2 dishonest.

shaft n 1 the long handle of any tool or weapon. 2 a deep tunnel leading down to a mine. 3 a ray of light.

shag'gy adj 1 having rough hair. 2 rough.

shake vb (pt **shook**, pp **shak'en**) 1 to move quickly and up and down or to and fro. 2 to tremble. 3 to make weaker or less firm:—n 1 trembling. 2 a sudden jerk. 3 a shock.

shak'y adj 1 not steady. 2 weak after illness.

shal'low adj 1 not deep. 2 not thinking deeply:—n a place where water is not deep.

sham n 1 a person pretending to be what he or she is not. 2 a thing made to look like something else. 3 a pretence:—adj not real, pretended:—vb (**shammed'**, **sham'ming**) to pretend.

sham'ble vb to walk clumsily.

sham'bles npl a scene of great disorder and confusion.

shame n a feeling of sorrow for wrongdoing or for inability to do something, disgrace:—vb to make ashamed, to disgrace.

shame'-faced adj showing shame or embarrassment.

shame'ful adj disgraceful, shocking.

shame'less adj not easily made ashamed.

shampoo' vb to wash and rub:—n 1 act of shampooing. 2 a preparation used for shampooing.

shape n 1 the form or outline of anything. 2 (inf) condition, state:—vb 1 to form. 2 to give a certain shape to:—**in good shape** in good condition.

shape'less adj ugly or irregular in shape.

shape'ly adj well-formed.

share n part of a thing belonging to a particular person:—vb 1 to divide among others. 2 to receive a part of.

shark n a large flesh-eating fish.

sharp adj 1 having a thin edge for cutting with, having a fine point. 2 quick and intelligent. 3 hurtful, unkind. 4 stinging, keen. 5 in singing, higher than the correct note. 6 rather sour:—n a musical sign to show that a note is to be raised half a tone (#):—adv (of time) exactly.

sharp'en vb to make sharp.

sharp-sight'ed adj having keen eyesight.

sharp-wit'ted adj quick and clever.

shat'ter vb 1 to break into pieces, to smash. 2 to put an end to.

shave vb 1 to cut off hair with a razor. 2 to cut strips off the surface. 3 to pass very close to without touching:—n 1 act of shaving, esp the face. 2 a close hair cut. 3 a narrow escape.

shawl n a cloth folded and worn loosely over the shoulders by women.

sheaf n (pl **sheaves**) a number of things in a bundle.

shear vb (pp **shorn**) 1 to cut with shears. 2 to clip the wool from. 3 to cut or cause to break:—npl **shears** a pair of large scissors (e.g. for cutting off the wool of a sheep).

sheath n a close-fitting case or container.

sheathe vb to put into a sheath.

sheaves see **sheaf**.

shed¹ n (**shed, shed'ding**) 1 to let fall down or off. 2 to spread about.

shed² n a hut, an outhouse.

sheen n brightness.

sheep n 1 a common animal valued for its wool and its meat. 2 a person who follows the lead of others without protesting.

sheep'dog n a dog trained to look after sheep.

sheep'ish adj awkward or embarrassed because of having done something wrong.

sheer¹ adj 1 very steep. 2 (of material) very fine or transparent. 3 thorough, complete.

sheer² vb to swerve, to move suddenly in another direction.

sheet n 1 a broad thin piece of anything. 2 a covering of linen, etc, for a bed. 3 a broad stretch of water, flame, ice, etc.

shelf n (pl **shelves**) 1 a board fixed to a wall or fastened in a cupboard, used for placing things on. 2 a ledge, a long flat rock or sandbank.

shell n 1 a hard outer covering. 2 a thick metal case filled with explosive and fired from a gun:—vb 1 to take the shell off. 2 to fire shells at.

shell'fish n a fish with a shell covering.

shel'ter n 1 a place that gives protection from the weather or safety from danger. 2 protection:—vb to protect, to go for protection.

shelve vb 1 to put aside for a time. 2 to slope.

shelves see **shelf**.

shep'herd n a person who looks after sheep:—f **shep-herd'ess**:—vb to guide a flock or group.

sher'iff n the chief law enforcement officer of a county.

sher'ry n a fortified Spanish wine.

shew vb old form of **show**.

shield n 1 a piece of metal or strong leather held in front of the body to defend it against sword strokes, etc. 2 a protector or protection:—vb to defend, to protect.

shift vb 1 to change. 2 to move. 3 to remove, get rid of:—n 1 a change. 2 a group of workers who carry on a job for a certain time and then hand over to another group. 3 the period during which such a group works. 4 a simple dress or nightgown.

shift'y adj untrustworthy, deceitful.

shilly-shally vb to be unable to come to a decision, to keep on changing one's mind.

shim'mer vb to shine with a flickering light:—also n.

shin n the front part of the leg below the knee.

shine vb (pt, pp **shone**) 1 to give off light. 2 to direct a light or lamp. 3 to polish. 4 (inf) to be very good at:—n brightness, polish.

shin'gle¹ n 1 thin wedge-shaped roof tile. 2 a name plaque.

shin'gle² n loose gravel or pebbles.

shin'y adj bright, glossy, as if polished.

ship n a large seagoing boat:—vb (**shipped, ship'ping**) 1 to put or take, as on board ship. 2 to go on board a ship.

ship'building n the act of making ships.

ship'ping n 1 all the ships of a port, country, etc. 2 ships in general.

ship'per n one who imports or exports goods by sea.

ship'shape adj in good order, neat and tidy.

ship'wreck n the loss or destruction of a ship at sea:—also vb.

ship'yard n a place where ships are built or repaired.

shirk vb to avoid:—n **shirk'er**.

shirt n a kind of loose upper garment with a collar.

shiv'er¹ vb 1 to tremble. 2 to break into small pieces:—n 1 a shaking or trembling. 2 a small piece.

shiv'ery adj trembling, as with cold or fear.

shoal n 1 a large number of fish swimming together. 2 (inf) a crowd.

shock n 1 the sudden violent striking of one thing against another (e.g. in a collision). 2 weakness of body or confusion of mind caused by a violent blow or collision. 3 sorrow or a state of upset caused by sudden bad news, etc. 4 an involuntary movement of the body, caused by passing electricity through it:—vb 1 to cause sudden pain or sorrow. 2 to horrify, to disgust.

shock'ing adj very bad, disgusting, indecent.

shod adj wearing shoes.

shod'dy adj cheap, of poor quality

shoe n a covering for the foot.

shoot vb (pt, pp **shot**) 1 to fire a bullet from a gun. 2 to let fly. 3 to move suddenly or quickly. 4 to hit or kill with a bullet from a gun. 5 (in games) to kick or hit at a goal. 6 to begin to grow. 7 to make a motion picture:—n 1 a young branch or bud. 2 a sloping way down which water may flow or objects slide.

shooting star n what looks like a moving star but is really a glowing fragment of a heavenly body flying through space.

shop n 1 a place where goods are sold, a store. 2 a place where work is done with tools or machines:—vb (**shopped, shop'ping**) to visit stores to buy things.

shop'lifter n one who steals from the stores he or she is visiting.

shore¹ n the land beside the sea, a river, lake, etc.

shore² n a wooden prop or support:—vb to prop up or support.

shorn pp of **shear**.

short adj 1 not long or tall. 2 not enough. 3 without enough of. 4 not lasting long. 5 quick and almost impolite. 6 (of pastry, etc) crumbling easily:—adv **short'ly** briefly, soon:—npl **shorts** trousers reaching not lower than the knees:—**in short** in a few words.

short'age n a lack of, insufficiency.

short cut n a quicker way.

short'en vb to make less in length or time.

short-lived adj living or lasting for a short time only.

shorts see **short**.

short-sight'ed adj 1 unable to see clearly things that are distant. 2 lacking foresight.

short-tem'pered adj easily angered.

shot pt of **shoot**:—n 1 the firing of a gun, etc. 2 small lead bullets. 3 a solid metal ball fired from a gun. 4 a person able to shoot. 5 (inf) a single attempt at doing something. 6 a series of pictures of a scene taken at one time by a movie camera. 7 (inf) an injection.

shoul'der n 1 the joint connecting an arm, wing, or foreleg to the body. 2 anything jutting out like a shoulder:—vb 1 to push with the shoulder. 2 to put on to the shoulder. 3 to bear.

shout vb to utter a loud cry:—n a loud cry.

shove [shuv] vb (inf) to push:—also n.

shov'el n a spade with a broad blade for lifting earth, gravel, etc:—vb to move with a shovel.

show vb 1 to let be seen, to display. 2 to point out. 3 to be in sight. 4 to prove:—n 1 a display. 2 a performance or entertainment. 3 pretense. 4 a gathering at which flowers, animals, etc, are displayed to the public.

show'er n 1 a short fall of rain. 2 a great number of things falling or arriving at one time. 3 a bath in which water is directed on to the body through a spray:—vb to give to or let fall on in large numbers.

show'ery adj rainy, marked by many showers.

show'room n a room or store in which things are on display to the public.

show'y adj bright and attractive but not necessarily good.

shred n (**shred'ded, shred'ding**) to tear or cut into small pieces:—n a scrap, a rag, a piece cut or torn off.

shrewd adj clever in practical matters, cunning, good at judging.

shriek vb to scream:—also n.

shrill adj high and piercing in sound.

shrimp n a small eatable shellfish:—vb to fish for shrimp.

shrine n 1 a box or tomb containing something connected with a holy person. 2 a place revered because of a connection with a holy person or event.

shrink vb 1 to make or become smaller. 2 to go back in fear, horror, etc.

shriv'el vb 1 to dry up and become smaller. 2 to become wrinkled.

shroud n 1 a garment or covering for a dead body. 2 pl the set of ropes supporting a mast of a ship:—vb 1 to put in a shroud. 2 to cover, to hide.

shrub n a short tree-like bush with a short trunk.

shrub'bery n a place where many shrubs are growing close together.

shrug vb (**shrugged, shrug'ging**) to raise one's shoulders in surprise, doubt, etc.

shud'der vb to tremble from fear, etc, to shiver with cold:—also n.

shuf'fle vb 1 to make a noise by moving the feet on the ground. 2 to mix cards before giving them out:—also n.

shun vb (**shunned', shun'ning**) to avoid, to keep away from.

shut vb (**shut, shut'ting**) to close.

shut'ter n a covering that can be placed or closed over a window or other opening to keep out light.

shy[1] adj timid, easily frightened, retiring in society:—vb to jerk or jump to the side in fear, etc:—n **shy'ness**.

shy[2] vb to throw:—n a throw.

sib'yl n in ancient times, a prophetess.

sick adj 1 ill. 2 bringing up food from the stomach by vomiting, about to vomit. 3 tired of through having too much.

sick'en vb 1 to make or become sick. 2 to disgust.

sick'ly adj 1 often ill. 2 pale. 3 over-sentimental.

sick'ness n 1 illness. 2 vomiting.

side n 1 one of the surfaces of a body, the part of the body between the shoulders and thighs. 2 edge, border. 3 slope. 4 one of two opposing parties or teams—on, at, or toward the other side:—vb to support one party against another.

side'board n a piece of furniture for storing dishes, cutlery, etc.

side'long adj to the side, slanting:—also adv.

side'show n a less important show at a fair, circus, exhibition, etc.

side'walk n a paved surface, esp a raised footway at the side of the road for pedestrians.

side'ways adv on or toward one side.

sid'ing n a short railroad track off the main line, used for shunting, etc.

si'dle vb to walk side first, to approach slowly.

siege n surrounding a fort, town, etc, with an army to take it or make its garrison surrender.

sieve [sêv] n a container with a network bottom or a bottom full of holes, used for separating small particles of anything from larger pieces:—vb to pass through a sieve.

sift vb 1 to pass through a sieve. 2 to examine closely:—n **sift'er**:—**sift out** to separate good from bad.

sigh [sî] vb a long, deep, easily heard breath expressing pain, sadness, unrequited love, etc:—vb 1 to draw such a breath. 2 (fml) to long for.

sight n 1 the power of seeing. 2 that which is seen. 3 something worth seeing. 4 the area within which things can be seen by someone:—vb to see, to notice:—**out of sight** too far away to be seen.

sight'less adj blind.

sight'seeing n going around the places of interest in a city, district, etc:—n **sight'seer**.

sign n 1 a mark, movement, gesture, etc, conveying an accepted meaning. 2 a mark or characteristic by which a person or thing can be recognized. 3 a notice to give directions or advertise:—vb 1 to write one's name on. 2 to convey meaning by a movement of the head, hands, etc.

sig'nal n 1 a sign to give information, orders, etc, at a distance. 2 a mechanism used to give such signs to drivers of railroad locomotives. 3 a message conveyed by such signals. 4 a turn signal:—adj notable, important:—vb to make signals to:—n **sig'naler**.

sig'nature n one's name written by oneself.

signature tune n a tune used to introduce a particular program on radio or TV.

signif'icance n meaning, importance.

signif'icant adj full of meaning, important.

sig'nify vb 1 to show by a sign. 2 to mean. 3 to be important.

sign'post n a post indicating the direction and sometimes also the distance to a place.

si'lence n absence of sound, quietness:—vb to cause to be quiet.

si'lencer n a device for reducing the noise of an engine, gun, etc.

si'lent adj 1 making no sound. 2 not talking, speaking little. 3 with no sound

silhouette [si'-lŏ-et] n 1 the dark outline and flat shape of an object as seen with a light behind it. 2 a solid outline drawing, usu in solid black on white, esp of a profile:—also vb.

sil'ica n a colorless mineral found as quartz or in fling, etc.

sil'icon n an element found in silica and used widely in transistors, etc, and in glass, etc.

silk n 1 the fine thread produced by the silkworm. 2 a soft material woven from this.

silk'en adj (lit) made of silk.

silk'worm n a caterpillar that spins silk thread to enclose its chrysalis.

silk'y adj 1 made of silk. 2 soft, smooth.

sill n the ledge of stone or wood at the foot of a window.

sil'ly adj foolish, unwise.

silt n the earth, sand, etc, deposited by a moving river:—vb to block or become blocked with silt.

sil'ver n 1 a precious metal of a shining white color. 2 coins, dishes, etc, made of silver:—adj made of silver.

sil'verware n dishes and utensils made of silver, knives, forks, spoons, etc.

silver wedding n the twenty-fifth anniversary of marriage.

sil'very adj 1 like silver. 2 clear in tone.

sim'ilar adj like, resembling.

similar'ity n likeness, resemblance.

simile [sim'-i-li] n a striking comparison of one thing with another.

sim'mer vb to keep on boiling slowly without boiling over.

sim'per vb to smile in a silly or insincere way:—also n.

sim'ple adj 1 unmixed, without anything added, pure. 2 not complicated. 3 plain. 4 trusting, innocent and inexperienced. 5 foolish, easily tricked:—n (old) a herb used as medicine.

simple fraction *n* a fraction other than a decimal fraction (e.g. ⁵/8).

simpli'city *n* 1 easiness. 2 sincerity. 3 plainness. 4 innocence.

sim'plify *vb* to make easier to do or understand.

sim'ply *adv* 1 in a clear way. 2 absolutely. 3 plain. 4 just, merely.

simulta'neous *adj* taking place at the same time.

sin *n* 1 a thought, word, or action that breaks the law of God. 2 a wicked act:—*vb* (**sinned'**, **sin'ning**) 1 to do wrong. 2 to commit sin:—*n* **sin'ner**.

since *prep* from (a certain time till now):—*adv* ago:—*conj* 1 from the time that. 2 because.

sincere' *adj* real, genuine, meaning what one says, frank.

sincer'ity *n* honesty of mind, freedom from pretense.

sin'ful *adj* full of sin, wicked.

sing *vb* (*pt* **sang**, *pp* **sung**) to make music with the voice, with or without words:—*n* **sing'er**.

singe *vb* to burn slightly, to burn the surface or ends of:—*also n*.

sin'gle *adj* 1 one only, alone. 2 unmarried:—*vb* to pick out one (for special attention, etc.).

sin'gle-mind'ed *adj* concentrating on one main purpose.

sin'gular *adj* 1 (*fml*) remarkable, unusual, odd, strange. 2 (*in grammar*) referring to one only.

singular'ity *n* 1 peculiarity, strangeness. 2 an unusual characteristic.

sin'gularly *adv* (*fml*) strangely, remarkably.

sin'ister *adj* 1 evil-looking. 2 threatening harm or evil.

sink *vb* (*pt* **sank**, *pp* **sunk**) 1 to go slowly down. 2 to go below the surface of water. 3 to become worse or weaker. 4 (*of an idea*) to be understood gradually. 5 to dig. 6 to cause to go underwater:—*n* a basin with a drainpipe leading from it, used when washing.

sinusi'tis *n* illness caused by an infection of the nasal sinus.

sip *vb* (**sipped'**, **sip'ping**) to drink in small mouthfuls:—*also n*.

sir *n* 1 a word of respect used to men. 2 the title given to a knight or baronet.

si'ren *n* 1 an attractive but dangerous woman. 2 a loud hooter sounded as a time signal or as a warning of danger.

sis'ter *n* 1 a female born of the same parents as another person. 2 a nun.

sis'terhood *n* a society of women, usu carrying out religious or charitable works.

sis'ter-in-law *n* 1 the sister of a husband or wife. 2 the wife of one's brother.

sis'terly *adj* like a sister.

sit *vb* (**sat**, **sit'ting**) 1 to take a rest on a seat. 2 to rest upon eggs to hatch them. 3 (*of parliament, courts, etc*) to meet to do business. 4 to rest upon:—**sit up** 1 to sit straight. 2 to stay out of bed when it is time to sleep.

site *n* the ground on which a building or number of buildings stands or is to stand:—*vb* to choose a place for.

sitting room *n* the room in which a family sit when not working.

sit'uated *adj* placed.

situa'tion *n* 1 a place or position. 2 (*fml*) a job. 3 circumstances.

size *n* bigness, bulk:—*vb* to arrange in order according to.

siz'zle *vb* to make a hissing or spluttering sound, as when frying.

skate *n* a steel blade fastened to a boot to allow a gliding movement on ice:—*vb* to move on skates or roller skates.

skat'ing rink *n* an area of ice prepared for skating.

skep'tical *adj* having doubts.

skel'eton *n* 1 the bony framework of a body. 2 an outline of a plot or plan.

sketch *n* 1 a rough drawing or painting, sometimes to be finished later. 2 an outline or short account. 3 a short amus-

ing play:—*vb* 1 to make a quick or rough drawing. 2 to give a short account or outline of, to draw.

sketch'y *adj* incomplete, leaving out details.

ski *n* a long shaped strip of wood, metal, etc, fixed to the feet to allow gliding movements over snow:—*ns* **ski'er**, **ski'ing**.

skid *n* 1 a sideways movement of a wheel on the ground. 2 a block put under a wheel to stop it turning. 3 a runner fixed to the under part of an airplane:—*vb* (**skid'ded**, **skid'ding**) 1 to move sideways on wheels that fail to turn. 2 to stop turning by placing a block under (a wheel).

skill *n* ability gained by practice, natural cleverness at doing something.

skilled' *adj* expert.

skil'ful *adj* expert, clever.

skim *vb* (**skimmed'**, **skim'ming**) 1 to remove anything floating on the surface of a liquid. 2 to pass quickly over the surface of. 3 to read quickly and without attention.

skim milk *n* milk from which the cream has been skimmed.

skimp'y *adj* insufficient.

skin *n* 1 the natural outer covering of an animal or vegetable. 2 a thin layer or covering. 3 a container made of skin:—*vb* (**skinned'**, **skin'ning**) to take the skin off.

skin'ny *adj* (*inf*) very thin.

skip *vb* (**skipped'**, **skip'ping**) 1 to jump about lightly. 2 to keep on jumping over a rope swung over the head and then under the feet alternately. 3 to leave out parts of a book when reading it:—*n* a light jump.

skip'per *n* the captain of a ship or team.

skir'mish *n* 1 a fight in which the main armies are not engaged. 2 a fight broken off before serious harm is done to either side:—*vb* to fight in small parties.

skirt *n* 1 the part of a garment below the waist. 2 a woman's garment stretching from the waist down. 3 the border or outer edge:—*vb* to pass along the edge or border.

skirting board *n* a board round the bottom of a room wall.

skull *n* the bony case that contains the brain.

skunk *n* 1 a weasel-like animal that gives out an evil-smelling fluid when attacked. 2 (*inf*) a mean or contemptible person.

sky *n* the space around the earth as visible to our eyes.

sky'-blue *adj* light blue, azure.

sky'light *n* a window in the roof of a building.

sky'line *n* the horizon.

sky'scraper *n* a very tall building.

slab *n* a large flat piece of anything.

slack¹ *adj* 1 loose, not tight. 2 careless, lazy. 3 not busy:—*n* the loose part of a rope, etc:—*vb* to work lazily or carelessly.

slack² *n* coal dust and tiny pieces of coal.

slack'en *vb* 1 to loosen. 2 to lose force or speed. 3 to become less.

slack'ness *n* 1 looseness. 2 carelessness.

slake *vb* to satisfy (thirst).

slam *vb* (**slammed'**, **slam'ming**) to shut or put down noisily:—*n* a bang.

slan'der *n* an untrue story put about to injure a person's character:—*vb* to spread such a story.

slan'derous *adj* harmful to the reputation.

slang *n* words and phrases in common use but not accepted as good English:—*vb* to scold, to abuse.

slant *n* slope:—*vb* 1 to slope or cause to slope. 2 to express or describe something in such a way as to emphasize a certain point or show favor toward a particular point of view.

slap *n* a blow with the open hand:—*vb* (**slapped'**, **slap'ping**) to strike with the flat of the hand or anything flat.

slash *vb* 1 to make a sweeping cut at with a knife, etc, to make long cuts in. 2 to reduce sharply:—*n* a long cut.

slate *n* **1** a type of rock that splits easily into thin layers. **2** a shaped piece of slate for covering a roof or for writing on:—*vb* to cover with slate.

slat'ternly *adj* dirty, untidy.

slaughter [slä'-tėr] *n* **1** killing in great numbers. **2** the act of killing:—*vb* **1** to kill in great numbers. **2** to kill for food.

slave *n* **1** one who is the property of another person and has to work for him or her. **2** one who has to do the dirty or unpleasant work:—*vb* to work very hard.

sla'ver *vb* to let saliva drop from the mouth:—*n* saliva running from the mouth.

slav'ery *n* **1** the state of being a slave. **2** hard, unpleasant, and badly paid work. **3** absence of all freedom.

slay *vb* (*pt* **slew**, *pp* **slain**) to kill.

sled, sledge *n* a vehicle on runners for use in snow.

sleek *adj* **1** smooth and shiny. **2** well fed and cared for.

sleep *vb* to rest the body, with the eyes shut, unaware of one's surroundings:—*n* a complete rest for the body, as at night.

sleep'er *n* **1** one who is asleep. **2** a railroad tie. **3** a car on a train with bunks for sleeping passengers.

sleep'less *adj* **1** unable to sleep. **2** without sleep.

sleep'walker *n* one who walks about in his or her sleep.

sleep'y *adj* wanting to sleep, drowsy.

sleet *n* falling snow mixed with rain or hail:—*adj* **sleet'y**.

sleeve *n* the part of a garment that covers the arm:—**laugh up one's sleeve** to be amused without showing it.

sleigh [slä] *n* a vehicle on runners for use in snow, a sledge.

slen'der *adj* **1** thin, scanty, only just enough. **2** slim.

sleuth [slöth] *n* a detective.

slice *vb* **1** to cut into thin pieces. **2** to strike a ball a glancing blow that makes it spin:—*n* **1** a thin broad piece cut off. **2** a flat utensil for serving food.

slick *adj* **1** quick and clever. **2** smart but deceitful.

slide *vb* (*pt, pp* **slid**) to move smoothly over a surface, as of ice, to slip:—*n* a slope or track for sliding on.

slight *adj* **1** small, lightly built. **2** small, not great, not serious:—*n* an insult:—*vb* to treat as unimportant, to treat insultingly.

slim *adj* thin, lightly built, small:—*vb* (**slimmed'**, **slim'ming**) to reduce weight by exercises, not eating certain foods, etc.

slime *n* sticky mud.

slim'y *adj* **1** covered with slime, slippery. **2** untrustworthy.

sling *vb* (*pt, pp* **slung**) **1** to throw with the outstretched arm. **2** to cause to hang from:—*n* **1** a strap or band used for hurling stones. **2** a bandage hanging from the neck to support an injured arm. **3** a band passed around something to help to lift or support it.

sling'shot *n* a Y-shaped stick with elastic for shooting stones, etc.

slink *vb* (*pt, pp* **slunk**) to go away quietly as if ashamed.

slip *vb* (**slipped'**, **slip'ping**) **1** to move smoothly along. **2** to go quietly or unseen. **3** to lose one's footing. **4** to escape (the memory):—*n* **1** the act of slipping. **2** a careless mistake. **3** a narrow piece of paper. **4** a loose cover (e.g. a pillowcase).

slip'knot *n* a knot that can be moved.

slip'per *n* a loose shoe for wear in the house.

slip'pery *adj* **1** hard to stand on without sliding or falling. **2** hard to hold without losing one's grip slightly. **3** (*inf*) untrustworthy.

slit *vb* (**slit'ted, slit'ting**) to make a long cut in:—*n* a long narrow cut or opening.

slith'er *vb* to slide clumsily or without control.

sliv'er *n* a thin piece cut off, a splinter.

slob'ber *vb* to let saliva run or fall from the mouth.

slog *vb* (**slogged'**, **slog'ging**) (*inf*) to work hard.

slo'gan *n* **1** a war cry. **2** a party cry or catchword. **3** an easily memorized saying used to advertise a product or campaign.

slope *n* **1** a rise or fall from the level. **2** a slant:—*vb* **1** to rise or fall from the level. **2** to slant.

slop'py *adj* (*inf*) **1** wet, muddy. **2** careless and untidy. **2** foolishly sentimental.

slot *n* a narrow oblong opening or hole, esp one made to receive coins.

sloth *n* laziness

sloth'ful *adj* very lazy.

slouch *vb* to stand, walk, or sit with bent back and head and shoulders sloping.

slough [sluf] *vb* **1** to cast off. **2** to throw off.

slov'enly *adj* dirty and untidy, very careless.

slow *adj* **1** not quick or fast. **2** taking a long time to do things. **3** not clever. **4** behind the correct time:—*vb* to go or cause to go less quickly.

slug *n* a shell-less snail, harmful to plants.

slug'gish *adj* slow-moving.

sluice [slös] *n* **1** a sliding gate to control the flow of water. **2** the waterway so controlled:—*vb* to wash out with running water.

slum *n* part of a town in which people live in overcrowded, dirty, and unhealthy houses.

slum'ber *vb* to sleep:—*n* sleep.

slump *n* a sudden fall in prices, wages, etc:—*vb* **1** to go suddenly down in price, etc. **2** to fall suddenly or heavily.

slur *vb* (**slurred'**, **slur'ring**) **1** to pass over quickly or without attention. **2** to make (sounds) indistinct by running them together:—*n* **1** a bad point in one's character or reputation. **2** (*mus*) a curved mark over two notes to be played smoothly one after the other.

slush *n* **1** half-melted snow, soft mud. **2** (*inf*) sentimental language:—*adj* **slush'y**.

slush fund *n* a fund of money used secretly to bribe, etc.

slut *n* a dirty and untidy woman:—*adj* **slut'tish**.

sly *adj* cunning, deceitful, doing things in a secret and deceitful way.

smack *vb* **1** to hit with the flat of the hand. **2** to part the lips so as to make a sharp noise:—*n* **1** a slap. **2** a loud kiss.

small *adj* **1** little. **2** not much:—*n* the narrow part of the back.

smart *adj* **1** quick, clever. **2** well-dressed:—*vb* to feel or cause a quick keen pain.

smart'en *vb* to make smart or smarter.

smash *vb* to break into pieces:—*n* **1** act of breaking into pieces. **2** the noise caused by breakage. **3** an accident involving one or more vehicles. **4** a disaster.

smear *vb* **1** to spread (something sticky or dirty) over the surface. **2** to smudge, to make or become blurred:—*n* **1** a dirty mark, a blot. **2** a story intended to harm a person's good name.

smell *n* **1** the sense that enables animals to perceive by breathing in through the nose. **2** scent, odor:—*vb* (*pt, pp* **smelled'** or **smelt**) **1** to perceive by smell. **2** to give off an odor:—**smell a rat** to be suspicious.

smell'y *adj* (*inf*) having an unpleasant odor.

smile *vb* **1** to show joy, amusement, etc, by a movement of the lips. **2** to be favorable:—*n* a look of pleasure or amusement.

smirk *vb* to smile in a silly or unnatural manner:—*n* a smug or scornful smile.

smith *n* one who works in metals.

smith'y *n* the workshop of a blacksmith.

smock *n* **1** a loose overall worn to protect one's clothes. **2** a woman's loose dress.

smog *n* a smoky fog.

smoke *n* the sooty vapor rising from a burning substance:—*vb* **1** to give off smoke. **2** to draw in the tobacco smoke from a cigarette, pipe, etc. **3** to preserve in smoke. **4** to drive out by

smok'y adj 1 full of smoke. 2 giving off smoke.

smol'der vb to burn without flame.

smooth adj 1 having an even surface, not rough. 2 free from difficulties. 3 having good yet not pleasing manners:—vb to make smooth or level.

smooth'-tongued adj able to speak in a very polite or flattering manner.

smoth'er vb to kill by keeping air from.

smudge n a dirty mark, a stain:—vb 1 to make a dirty mark on. 2 to make or become blurred or smeared:—adj **smudg'y**.

smug n self-satisfied, too pleased with oneself.

smug'gle vb 1 to bring goods into the country secretly, without paying customs duties on them. 2 to bring in or pass secretly.

smug'gler n one who smuggles goods.

smut n 1 a flake of soot. 2 a dirty mark or stain. 3 dirty or indecent talk:—adj **smut'ty**.

snack n a light quick meal.

snag n an unexpected difficulty or hindrance.

snail n a slow-moving soft-bodied creature with a shell on its back.

snake n 1 a long crawling creature with no legs and a scaly skin, a serpent. 2 an untrustworthy person.

snap vb (**snapped'**, **snap'ping**) 1 to bite or seize suddenly. 2 to break with a sharp sound. 3 to speak in a quick, angry manner. 4 to take a photograph of with a hand camera:— n 1 a sudden bite. 2 a short sharp sound. 3 a spell of weather. 4 a card game. 5 a snapshot.

snare n a trap for catching birds or animals, esp one made with a running noose.

snarl vb 1 to growl angrily and show the teeth. 2 to speak angrily:—also n.

snatch vb to seize quickly or suddenly:—n 1 a sudden seizing. 2 a small part.

sneak vb 1 to go quietly, as a thief. 2 to tell of another's wrongdoing to one in authority:—n 1 a telltale. 2 a mean person:— adj **sneak'y**.

sneak'ers npl light rubber-soled shoes.

sneer vb to show contempt by a look or remark:—n a mocking smile or remark.

sneeze vb to expel air noisily through the nose:—n the act or sound of sneezing.

snick'er same as **snigger**.

sniff vb 1 to breathe noisily inward. 2 to smell:—n 1 the act or sound of sniffing. 2 a slight smell.

snig'ger vb to giggle nervously or unpleasantly:—also n.

snip vb (**snipped'**, **snip'ping**) to cut as with scissors, to cut off with one sharp movement.

snip'pet n 1 a small piece cut off. 2 a short item of news.

snob n one who looks down on others because they are less wealthy or of lower rank in society:—n **snob'bery**.

snob'bish adj behaving like a snob.

snook'er n a billiards game in which players have to knock, with a white cue ball, 15 red and then in order 6 colored balls into pockets on a table.

snoop vb to go about secretly or stealthily in order to find out something:—n **snoop'er**.

snore vb to breathe noisily while asleep, as if grunting:—n the noise so made.

snort vb to blow air out noisily through the nose:—also n.

snout n 1 the long nose and mouth of an animal. 2 the nozzle of a pipe.

snow [snō] n 1 vapor frozen in the air and falling in flakes:—vb to fall as snow, to cover as with snow.

snow'ball n snow pressed into a hard ball.

snow'bound adj cut off by snow.

snow'drift n snow heaped up by the wind to form a bank.

snow'flake n a single piece of snow.

snow'y adj 1 of or like snow. 2 pure white.

snub vb (**snubbed'**, **snub'bing**) to show dislike or disapproval of a person by taking no notice of or speaking rudely to him or her:—n rude lack of notice, an unfriendly act or speech:—adj (of a nose) short and turned up.

snug adj warm and comfortable, cozy.

snug'gle vb to lie close for warmth, to settle comfortably.

so adv 1 in this or that manner. 2 to that extent. 3 thus. 4 very:—conj therefore.

soak vb 1 to wet thoroughly. 2 to steep. 3 to suck up.

soap n a substance made of oil or fat and certain chemicals, used in washing:—vb to rub with soap.

soar vb 1 to fly upward. 2 to tower up.

sob vb (**sobbed'**, **sob'bing**) to draw the breath noisily when weeping or short of breath:—also n.

so'ber adj 1 not drunk. 2 serious, quiet. 3 dark in color.

so'-called adj given a name or title to which one has no right.

soc'cer n a game played on a field between two teams of 11 players with a round ball.

so'ciable adj fond of company.

so'cial adj 1 having to do with society. 2 living in an organized group.

so'cialism n the belief that the means of production are the property of the community:—n **so'cialist**.

soci'ety n 1 a group of people living together in a single organized community. 2 a group of people who meet regularly for a special purpose, mixing with other people. 3 the wealthy or high-ranking members of a community.

sock n a short stocking.

sock'et n a hole or hollow for something to fit into or turn in.

so'da n 1 an alkali (carbonate of soda) made into a powder and used in washing, baking, etc. 2 a nonalcoholic drink, often carbonated. 3 soda water.

soda water n water containing bicarbonate of soda and made fizzy by gas.

sod'den adj wet through, soaking.

so'fa n a couch with cushioned seat, back, and arms.

soft adj 1 not hard. 2 easily reshaped by pressing. 3 not loud. 4 (of color) not bright. 5 gentle. 6 not strict. 7 not alcoholic. 8 foolishly kind:—adv quietly, gently.

soften [sä'-fēn] vb 1 to make or become soft. 2 to become less harsh or angry.

soft'ware n the programs used in computers.

sog'gy adj soft and wet.

soil n the ground, earth, esp that in which plants are grown:— vb to dirty, to spoil.

sol'ace vb to cheer, to comfort:—n that which gives cheer or comfort.

so'lar adj having to do with the sun.

solar system n the sun and the planets that move around it.

sold pt of **sell**.

sol'dier n a person serving in an army.

sole[1] n the underside of the foot, stocking, or shoe:—vb to put a sole on (a shoe).

sole[2] n a small flatfish.

sole[3] adj only, single:—adv **sole'ly**.

sol'emn adj 1 serious in manner or appearance. 2 slow, stately.

sol'-fa n the use of the sounds doh, ray, me, fah, soh, lah, te in singing the scale:—also adj.

soli'cit vb to ask earnestly or repeatedly:—n **solicita'tion**.

soli'citor *n* 1 one who solicits, esp for gifts of money. 2 a legal adviser to certain parts of the public service.

sol'id *adj* 1 not hollow, consisting of hard matter throughout. 2 not liquid or gaseous. 3 firm. 4 reliable:—*n* a body consisting of hard matter throughout.

solid'ify *vb* to make or become solid.

sol'itary *adj* 1 alone, without companions. 2 living or being alone by habit or preference. 3 lonely, secluded.

sol'itude *n* loneliness, being alone, a lonely place.

so'lo *n* 1 a piece of music for a single performer. 2 a performance by one person.

sol'uble *adj* able to be melted or dissolved in liquid:—*n* solubil'ity.

solu'tion *n* 1 a liquid containing another substance dissolved in it. 2 the answer to or explanation of a problem, etc.

solve *vb* to find the right answer to or explanation of.

sol'vent *adj* 1 able to pay one's debts. 2 able to dissolve:—*n* a liquid able to dissolve another substance.

som'ber *adj* dark, gloomy, cheerless.

some *adj* a certain number or amount (of):—*pron* 1 certain people. 2 a little:—*ns and prons* **some'one**, **some'thing**.

some'body *n and pron* 1 some person. 2 a person of importance.

some'how *adv* in some way or other.

somersault [sum'-èr-sålt] *n* a leap or roll in which the heels turn completely over the head.

some'times *adv* now and then.

some'what *adv* in some degree, a little.

some'where *adv* in some place.

sonar' *n* an apparatus that detects objects underwater by reflecting sound waves.

song *n* 1 words set to music for the voice. 2 the sounds uttered by a bird.

son'-in-law *n* the man married to one's daughter.

soon *adv* 1 in a short time. 2 early. 3 willingly.

soot *n* black particles that rise with the smoke from burning matter.

soothe *vb* to calm, to comfort.

sop *n* 1 a piece of bread dipped in liquid before being eaten. 2 a money gift or bribe given to make less angry or unfriendly:—*vb* (**sopped'**, **sop'ping**) to soak.

sophis'ticated *adj* 1 (*fml*) not natural. 2 having a great deal of experience and worldly wisdom, knowledge of how to dress elegantly, etc:—*n* sophistica'tion.

sop'py *adj* 1 wet through. 2 foolishly sentimental.

sor'cerer *n* one who works magic, an enchanter.

sor'cery *n* magic, witchcraft.

sor'did *adj* mean, dirty, disgusting.

sore *adj* painful, hurtful:—*n* a painful cut or growth on the body.

sore'ly *adv* very much.

sor'row *n* sadness caused by loss or suffering, grief:—*vb* to mourn, to grieve:—*adj* **sor'rowful**.

sor'ry *adj* 1 feeling pity or regret, sad because of wrongdoing. 2 wretched.

sort *n* a kind, class or set:—*vb* to arrange in classes or sets:—**out of sorts** not well.

so'-so' *adj* fairly good, not bad.

sot *n* a drunkard.

sought *pt of* **seek**.

soul *n* 1 the spiritual part of a person. 2 (*inf*) a person.

soul'ful *adj* full of feeling.

soul'less *adj* lacking nobility of mind, mean-spirited.

sound[1] *adj* 1 healthy. 2 strong. 3 without serious error or weakness:—*adv* completely.

sound[2] *n* 1 a noise. 2 that which is heard:—*vb* 1 to make a noise. 2 to touch or strike so as to cause a noise.

sound[3] *n* a long narrow piece of water between two land masses, a strait:—*vb* 1 to find depth by lowering a lead weight on a cord. 2 to try to discover someone's opinion by questioning.

sound barrier *n* speed in motion equal to or greater than the speed of sound.

soup [söp] *n* a liquid food made by boiling meat, vegetables, etc.

sour *adj* 1 sharp or bitter in taste. 2 ill-tempered and hard to please.

source *n* 1 that from which anything begins. 2 the spring from which a river flows. 3 origin or cause.

south *n* 1 one of the four cardinal points of the compass, opposite north. 2 the position of the sun at noon. 3 (*with cap*) the states lying south of Pennsylvania and east of the Mississippi river:—*adj* being in the south, facing south:—*also* *adv*:—*adj and adv* **south'ward**.

south'east' *n* the point midway between south and east:—*also adj*:—*adjs* **southeast'erly**, **southeast'ern**.

sou'therly *adj* lying toward or coming from the south.

south'ern *adj* in or of the south.

south'west' *n* the point midway between south and west:—*also adj*:—*adjs* **southwest'erly**, **southwest'ern**.

sou'venir *n* an object kept to remind one of a person or event.

sou'wester' *n* a waterproof hat with a large flap at the back to cover the neck.

sov'ereign *n* ruler, a king or queen:—*adj* 1 supreme in authority or rank. 2 (*country, etc*) independent.

sov'ereignty *n* supreme power.

sow[1] [sou] *n* a female pig.

sow[2] [sö] *vb* (*pp* **sown**) 1 to scatter. 2 to plant with seeds.

soy'bean *n* a type of bean grown in the East, used for making flour or oil, as fodder for cattle, and in food that is free of dairy products, such as **soy milk**.

space *n* 1 the whole extent of the universe not occupied by solid bodies. 2 the distance between one body or object and another. 3 the place occupied by a person or thing. 4 a length of time:—*vb* to arrange with intervals between.

spa'cious *adj* roomy.

spade *n* 1 a tool with a broad blade, used for digging. 2 *pl* a suit of playing cards.

spaghetti [spä-ge'-ti] *n* long thin tubes of paste made from flour.

span *n* 1 the distance between the tip of the thumb and the little finger fully extended (about 9 inches in an adult). 2 the spread of an arch. 3 the distance from end to end of a bridge. 4 a space of time:—*vb* (**spanned'**, **span'ning**) 1 to extend from one point in space or time to another. 2 to measure with outstretched fingers.

span'gle *n* a small glittering metal ornament.

spaniel [span'-yèl] *n* a sporting or pet dog with long silky hair and drooping ears.

spank *vb* to slap with the hand.

span'ner *n* a wrench.

spare *adj* 1 scarce. 2 thin. 3 more than is needed, kept in reserve:—*vb* 1 to let off punishment or suffering, to show mercy to. 2 to do without. 3 to use up slowly and carefully.

spark *n* a tiny piece of burning matter.

spark'le *vb* 1 to seem to give off sparks, to glitter. 2 to be lively and intelligent:—*n* glitter, liveliness, brilliance.

spar'row *n* a common small bird.

sparse *adj* 1 thinly scattered. 2 scanty, scarcely enough:—*n* spar'sity.

spasm n **1** a sudden involuntary movement of the body, caused by a tightening of muscles, as in cramp, a fit. **2** a feeling or activity that does not last long.

spasmod'ic adj done occasionally for short periods.

spate n **1** a flood, the overflow of a river. **2** a large number or amount.

spat'ter vb to throw or scatter (liquid, mud, etc) in drops, to splash.

spawn n the eggs of fish, frogs, etc:—vb **1** to produce spawn. **2** to produce, usu in large numbers.

speak vb (pt **spoke**, pp **spok'en**) **1** to utter words, to talk. **2** to make a speech. **3** to pronounce.

spear n a weapon with a long straight handle and a pointed metal head.

spe'cial adj **1** having to do with one particular thing, person, or occasion. **2** not common or usual, distinctive.

spe'cialist n one who makes a particular study of one subject or of one branch of a subject.

special'ty n **1** a special field of work or study. **2** something made or sold only by a certain trader.

spe'cies n kind, sort, a group of things (e.g. plants, animals) with certain characteristics in common.

specif'ic adj **1** definite. **2** particular:—n a remedy for a particular disease.

specif'y vb to state exactly or in detail.

spec'imen n a sample, a part taken as an example of the whole.

speck n a tiny particle, spot, or stain.

speck'le n a small spot on a differently colored background:—adj **speck'led**.

spec'tacle n **1** something worth looking at, a wonderful or magnificent sight. **2** pl glasses worn in front of the eyes to assist the eyesight.

spectac'ular adj **1** magnificent or splendid to look at. **2** impressive, dramatic.

specta'tor n one who looks on.

spec'trum n a band of colors, as in a rainbow, produced by passing light through a prism.

spec'ulate vb to think about, to guess without having the necessary facts.

specula'tion n **1** act of speculating. **2** a guess or theory.

speech n **1** the ability to speak. **2** a talk given in public.

speech'less adj unable to speak for love, surprise, fear, etc.

speed n **1** quickness of movement. **2** haste:—vb (pt **sped**) **1** to go fast. **2** to drive an automobile very fast, often illegally fast. **3** to cause to happen faster.

speedom'eter n an indicator to show how fast an automobile, motorcycle, etc, is traveling.

speed'well n a plant with small blue flowers.

speed'y adj fast, quick-moving.

spell vb (pt, pp **spelt** or **spelled'**) to say or write the letters of a word in order.

spell n certain words uttered in order to make something happen by magic, a charm, a strange or magical power.

spell n **1** a length of time. **2** a turn at doing work.

spell'bound adj fascinated, made still by wonder or magic.

spend vb (pt, pp **spent**) **1** to pay out (money). **2** to use or use up. **3** to pass (time).

spend'thrift n one who spends money wastefully and carelessly.

spent adj **1** tired out. **2** used up.

spew vb **1** (inf) to vomit. **2** to come out in a flood.

sphere n **1** a ball. **2** a sun, star, or planet. **3** the extent of one's work, knowledge, influence, etc.

spher'ical adj round like a sphere.

spice n **1** a sharp-tasting substance used to flavor food. **2** something exciting or interesting:—vb to flavor with spice, etc.

spic'y adj sharp-tasting.

spick'-and-span' adj neat and tidy, smart.

spi'der n an eight-legged creature that spins a web to catch the insects on which it lives.

spike n a short piece of pointed metal, a large nail:—vb **1** to fasten with spikes. **2** to pierce with a spike.

spill vb (pt, pp **spilled'** or **spilt**) to let run out or overflow:—n **1** a fall. **2** something spilled.

spin vb (**spun, spin'ning**) **1** to draw out (wool, cotton, etc) and twist into threads. **2** to turn quickly around and around one point. **3** (inf) to make up:—n **1** a short or rapid trip. **2** a dive made by an airplane turning around and around at the same time.

spin'ach n a vegetable whose leaves are eaten as food.

spin'al adj having to do with the spine.

spin'dle n in a spinning machine, the bar on to which the newly made thread is wound.

spind'ly adj long and thin.

spin'drift n the spray blown from the tops of waves.

spine n **1** the backbone. **2** a pointed spike on an animal or fish. **3** a thorn.

spine'less adj **1** having no spine. **2** weak, lacking determination.

spir'al adj winding around and around like the thread of a screw:—n **1** a spiral line or shape. **2** a continuous expansion or decrease:—vb **1** to move up or down in a spiral curve. **2** to increase or decrease steadily.

spire n a tall tower, tapering to a pointed top.

spir'it n **1** the soul. **2** a ghost. **3** courage, liveliness. **4** mood. **5** the intention underlying. **6** pl strong alcoholic liquor.

spir'ited adj **1** lively. **2** showing courage.

spir'itual adj **1** having to do with the soul or spirit. **2** religious, holy.

spir'itualism n the belief that the soul or spirit only has real existence, the belief that it is possible to communicate with the souls of the dead:—n **spir'itualist**.

spit n a long thick pin on which meat is roasted over a:—vb (**spit'ted, spit'ting**) to put on a spit, to pierce.

spit vb (**spat, spit'ting**) **1** to blow from the mouth. **2** to put saliva, etc, out of the mouth:—n a quantity of spit put out of the mouth.

spite n ill-feeling against another, a desire to hurt or harm another:—vb to do something to hurt or harm another:—in **spite of** without paying attention to.

spite'ful adj desiring or intended to hurt or harm another.

splash vb to throw or scatter drops of mud or liquid on to:—n **1** act of splashing. **2** the sound made by a heavy body striking water. **3** a spot of mud or liquid.

splay vb to slope or turn outward:—adj (of feet) turned outward and flat.

splen'did adj **1** bright, shining, brilliant. **2** excellent.

splen'dor n brightness, magnificence.

splint n a piece of wood to keep a broken bone in position.

splin'ter n a sharp-edged piece of glass, wood, metal, etc, broken off a larger piece:—vb to break into small pieces.

split vb (**split, split'ting**) **1** to cut or break from end to end. **2** to separate into parts or smaller groups:—n **1** a long break or crack. **2** a division. **3** pl the trick of going down upright on the ground with the legs spread out at right angles to the body.

splut'ter vb **1** to utter confused, indistinct sounds. **2** to make a spitting noise:—also n.

spoil vb (pt, pp **spoiled'** or **spoilt**) **1** to make or become useless or unpleasant. **2** to rob, to plunder. **3** to harm someone's

spoil'sport n one who spoils the pleasure of others.

spoke[1] pt of **speak**:—pp **spok'en**.

spoke[2] n one of the bars running from the hub to the rim of a wheel.

spokes'man, spokes'woman, spokes'person n one who speaks for others.

sponge [spunj] n 1 a type of sea animal. 2 a kind of light absorbent washcloth made from the soft frame of a sponge. 3 one who lives on the money or favors of another:—vb 1 to wipe with a sponge. 2 to live on the money or favors of another.

spongy [spun'-ji] adj soft and absorbent.

spon'sor n 1 one who introduces someone or something and takes responsibility for it. 2 a business that pays for an event, show, etc, in return for advertising. 3 a person who agrees to pay someone money for charity if he or she completes a specified activity:—vb 1 to put forward and support. 2 to act as a sponsor.

sponta'neous adj 1 done willingly. 2 not caused by an outside agency. 3 done without previous thought:—n spontane'ity.

spool n a reel on which thread, film, etc, may be wound:—vb to wind on a spool.

spoon n a domestic utensil consisting of a shallow bowl and a handle, used in cooking or feeding:—vb to lift with a spoon.

spoon'ful n the amount that a spoon contains.

sport n 1 outdoor or athletic indoor games in which certain rules are obeyed. 2 one of these games. 3 (fml) something done for fun or amusement. 4 (inf) a person regarded as fair abiding by the rules:—vb to play, to have fun.

sport'ing adj 1 fond of sports. 2 used in sport. 3 fair-minded and generous, esp in sports.

sports'man, sports'woman, sports'person n one who takes part in a sport.

sports'manship n the spirit of fair play.

spot n 1 a small mark, stain, or blot. 2 a tiny piece. 3 a pimple. 4 the exact place where something happened:—vb (spot'ted, spot'ting) 1 to stain. 2 to see or catch sight of.

spot'less adj unmarked, very clean.

spot'light n a strong beam of light shone on a particular person or place on a stage.

spot'ty adj covered with spots.

spout n 1 a long tube sticking out from a pot, jug, pipe, etc, through which liquid can flow. 2 a jet or gush of liquid:—vb 1 to gush or make to gush in a jet. 2 (inf) to talk at length.

sprain n the painful twisting of a joint in the body, causing damage to muscles or ligaments:—vb to twist a joint in such a way.

sprawl vb 1 to sit or lie with the limbs spread out awkwardly. 2 to be spread out untidily.

spray[1] n 1 a twig or stem with several leaves or flowers growing on it. 2 an arrangement of flowers.

spray[2] n 1 a cloud of small drops of liquid moving through the air. 2 liquid to be sprayed under pressure. 3 a can or container holding this:—vb 1 to sprinkle with fine drops of liquid.

spread vb (pt, pp **spread**) 1 to lay out over an area. 2 to grow bigger, so covering more space. 3 to make or become more widely known or believed. 4 to affect more.

sprig n a small shoot or twig.

spring vb (pt **sprang**, pp **sprung**) 1 to jump. 2 to flow up from under the ground. 3 to be caused by:—n 1 a jump. 2 a piece or coil of metal that after being compressed returns to its earlier shape or position. 3 water flowing up from under

the ground. 4 the season following winter when plants begin to grow again.

spring'y adj having elasticity.

sprin'kle vb to scatter in small drops or tiny pieces.

sprin'kling n a very small number or quantity.

sprint vb to run as fast as possible for a short distance:—n 1 a short foot race. 2 a short fast run.

sprout vb to begin to grow, to bud:—n a young plant, a shoot of a plant.

spruce[1] adj neat, smart and tidy.

spruce[2] n a type of fir tree, valued for its white timber.

spry adj quick and active, lively.

spur n 1 a pointed instrument or spiked wheel attached to a rider's heel and dug into the horse's side to make it move more quickly. 2 encouragement. 3 a hard sharp projection. 4 a line of hills running out at an angle from a larger hill:—vb (**spurred', spur'ring**) 1 to prick with a spur. 2 to urge to greater effort:—**on the spur of the moment** without previous thought.

spu'rious adj false.

spurn vb to refuse with contempt.

spurt vb to burst out in a jet:—n 1 a gush of liquid. 2 a special effort. 3 a sudden short burst of extra speed.

spy n 1 one who tries to obtain secret information about one country on behalf of an enemy country. 2 one who tries to find out another's secrets:—vb 1 to catch sight of. 2 to act as a spy.

squab'ble vb to quarrel over unimportant matters:—also n.

squad n a small party of soldiers or workers.

squal'id adj dirty and unpleasant, unclean.

squall vb to scream loudly:—n 1 a loud scream. 2 a sudden violent gust of wind.

squal'or n excessive dirt, filth.

squan'der vb to spend wastefully, to use up needlessly.

square adj 1 having four equal sides and four right angles. 2 forming a right angle. 3 just, fair. 4 even, equal:—n 1 a square figure. 2 an open space in a town with buildings on its four sides. 3 the number obtained when a number is multiplied by itself. 4 an L- or T-shaped instrument for drawing right angles:—vb 1 to make square. 2 to pay money due. 3 to bribe. 4 to multiply (a number) by itself.

squash[1] vb 1 to crush, to press or squeeze into pulp. 2 to speak sharply to someone to silence him or her:—n 1 a crowd, a crush. 2 a game played in a walled court with rackets and a rubber ball.

squash[2] n a widely grown vegetable.

squat vb (**squat'ted, squat'ting**) 1 to sit down on the heels. 2 to make one's home on a piece of land or in a building to which one has no legal right:—adj short and broad.

squawk vb to utter a harsh cry:—also n.

squeak vb to utter a short, high-pitched sound:—also n:—**narrow squeak** an escape that almost fails.

squeal vb to cry with a sharp shrill voice:—also n.

squeam'ish adj easily made sick.

squeeze vb 1 to press from more than one side. 2 to hug. 3 to push through a narrow space:—n 1 the act of squeezing. 2 a hug. 3 a tight fit.

squelch vb to make a sucking noise, as when walking over sodden ground:—also n.

squib n a small firework.

squint vb to have eyes that look in different directions. 2 to look sideways without turning the head:—n 1 eyes looking in different directions. 2 (inf) a quick look.

squire n 1 a landowning country gentleman. 2 (old) one who attended on a knight:—vb to accompany (a woman) in public.

squirm *vb* to wriggle about.

squir'rel *n* a small bushy-tailed animal living in trees.

squirt *vb* to force or be forced out in a thin fast stream:—*n* 1 a jet. 2 an instrument for throwing out a jet of liquid.

stab *vb* (**stabbed'**, **stab'bing**) to wound with a pointed weapon:—*n* 1 a wound made with a pointed weapon. 2 a thrust with a dagger or pointed knife. 3 a sharp feeling.

stabil'ity *n* steadiness, security.

sta'ble[1] *n* a building or shelter for horses, cattle, etc:—*vb* to keep in a stable.

sta'ble[2] *adj* 1 firm, secure, not easily upset or changed. 2 likely to behave reasonably.

stack *n* a large orderly pile of hay, wood, etc:—*vb* to pile together.

sta'dium *n* a large ground for sports and athletics.

staff *n* 1 a stick or rod used as a support. 2 the set of five parallel lines on and between which musical notes are written. 3 any body of employees:—*vb* to provide with workers or employees.

stag *n* a male red deer.

stage *n* 1 a raised platform for actors, performers, speakers, etc. 2 the theater. 3 a halting place. 4 the distance that may be traveled after paying a certain fare. 5 a certain point in development or progress:—*vb* to produce (a play) on a stage.

stage'coach *n* formerly, a coach providing a regular service for passengers.

stag'ger *vb* 1 to walk unsteadily, to lurch to the side, to reel. 2 to amaze.

stag'nant *adj* 1 not flowing. 2 unchanging, dull.

stagnate *vb* 1 to cease to flow. 2 to cease to develop or be active:—*n* **stagna'tion**.

staid *adj* serious, steady, unwilling to move with the times.

stain *vb* 1 to make dirty. 2 to change the color of. 3 to make marks of a different color on. 4 to spoil, to disgrace:—*n* 1 a dirty mark or discoloration that cannot be removed. 2 a paint or dye. 3 disgrace.

stain'less *adj* 1 not easily stained or rusted. 2 without fault or disgrace.

stair *n* a series of connected steps leading from one place to another on a different level.

stake[1] *n* a stout piece of wood pointed at one end for driving into the ground. 2 formerly, the post to which was tied a person condemned to death by burning:—*vb* to mark with stakes.

stake[2] *n* the amount of money bet:—*vb* to bet (money), to risk:—**at stake** able to be lost.

stale *adj* 1 not fresh. 2 not new. 3 uninteresting.

stalk[1] [stâk] *n* the stem of a plant.

stalk[2] [stâk] *vb* 1 to walk holding oneself stiffly upright. 2 to hunt (game, prey) stealthily:—*n* **stalk'er**.

stall *n* 1 a division of a stable or byre in which one animal is kept. 2 a counter on which goods are laid out for sale. 3 a small, sometimes temporary, store set up in an open place. 4 a ground-floor seat in a theater. 5 a seat in the choir of a church:—*vb* 1 (*of an engine*) to stop working. 2 to avoid giving a direct answer.

stal'wart *adj* tall and strong.

sta'men *n* one of the little pollen-bearing stalks in the middle of a flower.

stam'ina *n* staying power, ability to endure.

stam'mer *vb* to have difficulty in uttering the sounds at the beginning of words, sometimes attempting them several times before succeeding:—*n* such difficulty in speaking.

stamp *vb* 1 to strike the foot forcefully or noisily downward. 2 to print a mark on. 3 to put a postage stamp on:—*n* 1 a forceful or noisy downward movement of the foot. 2 a mark or paper affixed to a letter or package to show that postage

has been paid. 3 a mark consisting of letters, numbers, a pattern, etc, printed on paper, cloth, coins, etc. 4 a machine for making such a mark. 5 (*fml*) a kind or sort.

stampede' *n* a sudden panic-stricken rush of many people or animals:—*vb* to take sudden flight.

stand *vb* (*pt* **stood**) 1 to be upright on the feet, legs, or end. 2 to rise up. 3 to set upright. 4 to stop moving. 5 to stay motionless. 6 to be in a certain place. 7 to bear, to put up with. 8 to become a candidate for election. 9 (*inf*) to pay for:—*n* 1 a halt. 2 a small table, rack, etc, on which things may be placed or hung. 3 a structure with seats arranged in tiers for spectators. 4 a base or support on which an object may be placed upright. 5 resistance to an attack:—**stand by** to support, to be ready to help:—**stand out** 1 to be prominent. 2 to refuse to give in:—**stand up** to get to one's feet:—**stand up for** to defend:—**stand up to** to resist.

stan'dard *n* 1 a fixed measure. 2 an average level of accomplishment with which others' work is compared. 3 a large flag or banner. 4 an upright post, etc:—*adj* fixed. 2 fixed by rule. 3 usual. 4 standing upright.

stand'ing *n* rank, position, reputation:—*adj* 1 upright. 2 not flowing. 3 permanent, fixed.

stand-off'ish *adj* unfriendly, unwilling to mix with others.

stand'still *n* a stoppage.

star *n* 1 a heavenly body seen as a twinkling point of light in the night sky. 2 any object like a twinkling star in shape. 3 an asterisk (*). 4 a leading actor or actress:—*vb* (**starred'**, **star'ring**) to have the leading part in a play, etc.

starch *n* a vegetable substance found in potatoes, cereals, etc.

stare *vb* to look at fixedly, to look at with wide-open eyes:—*also n*.

stark *adj* 1 bare or simple, often in a severe way. 2 utter, complete:—*adv* completely.

star'ry *adj* full of stars, like stars.

start *vb* 1 to begin. 2 to set in motion. 3 to jump or make a sudden movement:—*n* 1 a beginning. 2 a sudden sharp movement.

start'er *n* 1 a device for starting a motor engine. 2 one who gives the signal to begin.

star'tle *vb* to frighten suddenly.

starve *vb* 1 to die of hunger, to suffer greatly from hunger. 2 to keep without food. 3 to suffer for want of something necessary:—*n* **starva'tion**.

state *n* 1 condition, circumstances. 2 the people of a country organized under a form of government. 3 the governmental institutions of a country:—*adj* 1 having to do with the government. 2 public:—*vb* 1 to say as a fact. 2 to put clearly into words, spoken or written.

state'ment *n* 1 a clear spoken or written account of facts. 2 an account of money due or held.

stat'ic *adj* motionless, at rest:—*n* electrical interference causing noise on radio or TV.

sta'tion *n* 1 (*old*) position, rank. 2 a regular stopping place for trains, buses, etc:—*vb* to put in or send to a certain place.

sta'tionary *adj* fixed, not moving.

sta'tionery *n* paper, pens, and all other writing materials.

station wagon *n* an extended automobile with a third seat or luggage platform.

statis'tics *n* 1 the science of turning facts into figures and then classifying them. 2 the study of figures in order to deduce facts. 3 figures giving information about something.

stat'ue *n* the carved or molded figure of a person or animal in stone, etc.

stat'ure *n* 1 height of the body. 2 importance, reputation.

sta'tus *n* rank, social position.

stat'ute n 1 a law. 2 a law passed by parliament.

stat'utory adj required by law or statute.

staunch[1] adj loyal, firm, reliable.

staunch[2], **stanch** vb to stop blood flowing from a cut, etc.

stave n 1 one of the strips of wood forming the sides of a barrel. 2 the set of five parallel lines on and between which musical notes are written:—vb to break inward:—**stave off** to keep away, to put off.

stay vb 1 to remain. 2 to live in a place for a time:—n time spent in a place.

stead'fast adj loyal, firm, unmoving.

stead'y adj 1 firm. 2 not easily changing. 3 regular. 4 reliable, sensible:—n **stead'iness**.

steak [stāk] n a slice of meat or fish for cooking.

steal [steel] vb (pt **stole**, pp **sto'len**) 1 to take what belongs to another. 2 to move slowly and quietly.

stealth'y adj quiet, sly, secretive.

steam the vapor of hot liquid, esp water:—vb 1 to give off steam. 2 to cook in steam. 3 to move by steam power. 4 to become extremely angry or emotional.

steam engine an engine driven by steam power.

steel n an alloy consisting of iron hardened by carbon:—adj made of steel.

steel'y adj hard, unsympathetic.

steep adj having a rapid slope up or down:—n a cliff or precipice.

steep'le n a tall church tower, sometimes tapering to a point.

steer vb to keep a moving object pointed in the desired direction, to guide or control.

stem[1] n the trunk of a tree, the stalk of a flower, leaf, etc

stem[2] vb (**stemmed**, **stem'ming**) to check, to stop (something) flowing.

stench n a foul smell.

step n 1 a pace taken by one foot. 2 the distance covered by such a pace. 3 a footprint. 4 the sound of a footfall. 5 a complete series of steps in a dance. 6 one of a series of rungs or small graded platforms that allow one to climb or walk from one level to another. 7 pl a flight of stairs. 8 pl a stepladder:—vb (**stepped**, **step'ping**) to walk:—**out of step** 1 out of time with others in performing a regular movement. 2 behaving or thinking differently from others:—**step out** to move boldly or quickly forward:—**step up** to increase:—**take steps** to take action.

step'child n the child of a husband or wife by a previous marriage:—also **step'daughter**, **step'father**, **step'mother**, **step'son**.

step'ladder n a portable self-supporting ladder.

ste'reotyped adj fixed and unchanging.

ster'ile adj 1 bearing no fruit or children, barren. 2 germ-free:—n **steril'ity**.

ster'ilize vb 1 to make sterile. 2 to get rid of germs (by boiling, etc).

ster'ling n British coinage:—adj genuine, of worth.

stern[1] adj severe, strict, harsh.

steth'oscope n an instrument by means of which one can listen to the sound of another's breathing or heartbeats.

stew vb to boil slowly in little liquid in a closed vessel:—n stewed meat and vegetables.

stew'ard n 1 one paid to manage another's land or property. 2 a manservant on a ship or airplane. 3 an official at a concert, race meeting, show, etc:—f **stew'ardess**.

stick[1] vb (pt, pp **stuck**) 1 to pierce or stab. 2 to fasten or be fastened to, as with glue. 3 to be unable to move.

stick[2] n 1 a rod, a long thin piece of wood, espe one carried when walking. 2 a bar of toffee, etc.

stick'y adj 1 smeared with glue, etc, for fixing to other things. 2 tending to fasten on by sticking. 3 (inf) difficult.

stiff adj 1 hard to bend. 2 firm. 3 unable to move easily. 4 cold and severe in manner. 5 difficult.

sti'fle vb 1 to smother. 2 to prevent from expressing. 3 to keep down by force.

stile n a set of steps over a fence or wall.

still[1] adj 1 at rest, motionless. 2 calm, silent:—n a single photograph out of a series taken by a movie camera:—vb to make still:—adv 1 even so. 2 up to this moment.

still[2] n an apparatus for distilling spirits.

still life n (pl **still lives**) inanimate objects (e.g. fruit, ornaments, etc) as subjects for painting.

still'y adj (lit) silent, peaceful.

stilt n one of a pair of poles with footrests so that one can walk some height above the ground.

stilt'ed adj 1 unnatural or pompous in manner. 2 awkwardly expressed.

stim'ulant n something that increases energy for a time:—also adj.

stim'ulate vb 1 to rouse or make more alert, active, etc. 2 to stir up, cause:—adj **stim'ulating**.

stim'ulus n (pl **stim'uli**) something that arouses one's feelings or excites one to action.

sting n 1 a sharp-pointed defensive organ of certain animals or insects by means of which they can inject poison into an attacker. 2 in plants, a hair containing poison. 3 the pain caused by a sting. 4 any sharp pain:—vb (pt, pp **stung**). 1 to pierce or wound with a sting. 2 to pierce painfully with a sharp point. 3 to drive or provoke (a person) to act.

stink vb (pt **stank** or **stunk**, pp **stunk**) to give off an unpleasant smell:—n an unpleasant smell.

stint vb to give or allow only a small amount of:—n limit, a set amount of work.

stir vb (**stirred**, **stir'ring**) 1 to move or set in motion. 2 to arouse:—n excitement, noisy movement, a sensation.

stir'ring adj rousing, exciting.

stir'rup n a metal foot support hung from the saddle for a horse-rider.

stitch n 1 a single complete movement of the needle in knitting, sewing, etc. 2 the thread, wool, etc, used in such a movement. 3 a sharp pain in the side as a result of running, etc:—vb to join by stitches.

stock n 1 the main stem of a plant, the trunk of a tree. 2 the families from which one is descended. 3 the wooden handle of a gun. 4 goods kept for selling. 5 the animals of a farm. 6 shares in a business. 7 liquid in which marrow bones, vegetables, etc, have been boiled. 8 pl (old) a frame with holes for the hands and feet into which lawbreakers could be fastened for punishment. 9 pl the wooden frame on which a ship rests while being built:—adj always in use or ready for use:—vb to provide with necessary goods, to keep a store of.

stock'ing n a close-fitting covering for the foot and leg.

stock'-still adj motionless, completely still.

stock'y adj short and broad.

stodg'y adj 1 dull. 2 (of food) heavy or hard to digest.

stoke vb to put fuel on a fire.

stole[1] n a long scarf worn round the shoulders by women.

stole[2] pt of **steal**.

sto'len pp of **steal**:—also adj.

stol'id adj dull, not easily moved, impassive:—n **stolid'ity**.

stomach [stum'-ak] n 1 the bag-like bodily organ that receives and digests food. 2 courage:—vb to bear with, to put up with.

stone n 1 a hard mass of rock. 2 a piece of rock, a pebble. 3 the hard center of some fruits. 4 a precious stone or gem. 6 a measure of weight (14 pounds):—*adj* made of stone:—*vb* 1 to throw stones at. 2 to remove the stones from (fruit).

Stone Age n an early period in history during which humans made tools, weapons, etc, of stone.

ston'y *adj* 1 like stone. 2 covered with stones. 3 hard, unsympathetic.

stood *pt* of **stand**.

stool n a low backless seat.

stoop vb 1 to bend forward and downward. 2 to agree to do something unworthy, to give in:—n a downward bending of the head and shoulders.

stop vb (**stopped'**, **stop'ping**) 1 to cease or prevent from moving or doing something. 2 to come or bring to a standstill. 3 to block or close up:—n 1 a pause. 2 a place where a bus, etc, halts to pick up passengers. 3 time spent standing still or doing nothing. 4 a punctuation mark at the end of a sentence (.). 5 one of the knobs controlling the flow of air in the pipes of an organ, so regulating the sounds produced.

stop'page n 1 a halt. 2 a ceasing of work. 3 something blocking a tube or pipe.

stop'per n something closing a small hole (e.g. in the neck of a bottle).

stop'watch n an accurate watch, used for timing events, that can be started or stopped at will.

stor'age n 1 the putting of goods in warehouses, etc, until they are required. 2 the storing of data in a computer memory, etc.

store n 1 a large quantity. 2 a supply of goods that can be drawn on when necessary. 3 a room or building where such goods are kept. 4 a place where many different kinds of articles are sold:—vb 1 to keep for future use. 2 to put in warehouses. 3 to put (data) into a computer memory or on to a storage device.

store'keeper n one who owns a store where goods are sold.

stork n a white wading bird of the heron family, with long legs and bill.

storm n 1 a spell of very bad weather (e.g. rain, wind, snow, etc). 2 a display of violent emotion, public anger:—vb 1 to make a sudden violent attack on a defended place. 2 to be angry. 3 to rain, snow hard.

storm'y *adj* 1 liable to or troubled by storms. 2 violent, marked by angry feelings.

stor'y¹ n an account of events, real or imagined.

stor'y² n any floor of a building from the first floor upward.

stout *adj* 1 strong or thick. 2 fat. 3 brave and resolute:— n a strong dark beer.

stove n a closed-in fireplace or metal apparatus for warming a room, cooking, etc.

stow'away n one who hides on a ship, etc, so as to travel without paying the fare.

strad'dle vb 1 to spread the legs wide apart. 2 to sit or stand with a leg on either side of.

strag'gle vb 1 to move in widely scattered formation. 2 to fall behind the main body.

strag'gler n one who wanders from the main body.

straight [strāt] *adj* 1 not curving or crooked. 2 honest. 3 (*of a drink*) not diluted:—*adv* directly, at once.

straight'en vb to make straight.

straightfor'ward *adj* 1 simple, not complicated. 2 honest.

strain'¹ vb 1 to stretch tightly. 2 to make the utmost effort. 3 to harm by trying to do too much with. 4 to put in a sieve to draw liquid off:—n 1 violent effort. 2 harm caused to muscles, etc, by straining them

strain² n breed, stock.

strained *adj* 1 stretched too far. 2 not natural.

strain'er n a small sieve or filter.

strait *adj* narrow, strict:—n 1 a strip of water between two land masses. 2 *pl* distress, difficulties.

strand' n land at the edge of water:—vb 1 to run aground. 2 to leave helpless without money, friends, etc.

strand² n one of the threads of a rope or string.

strange *adj* 1 unusual, odd. 2 unfamiliar. 3 peculiar, uncomfortable, unwell.

stran'ger n 1 one previously unknown. 2 a new arrival to a place, town, etc. 3 one who is unfamiliar with or ignorant of something.

strang'le vb to kill by pressing the throat tightly, to choke.

strap n a narrow band of leather or other material:—vb (**strapped'**, **strap'ping**) to fasten with a strap.

strap'ping *adj* tall and strong.

strata see **stratum**.

strat'egy n 1 the art of dealing with a situation in such a way as to gain from it the greatest advantage possible. 2 in war, the planning of a campaign.

straw n 1 the dried stalks of corn, etc. 2 one such stalk or something like it. 3 something of no worth.

straw'berry n 1 a wild or garden plant. 2 the juicy red fruit it bears.

stray vb to wander, to lose the way:—*adj* 1 lost, off the right path. 2 occasional:—n a lost or wandering person or animal.

streak n 1 a long narrow mark or stain, a stripe, a narrow band. 2 part of one's character:—vb to mark with streaks.

streak'y *adj* consisting of or marked with streaks.

stream n 1 a current of any liquid or gas. 2 a small river. 3 a succession of people moving in one direction:—vb 1 to move in a stream. 2 to flow freely.

stream'er n 1 a long narrow flag. 2 a narrow strip of ribbon or colored paper for flying in the wind.

street n a road lined with buildings in a town or city.

street'car n an electrically powered vehicle running on rails laid in the streets.

strength n 1 bodily power. 2 might, force. 3 the number of persons of a class, army, etc, present or on the roll.

strength'en vb to make or become stronger.

stren'uous *adj* requiring much energy or vigor.

stress vb 1 to point out the importance of. 2 to emphasize with the voice:—n 1 importance. 2 strain, pressure. 3 the special emphasis given in speaking to particular syllables, words, etc.

stretch vb 1 to make or become longer or broader by pulling. 2 to draw out to the fullest extent. 3 to put or reach out:— n a full length of time or space.

stretch'er n a light frame for carrying a sick or wounded person.

strict *adj* 1 severe. 2 demanding obedience to rules.

stride vb (*pt* **strode**) to walk with long steps:—n a long step.

strife n open disagreement, quarreling, fighting.

strike vb (*pt*, *pp* **struck**) 1 to hit. 2 (*of a clock*) to sound the hours or quarters. 3 to stop work to try to make employers grant better pay or conditions. 4 to come suddenly to mind. 5 to make and stamp (a coin or medal). 6 to take down (a flag or tent). 7 to light (a match) by rubbing. 8 to come upon by chance:—n a stopping of work.

strik'er n a worker on strike.

strik'ing *adj* attracting attention because fine or unusual.

string n 1 a cord or strong thread. 2 the cord or wire of a musical instrument. 3 a number of persons or things, one following the other).

strip *vb* (**stripped′, strip′ping**) 1 to pull off the outer covering. 2 to undress. 3 to take everything from:—*n* 1 a long narrow piece. 2 a runway.

stripe *n* a band or streak of different colour from those on either side of it.

striped *adj* having stripes.

strive *vb* (*pt* **strove**, *pp* **striv′en**) to try as hard as possible, to struggle.

stroke[1] *n* 1 a blow. 2 a sudden turn of luck, good or bad. 3 a sudden attack of illness, esp one affecting the brain. 4 a line made by a pen, pencil, etc.

stroke[2] *vb* to rub gently with the hand in one direction.

stroll *vb* to walk in a leisurely way:—*n* a short leisurely walk.

stroll′er *n* a wheeled chair for a small child in which it may be pushed.

strong *adj* 1 powerful. 2 healthy. 3 possessing bodily power or vigour.

strong′-minded *adj* determined.

struc′ture *n* 1 a building. 2 anything consisting of parts put together according to a plan. 3 the way in which a thing is put together:—*vb* 1 to organize, arrange. 2 to build up.

strug′gle *vb* 1 to try hard. 2 to fight:—*n* 1 a hard effort. 2 a fight.

strut *vb* (**strut′ted, strut′ting**) to walk stiffly, as if trying to look important.

stub *n* 1 a short piece left when the rest is cut off or used up. 2 the retained section of a check, ticket, etc, a counterfoil:—*vb* (**stubbed′, stub′bing**) to strike (the toes) against by accident.

stub′ble *n* 1 the stumps of the corn stalks left in the ground after reaping. 2 the short bristly hairs that grow on a man's face after he has shaved:—*adj* **stub′bly**.

stub′born *adj* unwilling to change one's point of view, not ready to give in, obstinate.

stud[1] *n* a nail with a large head or knob. 2 a fastener with a head at each end for linking two buttonholes:—*vb* (**stud′ded, stud′ding**) 1 to decorate with many small ornaments. 2 to cover with.

stud[2] *n* a number of horses kept for breeding.

stu′dent *n* one who studies.

stu′dio *n* 1 the room in which a painter, photographer, etc, works. 2 a building in which films are made. 3 a workshop in which records are made or from which programs are broadcast.

stu′dious *adj* fond of studying.

stud′y *vb* 1 to read about or examine in order to obtain knowledge. 2 to examine closely, to think deeply about:—*n* 1 the obtaining of information, esp by reading. 2 a subject studied. 3 an office, a room set aside for reading and learning. 4 a work of art done to improve one's skill.

stuff *n* 1 the material of which something is made. 2 materials, things:—*vb* 1 to fill full. 2 to fill something hollow with another material.

stuff′ing *n* 1 material used to stuff something hollow. 2 a paste of breadcrumbs, minced meat, etc, put inside fowls, etc, when cooking.

stuff′y *adj* hot and airless.

stum′ble *vb* 1 to trip and nearly fall. 2 to make an error, to do wrong. 3 to come upon by chance.

stump *n* 1 the part of a tree left above ground when the rest is cut down. 2 the part of a limb, tooth, that remains after the larger part is cut off or destroyed:—*vb* 1 to walk heavily. 2 (*inf*) to ask someone a question that he or she is unable to answer. 3 to campaign for an election.

stun *vb* (**stunned′, stun′ning**) 1 to knock senseless. 2 to amaze.

stunt *n* 1 a trick to display special skill or daring. 2 anything done to attract attention or gain publicity.

stunt′ed *adj* undersized.

stu′pefy *vb* 1 to make stupid, to make the senses less acute. 2 to amaze.

stu′pid *adj* foolish, not intelligent, slow to understand:—*n* **stupid′ity**.

stur′dy *adj* strong, well-built.

stut′ter *vb* to speak with difficulty, to repeat the first sound of a word several times before saying the whole word:—*n* a stammer.

sty[1] *n* an enclosure in which pigs are kept.

sty[2] *n* an inflamed swelling on the eyelid.

style *n* 1 manner of doing anything. 2 a way of writing, painting, etc, by which works of art can be recognized as the work of a particular artist, school, or period. 3 a fashion. 4 elegance.

styl′ish *adj* well-dressed, smart, fashionable.

sub- *prefix* under, below.

subcon′scious *adj* not fully aware of what one is doing:—*n* mental processes that go on without one's being fully aware of them.

subdivi′sion *n* a part of a larger part.

subdue′ *vb* to conquer, to force to be tame or obedient.

subdued′ *adj* not bright, not loud.

sub′ject *adj* 1 ruled by another. 2 liable to:—*n* 1 one who owes loyalty to a ruler or government. 2 that about which something is said or written. 3 something studied. 4 in a clause or sentence, the word with which the verb agrees grammatically:—*vb* **subject′** 1 to bring under the power of. 2 to expose to.

subjec′tive *adj* having to do with one's own ideas and feelings rather than with objects outside one.

subject matter *n* the ideas under consideration.

sublime′ *adj* noble, awe-inspiring, grand and lofty.

sub′marine *adj* under the surface of the sea:—*n* a ship that can travel under the surface of the sea.

submerge′ *vb* to put or sink under water:—*n* **submer′gence**.

submis′sion *n* surrender, obedience.

submis′sive *adj* willing to accept orders, ready to give in.

submit′ *vb* (**submit′ted, submit′ting**) 1 to give in. 2 to put forward for consideration.

subor′dinate *adj* 1 less important. 2 of lower rank:—*n* one who is lower in rank, one who is working under the orders of another:—*vb* 1 to place in a lower rank, to put under the command of. 2 to regard as less important:—*n* **subordina′tion**.

subscribe′ *vb* 1 to sign one's name under. 2 to agree with. 3 to give or promise to give money to a fund or collection:—*n* **subscrib′er**.

subscrip′tion *n* 1 a signature. 2 a sum of money given to a fund or collection.

sub′sequent *adj* following, later.

subside′ *vb* 1 to sink gradually down. 2 to become less, to disappear gradually.

sub′sidence *n* a gradual sinking down, esp of land.

subsid′iary *adj* of less importance.

sub′sidize *vb* to pay a subsidy to.

sub′sidy *n* money paid by the government to certain groups, trades, etc, to enable them to provide the public with necessary services without losing money.

subsis′tence *n* existence, that which is necessary to support life.

sub′soil *n* the layer of earth just below the surface.

sub′stance *n* 1 the material of which a thing is made. 2 that which really exists (not what is imagined). 3 the chief ideas in a speech or written work. 4 (*fml*) wealth.

substan'tial *adj* **1** really existing. **2** solid. **3** fairly large or important.

sub'stitute *vb* to put in place of:—*n* a person or thing put in the place of another:—*n* **substitu'tion**.

subtle [sut'-l] *adj* **1** cunning, clever. **2** difficult to understand completely. **3** faint or delicate.

subtract' *vb* to take (one number) from another:—*n* **subtrac'tion**.

sub'urb *n* an outlying part of a city:—*adj* **subur'ban**.

sub'way *n* **1** an underground passage. **2** an underground railroad.

succeed' *vb* **1** to do what one has attempted or desired to do. **2** to come after, to follow in order and take the place of.

success' *n* **1** the doing of what one has attempted or desired to do. **2** a favorable result or outcome. **3** a person or thing that does as well as was hoped or expected.

success'ful *adj* doing well, doing what was attempted or desired.

succes'sion *n* **1** a number of persons or things following one another in order. **2** the order in which people may inherit a title when it becomes vacant.

success'ive *adj* coming in order, following one after another.

success'or *n* one who comes after or takes the place of another.

suc'culent *adj* juicy.

succumb' *vb* **1** to give way to, to be overcome. **2** to die.

such *adj* of a like kind or degree, similar.

suc'tion *n* the act of sucking, the drawing up of a fluid into a tube, etc, by expelling the air so that the fluid fills the vacuum.

sud'den *adj* happening without warning, unexpected, hurried.

suds *npl* the froth on soapy water.

sue *vb* **1** to bring a case against in a court of law. **2** (*fml*) to beg for.

suede [swād] *n* a soft kind of leather made from undressed kidskin:—*also adj*.

suf'fer *vb* **1** to undergo pain or great anxiety. **2** to experience or undergo. **3** to put up with.

suf'fering *n* pain, great anxiety.

suffi'ciency *n* a big enough supply.

suffi'cient *adj* enough.

suf'fix *n* a syllable added to the end of a word (e.g. -ness, -ly).

suf'focate *vb* **1** to choke for lack of air. **2** to kill by preventing from breathing:—*n* **suffoca'tion**.

su'gar *n* a sweet substance manufactured from sugar cane, beet, etc.

sugar beet *n* a plant with a root from which sugar is obtained.

sugar'cane *n* a tall stiff reed from which sugar is obtained.

su'gary *adj* sweet.

suggest' *vb* **1** to put forward. **2** to hint. **3** to cause an idea to come into the mind.

sugges'tion *n* **1** a proposal. **2** a hint.

sugges'tive *adj* putting ideas into the mind.

su'icide *n* **1** the deliberate killing of oneself. **2** one who kills himself or herself deliberately.

suit *vb* **1** to please or satisfy. **2** to go well with. **3** to look nice on:—*n* **1** a set of clothes of the same material. **2** one of the four sets (hearts, clubs, etc) in a pack of playing cards. **3** the taking of a case to a court of law:—**follow suit 1** to play a card from the same suit. **2** to do the same as or follow the example of another.

suit'able *adj* what is wanted for the purpose, fitting the occasion.

suit'case *n* a portable traveling bag for clothes.

suite [sweet] *n* **1** a set of rooms or furniture. **2** a series of connected pieces of music.

sul'fate *n* a salt of sulfuric acid.

sul'fur *n* a yellow nonmetallic element.

sulfu'ric *adj* having to do with or containing sulfur.

sul'furous *adj* having to do with or like sulfur.

sulk *vb* to behave in an ill-humored, unfriendly way, to refuse to speak to others because of ill-temper.

sulks *npl* a silent ill-humored mood.

sulk'y *adj* ill-natured, not mixing with others because of ill-humor.

sul'len *adj* ill-natured, silently bad-tempered.

sul'ly *vb* to dirty, to stain, to spoil.

sul'try *adj* very hot and close.

sum *n* **1** the answer obtained by adding several numbers together. **2** the total or entire amount, esp of money. **3** a problem in arithmetic:—*vb* (**summed'**, **sum'ming**) to add up:—**sum up** to summarize.

sum'marize *vb* to give a brief account of the main points.

sum'mary *n* a brief account of the main points:—*adj* **1** short. **2** done quickly.

sum'mer *n* the warmest season of the year.

sum'mit *n* the highest point, the top.

sum'mon *vb* **1** to call upon to appear before an official. **2** to call upon to do something.

sum'mons *n* an order to appear for trial by a court of law:—*vb* to present with such an order.

sump'tuous *adj* splendid, very expensive, luxurious.

sun *n* **1** the heavenly body that gives light and heat to the earth and other planets in the same system. **2** the warmth or light given out by the sun.

sun'burn *n* a darkening of the skin's color caused by exposure to the sun:—*also vb*.

Sun'day *n* the first day of the week.

sun'der *vb* (*fml*) to part, to separate.

sun'dial *n* an instrument that tells the time by casting the shadow of an indicator on a face marked with the hours.

sun'dry *adj* (*fml*) several, of different kinds:—*npl* **sun'dries** odds and ends of different kinds.

sun'flower *n* a tall plant with a large yellow flower.

sun'ny *adj* **1** brightly lit by the sun. **2** cheerful, happy.

sun'rise *n* the first appearance of the sun in the morning.

sun'set *n* the disappearance of the sun below the horizon in the evening.

sun'shine *n* **1** the light or warmth of the sun. **2** cheerfulness.

sun'stroke *n* a severe illness caused by the effect of the sun's heat on the body.

super- *prefix* above, over.

superb' *adj* magnificent, excellent.

supercil'ious *adj* disdainful, scornful.

superfi'cial *adj* **1** on the surface. **2** not deeply felt or thought about. **3** shallow, incapable of deep thought or feeling:—*n* **superficial'ity**.

super'fluous *adj* more than enough, unnecessary:—*n* **superflu'ity**.

superhu'man *adj* more than human.

superintend' *vb* to watch others to see that they do their job properly, to direct, to be in charge of.

superinten'dent *n* **1** one who superintends. **2** a high-ranking police officer.

supe'rior *adj* **1** higher in rank. **2** better:—*n* **1** one higher in rank. **2** one better than others:—*n* **superior'ity**.

super'lative *adj* **1** excellent, above all others in quality. **2** expressing the highest degree.

su'perman *n* a man of extraordinary powers, the imagined perfect human being of the future.

su'permarket *n* a large store selling (usu by self-service) food and household goods.

supernat'ural adj 1 not to be explained by natural causes. 2 caused by direct divine intervention in human affairs:— n immortal beings existing outside the known universe and having the power to intervene in human affairs.

superson'ic adj faster than sound.

supersti'tion n 1 a tendency to believe that certain human beings or objects have more than natural powers. 2 belief in magic, luck, etc.

supersti'tious adj believing in magic, etc.

su'pervise vb 1 to watch others to see that they do their work properly. 2 to be in charge of:—n **supervi'sion**:— n **supervi'sor**.

sup'per n a light evening meal.

supplant' vb to gain the place or position of another, esp by deceit.

sup'ple adj bending or moving easily.

sup'plement n 1 something added to make up what is lacking. 2 an addition:—vb **supplement'** to make additions to.

supplemen'tary adj given in addition, given to make up what is lacking.

supply' vb to provide what is needed:—n 1 a store of what is needed. 2 pl stores.

support' vb 1 to help to hold up. 2 to give help or encouragement to. 3 to provide the necessities of life for. 4 o put up with:—n 1 a prop. 2 assistance, encouragement. 3 a person or thing that supports.

support'er n one who helps or encourages.

suppose' vb 1 to believe to be true without sure evidence. 2 to imagine. 3 to think probable.

suppress' vb 1 to put down, to crush. 2 to prevent from being known:—n **suppres'sion**.

supreme' adj 1 highest in power or authority. 2 greatest.

sure adj 1 certain. 2 convinced of. 3 unfailing.

sure'ly adv without doubt.

sure'ty n something given into the possession of another by a debtor until such time as the money due is paid.

surf n the foamy water caused by waves breaking on a sloping shore:—vb to ride on the surf on a special board:— n **surf'er**.

sur'face n 1 the outside or top part of anything. 2 outside appearance:—vb to rise to the surface.

sur'feit n too much of anything.

surge vb to rise, to well up, as a wave.

sur'geon n a doctor skilled in surgery.

sur'gery n the art or science of curing disease by cutting the body. 2 a doctor's consulting room.

sur'ly adj gloomy and ill-humored:—n **sur'liness**.

surmount' vb to overcome.

sur'name n a person's last name.

surpass' vb to do better than.

sur'plus n the amount by which anything is more than is required.

surprise' n 1 the feeling caused by what is sudden or unexpected. 2 a sudden or unexpected event, gift, piece of news, etc:—vb 1 to come upon when not expected. 2 to take unawares, to startle, to astonish.

surren'der vb 1 to stop fighting and accept the enemy's terms, to give up. 2 to hand over:—also n.

surround' vb to go, put, or be on all sides of.

surround'ings npl the objects or country around a person or place.

survey' vb 1 to look over. 2 to look at carefully. 3 to measure an area of land and make a plan of it:—n **sur'vey** 1 a general view. 2 the measuring of a piece of land.

surviv'al n 1 act of surviving. 2 a person or thing that has lived on from a past age.

survive' vb 1 to live on after. 2 to continue to live or exist.

survi'vor n one who has lived on, esp after a disaster.

suscep'tible adj easily influenced or affected by:—n **suscepti-bili'ity**.

suspect' vb 1 to think something is the case but have no proof. 2 to mistrust, to doubt the truth or genuineness of. 3 to believe to be guilty:—n **sus'pect** one who is suspected:— adj **sus'pect** not worthy of trust.

suspend' vb 1 to hang from. 2 to cause to stop for a time.

suspend'ers npl crossed straps for holding up pants.

suspense' n uncertainty or anxiety about what may happen in the future.

suspi'cion n a feeling of doubt or mistrust.

suspi'cious adj doubtful, mistrustful.

sustain' vb 1 to keep up, to support. 2 to give strength to. 3 to keep in existence over a long period. 4 to undergo.

sus'tenance n food, nourishment.

swag'ger vb to walk proudly, to behave boastfully:— also n.

swal'low¹ vb 1 to draw down the throat and into the stomach. 2 to enclose in something bigger. 3 to believe without question:—n the act of swallowing.

swal'low² n a bird with long wings and a forked tail that flies to a warmer country in winter.

swamp n wet, marshy ground:—vb 1 to flood. 2 to overwhelm by greater numbers or strength.

swamp'y adj soft and wet, marshy.

swan n a long-necked bird of the duck family.

swap vb (**swapped'**, **swap'ping**) to exchange (one thing for another).

swarm n 1 a large number of insects (e.g. bees) moving as a group. 2 a large closely packed crowd:—vb 1 to come together in large numbers. 2 (of bees, etc) to leave the hive in a body. 3 to climb, gripping with the arms and legs.

swar'thy adj dark-skinned.

swat vb (**swat'ted**, **swat'ting**) to hit sharply, to crush.

swath n a strip of cut grass or corn.

swathe [swäth] vb 1 to wrap up in bandages or clothing:— n **swathe** or **swath**.

sway vb 1 to move with a rocking motion from side to side or backward and forward. 2 to rule, to have influence over:— n 1 a rocking movement. 2 control, rule.

swear vb (pt **swore**, pp **sworn**) 1 to promise solemnly to tell the truth, calling on God as witness to one's good faith. 2 to declare something is true. 3 to use bad words or language insulting to God, to use words that are considered offensive and socially unacceptable.

sweat n the moisture that oozes from the body when it is overheated, perspiration:—vb to perspire.

sweat'er n a heavy woolen jersey.

sweat'y adj (inf) damp with perspiration.

sweep vb (pt, pp **swept**) 1 to clean with a brush or broom. 2 to move over swiftly and smoothly. 3 to remove with an extensive or curving movement:—n 1 an extensive or curving movement. 2 a quick look over. 3 one who cleans chimneys:—**sweep the board** to win everything offered or at stake.

sweep'ing adj 1 wide, extensive. 2 not taking sufficient account of exceptions.

sweet adj 1 tasting like honey or sugar. 2 having a pleasing smell. 3 pleasing to the senses. 4 gentle and likeable. 5 pretty:—n 1 a sweetmeat. 2 a pudding:—adv **sweet'ly**.

sweet'en vb to make or become sweet.

sweet'heart *n* one dearly loved, a lover.

swell *vb* (*pp* **swoll'en**) **1** to grow larger. **2** to make or become louder. **3** to bulge out. **4** (*of the sea*) to rise and fall in large waves that do not break:—*n* movement of the sea in large waves that do not break.

swell'ing *n* a lump raised for a time on the body by a bruise, infected cut, etc.

swel'ter *vb* to be very hot:—*adj* **swel'tering**.

swerve *vb* to turn or move suddenly to one side:—*also n*.

swift *adj* quick-moving, speedy:—*n* a bird like the swallow.

swill *vb* n liquid food for pigs.

swim *vb* (**swam**, **swim'ming**, *pp* **swum**) **1** to move through the water by moving the arms and legs. **2** to float in or on the top of. **3** to be dizzy:—*n* act of swimming, a bathe spent swimming:—*n* **swim'mer**.

swimming pool *n* an artificial pond made for swimming in.

swin'dle *vb* to cheat:—*n* a deception intended to cheat people, a fraud.

swind'ler *n* a cheat, one who tricks people out of money.

swine *n* (*pl* **swine**) **1** a pig. **2** (*inf*) a very nasty person.

swing *vb* (*pt, pp* **swung**) **1** to move to and fro, esp when suspended from above. **2** to whirl round. **3** to turn round when at anchor. **4** to walk quickly with a swaying movement:—*n* **1** a seat suspended by ropes, etc, on which a child can swing to and fro. **2** a swinging movement. **3** a long-range blow given with a curved arm.

swirl *vb* to flow or move with a circular motion:—*n* a circular motion of water.

swish *n* the sound made by a light or thin object moving through the air.

switch *n* **1** an easily bent stick. **2** a small lever for turning on and off electric current:—*vb* **1** to hit with a switch. **2** to turn electric current (on or off). **3** to change suddenly.

swiv'el *n* a ring that turns freely round a pin, so that what the one is connected to can remain stationary while the other turns:—*vb* to turn around, as on a swivel.

swoon *vb* to faint:—*n* a fainting turn.

swoop *vb* **1** to fly down upon with a sudden swift movement. **2** to come upon swiftly and suddenly:—*n* **1** a sudden downward rush. **2** a sudden attack.

sword [sord] *n* a weapon with a long blade and sharp point for cutting or thrusting.

syl'lable *n* a part of a word or a word containing one vowel sound.

syl'labus *n* a plan for a course of studies, giving subjects to be studied, times of classes, etc.

sylph'-like *adj* slim and graceful.

sym'bol *n* **1** an emblem or sign made to stand for or represent something else. **2** a sign that all recognize as bearing a certain meaning.

symbol'ic *adj* standing for or representing something else:—*adv* **symbol'ically**.

sym'bolism *n* the use of symbols.

sym'bolize *vb* to stand as a sign for.

symmet'rical *adj* **1** having a balanced or regular design. **2** graceful because the parts are in pleasing proportion to each other and to the whole.

sym'metry *n* **1** sameness between the two halves of a design. **2** a pleasing similarity or contrast between parts, beauty resulting from graceful proportions.

sympathet'ic *adj* showing or feeling understanding or pity.

sym'pathize *vb* **1** to feel with and for another. **2** to be in agreement with.

sym'pathy *n* **1** understanding of the sorrow or distress of another, pity. **2** agreement with the opinion of another.

sym'phony *n* a piece of music written for a full orchestra:—*adj* **symphon'ic**.

symp'tom *n* **1** a sign or mark by which something can be recognized. **2** one of the signs by which a doctor is able to recognize the disease affecting a patient:—*adj* **symptoma'tic**.

syn'agogue *n* a Jewish church.

syn'chronize *vb* **1** to happen or cause to happen at the same time. **2** to set to exactly the same time.

syn'copate *vb* to change the rhythm of music by beginning or ending notes slightly sooner or later than is strictly correct.

syn'dicate *n* **1** a group of persons or companies who are working together for business reasons or financial gain.

syn'onym *n* a word having the same or nearly the same meaning as another word.

synon'ymous *adj* having the same meaning.

synop'sis *n* a summary, a short account of the main happenings or ideas in a book.

synthet'ic *adj* made or put together by artificial means, not natural.

syringe *n* a tube filled with a piston by means of which fluid can be drawn up or squirted out:—*vb* to squirt or spray with a syringe.

syr'up *n* **1** a thick sweet-tasting liquid. **2** the liquid obtained when refining cane sugar.

syr'upy *adj* thick and sweet.

sys'tem *n* **1** a method by which a number of parts of different kinds are made to work together as a unified whole. **2** a regular method of doing things. **3** a plan.

systemat'ic *adj* methodical, arranged in an orderly or reasonable manner, following a plan.

T

tab *n* a small piece of paper, cloth, etc, sticking out from something larger, a small flap.

tab′by *n* a female cat.

ta′ble *n* 1 an article of furniture with legs and a flat top, used for placing or resting things on. 2 a list of figures, names, facts, etc, arranged in columns.

tableau *n* (*pl* tableaux [tab′-lōz]) a scene in which people stand motionless as if figures in a picture.

ta′blespoon *n* a large spoon used for serving at table or as a measure in cooking.

tab′let *n* 1 a piece of cardboard or flat piece of metal or stone with some writing or signs on it. 2 a small flat slab. 3 a pill.

tab′loid *n* a small-format newspaper usu with emphasis on photographs and news in condensed form.

taboo′ *adj* not to be touched or used, forbidden for religious reasons or because it is against social custom:—*n* an order not to touch or use something.

ta′citurn *adj* speaking little, silent by nature:—*n* tacitur′nity.

tack *n* 1 a small sharp nail with a broad head. 2 a long loose stitch. 3 the zigzag course of a sailing ship against the wind:—*vb* 1 to nail with tacks. 2 to sew with long loose stitches. 3 to change course to catch the wind.

tack′le *n* 1 all the equipment needed for some sport or game. 2 all the things necessary for a task:—*vb* 1 to struggle with, to seize and pull down. 2 (*in football*) to prevent from advancing with the ball. 3 to try to do.

tact *n* the ability to speak or behave without hurting the feelings of others, consideration:—*adjs* tact′ful, tact′less.

tac′tical *adj* having to do with tactics.

tac′tics *npl* any actions intended to gain an immediate advantage.

tad′pole *n* the young of a frog, toad, etc, just after it has come out of the egg.

tag *n* 1 the metal point at the end of a shoelace. 2 an address label:—*vb* (tagged′, tag′ging) to fasten on.

tail *n* 1 a long hanging part of an animal's body, situated at the end of the spine. 2 the back part of anything.

tail end *n* the last or back part.

tail′or *n* one who makes clothes, esp for men:—*vb* to make clothes.

tails *npl* the reverse side of a coin.

taint *vb* to spoil or make bad:—*n* 1 a stain. 2 a mark of shame or disgrace.

take *vb* (*pt* took, *pp* tak′en) 1 to seize or grasp. 2 to receive or accept. 3 to capture. 4 to carry. 5 to travel by (bus), etc. 6 to eat. 7 to be infected by. 8 to require (numbers, time, material, etc):—**take after** to be like:—**take down** to write (notes, etc):—**take for** to think to be:—**take in** 1 to deceive. 2 to understand. 3 to make (a garment) smaller:—**take off** 1 to remove. 2 to leave the ground when beginning to fly. 3 to imitate mockingly:—**take over** to get control of:—**take place** to happen:—**take to** to begin to like:—**take up** 1 to begin to do or study.

tak′ings *n* money received for goods, admission, etc.

talc′um *n* a fine powder made from talc.

tale *n* 1 a story. 2 (*old*) a number.

tale′-bearer, tale′-teller *ns* one who reports another's wrongdoings in order to get him or her into trouble.

tal′ent *n* special ability or skill

tal′ented *adj* very clever.

tal′isman *n* (*pl* tal′ismans) an object supposed to possess magic powers.

talk [tåk] *vb* to speak:—*n* 1 a conversation. 2 a lecture. 3 gossip:—**talk over** to discuss.

talk′ative *adj* fond of talking.

tall *adj* 1 high. 2 above the usual height.

tal′ly *n* 1 an account. 2 formerly, an account kept by cutting notches on wood. 3 a score or count:—*vb* to agree with, to fit.

tal′on *n* the claw of a bird of prey.

tambourine′ *n* a small one-sided drum with rattling metal disks around its sides, played by hand.

tame *adj* 1 not wild. 2 trained to be obedient. 3 dull:—*vb* to make tame.

tam′per *vb* to meddle with, to interfere with dishonestly or unlawfully.

tan *n* 1 bark of trees crushed for use in preparing leather. 2 a light-brown color. 3 suntan:—*vb* (tanned′, tan′ning) 1 to treat animal skins so as to turn them into leather. 2 to make or become brown from sunburn:—*adj* light brown in color.

tan′dem *adj* one behind the other:—*n* a bicycle for two persons, one sitting behind the other.

tang *n* a sharp taste.

tan′gent *n* a straight line touching a circle but not cutting.

tan′gible *adj* 1 able to be touched. 2 real.

tan′gle *vb* 1 to interweave in a confused way, difficult to undo. 2 to muddle:—*n* 1 a mass of confusedly interwoven thread, string, etc. 2 a muddle, a complication.

tank *n* 1 a large container for storing water, oil, etc. 2 a fighting vehicle protected by thick metal plates.

tank′er *n* a cargo ship with tanks for carrying oil.

tanned *adj* made brown by the sun.

tantrum *n* a fit of bad temper or ill-humor.

tap¹ *n* 1 a short pipe containing a stopper that can be opened by a handle to allow liquid to flow out. 2 a stopper:—*vb* (tapped′, tap′ping) 1 to draw liquid out of. 2 to obtain information from.

tap² *vb* (tapped′, tap′ping) 1 to strike lightly. 2 to knock gently:—*also n*.

tape 1 a long narrow strip of cloth, paper, or sticky material. 2 a sensitized strip for recording and transmitting sound or pictures:—*also vb*.

tape mea′sure *n* a strong tape of cloth, metal, etc, used for measuring.

ta′per *vb* to become narrow or thinner at one end.

tape record′er *n* a machine for recording and transmitting sounds on tape.

tap′estry *n* a large piece of cloth in which different colored threads are worked together to make a picture, sometimes hung on walls as a decoration.

tar *n* a thick black sticky substance obtained from wood or coal.

taran′tula *n* a large poisonous spider.

tar′dy *adj* (old) slow, late:—*n* tar′diness.

tar′get *n* 1 something set up for aiming or shooting at. 2 a goal or result that one hopes to achieve.

tar′iff *n* 1 the tax to be paid on an imported commodity. 2 a list of charges.

tar′mac, tarmaca′dam *ns* a road surface material made of tar and fragmented stone.

tar′nish *vb* 1 to make less bright, to discolor. 2 to spoil.

tarpaul′in *n* strong cloth or canvas covered with tar to make it waterproof.

tart¹ *n* a pastry containing jam or fruit.

tart² *adj* 1 sharp-tasting. 2 sour, biting, sarcastic.

tar'tan n a cloth with stripes and squares of different colors, esp. when worn as part of Scottish highland dress.

tar'tar n 1 a hard substance that forms on the teeth. 2 a hot-tempered person, a person who is hard to manage.

task n a piece of work to be done:—vb to lay upon as a burden.

tas'sel n an ornamental knot with loose threads hanging down from it.

taste n 1 the sense by which one judges whether food is pleasant or unpleasant. 2 the ability to distinguish what is fine, beautiful, or correct from what is not so. 3 the flavor of food when eaten:—vb 1 to eat to see whether pleasant or unpleasant. 2 to have a flavor (of).

taste'ful adj showing good taste or judgment.

taste'less adj 1 having no flavor. 2 showing bad taste or judgment.

tas'ty adj having a pleasing flavor.

tat'tered adj ragged.

tattoo' vb to make a colored design on the skin by pricking holes in it and filling them with colored matter:—also n.

taught pt of **teach**.

taunt vb to make fun of in order to hurt:—n a mocking or hurtful remark.

taut adj stretched tight.

tav'ern n an inn.

taw'dry adj showy but cheap or of bad quality.

taw'ny adj yellowish-brown.

tax n money paid to the government to help pay for public services:—vb 1 to raise a tax. 2 to charge a tax on. 3 to accuse. 4 to be a hard test for.

taxa'tion n 1 all the taxes paid. 2 the charging of taxes.

tax'i n an automobile for hire, esp one fitted with a machine (**tax'imeter**) showing the amount to be paid as a fare:—also **tax'i-cab**:—vb (of an airplane) to run along the ground.

tea n 1 a shrub found in India and China. 2 its leaves dried. 3 a drink made by pouring boiling water on dried tea leaves. 4 a light afternoon or evening meal.

teach vb (pt, pp **taught**) 1 to give information about. 2 to show how to do something. 3 to give lessons to.

teach'er n 1 one who teaches. 2 a schoolmaster or schoolmistress.

team n 1 a number of persons working together for the same purpose. 2 a set of players on one side in a game. 3 a number of horses, oxen, etc, harnessed together.

tear[1] [teer] n a drop of water appearing in or falling from the eyes.

tear[2] [tĕr]vb (pt **tore**, pp **torn**) 1 to pull apart or into pieces. 2 to pull with violence. 3 (inf) to rush:—n a hole or division made by tearing.

tear'ful adj weeping.

tease vb 1 to annoy by making fun of. 2 to pull apart wool, etc, into separate strands. 3 to comb wool to give it a hairy surface:—n one who annoys another by teasing.

tea'spoon n a small spoon for use with tea.

teat n 1 the part of the breast from which milk may be sucked or drawn. 2 a rubber attachment through which a baby sucks milk from a bottle.

tech'nical adj having to do with a particular art, science, or craft.

technical'ity n 1 a technical word or phrase. 2 a small detail or rule.

techni'cian n one skilled in a particular art or craft.

technique [tek-neek'] n the method of doing something that requires skill.

techno'logy n the study of methods of manufacturing:—n **techno'logist**.

ted'dy, ted'dy bear n a child's toy bear.

te'dious adj long and boring, tiresome.

te'dium n boredom, long-drawn-out dullness.

teem vb to be full of.

teen'ager n one aged between 13 and 19.

teens npl the ages from 13 to 19.

teeth see **tooth**.

teethe vb to grow one's first teeth.

teeto'tal adj taking no strong drink:—n **teeto'taler**.

tel'e- prefix far, at or to a distance.

tel'ephone n (abbr **phone**) an apparatus by means of which one may speak with a person at a distance by means of electric currents carried along wires:—vb to speak with or communicate by telephone.

teleph'onist n one who operates a telephone.

tel'escope n an instrument consisting of lenses set in a tube or tubes that, when looked through, makes distant objects appear larger:—vb 1 to slide together, one section fitting into another, as with a telescope. 2 to become shorter by one part sliding over the other.

tel'evise vb to transmit by television.

tel'evision n (abbr **TV**) the transmitting of pictures by sound waves so as to reproduce them on a screen.

tell vb (pt, pp **told**) 1 to give an account of. 2 to let another know of by speaking. 3 to count. 4 to have an effect.

tell'er n 1 a bank clerk who receives and pays out cash. 2 one appointed to count votes. 3 one who tells.

tell'ing adj very effective.

tell'-tale adj 1 giving information. 2 revealing what was secret:—n one who tells what another has done to get him or her into trouble.

tem'per vb 1 to mix in proper proportions. 2 to make less severe:—n 1 mood, state of mind. 2 anger.

tem'perament n 1 one's character. 2 the usual state of one's mind or feelings.

temperamen'tal adj easily excited, changing mood quickly.

tem'perate adj 1 taking neither too much nor too little. 2 neither too hot nor too cold.

tem'perature n 1 degree of heat or cold. 2 body heat above the normal.

tem'pest n a violent storm.

tem'ple[1] n 1 a place of worship. 2 a church.

tem'ple[2] n the side of the head above the end of the cheekbone and between the ear and the forehead.

tem'po n (pl **tem'pos** or **tem'pi**) the speed at which a piece of music is played.

tem'porary adj lasting for a time only, not permanent.

tempt vb to try to get someone to do what he feels he ought not to do:—ns **tempt'er**, **tempt'ress**.

tempta'tion n attraction to what is wrong.

ten'ancy n 1 the renting of property. 2 property for which a rent is paid. 3 the time during which one rents property.

ten'ant n one who occupies rented property.

tend[1] vb 1 to incline to. 2 to have a leaning toward.

tend[2] vb to care for, to look after.

ten'dency n a leaning toward, an inclination, liability to do certain things more than others.

ten'der[1] vb (fml) to offer or present:—n an offer, esp one to do work at a certain price.

ten'der[2] adj 1 soft, gentle and loving. 2 easily hurt:—n **ten'derness**.

ten'don n a strong cord-like band joining a muscle to a bone.

ten'nis n a game played across a net by striking a ball to and fro with rackets.

ten'on n the end of a piece of wood, etc, shaped to fit into a hole (mortise) cut in another piece.

tenpins npl a game in which one bowls a ball at ten pins to knock them down.

tense[1] n a set of forms of the verb that indicate time.

tense[2] adj **1** strained. **2** excited from expectation.

ten'sion n **1** act of stretching. **2** tightness, strain. **3** excitement due to expectation.

tent n a portable shelter of canvas, supported by a pole or poles and stretched and held in position by cords.

ten'tacle n a slender boneless limb of various creatures, used for feeling, gripping, or moving.

ten'tative adj done as an experiment or trial.

ten'terhook n:—**on tenterhooks** anxious or excited because of doubt or suspense.

tep'id adj lukewarm.

term n **1** a limited period of time. **2** a division of the school year. **3** a word or phrase used in a particular study. **4** pl conditions, charge, price:—vb to name, to call.

ter'minal adj having to do with the end or last part:—n **1** one of the screws to which an electric wire is attached to make a connection. **2** the station at the end of a line or route.

ter'minate vb to bring or come to an end.

termino'logy n the words, phrases, etc, special to a particular branch of study.

ter'minus n (pl **ter'mini** or **ter'minuses**) the station at the end of a line or route.

ter'race n **1** a raised bank of earth with a flat area on top. **2** a row of houses.

terrain' n a stretch of country.

ter'rapin n a type of tortoise.

terres'trial adj having to do with the earth.

ter'rible adj **1** frightening, causing dread. **2** very bad.

ter'rier n a small dog good at hunting.

terri'fic adj **1** frightening, causing dread. **2** exceptionally good.

ter'rify vb to make very frightened.

ter'ror n great fear, dread.

ter'rorism n ruling by fear, the use of fear to obtain obedience.

ter'rorist n one who believes in or uses terrorism:—also adj.

ter'rorize vb **1** to make very frightened. **2** to make do what is desired by causing fear.

terse adj short and to the point:—n **terse'ness**.

test n an examination or trial intended to reveal quality, ability, progress, etc:—vb **1** to try the quality of. **2** to examine.

tes'tify vb **1** to give evidence. **2** to say publicly what one believes to be true.

testimo'nial n **1** a letter stating a person's good qualities and abilities. **2** a gift presented as a sign of respect.

tes'timony n evidence, a public statement of belief.

test tube n a glass tube open at one end, used for scientific experiments.

tes'ty adj irritable, easily angered.

tet'anus n a disease causing cramp in the muscles and making the jaw so stiff that it cannot move.

tête-à-tête n a private talk between two people.

teth'er vb to tie an animal by a rope to a stake or peg:—n a stake, etc:—**at the end of one's tether** at the end of one's strength or endurance.

tet'ra- prefix four.

tet'ragon n a four-sided figure.

text n **1** the words actually written by the author (not including notes, drawings, etc). **2** subject, topic. **3** a short passage from the Bible.

text'book n a book about a subject written for those studying it.

tex'tile n a cloth made by weaving.

tex'ture n the way in which a fabric or cloth, etc, is woven.

thank vb to express pleasure to another for something done, etc, to express gratitude.

thank'ful adj grateful, full of gratitude.

thank'less adj ungrateful, for which one will receive no thanks.

thanks npl an expression of gratitude.

thatch n straw used as a cover for the roof of a house:—vb to put thatch on:—n **thatch'er**.

thaw vb to melt:—n a state of thawing.

the'ater n **1** a building or hall in which plays are acted. **2** a lecture hall. **3** an operating room. **4** a scene of action.

theat'rical adj **1** having to do with plays or the theater. **2** behaving as if acting in a play.

thee pron you (sing).

theft n act of stealing.

their, theirs poss adj and pron belonging to them.

theolo'gical adj having to do with theology.

theo'logy n the study of the existence of God and man's beliefs about God.

theorem [thee'-rĕm] n an idea that can be proved true by reasoning.

theoret'ical adj based on ideas, not on practice.

the'orize vb **1** to suggest explanations. **2** to put forward theories.

the'ory n **1** an explanation that seems satisfactory but has not been proved true. **2** a set of ideas or rules on how something should be done.

ther'apy n the treatment and cure of disease:—adj **therapeu'tic**.

there adv in that place.

there'fore adv for this or that reason.

therm'al adj having to do with heat, hot.

thermo'meter n an instrument for measuring degree of heat.

Ther'mos n trademark a flask for keeping hot liquid hot or cold liquid cold.

therm'ostat n an instrument that mechanically controls temperature.

thick adj **1** broad. **2** fat. **3** not easily seen through. **4** slow to understand:—n **thick'ness**.

thick'en vb to make or become thicker.

thick'et n a group of trees, shrubs, etc, growing close together.

thick'set adj broad and strong of body.

thick'-skinned adj slow to feel or resent insults.

thief n (pl **thieves**) one who steals.

thieve vb to steal.

thigh n the part of the leg above the knee.

thim'ble n a metal or plastic cap to protect the finger in sewing.

thin adj **1** not thick. **2** not fat, lean, skinny, slim. **3** not crowded. **4** not convincing:—vb to make or become thin:—n **thin'ness**.

thing n **1** any single existing object. **2** whatever may be thought of or spoken about. **3** a happening. **4** pl one's belongings.

think vb (**thought, thinking**) **1** to form ideas in the mind, to consider. **2** to believe.

think'ing adj able to think or reason.

thin'-skinned adj quick to feel or resent insult, easily upset.

third adj coming after second:—n one of three equal parts.

thirst n **1** the need or desire to drink. **2** a strong desire for anything:—vb to feel thirst, to desire strongly.

thirst'y adj 1 wanting or needing a drink. 2 dry. 3 causing thirst.

this'tle n a prickly plant with a purple head.

thorn n 1 a prickle on the stem of a plant. 2 a bush or plant with prickles:—**thorn in the flesh** a cause of trouble or difficulty.

thorough [thur'-ė] adj 1 complete. 2 doing work with great care:—n **thor'oughness**.

though [thô] prep despite the fact that.

thought pt of **think**:—n 1 the power or act of thinking. 2 what one thinks, an idea.

thought'ful adj 1 given to thinking. 2 considerate, thinking of others.

thought'less adj 1 not thinking before acting. 2 not thinking of others.

thou'sand adj and n ten hundred.

thrash vb to beat hard, to flog.

thread n 1 a fine strand of any substance (e.g. cotton, wool, etc) drawn out and twisted to make a cord. 2 the spiral ridge running around and around a screw, etc. 3 the main connected points running through an argument:—vb 1 to pass thread or fine cord through. 2 to make one's way through.

thread'bare adj (of clothes) having the fluffy surface worn off, shabby, frequently used and so no longer fresh or new.

threat n 1 a promise to hurt or punish another in future. 2 a warning of harm to come.

threat'en vb 1 to make threats to. 2 to be a sign of coming harm, evil, etc.

thresh'old n 1 the plank or stone one crosses when passing through a door. 2 the beginning.

threw pt of **throw**.

thrice adv three times.

thrift n care in spending or using up, the habit of saving and not wasting.

thrift'y adj careful in spending, saving.

thrill n a sudden feeling of excitement or emotion:—vb to excite, to cause a thrill in.

thrill'ing adj very exciting.

thrive vb 1 to do well. 2 to be or become strong or successful.

throat n 1 the front of the neck. 2 the opening downward at the back of the mouth and the pipe leading down from it.

throb vb 1 to beat, as the heart. 2 (of pain) to increase and decrease at short regular intervals:—also n.

throne n the chair occupied by a monarch or bishop.

throng n a crowd.

throt'tle n a valve controlling the flow of fuel to an engine:—vb 1 to control the speed of (an engine) using a throttle. 2 to choke or strangle.

through [thrŭ] prep 1 from end to end. 2 from beginning to end. 3 by means of. 4 because of:—adv from end to.

throughout' adv in every way or part:—prep right through.

throw vb (pt **threw**, pp **thrown**) 1 to fling or cast. 2 to make to fall on the ground (e.g. in wrestling):—also n.

thrush n a songbird.

thrust vb 1 to push with force. 2 to stab at or into. 3 to push forward:—n 1 a sudden or violent push. 2 a stab.

thud n a low dull sound, as of a muffled blow:—also vb (**thud'ded, thud'ding**).

thug n a ruffian.

thumb n the shortest and thickest of the.

thump n a dull heavy blow:—vb to beat heavily.

thun'der n 1 the sound that follows lightning. 2 any loud rumbling noise:—vb 1 to make thunder. 2 to make a loud noise.

thun'derstorm n a storm with thunder and lightning.

thun'derstruck adj amazed, astonished.

thun'dery adj (of weather) hot and close, as before a thunderstorm.

Thurs'day n the fifth day of the week.

thus adv in this way.

thwack vb to beat hard:—n a heavy blow.

thwart vb to prevent from succeeding:—n a rower's seat from side to side of a boat.

tia'ra n a jeweled band, like a small crown, worn on the head by women.

tick n 1 the sound made by a watch or clock. 2 a mark made when checking or correcting:—also vb.

tick'et n 1 a marked card giving its possessor the right to do something (e.g. travel by train, enter a theater, etc). 2 a label.

tick'le vb 1 to cause discomfort or make laugh by touching or prodding lightly a sensitive part of the body. 2 (inf) to please, to amuse:—adj **tick'lish**.

tid'bit n a tasty piece of food.

tide n 1 the regular rise and fall, or ebb and flow, of the sea. 2 time, season.

ti'dy adj neatly arranged, orderly:—vb to arrange neatly.

tie vb 1 to fasten with cord, rope, etc. 2 to connect. 3 to make a knot in. 4 (in a game or contest) to be equal with:—n 1 a band of cloth, usu colored, worn round the neck. 2 a connection, bond. 3 a match in a knockout competition. 4 a draw (i.e. an equal score). 5 a long rectangular block that supports railroad lines.

tier n one of a series of rows of seats arranged on the slope, so that each row is slightly higher than the one below it.

ti'ger n a large fierce striped animal of the cat family:—f **ti'gress**.

tight adj 1 close-fitting. 2 closely packed.

tight'en vb to make or become tight.

tight'rope n a tightly stretched rope on which an acrobat walks and performs.

tights npl pantihose.

tile n a thin slab of baked clay or other suitable material for covering roofs, floors, etc:—vb to cover with tiles.

till[1] n in a store, a drawer for money.

till[2] prep up to the time of:—conj up to the time when.

till[3] vb to plow and prepare for seed.

tilt vb to make to slope to one side, to lean.

tim'ber n 1 wood for building, carpentry, etc. 2 trees from which such wood can be obtained.

timbre [tim'-bėr] n (fml) the recognizable quality of a sound, voice, etc.

time n 1 the measure of the passage of past, present, and future. 2 the moment of the hour, day, year, etc. 3 a season. 4 an occasion. 5 the rhythm of a piece of music:—vb 1 to see how long something lasts. 2 to see that something happens at the right moment:—**for the time being** meanwhile.

time'table n 1 a schedule showing a planned order or sequence. 2 a list giving the times of arrival and departure of trains, buses, etc.

tim'id adj easily made afraid, shy:—n **timid'ity**.

tim'orous same as **timid**.

tin n a soft, light white metal. 2 a can or box made from thin iron coated with tin:—vb (**tinned', tin'ning**) 1 to coat with tin. 2 to put or pack in tins.

tinc'ture n 1 a shade of color. 2 a slight taste or flavor of something.

tin'foil n tin beaten into a very thin sheet and used for wrapping.

tinge vb to color slightly:—n a slight color.

tingle [ting'-gėl] vb to feel a prickly or thrilling sensation.

tink'er n (old) one who goes from door to door, mending pots, kettles, etc:—vb to mend roughly.

tinkle [ting'-kėl] vb to make soft, bell-like sounds:—also n.

tinned adj in a tin.

tin'sel n thin strips, threads, disks, etc, of shiny metal.

tint n 1 a shade of color. 2 a faint color:—vb to color slightly.

ti'ny adj very small.

tip n 1 a narrow end or point. 2 a light blow. 3 money given as a present or for special help. 4 a helpful hint. 5 a place where rubbish, etc, is heaped:—vb (**tipped', tip'ping**) 1 to put a tip on. 2 to make to tilt. 3 to give a money tip to. 4 to give a useful hint to. 5 to throw out (of).

tip'sy adj drunk, confused by strong drink.

tip'toe n the point of the toe:—vb 1 to walk on the points of the toes. 2 to walk very quietly.

tip'top' adj splendid, excellent.

ti'rade n a long angry speech, a violently critical speech.

tire[1] vb to make or become weary.

tire[2] n a ring of iron or rubber around the outside rim of a wheel.

tired adj weary.

tire'some adj boring, annoying.

ti'ro same as **tyro**.

tis'sue n 1 any fine woven material. 2 substance (fat, muscle, etc) of which the parts of animals and plants are made. 3 a complete connected set.

tis'sue paper n thin soft paper for wrapping.

tit[1] n a small bird.

tit[2] n:—**tit for tat** getting one's own back.

tit[3] same as **teat**.

ti'tle n 1 the name of a book, piece of writing or music, picture, etc. 2 a name or word used in addressing someone, to indicate rank, office, etc.

tit'ter vb to giggle:—also n.

toad n a frog-like animal that lives both on land and in water.

toad'stool n a poisonous fungus, like a mushroom in shape.

toast vb 1 to dry and brown by heat. 2 to warm at the fire. 3 to drink the health of:—n 1 sliced bread browned by heat. 2 a person whose health is drunk. 3 a sentiment or thing to which one drinks.

toast'er n 1 an electrical implement for toasting bread. 2 one who toasts.

tobac'co n the dried leaves of the tobacco plant, used for smoking or taken as snuff.

tobac'conist n one who sells tobacco, cigarettes, etc.

tobog'gan n a narrow sledge for sliding down snow-covered slopes:—vb to go on a toboggan.

today' adv on this day.

tod'dle vb to walk with short unsteady steps, as a small child.

tod'dler n a small child just beginning to walk.

toe n one of the five finger-like members at the end of the foot.

tof'fee n a sweetmeat made of sugar and butter.

togeth'er adv with another or others, in company.

toil vb to work hard:—n hard work.

toil'et n a lavatory.

to'ken n 1 a mark or sign. 2 an object often to help to remember. 3 something used instead of money.

told pt of **tell**.

tol'erable adj 1 able to be put up with. 2 fairly good.

tol'erance, tolera'tion ns 1 patience. 2 readiness to allow what is displeasing, strange, or different to continue to exist.

tol'erant adj ready to tolerate.

tol'erate vb 1 to put up with. 2 to allow.

toll[1] n a tax charged for the use of a bridge, road, etc.

toll[2] vb to ring slowly, as a bell at a funeral:—n a single stroke of a large bell.

toma'to n (pl **toma'toes**) 1 a plant with a soft eatable fruit. 2 the fruit of the tomato.

tomb [tōm] n 1 a grave. 2 a cellar in which dead bodies are placed.

tom'boy n an energetic girl who is fond of boyish games and sports.

tomb'stone n a stone placed over a grave giving the name, etc, of the person buried underneath.

tomor'row adv the day after today.

ton n 1 a measure of weight (= 2000 pounds). 2 (inf) a great quantity.

tone n 1 a sound. 2 the quality or pitch of a voice or sound. 3 the prevailing spirit or atmosphere. 4 a shade of color.

tongs npl an instrument with two arms between which things can be gripped for moving.

tongue [tung] n 1 an organ in the mouth with the help of which one speaks or tastes. 2 anything shaped like a tongue (e.g. a leather flap in a shoe). 3 a language. 4 the clapper of a bell.

tongue'-tied adj unable to speak because of excitement or nervousness.

tongue'-twist'er n a group of words that it is difficult to pronounce quickly.

ton'ic n a strengthening medicine.

tonight' adv on this night.

tonne n a metric ton (= 1000 kilograms).

ton'sil n one of the two glands at the back of the mouth.

took pt of **take**.

tool n an instrument for working with.

toot n the sound of a horn.—also vb.

tooth n (pl **teeth**) 1 one of the bony projections rooted in the jaw, used for biting or chewing. 2 any tooth-shaped projection, as on a saw, rake, etc:—**have a sweet tooth** to like eating sweet things.

tooth'ache n a pain in a tooth.

tooth'y adj having or showing large or sticking-out teeth.

top n 1 the highest part or place. 2 the summit. 3 a toy for spinning:—adj 1 highest. 2 most important:—vb (**topped', top'ping**) 1 to be at the top of. 2 to hit the top of. 3 to do better than.

top hat n a tall cylindrical hat covered with silk.

top'ic n a subject of discussion.

top'ical adj having to do with events of the present day.

top'most adj highest.

top'ple vb 1 to fall over, to overbalance. 2 to cause to fall.

top'sy-tur'vy adj confused, upside-down.

torch n 1 a flashlight. 2 (old) a piece of blazing wood carried or stuck up to give light.

tore pt of **tear**.

tor'ment n 1 great suffering or agony. 2 great anxiety:—vb **torment'** 1 to cause distress or suffering to, to torture. 2 to tease:—n **tormen'tor**.

torn pp of **tear**.

torna'do n (pl **torna'does**) a violent swirling wind or hurricane.

torpe'do n (pl **torpe'does**) 1 a long narrow shell that can be fired along the surface of the water to hit another ship and explode:—vb 1 to hit or damage a torpedo. 2 to spoil or ruin.

tor'rent n 1 a rushing stream. 2 a heavy downpour.

torren'tial adj flowing with great violence, falling heavily and steadily.

tor'so n the body without the head or limbs.

tor'toise n a four-footed reptile almost entirely covered by a hard shell.

tor'ture *vb* **1** to cause great suffering or anxiety to. **2** to cause pain to as a punishment or in order to obtain information from:—*n* extreme pain or anxiety.

toss *vb* **1** to throw upward, to jerk upward, as the head. **2** (*of a ship*) to roll about in rough seas. **3** to drink (off) quickly:—*n* **1** a throw. **2** a fall:—**toss up** to throw up a coin to decide something by chance.

tot *n* **1** a small child. **2** a small quantity:—*vb* (**tot'ted, tot'ting**) to add up.

total' *adj* **1** whole. **2** complete:—*n* **1** the whole amount. **2** the result when everything has been added up:—*vb* **1** to add up. **2** to add up to.

tot'ter *vb* to stand or walk unsteadily.

toucan [tŏ'-kan] *n* a South American bird with a huge bill.

touch *vb* **1** to come to rest against with any part of the body, esp the hand. **2** to be in contact. **3** to cause to feel emotion. **4** to make a difference to, to concern:—*n* **1** act of coming against or being in contact with. **2** the ability to do really well something requiring skill. **3** the sense of feeling:—**touch on** to mention briefly:—**touch up**, to improve by making small changes.

touch'ing *adj* moving the feelings, causing pity:—*prep* having to do with.

touch'y *adj* easily angered or hurt.

tough [tuf] *adj* **1** hard to cut, tear or chew. **2** hardy strong. **3** rough-mannered. **4** difficult to deal with:—*n* a street ruffian.

tough'en *vb* **1** to make tough. **2** to make better able to resist.

tour [tŏr] *n* a journey, made for pleasure, to various places, usu ending up at the starting point:—*vb* to go for a tour, to travel here and there.

tour'ism *n* the providing of hotels, routes, etc, for tourists.

tour'ist *n* one who travels for pleasure.

tour'nament *n* **1** a series of games between different competitors to see which is the best player or team. **2** in olden times, a display of fighting on horseback in which the warriors carried blunted arms.

tou'sle *vb* **1** to disarrange, esp the hair. **2** to make untidy.

tow[1] [tŏ]*vb* to pull along with a rope, chain, etc:—*n* **1** anything towed. **2** the act of being towed.

tow[2] [tŏ] *n* fibers of flax or hemp.

toward, towards *preps* in the direction of.

tow'el *n* a cloth for drying the body:—**throw in the towel** to admit defeat:—*vb* **1** to rub (oneself) with a towel.

tow'eling *n* material for making towels, etc.

tow'er *n* **1** a building much higher than it is broad. **2** a high part of another building, projecting above it. **3** a fortress:—*vb* to rise high into the air

tow'line, tow'rope *ns* the rope used in towing.

town *n* a group of houses, stores, etc, larger than a village but smaller than a city.

town hall *n* the offices in which the business of the town council is carried on.

town house *n* a house in a group of houses that share one or more walls.

tow'path *n* a path beside a canal for a horse towing a barge.

tox'ic *adj* poisonous.

toy *n* a plaything:—*vb* to play with.

trace *n* **1** a mark left behind. **2** a footstep. **3** a trace, a sign of something that has happened or existed. **4** one of the two straps by which a horse is joined to a carriage:—*vb* **1** to copy a drawing on to transparent paper laid on top of it. **2** to follow the tracks of.

tra'cing *n* a drawing made by copying another drawing on to transparent paper laid on top of it.

track *n* **1** a footprint. **2** the mark or rut left by a wheel. **3** a path made by coming and going. **4** a railroad line. **5** a course for races:—*vb* **1** to follow the marks left by. **2** to pursue or search for someone or something until found.

trac'tor *n* a heavy motor vehicle used for drawing other vehicles or farm implements.

trade *n* **1** the buying and selling of goods. **2** the exchanging of goods in large quantities:—*vb* **1** to buy and sell. **2** to exchange.

trade'mark *n* an officially registered mark or name put on goods to show who manufactured them and not to be used by any other party:—*also vb*.

trades'man *n* a skilled workman.

trade union *n* the banding together in an association of people engaged in a certain trade to protect their interests.

trade wind *n* a wind that is always blowing toward the equator (from northeast or southeast).

tradi'tion *n* **1** the handing down of knowledge, customs, etc, from age to age by word of mouth. **2** any story, custom, etc, so handed down.

tradi'tional *adj* according to or handed down by tradition.

traf'fic *n* **1** trade. **2** the carrying of goods or persons in vehicles, etc. **3** all the vehicles on the roads:—*vb* (**traf'ficked, traf'ficking**) to trade.

traffic circle *n* a meeting place of roads with a circular island around which vehicles must go until they turn off.

tra'gedy *n* **1** a sad event, a disaster. **2** a play showing the suffering caused by man's inability to overcome evil.

tra'gic *adj* **1** having to do with tragedy. **2** very sad.

trail *n* **1** the track or scent left by a moving creature. **2** a path or track made by coming and going:—*vb* **1** to drag along the ground. **2** to draw along behind. **3** to walk wearily. **4** to follow the tracks of.

trail'er *n* **1** a vehicle without an engine, often containing living quarters, towed by another. **2** a short filmed advertisement for a film or TV program.

train *vb* **1** to prepare or make to prepare by constant practice or teaching. **2** to aim. **3** to make to grow in a particular direction:—*n* **1** railroad coaches or trucks drawn by an engine. **2** part of a dress that trails behind the wearer. **3** (*old*) persons in attendance. **4** a series.

train'er *n* **1** one who trains people or animals to be physically fit for sport. **2** *pl* shoes with good support and thick soles for running and other sport.

train'ing *n* education, practice.

trai'tor *n* one who helps an enemy against his or her own country or friends:—*adj* **trai'torous**.

tram, tram'car *ns* a streetcar.

tramp *vb* **1** to walk heavily. **2** to travel on foot:—*n* **1** a journey on foot. **2** one who has no home and walks about the countryside begging. **3** the sound of heavy steps.

tram'ple *vb* to walk heavily on top of.

trance *n* a state in which one is unconscious of one's surroundings.

tran'quil *adj* **1** calm, peaceful. **2** still:—*n* **tranquil'ity, tranquil'lity**.

transac'tion *n* **1** a piece of business. **2** *pl* a written record of the doings of a society.

transatlan'tic *adj* across or crossing the Atlantic.

transfer' *vb* (**transferred', transfer'ring**) to send or remove from one place or owner to another:—*n* **trans'fer** act of transferring.

transfer'able *adj* that can be transferred.

trans'ference *n* act of transferring.

transform' *vb* 1 to change the form of. 2 to change completely:—*n* **transforma'tion.**

transfu'sion *n* 1 the act of transfusing. 2 the passing of the blood of one person into another.

transgres'sion *n* 1 fault. 2 wrongdoing.

trans'ient *adj* 1 not lasting for long, passing quickly. 2 not staying for long:—*n* **trans'ience.**

trans'it *n* 1 going or being moved from one place to another. 2 the passing of a planet between the sun and the earth.

transi'tion *n* changing from one state or condition to another.

trans'itive *adj*:—**transitive verb** a verb taking a direct object.

trans'itory *adj* passing quickly.

translate' *vb* to give the meaning of what is said or written in one language in another language:—*n* **transla'tor.**

transla'tion *n* a turning from one language into another.

translu'cent *adj* allowing light to pass through.

transmis'sion *n* 1 the act of sending messages, etc. 2 a radio or TV broadcast.

transmission tower *n* a hollow skeleton pillar for carrying overhead cables.

transmit' *vb* (**transmit'ted, transmit'ting**) 1 to send (a message, news, etc). 2 to send by radio or TV. 3 to send or pass from one person to another.

transmit'ter *n* a radio apparatus able to send messages or make broadcasts.

transpa'rent *adj* 1 that can be clearly seen through. 2 obvious:—*ns* **transpa'rence, transpa'rency.**

transpire' *vb* 1 to become known. 2 to happen.

transplant' *vb* 1 to uproot and plant in another place. 2 to replace an organ of the body by one belonging to someone else:—*vb* **trans'plant.**

transport' *vb* 1 to carry from one place to another. 2 (*old*) to convey to another country as a punishment:—*n* **trans'port** any means of carrying persons or goods from one place to another.

transporta'tion *n* 1 transport. 2 (*old*) the conveying of convicts to another country as a punishment.

transverse' *adj* lying across.

trap *n* 1 an instrument or device for catching wild animals and holding them alive or dead. 2 any device that, by its appearance, deceives one into advancing into unseen difficulties. 3 a light two-wheeled horse carriage:—*vb* (**trapped', trap'ping**) to catch in a trap or snare. 2 to deceive.

trap'door *n* a door covering in a floor, ceiling, or roof.

trapeze' *n* a bar suspended from two swinging ropes, some distance above the ground, and used in acrobatic exercises.

trape'zium *n* a four-sided figure of which two sides are parallel and unequal in length.

trapp'ings *npl* 1 finery, decoration. 2 ornamental harness for a horse.

trash *n* 1 rubbish. 2 (*inf*) something worthless:—*adj* **trash'y.**

trash can *n* a container for household trash.

trav'el *vb* 1 to make a journey. 2 to move on one's way.

trav'eler *n* 1 one who journeys. 2 one who goes from place to place to obtain orders for a business firm.

trav'erse *vb* 1 to go across. 2 to journey.

trav'esty *n* a silly imitation, a burlesque.

trawl'er *n* a fishing boat using a trawl.

tray *n* a flat piece of wood, metal, etc, with a rim, used for carrying dishes, etc.

treach'erous *adj* 1 faithless, disloyal, deceitful. 2 dangerous but seeming safe.

treach'ery *n* unfaithfulness to those who have placed trust in one, disloyalty.

tread *vb* (*pt* **trod,** *pp* **trod'den** *or* **trod**) 1 to step or walk. 2 to walk heavily on:—*n* 1 a step. 2 the sound of walking. 3 the flat part of the step of a stair. 4 the part of a tire that touches the ground.

tread'le *n* a pedal used for operating a machine.

trea'son *n* disloyalty to one's country or ruler.

trea'sure *n* 1 something greatly valued. 2 a store of great wealth:—*vb* to value greatly.

trea'sure trove *n* treasure found hidden and ownerless.

treat *vb* 1 to deal with. 2 to act toward. 3 to talk or write about. 4 to try to cure by certain remedies. 5 to pay for another's entertainment. 6 to discuss conditions for an agreement:—*n* 1 an entertainment. 2 something that gives great pleasure.

treat'ment *n* the way of treating anything.

trea'ty *n* an agreement between two nations.

treb'le *adj* threefold, three times:—*vb* to multiply by three:—*n* the highest part in singing, soprano.

tree *n* 1 a plant with a trunk and branches of wood. 2 a branching representation of something, such as a family tree:—**up a tree** in a difficult situation, stumped.

trek *vb* (**trekked', trek'king**) to journey on foot, often wearily:—*also n.*

trell'is *n* a light framework of crisscrossing bars of wood or metal for supporting climbing plants.

trem'ble *vb* 1 to shake with fear, cold, fever, etc. 2 to feel great fear.

tremen'dous *adj* 1 huge. 2 very great, impressive.

trem'or *n* a slight shaking or shivering.

trench *n* a long narrow hole or ditch dug in the ground:—*also vb.*

trend *n* 1 tendency. 2 a current style or fashion.

trepida'tion *n* fear.

tres'pass *vb* to go unlawfully on another's land:—*n* **tres'passer.**

tres'tle *n* a movable wooden stand for supporting a table top, platform, etc.

tri- *prefix* three.

tri'al *n* 1 a test. 2 hardship or distress undergone. 3 the examining of a prisoner in a court of law.

trian'gle *n* 1 a figure with three sides and three angles. 2 a musical instrument consisting of a triangle-shaped steel rod, played by striking it with a metal rod.

trian'gular *adj* having three sides and angles.

tribe *n* a group of people or families living together under the rule of a chief:—*adj* **trib'al:**—*n* **tribes'man.**

tribu'nal *n* 1 a court of justice. 2 a body appointed to look into and report on a matter of public interest.

trib'utary *adj* flowing into a larger stream or river:—*also n.*

trib'ute *n* deserved praise

trice *n*:—**in a trice** in a moment.

trick *n* 1 something said or done in order to deceive. 2 something done quickly and skillfully in order to amuse. 3 a special way of doing something. 4 cards played and won in a round:—*vb* to deceive, to cheat.

trick'ery *n* cheating, deceitful conduct.

trick'le *vb* to flow very slowly:—*n* a thin stream of liquid.

trick'ster *n* a cheat.

trick'y *adj* requiring skill.

tri'cycle *n* a three-wheeled cycle.

tried *pt* of **try:**—*adj* reliable, proved good.

tri'fle *n* 1 a thing of little value or importance. 2 a small amount:—*vb* 1 to treat without seriousness. 2 to idle.

tri'fling *adj* of no value or importance, insignificant.

trill *vb* in music, to play or sing in rapid succession two sounds that are close together:—*also n.*

trill'ion *n* a million million million.

tril′ogy n a series of three connected plays, novels, etc.

trim vb (**trimmed′**, **trim′ming**) 1 to make neat, esp by cutting. 2 to decorate. 3 to rearrange cargo so that a ship or airplane is properly balance. 4 to make ready for sailing:—adj neat, tidy.

trimes′ter n 1 an academic term. 2 three months.

trim′ming n something added as an ornament.

trin′ket n an ornament of little value, a piece of cheap jewelry.

tri′o n a set of three.

trip vb (**tripped′**, **trip′ping**) 1 (fml) to move with light quick steps (trip upstairs). 2 to stumble or fall over. 3 to cause to stumble or fall:—n 1 a stumble. 2 a short journey or outing.

tripe n 1 part of the stomach of a sheep, cow, etc, prepared as food. 2 (inf) nonsense, rubbish.

tri′ple adj made up of three parts, threefold:—vb to make or become three times as large or many.

trip′let n 1 a set of three. 2 one of three children born at one birth.

trip′licate adj threefold:—**in triplicate** with three copies.

tri′pod n a three-legged stand or support (e.g. for a camera).

trite adj often used, commonplace.

tri′umph n 1 joy at success or victory. 2 a great success or victory:—vb to gain a great success or victory.

trium′phant adj 1 successful, victorious. 2 joyous at success or victory.

triv′ial adj of small importance, trifling:—n **trivial′ity**.

troll n a dwarfish elf or goblin.

trol′ley n (pl **trol′leys**) 1 a small truck. 2 a type of handcart with two wheels. 3 a serving table on wheels. 4 a pole that conveys electric current from an overhead wire to a bus or tramcar.

trol′lop n a dirty and untidy woman.

trombone′ n a deep-toned type of trumpet with a sliding tube moved in and out when it is being played.

troop n 1 a collection or group of people or animals. 2 an organized group of soldiers, Scouts etc. 3 pl soldiers:—vb to move or gather in large numbers.

tro′phy n something given or kept as a reward for or reminder of success or victory.

trop′ic n one of two imaginary lines round the earth marking the farthest distance north and south of the equator at which the sun rises and sets during the year:—npl the hot regions north and south of the equator.

trop′ical adj 1 having to do with the tropics. 2 very hot.

trot vb (**trot′ted**, **trot′ting**) 1 to run with short steps. 2 (of a horse) to go at a pace between a walk and a gallop:—n a medium pace.

trot′ter n the foot of a pig or sheep.

trouble [trubl] vb 1 to cause anxiety, difficulty or distress to. 2 to disturb:—n 1 worry, anxiety, distress. 2 difficulty.

trou′blesome adj causing trouble.

trough [trof] n a long narrow vessel to hold water or food for animals.

trounce vb to beat severely.

troupe [trōp] n a company of actors or other performers.

trou′sers n a garment originally for men, reaching from waist to ankles and covering each leg separately.

trout n an eatable freshwater fish.

trow′el n 1 a tool with a flat blade used for spreading mortar, plaster, etc. 2 a tool with a curved blade used for gardening.

tru′ant n a child who stays off school without leave:—**play truant** to stay off school without leave.

truce n an agreement to stop fighting for a time.

truck n 1 a large motor vehicle for carrying goods. 2 a railroad freight wagon.

truck′er n one who drives a truck.

truck farm n a place where vegetables are grown for sale:—n **truck farm′er**.

truc′ulent adj quarrelsome, trying to find a cause for quarreling or fighting:—n **truc′ulence**.

trudge vb to walk, esp with heavy steps, to walk in a tired manner:—also n.

true adj 1 in agreement with fact, not false. 2 genuine. 3 honest. 4 faithful, loyal. 5 exact, close:—adv **tru′ly**.

trump n one of a suit of cards that, in a particular hand, beats a card of any other suit:—vb to play a trump on a card of another suit:—**trump up** to make up, to invent.

trum′pet n a metal wind instrument:—vb 1 to make known far and wide. 2 to make a noise, as an elephant.

trum′peter n one who plays the trumpet.

trun′cheon n a policeman's baton.

trun′dle vb to roll, push, or bowl along.

trunk n 1 the main stem of a tree. 2 the body without the head or limbs. 3 the long tube-like nose of an elephant. 4 a box or chest for clothes, etc. 5 the storage space at the back of an automobile.

truss n 1 a bundle of hay or straw. 2 a supporting bandage:—vb 1 to tie. 2 to tie up (a fowl) for cooking.

trust n 1 a firm belief that another person or a thing is what it claims or is claimed to be, confidence. 2 the holding and controlling of money or property for the advantage of someone. 3 care or responsibility:—vb 1 to rely upon, to have faith in. 2 to hope.

trustee′ n one appointed to hold and look after property on behalf of another:—n **trustee′ship**.

trust′ful, trust′ing adjs ready to trust.

trust′worthy adj deserving trust or confidence, reliable.

truth n that which is true.

try vb (**tried′**, **try′ing**) 1 to attempt. 2 to test. 3 to examine and judge in a court of law.

try′ing adj difficult, worrying, annoying.

tub n 1 a large open container used for bathing, washing clothes, growing things etc. 2 a bathtub.

tu′ba n a low-pitched brass wind instrument.

tub′by adj (inf) round and fat.

tube n 1 a pipe. 2 a hollow cylinder. 3 a device by which one can control the power of radio waves transmitted or received.

tub′ing n 1 a length of tube. 2 a series of tubes.

tub′ular adj 1 like a tube. 2 consisting of tubes.

tuck vb 1 to push, to stuff. 2 to put in a secure or private place:—n a fold in a garment:—**tuck in** 1 to cover up comfortably. 2 (inf) to eat hungrily.

Tues′day n the third day of the week.

tuft n 1 a bunch or clump of grass, hair, etc, growing together. 2 a bunch of threads, pile, feathers, etc.

tug vb (**tugged′**, **tug′ging**) 1 to pull with effort. 2 to pull sharply:—n 1 a strong sharp pull. 2 a small boat used to pull larger ones.

tug-of-war′ n a contest in which two teams pull opposite ways on a rope until one is pulled across a mark.

tui′tion n teaching.

tu′lip n a plant growing from a bulb and having a single brightly colored flower.

tum′ble vb 1 to fall. 2 to do acrobatic and jumping tricks:—n a fall.

tumbledown′ adj in a ruined state, falling apart.

tum′bler n 1 a drinking glass. 2 an acrobat.

tu′mor n a mass of diseased cells in the body causing swelling.

tu'mult n 1 noisy confusion, uproar. 2 disorderly behavior by a crowd.

tumul'tuous adj noisy and disorderly.

tun n a large cask.

tune n 1 the melody or air of a piece of music. 2 a short pleasing piece of music. 3 the correct relation of one musical note to others:—vb 1 to see that the strings of an instrument are adjusted to play the correct notes. 2 to adjust a radio, etc, until it is receiving as clearly as possible.

tu'nic n 1 a loose upper garment covering the body, sometimes to below the waist. 2 a soldier's uniform jacket.

tun'nel n an underground passage, esp one that enables a road or railroad to pass under or through an obstacle.

tur'ban n a headdress made by winding a band of cloth around and around the head.

tur'bid adj 1 muddy. 2 thick.

tur'bine n a type of wheel that, when moved by steam or water power, drives an engine.

tur'bot n a large eatable flatfish.

turf n 1 earth covered thickly with short grass. 2 a single piece of turf cut out:—vb to cover with turf.

tur'key n a large farmyard fowl.

tur'moil n noisy confusion, disorder.

turn vb 1 to move or cause to move round. 2 to shape wood by cutting it as it revolves. 3 to change. 4 (of milk) to become sour:—n 1 a change of direction. 2 (of a wheel) a revolution. 3 a bend. 4 an act. 5 a short walk. 6 a sudden feeling of sickness:—**turn down** to refuse:—**turn in** (inf) to go to bed:—**turn out** 1 to have (good or bad) results. 2 to attend a meeting:—**turn up** to appear unexpectedly:—**turn upon** to attack suddenly:—**in turn** one after the other, in the proper order.

turn'ing n 1 a bend in the road. 2 a corner leading off to another road.

tur'nip n a plant with a large eatable root.

turn'out n the number of people in an assembly.

turn'over n in business, the amount of money paid in and out in a certain period.

turn'pike n a road that travelers must pay a tax to use.

turn signal n one of the lights on a vehicle that flashes to show which way it is turning.

turn'stile n a revolving gate through which only one person can pass at a time.

turn'table n a round spinning surface on a record player on which a record is placed.

tur'pentine n 1 a resin obtained from certain trees. 2 an oil made from this.

tur'quoise n a greenish-blue precious stone or its color:—also adj.

tur'ret n a small tower forming part of a building.

tur'tle n a large sea tortoise.

tusk n a long pointed tooth sticking out from the mouth, as in an elephant, walrus, etc.

tus'sle n a short struggle, a disorderly fight:—vb to struggle.

tu'tor n a private teacher:—vb to teach, to act as tutor.

tuto'rial adj having to do with a tutor or teaching:—n 1 a group of students who study with a tutor. 2 study time spent with a tutor.

TV abbr for **television**.

twang n 1 the sound made by plucking a tightly stretched string or wire. 2 a tone that sounds as if one were speaking through one's nose:—vb to pluck a tightly stretched string or wire.

tweak vb to twist sharply, to pinch:—also n.

tweed n a rough woollen cloth.

twee'zers npl small pincers for pulling out hairs, lifting tiny things, etc.

twice adv two times.

twid'dle vb to play with.

twig n a small shoot or branch of a tree.

twi'light n the faint light just after sunset or before dawn.

twin n one of two children born at one birth:—adj born at one birth.

twine n strong string:—vb 1 to twist or wind around. 2 to twist together.

twinge n a sudden sharp pain.

twin'kle vb 1 to sparkle. 2 to shine with a light that very quickly increases and decreases:—n 1 a gleam of light. 2 a quick look of amusement in the eyes:—also n.

twirl vb to turn around rapidly:—also n.

twist vb 1 to turn quickly out of shape or position. 2 to wind strands around each other. 3 to put a wrong meaning on:—n 1 something made by twisting. 2 a sudden turning out of shape or position.

twitch n 1 a jerk. 2 a sudden quick movement:—vb 1 to pull sharply. 2 to make a quick movement unintentionally.

twit'ter vb to chirp, as a bird:—also n.

two [tö] adj and n one more than one.

two-faced' adj deceitful, not sincere.

type n 1 a person or thing possessing most of the qualities of a certain group, class, nationality, etc. 2 a class or kind. 3 a letter or symbol cut in metal, etc, and used for printing:—vb to use a typewriter.

type'writer n a machine operated by keys that, when struck, cause letters or symbols to be printed through an inked ribbon on to paper.

typ'ical adj 1 serving as an example of a class or group. 2 characteristic.

typ'ist n one who uses a typewriter.

tyran'nical, tyr'annous adjs cruel, ruling unjustly.

tyr'anny n cruel or unjust use of power.

ty'rant n 1 one who uses power cruelly. 2 an unjust ruler.

tyre same as **tire**².

ty'ro n a novice, a beginner.

U

ud′der *n* the organ containing the milk-producing gland of a cow, sheep, etc.

ug′ly *adj* 1 unpleasant to see or hear. 2 unpleasant, dangerous:—*n* **ug′liness**.

ukulele [u-kē-lā′-li] *n* a stringed musical instrument played by plucking the strings.

ul′cer *n* an infected sore containing poisonous matter.

ulte′rior *adj* secret, hidden.

ul′timate *adj* last, final:—*adv* **ul′timately**.

ultima′tum *n* a last offer of conditions, to be followed, if refused, by action without more discussion.

ul′tra- *prefix* 1 very, extremely. 2 beyond.

ultramarine′ *n* a brighty sky-blue color.

ultravi′olet *n* beyond the violet end of the spectrum.

um′brage *n*:—**take umbrage** to be offended or made angry by.

umbrel′la *n* a folding frame covered with waterproof material that can be opened out and held over the head at the end of a stick as protection against rain.

um′pire *n* one who acts as judge in a dispute or contest, a referee:—*also vb*.

un- *prefix* not.

unaccept′able *adj* unwelcome.

unaccount′able *adj* that cannot be explained.

unaccus′tomed *adj* not usual.

unaffect′ed *adj* 1 simple, sincere. 2 unmoved.

unanim′ity *n* complete agreement.

unan′imous *adj* 1 being all of the same opinion. 2 agreed to by all present.

unapproach′able *adj* unfriendly in manner.

unassum′ing *adj* modest, not boastful.

unaware′ *adj* not knowing, ignorant (of).

unawares′ *adv* unexpectedly.

unbal′anced *adj* 1 not steady. 2 mentally unstable.

unbecom′ing *adj* not suitable, not proper.

unbi′as(s)ed *adj* fair to all parties, just.

uncalled′-for *adj* unnecessary and rude.

uncan′ny *adj* strange, mysterious.

uncer′tain *adj* 1 not sure. 2 doubtful:—*n* **uncer′tainty**.

un′cle *n* 1 the brother of one's father or mother. 2 the husband of one's aunt.

uncoil′ *vb* to unwind.

uncom′fortable *adj* 1 uneasy. 2 giving no comfort.

uncom′promising *adj* firm, not ready to give in.

uncondi′tional *adj* without conditions.

uncon′scious *adj* 1 not knowing, unaware. 2 stunned, as by a blow, etc, and so unaware of what is going on.

unconven′tional *adj* not bound by custom.

uncouth′ *adj* rough in manner.

undaun′ted *adj* bold, fearless.

undecid′ed *adj* not having made up one's mind, doubtful.

undeni′able *adj* that cannot be argued against, certain.

un′der *prep* 1 below. 2 beneath. 3 subject to. 4 less good than:—*adv* in a lower condition, degree, or place.

undercharge′ *vb* to ask less than the correct price.

un′derclothes, un′derclothing *n* clothes worn under others or next to the skin.

undercut′ *vb* to offer to sell at a lower price (than).

underes′timate *vb* to have too low an opinion of.

undergo′ *vb* to bear, to suffer.

undergrad′uate *n* a university student who has not yet taken a degree.

underground′ *adj and adv* 1 beneath the ground. 2 secret:—*n* **un′derground** a railroad running through underground tunnels.

un′dergrowth *n* shrubs and low bushes growing among trees.

underhand′ *adj* sly, secret, dishonest.

underline′ *vb* 1 to draw a line under. 2 to emphasize.

undermine′ *vb* to destroy gradually, to seek to harm by underhand methods.

underrate′ *vb* to have too low an opinion of.

under′shirt *n* a garment worn next the skin.

undersized′ *adj* less than the normal size, very small.

understand′ *vb* 1 to see the meaning of. 2 to know thoroughly.

understand′ing *n* 1 intelligence, powers of judgment. 2 an agreement, esp an unwritten one.

understate′ *vb* to talk of something as smaller or less important than it really is.

un′derstudy *n* one who learns the same part as another actor in order to be able to take his or her place if necessary.

undertake′ *vb* to take upon oneself to do.

un′dertaker *n* one who manages funerals.

un′dertaking *n* 1 a task. 2 a promise.

un′dertone *n* a low voice.

un′derwear *n* underclothes.

undisguised′ *adj* open, not hidden.

undisturbed′ *adj* calm, tranquil.

undo′ *vb* to reverse what has been done, to untie or unfasten, to ruin.

undo′ing *n* ruin.

undoubt′ed *adj* certain, undeniable.

undress′ *vb* 1 to take one's clothes off. 2 to take off the clothes of.

undue′ *adj* greater than is necessary.

un′dulate *vb* 1 to rise and fall like waves. 2 to have a wavy appearance.

undu′ly *adv* more than is necessary, excessively.

unearth′ *vb* 1 to discover by searching. 2 to dig up.

unearth′ly *adj* weird, supernatural, ghostly.

uneas′y *adj* uncomfortable, anxious.

unemployed′ *adj* having no paid job, out of work.

une′ven *adj* 1 not flat, not smooth. 2 sometimes not so good as at other times.

unfamil′iar *adj* strange.

unfas′ten *vb* to undo, to unfix, to set loose.

unforeseen′ *adj* unexpected.

unfor′tunate *adj* unlucky.

unfurl′ *vb* to spread out.

ungain′ly *adj* clumsy, awkward.

ungrate′ful *adj* not showing due thanks.

unhap′piness *n* misfortune, misery.

unhap′py *adj* 1 miserable, sad. 2 unlucky.

unhealth′y *adj* 1 not having good health. 2 bad for health. 3 having a bad influence.

u′nicorn *n* in fables, an animal like a horse with a single straight horn on its head.

u′niform *adj* 1 unchanging. 2 of the one kind, shape, size, etc:—*n* distinctive clothing worn by all members of the same organization, institution, etc.

unilat′eral *adj* affecting one side or party.

un′ion *n* 1 a putting together to make one. 2 act of joining together. 3 a trade union.

unique [û-neek'] *adj* being the only one of its kind, unequalled.

u'nit *n* 1 the number 1. 2 a single person, thing, or group

unite' *vb* 1 to make or become one. 2 to join together, to act or work together.

u'nity *n* 1 oneness. 2 agreement.

univer'sal *adj* 1 total, whole. 2 affecting all, done by everyone.

u'niverse *n* 1 the whole of creation. 2 the world.

univer'sity *n* an educational institution in which advanced study in all branches of knowledge is carried on, and by which degrees are awarded to those showing merit in their subjects.

unkempt' *adj* (of hair) uncombed.

unlea'vened *adj* not mixed with yeast.

unless' *conj* if not.

unlim'ited *adj* as much as is wanted, that cannot be used up.

unload' *vb* to remove the load or burden from.

unmoved' *adj* firm, calm, not affected (by).

unnerve' *vb* to take away the strength or courage of.

unobtru'sive *adj* not attracting attention, modest.

unoc'cupied *adj* empty.

unor'thodox *adj* holding unusual views, differing from the accepted view.

unpop'ular *adj* widely disliked.

unpre'cedent'ed *adj* without a previous example of the same kind.

unpremed'itated *adj* done without forethought.

unprepossess'ing *adj* unattractive at first sight.

unpreten'tious *adj* modest, not attracting attention.

unqual'ified *adj* 1 not having the necessary training or skill. 2 complete.

unrav'el *vb* 1 to disentangle. 2 to solve.

unrelieved' *adj* 1 without relief (from pain, etc). 2 lacking variety.

unremitt'ing *adj* without pause, ceaseless.

unrequi'ted *adj* not rewarded, not returned.

unrest' *n* discontent, rebellion.

unru'ly *adj* disorderly, badly behaved.

unsani'tary *adj* dirty, causing disease.

unsa'voury *adj* unpleasant.

unscathed' *adj* unhurt.

unscru'pulous *adj* having no standards of good and evil, wicked.

unseem'ly *adj* not fitting, improper.

unset'tle *vb* to upset, to disturb.

unsight'ly *adj* ugly, unpleasant to look at.

unskilled' *adj* having no special skill or training.

unsophis'ticated *adj* simple, natural, innocent.

unsuspect'ing *adj* free from fear of danger or evil, trusting.

until' *prep* up to the time of:—*conj* up to the time when.

untold' *adj* 1 not related, not told. 2 vast.

untoward' *adj* awkward, unsuitable, undesirable.

untrue' *adj* 1 not true. 2 not loyal, faithless.

unu'sual *adj* rare, peculiar.

unut'terable *adj* that cannot be described in words.

unveil' *vb* to uncover, to reveal, to disclose to view.

unwiel'dy *adj* 1 huge. 2 hard to move. 3 clumsy.

unwill'ing *adj* not willing, reluctant.

unwit'ting *adj* not knowing.

unwor'thy *adj* 1 not deserving. 2 dishonourable.

up *adv* 1 in or to a higher place, amount, etc. 2 above:—*prep* from below to.

upbraid' *vb* to scold, to blame.

up'bringing *n* one's early training at home and school.

upheav'al *n* a great change.

uphill' *adv* in an upward direction:—*adj* 1 sloping upward. 2 very difficult.

uphold' *vb* 1 to support. 2 to defend as correct.

up'keep *n* 1 the money needed to keep anything in good condition. 2 the act of keeping in good health or condition.

up'per *adj* higher in place or rank:—*n* the upper part of a shoe.

up'right *adj* 1 standing straight up. 2 honest:—*n* a vertical post.

up'roar *adj* confused noise.

uproar'ious *adj* noisy.

upset' *vb* 1 to overturn, to knock over. 2 to spoil completely. 3 to cause to be sad, worried, etc:—*adj* 1 worried. 2 ill:—*n* **up'set** 1 disturbance. 2 trouble. 3 a sudden misfortune.

up'shot *n* result, outcome.

up'side-down *adv* with the top down and the bottom upward.

up'stairs' *adv* on an upper floor of a house with stairs.

up'start *n* one who has risen quickly to a position of wealth or importance.

ur'ban *adj* having to do with a city.

urbane' *adj* polite, refined, smooth:—*n* **urban'ity**.

ur'chin (old) a ragged street child.

urge *vb* 1 to press to do. 2 to suggest strongly.

ur'gent *adj* needing immediate attention:—*n* **ur'gency**.

u'rine *n* fluid passed from the kidneys and bladder.

urn *n* 1 a vase for the ashes of the dead. 2 a large container with a tap for making and serving tea, etc.

u'sage *n* treatment.

use *vb* 1 to do something with for a purpose. 2 to employ. 3 to consume:—*n* 1 the act of using, the state of being used. 2 advantage, benefit, value. 3 the power of using. 4 permission to use, the right to use:—**use up** to consume or exhaust, leaving nothing.

use'ful *adj* 1 of help. 2 able to be used.

use'less *adj* 1 of no help. 2 not any use.

u'sual *adj* common, normal.

uten'sil *n* a vessel or object in common household use.

u'tilize *vb* (fml) to make use of.

ut'most *adj* 1 the farthest. 2 the greatest.

ut'ter[1] *adj* complete, total.

ut'ter[2] *vb* to speak, to pronounce.

ut'termost *adj* 1 farthest. 2 greatest.

V

va'cancy n 1 an empty space. 2 a job to be filled.

va'cant adj 1 empty, not occupied. 2 unthinking.

vacate' vb 1 (fml) to leave empty. 2 to give up.

vaca'tion n a period of holiday:—vb 1 to go on a vacation. 2 to spend one's vacation.

vac'cinate vb to inject with vaccine or with fluids giving protection against diseases:—n **vaccina'tion**.

vac'cine n 1 fluid taken from a cow infected with cowpox and injected into a person's bloodstream to cause a mild attack of smallpox, so protecting against worse attacks later. 2 a substance made from the germs that cause a particular disease and given to someone to prevent the disease.

vac'uum n a space from which all the air has been taken.

vacuum bottle, vacuum flask n a container with two walls with a vacuum between them so that hot food keeps hot or cold food remains cold.

vacuum clean'er n a machine that cleans carpets, etc, by sucking dust into a bag.

vag'abond n one who wanders aimlessly from place to place:—adj wandering.

va'grant adj wandering:—n a wanderer or tramp:—n **va'grancy**.

vague adj not clear, not definite:—n **vague'ness**.

vain adj 1 having no meaning or value. 2 too proud of oneself. 3 useless:—**in vain** without result or effect.

val'ance n a short curtain hanging from a couch, bedstead, etc.

valedic'tion n 1 farewell. 2 a speech made at this time.

valedictor'ian n a student appointed on grounds of merit to deliver the valedictory oration on commencement day.

valedic'tory adj said, shown, performed, or done by way of valediction:—n a valedictory oration.

val'ence n the power of chemical elements to combine.

val'entine n 1 one chosen as a lover or beloved on St Valentine's day, February 14. 2 a card expressing love sent on this day.

val'et n 1 a man's personal servant. 2 a steward in a hotel or on board ship:—vb 1 to work as a valet. 2 to clean a car as a professional service.

valetudina'rian n (old) one who is always worrying about the state of his or her health.

val'iant adj brave.

val'id adj 1 correct according to law. 2 good, sound:—n **valid'ity**.

valise [va-leez'] n a traveling bag for holding belongings.

val'ley n the low ground between neighboring hills or mountains, often watered by a river.

val'or n bravery, courage:—adj **val'orous**.

val'uable adj 1 of great worth or importance. 2 costly.

valua'tion n the estimated worth, price, or importance of a thing.

val'ue n 1 worth, importance. 2 price, cost. 3 pl the standards by which one judges the worth of things.

valve n 1 a device that, when opened, allows gas, air, fluid, etc, to pass through in one direction only. 2 a device by which one can control the power of radio waves transmitted or received.

van¹ short for **vanguard**.

van² n a covered car or wagon for goods.

van'dal n one who purposefully and pointlessly destroys or damages public buildings or other property:—n **van'dalism**.

vane n a weathercock.

van'guard n (abbr **van**) 1 the front part of an army or fleet. 2 those leading the way.

vanil'la n a flavoring prepared from a tropical plant.

van'ish vb 1 to disappear. 2 to pass out of sight.

van'ity n 1 lack of meaning or value. 2 too great pride in oneself, conceit. 3 a built-in cupboard with a basin.

van'quish vb to defeat completely.

va'por n 1 the gas given off by a body when sufficiently heated. 2 mist.

va'riable adj 1 quick to change. 2 changing often or easily.

va'riance n:—**at variance with** in disagreement with.

varia'tion n change, difference.

vari'ety n 1 the state of being different. 2 a collection of different or slightly different things. 3 a class or species. 4 a theater show with performers of different kinds.

var'nish n a clear, sticky liquid used to give a shiny surface to wood, metal, paper, etc:—vb to coat with varnish.

va'ry vb to make or become different, to change.

vase [väz] n a vessel used for holding flowers or as an ornament.

vast adj 1 of great extent. 2 huge.

vat n a large tub or tank.

vaude'ville n a stage show with various acts, such as singing, dancing, and comedy.

vault¹ n 1 an arched roof. 2 a room, usu underground, with an arched roof (e.g. a cellar, a tomb).

vault² vb to jump over while resting the hand on something for support:—n a leap (over something).

veal n the flesh of a calf.

veer vb to change direction.

veg'etable n a plant grown for food.

vegeta'rian n one who eats only vegetable food, taking no meat.

veg'etate vb to lead a dull, inactive life.

vegeta'tion n 1 plants in general. 2 the plants of a particular region.

ve'hement adj 1 full of strong feeling, passionate. 2 having a forceful way of speaking:—n **ve'hemence**.

ve'hicle n any type of carriage, cart, etc, used on land for carrying people or things.

veil n 1 a cloth worn over the face to hide or protect it. 2 something that hides or conceals:—vb 1 to conceal. 2 to cover.

vein n 1 one of the blood vessels through which blood flows back to the heart. 2 a sap tube or small rib of a leaf. 3 a layer of mineral in a rock. 4 a mood.

velo'city n speed.

vel'vet n a thick silk fabric or substitute, with a soft pile on one side.

vel'vety adj soft and smooth, like velvet.

vend vb (old) to sell.

vendet'ta n a feud between two families in which each is bound to revenge the death of any of its members killed by the other.

ven'dor n one who sells.

veneer' n 1 a thin layer (of fine wood, plastic, etc) glued on the surface of another inferior one. 2 something that appears fine but is not deep or lasting:—vb to cover with veneer.

ven'erable adj worthy of respect because of age or goodness, old and honorable.

ven'erate vb to feel great respect for, to show one's respect for:—n **venera'tion**.

163

ven'geance n harm done in return for harm or injury received, revenge.

venge'ful adj desiring revenge.

ven'ison n the flesh of deer.

ven'om n 1 (fml) poison. 2 spite.

ven'omous adj 1 poisonous. 2 spiteful.

vent n a hole or opening through which air, smoke, etc, can pass. 2 an outlet. 3 expression:—vb to give free expression to.

ven'tilate vb 1 to allow fresh air to pass into or through. 2 to discuss freely:—n **ventila'tion**.

ven'tilator n any device to let in fresh air.

ventril'oquist n one able to speak without moving the lips, in such a way that the voice seems to come from another person:—n **ventril'oquism**.

ven'ture n an undertaking that may lead one into loss or danger:—vb 1 to dare. 2 to risk.

ven'ue n the place appointed for a trial or public event.

veran'da, veran'dah n a covered platform or open balcony along the wall of a house.

verb n a word that tells the action or state of the subject of a sentence.

verb'al adj 1 of or in words. 2 by word of mouth. 3 word for word:—adv **verb'ally**.

ver'dict n 1 the decision of a jury. 2 a considered opinion or judgment.

verge n 1 the edging of a road etc. 2 edge, brink:—also vb.

ver'ify vb 1 confirm. 2 to prove to be true:—n **verifica'tion**.

ver'itable adj (fml or hum) true, real, actual.

ver'min n 1 small animals that do harm (e.g. to crops), as rats, mice, etc. 2 insects connected with discomfort to human beings or dirt.

ver'satile adj able to do many different kinds of things:—n **versatil'ity**.

verse n 1 poetry. 2 writing set down in the form of poetry. 3 a section of poetry.

ver'sion n 1 an account or description peculiar to a particular person. 2 a translation.

ver'sus prep against.

ver'tebra n (pl **ver'tebrae**) one of the bones of the spine.

ver'tebrate adj having a backbone:—n an animal with a backbone.

ver'tex n (pl **vertices**) the highest point.

ver'tical adj upright, at right angles to the bottom or ground level.

ver'tigo n dizziness, giddiness.

ver'y adj true, real:—adv extremely.

ves'sel n 1 a container for holding things. 2 a ship or boat.

vest n 1 a waist-length, sleeveless garment worn immediately under a jacket, a waistcoat. 2 an undershirt.

vested interests npl rights that have been long held and will not readily be given up.

ves'tibule n a porch or small compartment between the outer and inner front doors of a house, a small entrance hall.

ves'tige n 1 a mark or trace. 2 a very small amount.

vet[1] short for **veteran**, **veterinarian**.

vet[2] vb (**vet'ted, vet'ting**) to approve, to pass as sound.

vet'eran n an old person having long experience, esp as a soldier:—also adj.

veterinar'ian n (abbr **vet**) an animal doctor.

vet'erinary adj having to do with the diseases of domestic animals.

ve'to n (pl **ve'toes**) the right to refuse or forbid:—vb to forbid.

vex vb to make angry, to annoy:—n **vexa'tion**.

via [vee'-a] prep by way of.

vi'able adj 1 able to exist or survive. 2 workable.

vi'brant adj 1 quivering. 2 full of energy.

vibrate vb 1 to move quickly backward and forward. 2 to shake, to quiver:—n **vibra'tion**.

vic'ar n the minister in charge of a parish.

vic'arage n the house of a vicar.

vice[1] n a fault, a bad habit.

vice[2] see **vise**.

vice- prefix in the place of, next in order to (vice-admiral, vice-chairman, etc).

vice versa [vī'-si ver'-sa] adv the other way round.

vicin'ity n neighborhood.

vi'cious adj wicked, evil, ill-tempered.

vic'tim n 1 one who suffers either from his or her own faults or from outside circumstances. 2 a person or animal killed and offered in sacrifice.

vic'timize vb to make to suffer, to treat unfairly:—n **victimiza'tion**.

vic'tor n one who wins or conquers.

victo'rious adj successful in a war, battle, or contest.

vic'tory n the winning of a battle, contest, or match.

vi'deo n the transmission or recording of TV programs or films using a TV set and a **video recorder** and **videotape**:—also vb.

vie vb to try hard to do better than.

view n 1 all that can be seen at one look or from one point, a scene. 2 opinion. 3 intention:—vb 1 to look at. 2 to examine, to consider.

view'point n 1 a place from which one can see the surroundings well. 2 the way in which one considers or thinks of something.

vi'gil n an act of staying awake all night or of remaining watchful.

vi'gilance n watchfulness, care.

vi'gilant adj watchful, careful.

vig'orous adj full of strength or energy, active.

vig'or n strength and energy, power of mind.

vile adj 1 wicked, evil. 2 disgusting, horrible.

vill'age n a group of houses, stores, etc, smaller than a town.

vill'ager n one who lives in a village.

vill'ain n a bad or wicked person, a scoundrel.

vill'ainy n wickedness.

vim n energy, strength, force.

vin'dicate vb 1 to show that charges made are untrue, to free from blame. 2 to prove that something is true or right, to justify:—n **vindica'tion**.

vindic'tive adj eager to obtain revenge, spiteful.

vine n a climbing plant that bears grapes.

vin'egar n a sour liquid made from wine or malt and used in cooking or for seasoning.

vineyard [vin'-yärd] n a field or area in which vines are cultivated.

vio'la n a large type of violin.

vi'olence n 1 great force. 2 harm, injury.

vi'olent adj 1 strong. 2 using force.

vi'olet n 1 a small bluish-purple flower. 2 a bluish-purple color:—adj bluish-purple.

violin' n a four-stringed musical instrument played with a bow:—n **vi'olinist**.

violoncello [vī-ê-lên-chel'-ō] n (abbr **cello**) a large violin giving deep notes:—n **violoncell'ist**.

vi'per n a poisonous snake.

vir'gin n a chaste unmarried girl or woman:—adj 1 pure. 2 still in its original condition:—n **virgin'ity**.

vir'ile adj manly, strong:—n **viril'ity**.

vir'tual *adj* being so in fact but not in name or title.

vir'tue *n* **1** goodness of life or character. **2** a good quality, power, strength.

vir'tuous *adj* morally good, of good character, leading a good life.

vir'ulent *adj* **1** powerful, dangerous. **2** full of hatred, spiteful:— *n* **vir'ulence**.

vi'rus *n* any of various types of germ that are smaller than bacteria and cause infectious diseases in the body.

visa [vee'-za] *n* a permit stamped on a passport, giving the owner the right to enter or leave a particular country.

vise, vice *n* an instrument for holding something (a piece of wood, metal, etc) steady while one is working on it.

visibil'ity *n* **1** clearness to sight. **2** the state of weather, atmosphere, etc, as they affect one's ability to see clearly.

vis'ible *adj* able to be seen.

vi'sion *n* **1** the ability to see, sight. **2** something imagined as in a dream. **3** something seen that has no bodily existence. **4** the power to foresee consequences.

vi'sionary *adj* imaginative:— *n* an imaginative person, an idealist.

vis'it *vb* **1** to go to see or stay with. **2** to call upon:— *n* **1** a call upon. **2** a short stay.

vis'itor *n* one who visits.

vi'tal *adj* **1** very important. **2** unable to be done without, necessary to life.

vital'ity *n* energy, vigor, liveliness.

vit'amin *n* one of several substances found in food, necessary to the health of the body.

vitriol'ic *adj* using violent language, full of hatred.

viva'cious *adj* lively, bright, and talkative.

viva'city *n* liveliness.

viv'id *adj* **1** bright, striking. **2** appearing true to life.

vix'en *n* **1** a female fox. **2** a bad-tempered woman.

viz *adv* (short for Latin *videlicet*) that is, namely.

vocab'ulary *n* **1** all the words used by a certain person or a certain work. **2** a list of words with their meanings.

vo'cal *adj* **1** having to do with the voice, spoken or sung. **2** intended to be heard.

vo'calist *n* a singer.

voca'tion *n* one's employment, profession, or trade. **2** the particular work one feels one is specially fitted for.

voca'tional *adj* concerned with one's profession or trade.

vod'ka *n* a strong drink, made from rye, originating in Russia.

vogue [vōg] *n* a popular or passing fashion.

voice *n* **1** the sound produced through the mouth when speaking or singing. **2** a vote, an opinion. **3** the right to speak or express an opinion:— *vb* **1** to say. **2** to express.

void *n* empty space.

volca'no *n* (*pl* **volca'noes**) a mountain with an opening at its summit through which molten rock, metals, etc, are occasionally forced up in a red-hot stream from beneath the surface of the earth:— *adj* **volcan'ic**.

voll'ey *n* **1** the firing of several guns or throwing of many things at the same time. **2** the speaking of a number of words in quick succession. **3** in tennis, the hitting of a ball before it touches the ground.

volt *n* the unit used in measuring electrical power or force.

volt'age *n* electrical power measured in volts.

vol'uble *adj* speaking much:— *n* **volubil'ity**.

vol'ume *n* **1** a book. **2** one of a series in a set of books. **3** the amount of space taken up by anything. **4** a large mass or amount. **5** level of sound.

volu'minous *adj* very big.

vol'untary *adj* done of one's own free will, not forced:— *n* an organ solo before or after a church service.

volunteer' *n* one who offers to do something without being asked or ordered:— *vb* **1** to offer one's services. **2** to give (information) unasked.

vom'it *vb* **1** to throw up from the stomach through the mouth, to be sick. **2** to put out in large clouds, e.g. of smoke.

voo'doo *n* a primitive form of worship, witchcraft.

vor'tex *n* **1** a whirlpool. **2** a whirlwind.

vote *n* **1** an expression of opinion for or against a proposal. **2** the support given by an individual to a person contesting an election:— *vb* **1** to give a vote. **2** to decide by vote:— *n* **vo'ter**.

vouch *vb* to speak (on behalf of) with confidence, to confirm, to guarantee.

vouch'er *n* a paper handed over in exchange for goods instead of cash.

vow *n* a solemn promise, a promise made to God:— *vb* to promise solemnly.

vow'el *n* **1** a simple sound (*a, e, i, o, u*) made by the voice without obstruction to the air passage. **2** the letter representing it.

voy'age *n* a long journey, esp by sea.

vul'gar *adj* coarse in manners or behavior, rude.

vulgar fraction *n* a simple fraction.

vulgar'ity *n* rudeness, coarseness.

vul'nerable *adj* **1** able to be wounded or hurt. **2** weakly defended against attack.

vul'ture *n* a large bird that feeds on the flesh of dead animals.

W

wad'dle *vb* to walk, rolling from side to side, as a duck:—*also n.*

wade *vb* 1 to walk through water. 2 to walk slowly and with difficulty. 3 to read through with difficulty.

wa'fer *n* a very thin cake or biscuit.

waf'fle *n* a thick pancake baked in a waffle iron.

waffle iron *n* a metal cooking utensil with two hinged parts that close and impress a square pattern on a waffle.

waft *vb* to bear along gently through the air.

wag *vb* (**wagged, wag'ging**) to shake up and down or to and fro:—*n* 1 a wagging movement. 2 one fond of telling jokes.

wage *n* money paid regularly for work done (*often pl*):—*vb* to carry on, e.g. war.

wa'ger *n* a bet:—*vb* to bet.

wag'gle *vb* to wag.

wag'on *n* 1 a four-wheeled cart. 2 a railroad truck.

waif *n* a homeless child or animal.

wail *vb* to cry aloud in grief, distress:—*n* a loud cry of grief, a moaning cry.

waist *n* the narrowest part of the human trunk, just below the ribs.

wait *vb* 1 to stay in a place in the hope or expectation of something happening. 2 to serve at table:—*n* time spent waiting.

wait'er *n* a person employed to serve food at table:—*f* **wait'ress**.

waive *vb* to give up, not to insist on.

wake[1] *vb* (*pt* **woke**, *pp* **wo'ken**) 1 to arouse from sleep. 2 to return to full consciousness after sleep:—*n* a watch kept over a dead body until the time of burial, sometimes with feasting.

wake[2] *n* the track left on water by a moving ship:—**in the wake of** behind, following.

wa'ken *vb* to wake.

walk *vb* 1 to advance step by step. 2 to go on foot:—*n* 1 an outing on foot. 2 one's manner of walking. 3 a road or path.

wall *n* 1 a barrier of stone, brick, etc. 2 one of the sides of a building, room, etc:—*vb* to provide with a wall.

wall'et *n* a flat pocketbook for bills, cards, etc.

wal'lop *vb* to thrash soundly, to strike heavily:—*also n.*

wall'paper *n* colored or decorative paper covering the walls of rooms.

wal'nut *n* 1 a tree whose wood is much used for making furniture. 2 its eatable nut.

wal'rus *n* a large tusked sea mammal that can live on both land and sea.

waltz *n* 1 a dance for two people. 2 music for such a dance:—*vb* to dance a waltz.

wand *n* 1 a long thin stick. 2 the rod of a magician or conjurer.

wan'der *vb* 1 to go purposelessly from place to place. 2 to lose one's way. 3 to talk in a disconnected manner. 4 to go off the point:—*n* **wan'derer**.

wane *vb* 1 to grow less or smaller. 2 to lose strength or power.

want *n* 1 need. 2 longing. 3 shortage. 4 poverty:—*vb* 1 to lack. 2 to need. 3 to desire.

war *n* 1 a state of fighting and enmity between nations or within a nation. 2 an active campaign against something:—*vb* (**warred, war'ring**) to make war.

ward *vb* (*with* **off**) 1 to defend oneself against. 2 to defeat (an attack) for the time being:—*n* 1 in a hospital, a large room containing several beds. 2 a division of a city for the purposes of local government. 3 a person under the legal care of another until he or she is old enough to manage his or her own affairs.

war'den *n* 1 an official. 2 a person in charge of a building or home. 3 a prison governor.

ward'robe *n* 1 a cupboard for hanging clothes. 2 all a person's clothes.

ware'house *n* a building for storing goods.

war'fare *n* the carrying on of fighting in war.

war'like *adj* fond of fighting.

war'lock *n* one having magical powers.

warm *adj* 1 quite hot. 2 affectionate. 3 sincere:—*vb* to make or become warm.

warmth *n* 1 gentle heat. 2 sincerity.

warn *vb* 1 to advise against possible danger or error. 2 to tell to be careful.

warn'ing *n* 1 advice to be careful. 2 advice that danger or trouble lies ahead.

warp *vb* 1 to twist out of shape. 2 to become twisted. 3 to spoil the nature or character of.

war'ren *n* many rabbit burrows in one place.

war'rior *n* one good at fighting.

wart *n* a hard dry growth on the skin.

war'y *adj* careful, cautious.

wash *vb* 1 to clean with water. 2 to flow against or over. 3 to carry away (on a rush of liquid). 4 to color lightly:—*n* 1 the act of cleaning with water. 2 a washing, the flow or dash of water. 3 a healing liquid. 4 a thin coat of color.

wash cloth *n* a small piece of material used for washing the face, etc.

wash'er *n* a ring of metal, rubber, etc, to keep a bolt, etc, firmly in position.

wash'ing *n* 1 dirty clothes or linen to be washed. 2 clothes newly washed.

wasp *n* a stinging winged insect, with black and yellow stripes on its body.

waste *vb* 1 to fail to put to a useful purpose. 2 to spend or use foolishly. 3 to destroy, to damage. 4 to make or become weaker:—*adj* 1 left over. 2 uncultivated, undeveloped:—*n* 1 what is left over as useless. 2 useless spending.

waste'basket *n* a container for waste paper.

waste'ful *adj* spending foolishly or uselessly.

waste pa'per *n* paper thrown away as useless.

watch *vb* 1 to look at or observe with care. 2 to look at. 3 to guard. 4 to look after. 5 (*old*) to stay awake:—*n* 1 a guard. 2 a careful look-out. 3 a four-hour spell of duty for half the crew on board a ship. 4 a clock carried in the pocket or on the wrist.

watch'ful *adj* keeping a lookout.

watch'maker *n* one who makes or repairs watches.

watch'man *n* a man employed to look after a building or site when it is unoccupied.

wa'ter *n* 1 the clear liquid that falls as rain and flows in streams and rivers. 2 a large area of water, as a lake, sea, etc:—*vb* 1 to supply with water. 2 to pour or sprinkle water on. 3 to mix water with illegally.

wa'terfall *n* a stream falling over steep rocks or stones to a lower level.

water lily *n* a plant with floating flowers and leaves, found in ponds, etc.

wa'terlogged *adj* soaked or filled with water.

water po'lo *n* a ball game for swimmers.

wa'terproof *adj* able to keep out water, that water cannot pass through:—*n* 1 waterproof cloth. 2 a raincoat.

wa'ter-ski *n* a board on which a person can stand and be towed over water by a speedboat:—*also vb*:—*n* **wa'ter-ski'er**.

wa'terspout *n* a column of water created by a whirlwind.

wa'tertight *adj* so tight that water can pass neither in nor out.

wa'tery *adj* 1 full of water. 2 tasteless, thin.

watt *n* a unit of measurement of electric power.

wave *n* 1 a moving ridge of water rising above the surface of the sea and then sinking down again. 2 any movement resembling this. 3 one of several ridges in the hair. 4 a moving of the hand as a signal:—*vb* 1 to move or make to move up and down or to and fro. 2 to shake in the air as a sign. 3 to put waves in hair. 4 to signal with one's hand.

wav'er *vb* 1 to be uncertain, to hesitate. 2 to move unsteadily. 3 to flicker.

wav'y *adj* 1 rising and falling in waves. 2 covered with waves.

wax *n* 1 a sticky yellow substance made by bees. 2 any material resembling this. 3 a substance used to seal letters, parcels, etc.

way *n* 1 a track, path, or road. 2 a method of doing something. 3 distance traveled. 4 the route to a place. 5 a custom or habit.

weak *adj* 1 not strong, feeble. 2 giving in too easily to others. 3 not good at.

weak'en *vb* to make or become weak.

weak'ness *n* 1 lack of strength or determination. 2 a bad point in one's character. 3 a foolish liking for.

weal *n* a raised mark on the skin caused by a blow from a whip, thin stick, etc.

wealth *n* 1 riches. 2 plenty.

wealth'y *adj* very rich.

wea'pon *n* any instrument that can be used in fighting or attack.

wear [wâr] *vb* 1 (*pt* **wore**, *pp* **worn**) 1 to have on the body as clothing. 2 to put or stick on one's clothes for show. 3 to damage or weaken by rubbing or use. 4 to tire out:—*n* 1 clothing. 2 damage caused by rubbing or use:—*n* **wear'er**:—**wear away** to become gradually less, to rub or be rubbed away:—**wear on** to pass slowly:—**wear off** to become gradually less:—**wear out** 1 to exhaust. 2 to make useless by using too often.

weary [wee'-ri] *adj* 1 tired by continued effort, exhausted. 2 fed up, bored.

wea'sel *n* a small reddish-brown animal that eats, mice, birds, etc.

wea'ther *n* the general conditions of the atmosphere (e.g. sunshine, rain, wind, etc) at any particular time:—*vb* 1 to come safely through. 2 to be damaged or discolored by the effects of weather.

wea'ther-beaten *adj* marred or colored by the effects of the weather.

wea'ther-bound *adj* held up or delayed by bad weather.

wea'thercock, wea'thervane *ns* a pointer, often in the shape of a cock, that shows the direction from which the wind is blowing.

weave *vb* (*pt* **wove**, *pp* **wov'en**) 1 to form cloth by intertwining threads. 2 to put together sticks, twigs, etc, by interlacing them. 3 to make up:—*n* **weav'er**.

web *n* 1 cloth made by weaving. 2 the net of fine threads made by a spider.

wed *vb* (**wed'ded, wed'ding**) to marry.

wed'ding *n* a marriage.

wedge *n* a piece of wood, metal, etc, thick at one end and narrowing to a sharp edge at the other:—*vb* to split open, fix, or fasten with a wedge.

Wednesday [Wed'-áns-dā] *n* the fourth or middle day of the week.

weed *n* a useless plant growing in a garden or field:—*vb* to pull up weeds.

week *n* a period of seven days.

week'day *n* any day of the week except Sunday and often Saturday.

weekend' *n* the period from the time one's work ceases on Friday or Saturday until one begins it again on Monday.

week'ly *adj* happening once a week:—*n* a newspaper or magazine published once a week.

weep *vb* (*pt, pp* **wept**) 1 to shed tears, to cry. 2 to mourn.

weigh [wā] *vb* 1 to measure the heaviness of. 2 to consider carefully. 3 to raise (anchor). 4 to be of a certain heaviness. 5 to have importance

weight [wāt] *n* 1 heaviness. 2 a piece of metal, etc, of known heaviness, used in finding how heavy another object is. 3 importance, influence. 4 a heavy load.

weight'y *adj* 1 heavy. 2 important, deserving careful consideration.

weird [weerd] *adj* 1 strange, eerie, unearthly. 2 odd, very strange:—*n* fate.

wel'come *adj* 1 pleasing. 2 allowed to use or take at any time:—*n* a kindly greeting or reception:—*vb* 1 to greet kindly. 2 to receive or hear with.

wel'fare *n* 1 happiness, success. 2 health, good living conditions. 3 assistance or financial aid granted to the poor, unemployed, etc:—*vb* 1 to do good to. 2 to be of advantage to.

well[1] *n* 1 a spring of water. 2 a hole in the ground from which water can be drawn. 3 a pit made in the ground to reach oil. 4 a fountain:—*vb* 1 to come up as from a spring. 2 to gush out.

well[2] *adv* 1 in a good way or style. 2 thoroughly. 3 rightly. 4 with approval:—*adj* 1 in good health. 2 all right:—**as well as** in addition to.

well'being *n* success, happiness.

well-known' *adj* famous.

well-off', well-to-do' *adjs* rich.

well'-wisher *n* a friendly supporter.

well-worn' *adj* much worn, much used.

wend *vb* (*vb*) to go, to make (one's way).

west *n* one of the four principal points of the compass, the direction in which the sun sets.

west'erly *adj* from or toward the west.

west'ern *adj* in or from the west.

west'ward *adv* toward the west.

wet *adj* 1 covered or soaked with water or other liquid. 2 not dry, moist. 3 rainy:—*n* rainy weather:—*vb* (**wet'ted, wet'ting**) to make wet.

whack *vb* (*inf*) to strike sharply, to beat severely:—*n* 1 a blow. 2 a share.

whale *n* a large sea mammal:—*vb* to hunt whales.

wharf *n* (*pl* **wharves**) a platform or quay at which ships are loaded and unloaded.

wheat *n* the grain from which bread flour is obtained.

wheat'en *adj* made from wheat.

wheed'le *vb* to try to please a person in order to get him or her to do something, to coax.

wheel *n* a round frame, often strengthened by spokes, turning on an axis:—*vb* 1 to move on wheels. 2 to turn like a wheel.

wheel'barrow *n* a handcart, usu with one wheel, two legs, and handles.

wheeze *vb* to breathe with a hoarse or hissing sound:—*also n*:—*adj* **wheez'y**.

when *adv, conj* at what or which time.

whence *adv, conj* from what place.

whenev'er *adv, conj* at no matter what time.

where *adv, conj* at, to, or in what place.

where'abouts *n* the place one is in.

whereas' *conj* since, although.

whereby adv, conj by which.

whereupon adv, conj after which.

wherev'er adv, conj at, to, or in whatever place.

whet vb **1** to sharpen. **2** to make (a desire) more strongly felt.

wheth'er conj if—from which of two.

whey n the watery part of the milk, separated from the curd.

whiff n **1** a puff of air or smoke. **2** a quick or slight smell:—vb **1** to puff. **2** to smell.

while n a space of time:—conj during the time that:—vb to pass (time) in pleasure or leisure.

whilst conj while.

whim n a sudden strange desire or idea.

whim'per vb to cry brokenly, to whine:—also n.

whine n a long cry of complaint, a wail:—vb **1** to utter a sad or complaining cry. **2** to speak in a complaining voice.

whin'ny n the high-pitched cry of a horse:—also vb

whip n a cord attached to a stick for beating or driving animals:—vb (**whipped'**, **whip'ping**) **1** to strike with a whip. **2** to beat eggs, cream, etc, into a froth. **3** to take or move (something) quickly.

whir vb (**whirred'**, **whir'ring**) to move through the air or spin with a buzzing or clicking sound:—also n.

whirl vb to move quickly around and around, to spin quickly:—n a quick round-and-round movement, confusion.

whirl'pool n a current of water turning around and around with a circular motion.

whirl'wind n a violent wind blowing around and around in a circle.

whisk vb **1** to knock or brush with a quick light movement. **2** to beat lightly into a froth. **3** to take with a quick movement:—n **1** a quick or jerky movement. **2** an implement for beating eggs, etc.

whis'ker n **1** the hair growing on the cheeks, the stiff hairs growing on the cheeks of men. **2** the stiff hairs growing above the mouth of certain animals.

whis'key n an alcoholic drink distilled from barley in Ireland and corn or rye in North America.

whis'ky n an alcoholic drink made in Scotland from barley, rye, etc.

whis'per vb **1** to speak very softly, using the breath instead of the voice. **2** to rustle:—n **1** a very soft voice. **2** what is whispered. **3** a rumor.

whistle [whis'-el] vb **1** to make a high, shrill sound with the lips or a special instrument. **2** to play a tune by whistling:—n **1** a shrill sound made with the lips or a special instrument. **2** an instrument that makes a whistling sound when blown.

whit n a tiny piece.

white adj **1** of the color of clean snow or milk. **2** pale. **3** having a pale skin (as opposed to yellow, brown, or black):—also n.

white lie n a harmless lie told for politeness.

whit'en vb to make or become white.

whith'er adv and conj to which or what place.

whit'tle vb **1** to make smaller or thinner. **2** to cut down or reduce a little at a time.

whiz vb (**whizzed'**, **whiz'zing**) to make a hissing or swishing sound when moving through the air:—also n.

who pron which person.

whole adj [hōl] adj **1** complete, entiare **2** unharmed:—n the total, all.

wholeheart'ed adj enthusiastic, keen.

whole'sale n the selling of goods in large quantities to those who will resell them to others:—adj on a large scale.

whole'some adj **1** having a good effect on health. **2** healthy, morally healthy.

whol'ly adv completely.

whoop n a loud shout:—vb to make a whoop.

whosoev'er pron whoever who, any person concerned.

why adv, conj, interj for what reason.

wick n the thread in a candle, in an oil-lamp or oil heater, the band of cloth that draws up the oil and is burned to give light.

wick'ed adj bad, sinful, evil:—n **wick'edness**.

wick'et n **1** a small gate, a small door in or near a larger one. **2** in croquet, any of the small wire arches through which the balls must be hit. **3** in cricket, the sticks that the batsman stands at and defends.

wide adj broad, extending far in all directions:—adv **1** missing the target by passing beside it. **2** fully.

wid'en vb to make or become wide.

wide'spread adj occurring or found far and wide.

wid'ow n a woman whose husband is dead.

wid'ower n a man whose wife is dead.

width n breadth.

wield vb **1** to use with the hands. **2** to use or put into practice.

wife n (pl **wives**) a married woman.

wig n an artificial covering of hair for the head.

wig'gle vb to wag, to shake from side to side.

wild adj **1** not tamed or civilized. **2** not cultivated. **3** savage. **4** uncontrolled. **5** very.

wil'derness n a desert, an uncultivated or uninhabited area.

wile n a trick.

will n **1** one's power to make decisions or choices, self-control. **2** desire. **3** a written document made by a person to say what is to be done with his or her property after death:—vb **1** to desire. **2** to leave property to others by a signed will.

will'ful adj always wanting one's own way, done deliberately.

will'ing adj ready, eager.

will'ow n a tree with slender, easily bent branches

wilt vb **1** to droop. **2** to lose freshness or vigor.

wil'y adj cunning.

win vb (**won**, **winning**) **1** to be successful in a match or contest, to be victorious. **2** to obtain in a competition:—n **1** a success. **2** a victory:—n **win'ner**.

wince vb to twist the face from pain.

wind[1] [wind] n **1** air moving. **2** a current of air, a breeze or gale. **3** breath:—vb (pt, pp **win'ded**) to put out of breath by a blow in the stomach.

wind[2] [wīnd] vb (pt, pp **wound**) **1** to twist. **2** to coil. **3** to gather up by turning. **4** to follow a twisting course:—**wind up 1** to bring to an end. **2** to turn a handle to tighten a spring in a machine. **3** to bring to an end.

wind[3] [wīnd] vb (pt, pp **wind'ed** or **wound**) to blow (a horn).

wind'fall n **1** fruit blown down. **2** a piece of unexpected luck, an unexpected gift of money.

wind'mill n a mill with sails driven by wind.

win'dow n an opening in the wall of a house, etc, to let in light (usu filled with a sheet of glass).

wind'pipe n the air passage from the mouth to the lungs.

wind'shield n the protective glass panel at the front of a motor vehicle.

wind'y adj open to the winds, breezy, gusty.

wine n a strong drink made from the fermented juice of grapes.

wing n **1** the limb with the help of which birds, insects, etc, fly. **2** a side part or extension of a building, stage, etc. **3** the supporting parts of an airplane. **4** the side part of an army when drawn up for battle:—vb **1** to fly. **2** to wound in the wing.

wink vb **1** to shut and open one eyelid with a quick movement. **2** to flicker, to twinkle. **3** (fml) (usu with **at**) to pretend not to see:—n the act of winking.

winner see win.

win'ning adj 1 successful. 2 charming.

win'ter n the cold season of the year:—vb to spend the winter.

win'try adj like winter, cold, stormy.

wipe vb to clean or dry by gentle rubbing:—n a rub intended to clean or dry:—**wipe out** to destroy, to cause to cease to exist.

wire n 1 a thread or cord of metal. 2 a telegram:—vb 1 to provide with wire. 2 to send a telegram.

wire'less n (old) a radio:—adj without wires.

wi'ry adj thin but muscular.

wis'dom n the ability to make good use of one's knowledge and experience.

wise adj 1 having or showing wisdom. 2 sensible.

wish vb to have a desire, to want (to do), to long:—n 1 a desire. 2 the thing wanted.

wishful thinking n something believed in spite of the facts because one wants it to be true.

wish'y-wash'y adj weak and pale, feeble.

wisp n a small bundle of straw, hay, etc.

wist'ful adj thoughtful, longing.

wit n 1 intelligence, understanding. 2 the ability to say things shortly, neatly, and cleverly. 3 one having this ability.

witch n a woman believed to have magical powers granted by the devil.

witch'craft n magic performed with the aid of the devil.

witch'doctor n a man believed to be able to control evil spirits and cure illness by magic.

withdraw' vb 1 to draw or pull back, to retreat. 2 to take back (something said) as not meant. 3 to take money, etc, from one's bank or stock:—n **withdraw'al**.

with'er vb to make or become dry and faded, to shrivel, to rot away.

withhold' vb to refuse to grant or give, to keep back.

within' prep inside:—adv 1 indoors. 2 inwardly.

without' prep not having.

withstand' vb to resist, to oppose.

wit'ness n 1 a person who sees an event taking place. 2 one who tells in a court of law what took place on an occasion at which he or she was present:—vb 1 to see happening. 2 to sign a document to confirm that another has signed it in one's presence.

wit'ty adj able to say clever things briefly and often amusingly:—adv **witti'ly**.

wives see **woman**.

wiz'ard n 1 a man who claims magical powers. 2 a conjurer.

wiz'ened adj dried up and wrinkled.

wob'ble vb to sway from side to side, move unsteadily:—also n.

wob'bly adj unsteady.

woke pt of **wake**.

wolf n (pl **wolves**) a fierce wild animal of the dog family.

wo'man n (pl **wo'men**) a grown-up female human being.

wo'manhood n the state or qualities of a woman.

wo'manish adj 1 having the qualities of a woman. 2 unmanly.

women see **woman**.

won pt of **win**.

won'der n 1 great surprise or astonishment. 2 anything giving rise to such feelings, a marvel or miracle:—vb 1 to feel surprise or astonishment. 2 to think about the reasons for something.

won'derful adj very surprising, extraordinary.

woo vb to make love to, to seek to marry:—n **woo'er**.

wood n 1 a large collection of growing trees. 2 the hard substance of which the trunks and branches of trees are made, timber.

wood'ed adj covered with trees or woods.

wood'en adj 1 made of wood. 2 dull, lacking feeling.

wood'land n country covered with woods.

wood'pecker n a bird that taps holes in trees with its long pointed beak and takes out insects from them with its tongue.

woods'man n a man who works in woods or forests, one who cuts down trees.

wood'work n 1 the art of making objects out of wood. 2 objects so made.

wood'worm n a grub that eats its way into wood and destroys it.

wood'y adj 1 made of wood. 2 covered with woods.

wool n 1 the soft, wavy hair covering the body of certain animals (e.g. sheep, goats, etc). 2 thread or cloth made from wool.

wool'en adj made of wool:—also n.

wool'ly, wool'ly adj 1 covered with wool. 2 like wool.

word [wèrd] n 1 a sound or group of sounds expressing an idea. 2 a message, information. 3 a promise:—**have words with** to quarrel with:—**word for word** in exactly the same words as those used before.

word-per'fect adj able to say without an error the words of something learnt.

word'y adj using more words than are necessary.

wore pt of **wear**.

work n 1 effort. 2 a task, tasks. 3 that which one does for a living. 4 a book, picture, piece of music, etc. 5 pl a factory. 6 pl the parts of a machine that make it go:—vb 1 to labor, to toil. 2 to be in a job. 3 to make to do work. 4 to have the desired effect or result. 5 to cause, to bring about. 6 to give shape to.

work'er n 1 a person who works. 2 an insect (e.g. a bee) that does all the work.

work'man n one who works, esp with the hands.

work'manship n 1 the skill of a worker. 2 the quality of a piece of work.

work'shop n a building or room in which work is carried on.

world n 1 the earth on which we live. 2 any planet or star. 3 the universe and all created things. 4 all human beings. 5 any sphere of activity, study, etc. 6 a great amount.

world'ly adj 1 having to do with this world or life. 2 interested only in the things of this life.

worldwide' adj spread throughout or found everywhere in the world.

worm n 1 a small creeping animal without a backbone. 2 (inf) a despicable person:—vb 1 to wriggle or crawl along. 2 to do something slowly and secretly. 3 to persuade to tell by persistent questioning.

worn pp of **wear**:—adj showing signs of wear.

wor'ry vb 1 to feel anxiety. 2 to trouble, to vex. 3 to tear with the teeth:—n 1 anxiety, trouble. 2 a cause of anxiety.

worse adj more bad, less good, more ill or sick:—adv more badly.

wors'en vb to make or become worse.

wor'ship n 1 a religious service. 2 great love or reverence for. 3 a title of respect for magistrates:—vb (**wor'shipped, wor'shipping**) 1 to pray to. 2 to honor greatly. 3 to join in a religious service:—n **wor'shipper**.

worst adj most bad or ill:—adv most badly:—n the greatest evil or ill possible:—vb to defeat.

worth adj 1 equal in value to. 2 deserving of. 3 having such-and-such an amount of money or property:—n 1 value. 2 price. 3 merit, excellence.

worth'less adj of no use or value.

worthwhile' adj profitable, repaying the money, work, etc, expended.

worth'y adj deserving respect:—n (inf) a worthy person.

would'-be adj wishing to be, intending.

wound¹ [wōnd] *n* a hurt, cut, or bruise, an injury:—*vb* **1** to injure, to cause a wound to. **2** to hurt the feelings of.

wound² [woond] *pt of* **wind**:——**wound-up** over-excited.

wove *pt of* **weave**:——*pp* **woven**.

wran′gle *vb* to quarrel, to argue angrily:—*n* a quarrel, a dispute:—*n* **wrang′ler**.

wrap *vb* (**wrapped′, wrap′ping**) to fold paper, cloth, etc, around so as to cover:—*n* a shawl.

wrap′per *n* **1** a loose outer garment for wear indoors. **2** a cover for books, etc.

wrath *n* great anger, rage.

wreath *n* flowers, leaves, etc, woven together to form a ring or crown.

wreathe *vb* **1** to put a wreath on or around. **2** to weave together to make a wreath.

wreck *n* **1** destruction, esp of a ship at sea. **2** a ruin. **3** the remains of a ship destroyed by the sea:—*vb* to ruin, to destroy.

wreck′age *n* the broken parts of a wrecked ship.

wren *n* a very small songbird.

wrench *n* **1** a violent twist. **2** the sorrow caused by parting from or giving away. **3** a tool for gripping nuts, bolts, etc:—*vb* **1** to give a sudden twist or pull to. **2** to sprain.

wrest *vb* to twist, to pull violently from.

wres′tle *vb* to struggle with another by gripping and trying to throw down.

wrest′ler *n* one who wrestles for sport.

wrest′ling *n* the sport of wrestling.

wretch′ed *adj* **1** miserable. **2** worthless.

wrig′gle *vb* **1** to twist from side to side. **2** to move with a wriggling movement:—*also n*.

wring *vb* (*pt, pp* **wrung**) **1** to twist tightly. **2** to get by pressure or persuasion.

wrink′le *n* a fold or furrow in the skin, or in cloth, etc:—*vb* to make wrinkles in.

wrist *n* the joint between the hand and the arm.

wrist′watch *ns* a watch attached to a band worn around the wrist.

write *vb* (*pt* **wrote**, *pp* **writ′ten**) **1** to make marks standing for sounds, letters, or words on paper, etc, with a pen or pencil. **2** to make up stories, poems, etc, for publication. **3** to write a letter to.

writ′er *n* **1** an author. **2** one who writes.

writhe *vb* to twist and turn the body about.

wrong *adj* **1** not correct, false. **2** incorrect in one's opinion, etc. **3** not good, not morally right, evil:—*vb* **1** to treat unjustly. **2** to do harm to:—*n* **1** an injustice. **2** harm.

wrong′doer *n* a criminal, a sinner:—*n* **wrong′doing**.

wrong′ful *adj* **1** unjust. **2** criminal, wrong.

wrote *pt of* **write**.

wry *adj* **1** twisted, turned to one side. **2** slightly mocking.

XYZ

Xe′rox *n trademark* a photocopying process:—*vb* to make photocopies by machine.

Xmas [ex′-mès] *short for* **Christmas**.

X′-rays *npl* electric rays that are able to pass through solid substances and so can be used in photographing broken bones or other objects hidden behind a solid surface.

xylophone [zī′-lō-fōn] *n* a musical instrument of hanging wooden bars that give notes when struck with a wooden hammer.

yacht [yot] *n* a ship, esp a sailing ship, used for pleasure or racing.

yak *n* a type of ox with long silky hair, found in Tibet.

yank *vb* to move suddenly or with a jerk.

yap *vb* (**yapped′**, **yap′ping**) to yelp, to bark shrilly.

yard *n* **1** a measure of length (=3 feet). **2** an enclosed piece of ground near or behind a building. **3** a piece of ground enclosed for a particular purpose.

yard′stick *n* a standard by which one measures or judges other things.

yarn *n* **1** any type of spun thread. **2** (*inf*) a made-up or improbable story.

yawl *n* a small sailing ship.

yawn *vb* **1** to open the mouth wide because of tiredness or boredom. **2** to be wide open:—*n* act of yawning.

ye *pron* old form of you (*pl*).

year *n* the time taken by the earth to travel once around the sun, 365 days, esp from January 1 to December 31, twelve months.

year′ly *adj* **1** happening once a year. **2** happening every year:—*also adv*.

yearn *vb* to desire greatly, to long (for).

yearn′ing *n* a strong desire, a longing.

yeast *n* a frothy substance used for making bread rise and in making beer, etc.

yell *vb* to scream, to shout loudly and suddenly:—*also n*.

yell′ow *n* a bright golden color, as of daffodils:—*adj* **1** of golden color. **2** (*inf*) cowardly.

yellow jacket *n* an American hornet or wasp with yellow markings.

yelp *vb* to utter a sharp cry, as a dog in pain:—*also n*.

yes′terday *n* the day before today:—*also adv*.

yet *adv* **1** still. **2** in addition. **3** up to the present. **4** however. **5** all the same.

yew [yū] *n* a large evergreen tree often grown in churchyards.

yield *vb* **1** to produce (fruit, crops, profit, etc). **2** to give in, to surrender. **3** to give way:—*n* **1** the amount produced or made in profit. **2** a crop.

yogurt, yoghurt [yō′-gèrt] *n* a food made from fermented milk.

yolk *n* the yellow part of an egg.

yon, yon′der *adjs* (*old*) that (one) over there:—*adv* **yon′der** over there.

yore *n* (*old*) olden times:—**of yore** (*old*) in olden times.

young *adj* not old, not grown up, childish, youthful:—*n* **1** all the children or offspring (of). **2** young people in general.

young′ster *n* a young person.

youth *n* **1** the early part of one's life. **2** a young man. **3** young people.

youth′ful *adj* young, young-looking.

yowl *vb* to cry or howl like a dog:—*also n*.

Yule *n* Christmas.

za′ny *adj* crazy.

zeal *n* keenness, eagerness, enthusiasm.

zea′lous *adj* very keen, eager.

zeb′ra *n* a striped horse-like animal of Africa.

zen′ith *n* the highest point.

ze′ro *n* **1** the figure 0. **2** the 0-mark on a measuring scale.

zero hour *n* the time fixed for the beginning of something, such as a military attack.

zest *n* enthusiasm:—*adj* **zest′ful**.

zig′zag *adj* turning sharply to the left, following a straight line, then turning sharply to the right, and so on:—*n* a zigzag line or course:—*vb* (**zig′zagged**, **zig′zagging**) to follow a zigzag course.

zinc *n* a bluish-white metal.

zip *vb* (**zipped′**, **zip′ping**) **1** (*inf*) to whiz. **2** to fasten with a zip.

zip code *n* a US postal code that uses digits to denote an area.

zip-fas′tener, zip′per *ns* a sliding fastener that causes two strips of metal teeth to engage in or disengage from each other as it moves.

zith′er *n* a flat stringed musical instrument played with the fingers.

zo′diac *n* the band of the heavens within which the sun, moon, and planets seem to move, and containing the twelve groups of stars known as the signs of the zodiac.

zone *n* **1** a belt or stripe. **2** any region with distinctive characteristics of its own.

zoo *n* a park in which animals are kept in cages, enclosures, ponds, etc, for show.

zoolo′gical *adj* having to do with the study of animals.

zoological gardens *n* a zoo.

zool′ogist *n* one who studies animals.

zool′ogy *n* the study of animals.

zoom *vb* **1** to climb rapidly at a steep angle. **2** (*inf*) to increase rapidly. **3** (*inf*) to move very quickly.

zu′cchini *npl* a kind of long squash with a smooth green skin.

APPENDIX I

Weights and Measures: Conversions and Equivalents

Measurement of mass or weight

avoirdupois *metric equivalent*

	1 grain (gr)		= 64.8 mg
	1 dram (dr)		= 1.772 g
16 drams	= 1 ounce (oz.)		= 28.3495 g
16 oz (= 7000 gr.)	= 1 pound (lb)		= 0.4536 kg
100 lb	= 1 short hundredweight		= 45.3592 kg
112 lb	= 1 long hundredweight		= 50.8024 kg
2,000 lb	= 1 short ton		= 0.9072 kg
2,240 lb	= 1 long ton		= 1.01605 tonnes

metric *avoirdupois equivalent*

	1 milligram (mg)	0.015 gr
10 mg	= 1 centigram	0.154 gr
10 cg	= 1 decigram (dg)	1.543 gr
10 dg	= 1 gram (g)	15.43 gr = 0.035 oz
10 g	= 1 decagram (dag)	= 0.353 oz
10 dag	= 1 hectogram (hg)	= 3.527 oz
10 hg	= 1 kilogram (kg)	= 2.205 lb
1000 kg	= 1 tonne (metric ton)	= 0.984 (long) ton
		= 2204.62 lb

Troy weight

metric equivalent

	1 grain	= 0.065 g
4 grains	= 1 carat of gold or silver	= 0.2592 g
6 carats	= 1 pennyweight (dwt)	= 1.5552 g
20 dwt	= 1 ounce (oz)	= 31.1035 g
12 oz	= 1 pound (lb)	= 373.242 g
25 lb	= 1 quarter (qr)	= 9.331 kg
100 lb	= 1 hundredweight (cwt)	= 37.324 kg
20 cwt	= 1 ton of gold or silver	= 746.68 kg

Note: the grain troy is the same as the grain avoirdupois, but the pound troy contains 5760 grains, the pound avoirdupois 7000 grains. Jewels are not weighed by this measure.

Linear measure

		metric equivalent
	1 inch (in)	= 25.4 mm
12 in	= 1 foot (ft)	= 0.305 m
3 ft	= 1 yard (yd)	= 0.914 m
2 yds	= 6 ft = 1 fathom (fm)	= 1.829 m
5.5 yds	= 16.5 ft = 1 rod	= 5.029 m
4 rod	= 22 yds = 66 ft = 1 chain	= 20.12 m
10 chain	= 220 yds = 660 ft = 1 furlong (fur.)	= 0.201 km
8 fur.	= 1760 yds = 5280 ft = 1 (statute) mile (mi)	= 1.609 km
3 mi	= 1 league	= 4.827 km

metric		U.S. equivalent
	1 millimeter (mm)	= 0.0394 in
10 mm	= 1 centimeter (cm)	= 0.3937 in
10 cm	= 1 decimeter (dm)	= 3.937 in
10 dm	= 1 meter (m)	= 39.37 in
10 m	= 1 decameter (dam)	= 10.94 yds
10 dam	= 1 hectometer (hm)	= 109.4 yds
10 hm	= 1 kilometer (km)	= 0.621 mi

Surveyor's measure

Surveyor's linear units		metric equivalent
1 link	= 7.92 in	= 20.117 cm
25 links = 1 rod	= 5.50 yds	= 5.029 m
100 links = 1 chain	= 22 yds	= 20.12 m
10 chains = 1 furlong (fur.)	= 220 yds	= 0.201 m
80 chains = 8 fur.	= 1 mile (mi)	= 1.609 km

Surveyor's square units	metric equivalent
100 x 100 links or 10,000 sq. links	= 1 sq. chain = 484 sq. yds = 404.7 m^2
4 x 4 poles or 16 sq. poles	= 1 sq. chain
22 x 22 yds or 484 sq. yds	= 1 sq. chain
100,000 sq. links or 10 sq. chains	= 1 acre = 4840 sq. yds. = 0.4047 ha

Square measure

		metric equivalent
	1 square inch (sq. in)	= 6.4516 cm^2
144 sq. in.	= 1 square foot (sq. ft)	= 0.0929 m^2
9 sq. ft.	= 1 square yard (sq. yd)	= 0.8361 m^2

metric equivalent

30¼ sq. yds.	= 1 square perch	= 25.29 m²
40 sq. perch	= 1 rood	= 0.1012
4 roods or 4840 sq. yds	= 1 acre	= 04.047 ha
640 acres	= 1 square mile (sq. mi)	= 2.5900 km²

metric units   *U.S. equivalent*

	1 square millimeter (mm²)	= 0.0016 sq. in
100 mm²	= 1 square centimeter (cm²)	= 0.1550 sq. in
100 cm²	= 1 square decimeter (dm²)	= 15.500 sq. in
100 dm²	= 1 square meter (m²)	= 10.7639 sq. ft
		(= 1.1959 sq. yds)
100 m²	= 1 square decameter (dam²)	= 1076.3910 sq. ft
100 dam²	= 1 square hectometer (hm²)	= 0.0039 sq. mi
100 hm²	= 1 square kilometer (km²)	= 0.3861 sq. mi

*Note: The square hectometer is also known as a *hectare* (ha.).

The hectare can be sub-divided into *ares*:
metric units

100 m²	= 1 are	= 119.59 sq. yds
1000 m²	= 10 ares = 1 dekare	= 1195.9 sq. yds
10,000 m²	= 100 ares = 1 hectare	= 2.471 acres

Cubic measure

metric equivalent

	1 cubic inch (cu. in)	= 16.39 cm³
1728 cu. in	= 1 cubic foot (cu. ft)	= 0.0283 m³
27 cu. ft	= 1 cubic yard (cu. yd)	= 0.7646 m³

metric units

1000 cubic millimeters (mm³)	= 1 cubic centimeter (cm³)	= 0.0610 cu. in
1000 cubic centimeters (cm³)	= 1 cubic decimeter (dm³)	= 610 cu. in
1000 cubic decimeters (dm³)	= 1 cubic meter (m³)	= 35.3147 cu. ft

The *stere* is also used, in particular as a unit of measurement for timber:

1 cubic meter	= 1 stere	= 35.3147 cu. ft
10 decisteres	= 1 stere	= 35.3147 cu. ft
10 steres	= 1 decastere	= 353.1467 cu. ft
		(= 13.0795 cu. yds)

Liquid measure

		metric equivalent
	1 fluid ounce (fl. oz)	= 29.573 ml
4 fl. oz	= 1 gill	= 118.291 ml
4 gills	= 1 pint (pt)	= 473.163 ml
2 pt	= 1 quart (qt)	= 0.946l
4 qt	= 1 gallon (gal)	= 3.785l

U.S. and British equivalents

U.S.	British
1 fluid ounce	1.0408 fl oz
1 pint	0.8327 pt
1 gallon	0.8327 gal

metric units

10 milliliters (ml)	= 1 centiliter (cl)	= 0.0211 pt
10 cl	= 1 deciliter (dl)	= 0.211 pt
10 dl	= 1 liter (l)	= 2.11 pt
		(= 0.264 gal)
10l	= 1 decaliter (dal)	2.64 gal
10 dal	= 1 hectoliter (hl)	26.4 gal
10 hl	= kiloliter (kl)	264.0 gal

Temperature

Equations for conversion

°Fahrenheit = $(9/5 \times x°C) + 32$ °Centigrade = $5/9 \times (x°F - 32)$
°Kelvin = $x°C + 273.15$

Some equivalents

	Centigrade	Fahrenheit
Normal temperature of the human body	36.9°C	98.4°F
Freezing point	0°C	32°F
Boiling point	100°C	212°F

Table of equivalents

Fahrenheit	Centigrade	Centigrade	Fahrenheit
100°C	212°C	30°C	86°F
90°C	194°F	20°C	68°F
80°C	176°F	10°C	50°F

Fahrenheit	*Centigrade*	*Centigrade*	*Fahrenheit*
70°C	158°F	0°C	32°F
60°C	140°F	−10°C	14°F
50°C	122°F	−20°C	4°F
40°C	104°F	−30°C	−22°Fc

APPENDIX II

The International System of Units (SI units)

Quantity	Symbol	Unit	Symbols
acceleration	a	metres per second squared	ms-2 or m/s2
area	A	square metre	m2
capacitance	C	farad	F(1F = 1 AsV-1)
charge	Q	coulomb	C(1C = 1 As)
current	I	ampere	A
density	r	kilograms per cubic metre	kgm-3 or kg/m3
force	F	newton	N(1N = 1 kg ms-2)
frequency	f	hertz	Hz(1Hz = 1s-1)
length	l	metre	m
mass	m	kilogram	kg
potential difference	V	volt	V(1V = 1JC-1 or WA-1)
power	P	watt	W(1W = 1Js-1)
resistance	R	ohm	½ (1½ = 1VA-1)
specific heat capacity	c	joules per kilogram kelvin	Jkg-1 K-1
temperature	T	kelvin	L
time	t	second	s
volume	V	cubic metre	m3
velocity	v	metres per second	ms-1 or m/s
wavelength	l	metre	m
work, energy	W, E	joule	J(1J = 1Nm)

Useful prefixes adopted with SI units

Prefix	Symbol	Factor
tera	T	10^{12}
giga	G	10^{9}
mega	M	10^{6}
kelo	k	10^{3}
hecto	h	10^{2}
deda	da	10^{1}
deci	d	10^{-1}
centi	c	10^{-2}
milli	m	10^{-3}
micro	μ	10^{-6}
nano	n	10^{-9}
pico	p	10^{-12}
femto	f	10^{-15}
atto	a	10^{-18}

APPENDIX III

Chemical elements listed by symbol

Symbol	Element	Symbol	Element
Ac	Actinium	Mo	Molybdenum
Al	Aluminum	N	Nitrogen
Am	Americium	Na	Sodium
Ar	Argon	Nb	Niobium
As	Arsenic	Nd	Neodymium
At	Astatine	Ne	Neon
Au	Gold	Ni	Nickel
B	Boron	No	Nobelium
Ba	Barium	Np	Neptunium
Be	Beryllium	O	Oxygen
Bi	Bismuth	Os	Osmium
Bk	Berkelium	P	Phosphorous
Br	Bromine	Pa	Protactinium
C	Carbon	Pb	Lead
Ca	Calcium	Pd	Palladium
Cd	Cadmium	Pm	Promethium
Ce	Cerium	Po	Polonium
Cf	Californium	Pr	Praseodymium
Cl	Chlorine	Pt	Platinum
Cm	Curium	Pu	Plutonium
Co	Cobalt	Ra	Radium
Cr	Chromium	Rb	Rubidium
Cs	Caesium	Rh	Rhodium
Cu	Copper	Rn	Radon
Dy	Dysprosium	Ru	Ruthenium
Er	Erbium	S	Sulphur
Es	Einsteinium	Sb	Antimony
Eu	Europium	Sc	Scandium
F	Fluorine	Se	Selenium
Fe	Iron	Si	Silicon
Fm	Fermium	Sm	Samarium
Fr	Francium	Sn	Tin
Ga	Gallium	Sr	Strontium
Gd	Gadolinium	Ta	Tantalum
Ge	Germanium	Tn	Terbium
H	Hydrogen	Tc	Technetium
He	Helium	Te	Tellerium
Hf	Hafnium	Th	Thorium

Symbol	Element	Symbol	Element
Ho	Holmium	Ti	Titanium
I	Iodine	Tl	Thallium
n	Indium	Tm	Thulium
In	Iodine	U	Uranium
Ir	Iridium	V	Vanadium
Kr	Krypton	W	Tungsten
La	Lanthanum	Xe	Xenon
Li	Lithium	Y	Yttrium
Lu	Lutetium	Yb	Ytterbium
Md	Mendelevium	Zn	Zinc
Mg	Magnesium	Zr	Zirconium
Mn	Manganese		

APPENDIX IV

The United States of America

The States: area, population, motto, capital, state flower, state bird, nicknames

Alabama (AL)
Area (sq miles): 51,705; (sq km): 133,915
Population: 4,352,000
Motto: Crossroads of America
Capital: Montgomery
State flower: Camellia
State bird: Yellowhammer
Nicknames: Heart of Dixie; Camellia State

Alaska (AK)
Area (sq miles): 591,004; (sq km): 1,530,693
Population: 614,000
Motto: North to the future
Capital: Juneau
State flower: Forget-me-not
State bird: Willow ptarmigan
Nickname: The Last Frontier

Arizona (AZ)
Area (sq miles): 114,000; (sq km): 295,259
Population: 4,668,000
Motto: *Diat Deus* ('God enriches')
Capital: Phoenix
State flower: Saguaro
State bird: Cactus wren
Nickname: Grand Canyon State

Arkansas (AR)
Area (sq miles): 53,187; (sq km): 137,754
Population: 2,538,000

Motto: *Regnat Populus* ('The people rule')
Capital: Little Rock
State flower: Apple blossom
State bird: Mockingbird
Nickname: Land of Opportunity

California (CA)
Area (sq miles): 158,706; (sq km): 411,047
Population: 32,670,000
Motto: *Eureka* ('I have found it')
Capital: Sacramento
State flower: Golden poppy
State bird: California valley quail
Nickname: Golden State

Colorado (CO)
Area (sq miles): 104,091; (sq km): 269,594
Population: 3,971,000
Motto: *Nil sine numine* ('Nothing without providence')
Capital: Denver
State flower: Blue (Rocky Mountain) columbine
State bird: Lark bunting
Nickname: Centennial State

Connecticut (CT)
Area (sq miles): 5,018; (sq km): 12,997
Population: 3,275,000
Motto: *Qui transtulit sustinet* ('He who

transplanted still sustains')
Capital: Hartford
State flower: Mountain laurel
State bird: American robin
Nicknames: Constitution State; Nutmeg State

Delaware (DE)
Area   (sq miles): 2,044; (sq km): 5,294
Population: 745,000
Motto: Liberty and independence
Capital: Dover
State flower: Peach blossom
State bird: Blue hen chicken
Nicknames: First State; Diamond State

District of Columbia (DC)
Area   (sq miles): 68; (sq km): 108.8
Population: 606,900
Motto: *Justitia omnibus* ('Justice for all')
Capital: Washington
State flower: American beauty rose
State bird: Wood thrush
Nickname: Capital City

Florida (FL)
Area   (sq miles): 58,664; (sq km):
151,939
Population: 14,916,000
Motto: In God we trust
Capital: Tallahassee
State flower: Orange blossom
State bird: Mockingbird
Nickname: Sunshine State

Georgia (GA)
Area   (sq miles): 58,910; (sq km):
152,576
Population: 7,643,000
Motto: Wisdom, justice and moderation
Capital: Atlanta
State flower: Cherokee rose
State bird: Brown thrasher
Nicknames: Peace State; Empire State of the
South

Hawaii (HI)
Area   (sq miles): 6,471; (sq km): 16,760
Population: 1,194,000
Motto: The life of the land is perpetuated in
righteousness
Capital: Honolulu
State flower: Hibiscus
State bird: Nene goose/Hawaiian goose
Nickname: Aloha State

Idaho (ID)
Area   (sq miles): 83,564; (sq km):
216,430
Population: 1,229,000
Motto: *Esto perpetua* ('It is perpetual')
Capital: Boise
State flower: Syringa
State bird: Mountain bluebird
Nickname: Gem State

Illinois (IL)
Area   (sq miles): 57,871; (sq km):
149, 885
Population: 12,046,000
Motto: State sovereignty — national union
Capital: Springfield
State flower: Native violet
State bird: Cardinal
Nickname: Prairie State

Indiana (IN)
Area   (sq miles): 36,413; (sq km): 94, 309
Population: 5,900,000
Motto: Crossroads of America
Capital: Indianapolis
State flower: Peony
State bird: Cardinal
Nickname: Hoosier State

Iowa (IA)
Area   (sq miles): 56,275; (sq km):
145,752
Population: 2,863,000
Motto: Our liberties we prize and our rights

we will maintain
Capital: Des Moines
State flower: Wild rose
State bird: Goldfinch
Nickname: Hawkeye State

Kansas (KS)
Area   (sq miles): 82,277; (sq km): 213,096
Population: 2,629,000
Motto: *Ad astra per aspera* ('To the stars through difficulties')
Capital: Topeka
State flower: Sunflower
State bird: Western meadowlark
Nickname: Sunflower State

Kentucky (KY)
Area   (sq miles): 40,409; (sq km): 104,659
Population: 3,937,000
Motto: United we stand, divided we fall
Capital: Frankfort
State flower: Goldenrod
State bird: Kentucky cardinal
Nickname: Bluegrass State

Louisiana (LA)
Area   (sq miles): 47,752; (sq km): 123,677
Population: 4,369,000
Motto: Union, justice, and confidence
Capital: Baton Rouge
State flower: Magnolia
State bird: Eastern brown pelican
Nickname: Pelican State

Maine (ME)
Area   (sq miles): 33,265; (sq km): 86,156
Population: 1,245,000
Motto: *Dirigo* ('I direct')
Capital: Augusta
State flower: White pine cone and tassel

State bird: Chickadee
Nickname: Pine Tree State

Maryland (MD)
Area   (sq miles): 10,460; (sq km): 27,091
Population: 5,135,000
Motto: *Fatti maschii, parole femine* ('Many deeds, womanly words')
Capital: Annapolis
State flower: Black-eyed Susan
State bird: Baltimore oriole
Nicknames: Old Line State; Free State

Massachusetts (MA)
Area   (sq miles): 8,284; (sq km): 21,455
Population: 6,148,000
Motto: *Ense petit placidam sub libertate* ('By the sword we seek peace, but peace only')
Capital: Boston
State flower: Mayflower
State bird: Chickadee
Nicknames: Bay State; Colony State

Michigan (MI)
Area   (sq miles): 97,102; (sq km): 251,493
Population: 9,818,000
Motto: *Si quaeris peninsulam amoenam* ('If you seek a pleasant peninsula, look about you')
Capital: Lansing
State flower: Apple blossom
State bird: Robin
Nicknames: Great Lake State; Wolverine State

Minnesota (MN)
Area   (sq miles): 86,614; (sq km): 224,329
Population: 4,726,000
Motto: *L' Žtoile du nord* ('Star of the north')
Capital: St Paul
State flower: Pink and white lady's slipper
State bird: Common loon
Nicknames: North Star State; Gopher State

Mississippi (MS)
Area   (sq miles): 47,689; (sq km): 123,514
Population: 2,752,000
Motto: *Virtute et armis* ('By valor and arms')
Capital: Jackson
State flower: Magnolia
State bird: Mockingbird
Nickname: Magnolia State

Missouri (MO)
Area   (sq miles): 69,697; (sq km): 180,415
Population: 5,439,000
Motto: *Salus populi suprema lex esto* ('The welfare of the people shall be the supreme law')
Capital: Jefferson City
State flower: Hawthorn
State bird: Bluebird
Nickname: Show-Me-State

Montana (MT)
Area   (sq miles): 147,046; (sq km): 380,847
Population: 881,000
Motto: *Oro y plata* ('Gold and silver')
Capital: Helena
State flower: Bitterroot
State bird: Western meadowlark
Nickname: Treasure State

Nebraska (NE)
Area   (sq miles): 77,355; (sq km): 200,349
Population: 1,663,000
Motto: Equality before the law
Capital: Lincoln
State flower: Goldenrod
State bird: Western meadowlark
Nickname: Cornhusker State

Nevada (NV)
Area   (sq miles): 110,561; (sq km): 286,352
Population: 1,745,000
Motto: All for our country
Capital: Carson City
State flower: Sagebrush
State bird: Mountain bluebird
Nicknames: Sagebrush State; Battle-Born State

New Hampshire (NH)
Area   (sq miles): 9,279; (sq km): 24,032
Population: 1,185,000
Motto: Live free or die
Capital: Concord
State flower: Purple lilac
State bird: Purple finch
Nickname: Granite State

New Jersey (NJ)
Area   (sq miles): 7,787; (sq km): 20,168
Population: 8,116,000
Motto: Liberty and prosperity
Capital: Trenton
State flower: Purple violet
State bird: Eastern goldfinch
Nickname: Garden State

New Mexico (NM)
Area   (sq miles): 121,593; (sq km): 314,924
Population: 1,737,000
Motto: *Crescit eundo* ('It grows as it goes')
Capital: Santa Fe
State flower: Yucca
State bird: Roadrunner
Nickname: Land of Enchantment

New York (NY)
Area   (sq miles): 52,735; (sq km): 136,583
Population: 18,176,000
Motto: *Excelsior* ('Ever upward')
Capital: Albany

State flower: Rose (any color)
State bird: Bluebird
Nickname: Empire State

North Carolina (NC)
Area   (sq miles): 52,669; (sq km):
136,412
Population: 7,547,000
Motto: *Esse quam videri* ('To be rather than
to seem')
Capital: Raleigh
State flower: Dogwood
State bird: Cardinal
Nicknames: Tar Heel State; Old North State

North Dakota (ND)
Area   (sq miles): 70,702; (sq km):
183,117
Population: 639,000
Motto: Liberty and union, now and forever,
one and inseparable
Capital: Bismarck
State flower: Wild prairie rose
State bird: Western meadowlark
Nickname: Peace Garden State

Ohio (OH)
Area   (sq miles): 44,787; (sq km):
115,998
Population: 11,210,000
Motto: With God all things are possible
Capital: Columbus
State flower: Scarlet carnation
State bird: Cardinal
Nickname: Buckeye State

Oklahoma (OK)
Area   (sq miles): 69,956; (sq km):
181,185
Population: 3,347,000
Motto: *Labor omnia vincit* ('Labor conquers
all things')
Capital: Oklahoma City
State flower: Mistletoe

State bird: Scissor-tailed flycatcher
Nickname: Sooner State

Oregon (OR)
Area   (sq miles): 97,073; (sq km):
251,418
Population: 3,282,000
Motto: The union
Capital: Salem
State flower: Oregon grape
State bird: Western meadowlark
Nickname: Beaver State

Pennsylvania (PA)
Area   (sq miles): 46,063; (sq km):
119,251
Population: 12,002,000
Motto: Virtue, liberty and independence
Capital: Harrisburg
State flower: Mountain laurel
State bird: Ruffed grouse
Nickname: Keystone State

Rhode Island (RI)
Area   (sq miles): 1,212; (sq km): 3,139
Population: 989,000
Motto: Hope
Capital: Providence
State flower: Violet
State bird: Rhode Island hen
Nicknames: Little Rhody; Ocean State

South Carolina (SC)
Area   (sq miles): 31,113; (sq km): 80,852
Population: 3,836,000
Motto: *Dum spiro spero* ('While I breathe, I
hope')
Capital: Columbia
State flower: Carolina jessamine
State bird: Carolina wren
Nickname: Palmetto State

South Dakota (SD)
Area   (sq miles): 77,116; (sq km):

199,730
Population: 739,000
Motto: Under God, the people rule
Capital: Pierre
State flower: Pasque flower
State bird: Ring-necked pheasant
Nicknames: Coyote State; Sunshine State

Tennessee (TN)
Area   (sq miles): 42,144; (sq km):
109,152
Population: 5,431,000
Motto: Agriculture and commerce
Capital: Nashville
State flower: Iris
State bird: Mockingbird
Nickname: Volunteer State

Texas (TX)
Area   (sq miles): 266,807; (sq km):
691,027
Population: 19,760,000
Motto: Friendship
Capital: Austin
State flower: Bluebonnet
State bird: Mockingbird
Nickname: Lone Star State

Utah (UT)
Area   (sq miles): 84,899; (sq km):
219,887
Population: 2,010,000
Motto: Industry
Capital: Salt Lake City
State flower: Sego lily
State bird: Seagull
Nickname: Beehive State

Vermont (VT)
Area   (sq miles): 9,614; (sq km): 24,900
Population: 591,000
Motto: Freedom and unity
Capital: Montpelier
State flower: Red clover

State bird: Thrush
Nickname: Green Mountain State

Virginia (VA)
Area   (sq miles): 40,767; (sq km):
105,586
Population: 6,792,000
Motto: *Sic semper tyannis* ('Thus always to
tyrants')
Capital: Richmond
State flower: Flowering dogwood
State bird: Cardinal
Nickname: Old Dominion

Washington (WA)
Area   (sq miles): 68,139; (sq km):
176,479
Population: 5,690,000
Motto: *Alki* ('By and by')
Capital: Olympia
State flower: Rhododendron
State bird: Willow goldfinch
Nickname: Evergreen State

West Virginia (WV)
Area   (sq miles): 24,231; (sq km): 62,758
Population: 1,812,000
Motto: *Montani semper liberi* ('Mountain-
eers are always free')
Capital: Charlestown
State flower: Rhododendron
State bird: Cardinal
Nickname: Mountain State

Wisconsin (WI)
Area   (sq miles): 66,215; (sq km):
171,496
Population: 5,224,000
Motto: Forward
Capital: Madison
State flower: Wood violet
State bird: Robin
Nickname: Badger State

Wyoming (WY)
Area   (sq miles): 97,809; (sq km):
253,324
Population: 481,000
Motto: Equal rights
Capital: Cheyenne
State flower: Indian paintbrush
State bird: Meadowlark
Nickname: Equality State

Commonwealth: **Puerto Rico** (PR)
Area   (sq miles): 3,349; (sq km): 8,647
Population: 3,829,000
Motto: *Joannes est nomen eius* ('John is his
name')
Capital: San Juan
State flower: Maga
State bird: Reinita
Nickname: Equality State

APPENDIX V

Presidents and Vice Presidents of the United States

President	Term	Year of Birth–Death	Party	Vice President	Year of Birth–Death	Congresses
1. George Washington	4/30/1789–3/3/1797	1732–1799	F	John Adams	1735–1826	1, 2, 3, 4
2. John Adams	3/4/1797–3/3/1801	1735–1826	F	Thomas Jefferson	1743–1826	5, 6
3. Thomas Jefferson	3/4/1801–3/3/1805	1743–1826	D–R	Aaron Burr	1756–1836	7, 8
	3/4/1805–3/3/1809			George Clinton	1739–1812	9, 10
4. James Madison	3/4/1809–3/3/1813	1751–1836	D–R	George Clinton	1739–1812	11, 12
	3/4/1813–3/3/1817			Elbridge Gerry	1744–1814	13,14
5. James Monroe	3/4/1817–3/3/1825	1758–1835	D–R	Daniel D. Tompkins	1774–1825	15, 16, 17, 18
6. John Quincy Adams	3/4/1825–3/3/1829	1767–1848	D–R	John C. Calhoun	1782–1850	19, 20
7. Andrew Jackson	3/4/1829–3/3/1833	1767–1845	D	John C. Calhoun	1782–1850	21, 22
	3/4/1833–3/3/1837			Martin Van Buren	1782–1862	23, 24
8. Martin Van Buren	3/4/1837–3/3/1841	1782–1862	D	Richard M. Johnson	1780–1850	25, 26
9. William Henry Harrison	3/4/1841–4/4/1841	1773–1841	W	John Tyler	1790–1862	27
10. John Tyler	4/6/1841–3/3/1845	1790–1862	W	(No Vice President)		27, 28
11. James K. Polk	3/4/1845–3/3/1849	1795–1849	D	George M. Dallas	1792–1864	29, 30
12. Zachary Taylor	3/4/1849–7/9/1850	1784–1850	W	Millard Fillmore	1800–1874	31
13. Millard Fillmore	7/10/1850–3/3/1853	1800–1874	W	(No Vice President)		31, 32
14. Franklin Pierce	3/4/1853–3/3/1857	1804–1869	D	William R. King	1786–1853	33, 34
15. James Buchanan	3/4/1857–3/3/1861	1791–1868	D	John C. Breckinridge	1821–1875	35, 36
16. Abraham Lincoln	3/4/1861–3/3/1865	1809–1865	R	Hannibal Hamlin	1809–1891	37, 38
	3/4/1865–4/15/1865			Andrew Johnson	1808–1875	39
17. Andrew Johnson	4/15/1865–3/3/1869	1808–1875	D	(No Vice President)		39, 40
18. Ulysses S. Grant	3/4/1869–3/3/1873	1822–1885	R	Schuyler Colfax	1823–1885	41, 42
	3/4/1873–3/3/1877			Henry Wilson	1812–1875	43, 44
19. Rutherford B. Hayes	3/4/1877–3/3/1881	1822–1893	R	William A. Wheeler	1819–1887	45, 46
20. James Garfield	3/4/1881–9/19/1881	1831–1881	R	Chester A. Arthur	1829–1886	47
21. Chester A. Arthur	9/20/1881–3/3/1885	1829–1886	R	(No Vice President)		47, 48
22. Grover Cleveland	3/4/1885–3/3/1889	1837–1908	D	Thomas A. Hendricks	1819–1885	49, 50
23. Benjamin Harrison	3/4/1889–3/3/1893	1833–1901	R	Levi P. Morton	1824–1920	51, 52
24. Grover Cleveland	3/4/1893–3/3/1897	1837–1908	D	Adlai E. Stevenson	1835–1914	53, 54
25. William McKinley	3/4/1897–3/3/1901	1843–1901	R	Garret A. Hobart	1844–1899	55, 56
	3/4/1901–9/14/1901			Theodore Roosevelt	1858–1919	57
26. Theodore Roosevelt	9/14/1901–3/3/1905	1858–1919	R	Charles W. Fairbanks	1852–1918	57, 58
	3/4/1905–3/3/1909			Charles W. Fairbanks	1852–1918	59, 60
27. William H. Taft	3/4/1909–3/3/1913	1857–1930	R	James S. Sherman	1855–1912	61, 62
28. Woodrow Wilson	3/4/1913–3/3/1921	1856–1924	D	Thomas R. Marshall	1854–1925	63, 64, 65, 66
29. Warren G. Harding	3/4/1921–8/2/1923	1865–1923	R	Calvin Coolidge	1872–1933	67, 68
30. Calvin Coolidge	8/3/1923–3/3/1925	1872–1933	R	Charles G. Dawes	1865–1951	68
	3/4/1925–3/3/1929			Charles G. Dawes	1865–1951	69, 70
31. Herbert C. Hoover	3/4/1929–3/3/1933	1874–1964	R	Charles Curtis	1860–1936	71, 72
32. Franklin D. Roosevelt	3/4/1933–1/20/1941	1882–1945	D	John N. Garner	1868–1967	73, 74, 75, 76
	1/20/1941–1/20/1945			Henry A. Wallace	1888–1965	77, 78
	1/20/1945–4/12/1945			Harry S. Truman	1884–1972	79
33. Harry S. Truman	4/12/1945–1/20/1949	1884–1972	D	Alben W. Barkley	1877–1956	79, 80
	1/20/1949–1/20/1953			Alben W. Barkley	1877–1956	81, 82
34. Dwight D. Eisenhower	1/20/1953–1/20/1961	1890–1969	R	Richard M. Nixon	1913–1994	83, 84, 85, 86
35. John F. Kennedy	1/20/1961–11/22/1963	1917–1963	D	Lyndon B. Johnson	1908–1973	87, 88
36. Lyndon B. Johnson	11/22/1963–1/20/1965	1908–1965	D	Hubert H. Humphrey	1911–1978	88
	1/20/1965–1/20/1969			Hubert H. Humphrey	1911–1978	89, 90
37. Richard M. Nixon	1/20/1969–1/20/1973	1913–1994	R	Spiro T. Agnew	1918–1996	91, 92
	1/20/1793–8/9/1974			Spiro T. Agnew*	1918–1996	93
				Gerald R. Ford	1913–	93
38. Gerald R. Ford	8/9/1974–1/20/1977	1913–	R	Nelson A. Rockefeller	1908–1979	93, 94
39. James (Jimmy) Carter	1/20/1977–1/20/1981	1924–	D	Walter F. Mondale	1928–	95, 96
40. Ronald Reagan	1/20/1981–1/20/1989	1911–	R	George H. W. Bush	1924–	97, 98, 99, 100
41. George H. W. Bush	1/20/1989–1/20/1993	1924–	R	J. Danforth Quayle	1947–	101, 102
42. William Clinton	1/20/1993–1/20/2001	1946–	D	Albert A. Gore, Jr.	1948–	103, 104, 105, 106
43. George W. Bush	1/20/2001–	1946–	R	Richard Cheney	1941–	107

* Spiro T. Agnew resigned on October 10, 1973. Gerald R. Ford was inaugurated December 6, 1973.

F: Federalist   D–R: Democratic Republican   D: Democratic   W: Whig   R: Republican